Introduction to

AGRICULTURAL ECONOMICS

Prentice-Hall
A Division of Simon & Schuster, Inc.
Englewood Cliffs, New Jersey

USDA Photo by Doug Wilson

Introduction to

AGRICULTURAL ECONOMICS

John B. Penson, Jr.
Professor
Department of Agricultural Economics
Texas A&M University

Rulon D. Pope
Associate Professor
Department of Economics
Brigham Young University

Michael L. Cook
President
California Rice Growers Association
West Sacramento, California

0-13-477712-3

Published by
Prentice-Hall
A Division of Simon & Schuster, Inc.
Englewood Cliffs, New Jersey 07632

10 9 8 7 6 5 4 3 2 1

Printed in the United States of America.

Part Opening Photo Credits:

Part I: USDA Photo
Part II: USDA Photo by Jim Pickerell
Part III: USDA Photo
Part IV: USDA Photo by Doug Wilson
Part V: USDA/SCS Photo by H. E. Alexander

Figure 6.1: Reprint with permission of Commodity Research Bureau, a Knight-Rider
Business Information Service.

Page 363: Cartoon reprinted with permission from the *San Diego Union.*

Page 510: Newspaper clipping reprinted with permission from the *Des Moines Register.*

Page 495: Photograph provided courtesy of the Food and Agriculture Organization of
the United Nations, Rome, Italy.

CONTENTS

part II

UNDERSTANDING CONSUMER AND PRODUCER BEHAVIOR

PREFACE

The purpose of this book is to provide beginning students in agriculture with a systematic introduction to the basic concepts and issues in economics as they relate to agriculture at the firm, national, and international levels. The book is oriented primarily toward commercial agriculture and the economic environment in which it operates.

We begin the book by answering the question raised by the title of Chapter 1; namely, "What is agricultural economics?" We do this by first defining the field of economics and then developing a definition of agricultural economics based on the role that agricultural economists play at both the micro and macro levels. A discussion of the changing structure of agriculture during the post–World War II period and the structure of those sectors in the economy that supply farm inputs and process farm output is presented in Chapter 2.

Part II focuses on gaining an understanding of the economic decisions made by consumers and producers. The topics covered here include consumer behavior (Chapter 3), the technology of production (Chapter 4), production decisions for a competitive firm (Chapter 5), farm marketing options (Chapter 6), growth of the competitive firm (Chapter 7), and decision making in an uncertain world (Chapter 8). Heavy emphasis is placed on those chapters traditionally found in "introductory" textbooks (Chapters 3, 4, and 5). Empirical examples are presented where possible to illustrate the magnitude and applicability of the relationships involved. The scope of these chapters has also been expanded beyond the coverage normally found to include several important topics of which students should be aware. For example, an entire chapter in Part II is devoted to a discussion of the marketing options available to farmers, including the advantages and disadvantages associated with the use of futures contracts. In addition, recognition of the existence of uncertainty in agriculture and how it can affect the farmer's production, marketing, and investment decisions is normally relegated to more advanced textbooks. The experience of the seventies and early eighties, however, suggests that beginning students should at least (1) be aware that uncertainty exists in agriculture, and (2) understand some of the ways in which farmers can respond to this uncertainty.

Part III introduces the concepts of market equilibrium and general equilibrium. Chapter 9 presents a discussion of the determination of the equilibrium price and quantity in the market for raw agricultural products and the market intermediaries involved as the product leaves the farm gate and moves through the marketing channel to the retail level. The relationship between this market equilibrium and farm policy is explored in Chapter 10, where the objectives of government supply constraint and demand expansion programs are made clear. This part of the book concludes with Chapter 11, where multimarket relationships and the concept of general equilibrium are introduced. A description of the interrelationships between agriculture and the rest of the U.S. economy is presented. This chapter also highlights the relationship between sector output and the nation's total output or gross national product, making the point that the nation's output is *not* found by simply adding up the output of all the sectors in the economy.

Part IV focuses on U.S. macroeconomic policy and how agriculture is affected by policy responses to business fluctuations. Chapter 12 begins Part IV by discussing measures of macroeconomic performance at the economy-wide and sector level. It also discusses the nature of business fluctuations in the economy and their major consequences: unemployment and inflation. Chapters 13 and 14 stress the effects that national economic policies (both fiscal and monetary) have on aggregate demand in the economy and the attainment of the economy's current potential output. Chapter 15 then focuses on how these policies are applied to eliminate inflation or unemployment and how these actions are transmitted to agriculture. The chapter concludes with a discussion of the problems that variable macroeconomic policies can cause for agriculture. *Importantly, the discussion in Chapter 15 is presented in such a way that Chapters 11 through 14 can be skipped if desired without jeopardizing the reader's understanding of the relationships between agriculture and the general economy.* Chapter 16 inventories the scarce resources used by farmers to produce raw agricultural products and discusses such issues as the conservation of natural resources and environmental regulations. The last chapter in Part IV presents a discussion of the lenders that supply loan funds to agriculture, a major link between this sector and the rest of the economy.

Part V contains three chapters, the first two of which focus on the major concepts and issues in international agricultural trade. This discussion focuses on the factors affecting the export supply and import demand for farm products as well as the welfare implications of tariff and nontariff policies. The final chapter focuses on the future climate for international agricultural trade.

Each chapter concludes with a restatement of the purpose of the chapter and a point-by-point listing of the major concepts and issues covered. In addition, there is a section containing definitions of the key terms used in the chapter. There is also a list of references and further readings on the subject covered in the chapter and a set of questions for further study. Most chapters also contain a discussion of one or more advanced topics that extend the coverage presented in the chapter.

There are numerous ways in which this book can be used in the classroom. We would like to take this opportunity to outline three potential approaches to using this book in a one-semester introductory course: (1) a *micro* approach, (2) a *macro* approach, and (3) a blend of *micro and macro* approaches. One potential combination of chapter assignments for each of these three approaches is as follows:

Micro	Macro	Both
1	1	1
3	2	2
4	9	3
5	10	4
6	11	5
7	12	6
8	13	7
9	14	9
10	15	10
11	16	11
16	17	12
17	18	15
18	19	18
	20	

Introductory courses are traditionally highly micro in scope. Little is normally said about multimarket relationships, national economic policies, and how these policies affect, both directly and indirectly, the performance and structure of agriculture. The micro approach suggested above reflects this orientation. There has been an increasing interest in introductory courses in the *macroeconomics of agriculture.* The macro approach suggested above begins with the concepts of market and general equilibrium and agriculture's contribution to the nation's total output before discussing aggregate demand and supply and the effects of alternative macroeconomic policies. Some instructors may desire a *mixture* of micro and macro concepts in a one-semester course. The approach suggested above omits specific topics included in the first two approaches (Chapters 8, 13, and 14), which some instructors may wish to retain if time permits. Finally, there is sufficient coverage of micro and macro concepts in this book to justify its use in a two-semester sequence emphasizing the micro- and macroeconomics of agriculture.

John B. Penson, Jr.
Rulon D. Pope
Michael L. Cook

part I
INTRODUCTION

1

WHAT IS AGRICULTURAL ECONOMICS?

If you were to answer this question by saying that agricultural economics is the application of economic principles to agriculture, you would be technically correct. This definition, however, glosses over the nature and scope of the issues typically addressed by agricultural economists. Before advancing a more descriptive definition, let us first take a moment to examine the scope of economics and the role that agricultural economists play in today's economy. This will place us in a better position to propose a more definitive answer to the question raised by this chapter's title. An appendix to this chapter presents a discussion of how to construct and interpret graphs. If you are unfamiliar with graphical analysis, study this material carefully before proceeding with the remaining chapters.

SCOPE OF ECONOMICS

Because we—individually or collectively—cannot have everything we desire, we must make choices. Consumers, for example, must make expenditure decisions with a budget in mind. Their objective is to maximize the satisfaction they derive from (1) allocating their time between work and leisure, and (2) allocating their available income to consumption and saving given the current prices and interest rates. Farmers must also make production, marketing, and investment decisions with a budget in mind. Their objective might be to maximize the profit of their firm given its current resources (e.g., its tillable land, feedlot capacity, borrowing ability, etc.) and the current prices and interest rates. The scarcity of resources plays a major role in determining the level of prices and interest rates that both consumers and producers encounter in the marketplace. Finally, society must collectively make choices as to how best to allocate its scarce resources among different government programs after considering all the costs and benefits involved.

Two terms were alluded to several times in the preceding paragraph: "scarce resources" and "choice." Let us examine these two terms more closely.

Scarce Resources

The term *scarcity* refers to the fact that there is only a finite quantity of resources available to meet society's needs.[1] That is, nature does not freely provide as much of these resources as we may want. A discussion of scarce resources can be broken down into the following categories: *natural resources, human resources,* and *manufactured resources.*

Natural resources.   Land and the mineral deposits it contains probably come to mind first when the topic of resource scarcity is brought up. The quality of these natural resource in the United States differs greatly from one region to the next. Some land is incapable of growing anything in its natural state, whereas other lands are extremely fertile. Still other areas are rich in coal deposits or oil and natural gas reserves. In recent years our society has also become aware of the increasing scarcity of fresh water. Whereas energy-related natural resources have represented the critical scarce resources of the seventies and early eighties, water could well become the critical scarce natural resource as we approach the end of this century.

Human resources.   The services provided by laborers and management to the production of goods and services are *human resources,* and are also considered scarce. Laborers, for example, provide services which, combined with scarce nonhuman resources, produce economic goods.[2] Steel workers, for example, provide the labor input to producing steel. Farm laborers provide the labor input to producing raw food and fiber products. Labor is considered scarce even when the country's labor force is not "fully employed" (e.g., the unemployment rate is 10 percent). Laborers supply services in response to the going wage rate as well as "returns" that they derive from leisure. In short, businesses may not be able to hire all the labor services they desire at the wage they wish to pay.

---

[1] Resources can be defined as the inputs or factors used in the production of the goods and services we desire.

[2] Goods and services produced from scarce resources are also scarce and are referred to as *economic goods.* Economic goods are in contrast to *free goods,* where the quantity desired is available at a price of zero. Air has long been a free good, but pollution making the air unfit to breath is changing this notion in some areas of the country.

USDA Photo

A resource is said to be scarce when it exists only in finite quantity. Land and its mineral deposits constitute a major natural resource in agriculture. The population growth in this country and subsequent increasing demand for land for commercial and residential uses has resulted in the permanent loss of fertile farmland from agricultural use. Water is another natural resource that is available in finite quantity. Human resources and manufactured resources represent two additional categories of natural resources.

Management, another form of human resource, provides entrepreneurial services. These services may entail the formation of a new firm, the renovation or expansion of an existing firm, the taking of such risks as losing money and going bankrupt, and the use of the firm's existing resources in such a way that its objectives can be met. Without entrepreneurship, large-scale business would cease operating efficiently.

Manufactured resources. The third major category of resources is manufactured resources, or *capital.* These resources take the form of machines, equipment, and structures. Examples in farming include tractors, combines, storage sheds, glass-lined silos, and cattle feedlots. Improvements to natural resources, such as irrigation ditches, fences, and tilling, are also considered a manufactured resource. A product produced during the year which has not been used up is also considered as a manufactured resource. For example, inventories of corn raised but not fed to livestock or sold to other sectors represent a manufactured resource.

Nations with high per capita incomes and wealth face the problem of scarcity just as do nations with low per capita incomes and wealth. Scarcity is a *relative* concept. That is, even though consumers and producers in the United States enjoy a higher per capita income and wealth than, say, their counterparts in India, they typically (1) still want more than they have, or (2) need more time to do what they want to do. The terms "scarcity" and "poverty" are therefore not synonymous. All societies face the universal problem of scarcity because they cannot obtain everything from existing resources without making some sacrifices, and these sacrifices force us to make choices among alternatives.

Making Choices

The mere fact that resource scarcity exists forces consumers and producers to *make choices.* These choices have a time dimension. The choices consumers make today will have an effect on how they will live in the future. The choices farmers make today will have an effect on the future profitability of their firms. Your decision to go to college rather than get a job was probably based in part on your desire to increase your *future* earning power or eventual wealth.

The choices one makes also have an associated *opportunity cost.* The opportunity cost of going to college now is the income you are currently foregoing by not getting a job at this time. The opportunity cost of a consumer taking $1,000 out of his or her savings account to buy a new stereo system is the interest income this money would have earned if left in the bank. A farmer considering the purchase of a new tractor with a limited amount of money to spend must also consider the income he could have received by using this money for some other purpose. More will be said about the concept of opportunity cost in Chapter 7.

Sometimes the choices we make are constrained not only by resource scarcity but by noneconomic constraints as well. These forces may be political, legal, or moral in nature. For example, some states have "blue laws" that prohibit the sale of specific commodities on Sundays. Many lenders serving agriculture are constrained by legal lending limits when lending to their large customers.

Most resources are best suited for a particular use. The instructor of this course is probably better suited for this task than, say, performing open-heart surgery. By focusing the use of our resources on a specific task, we are engaging in what is known as *specialization*. With a given set of human and nonhuman resources, specialization of effort generally results in a higher total output. Individuals and even nations should be doing what they do comparatively better than others, given their endowment of resources. Individuals might specialize in professional athletics, law, or agricultural economics. As we shall explore in Chapter 18, a nation may find it to its advantage to specialize in the production of coffee, rice, or computers and import other commodities for which its endowment of natural, human, and manufactured resources is ill suited.

Society as a whole must make choices that might alter the allocation of resources from that which individuals collectively might have desired. For example, all nations normally allocate some resources to military uses. Society as a whole must therefore decide how best to allocate resources between the production of civilian goods versus production of military goods (i.e., the "guns versus butter" argument).

DEFINITION OF ECONOMICS

With the foregoing concepts of resource scarcity and choice in mind, we are now in a position to define the nature and scope of the field of economics. This definition is as follows: *Economics is a social science that studies how consumers, producers, and societies choose among the alternative uses of scarce resources in the process of producing, exchanging, and consuming goods and services.*

Microeconomics versus Macroeconomics

As with most disciplines, the field of economics can be divided into several branches. There are two major branches of economics: (1) *microeconomics*, and (2) *macroeconomics*. Microeconomics focuses on the economic actions of individuals or specific groups of individuals. For example, we may be concerned with the economic behavior of consumers or producers of farm products and with the determination of price in that particular market. By assuming that other events taking place in the economy outside the market will remain constant, microeconomics ignores the interrelationships among markets.

Macroeconomics, on the other hand, focuses on broad aggregates such as the growth of gross national product (GNP), the gaps between the economy's potential GNP and its current GNP, and trade-offs between unemployment and inflation. For example, macroeconomics is concerned with identifying the monetary and fiscal policies that would eliminate the GNP gap discussed above, eliminate inflation, and promote the growth of the nation's economy. Such analyses explicitly account for the interrelationships between the labor, product, and money markets.

Despite this contrast between micro- and macroeconomics, there is no conflict between these two branches. After all, the economy in the aggregate is certainly affected by the events taking place in individual markets. The difference is one of emphasis. Microeconomists studying the demand for pork, for example, might assume that the prices of many other products are fixed. They might also assume that consumer income is given, or known in advance. Macroeconomists, on the other hand, might limit their focus to a single price index for *all* goods and services when studying aggregate demand in the economy. They would also view the aggregate level of income as a key variable to be determined in the analysis rather than something to be taken as given.

Positive versus Normative Economics

The study of economics can also be divided along other lines. A prime example is the division between *positive* economics and *normative* economics. Positive economics focuses on "what is" and "what would happen if" questions and policy issues. No value judgments or prescriptions are made. Instead, the economic behavior of producers and consumers is explained or predicted. For example, policymakers may be interested in knowing how consumers and producers might respond if a tax cut were passed.

Normative economics, on the other hand, interjects the values associated with specific goals or objectives. The focus of normative economics is on determining "what should be" or "what ought to be." For example, policymakers might inquire which of several alternative policies *should be* adopted to maximize the economic welfare of producers and consumers. At the micro level, a farmer might be interested in knowing the combination of crops that *should be* planted to maximize his profit.[3]

Economic Systems

An economic system can be defined as the institutional means by which resources are used to satisfy human desires, where the term "institutions" refers to the laws, habits, ethics, and customs of the nation's citizens. *Capi-*

---

[3] For a more in-depth discussion of positive and normative economics, see Milton Friedman, *Essays in Positive Economics* (Chicago: University of Chicago Press, 1974), Chap. 1.

talism, for example, is an economic system where individuals own resources and have the right to employ their time and resources however they choose, with minimal legal constraints from government. Prices signal the value of resources and economic goods. This system differs sharply from *socialism,* where resources are generally collectively owned and where government decides through central planning how human and nonhuman resources are to be utilized across the various sectors of the economy. Prices are largely set by government and administered to consumers and farmers.

In the United States, we have what is commonly referred to as a *mixed economic system.* That is, markets are not entirely free to determine price in some markets but are in others. Government's intervention in agriculture, for example, is well known. The use of supply constraint programs to influence the supply of specific farm products and demand expansion programs to influence the demand for farm products will be explored extensively in Chapter 10. Agriculture is not the only sector in which government has intervened, however. Loan guarantees to large firms such as Lockheed and Chrysler are forms of government intervention in the private sector. Another example is the windfall-profits tax on oil recently enacted. Government also controls numerous aspects of transportation, communications, education, and finance. Welfare programs are also indicative of a mixed economic system.

The U.S. economy is therefore not a "pure" capitalistic system. Nor does it represent a political system where government regulates all aspects of human and nonhuman resource use. Instead, it is a mixed system where producers and consumers as well as government influence what happens in the marketplace.

ROLE OF THE AGRICULTURAL ECONOMIST

Now that we have advanced a definition of the field of economics and introduced the notion that the U.S. economy represents a market economy—where prices signal resource scarcity to consumers and producers—with some government control and intervention, let us examine the role that agricultural economists play in our economy. From this we will synthesize a definition of agricultural economics.

Role at the Micro Level

The application of economics to agriculture is greatest by far at the micro level. A review of the curriculums at universities offering degrees in agricultural economics will support this contention, as most undergraduate courses focus on marketing, farm management, agribusiness management, and finance. Even policy courses normally have a decidedly micro flavor. Students majoring in other fields in agriculture also normally limit their course selections in economics to one or more of the micro topics just mentioned.

Agricultural economists at the micro level are concerned with issues related to resource use in the production, processing, distribution, and consumption of products originating in agriculture. Production economists, for example, examine resource demand by farm businesses and their supply response. Market economists focus on the flow of food and fiber through market channels to its final destination and the determination of prices at each stage. Financial economists are concerned with issues related to the financing of farm businesses and the supply of loan funds to these firms. Resource economists focus on the use and preservation of our nation's natural resources. Others are interested in the formation of government programs for specific commodities that will support the incomes of farmers. The latter group of economists is also concerned with the performance and structure of agriculture and the economic well-being of farmers and consumers.

Some agricultural economists trained to conduct research at the micro level utilize a variety of mathematical computer models for a particular type of farm to identify optimal management strategies under specific sets of assumptions. Others may develop models that account for those factors which influence the demand and supply of a particular commodity or group of commodities. These models may then be used to forecast future commodity prices, for example. Upon graduation, some undergraduate students majoring in agricultural economics go back to the family farm. Many, however, take positions with agribusiness firms and financial institutions, frequently entering training programs sponsored by these firms.

Role at the Macro Level

Agricultural economists involved at the macro level are interested in the role agriculture plays in domestic and world economies and how the events taking place in other sectors affect agriculture, and vice versa. Agricultural economists employed by the Federal Reserve System, for example, must evaluate events in agriculture in a broad context that extends well beyond the farm gate. Macroeconomists with a research interest in agriculture may use computer-based models to analyze the direct and indirect effects that specific monetary or fiscal policy proposals would have on this sector. Others might use macroeconomic models to examine foreign trade relationships for food and fiber products as well as issues in the area of international development. Unfortunately, few undergraduate students are sufficiently trained in macroeconomic analysis to play a significant role in this branch of economics.

In summary, agricultural economists can be found at work throughout our mixed economic system; on farms and ranches, with lending institutions, grain companies, machinery and equipment manufacturers, in government, at universities, and in many other employment situations.

DEFINITION OF AGRICULTURAL ECONOMICS

We can define the field of agricultural economics by the activities of agricultural economists identified above. One possible definition reads as follows: *Agriculture economics is (1) the study of the production, processing, marketing, and consumption of food and fiber products, and (2) the study of the interrelationships between agriculture and the general economy and the direct and indirect effects of macroeconomic policies.*

Now that we have a more complete understanding of the breadth of the agricultural economics profession, let us move on to an examination of the structure and performance of the U.S. food and fiber system.

SUMMARY

The purpose of this chapter was to define the field of agricultural economics as a subset of the general field of economics. The major points made in this chapter may be summarized as follows:

1. *Scarce resources* are those human and nonhuman resources that exist in a finite quantity. Scarce resources can be subdivided into three groups: (1) natural resources, (2) human resources, and (3) manufactured resources.

2. The fact that resource scarcity exists forces both consumers and farmers to make choices.

3. Most resources are best suited to a particular use. Specialization of effort may lead to a higher total output.

4. The field of economics can be subdivided into *microeconomics* and *macroeconomics*. Microeconomics focuses on the actions of individuals, being concerned with the economic behavior of consumers and farmers. Microeconomic analysis is largely *partial equilibrium* in nature; events outside the market in question are assumed to be constant. Macroeconomics focuses on broad aggregates, including the nation's aggregate performance as measured by GNP, unemployment, and inflation. Macroeconomic analysis is normally *general equilibrium* in nature; events in all markets are allowed to vary.

5. *Positive economic analysis* focuses on "what is" and "what would happen if" questions and policy issues. *Normative economic analysis*, on the other hand, focuses on "what should be" policy issues.

6. *Capitalism* and *socialism* represent economic systems at the opposite ends of the spectrum. The U.S. economy represents a *mixed* economic system. Some markets are free to determine price, whereas other market prices are regulated.

7. Agricultural economists at the micro level are concerned with issues related to resource use in the production, processing, distribution, and consumption of farm output. Agricultural economists at the macro level are concerned with agriculture's role in the general economy, its interrelationships with other sectors, and the effects of macroeconomic policies.

DEFINITION OF TERMS

Scarce resources: a resource is said to be scarce if only a finite quantity of the resource exists. Nature does not freely provide as much of these resources as we would like.

Natural resources: includes such resources as land and its mineral deposits that are available without additional effort on the part of the owners.

Human resources: the services provided by laborers and the entrepreneurship services provided by management represent the two major forms of human resources.

Manufactured resources: often referred to as capital, these resources consist of plows, tractors, tools, buildings, and other improvements to land that are manufactured by human beings.

Specialization: the separation of productive activities between persons or geographical areas in such a manner that none of these persons or regions is completely self-sufficient. For example, some people specialize by learning to be plumbers. Others choose to be lawyers or even agricultural economists.

Economics: a social science that studies how consumers, producers, and societies choose among the alternative uses of scarce resources in the process of producing, exchanging, and consuming goods and services.

Agricultural economics: the study of (1) the production, processing, marketing, and consumption of food and fiber products, and (2) the interrelationship between agriculture and the general economy and the direct and indirect effects of macroeconomic policies.

Microeconomics: branch of economics that focuses on the economic actions of individuals or specific groups of individuals.

Macroeconomics: branch of economics that focuses on broad aggregates such as the growth of gross national product and the money supply as well as the stability of prices and the level of employment.

Positive economics: focuses on "what is" and "what would happen if" questions and issues. Does not involve value judgments or policy pre-scriptions to reach a particular objective.

Normative economics: focuses on determining "what should be" or "what ought to be" issues and questions. Unlike positive economics, it inter-jects the values with specific goals or objectives.

Capitalism: an economic system where individuals own resources and have the right to employ their time and resources however they choose, with minimal legal constraints from government.

Mixed economic system: markets are not entirely free to determine price in some markets but are in others. Government controls in selected mar-kets and welfare programs are indicative of a mixed economic system.

Socialism: resources are generally collectively owned and government de-cides through central planning how human and nonhuman resources are to be utilized in different sectors of the economy. Prices are largely set by the government and administered to consumers and producers.

ADDITIONAL READINGS

FRIEDMAN, MILTON, *Essays in Positive Economics.* Chicago: University of Chicago Press, 1974.

HEILBRONER, ROBERT, *The Making of Economic Society,* 6th ed. Englewood Cliffs, N.J.: Prentice-Hall, Inc., 1980.

MARTIN, LEE R., *A Survey of Agricultural Economics Literature: Traditional Fields of Agricultural Economics,* Vol. 1. Minneapolis, Minn.: University of Minnesota Press, 1977.

SAMUELSON, PAUL A., *Economics,* 12th ed. New York: McGraw-Hill Book Company, 1980.

SCHUH, G. EDWARD, "The New Macroeconomics of Agriculture," *American Journal of Agricultural Economics,* 1976, pp. 802–811.

QUESTIONS

1. Discuss what is meant by the term "capital" and how it relates to the concept of manufactured resources.
2. The point was made in this chapter that the terms "scarcity" and "poverty" are not synonymous. Why is this so?
3. Define and contrast the fields of economics and agricultural economics. Identify the roles played by agricultural economists at the micro and macro levels.
4. Contrast the essential differences between capitalism and socialism. Why do we say that the United States is characterized by a mixed economic system?

A REVIEW OF GRAPHICAL ANALYSIS

It is essential in many of the chapters to follow that you be able to understand the construction and interpretation of graphs. We begin with the construction of a graph from the numbers in a table documenting the relationship between two variables. Once you understand how a table or a relationship can be converted to a graph, you will understand what graphs are and how to interpret them.

Constructing a Graph

Two variables can be related in different ways. For example, there is a *direct* relationship between yields and fertilizer usage (at least over some relevant range). The higher the application of fertilizer, the higher the yield. In more general terms, the *increase* in one variable may be associated with an *increase* in another variable. Two variable can also be *inversely* related. As the price of gasoline increases, individuals will find ways to reduce their consumption of this product. Here, an *increase* in one variable is associated with a *decrease* in another variable. Finally, you will encounter instances later in this book where the relationship between two variables is *mixed*. For example, take the relationship between yields and rainfall. Yields will increase sharply as we move from a situation of no rainfall to some "normal" amount. Beyond this level of rainfall, however, yields may actually begin to decline as a result of farmers not being able to get into the fields at the proper time, low-lying areas being washed out, and so on. This suggests that there is a *maximum* point beyond which this curve begins decreasing instead of increasing.

To illustrate how to graph two related variables, let us assume that your local farm cooperative has noted the following relationship between the price they charge for work gloves and the number of pairs of work gloves they sell during the week:

Price per pair	Quantity sold during the week	Location on graph
$9	20	A
8	30	B
7	40	C
6	50	D
5	60	E
4	70	F

These data should suggest to you that there is an *inverse* relationship between the price of a pair of work gloves and the number of pair sold. Price is *decreasing* at the same time the quantity is *increasing*.

Each of the price–quantity relationships noted above can be viewed as coordinates in a graph. In economics, it is customary to put the dollar values (price in this instance) on the vertical or *y* axis and quantity on the horizontal or *x* axis. Figure 1.1 shows the location of these price–quantity coordinates on a graph. Point *A*, for example, represents the observation that 20 pairs of gloves will be sold if the price per pair is $9. Let us assume for the moment that the sales of work gloves are perfectly divisible. That is, we can sell 1/4 or 1/8 of a work glove. This allows us to have a quantity relationship at every possible price between the $4 to 9 range cited above, and also allows us to connect points *A* through *F* in Figure 1.1 with a *solid* line. This line is normally referred to as a *linear curve* by economists even though this line does not curve at all. The term *nonlinear curve* is used to distinguish between a true curve and a straight line. Panel a in Figure 1.2 again illustrates the shape of a linear curve, and panel b shows the shape of a nonlinear curve.

Slope of a Linear Curve

An important feature of a curve to an economist is its slope, or how fast the plotted relationship is increasing or decreasing. To illustrate the calculation

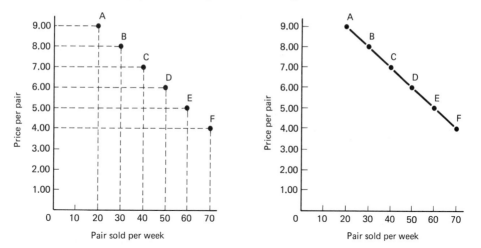

Figure 1.1 *Graphing Relationship between Price and Quantity.* The relationship between two variables can often be better understood if it can be visualized with the aid of a graph. The first step in graphing this relationship is to plot the relationship in an appropriately labeled graph. In our "work glove" example the price per pair of gloves is captured on the vertical or *y* axis and the quantity of gloves sold per week is captured on the horizontal or *x* axis. The quantity of gloves sold if the price of gloves is $9 is located on the vertical axis. This combination is then plotted (see point *A*). We can generalize the relationship between the price per pair of gloves and the quantity purchased per week by drawing a line connecting the series of points plotted above. The slope of this "linear curve" is equal to the change in the price of the gloves divided by the change in the quantity demanded per week.

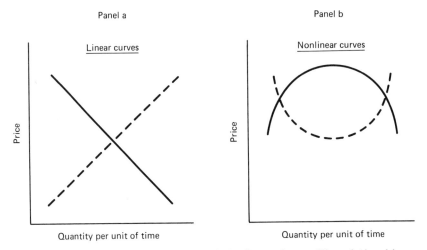

Figure 1.2 *Illustration of Linear and Nonlinear Curves.* The relationship between two variables (e.g., price and quantity) can take on numerous forms. Panel a shows, for example, that these relationships can either be downward sloping (solid line) or upward sloping (dashed line). Panel b also illustrates the fact that the relationship between two variables can be nonlinear (i.e., not a straight line).

of the slope for a linear curve, let us go back to the price–quantity relationship observed for work gloves referred to earlier. The slope of the linear curve plotted in Figure 1.1 would be found by dividing the change in the values on the y or vertical axis by the corresponding change in the values on the x or horizontal axis. For example, as we move from point A to point B on this curve, we note that the price per pair of work gloves falls by $1 since we moved from $9 a pair to $8 a pair. The corresponding change in quantity of gloves sold per week was 10 pairs, or 30 pairs minus 20 pairs. The slope of this curve therefore would be

$$
\begin{aligned}
\text{slope} &= \text{change in price} \div \text{change in quantity} \\
&= \$1.00 \div 10 \text{ pairs} \\
&= \$0.10 \text{ per pair}
\end{aligned}
\tag{1.1}
$$

Thus the slope of this linear curve at *all* points along this curve is $0.10. A specific property of a linear curve (which you should prove to yourself by examining other points along the curve) is that its slope is the same between any two points (i.e., its slope is *constant*). This conclusion is not affected by whether the linear curve is downward sloping (an inverse relationship) as was the case in both Figure 1.1 and the solid linear curve in panel a of Figure 1.2, or is upward sloping (a direct relationship) as illustrated by the dashed linear curve in panel a.

Slopes of Nonlinear Curves

Figure 1.2 also illustrates two possible forms that nonlinear curves can take. The solid nonlinear curve in panel b, for example, rises at first, reaches a peak, and then begins to decline. Unlike the linear curve, a nonlinear curve will have different slopes at specific intervals along the curve. That is, the slope will be changing as you move along a nonlinear curve.

Because the slopes differ, economists prefer to discuss the slope *at a particular point.* The slope at a particular point along a nonlinear curve is equal to the slope of a line drawn *tangent* to the curve at that point.[4] Panel a in Figure 1.3 illustrates the point of tangency (point *A*) between this line and the original nonlinear curve. To calculate the slope at point *A,* you simply divide the change in the value per unit noted on the *y* axis from point *A* to point *B* by the corresponding change in quantity observed on the *x* axis.

A nonlinear curve has a property that a linear curve does not; it has either a *maximum point* or a *minimum point.* Panel b in Figure 1.3 illustrates the location of the maximum point (point *C*) for this particular nonlinear curve, and panel c illustrates the location of the minimum point (point *D*). The slope of these curves at the maximum (panel b) and minimum (panel

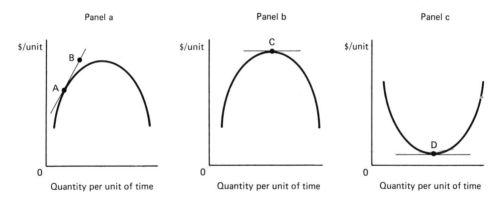

Figure 1.3 *Slope, Maximum, and Minimum Points of Nonlinear Curves.* Nonlinear relationships between two variables have several unique properties. For example, nonlinear curves will have different slopes at specific intervals along the curve. The slope at a particular point on a nonlinear curve can be found by drawing a line tangent to the nonlinear curve at that particular point (see point *A* in panel a) and then determine the slope of the line formed by points *A* and *B*. Nonlinear curves also frequently have maximum points, as illustrated panel b, and minimum points, as depicted in panel c.

[4]You should realize that every point on a nonlinear curve will have a *different* tangent line associated with it.

c) points in both cases is equal to *zero*. You can prove this to yourself by noting that the change in the value per unit at any point along these tangent lines is equal to zero.

Finally, you should realize that there are many kinds of nonlinear curves. Some may have both a maximum *and* a minimum point; in fact, they may have several.[5] Others may have neither. Two common nonlinear curves that have neither are illustrated in Figure 1.4. Panel a here shows a *nonlinear direct* relationship between *y* and *x*, and panel b shows a *nonlinear inverse* relationship between *y* and *x*. As you will note in subsequent chapters, a supply curve for a particular product frequently is illustrated like the nonlinear curve in panel a, while the demand curve takes on the form illustrated in panel b.

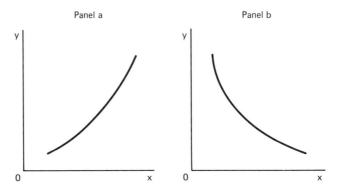

Figure 1.4 *Nonlinear Curves with No Maximum or Minimum Points.* Not all nonlinear curves have a maximum or a minimum point like those illustrated in Figure 1.3. Panel a illustrates a nonlinear *direct* relationship between two variables, and panel b illustrates a nonlinear *inverse* relationship between two variables. The nonlinear relationships depicted in panels a and b can be thought of as the nonlinear counterparts to the linear upward-sloping curve and linear downward-sloping curve depicted in Figure 1.2.

[5]We shall not stress such complex nonlinear curves in this text.

2

THE U.S. FOOD AND FIBER
SYSTEM

Farmers have played an important role in the development of the U.S. economy. Their efficient use of this country's resources in the early stages of its development freed labor and capital for use in other sectors of the economy. As the nonfarm business sectors of the economy developed, they began to supply farmers with machinery, improved seeds, fertilizer, and other manufactured resources. The tremendous technological advances embodied in these manufactured resources further enhanced the ability of farmers to supply raw agricultural products.

Farmers today are a highly integrated partner in the U.S. economy. Their ties to other sectors in the domestic economy include not only the markets where they sell their output, but also the financial markets where they invest in financial assets and borrow funds, the labor markets where they hire labor and seek off-farm employment, the manufactured input markets where they purchase chemicals, fertilizers, and equipment, and other markets as well. Farmers in the United States have also come to depend increasingly on foreign markets as outlets for specific commodities such as wheat and soybeans.

The purpose of this chapter is to (1) define the makeup of the "food and fiber system" in the United States, (2) acquaint you with recent trends in the structure and performance of farm businesses in general during the post-World War II period, and (3) describe briefly the nature of the other sectors comprising the food and fiber system as it relates to the markets in which they interact with farm businesses.

WHAT IS THE FOOD AND FIBER SYSTEM?

The term *agriculture* means different things to different people. Some might think solely of farm businesses when they use this term; others might include such "agribusiness" firms as Farmland Industries in their definition. In recent years, many agricultural economists have referred to the *food and fiber system* when describing the agricultural scene. The food and fiber system includes both farm and nonfarm businesses. Since we wish to distinquish between these two broad categories of firms and yet understand the relationship between them, we shall adopt the use of this term in this book.[1] *The food and fiber system therefore consists of those business entities that are involved in one fashion or another with the supply of food and fiber products to consumers.*

As Figure 2.1 suggests, the farm business sector, which represents an aggregation of firms that produce raw agricultural products, is one of four

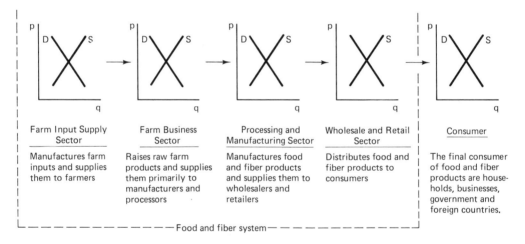

Figure 2.1 *The Food and Fiber System.* The food and fiber system consists of the farm input supply sector, the farm business sector, the processing and manufacturing sector, and the wholesale and retail sector. These sectors are linked together by a series of markets in which farmers purchase production inputs and sell their raw product to processors and manufacturers, which, in turn, create food and fiber products that are distributed to consumers in wholesale and retail markets. The symbols p and q represent the prices and quantities observed in each market. The solid lines denoted by D and S represent the traditional downward-sloping demand curve and upward-sloping supply curve, topics of discussion in future chapters.

[1] From time to time we shall use the term "agriculture" for ease of exposition. When this occurs, we are referring to the narrower focus identified above. namely, firms that produce raw food and fiber products.

principal sectors comprising the food and fiber system. Other sectors include such firms as John Deere, DeKalb Seed, and Ralston-Purina, which supply the goods and services farm businesses need to produce their product. Still other sectors include such firms as Swift and Green Giant, which use raw agricultural products as an input in their own manufacturing and processing operations, as well as such firms as Kroger and Safeway, which distribute the finished goods at the wholesale and retail level.

CHANGING COMPLEXION OF FARMING

Figure 2.1 defined the farm business sector to specifically *exclude* the activities of input suppliers as well as the activities of processors, wholesalers, and retailers. Although we shall discuss the nature of these other farm-related sectors later in this chapter (it would be incorrect to ignore them), our major focus is on the collective structure and performance of farm businesses, and on the changing complexion of farming activities in the United States. We can assess these attributes by examining recent trends in the (1) physical structure, (2) financial structure, (3) productivity, and (4) profitability of farm businesses in general.

Physical Structure

An examination of the *physical structure* of the farm business sector must necessarily focus on such things as the number and size of farm businesses, their ownership and control, and the ease of entry into the farm business sector.

Number and size of farms.   As Figure 2.2 illustrates, we have seen a trend toward fewer but larger farms during the post-World War II period. The number of farms has declined from 5.6 million in 1950 to about 2.4 million by the early eighties (U.S. Department of Agriculture, 1981). This represents a 50 percent decline in the number of farms in the last 30 or so years. The rate of decline in farm numbers slowed considerably during the seventies, however.

Where did the farmland go when these farms left the sector? Some 3 million acres are removed from the sector each year for nonagricultural uses.[2] About 1 million of these acres are considered to be prime farmland. This may appear to be an insignificant amount when we consider that there are still 413 million acres of cropland and another 127 million acres that could be converted to cropland. However, it is projected that we will need 462 million acres to meet demand by the year 2030. If the loss of prime

[2] U.S. Department of Agriculture, *National Agricultural Land Use Study–Final Report* (Washington, D.C.: U.S. Government Printing Office, 1981).

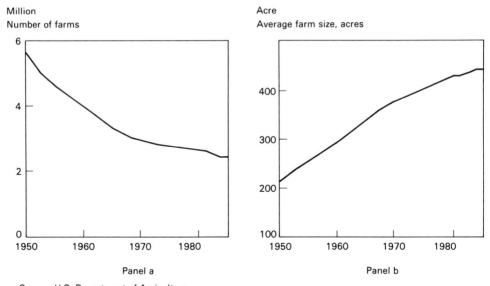

Source: U.S. Department of Agriculture.

Figure 2.2 *Trends in the Number and Average Size of Farms.* Two significant trends in the changing structure of the farm business sector is the declining number of farms and the rising average size of farms. Panel a shows that the number of farms in this country has declined from nearly 6 million farms in 1950 to roughly 2.5 million farms in the early eighties. Panel b shows that the average size of farm has roughly doubled during this period. This suggests that the land sold by farmers leaving the sector during this period has largely remained in agriculture.

farmland continues at 1 million acres per year, we would lose nearly 50 million acres by then. It is estimated that yields would have to increase by 1.1 percent per year to avoid being short of the cropland needed by 2030.

The majority of the land sold by farmers leaving the sector, however, is purchased by other farmers, who wish to expand their operations. The average farm size during the post–World War II period has doubled, from about 200 acres to over 400 acres per farm, as shown in panel b. National averages can, however, give a somewhat misleading picture of the physical structure of the farm business sector. For example, let us examine more closely the 400-acre-average-size statistic mentioned above. Roughly 250,000 farms in the United States have 50 acres or less, while approximately 150,000 farms have 1,000 acres or more.[3] Thus the 400-acre average cited above does not give an accurate representation of many of today's farming operations.

It is also interesting to note that the share of total farm receipts earned by the 50,000 *largest* farm businesses has been increasing over the last 30

[3] L. P. Schertz, "Farming in the United States," in Penn et al. (1979).

years. These farm businesses accounted for 36 percent of total sales in the early eighties compared to 30 percent in 1967 and only 23 percent in 1960. This is an amazing statistic when you stop to consider that these 50,000 farms represent only *2 percent* of the total number of farms in this country.[4] These farms have average assets totaling over $1 million. They also receive the majority of all direct government payments. The data above suggest, therefore, that *a large share of the resources and production is concentrated in a relatively small number of large farming operations.*

Tenure and business organization.   There have also been some interesting trends in the tenure relationships in agriculture. For example, while the number of full owners, part owners (they own part and rent part of the land they farm), and full tenants have been declining, there are now more part owners than full tenants. Both part owners and full tenants on average operate larger farms than do full owners. In the early eighties, for example, part owners on average operated farms about *three times the size* of those operated by full owners.

Corporate farming has attracted much attention in the press in recent years. As the data presented in Table 2.1 indicate, farm corporations play a minor role in the production of some food and fiber products (e.g., grain and dairy products) but a relatively important role in others (e.g., nursery and forest products, vegetables, and fruits and nuts). Family farm corporations, which are farm businesses that have been incorporated primarily for estate planning purposes, are shown in Table 2.1 to far outnumber the other forms of farm corporations. It is interesting to note, however, that while publicly held corporations active in farming—the corporate form people express the most concern about—are small in number, they do account for one-half of the total output produced by farm corporations. Thus, while small in number, publicly held corporations represent relatively large operations.

When *all* types of business organizations are taken into account, Table 2.1 shows that farm corporations are relatively small in number. Individuals or sole proprietors represent by far the major form of business organization in the farm business sector. These sole proprietors also control the majority of U.S. farmland and contribute the largest share to the sector's total output. As Table 2.1 suggests, however, the average size of publicly held corporations is almost 10 times greater than the average sole proprietorship.

The specter of foreigners investing in U.S. farmland has also received a lot of coverage in the press in recent years. Foreigners, however, hold only 13.5 million acres or slightly more than 1 percent of the approximately 1.25 billion acres of privately owned cropland, pastureland, and forestland in this country (U.S. Department of Agriculture, 1981). Foreign-owned farmland equals or exceeds 1 percent of the privately owned acreage in only nine states. These states are concentrated primarily in the West and South.

[4] Ibid.

Percentage of total output produced:			
Cattle	33		
Dairy products	6		
Fruits and nuts	32		
Grain production	5		
Nursery and forest products	60		
Poultry	28		
Vegetables	37		

Percentage distribution of alternative forms of farm corporations:	Number	Sales
Nonfamily privately held corporations	21	31
Family farm corporations	76	50
Publicly held corporations	3	19
	100	100

Percentage distribution of alternative forms of business organizations:	Number	Acres	Sales
Farm corporations	2	11	18
Sole proprietorships	89	75	67
Partnerships	9	14	15
	100	100	100

Source: L.P. Schertz, "Farming in the United States," *Structure Issues of American Agriculture,* USDA ERS Agricultural Economics Report 438 (Washington, D.C.: U.S. Government Printing Office, November 1979).

TABLE 2.1 RELATIVE IMPORTANCE OF CORPORATE FARMING. Corporate farms play a relatively minor role in the production of grain and dairy products. They are a significant producer of nursery, fruit, and vegetable products, however. Most corporate farms are small privately held corporations rather than large publicly held corporations. Farm corporations represent only 2 percent of the total number of farms, farm 11 percent of the total land in farms in this country, and account for 18 percent of total farm output.

Capital versus labor.   While the amount of land farmed in the United States has remained relatively stable over time, we have witnessed a large expansion in the use on farms of such manufactured resources as machinery and chemicals. Embodied in these resources are new technologies which have enabled farmers to expand their production substantially over time. For example, there has been a substantial increase in tractor horsepower on farms during the post–World War II period. A surprising statistic to some is the fact

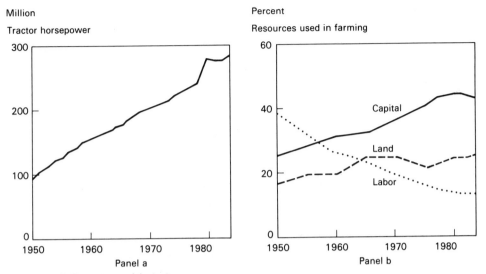

Panel a

Panel b

Source: U.S. Department of Agriculture.

Figure 2.3 *Changing Use of Resources in Farming Activities.* There has been a rapid expansion of the use of manufactured resources (capital) in the farm business sector during the post–World War II period. The new technologies embodied in these resources have enabled farmers to raise their output while cutting back on their use of human resources (labor). The contribution of farmland has been relatively constant during this period.

that there is an aggregate of almost twice as much buildings and machinery per worker in agriculture as there is for businesses in general. Fertilizer use has increased more than fivefold during this same period. Thus farming is a highly capital-intensive business activity.

In sharp contrast to the increased use of manufactured resources in the farm business sector is the *declining relative contribution of labor.* While manufacturerd resources increased in relative terms, Figure 2.3 shows that labor declined. Labor accounted for almost 40 percent of the value of all resources used in farming activities in 1950 but fell below 15 percent by the end of the seventies. Most farms today rely solely on the farm operator family as a source of labor; that is, little hired labor is used.

This shift in the relative use of capital and labor reflects (1) the changing relative productivity of these resources and (2) their relative prices. Improvements in farm machinery have led to an increase in production per unit of labor input, and have fostered the growth of large-scale, specialized farms.[5]

[5] Specialization in the production of farm commodities has become increasingly apparent during the post–World War II period. This has come about primarily as the result of the development of capital-intensive, specialized production technologies and government programs that have reduced the need for farm diversification as a method of reducing exposure to risk. For a further discussion, see David H. Harrington et al. (1983).

A farmer can cover more acreage today than ever before. In the early eighties, for example, farmers—who comprise only 3 percent of the nation's total civilian labor force—were producing enough output to feed our nation's population and still have enough left over to account for 20 percent of our nation's total export revenue.

Advances in machinery technology as well as achievements in farm chemicals have affected regional production patterns as well as once-conventional cropping practices. For example, farmers used to practice crop rotation and diversification to conserve their soil and control pests. Now farm chemicals allow farmers to grow one crop exclusively year after year. Disease-control techniques have also allowed livestock farms to specialize in one particular type of livestock and to utilize confinement production practices.

Hired farm labor continues to represent a significant production resource in areas where fruit and vegetable production are extensive, although some substitution of capital for labor (i.e., greater use of manufactured resources and less reliance on human resources) has taken place here as well.

Water. In the early eighties, approximately 50 million acres of cropland in the United States were irrigated (U.S. Department of Agriculture, 1981). Most of this land was harvested cropland (e.g., cotton, vegetables, fruits), but there were several million acres of irrigated pastureland as well. Almost one-half of the acreage irrigated with on-farm-pumped water was pumped using electricity as a source of power. Other sources of energy used to pump water include natural gas and diesel fuel. The rising cost of energy in the seventies, however, had an adverse affect on the cost of production for those farmers operating pump-irrigated farmland, forcing some to leave farming.

Some of the critical water problems facing agriculture in the eighties will include (1) inadequate surface water, particularly in the Great Plains and Southwest; (2) an overdraft of groundwater in key agricultural states (e.g., California, Texas, Illinois, Wisconsin, and North Carolina); (3) water pollution in all states; and (4) water-caused erosion and sedimentation in the East and parts of Utah, Arizona, and New Mexico. With respect to the groundwater overdraft occurring in key geographical areas, it is likely that pump-irrigated cropping practices will be sharply curtailed due to increasing costs (including rising energy prices) and depleted groundwater stocks.

Energy. Farm uses of energy accounted for approximately 2.5 percent of all energy used in the United States in 1980.[6] Thus the farm business sector is a relatively insignificant user of energy compared with other types of businesses and households. About 37 percent of the energy utilized in raising food and fiber products was in the form of petrochemicals (i.e., pesticides

---

[6] D. L. Van Dyne, R. D. Reinsel, T. J. Lutton, and J. A. Barton, "Energy Use and Energy Policy," in Penn et al. (1979).

and fertilizers). Another 22 percent is consumed through the operation of farm machinery.

The fifties and sixties represented a period of relatively low costs for energy and fertilizer. As a result, a farm business sector has evolved which is an intensive user of these products and manufacturerd resources in general. All of this began to change in 1973–1974. The OPEC oil embargo, coupled with the national economic policies in existence at that time, had a substantial effect on the prices farmers had to pay for oil and other energy-related products. The future energy price increases some experts forecast for the mid-eighties, if not accompanied by increases in the prices for raw and food and fiber products, will have a depressing effect on net farm income. This, if it occurs, could lead to fewer and larger farms in those areas most suitable for the use of energy-efficient manufactured resources and alter the production choices of farmers in those regions currently utilizing pump-irrigation practice.

Barriers to entry. The cost and availability of resources utilized in farming activities can represent a barrier to entry for would-be farmers, as will other factors that influence the number and size of farms. Technology is one example. Technological advances that allow farmers to operate larger acreages add to the competition for farmland, thereby placing upward pressures on land prices. Higher land values, together with higher prices for capital embodying new technologies, increase the capital needed to start an adequate-sized farm and thus may bar entry into the sector for some potential farmers. The expected low returns to effort during a new entrant's early years in farming, as well as the existence of risk and uncertainty, also discourage entry. Inheritance continues to ease the problems of entry for some. More than 80 percent of today's farmers inherited farm property from their parents.[7]

Productivity

Earlier we said that the total quantity of resources used in producing raw agricultural products has remained relatively stable during the post–World War II period. In contrast, column (1) in Table 2.2 indicates that the total output of raw agricultural products in 1982 represented an 88 percent increase over the level of output achieved in 1950 [i.e., 0.88 = (139 − 74) ÷ 74]. Total output of crops, shown in column (2), increased by 103 percent during this period [i.e., 1.03 = (154 − 76) ÷ 76], while total livestock and livestock products, shown in column (6), increased by 51 percent [i.e., 0.51 = (113 − 75) ÷ 75]. Thus *productivity,* or the *level of output per unit of input,* in the

---

[7] J. B. Penn, "The Structure of Agriculture: An Overview of the Issue," in Penn et al. (1979).

Year	Farm output						Productivity indicator	
		Crop[a]				Live-stock and prod-ucts[a]	Farm output per unit of total input	Crop pro-duction per acre[d]
	Total[b]	Total[c]	Feed grains	Food grains	Oil crops			
	(1)	(2)	(3)	(4)	(5)	(6)	(7)	(8)
1929	53	62	48	52	11	53	52	56
1940	60	67	52	52	29	60	60	62
1950	74	76	64	65	46	75	71	68
1960	91	93	87	87	68	87	90	89
1970	101	100	89	91	117	105	102	102
1971	110	112	116	107	121	106	110	112
1972	110	113	112	102	131	107	110	115
1973	112	119	115	114	155	105	111	116
1974	106	110	93	120	127	106	105	104
1975	114	121	114	142	153	101	115	112
1976	117	121	120	141	132	105	115	111
1977	119	129	126	132	175	106	114	116
1978	122	131	135	125	182	106	116	121
1979	129	144	148	144	219	109	119	129
1980	123	130	122	158	173	114	115	115
1981	140	150	152	190	200	116	131	131
1982	139	154	156	185	221	113	132	135

[a]Gross production.
[b]Farm output measures the annual volume of net farm production available for eventual human use through sales from farms or consumption in farm households.
[c]Includes items not included in groups shown.
[d]Computed from variable weights for individual crops produced each year.
Source: U.S. Department of Agriculture.

TABLE 2.2 FARM OUTPUT AND PRODUCTIVITY. The productivity or level of farm output per unit of farm input has increased sharply during the post–World War II period. Column (7) shows that farm output per unit of input has risen 77 percent since 1950. Yields per crop acre, another measure of productivity, have risen 94 percent over the same period. One reason for this rising productivity has been the technological advances embodied in farm inputs (e.g., new seed varieties and labor-saving manufactured inputs) which have either boosted farm output or reduced input requirements.

farm business sector has increased rather dramatically during the post–World War II period.

We can illustrate these productivity gains in several ways. For example, column (7) in Table 2.2 reports the index of farm output per unit of farm inputs. This index shows that the productivity of the farm business sector was 86 percent higher in 1982 than it was in 1950 [i.e., 0.86 = (132 – 71) ÷ 71]. The index of crop production per acre can also be used to highlight trends in the productivity of crop production activities. Column (8) in Table 2.2 shows that this index was 99 percent higher in 1981 than it was in 1950 [i.e., 0.99 = (135 – 68) ÷ 68]. The index reflects both the productivity of the land as well as the changing productivities and amounts of other inputs used with land to produce crops. Year-to-year variations in this index, as was the case for the index of crop output, reflect unusual weather patterns in addition to other factors. For example, the unusual weather experienced in 1974 (wet spring dry summer, early frost) had a disastrous effect on feed grain and oilseed crops. This, in turn, lowered both of the measures of productivity discussed above in that particular year.

Profitability

Gross income from farming activities and related production expenses were relatively stagnant from the mid-fifties to the early seventies. Beginning in 1972, however, gross income from farming activities has risen erratically while production expenses have risen steadily. This variability has led to volatile shifts in net farm income from the mid-seventies through the early eighties. Panel a in Figure 2.4 shows the sharp increase in both gross *and* net income in 1973. After 1973, production expenses began to increase persistently due in part to the rising prices for petroleum and rising interest rates on loan funds. This resulted in lower levels of net farm income in the late seventies and early eighties. If we adjusted the levels of net farm income in 1982 and 1983 for the effects of inflation, we would see that the *purchasing power* of these net income figures would be the lowest experienced since the depression years of the thirties. The levels of net farm income adjusted for inflation since 1965 are illustrated in panel b of Figure 2.3.

The off-farm income earned by farm families has increased steadily during the last several decades. In 1983, for example, off-farm income raised the average family income of all farmers taken together above the national median family income. Off-farm income constituted almost 70 percent of total farm family income that year. Again, national totals can be somewhat misleading. Much of this off-farm income is earned by farm operator families operating smaller farms, where one or more family members have a full-time job in the city.

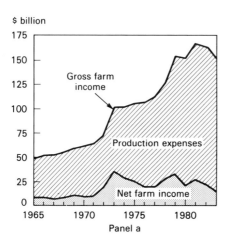

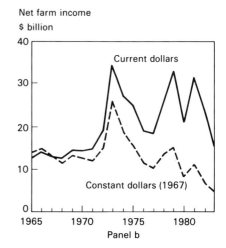

Panel a   Panel b

Source: U.S. Department of Agriculture

Figure 2.4 *Income from Farming Activities.* One of the key economic statistics watched by both policymakers and farmers is net farm income. This value, in turn, is affected by what is happening to gross farm income and farm production expenses (net farm income is equal to gross farm income minus farm production expenses). The purchasing power of net farm income, illustrated in panel b by the dashed line, reflects what today's net farm income would have been able to purchase in 1967. Thus we see that farmers are able to buy fewer goods and services with their net farm income in the early eighties than they were able to purchase in the mid-sixties.

Finally, let us compare the returns on investment in farm business assets with the returns on investment in the stock market. The annual average earnings from investments in farming of 4.7 percent during the seventies represented a 35 percent increase over the annual earnings rate one decade earlier:

	Annual earnings	Capital gains
Farm business assets		
The sixties	3.46	4.53
The seventies	4.69	11.59
Common stock		
The sixties	3.19	6.99
The seventies	3.92	0.72

The annual average capital gains on farm assets (e.g., appreciation of farmland values) of 11.6 percent during the seventies was also substantially above the 4.5 percent average achieved during the sixties.[8] A comparison of the returns to capital in farming with the returns to capital in common stock underscores the relative adverse trend in capital gains on common stock during the seventies.[9] While the total returns to capital invested in common stock were higher in the sixties than on capital invested in farming, the returns during the seventies were considerably lower. *This relative profitability of capital in farming helps explain the investment in farmland by both farm and nonfarm investors during the seventies.* This picture appears substantially less bright for the eighties given the reduced annual earnings achieved thus far as well as the declines in farmland values observed in many areas. In contrast, the returns on investment in the stock market have been relatively favorable in the early eighties.

Financial Structure

The financial structure of farm businesses in general can be assessed by examining the balance sheet for the farm business sector (U.S. Department of Agriculture, *Economic Indicators of the Farm Sector*). This balance sheet, which is published each year by the U.S. Department of Agriculture, indicates the value of the real estate assets (i.e., farmland and buildings) and non-real estate assets (i.e., machinery, trucks, and crop and livestock inventories) on farms as well as the financial assets and liabilities of farm businesses. Table 2.3 presents these balance sheet items for selected years during the 1950–1984 period. Examining this table, we see that real estate represents a somewhat larger proportion of the total value of all farm business assets today (76 percent) than it did in 1950 (62 percent). On the other hand, financial assets represent a smaller proportion of total farm assets (4 percent) today than they did in 1950 (9 percent). Turning to farm debt, we see that real estate debt is almost 22 times larger today than it was in 1950, while non-real estate debt is 15 times larger. Net worth, which is equal to total assets minus total debt, has grown almost eight times larger than the $94.6 billion recorded in 1950. This consists largely of the gains in land values accruing

[8] In doing so, it is important to recognize that returns on investment take two forms: (1) annual net earnings generated by use of the assets, and (2) capital gains income that would be earned if the asset were sold when its current market value exceeded its original purchase price less any accumulated depreciation where applicable. The annual dividend rate on common stock, for example, represents the annual earnings on investment in these assets. The annual earnings on investment in a farm business is found by dividing net farm income by the farmer's net worth tied up in these assets. The capital gains rate on both types of assets can be approximated by dividing the sales price minus the asset's original cost and accumulated depreciation (where applicable) by the farmer's net worth tied up in these assets.

[9] Schertz, op. cit.

Year	Real estate assets	Non-real estate assets	Financial assets	Total assets	Real estate debt	Non-real estate debt	Net worth
1950	65.5	31.3	9.1	105.8	4.7	6.5	94.6
1960	120.1	42.2	10.4	172.9	10.6	11.9	150.4
1970	194.2	62.8	13.6	270.5	26.2	22.7	221.6
1971	201.2	64.4	14.5	280.2	27.4	23.2	229.7
1972	216.4	71.2	15.5	303.0	29.1	23.6	247.7
1973	241.8	83.0	16.8	341.4	31.7	28.5	281.2
1974	297.1	103.9	18.0	418.9	35.8	32.3	350.8
1975	326.9	96.9	18.2	442.1	40.5	35.3	366.3
1976	381.0	108.8	20.4	510.2	45.1	40.0	425.1
1977	453.5	115.2	21.8	590.6	50.3	46.5	493.8
1978	507.6	127.0	22.5	657.1	57.8	56.8	542.3
1979	600.9	158.0	25.5	784.4	65.4	66.3	652.7
1980	695.1	185.7	28.1	909.0	78.4	76.6	754.1
1981	762.5	193.5	30.2	986.1	87.7	82.4	816.1
1982	754.6	192.9	32.3	979.8	97.0	91.5	791.3
1983	709.2	200.1	34.7	944.0	100.8	102.0	741.2
1984	705.2	187.0	36.4	928.6	102.8	98.1	727.6

Note: Values in billions of dollars.

Source: U.S. Department of Agriculture.

TABLE 2.3 BALANCE SHEET OF THE FARM BUSINESS SECTOR. The value of farm real estate assets (e.g., farmland and buildings) and non-real estate assets (e.g., farm machinery and equipment) has risen dramatically during the 1950–1981 period. Much of the rise in real estage assets is attributable to the appreciation of farmland values during this period. Farm holdings of financial assets (e.g., checking account balances and savings accounts) continue to represent a small proportion of total farm assets according to published U.S. Department of Agriculture reports. Loans to buy real estate and non-real estate farm assets have also risen sharply over this period, increasing some 22-fold and 15-fold, respectively. The primary factor explaining the rising net worth (i.e., total assets minus total debt) during this period was the appreciation of farmland values reflected in the first column of this table. The declines in farmland values and net worth since 1981 reflect the declining economic conditions in the farm business sector.

to landowners.[10] Finally, the declines in real estate values coupled with continued growth in farm debt contribute to the declines in net worth shown in Table 2.3 since 1981.

The aggregated balance sheet presented in Table 2.3 can be disaggregated by size of farm (i.e., gross sales) to illustrate further, the financial

[10] Approximately 70 percent of these capital gains accrue to farm owner-operators, while the remaining 30 percent accrue to nonoperator landlords, or those who own farmland but do not farm it themselves.

structure of the farm business sector. Figure 2.5 illustrates the growth of farm assets and debt during the seventies for five different sizes of farms. Although all sizes of farms exhibited growth in their total assets, farms in the "$40,000–$99,999" category and the $100,000 and over" category gained a larger share of the sector's total assets.

Lumping the two largest size categories together for the moment, it is interesting to note that farms with over $40,000 in gross sales represent only 19 percent of the total number of farms in the sector. Yet these farms account for slightly more than one-half of all farm business assets in the sector. Furthermore, these farm businesses account for over 70 percent of the sector's total farm debt outstanding and over 80 percent of the total equity in farming assets.[11]

The growth in farm debt during the seventies and early eighties and subsequent declines in net farm income has resulted in severe cash flow stress for highly indebted farmers. The USDA estimated in 1985 that 6.3 percent of all farms were insolvent. Another 7.4 percent are moving rapidly toward insolvency. The USDA also showed that one-third of all farmers owned over two-thirds of all farm debt.

Summary

This section illustrated the changes that have taken place in the structure and performance of the farm business sector during the post–World War II period. It was shown, for example, that there has been a trend toward fewer but larger farms. Today, a large share of the resources and production is concentrated on a relatively small number of large farms. Farmers have increasingly been renting land from nonfarm landlords when expanding the size of their farming operations. The use of manufactured resources has also increased in the sector, while the relative use of labor has declined. These changes reflect farmers' desire to take advantage of the technological progress embodied in capital and to avoid the relatively high cost of hired labor. The high cost of acquiring the necessary capital to begin farming, however, increasingly represents a barrier to entry for some would-be farmers.

Productivity, or the level of output per unit of input, has also increased dramatically during the post–World War II period. In contrast, net farm income, particularly after accounting for inflation, has been extremely variable, reaching all-time highs in the early seventies and depression-level lows in the early eighties. Finally, trends in the financial structure of farmers in general show a decline in the proportion of farmers' total assets accounted for by financial assets. This suggests a declining liquidity in the sector, or ability of farmers to cover their current liabilities quickly without disrupting the ongoing nature of their business.

[11] For a further discussion of the sector's financial structure, see D. A. Lins, "Credit Availability Effects on the Structure of Farming," in Penn et al. (1979).

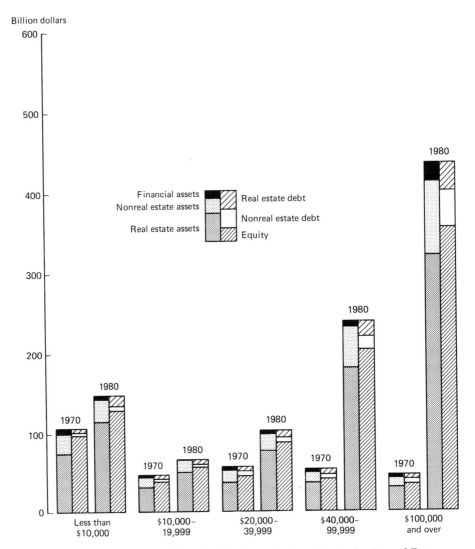

Figure 2.5 *Balance Sheet for the Farm Business Sector by Size of Farm.* Although all size-of-farm categories illustrated above exhibited growth during the decade of the seventies, the greatest growth was recorded by farms in the larger size categories. For example, total assets of farms in the "$100,000 and over" gross sales category were less than total assets on farms in most other categoreis. By the end of this decade, however, this situation had changed dramatically. While part of this "growth" can be explained by rising price levels, it also underscores the growing size of farms in the sector, as indicated in Figure 2.2.

OTHER SECTORS IN THE FOOD AND FIBER SYSTEM

It should be clear from the wide fluctuations in net farm income during the seventies and early eighties that the farm business sector is directly affected by the economic health of the rest of the economy, both domestic and foreign. In turn, the nonfarm business sectors in the food and fiber system illustrated in Figure 2.1 are also dependent on a healthy farm business sector. Farm input suppliers such as John Deere Company and the duPont Chemical Company, for example, are dependent on a healthy farm business sector for a strong market for their products. Similarly, food processors and manufacturers are dependent on the farm business sector for inputs to their production processes.

In Figure 2.1 we distinguished between farm businesses and other businesses involved in supplying food and fiber products to consumers. Let us look more closely now at some of the characteristics of the *other* firms involved in the U.S. food and fiber system.

Farm Input Suppliers

Farm input suppliers play an important role in providing farmers with the inputs they need in their farming operations. In 1981, for example, total sales of manufacturing inputs by farm input suppliers to the farm business sector totaled $74.1 billion. There are four broad categories of farm input suppliers: (1) the feed manufacturing industry, (2) the fertilizer industry, (3) the agricultural chemical industry, and (4) the farm machinery and equipment industry. Feed manufacturing represents the largest farm input supply industry. Of the some 6,500 feed manufacturing firms in the United States, 26 percent are cooperatives.[12] Perhaps the most dramatic structural change in this industry has been the movement of some feed manufacturers into direct participation in poultry production. Whereas broiler production used to be prevalent on a large number of farms operating on a small scale, feed manufacturers have helped foster large-scale, highly capitalized systems. The result has been a more standardized, less expensive product to consumers.

Conglomerate firms producing a wide variety of products are found in the fertilizer industry (e.g., petroleum producers and refiners as well as chemical companies). This industry from time to time during the sixties and seventies experienced either an excess supply of fertilizer products and falling prices, or input shortages and rising prices. This industry is fairly competitive, although less so than the feed manufacturing industry (see Table 2.4). In the late seventies, for example, the top four firms producing nitrogen accounted for only one-fourth of the market. The top four firms producing potash, however, accounted for slightly over one-half of the market. A similar market share was noted for manufacturers of phosphate fertilizer.

[12] L. G. Hamm, "Farm Inputs Industries and Farm Structure," in Penn et al. (1979).

| | Market share (%) | |
Input	Four largest firms	Eight largest firms
Fertilizer	35	45
Hybrid corn	57	71
Pesticides	57	79
Tractors		
Two-wheel drive	80	na
Four-wheel drive	68	na
Combines	83	na

Note: na, not available.

Source: R. F. Leibenluft, *Competition in Farm Inputs; Examination of Four Industries,*
Federal Trade Commission (Washington, D.C.: U.S. Government Printing Office,
February 1981).

TABLE 2.4 MARKET CONCENTRATION FOR SELECTED FARM INPUTS. The
markets for most manufactured inputs used in agriculture are characterized on the supply
side by a small number of firms accounting for a large proportion of total sales. For
example, 83 percent of total combine sales were accounted for by the four largest manufacturers of combines. Other manufactured products, such as fertilizer, are somewhat
more competitive. In general, however, in these input markets farmers are confronted
by sellers who have a great deal of market power in setting the price for their product.

The agricultural chemicals industry is also characterized by conglomer-
ates which produce a wide variety of chemical products. A prime example is
DuPont, which manufactures a variety of non-farm-oriented products
(e.g., paints) in addition to their line of agricultural chemical products. The
concentration of firms in this industry is apparently quite high. For example,
the four leading brands of corn insecticide accounted for over three-fourths
of total sales in the late seventies.[13]
The farm machinery and equipment industry is comprised of some
rather large firms that offer a full line of machinery and a somewhat more
diverse group of manufacturers that supply specialized equipment (e.g., irrigation equipment, grain-handling equipment, etc.). In the late seventies, for
example, about 80 percent of all two-wheel-drive tractor and nearly the same
proportion of all combined sales were accounted for by the four top firms.
Thus farm businesses are confronted by sellers who have a great deal of market power in the markets in which farmers purchase most of their production inputs. This generally means that farmers are "price takers" rather than
"price setters" in these markets.

[13] Ibid.

USDA Photo

The food and fiber system is the nation's largest employer, with nearly 23 million people working in agriculturally related jobs. Furthermore, it accounts for 20 percent of our gross national product. In addition to the input supply sector, processors such as the food canning operation depicted above and manufacturers play an important role in transforming raw agricultural products into their final form for distribution to consumers. These sectors as well as the food wholesaling and retailing sectors are characterized by a small number of large firms accounting for a significant fraction of total industry sales. The 50 largest food manufacturing firms, for example, own almost two-thirds of the total food manufacturing assets in this country.

Food Manufacturers and Retailers

The majority of marketed farm output is utilized as an input by food manufacturers.[14] The farm value of domestically produced food totaled $83.5 billion in 1982. Sales by grocery retailers accounted for about two-thirds of the $276.6 billion in expenditures on domestically produced food by consumers in 1982. Thus food manufacturing and retailing represent the major channel for the marketing of farm products.

Farm businesses are confronted by rather powerful buyers when marketing their output. In the late seventies, for example, the 50 largest food manufacturing firms owned almost two-thirds of all food manufacturing as-

[14] J. M. Connor, "Manufacturing and Food Retailing," in Penn et al. (1979).

sets. These firms accounted for three-fourths of total media advertisements and nearly all of network television advertisement for these products. Concentration was particularly high in industries marketing such products as breakfast cereals, beer, candy, and soft drinks. In contrast to other industries, where the number of firms is increasing, the number of food manufacturing firms has been decreasing. This has been accomplished in part through mergers and acquisitions of smaller firms by the industry leaders.

Food retailing has also showed increased concentration of production during the post-World War II period (Marion et al., 1979). "Mom and Pop" grocery stores have given way to large supermarket and convenience store chains. The number of grocery stores, for example, has declined by almost 40 percent since the early fifties. The chain stores, by combining wholesaling, retailing, and (in some cases) processing operations, were able to lower their costs and price the smaller independent stores out of business. In 1980, for example, companies with 11 or more stores accounted for approximately one-half of all retail foods store sales. The dominance of chain eating establishments was less evident (less than one-fourth of the market).

SUMMARY

The purpose of this chapter was to acquaint you with the structure and performance of the farm business sector during the post–World War II period and its role in the nation's food and fiber system. The major points made in this chapter can be summarized as follows:

1. The U.S. *food and fiber system* consists of different groups of business entities called *sectors*, which are in one way or another associated with the supply of food and fiber products to consumers. The *farm business sector,* which consists of firms that produce raw agricultural products, is one of four sectors comprising the U.S. food and fiber system. The other three sectors include firms that supply manufactured inputs to farm businesses, firms that process raw food and fiber products, and firms that distribute food and fiber products to consumers.

2. Among the physical structural changes taking place in the farm business sector during the post–World War II period is the trend toward fewer but larger farms. We have also seen a tremendous expansion in the use of manufactured inputs such as machinery and chemicals and a decline in labor use. Rising capital requirements in general during this period have increasingly represented a *barrier to entry* for would-be farmers.

3. While the total quantity of inputs used in producing raw agricultural products has remained relatively stable during the post–World War II period, the total quantity of output increased substantially. These

results taken together imply an increase in *productivity,* or the ratio of output to inputs.

4. Gross farm income has increased erratically during the post–World War II period, while production expenses increased steadily. The result is a highly variable level of profits, or *profitability,* from one year to the next. During the early eighties, net farm income after adjustments for the *purchasing power of money* fell to depression-era levels.

5. The financial structure of the farm business sector during the post–World War II period shows that financial assets represent a considerably smaller portion of total farm business assets now than was true 20–30 years ago. The use of loan funds to finance farm business expansion over this period has increased substantially.

6. The sectors of the food and fiber system that supply inputs to farm businesses and process their output are characterized by a relatively high proportion of market sales accounted for by a relatively small number of firms.

DEFINITION OF TERMS

Food and fiber system: consists of business entities that are involved in one way or another with the supply of food and fiber products to consumers.

Farm business sector: one of the sectors comprising the food and fiber system is the farm business sector. This sector represents an aggregation of firms that produce raw agricultural products (i.e., farms and ranches).

Balance sheet: a financial statement reporting the value of real estate (land and buildings), non-real estate (machinery, breeding livestock, and inventories), and financial (cash, checking account balance, and common stock) assets owned by farm businesses as well as these firms' debt outstanding. The difference between total farm assets and total farm debt outstanding represents the firms' net worth.

Purchasing power: the purchasing power of money reflects what $1 today would have purchased in goods and services in a particular base period. Inflation is said to erode the purchasing power of money over time.

Asset: something of value *owned* by a farm business. Assets are generally divided into either (1) physical and financial assets, or (2) current (short-term) and fixed (intermediate- and long-term) assets.

Liability: a liability or debt outstanding refers to the amount *owed* by the farm business to others.

Gross farm income: annual level of income received from farming activities before farm expenses, taxes, and withdrawals have been deducted.

Net farm income: gross farm income minus farm expenses and taxes.

Constant dollars: the valuation of assets and income in terms of some base period's prices (i.e., 1967) as opposed to today's prices (see also purchasing power).

Current dollars: the valuation of assets and income in terms of current or this year's prices as opposed to some base period's prices.

Productivity: level of output per unit of input. Crop yields per acre are a measure of productivity.

Technological change: also referred to as technical change and technical progress, technological change reduces the quantity of inputs required to produce a given level of output.

Profitability: returns on capital invested in farm business assets represents a measure of profitability. Profitability may be expressed in dollar terms (i.e., net farm income) or in percentage terms (i.e., rate of return on farm capital).

Capital gains: the gain in the value of an asset (sales price minus basis for tax purposes). This gain is considered a capital gain rather than as ordinary income if the asset is held for a specific length of time (usually 12 months).

Structure: the composition or makeup of a sector can be assessed by examining its physical and financial structure. Physical structure is assessed by looking at such things as the number and size of farms, their ownership and control, and the ease of entry and exit from the sector. Financial structure is evaluated by looking at the composition of a sector's balance sheet.

Performance: the efficiency and profitability of a farm business's production activities are typical barometers of a sector's performance.

Concentration: refers to the number and market power of firms marketing their products in a particular market. A market characterized by a small number of firms accounting for the majority of total sales is said to have a high degree of concentration.

REFERENCES

HARRINGTON, DAVID H., DONN A. REIMUND, KENNETH H. BAUM, and R. NEAL PETERSON, *U.S. Farming in the Early 1980's: Production and Financial Structure,* ERS-USDA, Agricultural Economics Report 504, September 1983.

MARION, B. W., et al., *The Food Retailing Industry: Structure, Profits and Prices*. New York: Praeger Publishers, 1979.

PENN, J. B., et al., *Structure Issues of American Agriculture*, U. S. Department of Agriculture, Agricultural Economic Report 438, November 1979.

U.S. Department of Agriculture, *Economic Indicators of the Farm Sector, Income and Balance Sheet Statistics*, ERS-USDA Statistical Bulletin Series. Washington, D.C.: U.S. Government Printing Office, selected issues.

U.S. Department of Agriculture, *Agricultural Statistics*. Washington, D.C.: U.S. Government Printing Office, 1981.

ADDITIONAL READINGS

BREIMYER, H. F., and WALLACE BARR, "Issues in Concentration versus Dispersion," in *Who Will Control U.S. Agriculture?*, North Central Regional Extension Publication 32. Urbana, Ill. University of Illinois, 1972, pp. 13–22.

BROOKS, R. C., "Structure and Performance of the U.S. Broiler Industry," in *Farm Structure*. Washington, D.C.: Committee on Agriculture, Nutrition and Forestry, U.S. Senate, April 1980, p. 197.

HEFFERMAN, W. D., "Agriculture Structure and the Community," in *Can the Family Farm Survive*, Special Report 219. Columbia, Mo.: University of Missouri, 1972, pp. 481–499.

LEIBENLUFT, R. F., *Competition in Farm Inputs: An Examination of Four Industries*, Federal Trade Commission. Washington, D.C.: U.S. Government Printing Office, February 1981.

RHODES, J. V., and L. R. KYLE, "A Corporate Agriculture," in *Who Will Control U.S. Agriculture?*, North Central Regional Extension Publication 32. Urbana, Ill.: University of Illinois, 1972.

U.S. Department of Agriculture, *A Time to Choose: Summary Report on the Structure of Agriculture*. Washington, D.C.: U.S. Government Printing Office, pp. 38–39.

U.S. Department of Agriculture, *National Agricultural Land Use Study—Final Report*. Washington, D.C.: U.S. Government Printing Office, 1981.

QUESTIONS

1. Describe the relationship between the farm business sector and the other sectors that make up the U.S. food and fiber system.

2. What has happened to the number and average size of farms during the post–World War II period? What is the significance of the fact that about 1 million acres of prime farmland are lost each year to nonagricultural uses?

3. How significant is corporate activity in the production of raw agricultural products? What is the predominant form of business organization found in the farm business sector?

4. Describe the trends in the use of manufactured resources in the farm business sector during the post–World War II period. What has happened to the role played by labor during this period? Why?

5. Describe the meaning and measurement of productivity.

6. Describe the concentration of market power in the markets in which the farm business sector buys its inputs and sells its products. What effect is this likely to have on the sector's ability to influence the prices they pay and receive?

ADVANCED TOPICS

Two advanced topics are covered in this section. The first topic has to do with the development and interpretation of an *index*. The second topic pertains to the difference between *current dollars and constant dollars*.

What Is an Index?

Table 2.2 reported trends in output and productivity through the aid of index values. An *index* is nothing more than a percentage comparison from a fixed point of reference or benchmark. By comparing, say, output of wheat in ensuing years with a benchmark output, economists can describe how much wheat output has increased or decreased relative to the benchmark or *base period*.

The index value for wheat output in year 1 (i.e., the first year after the base year, which is year 0) is found as follows:

$$I_{W,1} = \frac{Y_{W,1} \times P_{W,0}}{Y_{W,0} \times P_{W,0}} \tag{2.1}$$

where $I_{W,1}$ represents the index value in year 1, $Y_{W,1}$ represents the output of wheat in year 1, $Y_{W,0}$ is the output of wheat in the base period, and $P_{W,0}$ is the price of wheat in the base period. For year 2, the index value for wheat output would be given by

$$I_{W,2} = \frac{Y_{W,2} \times P_{W,0}}{Y_{W,0} \times P_{W,0}} \tag{2.2}$$

If only one commodity is involved, we can drop the price term ($P_{W,0}$) from both the numerator and denominator, since they cancel each other.

To illustrate the use of equations (2.1) and (2.2), assume the following values:

Year	Wheat output (billion bushels)	Price of wheat (dollars/bushel)	Output index	Price index
0	10	4.50	1.0	1.0
1	12	5.00	1.2	1.1
2	15	5.85	1.5	1.3

Substituting the appropriate values into equation (2.1), for example, we see that the index value for wheat output in year 1 is equal to

$$I_{W,1} = \frac{12 \times 4.50}{10 \times 4.50} = 1.2 \tag{2.3}$$

Similarly, equation (2.2) would tell us that the output index value for wheat in year 2 would equal

$$I_{W,2} = \frac{15 \times 4.50}{10 \times 4.50} = 1.5 \tag{2.4}$$

These index values reflect the movements of wheat output relative to the base year, which by definition is always equal to 1.0.

Note we have also calculated the *price index* for wheat. This was done by holding the output levels constant and allowing the price to vary over time. As mentioned above, we can drop the price terms in the equations if only one commodity is involved, since the $4.50 in both the numerator and denominator cancel. Also, it is common practice to express index values as a percentage, or to multiply the index value by 100. Thus both the output index and price index in the base year would be equal to 100 rather than 1.0.

The output index values reported in Table 2.2 reflect movements in more than one commodity, however. For example, the third column in this table reports index values for feed grains. To construct an index for more than one crop (say, wheat and corn), equation (2.1) must be restated as follows:

$$I_{WC,1} = \frac{(Q_{W,1} \times P_{W,0}) + (Q_{C,1} \times P_{C,0})}{(Q_{W,0} \times P_{W,0}) + (Q_{C,0} \times P_{C,0})} \tag{2.5}$$

where $I_{WC,1}$ represents the output index for wheat and corn in year 1, $Q_{W,1}$ represents the output of wheat in year 1, $P_{W,0}$ represents the price of wheat in year 0, $Q_{C,1}$ represents the output of corn in year 1, and $P_{C,0}$ represents the price of corn in year 0.

The numerator and denominator now consist of the sum of two (or more) products where the quantity for each crop is multiplied by its price. The resulting set of numbers represent an output index for wheat and corn. We could, instead, have calculated the price index for both crops taken together by allowing their prices to vary and holding quantities constant at their base-period level.[15] Finally, the index values expressed in equations (2.1) and (2.5) are pure numbers. That is, they are not expressed in either price or quantity units. Instead, they reflect the movements in quantity units (or price units) *relative* to a particular base period. For example,

[15] This form of index is known as Laspeyre's index. Two other approaches to computing an index, not discussed here, are Paasche's index and Fisher's index.

according to column three in Table 2.2, feed grain output in 1973 was 15 percent higher than it was in the base year.

Current versus Constant Dollars

When discussing the profitability of farming operations in this chapter, we referred to net farm income measured in *current dollars* and net farm income measured in *constant dollars.* Panel b in Figure 2.4, for example, utilized both terms. You probably also noted that the term "constant dollars" in this figure had the year 1967 in parentheses immediately following it. Finally, the term "purchasing power" was used when discussing the trends reported in panel b of this figure. What does all this mean?

To begin with, net farm income measured in *current* dollars simply refers to the fact that the receipts and expenditures used in calculating net farm income were valued in today's prices. Thus the points along the "current dollar" curve in panel b of Figure 2.4 reflect the prices that farmers incurred *in those years* (i.e., current dollars in 1959 reflect 1959 prices, current dollars in 1983 reflect 1983 prices, etc.). Net farm income measured in *constant* dollars, on the other hand, reflects the prices associated with receipts and expenditures in a specific base period (i.e., 1967 in Figure 2.4).

The approach to measuring net farm income in constant dollars is to divide net farm income expressed in current dollars by an index of prices paid by farmers, or

$$\text{net farm income in constant dollars} = \frac{\text{net farm income in current dollars}}{\text{index of prices paid by farmers}} \qquad (2.6)$$

For example, if net farm income is $25 billion in a particular year and the index of prices paid by farmers in that year was equal to 180 (i.e., 1.80 X 100), net farm income in that year expressed in constant dollars would be $13.9 billion (i.e., $25 billion ÷ 1.80). This suggests that the purchasing power of net farm income in the year in question is only slightly more than one-half (i.e., 55.6 percent) as much as the net farm income received in the base period. In Part IV, more will be said about the purchasing power of money and the impact of inflation.

part II

UNDERSTANDING
CONSUMER AND
PRODUCER BEHAVIOR

3

CONSUMER BEHAVIOR

The biological process of *photosynthesis,* where the addition of light to a plant's environment results in plant growth, can be thought of in a stimulus–response context. The stimulus is the addition of light, and the response is the growth of the plant. This process can be studied in a controlled environment using sophisticated measuring devices.

Economic behavior can also be thought of in a stimulus–response context. For example, as the price of milk falls, it acts as a stimulus to consumers. The nature of this stimulus can be measured and recorded. The normal response to this stimulus would see consumers purchasing more milk. These purchases of milk can also be measured and recorded. In most respects, however, any similarities end here. Whereas the complex process of photosynthesis can be examined and studied directly, most economic behavior processes cannot.

It is true that we can examine the technical relationships of converting inputs to outputs in a production process, but we cannot observe the process of connecting the economic stimulus to an economic decision. Why does Jane purchase more milk than Sue even when both face the same prices and have the same income? Although we may conjecture and ask questions about how individuals process information and behave, the approach of most social sciences is to *theorize about the process and see if observed behavior is consistent with the theory.*

The most prominent economic theories of consumer behavior assume that consumers are rational and seek to maximize their satisfaction while staying within their budget. In this chapter we discuss consumer theory in such a way that it can be used to understand the purchasing behavior of consumers. We begin with a discussion of the amount of funds the consumer has available to finance expenditures, known as the budget constraint. The concept and measurement of the utility provided by a good or service is presented next, followed by a discussion of the conditions for consumer equilibrium. We conclude with a discussion of the law of demand and the market demand curve.

The amount of funds the consumer has available to spend on consumer goods and services is referred to as the "budget constraint." The average family in the United States spends less than 17 percent of its budget on food items. By way of contrast, the average family in Japan spends 25 percent of its income on food. In the Soviet Union, the average family spends approximately one-half of its income on food items.

THE BUDGET CONSTRAINT

We often hear the phrase "I wanted to purchase it, but I just could not afford it." This underscores a fact of life: we are all faced with what economists call a *budget constraint.* That is, a consumer's purchases cannot exceed his or her income or income plus borrowing. If consumption decisions are made as a family, income should encompass all forms of family income. It should also *exclude* tax obligations, to reflect the family's *disposable* income.[1] Finally, we must have a unit of time in mind when we discuss the budget constraint. We may, for example, wish to focus on the maximum expenditures per day, per week, and so on.

The total expenditures made by a consumer on a number of items can be determined by multiplying the total quantity of goods and services purchased times their respective prices. For example, if your consumption was limited to purchases of hamburgers and tacos, your total expenditures would be equal to the price of hamburgers times the quantity of hamburgers consumed *plus* the price of tacos times the quantity of tacos consumed.

Since expenditures cannot exceed income or income plus borrowing, the budget constraint for *n* commodities must satisfy the following condition:

expenditures + expenditures + ... + expenditures ⩽ income plus (3.1)
  on good 1   on good 2   on good *n*   borrowing

where the symbol "⩽" means that everything to the left of this symbol must sum up to a value that is *less than or equal to* the value on the right. Thus this equation simply states that total expenditures must be less than or equal to income and borrowing. For most purposes it is helpful to assume that the consumer spends all of his or her income.[2] This implies that the budget constraint in equation (3.1) would be an *equality* instead of an inequality (i.e., the symbol "⩽" would be replaced by "=").

To illustrate, suppose that you have $5 a day to divide between tacos and hamburgers. Tacos cost $0.50 each and hamburgers cost $1.25 each. We shall assume for convenience that tacos and hamburgers are perfectly divisible, so that any fraction of each can be purchased. The expenditure equation, including the budget constraint in this case, would read as follows:

$1.25 × quantity of + $0.50 × quantity of = $5.00   (3.2)
        hamburgers   tacos

---

[2] One of the goods may be thought of as saving. Alternatively, savings may have already been substracted from income.

[1] Disposable income is defined as income minus tax obligations.

Thus your choice of how many hamburgers and tacos to consume must be such that the entire $5 is spent.

What effect does inflation have on the budget constraint? A *doubling* of the income and price levels in equation (3.2) yields

$$\$2.50 \times \text{quantity of hamburgers} + \$1.00 \times \text{quantity of tacos} = \$10.00 \qquad (3.3)$$

Note, however, that dividing both sides of equation (3.3) by 2 would give the *same* budget constraint expressed in (3.2). Economists assess this situation by concluding that *only changes in relative prices are relevant.*

The budget constraint is illustrated graphically in Figure 3.1. The constraint is normally referred to in this context as the *budget line*. We know from equation (3.2) that if just hamburgers are desired, taco consumption would be zero while the quantity of hamburgers consumed would be 4.0 [i.e., total income ($5.00) ÷ price of hamburgers ($1.25)]. In other words, the consumer could purchase a maximum of 4 hamburgers per day. This is indicated by point A in panel a of Figure 3.1. If only tacos are consumed (i.e., hamburger consumption is zero), a maximum of 10 tacos could be consumed [i.e., income ($5.00) ÷ price of tacos ($0.50)]. This is indicated by point B in panel a of Figure 3.1. *All feasible consumption possibilities would thus appear along the budget line AB.* For example, the consumption of 2 hamburgers and 5 tacos also requires an income of $5, as indicated by point C in panel a of Figure 3.1.

The slope of the budget line is equal to the negative of the price ratio, or

$$- \frac{\Delta \text{tacos}}{\Delta \text{hamburgers}} = \frac{\text{price of hamburgers}}{\text{price of tacos}} \qquad (3.4)$$

The symbol "Δ" in this equation represents the "change" in the consumption of a particular good. For example, Δtacos represents the change in the quantity of tacos consumed. If taco consumption increased from 2 tacos to 5 tacos, the value of Δtacos would be 3 tacos.[3]

Equation (3.4) indicates that for every unit increase in hamburger consumption, taco consumption must fall by the value of the negative of the

---

[3] We can derive the slope of the budget line from panel a in Figure 3.1. If a consumer initially purchased the combination of tacos and hamburgers represented by point B and then switched to the combination represented by point C, he or she has decided to buy more hamburgers and less tacos. Since the total expenditure at point B is identical to the total expenditure at point C, we can state that

$$- \Delta \text{ tacos} \times \text{price of tacos} = + \Delta \text{ hamburgers} \times \text{price of hamburgers}$$

Equation (3.4) simply represents a rearrangement of this equality.

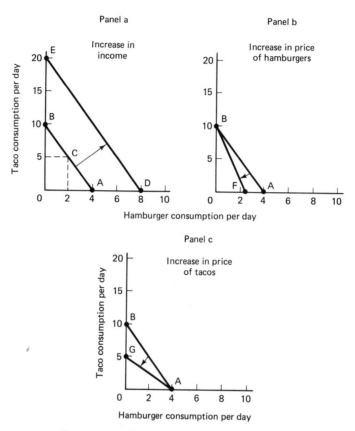

Figure 3.1 *Illustration of Budget Constraint.* Let the line connecting points *A* and *B* in all three of the panels represent the original budget constraint or "budget line." This line suggests that the consumer could spend his or her entire daily food budget of $5 to buy 4 hamburgers costing $1.25 each, 10 tacos costing $0.50 each, or some combination of these two food items that appears along line *AB*. Panel a shows that a doubling of the consumer's daily food budget to $10 would result in an outward parallel shift of this budget line to line *DE*. Panel b shows that an increase in the price of hamburgers would reduce the maximum number of hamburgers that can be bought and shift the budget line to *FB*. Panel c shows that an increase in the price of tacos would cause an inward shift of the budget line to line *AG*.

price ratio. In our example above, the value of the negative price ratio is equal –2.5 [i.e., –($1.25 ÷ $0.50)]. Thus for every additional hamburger consumed (i.e., Δhamburgers = +1.0), taco consumption must fall by 2.5 tacos (i.e., Δtacos = –2.5) if this consumer is to stay within the budget constraint given in equation (3.2).

What will happen to the budget line if income changes while prices remain unchanged? The answer is that the budget line will move in a parallel fashion as illustrated in panel a of Figure 3.1. Suppose that income increases to $10. When this occurs, maximum hamburger consumption will shift from 4 hamburgers at point A to 8 hamburgers (i.e., 8 = $10.00 ÷ $1.25) at point D. Maximum taco consumption would change from 10 tacos at point B to 20 tacos (i.e., 20 = $10.00 ÷ $0.50) at point E. Thus line DE would represent the new budget constraint. Note that line DE represents a parallel shift to the right from the original budget line AB as a result of the income increase. The budget line would take a parallel shift inward (leftward) if income decreases.

Changes in the price ratio for consumers with a fixed income will change the slope of their budget line, as indicated by equation (3.4). For example, if the price of hamburgers increases, the budget line will rotate to the left of line AB about point B as illustrated in panel b of Figure 3.1. This indicates that fewer hamburgers can be purchased for any given level of taco consumption. If the price of hamburgers decreases, the budget line will rotate the budget line to the right of line AB about point B. In both instances, therefore, the budget lines continue to have point B in common. At point B, only tacos are consumed and therefore a price change in hamburgers would have absolutely no effect. Similarly, changes in the price of tacos would rotate the budget line about point A as illustrated in panel c of Figure 3.1. A leftward rotation indicates a rise in the price of tacos, while a rotation in the opposite direction signifies a drop in taco prices.

To illustrate, assume that the price of hamburgers increases to $2. If all income is spent on hamburgers, 2.5 hamburgers can be purchased indicated by point F in panel b. Hence line FB represents the new budget line and has a slope of –4 (i.e., –$2.00 ÷ $0.50). This means that consumption of 4 tacos is forgone (acquired) for every 1-unit increase (decrease) in hamburger consumption. If the price of tacos were to increase to $1, a line connecting points G and A as shown in panel c would represent the relevant budget line.

To summarize, the slope of the budget line is given by the negative of the price ratio. This ratio indicates that the forgone consumption of tacos associated with a 1-unit increase in consumption of hamburgers is equal to the price of hamburgers divided by the price of tacos. An increase (decrease) in income will shift the budget line outward (inward) from the origin. This shift will be parallel in nature as long as the price ratio does not change.

UTILITY THEORY

Having discussed the nature of the feasible choices facing consumers, let us now turn our attention to the development of a theoretical framework that will help us understand the choices they make. In the discussion to follow, we shall assume that consumers are rational and can be thought of as maximizing their satisfaction or *utility*.

Total Utility

When a consumer purchases a good or service, it is because of the satisfaction he or she expects to receive. Early researchers of consumer behavior argued that utility was *cardinally* measurable.[4] They also argued that the utility derived from a given commodity is independent of the utility derived from other commodities. The latter belief suggests that the consumer can determine the utility of taco consumption independently from hamburger consumption. Total utility accordingly would be equal to the total utility derived from each of the individual commodities. The psychological units of satisfaction derived from consumption are referred to as *utils*.

A *utility function* allows us to order or rank consumption bundles by the total utility they provide, where the term "consumption bundles" is commonly used to refer to a particular combination of goods being considered.[5] The utility function describes the *total utility* derived from consuming a particular "bundle."

To clarify the meaning and use of the utility function, consider a consumer who has the following utility function:

$$\text{total utility} = (\text{quantity of hamburgers} \times \text{quantity of tacos}) \qquad (3.5)$$

Let us suppose, for example, that consumption bundle A consists of 2.5 hamburgers and 10 tacos. The consumer with a utility function like equation (3.5) would therefore derive a total utility of 25.0 from the consumption of this bundle (i.e., 2.5 × 10.0). Suppose that we wanted to know whether bundle B, which consists of 3 hamburgers and 7 tacos, is preferred, not preferred, or indifferent to bundle A. To begin with, we know from equation (3.5) that the utility this consumer derives from the consumption of bundle B would be 21.0 (i.e., 3.0 × 7.0). This consumer would therefore *prefer* bundle A to bundle B since the utility provided by bundle A (25.0) is greater than the utility provided by bundle B (21.0). Suppose that bundle C consists of 2 hamburgers and 12.5 tacos. The utility derived from consuming this bundle would also equal 25.0. This suggests this consumer would be *indifferent* between bundles A and C. These three bundles and the total utility they provide are summarized on chart on page 54.

Although the notion of a utility function may seem mysterious to you, it is the foundation of consumer economic analysis. It performs a role much like the production function for a farm business, as we will see in Chapter 4.

---

[4] We shall use the term *cardinally measurable* in the same sense that a ruler measures distances. *Ordinally measurable,* on the other hand, implies a ranking of distance such as longest to the shortest.

[5] There are two basic consumer axioms that serve as the building blocks for constructing a utility function. The interested reader is referred to the Advanced Topics section at the end of this chapter for a discussion and an illustration of these axioms.

Bundle	Tacos	Hamburgers	Total utility
A	2.5	10.0	25.0
B	3.0	7.0	21.0
C	2.0	12.5	25.0

Marginal Utility

If utility is measurable, it is appropriate to question how total utility *changes* as more of a particular good is consumed. The *marginal utility (MU)* associated with specific changes in the consumption of hamburgers is given by

$$MU_{hamburgers} = \frac{\Delta \text{ utility}}{\Delta \text{ hamburgers}} \tag{3.6}$$

or the change in utility associated with a change in the consumption of hamburgers. This value will always be greater than zero if we assume that the consumer never becomes total satiated, but will fall as hamburger consumption increases.

A Numerical Example

To illustrate the notion of marginal utility, let us assume that the data presented in Table 3.1 reflect the utility associated with consuming hamburgers. The first column in this table indicates the quantity of hamburgers consumed. The second column represents the total utility associated with each specific consumption level. Finally, the third column presents the levels of marginal utility. Note that each successive increment of hamburgers increases utility by a *smaller* amount. As consumption of hamburgers increases from 2 to 3, utility increases by 9 utils; as consumption of hamburgers increases from 8 to 9, utility increase by only 3 utils. Figure 3.2 shows the shape of the total and marginal utility curves associated with the data presented in Table 3.1.

Do you think it is reasonable that marginal utility should diminish like this? Suppose that you consume one hamburger, then another, and another. Doesn't it seem reasonable that the third hamburger gives you less satisfaction than the second? There is considerable appeal to this notion, so much so in fact that it has been given "law-like" status. The *law of diminishing marginal utility* suggests that as consumption per unit of time increases, marginal utility tends to decrease. However, does it seem logical to assume that utility (or marginal utility) provided by different commodities are independent? Wouldn't the utility you derive from hamburger consumption depend on the amount of soft drinks, french fries, and tacos you consume? Since most people would answer in the affirmative, we must take the consumption of

Quantity of hamburgers	Total utility	Marginal utility
1	20	
		10
2	30	
		9
3	39	
		8
4	47	
		7
5	54	
		6
6	60	
		5
7	65	
		4
8	69	
		3
9	72	
		2
10	74	

TABLE 3.1 CALCULATION OF MARGINAL UTIL-
ITY. The law of diminishing marginal utility suggests
that the marginal utility, or additional utility received
by consuming another unit of a product, decreases as
the number of units consumed during a specific period
of time increases. We see above, for example, that the
marginal utility derived from increasing consumption of
hamburgers from 1 to 2 is 10 utils, while the marginal
utility derived from increasing consumption from 8 to
9 hamburgers is only 3 utils.

other commodities into account in Table 3.1 before it can tell us much about
consumer behavior.

Indifference Curves

Modern consumption theory dismisses the notion that utility is cardinally
measurable and chooses instead to measure utility in ordinal terms.[6] The

---

[6] This is because cardinal measurement is both unreasonable and unnecessary.
Cardinality implies that society can add utils just as it can add distances. It was argued
that, if a dollar taken from John Doe would reduce his welfare by 0.5 util while a dollar
given to John Smith would increase his welfare by 0.75 util, society would benefit from
this redistribution.

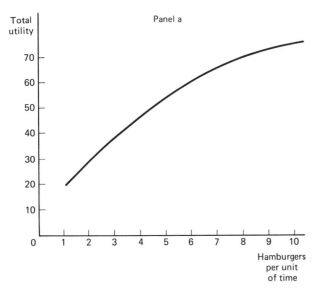

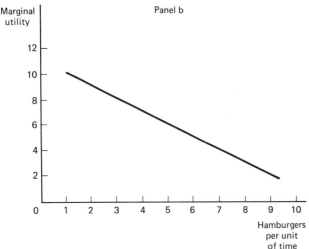

Figure 3.2 *Graphical Illustration of Total and Marginal Utility.* Panels a and b represent the shape of the total and marginal utility curves for the numerical example presented in Table 3.1. Panel a shows that the consumer's total utility continues to increase as the number of hamburgers consumed increases. At the same time, however, panel b shows that the marginal utility from increasing consumption per unit of time declines.

idea that bundle *M* yields a utility of 100 and bundle *N* provides a utility of 200 does not necessarily mean that bundle *N* provides twice as much satisfaction as bundle *M*. Instead, utility can be viewed as being ordinally measurable; that is, it can be thought of as a personal index of satisfaction where its magnitude is used only to rank consumption bundles. This suggests that all we really need know is that bundle *N* is preferred to bundle *M*, and not by how much.

The basic building block of modern consumption theory is the notion of an "isoutility" curve which accounts for substitution in consumption for two products. The term "iso" is of Greek origin and means "equal."[7] An isoutility curve is often referred to as an *indifference curve.* All consumption bundles that yield an *equal level of satisfaction or utility* can be plotted as an indifference curve.

The different combinations of goods where indifference occurs has special significance since total utility is "equal" or the same at all points a-long the indifference curve. The combinations of hamburgers and tacos that represent specific levels of utility are graphed in Figure 3.3. The curve labeled I_2, for example, illustrates specific combinations of these two goods that would yield a certain level of utility. Changes in utility would be indicated by outward (inward) shifts of an indifference curve. The indifference curve denoted by I_7, for example, represents a higher level of utility than the indifference curve labeled I_2.

Several properties of indifference curves must be understood. For example, *indifference curves cannot intersect.* To illustrate, are all three indifference curves in Figure 3.3 "legitimate"? Bundle M is said to be indifferent to bundle N and bundle O along curve I_0 and bundle N is said to be indifferent to bundle P along curve I_7. There is an obvious contradiction here, however. Bundle O is clearly preferred to bundle P because it contains *more* tacos and hamburgers than bundle P. Thus we cannot have indifference curves that cross or intersect.

Do indifference curves slope downward or upward? If more goods are preferred to less, it seems clear that indifference curves are downward sloping. If indifference curves were upward sloping, they would suggest, for example, that 2 hamburgers and 3 tacos might give the *same* satisfaction as 4 hamburgers and 5 tacos. Hence indifference curves generally slope downward, reflecting the notion that if the consumer reduced his or her taco consumption, hamburger consumption must increase in order to leave utility unchanged.

Marginal Rate of Substitution

The rate at which the consumer is willing to substitute one good for another is called the *marginal rate of substitution.* The marginal rate of substitution of hamburgers for tacos, for example, represents the number of tacos the consumer would be willing to give up for an additional hamburger to maintain the *same* level of satisfaction, or

$$\begin{array}{c} \text{marginal rate of} \\ \text{substitution of} \\ \text{hamburgers for tacos} \end{array} = \frac{\Delta \text{ tacos}}{\Delta \text{ hamburgers}} \qquad (3.7)$$

The marginal rate of substitution associated with moving from bundle M to

[7] For example, consider an isoceles triangle, where all angles are equal.

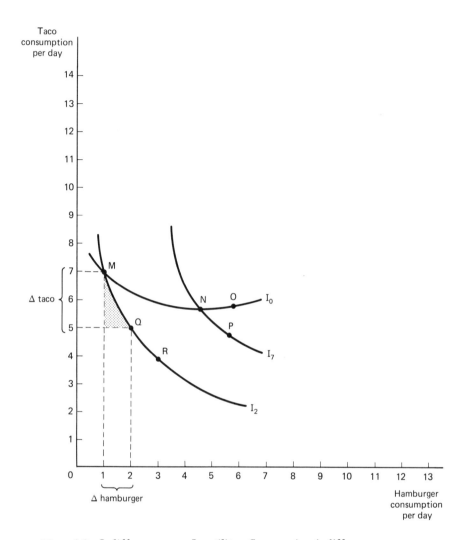

Figure 3.3 *Indifference or Isoutility Curves.* An indifference curve represents the combination of two goods that yield an equal level of satisfaction or utility. In other words, the total utility derived from consumption is equal at all points along an indifference curve. For example, the utility associated with consuming 7 tacos and 1 hamburger per day (point *M*) is equal to the utility associated with consuming 5 tacos and 2 hamburgers (point *Q*). Indifference curves I_2 and I_7 are legitimate, whereas the curve I_0 is not (indifference curves cannot intersect). Finally, curve I_7 represents a higher level of utility than curve I_2.

bundle Q in Figure 3.3 would be approximately (i.e., $-2 \div 1$). In other words, the consumer would be willing to give up 2 tacos for 1 additional hamburger. If we instead moved from bundle M to bundle R, we see that the marginal rate of substitution would fall to about -1.5 [i.e., $(-3) \div (+2)$].

The marginal rate of substitution represents the negative of the slope of the indifference curve. In other words, the cutback in taco consumption times the marginal utility of tacos is *identical* to the increase in hamburger consumption times the marginal utility of hamburgers. Therefore, we can also equate the marginal rate of substitution of hamburgers for tacos in equation (3.7) with the ratio of their marginal utilities, or

$$\frac{\Delta \text{ tacos}}{\Delta \text{ hamburgers}} = \frac{MU_{\text{hamburgers}}}{MU_{\text{tacos}}} \qquad (3.8)$$

The loss in utility from consuming fewer tacos is just matched by the gain in utility from consuming more hamburgers.

Why does the marginal rate of substitution fall as we move down the indifference curve? Perhaps the most intuitive explanation we can offer at this point relies on the notion of diminishing marginal utility discussed earlier. As taco consumption falls, its marginal utility rises. As hamburger consumption increases, its marginal utility falls. Thus the marginal rate of substitution *falls* as one moves *down* an indifference curve (e.g., increasing hamburger consumption and reducing taco consumption).

CONSUMER EQUILIBRIUM

In this section the concepts of the budget constraint and marginal utility developed in the preceding two sections are merged to develop a theory of consumer economic behavior. The goal is to understand how the consumer will react to changes in prices and income when deciding on the consumption of specific commodities. The two-commodity example presented above will be used to illustrate the concept of consumer equilibrium.

Conditions for Equilibrium

If there were no budget constraint, the consumer would choose the consumption levels where marginal utility of each good is zero.[8] With the budget constraint, modern consumer theory can be thought of as the process of choosing between hamburgers and tacos in such a way that the total utility the consumer derives from consumption is maximized subject to the size of his or her budget constraint.

[8] To go beyond this implies a reduction in total utility since the marginal utilities are negative.

Let us initially characterize the conditions for maximazation of utility graphically. Look at the budget constraint and the set of indifference curves illustrated in Figure 3.4. If utility is to be maximized subject to the budget constraint, we must find the point on the budget line that yields the *highest* utility. Figure 3.4 shows that this occurs at point *A*, where the indifference curve I_2 is tangent to the budget line. Point *C* would not exhaust the consumer's available income. Point *B* represents a higher utility than point *A*, but requires more income than this consumer has available. Thus point *A*, which consists of 5 tacos and 2 hamburgers, represents *consumer equilibrium.* There is economic incentive for the consumer to move to point *A* if he or she were located elsewhere on this graph (e.g., point *C*). Only at point *A* is the slope of the budget line is equal to the slop of the indifference curve.

We can use equations (3.4) and (3.8) to express the conditions for consumer equilibrium in mathematical terms. Setting these equations—which represent the slope of the budget line and the slope of the indifference curve—equal to each other, we see that consumer equilibrium in the case of tacos and hamburgers is reached when

$$\frac{\text{price of hamburgers}}{\text{price of tacos}} = \frac{MU_{\text{hamburgers}}}{MU_{\text{tacos}}} \qquad (3.9)$$

The first term in equation (3.9) represents the rate at which *the market* is willing to exchange tacos for hamburgers. The second term in this equation represents the rate at which *the consumer* is willing to exchange tacos for hamburgers given his or her tastes and preferences. When the equality expressed in equation (3.9) holds, the consumer is in equilibrium. We can also use equation (3.9) to restate the condition for consumer equilibrium as follows:

$$\frac{MU_{\text{hamburgers}}}{\text{price of hamburgers}} = \frac{MU_{\text{tacos}}}{\text{price of tacos}} \qquad (3.10)$$

which suggests that the marginal utility derived from the last dollar spent on each good are equal. The equilibrium condition expressed in equation (3.10) can be expanded to include all goods and services purchased by the consumer.

CHANGES IN EQUILIBRIUM

The condition stated above for consumer equilibrium suggests that the demand for each good is influenced by the consumer's income and all prices. Indeed, there is a *causal relationship* which suggests that the demand for hamburgers "is a function" of the price of hamburgers, the price of tacos, and the consumer's available income. In other words, changes in prices and income will *cause* the consumer's demand for hamburgers to change.

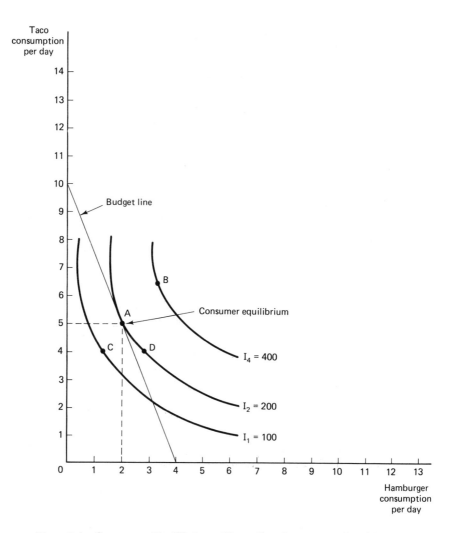

Figure 3.4 *Consumer Equilibrium.* The rational consumer is said to be in equilibrium with regard to the consumption of two goods when the slope of the budget line (the budget constraint) is equal to the slope of the indifference curve. In the example above, this occurs at point A. The indifference curve I_2 represents the highest utility curve attainable given the nature of the budget constraint. At point A, where the budget line is tangent to indifference curve I_2, the consumer is purchasing 5 tacos and 2 hamburgers. The cost of these items completely exhausts the consumer's budget of $5.

Changes in Quantity Demanded

It is often of interest to economists to evaluate the effects on demand of changes in income and prices, holding everything else fixed. The approach to measuring these *ceteris paribus* effects are examined below. Let us first focus on the effects of changes in the price of the product.

Change in own price. Suppose that the price of a hamburger is varied, leaving the price of tacos and income unchanged. If the price of hamburgers is $1.25, the price of tacos is $0.50, and income is $5., consumer equilibrium would be 2 hamburgers and 5 tacos. This equilibrium is denoted by point *A* in Figure 3.5. If the price of a hamburger were to fall to $1., the new equilibrium would be indicated by point *B,* where the consumer prefers to purchase 3 hamburgers and 4 tacos. If the price of a hamburger were varied further, other equilibriums, such as point *C,* would be identified. If the price were continuously varied, a full set of price and quantity pairs could be identified. This assumes, of course, that hamburgers can be marketed in fractions of their current size. If we graphed this series of points, we would get a downward-sloping *demand curve.* This curve would indicate what the quantity of hamburgers demanded by this consumer would be at any price.

The consumer's demand curve for hamburgers in this hypothetical example is derived in Figure 3.6. This demand curve shows, for example, that if the price of a hamburger is $1.25, 2 hamburgers would be demanded by this consumer (see point *A*). *Point A in both Figures 3.5 and 3.6 therefore represents the same quantity demanded.* The same relationship holds for points *B* and *C* in these two figures as well. Finally, Figure 3.6 suggests that if the price of hamburgers rises much above $6., the quantity of hamburgers demanded by this consumer would fall to zero (see point *D*).

Own-price elasticity of demand. It is convenient to measure the response of the quantity demanded to a change in the price of a good in percentage terms. The *own-price elasticity of demand* is defined as follows:[9]

$$\text{own-price elasticity of demand} = \frac{\text{percentage change in quantity}}{\text{percentage change in price}} \qquad (3.11)$$

where the percentage change in the quantity of tacos, for example, would be equal to Δ tacos divided by the average quantity of tacos over this range. To illustrate the calculation of this elasticity, let's return to Figure 3.6. As we move from point *B* to point *A* in Figure 3.6, consumption decreases from 3 hamburgers to 2 hamburgers while price increases from $1. to $1.25 per hamburger. The average quantity over this range would be equal to 2.5

[9] The elasticity of demand defined above is an arc elasticity which applies to discrete changes in price. As the changes approach zero, a point elasticity of demand can be defined.

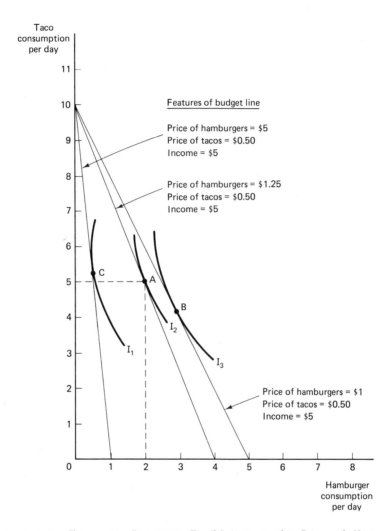

Figure 3.5 *Change in Consumer Equilibrium as the Price of Hamburgers Changes.* The consumer's equilibrium position in consumption can change as the budget line changes (see also Figure 3.1). Beginning with the consumer equilibrium at point *A*, where the consumer has $5 to spend on tacos and hamburgers, we see that the consumer would purchase 5 tacos and 2 hamburgers, as illustrated in Figure 3.4. If the price of hamburgers were to fall to $1, the budget line would rotate to the right and the new equilibrium would occur at point *B*. If the price rose to $5, the consumer would shift to point *C*.

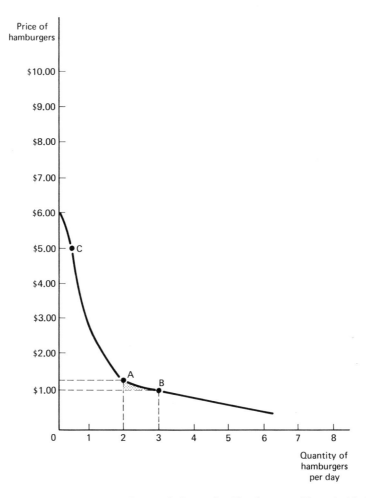

Figure 3.6 *Consumer's Demand Curve for Hamburgers.* If we hold the price of tacos constant at $0.50 and the budget constraint constant at $5, we can derive the consumer's demand curve for hamburgers by examining the quantities of hamburgers consumed given in Figure 3.5. For example, point *A* in Figure 3.6 corresponds to point *A* in Figure 3.5, where, at a price of $1.25, two hamburgers were purchased. If the price were to fall to $1 we see in both figures that 3 hamburgers would be desired (point *B*). Point *C* in both figures also indicates that the consumer would consume only one hamburger every other day if the price rose to $5. Finally, at a price of $6 per hamburger, the consumer would purchase no hamburgers. A line connecting these and other price–quantity combinations represents the consumer's demand curve.

[i.e., (2 + 3) ÷ 2], while the average price would be $1.125 [i.e., ($1.25 + $1.00) ÷ 2]. In this case, therefore, the own price elasticity of demand would be

$$\begin{array}{l} \text{own-price} \\ \text{elasticity} \\ \text{of demand} \end{array} = \frac{(2.0 - 3.0) \div 2.5}{(\$1.25 - \$1.00) \div \$1.125} \qquad (3.12)$$

$$= -1.8$$

Thus a 1 percent fall (rise) in the price of a hamburger will increase (reduce) demand by 1.8 percent. Often the minus sign is ignored (i.e., we might simply say that the own-price elasticity is 1.8).

When the price elasticity of demand for a good exceeds 1 (in absolute value), we call the response *elastic*. That is, the percentage change in quantity demanded exceeds the percentage change in price. If the price elasticity of demand is equal to 1 the curve would represent a *unitary elastic* demand. When the price elasticity of demand for a good is less than 1 (in absolute value), the demand is called *inelastic*. This means that the percentage change in the quantity demanded is less than the percentage change in the product's price.[10]

The effects of a change in the price of a good on the demand for this good can be summarized as follows:

If the own-price elasticity is:	Demand is said to be:
Greater than 1	Elastic
Equal to 1	Unitary elastic
Less than 1	Inelàstic

Along the demand curve, the elasticity may be changing. Consider the case of the *linear* demand curve for a hypothetical product illustrated in Figure 3.7. The consumer's demand response is elastic along the upper portion of this curve, as we see from the elasticities calculated using equation (3.11), which are presented in column (6) of Table 3.2. The curve is shown in this table to be unitary elastic at the midpoint of this curve. The curve is also shown to be inelastic to the right of this point and elastic to the left of this point.

Why does this elasticity change along a linear demand curve since the change in quantity divided by the change in price is constant? The answer lies in the fact that the ratio of price to quantity is continuously changing

---

[10] If the demand curve is perfectly flat or horizontal, the curve would represent a *perfectly elastic* demand; and if the demand curve is perpendicular to the horizontal axis or completely vertical, the curve would represent a *perfectly inelastic* demand.

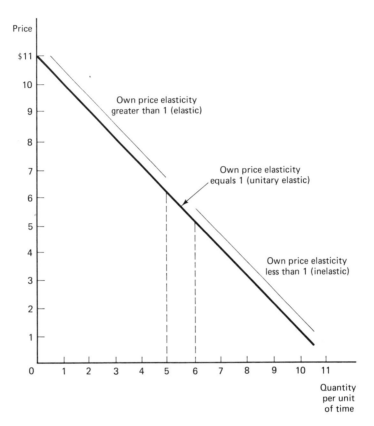

Figure 3.7 *Changing Own-Price Elasticity along the Demand Curve.* The own-price elasticity of demand tells us something about how the quantity demanded by the consumer will change if the price of the product changes. This elasticity will be different all along the demand curve, whether it is shaped like the nonlinear demand curve derived in Figure 3.6 or the linear demand illustrated above. In the case of a linear demand curve, if the demand curve is linear or a straight line, own-price elasticity of demand will be greater than 1.0 or elastic above the midpoint on this curve and less than 1.0 or inelastic below this point. When this elasticity is equal to 1.0, demand is said to be unitary elastic.

as we move down the demand curve. In fact, the ratio of price to quantity approaches zero as price approaches zero. Therefore, we can conclude that the *own-price elasticity of demand falls (rises) as the product's price falls (rises).*

Besides quantifying the relative responsiveness of the quantity demanded to a price change, the own-price elasticity of demand is also useful as a device to study how consumer expenditures change as price changes. The following relationship approximates the percentage change in expenditures:

$$\text{percentage change} \atop \text{in expenditures} = {\text{percentage change} \atop \text{in price}} + {\text{percentage change} \atop \text{in quantity demanded}}$$

$$(3.13)$$

If price increases by 6 percent and the quantity demanded falls by 4 percent, total consumer expenditures would rise by 2 percent. For an inelastic demand, an increase in price would lead to an increase in consumer expenditures since the percentage change in price is *greater than* the percentage change in quantity. If price were to fall by 6 percent and quantity increased by 4 percent, the percentage change in expenditures would be –2 percent. For the case of an elastic demand, the percentage change in price will be *less than* the percentage change in quantity, causing consumer expenditures to rise as price falls. The opposite conclusion holds for a price rise: namely, expenditures will fall as price increases. When the elasticity is 1, the percentage change in price will be *equal to* the percentage change in quantity. Thus there would be no change in consumer expenditures as price changes.

This concept is also illustrated in Table 3.2. For example, note that total expenditures made by the consumer would be $18 if the price was equal to $9. Total expenditure would be $28 if the price fell to $7. Total expenditures therefore would have risen by $10 (i.e., $28 – $18) if the price were to fall by $2 (i.e., $9 – $7). This relationship will always hold whenever the change in price takes place in the *elastic* portion of the demand curve. If the price were to fall from $4 to $2, total expenditures would fall by $10 (i.e., $28 – $18). This change in total expenditures took place in the *inelastic* portion of the demand curve. The opposite conclusion holds for the case of a price rise; namely, a rise in price raises (lowers) expenditure if demand is inelastic (elastic).

Changes in Demand

Earlier we said that the demand for hamburgers is a function of the price of hamburgers, the price of tacos, and the level of income. It is often convenient to think of a demand curve as being shifted by changes in income and other prices. We shall distinguish a *shift* in the curve, which is referred to as a *change in demand,* from a *movement along* the curve, which is referred to as a *change in the quantity demanded.*

Change in income. When prices are held fixed and income is varied, the effects that changes in income have on the consumer's demand for a particular product can be assessed. This impact has led economists to classify goods into two categories: (1) normal goods and (2) inferior goods. *Normal goods* are those goods where a rise (fall) in income will lead to increased (decreased) consumption. The demand for an *inferior good* falls (rises) when income rises (falls).

(1) Price	(2) Quantity demanded	(3) Total expenditure, (1) X (2)	(4) Percentage change in quantity % Δ (2)	(5) Percentage change in price % Δ (1)	(6) Own price elasticity (4)/(5)
$11	0	$ 0			
			1/0.5	1/10.5	21.00
10	1	10			
			1/1.5	1/9.5	6.33
9	2	18			
			1/2.5	1/8.5	3.40
8	3	24			
			1/3.5	1/7.5	2.14
7	4	28			
			1/4.5	1/6.5	1.44
6	5	30			
			1/5.5	1/5.5	1.00
5	6	30			
			1/6.5	1/4.5	0.69
4	7	28			
			1/7.5	1/3.5	0.67
3	8	24			
			1/8.5	1/2.5	0.29
2	9	18			
			1/9.5	1/1.5	0.14
1	10	10			

TABLE 3.2 CONSUMPTION EXPENDITURES AND THE OWN-PRICE ELASTICITY. We can also illustrate the changing nature of the own-price elasticity of demand by examining the price–quantity relationships plotted in Figure 3.7. Column (4) reports the percentage change in the quantity demanded. As quantity rises from 3 to 4 units, for example, the percentage change in quantity would be (4 – 3) ÷ 3.5, where 3.5 is the average quantity over this range [i.e., (3 + 4) 4 ÷ 2]. Column (5) reports the percentage change in price. As price falls from $9 to $8, for example, the percentage change in price would be (9 –8) ÷ 8.5, where 8.5 is the average price over this range [i.e., (9 + 8) ÷ 2]. The own-price elasticity of demand reported in column (6) is equal to the percentage change in quantity reported in column (4) divided by the percentage change in price reported in column (5). Note that the value of the elasticity reported in column (6) declines as price falls and quantity demanded increases (i.e., as we move down the demand curve). Also note that demand is elastic only when quantity demanded falls below 6 units.

Examples of normal goods are a physician's services, housing, and steak. Some inferior goods are whole milk, 1967 Chevrolet station wagons, and hamburger. One must, however, be cautious about classifying a commodity as either normal or inferior; this classification generally depends on the level of prices and income itself.

Figure 3.8 suggests that hamburgers and tacos are both normal goods

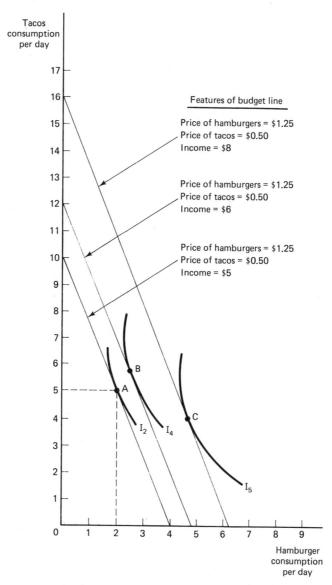

Figure 3.8 *Effect of Change in Income on Consumer Equilibrium.* We noted in Figure 3.1 that an increase in income would shift the budget line in a parallel fashion to the right. If the consumer's budget increased from $5 to $6 per day, he or she could attain a higher indifference curve (I_4) and new equilibrium position (point *B*). If the consumer's budget rose to $8, his or her equilibrium position would shift to point *C*. The nature of these changes in demand as income changes is summarized by the income elasticity of demand, or the percentage change in quantity divided by the percentage change in income.

when the consumer's income increases from \$5. to \$6. This increase in consumer income increased the equilibrium consumption of hamburgers from 2.0 (point *A*) to 2.6 (point *B*). Taco consumption would change from 5.0 to 5.5. However, if income were to rise to \$8, taco consumption would fall to 3.5 and hamburger consumption would rise to 5.0 (point *C*). This consumer obviously has a strong preference for hamburgers as income increases. Although tacos were initially considered a normal good when income expanded, they became an inferior good at higher income levels.[11]

As noted earlier, it is useful to assess the effects of changes in income in percentage terms. The income elasticity of demand is defined as

$$\begin{matrix} \text{income} \\ \text{elasticity} \\ \text{of demand} \end{matrix} = \frac{\text{percentage change in quantity}}{\text{percentage change in income}} \qquad (3.14)$$

An income elasticity greater than 1.0, for example, implies that a 1 percent increase in income will lead to a rise in consumption of greater than 1 percent. Such goods are called *luxuries* by economists. When the income elasticity is less than 1.0, the good is called a *necessity*.

If the income elasticity is:	The good is classified as:
Greater than 1	A luxury
Less than 1	A necessity
Greater than zero	A normal good
Less than zero	A inferior good

Typically, most foods are necessities (e.g., bread and eggs), while most non-food products, such as furniture, a physician's services, recreation, and eating away from home, are considered luxuries.

Changes in other prices. The demand curve for hamburgers will probably also shift if the price of a taco changes. If hamburgers and tacos are *substitutes,* a rise in the price of tacos would cause consumers to substitute hamburgers for tacos. Thus the demand curve for hamburgers would shift to the right (left) as the price of tacos rises (falls). If, instead, we consider the relationship between cokes and hamburgers, we may find that a rise in the price of cokes causes fewer hamburgers to be consumed. In this case, hamburgers and cokes are said to be *complements.* Finally, a rise in the price

[11] If income is varied continuously and we record the equilibrium choices, such as *A, B,* and *C* in Figure 3.8, we can plot a curve relating income to consumption of a good. Such a curve is called an Engel curve, named after a nineteenth-century German statistician, Ernst Engel. In our example, a larger proportion of an income change is devoted to the purchase of hamburgers as income increases.

of salt may cause no change in hamburger consumption. Hamburgers and salt are said to be *independent.*

Cross-price elasticity. We can measure the effects of changes in the price of tacos on the demand for hamburgers by calculating the *cross-price elasticity of demand* as follows:

$$\begin{matrix} \text{cross-price} \\ \text{elasticity} \\ \text{of demand} \end{matrix} = \frac{\text{percentage change in quantity of hamburgers}}{\text{percentage change in price of tacos}} \qquad (3.15)$$

This elasticity measures the relative responsiveness of the consumption of one good (hamburgers) to another good's (tacos) price. It is convenient to distinguish between the three different effects that a change in the price of one good can have on the demand for another good.

If the cross-price elasticity is:	The good is classified as:
Positive	Substitute
Negaitve	Complement
Zero	Independent

Substitution effects are of great interest to agricultural economists. As the price of beef increases, they want to know what will happen to the demand for other products, such as poultry, fish, and pork.

THE LAW OF DEMAND

So far we have focused on the behavior of an individual consumer. In this section the concept of market demand is introduced and some general principles governing individual market demand functions are discussed.

Market Demand

The economy is composed of a myriad of consumers who make expenditures on many goods. Thus it is the sum total over all relevant consumers that comprises *market demand.*

To illustrate the concept of market demand, suppose that there are two consumers in a market, consumer A and consumer B. The demand curves for each are represented in panels a and b of Figure 3.9. The market demand curve is the horizontal summation of the two individual demand curves, as shown in panel c. At a price of a hamburger equal to $2.50, the quantity de-

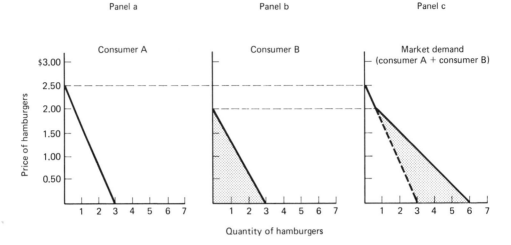

Figure 3.9 *Individual Consumer and Market Demand Curves.* The market demand for hamburgers or any other consumer good is given by the summation of the quantities demanded by individual consumers at a particular price. Let panel a represent consumer *A*'s demand curve and panel b represent consumer *B*'s demand curve. Further assume that these are the only two consumers in the economy. At a price of $2.50, neither consumer would desire to purchase hamburgers. Therefore, the market demand would be zero. If the price were $2 however, consumer *A* would desire to purchase 1 hamburger. Since consumer *B* would still defer from hamburger consumption, the market demand curve should reflect a quantity of 1. This process is then repeated for lower price levels, until the entire market demand curve is revealed.

manded by consumer *A* would be 3 hamburgers, while consumer *B* would purchase none at this price. The combination of a price of $2. and quantity of 1 hamburger thus represents one point on the market demand curve. If the price of hamburgers were $1.50, the market demand would be 3 hamburgers (i.e., 2 + 1). By varying the price in this way, a continuous market demand curve can be constructed, as shown in panel c.[12]

The concepts of price elasticity, cross-price elasticity, and income elasticity apply at the market or aggregate level just as they did earlier when we focused on an individual consumer. If tacos and hamburgers are substitute goods for both consumers, a rise in the price of tacos will shift each demand curve for hamburber to the right. Thus the market demand curve for hamburgers will shift to the right as well. Similar reasoning applies to changes in

[12] In some cases, horizontally adding market demands is in error. Suppose that consumer *A*'s demand curve depends on consumer *B*'s demand, or market demand. Then one cannot simply add the individual demand curves independently to obtain the market demand curve.

income; if the good is normal, increases in individual consumer incomes imply outward shifts of the individual and hence market demand curves.

General Properties of Demand

We have drawn demand curves sloping downward, suggesting that consumers demand more at a lower price. This occurs with such regularity that it is referred to as the law of demand.[13] In other words, as a general rule or *law*, demand curves have a negative or downward slope.

Demand curves have other properties that we can make some general statements about. For example, the larger (smaller) the number of substitutes, the more (less) elastic the demand curve will be. Thus a commodity such as salt is likely to be inelastic, whereas a commodity such as Hunt's catsup is likely to be very elastic. This is because there are more substitutes for Hunt's catsup (e.g., other brands of catsups). This also illustrates the principle that aggregates are generally more inelastic than their components. For example, the demand for food is more inelastic than, say, the demand for hamburgers.

Another general property worth mentioning has to do with the *budget share* of the commodity. Salt expenditures comprise a relatively small proportion of consumers' total expenditures. Thus salt is not likely to exhibit a high elasticity of demand (see Table 3.3). The demand for cabbage is also inelastic by virtue of its negligible budget share. On the other hand, there are relatively few substitutes for housing services, the budget share of housing is large and, the elasticity of demand for housing services, is relatively large compared to that for cabbage or salt. Houthakker and Taylor, for example, estimate that the own-price elasticity of demand for housing is approximately equal to 1 whereas the own-price elasticity of demand for cabbage is about 0.4.

A final general property of demand curves is that *short-run demand is more inelastic than longer-run demand*. With the passage of time, consumers find that they are better able to adjust. For example, if the price of automobiles fell, the consumer may have to save in order to purchase a new car. Also, habits are not quickly relinquished. If the price of coffee suddenly increased, with the passage of time consumers may substitute for tea. To illustrate this concept numerically, residential electricity has an estimated short-run elasticity of 0.13 and a long-run elasticity of 1.90 (Houthakker and Taylor, 1970).

---

[13] Is there a logical or empirical possibility of an upward-sloping demand curve? The answer to this question is yes. When this occurs, these goods are called *Giffen goods*. Although we shall not develop the argument here, normal goods will never be Giffen goods. Indeed, a good must be sufficiently inferior in order for a good to be a Giffen good. In reality, such goods are extremely rare. Even if some individuals have upward-sloping demand curves, however, the sum over all individuals would probably yield a downward-sloping market demand curve.

Item	Estimated elasticity
Cabbage	0.4
White potatoes	0.3
Green peas	
Fresh	2.8
Canned	1.6
Tomatoes	
Fresh	4.6
Canned	2.5
Salt	0.1
Newspapers and magazines	0.1
Shoes	0.4
Gasoline and oil products	
Short run	0.2
Long run	0.7
Tires	
Short run	0.4
Long run	0.6
Kitchen appliances	0.6
Radios and televisions	1.2
Sports equipment	
Short run	0.6
Long run	1.3
Housing	1.0
Residential electricity	
Short run	0.1
Long run	1.9
Legal services	0.5
Physicians' services	0.6
Foreign travel	
Short run	0.7
Long run	4.0

Source: H. Houthakker and L. Taylor, *Consumer Demand in the United States: Analyses and Projections* (Cambridge, Mass: Harvard University Press, 1979).

TABLE 3.3 EMPIRICAL ESTIMATES OF OWN-PRICE ELASTICITIES OF DEMAND. The elasticities reported are expressed in absolute terms (i.e., the negative sign has been dropped). A 1 percent increase in the price of cabbage, for example, will result in an estimated decline in the quantity of cabbage by 0.4 percent. The long-run elasticity (more than 1 year) is normally higher than the short-run elasticity of demand for a variety of reasons, including time lags in the consumer's recognition of market conditions as well as the elimination of short-term budgetary constraints.

Some Empirical Examples

There have been a number of studies that have estimated these specific elasticities associated with demand (i.e., own price, cross price, and income) for farm products.

Own-price elasticity.   The price elasticity of demand for farm products in general in the United States has been found to be very small. Early estimates of this elasticity at the retail level ranged from a high of –0.34 reported by Brandow (1961) to a low of –0.24 reported by Waugh (1964). Accounting for the growing importance of export demand during the seventies (which has been found to be more elastic than domestic demand), Tweeten discussed the importance of a short-run own price elasticity for farm products of –0.24 and a long-run elasticity of –0.63. A short-run price elasticity of –0.24 means that a 10 percent decrease in the price of farm products would have a very small (2.4 percent) effect on the quantity demanded by others.[14]

What does this mean for farmers? If we calculate the *price flexibility* or reciprocal of the price elasticity (i.e., 1.0/–0.24), we see that the short-run own-price elasticity estimate discussed by Tweeten implies that a 1 percent increase in the quantity marketed by farmers in the short run would reduce the price they received by 4.17 percent. More will be said about this startling observation in Chapter 10 when we discuss the relationship between the inelastic demand for farm products and farm policy.

With respect to specific commodities, George and King (1971) found that the price elasticity of demand for beef at the retail level, for example, was –0.64. Thus a 1 percent decline in the retail price of beef would increase the demand for beef at the retail level by 0.64 percent. Tweeten suggests that the short-run own-price elasticity of demand for wheat and soybeans during the seventies was –0.475 and –0.347, while the corresponding long-run elasticities for these commodities were actually greater than 1 (–1.220 and –1.002).

Cross-price elasticity.   Brandow (1961) found that the cross-price elasticity for beef with respect to the price of lamb was 0.04. Thus a 1 percent increase in the price of lamb would have virtually no effect on the demand for beef (i.e., lamb is not a close substitute for beef). The cross-price elasticity for lamb with respect to the price of beef according to Brandow is 0.62. Thus we can conclude that beef is a closer substitute for lamb than lamb is for beef when the prices for these products change. An increase in the price of lamb would shift the demand curve for beef to the right far less than an increase in the price of beef would shift the demand curve for lamb to the right.

[14] Luther Tweeten, "Economic Instability in Agriculture: The Contributions of Prices, Government Programs and Exports," Oklahoma Agricultural Experiment Station, 1983.

Income elasticity. Schultze (1971) found that the income elasticity for farm products in this country is only 0.08. This elasticity in other countries varies from 0.15 in Canada to 0.75 in both West Germany and France. As a result of the relatively low income elasticity in the United States, *a 10 percent increase in income would expand the demand for farm products by less than 1 percent.* Thus more would be spent proportionately on *nonfarm* products than in other developed countries.

At the commodity level, the income elasticity for food products is uniformally low. For example, Brandow found that the income elasticity for margarine is almost zero. Thus a doubling of income would not cause the consumption of margarine to change appreciably. Would you put more margarine on your bread if your income doubled?

SOME OTHER CONSIDERATIONS

Recent developments and applications of consumer theory have recognized that consumption goods are generally produced by the household. Labor time and effort, food, utensils, and appliances are all combined to produce a meal at home. A meal consumed away from home (say, at a restaurant) must include travel time and expenses. This has led many economists to argue that the resource *time* is extremely important in understanding much of observed economic behavior. For example, as money wages increase and more wives work outside the home, will this alter consumption patterns due not only to increase family income but also because food preparation time is more costly? Or consider the demand for children. As more wives realize increased off-farm employment opportunities and wages, how does this affect the rural population? Such questions have expanded the conceptual framework discussed in this chapter and enlarged the scope of consumption analysis.

This extension of consumption theory is discussed briefly in this section to stimulate your thinking on some of these issues.[15] The basic building block of this theory is that time is allocated between consumption-related or household production activities and working for a money wage. This constraint when integrated with equation (3.1) implies that one gives up the hourly money wage for every hour used in household production activities. Suppose that one is deciding whether to consume a meal away from home or to consume a similar meal at home. At least one factor in this decision

[15] Some examples of studies using this framework, see B. Gardner, "Economies of Size of North Carolina Rural Families," *Journal of Political Economy,* 1973, pp. 99–122. See also W. Huffman, "Farm and Off-Farm Work Decisions: The Role of Human Capital," *Review of Economics and Statistics,* 1980, pp. 14–23; and D. Sumner, "The Off-Farm Labor Supply of Farmers," *American Journal of Agricultural Economics,* 1982, pp. 499–509.

is the time factor involved in these two consumption choices. If eating at a fast-food restaurant is less "time intensive" than eating at home, this represents a relative benefit to eating away from home. In each case, the money wage multiplied by the amount of time involved in the activity measures the costs associated with time. Of course, there are other factors that must also be weighed in the consumer's decision, but one must explain this basic fact: average household expenditures on food away from home in constant dollars has risen by $130 between 1960–1961 and 1973–1974.[16] Recent studies have found that age, family size, urbanity, education, sex, working wife in the household, ethnic origin, and income and its compossition are important socioeconomic variables in "explaining" the consumptionof food away from home.[17]

As our earlier discussion suggests, the wages of women and the availability of time for household production activities have been found to be crucial determinants of these expenditures. As expected, the wife working for a money wage has a significantly large positive effect on the consumption of food away from home.

With regard to rural population growth, we can already see that part of the cost of having children is the money wage forgone while the parents carry, bear, and nurture the child. As the money wage increases, so does the cost of having children. Rural fertility, however, involves some special considerations. To quote Becker,

> The evidence over hundreds of years indicates that farm families have been larger than urban families. . . . Part of the explanation is that food and housing, important inputs in the rearing of children, have been cheaper on farms. The net cost of children is reduced if they contribute to family income by performing household chores, working in the family business, or working in the market place. . . . The contribution of farm children has declined as agriculture has become more mechanized and complex in the course of economic development. Both of these elements have encouraged farm families to extend their children's schooling. Since rural schools are too small to be efficient, and since the cost in time and transportation of attending school is greater to farm children. . . . the cost advantage of raising children on harms has narrowed, and possibly has been reversed as farm children have increased the time they spend in school. Not surprisingly, therefore, urban-rural fertility differentials have narrowed greatly in developed countries during this century and rural fertility is now slightly less than urban fertility in some countries.[18]

---

[16] See B. Sexaurer, "The Effect of Demographic Shifts and Changes in the Income Distribution on Food Away from Home Expenditures," *American Journal of Agricultural Economics,* 1979, pp. 1046–1057.

[17] Ibid.; J. Kinsey, "Working Wives and the Marginal Propensity to Consume Food Away From Home," *American Journal of Agricultural Economics,* 1983, pp. 10–19.

[18] See G. Becker, *A Treatise on the Family* (Cambridge, Mass.: Harvard University Press, 1981).

SUMMARY

The purpose of this chapter was to present consumer theory in such a way that it can be used to understand the purchasing behavior of consumers. The major points made in this chapter can be summarized as follows:

1. The *budget constraint* represents the amount of income the consumer has to commit to consumption in the current period. A proportional change in all prices and income has *no effect* on the budget constraint. For this reason, economists argue that only relative price changes matter. When presented graphically, the budget constraint is frequently referred to as the *budget line.* The *slope* of the budget line, which tells us the rate of exchange between two goods as their prices change, is given by the negative of the price ratio. Finally, an increase (decrease) in income will shift the budget line to the right (left).

2. The assumption was made that consumers are rational and maximize their satisfaction, or *utility.* Thus consumers are assumed to be able to rank all their choices and that more of a good is preferred to less. Furthermore, consumers are assumed to be willing to substitute among inputs of equal value.

3. Early researchers of consumer behavior argued that utility could be measured. The term *utils* was used as a unit of measure. A hamburger might yield 10 utils, a coke 4 utils, and so on. *Marginal utility* describes the change in utility or utils as more of a good is consumed, and is thought to diminish as consumption increases but not reach zero according to the assumption of nonsatiation.

4. Today no one really believes that utility can be measured in utils. Instead, utility is thought of in the context of a personal index of satisfaction. The magnitude of this index (or function) serves to order the *consumption bundles,* or combinations of goods the consumer faces.

5. All consumption points that provide the same utility form an *isoutility* or *indifference curve.* Increases (decreases) in utility are indicated by a shift in an indifference curve to the right (left). The negative of the slope of this curve is known as the *marginal rate of substitution* (MRS). This rate indicates the consumer's willingness to substitute one good for another. The declining rate as one moves down an indifference curve indicates a diminishing marginal utility. The consumer is at *equilibrium* when the MRS is equal to the slope of the budget line.

6. The *income elasticity of demand* measures the percentage change in a good for a 1 percent change in income. A good is considered a *normal good* if an increase in income leads to increased consumption. This occurs when the income elasticity of demand is greater than zero. When the opposite occurs, a good is considered an *inferior good.* The income elasticity of demand in this case will be negative.

7. The *price elasticity of demand* measures the percentage change in the quantity demanded for a good given a 1 percent change in its price. If this elasticity is greater than 1, demand is said to be *elastic* (i.e., the percentage change in quantity exceeds the percentage change in price). If this elasticity is less than 1, demand is said to be *inelastic* (i.e., quantity changes by a smaller percentage than price). Finally, if this elasticity is equal to 1, demand is said to be *unitary elastic* (i.e., quantity changes by the same percentage as price).

8. If demand is inelastic, a rise (reduction) in price will lead to increased (decreased) consumer expenditures. If demand is elastic, a rise (reduction) in price will lead to a reduction (increase) in consumer expenditures. Finally, if demand is perfectly elastic, expenditures are unchanged as price changes.

9. Movement along a demand curve is referred to as a *change in the quantity demanded,* while a shift in the demand curve resulting from a change in prices of other goods, income, and/or tastes is referred to as a *change in demand.*

10. A *cross-price elasticity* measures the change in the demand for one good in light of a 1 percent change in the price of another good. If this elasticity is positive (negative), the two goods are said to be substitutes (complements). If this elasticity is equal to zero, the two goods are *independent* in demand.

11. The *market demand* for a good is equal to the sum total of all individual demands for the good. As a general law, demand curves are presumed to have a negative slope as a consequence of the *law of diminishing marginal utility.*

DEFINITION OF TERMS

Consumption bundles: quantities of various goods or services that a consumer might potentially consume.

Total utility: the total satisfaction derived from consuming a given bundle of goods and services.

Utility function: a mathematical or functional representation of the satisfaction that a consumer derives from a consumption bundle.

Budget constraint: defined by the income available for consumption and the prices that a consumer faces. This constraint defines the feasible set of consumption choices facing a consumer.

Marginal utility: the increment to utility or satisfaction as consumption of a good is increased by 1 unit.

Marginal rate of substitution: the subjective rate of exchange of paris of consumption goods or services so as to leave utility or satisfaction unchanged, or the absolute value of the slope of an indifference curve.

Normal goods: goods whose consumption rises (falls) as a consumer's income increases (decreases).

Inferior goods: goods whose consumption falls (rises) as a consumer's income increases (decreases).

Indifference curve: a graph of the locus of consumption bundles that provide a consumer a given level of satisfaction.

Own-price elasticity: a measure of the relative response of consumption of a good or service to changes in its price. It is defined as the percentage change in the quantity demanded divided by the percentage change in price.

Cross-price elasticity; a measure of the response of consumption of a good or service to changes in the price of another good or service. It is defined as the percentage in the quantity of good A demanded divided by the percentage change in the price of good B.

Substitutes: goods A and B are substitutes if the cross-price elasticity of demand is positive.

Complements: goods A and B are complements if the cross-price elasticity of demand is negative.

Income elasticity: a measure of the relative response of demand to income changes. It is defined as the percentage change in the quantity demanded divided by the percentage change in income.

Law of diminishing marginal utility: marginal utility declines as more of a good or service is consumed during a specified period of time.

Change in demand: a shift in the demand curve caused generally by changes in the prices of complements or substitutes, income, and tastes.

Utils: units of satisfaction derived from consumption of goods or services.

Consumer equilibrium: the consumption bundle that maximizes total utility and is feasible as defined by the budget constraint. The marginal utilities per dollar spent on good or service must be equal.

REFERENCES

BRANDOW, GEORGE E., *Interrelations among Demand for Farm Products and Implications for Control of Market Supply,* Bulletin 680. University Park, Pa.: Pennsylvania Agricultural Experiment Station, August 1961.

BRANDOW, GEORGE E., "American Agriculture's Capacity to Meet Future Demands," *American Journal of Agricultural Economics,* 1974, pp. 1093–1102.

GEORGE, S., and G. A. KING, *Consumer Demand for Food Commodities in the United States with Projections for 1980,* Giannini Foundation Monograph 26. Davis, Calif.: California Agricultural Experiment Station, March 1971.

HOUTHAKKER, H., and L. TAYLOR, *Consumer Demand in the United States: Analyses and Projections.* Cambridge, Mass.: Harvard University Press, 1970.

JUST, RICHARD E., DARRELL L. HUETH, and ANDREW SCHMITZ, *Applied Welfare Economics and Public Policy.* Englewood Cliffs, N.J.: Prentice-Hall, Inc., 1982.

SCHULTZE, CHARLES L., *The Distribution of Farm Subsidies: Who Gets the Benefits?* Washington, D.C.: The Brookings Institution, 1971.

WAUGH, FREDRICK V., *Demand and Price Analysis,* USDA ERS Technical Bulletin 1316, November 1964.

YEH, C., "Prices, Farm Outputs and Income Projections under Alternative Assumed Demand and Supply Conditions," *American Journal of Agricultural Economics,* 1976, pp. 703–711.

ADDITIONAL READINGS

BREDAHL, MAURY, WILLIAM MEYERS, and KEITH COLLINS, "The Elasticity of Foreign Demand for U.S. Agricultural Products," *American Journal of Agricultural Economics,* 1979, pp. 58–63.

KOHLER, H., *Intermediate Microeconomics: Theory and Applications.* Glenview, Ill.: Scott, Foresman and Company, 1982.

PETERSON, WILLIS L., *Principles of Economics: Micro,* 4th ed. Homewood, Ill.: Richard D. Irwin, Inc., 1980.

PHLIPS, L., *Applied Consumption Analysis.* New York: North Holland/American Elsevier, 1974.

TWEETEN, LUTHER, "Economic Instability in Agriculture: The Contributions of Prices, Government Programs and Exports," Oklahoma Agricultural Experiment Station, 1983.

QUESTIONS

1. Given that your marginal rate of substitution between tacos and hamburgers is 2.0 and the prices of tacos and hamburgers are $1 and $1.50, respectively, how would you adjust your consumption of each good so as to maximize your utility?

2. If the income elasticity of demand for steak is 0.98, steak can be classified as what type of good?

3. Would you expect the own-price elasticity of demand to be lower for catsup in general than for a specific brand of catsup? Why?

4. If a consumer can purchase a dollar's worth of food stamps for $0.70, how will this alter the budget constraint when food and "all other goods" are considered in this budget?

5. Suppose that your parents offer to grant you an allowance of $30 as a daily "living allowance" to be used only for rent and food. Show how you would be better off, or at least no worse off, if you accept this offer with "no strings attached."

6. Which of the following goods are substitutes?
   (a) Bread and jelly
   (b) Home computers and printers
   (c) Introduction to agricultural economics and art history on your degree plan
   (d) Having children and vacations abroad

7. The cross-price elasticity of demand measuring the response of automobile consumption to a change in the price of gasoline is not in general equal to the cross-price elasticity of demand measuring the response of oil consumption to a change in the price of automobiles. Why? Speculate on the magnitudes of the two cross-price elasticities.

8. The price of Florida oranges is $0.30 per pound. Suppose that a freeze destroys 1 million pounds of oranges. The Secretary of Agriculture estimates that Florida farmers will lose $300,000 of income. If the own-price elasticity of demand is 0.8, will the Secretary's estimate be too high or too low?

9. Your boss states that he will pay all of your lunch bill beyond $4. How will this change your behavior? Illustrate your new consumer equilibrium using budget constraints and indifference curves. How will it compare with your previous equilibrium?

10. Given that the income elasticity for food declines as income increases, why might economic growth in third-world countries affect the food and fiber system in that country? What would you expect would occur in highly developed countries?

11. Fads suggest that the marginal utility in the consumption of some goods is positively related to market consumption of these same goods. Goods which have snob appeal imply that a person's marginal utility may be negatively related to market consumption. How would you describe bequests to children in terms of their utility function?

ADVANCED TOPICS

Two additional topics are presented in this section which go beyond the normal coverage found in introductory textbooks. The first has to do with factors underlying the consumer's utility function, and the second has to do with the concept of consumer surplus.

Consumer Axioms

To help us understand the meaning of the term "rationality" when discussing consumer behavior, two basic *consumer axioms* must be understood.[19] Let us assume that consumers know their preferences and are able to rank their consumption choices. Let M and N be two *consumption bundles.* These bundles represent specific quantities of all consumption goods the consumer might desire. For example, let bundle M represent 4 hamburgers and 10 tacos, and let bundle N be 3 hamburgers and 7 tacos.

[19] An "axiom" can be defined as a statement universally accepted as being true, or self-evident. A famous axiom by Euclid is that "things equal to the same thing are also equal to each other."

The *completeness axiom* states that a consumer must be able to rank all consumption bundles. Three alternative decisions are possible when ranking the two bundles described above: bundle *M* could be preferred over bundle *N*, (2) bundle *N* could be preferred over bundle *M*, or (3) the consumer could be indifferent between these two bundles.[20] Some decisions are obvious. Since bundle *M* consists of 4 hamburgers and 10 tacos and bundle *N* consists of 3 hamburgers and 7 tacos, bundle *M* would obviously be preferred to bundle *N* since it has both more tacos and more hamburgers. This, of course, presumes that *more* of each good is preferred to *less*. This assumption is referred to as *nonsatiation*.[21]

The second axiom is referred to as the *transitivity axiom*. To help define the nature of this axiom, let *M, N,* and *O* represent three different consumption bundles. If bundle *M* is preferred over bundle *N* and bundle *N* is preferred over bundle *O*, we know that bundle *M* must also be preferred over bundle *O*. Similarly, if the consumer is indifferent between bundle *M* and bundle *N*, and is indifferent between bundle *N* and bundle *O*, he or she would also be indifferent between bundle *O* and bundle *M*. For example, if a consumer is willing to exchange $30 for a video game and $30 for 24 hamburgers, the consumer should also be willing to exchange 24 hamburgers for the video game.

Consumer Surplus

An examination of the demand curve presented in Figure 3.10 reveals that the consumer pays $6 each for 5 units of this product. The consumer, however, was *willing to pay* $10 for 1 unit, $9 for 2 units, and so on. Thus, while the consumer actually pays $6 per unit to consume 5 units, he or she was willing to pay must more. If one pursues this line of reasoning, it can be argued that the area *ABC* in Figure 3.10 is a measure of the excess that the consumer is willing to pay to consume 5 units of this product. This difference between willingness to pay and the amount actually paid is referred to as *consumer surplus*. Although not without controversy, it is a "bread and butter" tool of economic policy analysis.[22]

Using this approach, the *increase* in consumer welfare when the price of hamburgers falls from $6 to $5 per unit is given by area *ACED*. The *loss* in consumer surplus would be equal to area *ACED* if the price were to rise from $5 to $6. Thus a policy that would bring about a decline in price from $6 to

---

[20] This does not mean that the consumer cannot make up his or her mind, but that the bundles *M* and *N* provide equal satisfaction or utility.

[21] It is easy to think of cases that suggest satiation. Consuming 10 tacos in one day might satiate your appetite. However, we will see that the budget constraint seldom allows points of satiation to occur.

[22] See Just et al. (1982) The issue is whether area *ABC* represents the consumer's actual willingness to pay for the privilege of purchasing the commodity at $6 each or only an approximation of it.

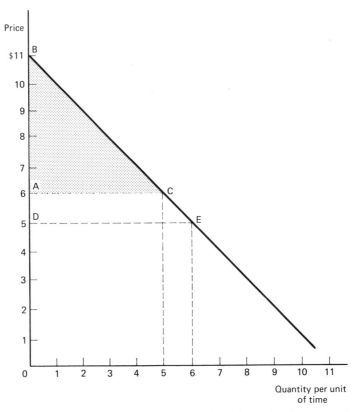

Figure 3.10 *Concept of Consumer Surplus.* The change in the economic welfare of consumers can be approximated by the concept of consumer surplus. This surplus is equal to the difference between what the consumer was "willing to pay" for a product and he or she had to pay. This figure shows that the consumer was willing to buy 5 units if the price per unit was $6 (see point *C*). Yet this figure shows that the consumer would have been willing to pay a higher price if fewer quantities were involved. Thus the shaded area *ABC* represents the difference between the price per unit for a smaller number of quantities and the $6 per unit price. If the price of the product were to fall to $5 per unit, the consumer would realize a gain in his or her consumer surplus equal to the area *ACED*.

$5 would increase consumer welfare by the sum of money equal to area *ACED*. The concept of consumer surplus thus places a monetary value on changes in utility.

Often, policies change many prices, in which case consumer surplus changes summed over all markets represents the economic benefits to consumers of the policy change. The concept of consumer surplus will be discussed further in Chapter 10.

4

TECHNOLOGY

OF PRODUCTION

It should be apparent from reading Chapter 2 that the economic world is both complex and interdependent. Farmers purchase goods and services from, and sell products to, many other sectors in the economy. For example, the production of crop products by farm businesses requires the services of soil, fertilizer, chemicals, machinery, labor, and other inputs. These service flows are often referred to by economists as *factors of production,* or simply *inputs*. The resulting product, on the other hand, is generally referred to as the *output*.

In this chapter we focus on the physical relationships between inputs and outputs. We place particular emphasis on those concepts that are important to agricultural economic decision making. These concepts include (1) a classification of inputs and outputs, (2) a demonstration of what is meant by technical efficiency, and (3) the identification of specific concepts that relate to how changes in inputs affect output.

CLASSIFICATION OF INPUTS

It is helpful to have some broad classifications in mind when discussing production relationships. These classifications are not only for efficient communication but also help us conduct economic analyses.[1] Although not

[1] Such jargon often comes under attack by those outside a discipline of study. For example, Edwin Newman in *Strictly Speaking* (New York: Warner Books, Inc., 1980) has satired the excessive use of such language. Economics seems to be no better or worse than

uniformly accepted, classification of inputs into the following four groups has proven useful: (1) land, (2) labor, (3) capital, and (4) management.

Land Input

Land includes not only the land forms associated with the earth's crust but also such resources as minerals, forests, groundwater, and other resources given by nature. Such resources are classified as either (1) renewable (e.g., forests) or (2) nonrenewable resources (e.g., minerals). An example of a key land input is productive topsoil. Indeed, it has many of the attributes of a nonrenewable resource.

Labor Input

Labor includes all labor services used in production with the exception of managerial functions. In crop production, for example, this includes preharvest, harvest, and postharvest labor activities. The typical crop budget includes expenditures for labor associated with seedbed preparation, planting, irrigation (if any), chemical applications, harvesting, and other functions.

Capital Input

Capital inputs are manufactured goods that provide productive services. Two key aspects of capital goods are: (1) they do not provide consumer satisfaction directly but rather aid in the production of consumer goods, and (2) they are not entirely consumed during the current production period but rather are consumed with the passage of time and by usage. To illustrate, consider a farm tractor—a common agricultural capital input. Consumers do not derive direct satisfaction from the possession or consumption of farm tractors. Instead, tractors are used to produce a product which, after further processing, does go to consumers, who derive satisfaction from consumption of the final product. The farm tractor is not "consumed" during the current period. Yet it clearly may not have the same value *after* the season as it did *prior* to its current usage. For this reason, agricultural economists distinguish between the *stock* of capital goods (e.g., farm tractors) and the flow of services provided by these capital goods during the period (which is proportional to the size of the tractor and hours of use).

Management Input

The final input category is management. Its functions are varied and are easier to conceptualize than measure. Farmers must make policy decisions as

---

other disciplines. Indeed, in most introductory classes, learning the "jargon" is an important portion of the course.

USDA Photo

The production of raw agricultural products involves the combination of land, labor, capital, and management inputs. Although the first two input categories are no doubt familiar to you, the last two may require definition. Capital inputs consists of manufactured resources, which may provide productive services over a multiyear period. Management differs from labor in that it encompasses the decision-making and risk-taking aspects of the farm business, which given the firm direction and directly affect its survival.

to how, when, and what to produce when organizing their inputs. This necessarily involves taking risks, since weather and other factors generate uncertainty as to the eventual yield and price of crops as well as livestock. A crucial component of risk taking is the adoption and innovation of new techniques of production and the organization of production systems. This and other facets of decision making in an uncertain world will be examined in Chapter 8.

Having classified these inputs, it is important to note that these classifications serve to highlight special characteristics of inputs. For example, it is clear that the decision to purchase a tractor must be based on projections of future benefits and costs, since it has a useful life extending over several years. Each category has special economic problems associated with its measurement and economic incentives for its use. Indeed, there are branches of economic study that focus on each of these four inputs regardless of which sector is being studied: (1) land, natural resource economics and land economics; (2) capital, investment economics; (3) labor, labor economics; and (4) management, broadly covered by all economic study but specifically focused on in managerial economics.

In this chapter we abstract from most of their differences and instead highlight some concepts common to all inputs. In particular, we focus technical relationships. Input and product prices will be meshed with these technical relationships in Chapter 5 when we discuss those input–output combinations that achieve a specific economic goal, such as profit maximization.

INPUT-OUTPUT RELATIONSHIPS

Several key relationships between the level of output and the level of input use must be understood before we consider the prices of these inputs and outputs. These relationships include the concept of a production function that reflects this input–output relationship, as well as the concepts of marginal and average product. Each is discussed in turn below.

The Production Function

A production function characterizes the *causal relationship* between input and output. Consider the following example, which has been of both current and long-standing interest to agronomists as well as agricultural economists. A corn farmer knows that as fertilizer use is varied (pounds per acre), yields (output of corn in bushels per acre) also vary in a systematic way. Before you as an agricultural economist can recommend what quantity of fertilizer the farmer should apply, you must have some knowledge of the causal relationship between yields and fertilizer use. If the application of fertilizer has no effect on crop yields, a profit-maximizing farmer obviously should not apply any fertilizer. Thus the agricultural economist, although not focusing on the details of the agronomic relationship between fertilizer and yields, must be aware of such technical relationships.

Of course, there are other inputs besides fertilizer which are used to produce corn. In the general case, where there are n identifiable inputs, a production function may be expressed in the following general form:

$$\text{output} = f(\text{quantity of input 1, quantity of input 2,} \ldots, \text{quantity of input } n) \qquad (4.1)$$

For example, in a traditional agricultural setting, output is a "function" of the services provided by labor, land, seeds, and hand implements.

A production function is a rule associating an output to given levels of the inputs used. If the first input varies while all the other inputs are held fixed, we can write equation (4.1) as follows:

$$\text{output} = f(\text{quantity of input } 1 \mid \text{quantity of input } 2,$$
$$\ldots, \text{quantity of } n \text{ used}) \qquad (4.2)$$

where the bar separating the first input from all other inputs indicates that only the first input is being varied while the other inputs are held fixed. It should be stressed that output is measured in *physical units.*

To illustrate the concept of the total physical product curve, consider the hypothetical data presented in Table 4.1, where one input (fertilizer) varies while other inputs are held fixed. The first column indicates the level of fertilizer use. The second column presents the levels of output corresponding to specific quantities of input use. For example, if the use of fertilizer is 0.50, output will be 10.0. If we were to connect with a smooth curve, this and other combinations of output and fertilizer use reported in columns (1) and (2) in Table 4.1, we would obtain the total physical product curve presented in Figure 4.1.

Point on Fig. 4.1	(1) Use of input	(2) Total physcial product, level of output	(3) Marginal physical product, $\Delta(2) \div \Delta(1)$	(4) Average physical product, $(2) \div (1)$
a	0.5	10.0		20.0
			30.0	
b	1.0	25.0		25.0
			35.0	
c	2.0	60.0		30.0
			15.0	
d	3.0	75.0		25.0
			5.0	
e	4.0	80.0		20.0
			2.0	
f	5.0	82.0		16.4
			1.0	
g	6.0	83.0		13.5
			0.5	
h	7.0	83.5		11.9
			−0.5	
i	8.0	83.0		10.4

TABLE 4.1 TOTAL, MARGINAL, AND AVERAGE PHYSICAL PRODUCT. This table shows the relationships between input use and several important output concepts. As additional inputs are employed, output increases in incremental amounts. The change in output for a given change in input use is known as the marginal physical product. The level of output for a given level of input use is known as the average physical product. At some level of input use, the level of output may crease increasing and may begin to decline. When this occurs, the marginal physical product will fall to zero and become negative.

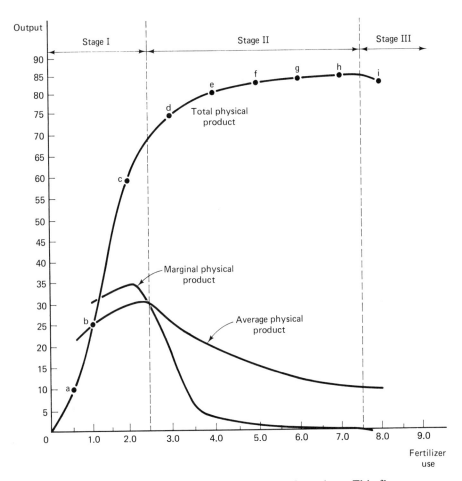

Figure 4.1 *Total, Marginal, and Average Physical Product.* This figure illustrates the nature of the input–output relationships for the numerical example presented in Table 4.1. Several relationships are made clearer here. For example, the marginal physical product curve intersects the average physical product curve from the top at the peak of the average physical product curve. The marginal physical product curve also crosses the horizontal axis (i.e., becomes negative) when the total physical product curve has reached its peak and begun to decline. This marks the start of stage III of production. Only stage II should be of interest to rational farmers.

To summarize our understanding of production functions, we stated that the production function expresses the relationship between output and inputs. This relationship is presumed *causal* in nature. That is, the quantities of inputs "cause" a particular level of output to occur. When one input is varied while all others are fixed, the production function generates points along the total physical product curve.

Marginal Physical Product

If the farmer adds another pound of fertilizer per acre, how will corn yields change? Does this response depend on the quantity of fertilizer and other inputs in current use on the farm? These questions give rise to an important concept, that of marginal physical product.[2] The marginal physical product for an input is the incremental response of output to an incremental change in the input with all other inputs remaining fixed at any particular level. Stated in equation form, the marginal physical product is equal to

$$\text{Marginal physical product} = \frac{\Delta \text{ output}}{\Delta \text{ input}} \tag{4.3}$$

The numerical value of the marginal physical product in the example introduced above is reported in column (3) of Table 4.1. There may be some confusion regarding which level of output to associate with a marginal physical product. In each case, the *intermediate* level of input use will be satisfactory. For example, the marginal physical product when the level of fertilizer use changes from 0.5 to 1.0 would be 30 [i.e., 30.0 = (25.0 – 10.0) ÷ 0.5]. This value is listed in the row associated with an input level of 1.0. If 3.0 units of fertilizer were used, the marginal physical product would be 15 [i.e., 15.0 = (75.0 – 60.0) ÷ (3.0 – 2.0)], and so on. Figure 4.1, which highlights the values from Table 4.1, presents smooth curves for the total and marginal physical product.

An important relationship exists between the total and marginal physical products. The slope of the total physical product curve with respect to the use of fertilizer is approximately equal to the marginal physical product. If the change in fertilizer use is very small, the marginal physical product is exactly equal to the slope of the total physical product curve. In other words, it measures the instantaneous rate of change in output in response to a change in the use of fertilizer.

There is a particular region of the graph presented in Figure 4.1 that should help illustrate the relationship between total and marginal physical product. Note that when the use of fertilizer is increasing from 7.0 to 8.0, the marginal physical product switches from positive to zero to negative. At the point where the marginal physical produce is equal to zero, the slope of the total physical product curve should also be equal to zero. This indicates that the maximum level of output has been reached. Indeed, an examination of Figure 4.1 indicates that the total physical product curve does level off and begin falling within the neighborhood of 7.5 units of fertilizer use.

Finally, when the slope of the total physical product curve, or the marginal physical product, is falling (i.e., becoming smaller), the total physical

---

[2] Some refer to this concept as marginal product. We will follow the time-honored tradition of using the word "physical" in our discussion. This makes it clear that the units of measurement are in physical units rather than dollars.

product curve is increasing at a *decreasing* rate. Before when the marginal physical product curve was increasing, the total physical product curve was increasing at an *increasing* rate. Note that if the use of fertilizer is expanded beyond 7.5 units, the marginal physical product becomes negative. This might indicate that so much fertilizer is being applied that it is "burning out" the crop. No rational farmer would ever want to use an input beyond the point where the marginal physical product becomes negative, since further *increases* in input would cause output to *fall*.

Average Physical Product

A final input–output relationship discussed here is the *average physical product*. The average physical product is related to the *level* of output relative to the *level* of fertilizer use instead of their incremental change. In the context of this discussion, the average physical product represents the yield in bushels per pound of fertilizer. In other words,

$$\text{average physical product} = \frac{\text{output}}{\text{input}} \tag{4.4}$$

or the ratio of the output level to the input level with all other input levels held fixed.

Column (4) in Table 4.1 presents the value of the average physical product for fertilizer use. An analogous smooth curve for the average physical product for fertilizer is presented in Figure 4.1. The average physical product curve is shown to rise and fall in a fashion similar to the movement of the marginal physical product curve. However, the marginal physical product curve peaks at a lower level of input use. A little reflection should convince you that if the marginal physical product curve is rising, the average physical product curve must be rising as well. Furthermore, it can be shown that the marginal physical product curve cuts the average physical product from above at that point where the average physical product curve reaches its maximum. Finally, when the average physical product curve is falling (i.e., getting smaller), the marginal physical product curve must be falling as well.

Stages of Production

It is often convenient to divide the graph in Figure 4.1 into three unique regions, often referred to as *stages of production*. Stage I is where the marginal physical product is rising but lies above the average physical product curve. Stage II consists of all applications of, say, fertilizer beginning at the end of stage I and continuing until the value of the marginal physical product becomes equal to zero. Finally, stage III consists of all applications of fertilizer to the right of stage II, or where the marginal physical product is negative.

Returning to the example presented in Table 4.1 and Figure 4.1, the stages of production are associated with the following levels of input use:

Stage	Usage of fertilizer	Operate?
I	Between 0 and 2.5	Irrational
II	Between 2.5 and 7.5	Rational
III	Greater than 7.5	Irrational

The significance of stage III has already been identified. No rational farmer would desire to operate in stage III. Would a farmer increase his use of fertilizer from 7.5 units to 8.0 units knowing full well that corn yields would fall? Clearly not. Stage I is also irrational, although it is more difficult to see why this is so. Under certain assumptions, it represents a stage III situation for the other inputs. It would be irrational to operate in this stage from the viewpoint of other inputs. Another consideration that underscores the irrational nature of stage I is that the farmer cannot be maximizing profit in this stage. We shall leave the support of this argument until Chapter 5. Suffice it to say that stage II appears to hold primary interest for a farmer who wishes to maximize his profits.

In stage II, the marginal physical product is falling. This phenomenon is so widely observed that it is called a law—the *law of diminshing returns.* This law states that *as successive units of a variable input are added to a production process with the other inputs held constant, the marginal physical product eventually falls.* Thus, in the region of greatest economic interest, we would expect to observe diminishing marginal physical product of a variable input.

An Empirical Example

Agricultural economists have devoted much time and money to the estimation of production relationships. Such relationships are estimated using experimental data or actual farm data. To illustrate some of the concepts discussed in this section, let us consider the study of lime applications by Hall and Free (1979). Lime is productive in many soils, mainly through its reduction of soil acidity. Experimental plots of alfalfa observed by Hall and Free held all other inputs fixed while applications of lime were varied. For lime application rates less than or equal to 3 tons of lime per acre, the following production function was estimated:

$$\text{alfalfa yield} = 0.902 + 1.794 \times (\text{lime}) - 0.290 \times (\text{lime})^2 \qquad (4.5)$$

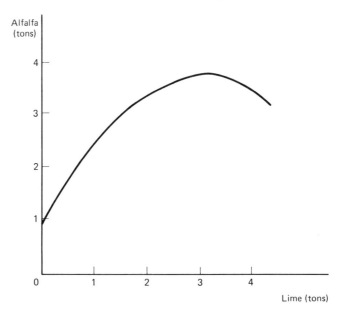

Figure **4.2** *Empirical Input–Output Relationships.* The input–output relationship between lime and alfalfa given in equation (4.5) is illustrated in this figure. As lime is increased beyond 3 tons per acre, we see that the total physical product curve peaks and begins to decline. No rational farmer would want to increase the use of lime beyond this point.

where the alfalfa yield (i.e., the total physical product per acre) and lime applications were measured in tons per acre and where (lime)² represents the quantity of lime used *squared*. The production relationship expressed in equation (4.5) is illustrated graphically in Figure 4.2.

Can you verify that the marginal physical product of lime is diminishing in this example? To begin with, the marginal physical product of lime when 1 ton is applied is about 1.2 tons of alfalfa. When 2 tons of lime is applied, the marginal physical product falls to about 0.60. Similar conclusions can be reached for the average physical product.

INPUT–INPUT RELATIONSHIPS

The fertilizer example cited above involved only one input. Let us now expand this discussion to include two variable inputs and the topic of input substitution. This requires shifting the "bar" appearing after the first input in equation (4.2) so that it appears after the second input. In this broader context we can now focus on the substitution between fertilizer and water in a cropping operation or between grain and hay in a livestock operation. In presenting this topic, however, let's illustrate input substitution in a way that is relevant both to U.S. agriculture and to agriculture throughout the world. In virtually every agricultural setting, a farmer can alter the combination of *capital* and *labor* used in production. For example, weeds can be pulled or hoed; or they can be covered by furrowing or killed with herbicides. At each stage of a product's development, there are usually a wide range of production practices that emerge to be more popular than others based on existing economic incentives.

Isoquants

If we attempted to graph the production function for two inputs, it would take three dimensions: two dimensions for the two inputs and one dimension for output. However, three-dimensional figures are difficult to draw and even more difficult to understand. For this reason it is convenient when discussing the concepts presented in this section to collapse a three-dimensional figure into two dimensions. This can be done by focusing on the two inputs for a specific level of output.

A curve that reflects the combinations of two inputs which result in a particular level of output is called an *isoquant* curve. The term "iso" here has the same meaning as it did in Chapter 3 when we were discussing isoutility curves. In the present context, an isoquant consists of a locus of points that correspond to "an equal" or identical level of output. Along any isoquant, an infinite number of combinations of labor and capital are possible. As the quantity of labor (capital) increases, less capital (labor) is necessary to produce a given level of output.

To illustrate this point, think of quantities of capital as being divisible units of machinery (e.g., tractor size as measured by horsepower). As the tractor and its complementary equipment are increased in quantity, fewer hours of labor would be required to produce a given level of output. Similarly, with less equipment used, more hours of labor would be required to produce the same output. We would conclude in this particular instance that capital and labor appear to be *technical substitutes.*

To determine the *rate* of substitution between two inputs, which by the way represents (the negative of) the *slope* of the isoquant, we can measure the *marginal rate of technical substitution.* The rate of substitution of capital for labor is determined as follows:

$$\frac{\Delta \text{ capital}}{\Delta \text{ labor}} = \frac{MPP_{\text{labor}}}{MPP_{\text{capital}}} \qquad (4.6)$$

where MPP_{capital} and MPP_{labor} represent the marginal physical products for capital and labor, respectively. The expression in equation (4.6) indicates that changes in labor must be compensated by changes in capital if the level of output is to remain unchanged.[3] For example, if the marginal rate of technical substitution of capital for labor was equal to 3.0, capital must be reduced by 3 units if labor is increased by 1 unit and if output is to remain unchanged.[4]

These concepts are illustrated in Figure 4.3. Two isoquants are drawn to illustrate the effects of two different output levels (i.e., 10 units and 20 units). Isoquants farther out from the origin (O) correspond to higher output levels. As we move from range A to range B on the isoquant corresponding to 10 units of output, we see that less capital and more labor is required. Consider three separate 1-unit changes in labor: Ranges A, B, and C each represent the values for the ratio of Δcapital to Δlabor at different locations on the isoquant associated with 10 units of output. We see in Figure 4.3 that the marginal rate of technical substitution of capital for labor falls from a value of approximately 4 in range A to 0.75 in range B and to 0.25 in range C.

These observations illustrate that as labor is substituted for capital along as isoquant (output remaining unchanged), the marginal rate of technical substitution of capital for labor falls. Declining marginal rates of technical substitution are a consequence of the law of diminishing returns discussed in the preceding section. As labor increases, its marginal physical product falls. Similarly, reductions in capital imply an increase in its marginal physical product.

How do the isoquants in Figure 4.3 relate to our earlier discussion of the stages of production? Focusing on the isoquant for 10 units of output, the marginal physical product of capital is negative above point G. Furthermore, the marginal physical product of labor is negative to the right of point H on this isoquant. You will recall that the marginal physical product in stage III was said to be negative. Since stage III is of no economic interest, the economic region of production is bounded by points G and H for the isoquant corresponding to an output of 10 units and by points D and F for the isoquant associated with an output of 20 units. Thus it should again be clear that only certain regions of input–output relationships are of interest to profit-maximizing farmers.

Figure 4.4 illustrates two input substitution relationships at opposite ends of the spectrum. Panel a illustrates the case where *no substitution* be-

---

[3] Since the loss in output due to the increase in labor must equal the gain in output resulting from the increase in capital if output is to remain unchanged (i.e., remain on the same isoquant), then

$$- \Delta \text{ labor} \times MPP_{\text{labor}} = + \Delta \text{ capital} \times MPP_{\text{capital}}$$

Equation (4.6) simply represents a rearrangement of this statement.

[4] Since the marginal rate of technical substitution is negative in all rational areas of production (i.e., stage II), most economists do not always bother to include the minus sign.

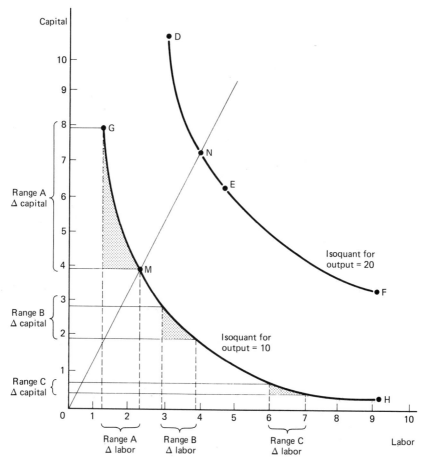

Figure 4.3 *Isoquants for Capital and Labor.* The relationship between two inputs for a given level of output is known as an isoquant. Different points along the same isoquant correspond to specific combinations of two inputs (labor and capital in this case). Higher levels of output for a given combination of inputs are found on isoquants lying farther to the right. The slope of an isoquant is known as the marginal rate of technical substitution. The value of this rate falls as we move down an isoquant (e.g., this rate is equal to 4.0 in range *A*, 0.75 in range *B*, and 0.25 in range *C*).

tween inputs is possible. The isoquants here have rectangular corners. Holding capital fixed at *C* while increasing labor will *not* increase the farmer's output. In terms of our definition of efficiency (i.e., least-cost input use for given level of output), only one input ratio *(C ÷ L)* is efficient for an output level of 10 units. At all other points on these isoquants, more of either capital or labor would be used than necessary to produce 10 units of output. It should

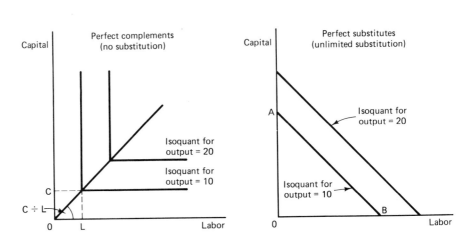

Figure 4.4 *Two Extreme Cases of the Substitution Relationships be-*
tween Inputs. Isoquants can take on many different shapes. Two extreme cases are depicted in panels a and b. In panel a, for example, no
substitution between capital and labor is possible; a fixed combination
of these two inputs is required to produce this product. In panel b,
however, we see there are no limits placed on substitution; that is,
these two inputs can be freely substituted for one another in production.

be clear after reviewing panel a that this ratio represents the efficient input
ratio for *all* output levels.[5]

At the other extreme is the production relationship depicted in panel b.
This isoquant is linear with a constant slope, suggesting *unlimited substitu-*
tion possibilities between capital and labor. Moving down from point *A* to
point *B* on the isoquant associated with 10 units of output, we see that there
is no reduction in the possibility of substituting labor for capital. For example, if the ratio of Δ capital to Δ labor is equal to -3.0, it is *always* possible
to reduce capital by 3.0 units and still keep output fixed *if* labor is increased
by 1 unit. This is in contrast to the case illustrated in Figure 4.3, where the
substitution possibilities diminished in the sense that increasing levels of
labor are required for a given reduction in capital as one moves down the
isoquant.

Neither the zero or constant marginal rates of substitution depicted
in Figure 4.4 are very descriptive of typical production processes found in
agriculture. Even if there is no substitution among inputs in the short run,

[5] This substitution relationship is occasionally referred to as inputs which are perfect
complements. That is, efficient production implies that an increase in capital must be
accompanied by an increase in labor, and vice versa. The marginal rate of substitution
here is zero.

the passage of time usually allows for some substitution possibilities. Thus diminishing marginal rates of technical substitution as illustrated in Figure 4.3 are typical of existing farm production relationships.

Increases in Production

As noted in Figure 4.3, increases in output are reflected by isoquants that lie farther away from the origin. In this figure the isoquant for an output of 20 units was farther from the origin than the isoquant associated with an output of 10 units. This brings up an interesting question. Is the isoquant associated with 20 units twice as far from the origin as the isoquant associated with 10 units? Consider a line denoted by *OMN* drawn from the origin in Figure 4.3. Along this line, all input ratios (i.e., capital to labor) are *fixed*. At point *M*, approximately 3.75 units of capital and 2.25 units of labor would produce 10 units of output. At point *N*, 7.0 units of capital and 4.25 units of labor would produce 20 units of output. Thus both inputs would increase by 189 percent [i.e., (7.0 ÷ 3.75) × 100 and (4.25 ÷ 2.25) × 100], while output would increase by 200 percent.

An Empirical Example

A recent study of swine production in the United States considered the relationship between the weight of swine, corn consumption, and protein supplement consumption (Sonka et al., 1976). Output in this case is the weight of the gain for swine, while the inputs are the corn and protein supplement. To illustrate, consider the isoquant corresponding to an initial weight of 60 pounds and a closing weight of 100 pounds (i.e., a weight gain of 40 pounds). The equation for this estimated relationship was estimated to be

$$\text{corn} = 6.1630 - 0.5898 \times (\text{protein supplement}) \qquad (4.7)$$

where each input is measured in pounds and expressed in logarithms.[6] This isoquant has the same general shape as the isoquant illustrated in Figure 4.3, as we see in Figure 4.5.

This figure shows, among other things, that the marginal rate of technical substitution of corn for the protein supplement is positive, indicating that the level of output would be unchanged if we decreased corn as long as we increased protein supplement by an appropriate amount. For example, the ending weight of the swine (100 pounds) can be achieved with 16 pounds of protein supplement and 92.5 pounds of corn (we have made the conversion from logarithms for the purposes of our discussion). This same weight gain can also be achieved using 25 pounds of protein supplement and 71.1 pounds of corn.

---

[6] To follow our discussion, it is not essential that you understand how to express units in logarithms.

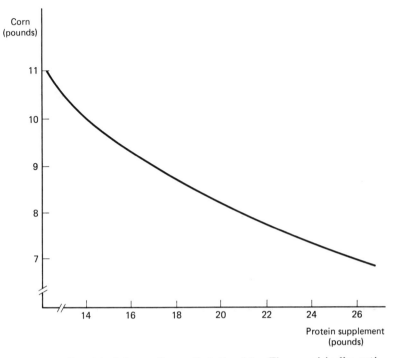

Figure 4.5 *Empirical Input–Input Relationship.* The empirically estimated relationship between corn and protein supplement in the production of hogs presented in equation (4.7) is depicted here. The shape of this isoquant suggests that these two inputs can readily be substituted for one another in the production of hogs.

We can calculate the marginal rate of technical substitution for different combinations of corn and protein given by equation (4.7) by substituting these values into equation (4.6). For example, this substitution rate is about 3.4 when 16 pounds of protein supplement and 82.5 pounds of corn is used. This substitution rate would fall to 1.7 if the protein supplement were increased to 25 pounds and corn were decreased to 71.1 pounds. Presumably, this drop in the rate of substitution occurred as a result of the decrease in the marginal physical product of the protein supplement and increase in the marginal physical product of corn as the use of the supplement was increased and corn use was decreased. This illustrated the principle of *diminishing marginal rate of substitution* of corn for the protein supplement.[7]

[7] Although the marginal rate of technical substitution is a useful measure of substitution as one moves *along* an isoquant, it is similar to the marginal physical product in that it is not free of the units of measurement, a problem that hampers comparisons of unlike physical quantities. A measure that *is* unit free is the *elasticity of substitution* because it is expressed in percentage terms. For two inputs on a particular isoquant and at a particular input ratio (e.g., capital to labor), this elasticity is given by the percentage change in the input ratio (i.e., the percentage change in labor divided by the percentage in capital) divided by the percentage change in the marginal rate of substitution of capital

OUTPUT-OUTPUT RELATIONSHIPS

In the preceding section we examined several types of input–input relationships. Our specific interest was the ease with which one input substituted for another in producing a given level of output. It is also necessary to understand the nature of output–output relationships or the substitution of one product for another. Although we have seen increasing specialization in agricultural production, most farm businesses produce more than one product, or are *diversified.*

Suppose that a farmer operating a 1,000-acre crop farm can produce either all corn, all wheat, or any combination of these two crops. As corn (wheat) acreage is increased, wheat (corn) acreage must be cut back. Thus there is a *substitution among products* in much the same sense that inputs were substitutes for one another in the preceding section.

These multiproduct relationships possess similar but different properties from those in the single-product case. Among the most important of these is how the expansion of one product leads to changes in the production of other products.

Production Possibilities Curve

Figure 4.1 stressed production efficiency by seeking to minimize input use for a *given level of output.* In the multiproduct case, we can now think of efficiency in terms of maximizing output with a *given level of inputs.* To facilitate the graphical presentations that follow, we shall assume that the farmer's production choices are limited to two products (corn and wheat).

Points *A* and *H* in Figure 4.6 represent production levels for corn and wheat on a 1,000-acre farm for a given complement of machinery and labor. Point *A*, for example, represents specialization in the production of corn. Point *H*, on the other hand, reflects a diversified production plan. Is point *H* efficient? We know that point *C* would result in the production of more of both commodities with the *same* quantity of inputs. Thus point *H* is inefficient. By similar reasoning, point *F* can also be ruled to be technically inefficient, leaving only points *A, B, C, D,* and *E* as the efficient production points. A smooth curve drawn through these points is called an isoproduct or *production possibilities curve.* This curve gives the product combinations that can be efficiently produced using a *given* quantity of inputs.

---

for labor. For the production process described by panel a in Figure 4.4, where the input ratio does not change, the elasticity of substitution would equal zero. For the production process in panel b of Figure 4.4, the elasticity of substitution is infinite. The production process depicted in Figure 4.4 obviously lies in between these two extremes. Of special interest is the elasticity of substitution between capital and labor in agriculture. For the United States as a whole, estimates indicate considerable substitution possibilities, with an aggregate elasticity of substitution often approaching 1.

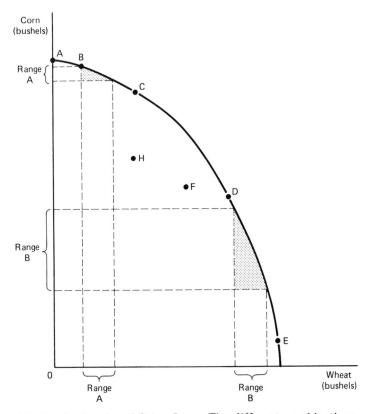

Figure 4.6 *Production Possibilities Curve.* The different combinations of products that can be produced efficiently with a given level of inputs are found on the production possibilities curve. As wheat production is increased, corn production must be cut back. Any combination of products lying within this "frontier" is technically inefficient since more output could be generated with the same quantity of inputs. The slope of the production possibilities curve is known as the marginal rate of production transformation.

As you proceed down the production possibilities curve, one of the first things you note is that as wheat production is increased, successively larger amounts of corn production must be sacrificed. The cutback in cotton production as wheat production is expanded increases sharply as we move from range *A* in Figure 4.6 to range *B*. A measure of this effect is the *marginal rate of product transformation.* In absolute terms, the marginal rate of product transformation represents the rate at which the production of corn must contract (expand) for a 1-unit increase (decrease) in the production of wheat. The marginal rate of transformation is given by

$$\begin{matrix} \text{marginal rate} \\ \text{of product} \\ \text{transformation} \end{matrix} = -\frac{\Delta \text{ corn}}{\Delta \text{ wheat}} \qquad (4.8)$$

Earlier we noted that in range A, the marginal rate of product transformation of wheat for corn is very small (i.e., Δ corn relative to Δ wheat is quite small). We also observed that the marginal rate of product transformation near point E would be much higher (i.e., Δ corn relative to Δ wheat is quite large). This *increasing* marginal rate of production transformation is a widely observed and measured phenomenon and has the same general "law-like" acceptance as the declining marginal rate of technical substitution discussed earlier for two inputs.[8]

The marginal rate of product transformation may not always be increasing as depicted in Figure 4.6. For example, the production possibilities curve may be "bowed in," indicating that increments in an output require successively smaller decreases in the production of the other product (Heady, 1952). Some agricultural economists would see this case as being descriptive of many production processes observed in the farm business sector.

Two cases at the opposite ends of the spectrum are illustrated in Figure 4.7. In panel a of Figure 4.7, the case where no output substitution is

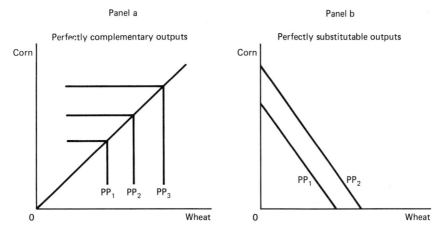

Figure 4.7 *Two Extreme Cases of Product Substitution.* The substitution relationship between two products can also take on many different forms. The two extreme cases are illustrated here. In panel a, for example, corn and wheat are not substitutes for one another in production. The farmer must either grow all corn or grow all wheat. In panel b, on the other hand, corn and wheat are perfect substitutes. This is, any combination of corn and wheat is technically possible for a given level of input use.

[8] To avoid a "units of measure" problem when examining output–output relationships, we can use the *elasticity of product transformation,* which measures the marginal rate of product transformation for two products in percentage terms. This elasticity is given by the ratio of the percentage change in the output ratio (i.e., the percentage change in wheat divided by the percentage change in cotton) divided by the percentage change in the marginal rate of product transformation.

possible is shown. In other words, the farmer can grow either all wheat or all corn, but not some combination of these two crops. Panel b in Figure 4.7 illustrates the case where perfect product substitution is possible. That is, these two crops are one-to-one substitutes for each other.

Increase in Input Use

Changes in the level of fixed inputs used in production will shift the production possibilities curve in much the same way as output changes shifted the isoquant in Figure 4.3. The production possibilities curve for a larger (smaller) quantity of fixed inputs than that associated with the curve plotted in Figure 4.6 would lie to the right (left) of this curve.

A Numerical Example

The substitution relationship between two products can be illustrated further by examining the numerical example presented in Table 4.2. As the farmer in this hypothetical example increases his production of wheat, he must cut back his production of corn. If he specialized in corn production, this farmer could raise 135,000 bushels of corn. If he specialized in wheat production, this farmer could raise 90,000 bushels of wheat. Column (3) in Table 4.2 reflects the increasing nature of the marginal rate of product transformation for these two products. We shall return to this example in Chapter 5 when we examine which of these combinations maximizes the farmer's profits.

PRODUCTION IN CONSUMPTION ACTIVITIES

All the examples examined thus far in this chapter refer to converting inputs to farm products. However, production activities take place in many other ways. Whenever we consume a good such as a movie, we are "producing" this consumption by using time and perhaps a vehicle. Thus an appropriate production function in this instance might be

$$\text{movie} = f(\text{time in minutes, vehicle-miles}) \qquad (4.9)$$

A housewife "producing" a meal uses capital (kitchen utensils and appliances), labor, and raw materials (unprepared food). To produce "grown children," capital, labor, management, and other inputs are required. Although we will not pursue the meaning of efficient production in this case, it is clear that the notion of efficient conversion of inputs into outputs is a pervasive concept. Marriage, divorce, sleeping, and even toothbrushing have lent themselves to economic analysis based on technical relationships that exist between inputs and outputs.

(1)	(2)	(3) Marginal rate of product transformation, $\Delta(1) \div \Delta(2)$
Corn	Wheat	
135,000	0	
		0.7
128,000	10,000	
		0.9
119,000	20,000	
		1.1
108,000	30,000	
		1.3
95,000	40,000	
		1.5
80,000	50,000	
		1.7
63,000	60,000	
		1.9
44,000	70,000	
		2.1
23,000	80,000	
		2.3
0	90,000	

TABLE 4.2 PRODUCTION POSSIBILITIES FOR A 1,000-ACRE FARM. The output levels for corn and wheat presented in columns (1) and (2) represent points on a hypothetical farmer's production possibilities curve. The marginal rate of product transformation stated in absolute terms is presented in column (3). These values represent the slope of the production possibilities curve at each one of the points on this curve given by the values reported in columns (1) and (2).

SUMMARY

The purpose of this chapter was to illustrate the various physical relationships that exist between inputs and outputs with which agricultural economists must be familiar. The major points of this chapter can be summarized as follows:

1. Farm inputs can be classified into four major categories: (1) land, (2) labor, (3) capital, and (4) management.
2. A *production function* captures the causal relationship between inputs and output. The levels of total output for alternative levels of input provide points on the *production possibilities curve.*

3. The *total physical product* reflects the level of output of a given level of input use. *Marginal physical product* represents the change in the level of output associated with a change in input use. Finally, *average physical product* reflects the level of output per unit of input use. In each case, all other inputs are held fixed at any particular level. The value of the marginal physical product represents the slope of the total physical product curve. No rational farmer would want to produce beyond the point where the marginal physical product equals zero since further input use would cause output to *fall*.

4. There are three *stages of production:* (1) stage I is where the marginal physical product curve for a particular input is rising but still lies above the average physical product curve; (2) stage II picks up where marginal physical product equals the average physical product and continues until the marginal physical product for the input in question reaches zero; and (3) stage III begins where stage II left off. Stage II is the range of an input–output relationship that holds primary interest for profit-maximizing farmers.

5. The *law of diminishing returns* states that as the use of an input increases, its marginal physical product will eventually fall.

6. An *isoquant* represents the input combinations for two inputs that would leave the output of the firm unchanged. The slope of an isoquant is the *marginal rate of technical substitution,* which declines as a consequence of the law of diminishing returns.

7. An *isoproduct* or *production possibilities curve* indicates the combinations of two outputs that can be efficiently produced using a *given* quantity of inputs. The slope of this curve is measured by the *marginal rate of product transformation*.

DEFINITION OF TERMS

Production function: a mathematical or functional relationship between the maximum possible output associated with a given level of input use.

Marginal physical product: the increment to efficient output, or total physical produce when an input is varied while other inputs are held fixed.

Average physical product: total physical produce or output divided by the input level.

Total physical product: efficient output for a given level of input use. As inputs are varied, the total physical product curve is traced out.

Isoquant: all input combinations that lead to a given level of output.

Marginal rate of technical substitution: the rate that the usage of one input must decline as another input expands by 1 unit so as to leave output unchanged.

Production possibilities curve: it shows the maximum possible output levels of two or more outputs when inputs are fixed.

Marginal rate of product transformation: measures the minimum possible reduction of the output of good *A* as the output of good is expanded by 1 unit.

Factors of production: the inputs in a production process.

Stages of production: classification of production as to whether marginal physical products as rising, falling, or are negative.

Law of diminishing marginal returns: eventually successive increments in an input lead to correspondingly lower increments (i.e., marginal physical products eventually fall with increased input quantities).

Technical efficiency: the maximum possible output for a given input level or the minimum possible input use for a given level of output.

REFERENCES

ALLEN, R. G. D., *Mathematical Analysis for Economists.* New York: St. Martin's Press, Inc., 1964.

BINSWANGER, H., "The Measurement of Technical Change Biases with Many Factors of Production," *American Economic Review,* 1974, pp. 964–976.

GRILICHES, ZVI, "Research Expenditures, Education and the Aggregate Agricultural Production Function," *American Economic Review,* 1964, pp. 961–974.

HALL, H., and W. FREE, "On Evaluating Crop Response to Lime in the Tennessee Valley Region," *Southern Journal of Agricultural Economics,* 1979, pp. 75–81.

HEADY, E. O., *Economics of Agricultural Production and Resource Use.* Englewood Cliffs, N.J.: Prentice-Hall, Inc., 1952.

KISLEV, Y., and W. PETERSON, "Prices, Technology and Farm Size," *Journal of Political Economy,* 1982, pp. 578–595.

SONKA, S. T., E. O. HEADY, and P. F. DAHM, "Estimation of Gain Isoquants and a Decision Model Application for Swine Production," *American Journal of Agricultural Economics,* 1976, pp. 466–474.

ADDITIONAL READINGS

HEADY, E. O., and J. DILLON, *Agricultural Production Functions.* Ames, Iowa: Iowa State University Press, 1961.

KOHLER, H., *Intermediate Microeconomics: Theory and Applications.* Glenview, Ill.: Scott, Foresman and Company, 1982.

QUESTIONS

1. Fill in the blanks in the following table.

Labor	Capital	Total product of labor	Average physical product of labor	Marginal physical product
0	1	0	–	
				_____
1	1	15	15	
				55
2	1	70	_____	
				10
3	1	80	_____	
				_____
4	1	_____	22	
				8
5	1	96	19	
				_____
6	1	100	17	
				–1
7	1	_____	14	

2. You are a member of an agricultural cooperative that distributes proceeds (output) equally among its members. Such cooperatives are common throughout much of the world. Which of the concepts—total physical product, average physical product, or marginal physical product—is most relevant to deciding how many members of the cooperative to have? If the labor input in problem 1 refers to the number of workers, how many cooperative members would be optimal from the point of view of each member?

3. A common historical argument was that production agricultural commodities in the antebellum South using slaves was less efficient than similar production in the North. Can you think of reasons why this argument may or may not be valid? Empirical evidence suggests that the argument is fallacious. You may wish to refer to the work of two economic historians, Robert W. Fogel and Stanley Engerman, in *Time on the Cross: The Economics of American Negro Slavery* (Boston: Little, Brown, 1974).

4. How would you characterize the efficiency of a professional athlete in the sport of your choice? Each athlete has particular strengths and weaknesses. How does this recognition relate to the concept of a production possibilities curve for a player and a team?

5. One input that appears to be very important in most production processes is education and training. Economists refer to such inputs as "human capital." Is it possible to substitute human and physical capital in most production processes, or is the marginal rate of substitution near zero throughout?

6. Give an intuitive discussion of why isoquants are thought generally to be downward sloping and bowed toward the origin (diminishing marginal rate of technical substitution).

7. Suppose that over time specialized equipment reduces output substitution possibilities. Illustrate this with a changing production possibilities curve.

8. If a new hybrid variety of corn is developed which increases yields by 15 percent, how do you think this would shift an isoquant that is graphed to capture capital and labor usage?

ADVANCED TOPICS

Four advanced topics are covered in this section. The first two have to do with the concepts of *partial* and *total production elasticities.* The third topic pertains to the concept of *technical change,* while the final topic focuses on the concept of *ridge lines.*

Partial Production Elasticities

Although marginal physical product is an extremely important notion, it is not always entirely useful because it depends on the units of measurement. For example, if fertilizer is measured in hundreds of pounds rather than pounds, the value of the marginal physical product will change. Further, it is not possible to compare marginal physical products of two inputs in the same production process. For example, the marginal physical product for labor might be expressed in bushels per worker-hour, while the marginal physical product for fertilizer may be in bushels per pound of fertilizer. Comparisons of the two is akin to the familiar adage of "comparing apples and oranges."

For this reason, economists seek measures that are free of the "units of measurement" problem. The simplest and most useful unit-free measure is an *elasticity.* It measures *relative changes.* In the context of our discussion, we are interested in the *partial production elasticity.* This elasticity measures the percentage change in output for a 1 percent change in the use of a particular input. As such, this elasticity represents the percentage equivalent of the marginal physical product. Returning to our examination of the role that fertilizer plays in the level of output, we can calculate the partial production elasticity for this input as follows:

$$\text{partial production elasticity for fertilizer} = \frac{\text{percentage change in output}}{\text{percentage change in fertilizer use}} \quad (4.10)$$

If this partial production elasticity was equal to 2.0 at a particular level of output, we would know that a 1 percent increase in the use of fertilizer would cause a 2 percent increase in output. Referring back to Table 4.1, the partial production elasticity for fertilizer when output is 80 would be 0.25, implying that a 4 percent increase in fertilizer would increase output by 1 percent.

In summary, *the partial production elasticity measures the percentage change in output in response to a given percentage change in the quantity of an input applied in the production process.*

To illustrate input–output relationships when several variable inputs are used, let's consider the classic production function study by Griliches (1964), in which he estimated a production function for the entire farm business sector. Griliches found the following production elasticities:

Input	Partial production elasticity
Machinery	0.250
Labor X education	0.311
Research and extension	0.050
Fertilizer	0.144
Land and buildings	0.158
Other inputs	0.349

Note that the education of farm laborers as well as government-sponsored research and extension activities contribute to farm output. This is in addition to the contribution of the more conventional inputs such as machinery, land, and fertilizer. Each of the foregoing elasticities indicates the percentage contribution to U.S. farm output resulting from a 1 percent change in the respective input. For example, a 10 percent increase in fertilizer use would increase farm output by slightly more than 1.4 percent.

Total Production Elasticities

The percentage change in output from a 1 percent change in all inputs is defined as the *total production elasticity*. This is also known as the *returns to scale*. Since the *partial* production elasticity indicates (in percentage terms) the impact of a 1-unit input change on output, the sum of these changes over all inputs must necessarily represent the total production elasticity.

For two inputs such as labor and capital, the total production elasticity can be defined as follows:

$$\begin{matrix} \text{total} \\ \text{production} \\ \text{elasticity} \end{matrix} = \begin{matrix} \text{partial produc-} \\ \text{tion elasticity} \\ \text{for labor} \end{matrix} + \begin{matrix} \text{partial produc-} \\ \text{tion elasticity} \\ \text{for capital} \end{matrix} \qquad (4.11)$$

If a farmer experiences a total production elasticity of 1.0 or *constant returns to scale*, a doubling or tripling of all inputs will double or triple output. In other words, the output–input ratios would be *constant*. Thus a 1 percent increase in all inputs would cause output to increase by 1 percent. If the total production elasticity was instead equal to 0.75, a 1 percent increase in all inputs would lead to a 0.75 percent increase in output. This case represents *decreasing returns to scale*. In this case, the input–output ratios would rise as output expands. Finally, a total production elasticity of greater than 1.0 implies *increasing returns to scale*. Here the input–output ratios would fall as output is expanded. The concept of returns to scale as it relates to the growth of the farm will be explored further in Chapter 7.

To illustrate the concept of total production elasticity, consider the estimated partial production elasticities found by Griliches reported earlier. Suppose that all inputs over which farmers have direct control are increased by 10 percent (we have excluded research and extension). The sum of the remaining partial production elasticities is approximately 1.2. This total indicates the presence of *increasing returns to scale*. Output would increase by almost 12 percent if these inputs were increased by 10 percent.

Technical Change

An important aspect of input–output relationships is how they evolve. Technology represents the amalgamation over time of "know-how" in converting inputs into outputs. For example, a new hybrid seed can have an enormous effect on crop yields. Innovations in disease control can also have a significant impact on farm output. These innovations represent changes in technology or *technical change*. Knowledge of technology and the introduction of these innovations into the production process alters the physical product curves presented in this chapter.

Before proceeding further, however, it is important to understand the difference between a change in the technique of production and technical change. A change in the *technique of production* is represented by a *movement along an isoquant*. Thus, in panel a of Figure 4.8, the movement from point D to point E on isoquant ISQ_2 is a move toward a more capital-intensive production technique, where intensity is measured by the capital/labor ratio. This shift represents a change in production technique. A *shift in an isoquant*, on the other hand, reflects a *technical change*. In panel a, for example, isoquants ISQ_1 and ISQ_2 both represent 10 units of output. Technical progress, as reflected by ISQ_2, has reduced the quantity of inputs required to produce a given level of output. Thus point D and point F have the same marginal rate of technical substitution.

Some years ago Hicks categorized technical change according to changes in the marginal rate of technical substitution for a given input ratio. Three categories of technical change identified by Hicks were:

1. *Neutral:* If technical progress for a given input ratio leaves the marginal rate of substitution of labor for capital unaltered, the change is said to be *input neutral*.

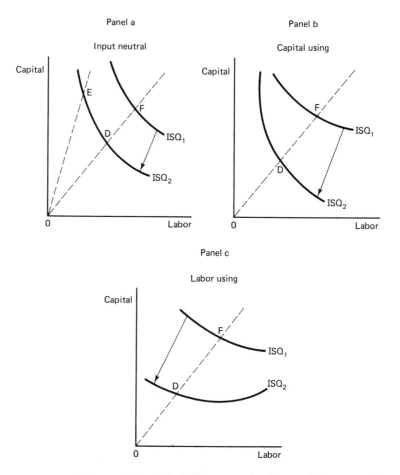

Figure 4.8 *Effects of Technical Change on the Shape of Isoquants.* The existence of technical change in production inputs can cause the shape of the isoquant for a given level of output to change. Assume that ISQ_1 represents the original isoquant before the technical change is introduced. If the technical change is neutral between two inputs, the shift in the isoquant after the technological improvement has been introduced will be in a parallel fashion (see panel a). If the technical change is capital using, the shift in the isoquant from adopting this new technology will be biased toward capital (see panel b). Finally, if the technical change is labor using, the shift will be biased toward labor (see panel c).

2. *Capital using:* If technical progress for a given input ratio decreases the marginal rate of substitution of labor for capital, the change is said to be *capital using.*

3. *Labor·using:* If technical progress for a given input ratio increases the marginal rate of substitution of labor for capital, the change is said to be *labor using.*

The neutral case is represented by the parallel shifts in the isoquants illustrated in panel a. Capital-using technical progress implies that capital's marginal physical product increases more than labor's does for a given ratio of capital to labor. Hence the marginal rate of technical substitution of labor for capital must fall. For a 1-unit increase in labor, a *smaller* reduction in capital would be required to keep output constant. This effect is illustrated in panel b, where the marginal rate of technical substitution falls as we move from point F on ISQ_1 to point D on ISQ_2. Finally, if we replace capital with labor in the discussions above, the labor-using case can be as illustrated in panel c. The marginal rate of technical substitution rises with technical progress as we move from point F on ISQ_1 to point D on ISQ_2.

The definitions above highlight the importance of innovations in technology-to-production relationships. U.S. agriculture has been quick to adopt numerous mechanical and biological innovations. In Chapter 2 we reported the index of farm output per unit of total input published by the U.S. Department of Agriculture (see Table 2.2). This measure attempts to illustrate changes in efficiency in farm production. As this table indicated, efficiency has increased dramatically in the twentieth century. In both relative and absolute terms, the decade of the fifties saw especially large gains in technical efficiency. The development of agronomic, genetic, mechanical, and other forms of innovations all contributed to these increases in efficiency. What is not apparent from these data is whether technical change was biased toward or away from particular inputs. In the former (latter) case, technical change implies greater (reduced) use of the input.

Although further study is under way, it appears that technical change has been biased toward greater fertilizer and machinery use and biased away from greater use of labor and land inputs (Binswanger, 1974). Indeed, it is noteworthy that the index of output per labor hour and machinery per labor hour employed in the farm business sector have risen dramatically since 1910. For example, the index of output per labor hour has risen from 14 in 1910 to over 200 in 1980. This has occurred partly because the machinery per labor hour has also increased dramatically during the same period of time due to machinery innovations increasing its marginal physical product.[9]

Ridge Lines

In this chapter we introduced the concept of "stages of production" and said that stage III represented an irrational range of behavior in a single input–output relationship since the marginal physical product was negative. We can expand the discussion of stage III production to input–input relationships by introducing the concept of *ridge lines*.

[9] An alternative view has been investigated by Kislev and Peterson (1982). Drawing on material to be presented in Chapter 5, perhaps the rise in nonfarm wages led labor to exit to urban centers of employment. This could lead to increased farm size and reduced farm labor, thereby suggesting increased output per worker.

Figure 4.9 presents a set of isoquants for two inputs associated with different levels of output, holding all other inputs fixed. The series of input combinations labeled A, B, C, and D in this figure represents the combination of X_1 and X_2 used in producing specific levels of output where the marginal physical product of X_1 *becomes equal to zero.* Conversely, points E, F, G, and H represent the combination of X_1 and X_2 used in producing specific levels of output where the marginal physical product of X_2 *becomes equal to zero.*[10]

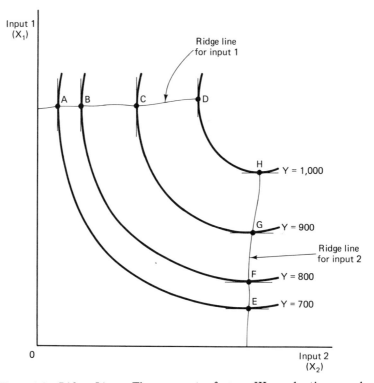

Figure 4.9 *Ridge Lines.* The concept of stage III production can be extended to the two-variable input case through the use of ridge lines. Points A, B, C, and D represent the combination of two inputs (X_1 and X_2), where the marginal physical product of input 1 or X_1 becomes zero. If more of this input were used, none of input 2 or X_2 would be replaced. Thus use of X_1 beyond the ridge line formed by these points associated with different levels of output would be irrational. Points E, F, G, and H represent the same concept for the use of X_2. Additional use of this input beyond the ridge line formed by these points would represent an irrational use of X_2 since none of X_1 would be replaced and output would remain unchanged.

[10] These results are obtained by varying X_1 while holding X_2 fixed at different levels and all other variables fixed at one level.

A line connecting these points is referred to as a ridge line and represents the end of stage II and beginning of stage III for X_1 and X_2, respectively. If the use of input X_1 is increased beyond the levels indicated by point A, B, C, or D, none of X_2 is replaced. Similarly, if the use of input X_2 is increased beyond the levels indicated by point E, F, G, or H, none of X_1 is replaced. Therefore, these two ridge lines represent the beginning of stage III for the use of X_1 and X_2, respectively. No rational farmer would want to operate beyond these two ridge lines.

Finally, on a related matter, diminishing returns (declining marginal physical product) is suggested by the spacing of the isoquants in Figure 4.9. The increasing nature of the gaps between these isoquants as we move out from the origin suggests that increasing larger quantities of these variables inputs are needed to produce the level of output.

5

PRODUCTION DECISIONS
FOR A COMPETITIVE FIRM

A thorough understanding of the technology of production does not necessarily imply that good economic decisions will be made. In recent years, numerous farms have failed despite the fact that the farmer was highly skilled in the technical aspects of production. This underscores the need to understand the *economic dimension* of production decisions. In this chapter the technology of production is assumed to be known. The relationships covered in Chapter 4 will be used as an input to determining optimal economic decisions. Such decisions might be the optimal quantity of fertilizer to apply to a crop, the optimal feed ration to feed livestock, or the optimal acreage or production of a crop or livestock. Thus we seek in this chapter to characterize *economic efficiency* given the knowledge of how to make *technically efficient* decisions gained in Chapter 4.

The assumption is made in this chapter that there are many buyers and sellers, each possessing all relevant market information. Producers understand the technology of production and each knows the prices in the marketplace. We shall also assume there are no barriers that would prohibit the free exchange of goods and services. These assumptions imply an economic system that economists call *competitive* and ensures that no single firm or consumer can influence price.[1]

We begin with a discussion of the determination of the least-cost level of input use for a given level of output and what happens if the prices of these inputs change. Next we examine the relationship between cost and

[1] The competitive case will be contrasted with the noncompetive decisionmaking in Chapter 9.

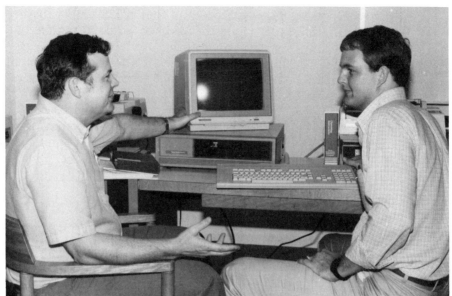

The use of microcomputers in farm decision making has been increasing rapidly in recent years. The development of software programs for these microcomputers has enabled farmers to improve their record-keeping systems and in some instances make analyses of their operations that would be impossible for them to do otherwise. Existing software programming packages include those designed to generate a set of financial statements for the farm business, determine the most economical feed ration to feed market animals, and identify the most profitable farm investments to undertake.

output in the short run. Having gained an understanding of the relationship between costs and the level of output, we will discuss the determination of the profit-maximizing level of output for a single-product firm. Finally, we examine the optimal combination of products for a farm with more than one product and the nature of the market input demand and product supply curves in agriculture.

DETERMINING LEAST-COST USE OF INPUTS

Let us suppose that a farmer asks the following question: "if I want to produce a particular level of output, how can I determine the input choices I must make to minimize my cost of production?" He may, for example, want to know the least-cost feed ration to feed the 100 cattle he has in his feedlot.

This question is relatively easy to answer *if* production involves only one variable input. To see this, let us return to the fertilizer example discussed in Chapter 4. Suppose that an output of 35 units is desired. Figure 4.1 shows that a level of 1.5 units of fertilizer would be required to produce this level of output. This level of fertilizer use represents the *least-cost* level of this input for 35 units of output. Since it also represents the only technically efficient input level, economic and technical efficiency coincide in the case of one variable input.

For the case of two or more variable inputs, however, the optimal choice of inputs requires further analysis. In all cases, however, economic efficiency with respect to *input choice* is defined as that input choice which minimizes the cost of producing a particular level of output.

The Isocost Line

Let us assume for the moment that a farmer uses one variable input (labor) and one fixed input (capital) to produce his farm products. The *total cost* of production in this case would be equal the wage rate times the units of labor used plus the rental rate on capital times the units of capital used. While the concept of wage rates paid to labor is something with which all of us are familiar, the rental rate on capital might require some further explanation. Think of capital as being measured by the number of hours a tractor is used. In this case, the per unit cost of capital would be the *rental cost per hour.* Even if the tractor is owned rather than rented, there is a rental cost associated with ownership. The owner of the tractor has the option of renting the tractor to others. The revenue forgone from *not renting* the tractor to others is a cost. Economists call it an *opportunity cost.* These two input prices are treated as fixed and do not vary with the level of input use.[2]

The farmer's total costs under the assumptions set forth above would be given by

$$\begin{matrix} \text{Total} \\ \text{cost} \end{matrix} = \begin{bmatrix} \text{wage} \\ \text{rate} \end{bmatrix} \times \begin{matrix} \text{units of} \\ \text{labor} \end{matrix} + \begin{bmatrix} \text{rental} \\ \text{rate} \end{bmatrix} \times \begin{matrix} \text{units of} \\ \text{capital} \end{matrix} \quad (5.1)$$

For a given level of total cost, we can determine the level of capital use corresponding to a particular level of labor use by modifying equation (5.1) as follows:

$$\text{units of capital} = \frac{\text{total cost}}{\text{rental rate}} - \frac{\text{wage rate}}{\text{rental rate}} \times \text{units of labor} \quad (5.2)$$

Since total cost in equation (5.2) is held fixed, we call the line given by alternative combinations of labor and capital use an *isocost line.* As an example, for a total cost of $1,000, a wage rate of $10, and a rental rate for capital of $100, the isocost line would be as follows:

---

[2] More will be said about the concept of opportunity cost in Chapter 7 when we introduce the analysis of investment opportunities and the growth of the firm.

$$\text{units of capital } = \frac{\$1,000}{\$100} - \frac{\$10}{\$100} \times \text{ units of labor} \qquad (5.3)$$

Thus the isocost line has an intercept of 10 and slope of –0.10, as illustrated by line *AB* in panel a of Figure 5.1.

Note that if these two input prices change by a constant proportion, the total cost will change. But the slope of the isocost line will remain constant. For example, suppose that the prices of all inputs doubled. Total costs would double but the isocost line would still have a slope of –0.10, as illustrated by line *CD* in panel a. Thus only changes in the *relative price* of inputs (or input price ratio) will alter the slope of the isocost line.

For a given total cost, if the price of capital rises (falls) relative to that of labor, the isocost line will rotate clockwise (counterclockwise). If labor's wage rises (falls), the cost line will rotate counterclockwise (clockwise). For example, suppose that the wage rate is $20 instead of $10. The new isocost line is steeper, as illustrated by line *AE* in panel b. It still intersects the "capital" axis at point *A,* however, since a maximum of 10 units of capital can be purchased if total cost is limited to $1,000. Similarly, if capital's price rose to $200 per unit, the isocost line if flatter, as illustrated by line *FB* in panel c.

The Least-Cost Input Choice

The least-cost use of inputs requires that we find the lowest cost of producing a given level of output. Technology and input prices are assumed known and unvarying. You will recall from Chapter 4 that the capital-labor ratios which produce a given level of output form what was called an *isoquant* (see Figure 4.3). The approach to finding the least-cost combination of inputs assumes that the isoquant is fixed at say 100 units of output. The focus of attention is centered on determining the lowest cost of producing that output. *Graphically, the least-cost combination of inputs is found by shifting the isocost line in a parallel fashion until it is tangent to (i.e., just touches) the isoquant.* This point of tangency represents the least-cost capital/labor combination of producing this level of output. If isocost lines *AB* and *MN* (which is parallel to line *AB*) reflect the existing input prices for labor and capital, the least-cost combination of input use would be indicated by point *G* in Figure 5.2, where 60 units of labor are combined with 14 units of capital to produce 100 units of output. Total cost at point *G* would be equal to $2,000 (i.e., $10 × 60 units of labor plus $100 × 14 units of capital).

If you are unsure that point *G* represents the lowest cost of producing 100 units of output, calculate the total cost at any other point on this isoquant. It should be clear that total costs at say point *H*, for example, would exceed total costs at point *G*. An isocost line passing through point *H* would be *farther from the origin* than an isocost line passing through point *G*. The total cost at point *H* would be $2,000 (i.e., $10 × 40 units of

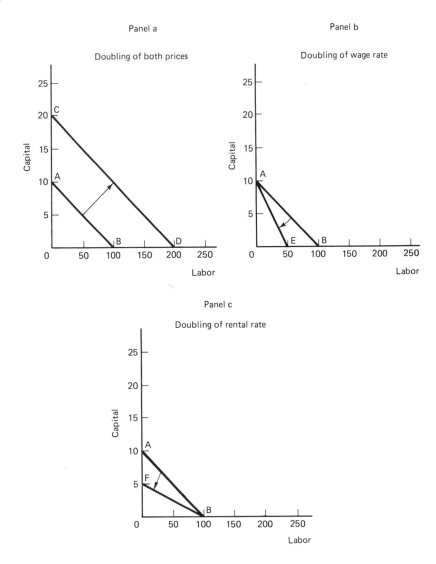

Figure 5.1 *Effects of Input Price Changes on Isocost Line.* The isocost line plays a key role in determining the least-cost combination of input use. Equation (5.2) showed that the intercept of the isocost line is given by the ratio of total cost to the rental rate of capital. The slope of the curve is given by the ratio of the wage rate for labor to the rental rate for capital. Panel a shows that a doubling of both input prices changes the intercept of the isocost line but not its slope. Panel b shows that a doubling of the wage rate (holding the rental rate constant) results in a steeper isocost curve. Finally, a doubling of the rental rate (holding the wage rate constant) makes this curve flatter.

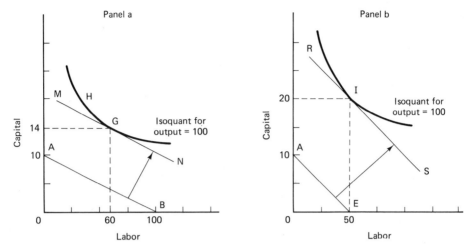

Figure 5.2 *Input Price Change and Least-Cost Input Choice.* The least-cost choice of input use is given by the point where the isocost curve is tangent to the isoquant for the desired level of output. If the isocost line is line *AB,* panel a shows that the least-cost combination would occur at point *G.* Panel b shows that if the isocost line shifts to line *AE* as the result of higher wage rates, the least-cost combination of input use would occur at point *I* instead. Thus labor use decreased from 60 to 50 units and capital increased from 14 to 20 units in response to the increase in the wage rate.

labor plus $100 × 18 units of capital). Thus costs are higher at point *H* than at point *G,* where total costs were $2,000. Point *G* therefore represents the least-cost input usage for input prices of $10 (labor) and $100 (capital) when an output level of 100 units is desired.

There is a very fundamental interpretation to the conditions underlying the least-cost combination of input use. To begin with, we know that the slope of the isoquant is equal to the slope of the isocost line at point *G.* At this point, the *marginal rate of technical substitution* of capital for labor (i.e., the negative of the slope of the isoquant) equals the *input price ratio* (i.e., the negative of the slope of the isocost line). Thus the least-cost combination of inputs in the example above requires that the market rate of exchange of capital for labor (i.e., the ratio of input prices) be equal to their rate of exchange in production (i.e., their marginal rate of technical substitution).

We can express the foregoing conditions for the least-cost combination of labor and capital in mathematical terms using the definitions of the marginal rate of technical substitution of capital for labor presented in equation (4.6) as follows:

$$\frac{MPP_{labor}}{MPP_{capital}} = \frac{\text{wage rate}}{\text{rental rate}} \qquad (5.4)$$

This equation states that to minimize cost subject to a given output level, the farmer must employ inputs in such quantities as to equate the ratio of the marginal physical products with their input price ratio. We can rearrange equation (5.4) to read as follows:

$$\frac{MPP_{\text{labor}}}{\text{wage rate}} = \frac{MPP_{\text{capital}}}{\text{rental rate}} \qquad (5.5)$$

Equation (5.5) suggests that the marginal physical product per dollar spent on labor must equal the marginal physical product per dollar spent on capital. This is entirely analogous to the condition for consumer equilibrium [see equation (3.10)] and represents a recurring theme in economics. In the present context, a farmer should allocate his expenditures on inputs such that the marginal benefits per dollar expended in competing acivities are equal.[3]

The discussion presented above can be summarized as follows: *input use depends on input prices, output, and technology.* Such cost-minimizing input use is often referred to as *conditional demand* because it is conditioned by the level of output.

Effects of Input Price Changes

Now let us see what would happen to these conditional input demands if we allow the price of an input to change. Since total costs equal the sum of expenditures on each input, total cost clearly increases (decreases) with a rise (fall) in an input price. A fundamental principle of economic behavior suggests that farmers will substitute for resources that become more expensive.

Figure 5.2 shows that as the relative price of labor (price of labor divided by price of capital) rises, the isocost line becomes steeper, as illustrated by isocost lines AE and RS (which is parallel to line AE) in panel b. Based on our previous discussion, we know that the least-cost combination of input use for 100 units of output would shift from point G in panel a to point I in panel b. Thus as the price of labor rises (falls) relative to the price of capital, capital is substituted for labor and the capital/labor ratio rises. We can reason through this behavior another way. As the price of labor rises, the marginal benefit per dollar expended on labor is lower than the marginal benefit per dollar expended on capital. Because of diminishing

---

[3] Another way to think of this equilibrium is in the context that *marginal benefit equal marginal cost.* Suppose that the marginal benefit per dollar of labor usage (marginal physical product times the price of output) is $5 while the corresponding marginal benefit is $7 for capital. The opportunity cost of expending a dollar on increased labor usage is the $7 gain if this expenditure were instead used to purchase another unit of capital services. Thus the marginal benefit ($5) is less than marginal cost ($7) and labor usage should be reduced. If output is to remain constant as labor is reduced, capital must be expanded until marginal benefit equals marginal cost.

marginal products, equilibrium is attained by reducing labor use from 60 to 50 units and using more capital (20 units instead of 14 units).

An examination of Figure 5.2 indicates that the more sharply curved the isoquant, the less able the farmer will be to substitute capital (labor) for labor (capital). Indeed, in the case of the isoquant depicted in panel a in Figure 4.4, the farmer could not substitute at all. At the other extreme, the substitution among inputs is accomplished with ease in panel b of Figure 4.4.

An Empirical Example

Recall the empirical example of the isoquant relating corn and protein supplement for a particular weight gain for swine presented in Chapter 4 [see equation (4.7)]. We can use this equation to calculate the *least-cost feed ration* for feeding swine out to 100 pounds. If the ratio of the price of protein supplement to the price of corn is 2.0, we know from equation (5.4) that the least-cost feed ration will occur where the marginal rate of technical substitution of corn for the protein supplement is also equal to 2.0.

To determine the least-cost feed ration, consider the values of supplement use between 20 and 25 pounds together with their calculated marginal rates of technical substitution presented in Table 5.1. Applying the concept presented in equation (5.4), we see that the least-cost feed ration for this

	Corn use (pounds)	Protein supplement use (pounds)	Swine output (pounds)	Marginal rate of technical substitution of corn for protein supplement	Price ratio
	81.1	20.0	100.0	2.4	2.0
Least-	78.8	21.0	100.0	2.2	2.0
cost	76.7	22.0	100.0	2.0	2.0
ration	74.7	23.0	100.0	1.9	2.0
	72.9	24.0	100.0	1.8	2.0
	71.1	25.0	100.0	1.7	2.0

Note: These data were calculated using equation (4.7).

TABLE 5.1 EMPIRICAL EXAMPLE OF LEAST-COST FEED RATION. The empirical example presented in this table illustrates how to determine the least-cost combination of corn and protein supplement to use in feeding market hogs out to a certain weight (100 pounds of gain). At the point where the isocost line is tangent to the isoquant illustrated in Figure 5.2, the marginal rate of technical substitution (i.e., the slope of the isoquant) is equal to the price ratio (i.e., the slope of the isocost line) for these two inputs. Looking at the table, we see that this requirement is satisfied at 76.7 pounds of corn and 22 pounds of protein supplement. If the price of corn or protein supplement were to change, however, the least-cost feed ration would have to be recomputed.

weight occurs at 22 pounds of protein supplement and 76.7 pounds of corn. It is at this point and this point only that the equality expressed in equation (5.4) is met. If the price of the protein supplement were suddenly to fall to the point where the ratio of the price of the supplement to the price of corn was 1.8, minimization of costs would require that additional protein supplement be substituted for corn. The least-cost feed ration would now be 24 pounds of protein supplement and about 73 pounds of corn.

RELATIONSHIP BETWEEN COST AND OUTPUT

Since total cost is equal to the sum of input prices times the corresponding conditional input demands, it follows that total cost of production depends on the level of production, existing technology and the level of input prices. While input prices and technology are certainly important factors, let us hold them fixed for the moment and focus our attention on the relationship between cost and the level of output. This departs from the discussion in the preceding section, where we focused on the least-cost combination of inputs for a *particular level of output*.

Total Cost of Production

The total cost of production captures the costs associated with the use of *all* inputs to production. The higher the level of production, the greater total costs will be. The effects of *changing output levels* on total production costs can be seen by examining Figure 5.3. Let the per unit price of capital be $100 and the per unit price of labor be $2. The least-cost way to produce 200 units of output would require the use 6 units of capital and 150 units of labor. Total production costs in this instance would be $900. These results are represented by points A and B in panels a and b of Figure 5.3, respectively. If output were increased to 300 units, the least-cost combination of inputs would be 8 units of capital and 200 units of labor. Total production costs would rise to $1,200. These results are represented by points C and D in panels a and b, respectively.

Repeating this process for all other possible levels of output would result in a smooth curve formed by the tangencies of isocosts lines and isoquants. This curve is called an *expansion path* as noted in panel a. The corresponding smooth total cost curve in panel b of this figure represents the relationship between the farmer's total cost curve and output under these conditions. Since more resources are required to produce more output, total cost increases as output increases.

The foregoing discussion of the relationship between output and cost was presented in a long-run context since all inputs were considered variable. In many cases, however, some inputs in the short run are fixed. For example, a farmer might be limited to using his existing farm land and machinery

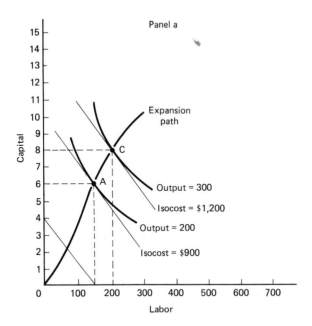

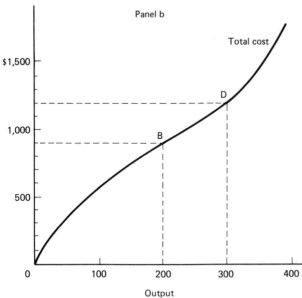

Figure 5.3 *Relationship between Inputs, Output, and Total Cost.* Point *A* in panel a represents the least-cost capital and labor use for producing 200 units of output given prices of $100 per unit of capital and $2 per unit of labor. Point *C* is the least-cost capital and labor use for producing 300 units of output given prices of $100 per unit for capital and $2 per unit for labor. Points *B* and *D* are representations of these input combinations when total cost is graphed against total output.

in the current period.[4] The cost-minimizing combination of those inputs that can be varied in the short run is determined in the same manner described above, with the exception that these variable inputs are chosen subject to a specific level of output and a given level of fixed inputs.

The freedom to employ all inputs at their long-run least-cost level can never increase total costs over what they would be in the short run where some inputs are held fixed. To illustrate, assume that the long-run least-cost combination of capital and labor for producing 200 units of output is 6 units of capital and 150 units of labor when the prices of capital and labor are $100 and $2, respectively. The total cost of production in this case would be $900. Suppose, however, that the availability of capital is limited to 4 units in the current period. The only way that 200 units of output could be produced under these circumstances would be to use more than 150 units of labor. Yet if labor use were doubled to 300 units, the farmer's total cost of production would increase to $1,000. Finally, short- and long-run total costs will coincide only when the fixed inputs such as farmland are at their long-run least-cost levels (e.g., capital is 6 units is employed in producing 200 units of output).

It is important to understand the various concepts of cost in the short run and their relationship to output. For example, a farmer's *total costs* in the short run can be divided into *fixed costs* (those costs associated with the fixed inputs) and *variable costs* (those costs associated with the variable inputs). Two additional cost concepts related to the level of output that must also be understood are *marginal costs* and *average costs*. Each of these cost concepts is addressed in the remainder of this section.

Total Fixed Costs

Those costs incurred by the farmer in his farming operations that *do not vary* with the level of production are referred to as *fixed costs*. These are costs the farmer must meet regardless of whether he chooses to produce. In our previous example, total fixed costs were $400 (i.e., $100 per unit of capital X 4 units of capital). Two examples of fixed costs are property taxes and the interest payments on the farmer's mortgage. Both costs must be paid in the current period and do not vary directly with the level of current production. As shown in panel a of Figure 5.4, the total fixed-cost curve is represented by a straight line running parallel to the horizontal axis.

Total Variable Costs

Those total costs that do not meet our definition of fixed costs are instead considered as *variable costs*. In our previous example, labor costs were

---

[4] These inputs may be fixed because of extremely large adjustment costs. Land is often treated as a fixed input in the short run. In the long run, however, all inputs are variable. The relationship between short-run and long-run costs will be addressed in more detail in Chapter 7 when we focus on the expansion of the farm.

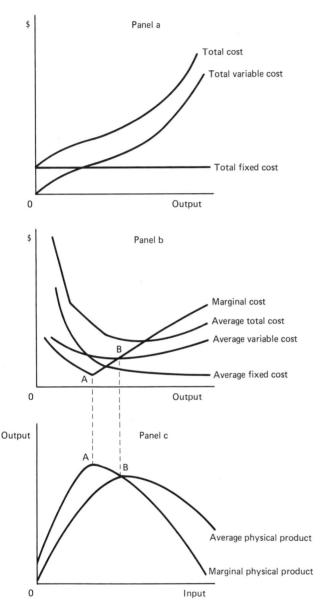

Figure 5.4 *General Cost and Production Relationships.* Panel a shows that the total cost is equal to total variable cost plus total fixed cost. Panel b further categorizes total, fixed, and variable costs using marginal and average concepts. The concept of average cost involves dividing the measures of cost in panel a by the appropriate level of output. Marginal cost is found by measuring the change in total cost as output changes. Finally, panel c illustrates the relationships between these cost curves and the physical product curves presented in Chapter 4 for the one-variable input case.

considered a variable cost since these costs *do vary* with the level of production. Further examples of variable costs are fuel expenses and – if applicable – herbicide, pesticide, and fertilizer expenses. The more acres the farmer plants, the more fuel he will need to power his tractor and other motorized machinery and the more herbicides, pesticides, and fertilizer he will need to achieve his output objectives. Panel b in Figure 5.4 illustrates the general nature of this relationship: *total variable costs increase as output increases.*

Short-Run Average Costs

Another important cost concept is that of *average cost.* This concept of costs involves measuring costs *per unit of output.* The three concepts of costs discussed thus far in this section (i.e., total costs, fixed costs, and variable costs) can be expressed as average costs as follows:

$$\text{average total costs} = \frac{\text{total costs}}{\text{output}} \tag{5.6}$$

$$\text{average fixed costs} = \frac{\text{total fixed costs}}{\text{output}} \tag{5.7}$$

$$\text{average variable costs} = \frac{\text{total variable costs}}{\text{output}} \tag{5.8}$$

Panel b in Figure 5.4 illustrates the general nature of these three short-run average-cost curves. While average fixed costs decline over the entire range of production levels, average variable costs normally decreases up to a certain output level and then increase as the farmer expands his output further. The *minimum point* on the average variable cost curve corresponds to the *maximum point* on the farmer's average physical product curve introduced in Chapter 4 when only one variable input is used (see point *B* in panels b and c of Figure 5.4).[5]

Marginal Cost

The final-cost concept discussed in this section is the change in the farmer's total costs per unit of change in output, or *marginal cost.* The concept of marginal cost is measured as follows:

$$\text{marginal cost} = \frac{\Delta \text{total cost}}{\Delta \text{output}} \tag{5.9}$$

where Δ represents "the change" in a particular item (e.g., costs, output) as

---

[5]This can be rationalized by noting that average variable cost is the price of the variable input divided by average product.

it did in the preceding two chapters. Marginal cost also represents the slope of the total cost and total variable cost curves.[6]

The general nature of the farmer's marginal cost curve is illustrated in panel b of Figure 5.4. Like average variable costs, the marginal cost of production first falls and then rises. In the case of one variable input, the *minimum point* on the marginal cost curve in panel b corresponds to the *maximum point* on the variable input's marginal physical product curve introduced in Chapter 4 (see point *A* in panel c). All other things constant, the more productive a variable input is (i.e., the greater its marginal and average physical product), the lower its marginal and average cost will be. When the use of a variable input is increased to the point where it adds little to output at the margin (i.e., where its marginal physical product approaches zero), its marginal cost will become quite large.[7]

Finally, marginal costs will equal average variable costs at the point where the marginal physical product is equal to the average physical product (see point *B* in both panels b and c). This helps illustrate why the statement is often made that the marginal and average variable cost curves are "mirror images" of the marginal and average physical product curves.

A Numerical Example

Perhaps the relationship between output and cost can be seen more readily if we examine the costs associated with the numerical production example presented in Chapter 4 (see Table 4.1 and Figure 4.1). Let us continue to assume that the use of one input (i.e., capital) is fixed in the current period at 1 unit, with each unit of this fixed input costing $100. The other input (fertilizer) is variable and is assumed to cost $2 per unit. Columns (1) through (5) in Table 5.2 repeat the physical product relationships reported in Table 4.1, while columns (6) through (12) apply the concepts of marginal, average, fixed, and variable costs to this production data.

Column (6) in Table 5.2 illustrates the constant nature of total fixed costs, and column (8) illustrates the increasing nature of total variable costs. Column (7) shows that these costs *do* decline over the range of production levels, while column (9) shows that these costs *do* decrease up to a certain output level and then increase as output is further expanded. Finally, column (11) shows that these costs *do* first fall and then rise. These relationships are graphed in a piecewise-linear fashion in Figure 5.5.

[6] Note that both total costs and total variable cost curves in Figure 5.4 have the same slope since they differ only by total fixed cost. Also note that we could have substituted Δtotal variable cost in the numerator of equation (5.9).

[7] It can be shown that marginal cost is equal to each input price divided by its marginal physical product. This can be seen by noting that equation (5.9) can be written as (Δtotal cost/Δinput)/(Δoutput/Δinput). Since the marginal physical product is in the denominator of this expression, there is an inverse relationship between marginal cost and marginal physical product.

TABLE 5.2 SHORT-RUN COST AND PRODUCTION RELATIONSHIPS

Point on Fig. 5.5	(1) Use of fixed input	(2) Use of variable input	(3) Total physical product (output)[b]	(4) Average physical product† (3)÷(2)[c]	(5) Marginal physical product Δ(3)÷Δ(2)[d]	(6) Total fixed cost	(7) Average fixed cost (8)÷(3)	(8) Total variable cost $2×(2)	(9) Average variable cost (8)÷(3)	(10) Total cost (6)+(8)	(11) Marginal cost Δ(10)÷Δ(3)	(12) Average cost (7)+(9)
a	1	0.5	10.0	20.0		$100.00	$10.00	$ 1.00	$0.10	$101.00		$10.10
					30.0						$0.07	
b	1	1.0	25.0	25.0		100.00	4.00	2.00	0.08	102.00		4.08
					35.0						0.06	
c	1	2.0	60.0	30.0		100.00	1.67	4.00	0.07	104.00		1.73
					15.0						0.13	
d	1	3.0	75.0	25.0		100.00	1.33	6.00	0.08	106.00		1.43
					5.0						0.40	
e	1	4.0	80.0	20.0		100.00	1.25	8.00	0.10	108.00		1.35
					2.0						1.00	
f	1	5.0	82.0	16.4		100.00	1.22	10.00	0.12	110.00		1.34
					1.0						2.00	
g	1	6.0	83.0	13.5		100.00	1.20	12.00	0.14	112.00		1.34
					0.5						4.00	
h	1	7.0	83.5	11.9		100.00	1.23	14.00	0.17	114.00		1.40
					0.5						–e	
i	1	8.0	83.0	10.4		100.00	1.25	16.00	0.19	116.00		1.44

[a]The data appearing in this column were obtained from column (1) in Table 4.1.
[b]The data appearing in this column were obtained from column (2) in Table 4.1.
[c]The calculations appearing in this column were originally made in column (4) of Table 4.1.
[d]The calculations appearing in this column were originally made in column (4) of Table 4.1.
[e]These marginal costs would be associated with earlier inputs in the neighborhood of 80 to 81 units of output and are not reported, to reduce potential confusion.

TABLE 5.2 SHORT-RUN COST AND PRODUCTION RELATIONSHIPS. The numerical example presented here further illustrates the relationship between selected physical product and cost concepts. The computational instructions given just below each column heading underscores these relationships. For example, marginal cost in column (11) is found by dividing the change in the level of total cost reported in column (10) by the change in the level of output reported in column (3).

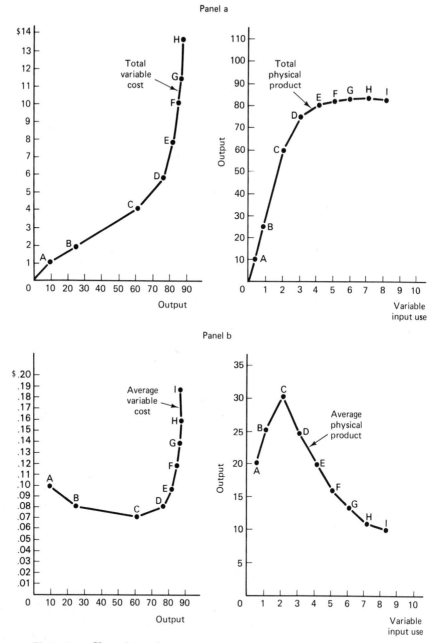

Figure 5.5 *Short-Run Cost and Production Relationships.* This figure illustrates the cost and production relationships presented in numerical example given in Table 5.2. These relationships also roughly resemble the cost and production curves presented for the general case in Figure 5.4. (*Continued on next page*)

Panel c

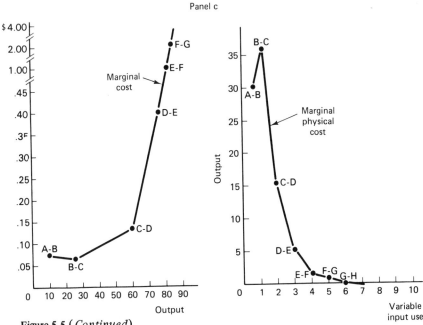

Figure 5.5 (*Continued*)

Let us compare the production and cost relationships presented in Figure 5.5 with the general relationships plotted in Figure 5.4. For example, we made the point earlier using Figure 5.4 that the total, marginal, and average cost curves are "mirror images" of the total, marginal, and average physical product curves. This can also be seen by comparing the cost curves in each panel on the left-hand side of Figure 5.5 with the corresponding panels on the right-hand side. In addition, an examination of panel b in Figure 5.5 reveals that average variable cost is minimized at 60 units of output and 2 units of variable input. We also see in panel b of Figure 5.5 that the average physical product is maximized at 30 units. These two observations correspond to points *B* of panels b and c in the general case depicted in Figure 5.4. Panel c of Figure 5.5 also shows that when the marginal physical product is increasing (decreasing), marginal cost is falling (rising). This observation was illustrated in general terms in panels b and c of Figure 5.4.

Finally, the marginal physical product in column (5) of Table 5.2 is maximized as output is expanded from 25 to 60 units. This corresponds to the change in output where marginal costs is minimized (see point *B-C* in panel c of Figure 5.5). These observations also correspond to point *A* in panels b and c for the general case illustrated in Figure 5.4.

In summary, there is a definite relationship between specific physical production relationships presented in Chapter 4 and the costs of production discussed in this chapter. It is essential that these relationships and their measurement illustrated by the numerical example presented in Table 5.2 and Figure 5.5 be clearly understood before proceeding with the remainder of this chapter.

DETERMINING PROFIT-MAXIMIZING LEVEL OF OUTPUT

The major concepts presented in this section involve the application of the following rule of thumb: "increase (decrease) the level of production as long as the marginal benefit from doing so is greater than (less than) the marginal costs. In this section we continue to focus the discussion on a farmer producing a *single product*. We also continue to assume that individual farmers are price takers in all markets.

Revenue

Total revenue is found by multiplying the price of the product by the level of output. If the price of a unit of output is $2, then $2 times the number of units produced represents the farmer's total revenue. Graphically, total revenue is represented by a straight line emanating from the origin as illustrated for the general case presented in panel a of Figure 5.4. The slope of this line is the unit price of the product. *Marginal revenue* is also equal to the price of the product. For every unit of output sold, total revenue increases by the price of the product (i.e., Δrevenue divided by Δoutput equals price). Price also represents the *average revenue* (i.e., revenue divided by output equal price). Thus both the marginal and average revenue are equal to the sales price of the product.

Profit-Maximizing Output

Profit is defined as total revenue minus total cost.[8] To maximize profit, the farmer must produce at the point where the *difference* between total revenue and total cost curves in panel a is greatest. There is another way of characterizing the profit-maximizing level of output for a competitive, single-product firm that is perhaps more intuitive and economically meaningful.

To begin with, we know that the marginal benefit of producing and selling 1 more unit of output is the marginal revenue, or product price. The marginal revenue curve represents the demand curve perceived by each individual farmer. It is perfectly flat, as shown in panel b of Figure 5.6, since the farmer is a *price taker*. Nothing he does will change the price he receives for his output. Expansion of the farmer's output is profitable as long as the marginal benefit exceeds the marginal cost. This logically leads to a profit-

---

[8] This represents the definition of *economic* profits. The distinction between economic profits and *accounting* profits is that the latter concept purposely does not account for the opportunity cost of capital or other inputs not explicitly priced.

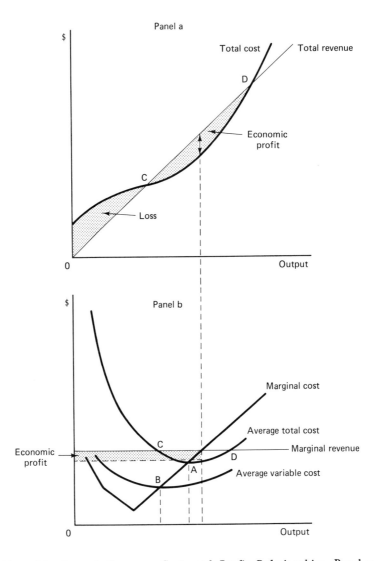

Figure 5.6 *General Revenue, Cost, and Profit Relationships.* Panel a shows that if the total cost curve in panel a of Figure 5.4 lies above the total revenue curve, economic losses will result. Farmers will prefer to operate in the output range where the total cost curve lies below the total revenue curve. In fact, they will want to operate at the point where the difference between these two curves is maximized. Panel b shows that this will occur at the point where the marginal revenue curve is equal to the marginal cost curve. Point *A* in panel b represents the "break-even" level of output while point *B* represents the "shutdown" level of output.

maximizing output level where the marginal revenue from the sale of another unit output equals the marginal cost of producing this unit. Looking at Figure 5.6, we see that the maximum difference between the total revenue and total cost curves in panel a occurs at the output where the marginal revenue curve intersects the marginal cost curve in panel b. The shaded area in panel b represents the profit achieved at this level of output. Note that this area is bounded, in part, by the distance between the firm's demand curve and its average total cost curve.

A Numerical Example

Let us expand our "fertilizer" example developed in Tables 4.1 and 5.2 to determine the *profit-maximizing level of output.* Table 5.3 shows that at a product price of $2 per unit, the profit-maximizing output would be approximately 82.5 units of output. Total revenue at this output level would be $165 [see column (3)], while total cost would be approximately $111. The total profit at this level of production if $54.

It is very important that you understand the economic rationale associated with this result. The marginal benefit of moving from 75 to 80 units of production is $10 in additional revenue, or 5 units of additional output valued at $2 per unit. The increment in cost is $2, or 5 additional output units costing $0.40 per unit. The marginal net benefit of moving from 75 to 80 units is therefore $1.60 per unit (i.e., $2 in additional revenue per unit minus $0.40 in additional cost). In other words, total profits will increase by $8 (i.e., 5 units of additional output netting $1.60 per unit). These considerations imply that production will increase until marginal benefit equals marginal cost or until marginal net benefit equals zero. Finally, total profits will fall if production is expanded beyond 82.5 units of output.

The relevant curves determining the profit-maximizing output in this example are depicted in Figure 5.7. Price equals marginal cost at about 82.5 units of output, as depicted in panel a. The distance between the total revenue and total cost curves, profit, is largest at this level of output, as shown in panel b. This level of profit can also be seen in panel a. Price minus average cost is the profit per unit (average profit). Thus the shaded area in panel a represents the same level of profit at 82.5 units as the level of total profit shown in panel b.

This numerical example helps underscore a fundamental conclusion: *price (marginal benefit) equals marginal cost* is the criterion that identifies the profit-maximizing level of output if it is profitable to produce at all.

The Firm's Supply Curve

The marginal cost curve represents the minimum price at which a particular level of output will be produced and sold. For an output of about 82.5 units

Point on Fig. 5.7	(1) Total physical product[a]	(2) Market price	(3) Total revenue (1) × (2)	(4) Total cost[b]	(5) Profit (3) – (4)	(6) Marginal cost $\Delta(4) \div \Delta(1)$	(7) Marginal revenue $\Delta(3) \div \Delta(1)$
a	10.0	$2.00	$ 20.00	$101.00	−$81.00		
						$0.07	$2.00
b	25.0	2.00	50.00	102.00	−52.00		
						0.06	2.00
c	60.0	2.00	120.00	104.00	16.00		
						0.13	2.00
d	75.0	2.00	150.00	106.00	44.00		
						0.40	2.00
e	80.0	2.00	160.00	108.00	52.00		
						1.00	2.00
f	82.0	2.00	164.00	110.00	54.00		
						2.00	2.00	← Profit maximization
g	83.0	2.00	166.00	112.00	54.00		
						4.00	2.00
h	83.5	2.00	167.00	114.00	53.00		
						−c	2.00
i	83.0	2.00	166.00	116.00	50.00		

[a]Data appearing in this column appeared previously in column (3) of Table 5.2.
[b]Data appearing in this column appeared previously in column (9) or Table 5.2.
[c]As was the case in Table 5.2, these marginal costs are not reported, to reduce potential confusion.

TABLE 5.3 DETERMINATION OF PROFIT-MAXIMIZING LEVEL OF OUTPUT. The empirical example presented in this table illustrates the calculation of the marginal costs [see column (6)] and marginal revenue [see column (7)]. Profit is maximized at 82 to 83 units of production. This represents the level of output corresponding to the profit-maximizing condition that marginal cost ($2) equal marginal revenue ($2).

in the example presented in Table 5.3, the *minimum* acceptable product price would be $2 since it would cost $2 to produce the eighty-third unit of output. The farmer would not produce this unit if the price of the product was less than $2, at least not under conditions of certainty. If output price fell to $1, approximately 81.5 units of output would be supplied. Thus, if it is profitable to produce at all, the marginal cost curve represents the minimum supply price. The marginal cost curve therefore represents the *supply curve of the firm*.

Point *A* on the marginal cost curve presented earlier in panel a of Figure 5.4 represents the *break-even point* of production. This is where price equals average cost. The farmer, however, can minimize his losses by continuing to produce if price were below point *A*. If the product price

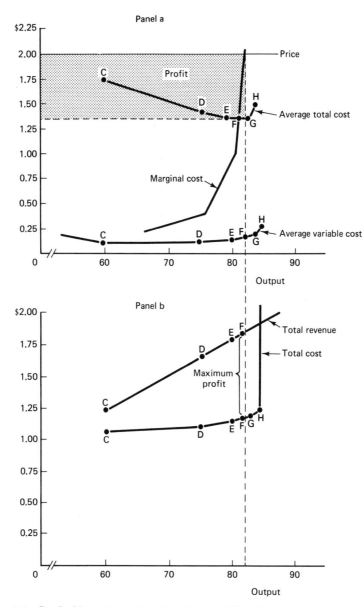

Figure 5.7 *Profit-Maximizing Level of Output.* This figure presents the determination of the profit-maximizing level of output for the numerical example presented in Table 5.3. Total revenue minus total cost is shown in panel b to be greatest when the price of the product ($2 in this case) equals marginal cost. This occurs at approximately 82.5 units of output. Total profit in panel b is given by the distance between the total revenue and total cost curves, while total profit in panel a is represented by the shaded area.

corresponding to the segment of the marginal cost curve lies between points *A* and *B*, the farmer can—by continuing to produce—cover some, though not all of his *fixed* costs. A rational competitive farmer will cease producing in the short run only when the product price falls below average *variable* costs of production, which occurs at point *B* in panel b of Figure 5.4. Operating when price is below point *B* on the marginal costs curve will only *add* to the firm's losses since the farmer is no longer covering all *variable* costs. Point *B* on the marginal cost curve is thus referred to as the *shutdown* point.

The farmer's break-even level of output occurs where profit is zero or where total revenue equals total cost (alternatively, where price equals average cost). In Figure 5.6 this occurs at the output associated with points *C* and *D*. For the numerical example in Table 5.3, this occurs for an output between 25 and 60 and when an output beyond 83.5 is attempted. In the latter case, further input use is costly but cannot increase output, so total cost becomes vertical, as noted in panel b of Figure 5.7.

It is often interesting to ask how low the product's price would have to fall before the farmer should cease operation. Zero profit is implied when price equals the minimum of average cost, which occurs at *A* in panel a of Figure 5.6. This corresponds to a price of $1.34 in our numerical example [see column (12) in Table 5.2]. Shutdown occurs when the price falls below point *B* in Figure 5.6. This would occur at a price of $0.07 per unit in our numerical example [see column (9) in Table 5.2].

The firm's supply curve is generally upward sloping since marginal costs increases, implying that the quantity supplied by the farmer increases with price. As was true when we discussed consumer behavior in Chapter 3, it is helpful to think of the behavioral response of the producer in the context of an elasticity. We can define a farmer's *elasticity of supply* as follows:

$$\text{elasticity of supply} \;=\; \frac{\text{percentage change in the quantity supplied}}{\text{percentage change in output price}} \qquad (5.10)$$

An elasticity of supply exceeding 1 indicates an *elastic* supply, while an elasticity of less than 1 suggests an *inelastic* supply. For example, if the elasticity of supply was 1.5, a 1 percent increase in output price would lead the farmer to increase his output. Since the percentage change in the farm's revenue is equal to the percentage change in price plus the percentage change in the quantity supplied, total farm revenue would increase by 2.5 percent. Thus the more (less) elastic the farmer's supply response is, the greater (lower) an impact of a price change will be on his total revenue, all other things constant.

PROFIT-MAXIMIZING INPUT DEMAND

We said when examining Table 5.3 that if the price of the product is $2 per unit, profit would be maximized at an output level of 82.5 units. The profit-maximizing choice of inputs, in turn, must therefore depend on the price of output, input prices, and technology. Given this output level, we can determine input demands given our knowledge of cost-minimizing (conditional) input demands. In this section we discuss an alternative approach for directly determining profit-maximizing input demands by comparing the marginal benefit associated with different levels of input use with the marginal *input* cost.

Since farm revenue is equal to the product price times output, it is clear that the marginal benefit from input use is equal to the change in total revenue per unit change in the input. This marginal benefit is called the *marginal value product,* and for labor is equal to[9]

$$\begin{matrix} \text{marginal value} \\ \text{product for} \\ \text{labor} \end{matrix} \quad = \quad MPP_{\text{labor}} \times \text{product price} \qquad (5.11)$$

The optimum or profit-maximizing level of input use occurs where the marginal value product equals the marginal input cost. For the case of labor, the optimal level of labor use is given by

$$MPP_{\text{labor}} \times \text{product price} = \text{wage rate} \qquad (5.12)$$

If additional labor was employed beyond this point, the marginal cost of doing so (i.e., the wage rate) would exceed the marginal benefits achieved (i.e., the marginal value product for labor).

A Numerical Example

Let us illustrate the determination of the profit-maximizing level of input use by applying equation (5.12) to the information presented in Table 5.4. This table assumes that the price of the product and the cost of the input are both equal to $2 per unit. Multiplying the marginal physical product [column (1)] by $2 gives us the marginal value product [column (3)]. For example, the addition of the second unit of input adds 35 units (bushels) of output. The value to the firm of these 35 bushels is $70 (i.e., $2 × 35 units). This represents the marginal benefit from adding the second unit of input.

Column (4) in Table 5.4 indicates that the farmer is a *price taker* in the market for the input since the firm's increased use of the input has no

---

[9] Some prefer to use the term "value of the marginal product" instead of "marginal value product."

(1) Use of input	(2) Marginal physical product[a]	(3) Marginal value product (2) × $2	(4) Marginal input cost	(5) Marginal net benefit (3) − (4)
0.0				
	30.0	$60.00	2.00	$58.00
1.0				
	35.0	70.00	2.00	68.00
2.0				
	15.0	30.00	2.00	28.00
3.0				
	5.0	10.00	2.00	8.00
4.0				
	2.0	4.00	2.00	4.00
5.0				
	1.0	2.00	2.00	0.00 — Optimal input use
6.0				
	0.5	1.00	2.00	−1.00
7.0				
	−0.5	−1.00	2.00	−3.00
8.0				

[a]Column (10) in Table 5.2.

TABLE 5.4 DETERMINATION OF PROFIT-MAXIMIZING LEVEL OF INPUT USE. The profit-maximizing level of input use occurs at the level of input use where the marginal value product (i.e., the marginal physical product multiplied by the price of the product) is equal to the marginal input cost. In the numerical example presented here, the farmer's profit-maximizing level of input use would be 6 units. The marginal benefit of increasing the use of this input any further would be negative, as illustrated in column (5).

effect on its cost. The cost of each additional unit of input is $2. The contribution to profit (net marginal benefit) is reported in column (5). This value is found by subtracting the marginal cost in column (4) from the marginal benefit reported in column (3). It is apparent from the information presented in Table 5.4 that the farmer should use 6 units of this input. The seventh unit would *reduce* profit by $2.

The marginal value product and marginal input cost relationships in the example above are plotted in Figure 5.8. Since the marginal value product curve is nothing more than the marginal physical product curve multiplied by a fixed product price, it is not surprising that the marginal value product curve in Figure 5.8 looks very much like a marginal physical product curve (i.e., like the one presented in panel c of Figure 5.3. As Table 5.4 suggests, the input use that maximizes profits is 6 units. This is also shown in Figure 5.8 to represent the input use level where the marginal value product curve intersects the marginal input cost curve.

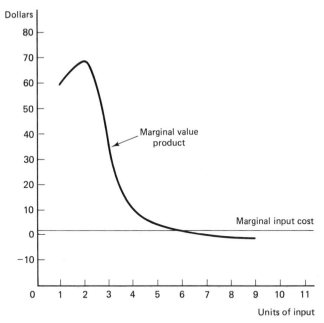

Figure 5.8 *Profit-Maximizing Level of Input Use.* The profit-maximizing level of input use determined numerically in Table 5.4 is illustrated graphically here. The marginal value product curve intersects the marginal input cost curve at 6 units of input. This figure also helps illustrate the point that an increase in the marginal input cost (which would shift this curve upward) will reduce input demand. What would happen to the profit-maximizing level of input use if the marginal input cost suddenly rose to $10?

The analysis presented in Table 5.4 and Figure 5.8 can be extended to *any input.* It represents a general way of characterizing the profit-maximizing level of input use. Profit maximization requires that the marginal value product (marginal benefit) of *each variable input* equal its marginal input cost. This concept intuitively leads to the conclusions we reached earlier when we discussed the least-cost combination of input use. For example, if an input's price should rise (fall) at this point, the marginal benefit would be less than (more than) the marginal cost. When this occurs, the farmer would decrease (increase) his use of the input.

An Empirical Example

In Chapter 4 we examined the impact of lime on alfalfa yields [see equation (4.5)]. Let us now examine the following question: Given this production function, what quantity of lime should the farmer apply if he wants to maximize his profit? The answer to this question will hinge on the impact of lime applied this year on *future* soil acidity. However, let us consider the simplest case possible; namely, the farmer leases theland for only one year. Thus, only *this year's* benefit is relevant to him. Table 5.5 presents the yields and marginal physical products calculated using equation (4.5) for selected quantities of lime. Looking at this table, we see that the marginal physical product of lime falls from 0.605 to 0.083 as lime use is increased from 2 tons per acre to 3 tons per acre. If the farmer wished to maximize his *yield,* more than 3 tons per acre would be applied (he would continue to apply

Lime use	Yield	Marginal physical product of lime per acre	Marginal value product	Marginal input cost
2.0	3.3300			
		0.605	18.15	10.00
2.1	3.3905			
		0.547	16.41	10.00
2.2	3.4452			
		0.489	14.67	10.00
2.3	3.4941			
		0.431	12.93	10.00
2.4	3.5372			
		0.373	11.19	10.00
2.5	3.5745			
		0.315	9.45	10.00
2.6	3.6060			
		0.257	7.71	10.00
2.7	3.6317			
		0.199	5.97	10.00
2.8	3.6516			
		0.141	4.23	10.00
2.9	3.6657			
		0.083	2.49	10.00
3.0	3.6740			

Optimal input use → 2.5

Note: These data are calculated using equation (4.5).

TABLE 5.5 EMPIRICAL EXAMPLE OF PROFIT-MAXIMIZING LEVEL OF LIME USE. Assume that the cost of lime is $10 per ton and that the price the farmer receives for alfalfa is $30 per ton. Using the example presented in Chapter 4 for the application of lime to alfalfa plantings, we see that the profit-maximizing application of lime on alfalfa would be approximately 2.5 tons per acre. Beyond this point, the marginal value product would be less than the marginal input cost.

lime until its marginal physical product was zero). However, lime is not free. Therefore, the farmer will want to weigh the costs and benefits of lime use.

   Assuming that the price received for alfalfa (net of other expenses) is $30 per ton and that the price of lime is $10 per ton, the profit-maximizing level of lime use is given by the point where the marginal physical product of lime times the price of alfalfa is equal to $10. The marginal value product of lime use is found by multiplying column (3) in this table by $30 (the price of alfalfa).[10] Suppose that alfalfa sells for $30 per ton. If lime use were to increase from 2.1 to 2.2 tons per acre, the marginal value product would

[10] Generally, the costs of other inputs are deducted from the price of the product so that the marginal benefit is expressed in *net* terms.

be $18.15, which exceeds the marginal input cost of $10. Hence profit can be increased by $8.15 by increasing lime use. Following this line of reasoning, we find the profit-maximizing lime use of 2.5 tons per acre. Adding lime beyond this point would lead to a situation where the marginal value of product of additional lime use is *less than* the marginal input cost, and profit would actually fall.

PROFIT-MAXIMIZING COMBINATION OF PRODUCTS

If a farmer produces several products but these products are independent of each other or *nonjoint,* all of the discussion presented in the preceding section applies to each product *considered separately.* This is because we can supposedly associate the use on an input with a particular product.

We know, however, that pesticides applied to one crop might affect the pest population in another crop. In this case, pesticide use is associated *jointly* with two or more products. With appropriate modifications, the single-product theory presented in the previous secitons is still useful. Profit maximization still implies that the price of each product equals marginal cost. However, if there is joint production of wheat and corn, the marginal cost of wheat will depend on the quantity of corn, and vice versa. Profit-maximizing output combinations in such cases must be simultaneously determined. In this section we show that this involves the calculation of the *isorevenue line* and then finding the point of tangency between this line and the production possibilities curve developed in Chapter 4.

Market Rate of Exchange

The *isorevenue line* represents the market rate of exchange of one product for another. The general nature of the isorevenue line for two products (corn and wheat) is illustrated in Figure 5.9. Like the approach taken to determining the isocost line discussed earlier in this chapter, the isorevenue line can be developed from the definition of total revenue (i.e., the sum of product prices multiplied by the respective quantities marketed). The isorevenue line for wheat and corn is equal to the negative of the price ratio of these two products, or

$$\begin{matrix} \text{units} \\ \text{of} \\ \text{corn} \end{matrix} = \frac{\text{total revenue}}{\text{price of corn}} - \frac{\text{price of wheat}}{\text{price of corn}} \times \text{units of wheat} \qquad (5.13)$$

The slope of this line, or the negative of the price of wheat to the price of corn, represents the rate at which the market is willing to exchange these two products. Suppose that the price of corn is $4.50 a bushel and the price of wheat is $4 per bushel. The slope of the isorevenue line therefore would

Figure 5.9 *The Isorevenue Line.* The isorevenue line plays an important role in the determination of the profit-maximizing combination of products. The slope of this line is equal to the negative of the price ratio for these two products as indicated by equation (5.13). The intercept of this line is equal to the quantity of corn produced if the farmer chose to specialize in this commodity. This value is found by dividing total revenue from the sale of corn by the price of corn [see equation (5.13)].

be −0.80 (i.e., −$4.00 ÷ $4.50). This suggests that 1 bushel of wheat is worth 4/5 of a bushel of corn.

Technical Rate of Exchange

The technical rate of exchange between corn and wheat is given by a production possibilities curve like the one illustrated in Figure 5.10. We know from equation (4.8) that the absolute value of the slope of this curve, called the *marginal rate of product transformation,* is equal to the ratio of the change in these two products. This slope is negative and falling, indicating an increasing opportunity cost of production. In other words, a marginal increase in wheat production requires a greater reduction in corn production.

Profit-Maximizing Choice

The profit-maximizing combination of products seeks to maximize the revenue for the least-cost combination of inputs. The only difference between this objective and the "cost-minimization" objective discussed in the first section of this chapter is that here we want to determine the *highest feasible isorevenue line.* This occurs at point *A* in Figure 5.10, where the slope of the production possibilities curve is equal to the slope of the isorevenue line. At this point, the marginal rate of product transformation equals the ratio of the price of wheat to the price of corn. We can therefore state the conditions for the profit-maximizing combination of products (e.g., wheat and corn) in mathematical terms as follows:

$$\frac{\Delta\,\text{corn}}{\Delta\,\text{wheat}} = \frac{\text{price of wheat}}{\text{price of corn}} \tag{5.14}$$

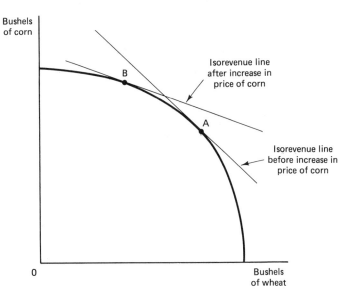

Figure 5.10 *Profit-Maximizing Choice of Products.* The profit-maximizing combination of corn and wheat is indicated by the point where the isorevenue line is tangent to the production possibilities curve. This is the only point where the slopes of these two curves are equal, the condition for profit maximization given in equation (5.14). The original optimal combination of products is given by point *A*. If the price of corn should increase, however, the farmer will wish to produce more corn and less wheat, as indicated by point *B*.

where the negative signs on both sides of the equation have been dropped for ease of presentation.

Let's assume that we are at point *A* in Figure 5.10 and the price of corn suddenly increases relative to the price of wheat. This will alter the slope of the isorevenue line. Let's assume that the new isorevenue line is tangent to the production possibilities curve at point *B*. We can see in Figure 5.10 that the profit-maximizing farmer will increase his corn production and decrease his wheat production. In other words, a farmer with a fixed amount of land will alter the allocation of his acreage among wheat and corn as their price ratio changes. The supply of wheat and corn will therefore depend on all input prices, fixed inputs, technology, the price of wheat, and the price of corn.

A Numerical Example

Let us expand the numerical example of the product–product relationship for corn and wheat presented in Chapter 4 to determine the *profit-maxi-*

mizing combination of these two products. Table 5.6 suggests that if the ratio of the price wheat to the price of corn is equal to 0.90, the profit-maximizing combination of these two products would be 119,000 bushels of corn and 20,000 bushels of wheat. At this combination, the marginal rate of product transformation (slope of the production possibilities curve) is equal to the price ratio (slope of the isorevenue curve). This satisfies the condition for profit maximization expressed in equation (5.14). If the price of wheat were to increase (decrease), the price ratio in column (4) of Table 5.6 would increase (decrease), as would the production of wheat relative to

(1)	(2)	(3) Marginal Rate of product transformation $\Delta(1) \div \Delta(2)$	(4) Price ratio $\$4 \div \$4.50$	
Corn	Wheat			
135,000	0			
		0.7	0.9	
128,000	10,000			
		0.9	0.9	Profit maximization
119,000	20,000			
		1.1	0.9	
108,000	30,000			
		1.3	0.9	
95,000	40,000			
		1.5	0.9	
80,000	50,000			
		1.7	0.9	
63,000	60,000			
		1.9	0.9	
44,000	70,000			
		2.1	0.9	
23,000	80,000			
		2.3	0.9	
0	90,000			

TABLE 5.6 PROFIT-MAXIMIZING COMBINATION OF PRODUCTS. Let's return to the numerical production possibilities example presented in Table 4.2. Columns (1) through (3) repeat columns (1) through (3) in Table 4.2 and represent the coordinates of points on the production possibilities curve [columns (1) and (2)] and the absolute value of the slope of this curve at each location [column (3)]. The absolute value of the slope of the isorevenue line is presented in column (4). We know from equation (5.14) that profit is maximized when production occurs where the slope of these two curves are equal. Looking at these data, we see that this occurs at 119,000 bushels of corn and 20,000 bushels of wheat. Any change in the price ratio in column (4), however, would alter this desired combination of corn and wheat.

corn. If the price of corn were to increase (decrease), the price ratio in column (4) would decrease (increase), as would the production of wheat relative to corn.

Cross-Price Elasticity of Supply

The substitution between products as prices change suggests the need to measure the farmer's *cross-price elasticity of supply*. Using wheat as an example, the cross-price elasticity of supply is defined as follows:

$$\begin{matrix} \text{cross-price} \\ \text{elasticity of supply} \\ \text{for wheat} \end{matrix} = \frac{\text{percentage change in wheat supply}}{\text{percentage change in corn price}} \qquad (5.15)$$

If the cross-price elasticity for these two products is equal to zero, the price of corn would have no impact on the farmer's production of wheat. If this elasticity is positive, the two products are *substitutes*. If it is negative, these products are *complements*. Suppose we know that the farmer's own price elasticity of supply for wheat is 0.8 and that his cross-price elasticity for corn is −0.6. This suggests that a policy which raises the price of corn by 10 percent will reduce this farmer's production of wheat by 6 percent.

In summary, optimal product choice is characterized by the equality of the marginal rate of product transformation and the product price ratio. This implies that the supply of each product depends on the prices of other products.

MARKET INPUT DEMAND AND PRODUCT SUPPLY

The market input demand and product supply curves are equal to the *horizontal summation* of all the farm level input demand and product supply curves, respectively. This approach is entirely analogous to the market demand curve for consumers discussed in Chapter 3 (see Figure 3.9) and is not repeated here. There is one aspect of the aggregation of individual behavior into a market-level response, however, which deserves mention.

Suppose that the price of wheat increases and each farm attempts to expand output at existing fixed input prices. Farm expansion would require more land. This would bid up the price of land. As land costs increase, the marginal cost of wheat production would increase. Thus each farm will end up producing less wheat than if the price of land had remained fixed. This will lead to a market supply curve that is more inelastic (less responsive or steeper) than the supply curve with a fixed land price.

In the remainder of this section, let us examine the nature of the market input demand and product supply elasticities estimated by agricultural economists.

Estimates of Input Demand Elasticities

We earlier stated that product supply and input demand at the firm level depends on the price of the product and all relevant input prices. To illustrate these interrelationships at the aggregate or sector level, consider the estimated elasticities for selected inputs in the United States presented in Table 5.7. These elasticities are not expressed in absolute-value terms. Thus the negative sign on the elasticities reported along the diagonal of this table indicates that they represent own-price elasticities, while the "off-diagonal" entries in this table represent cross-price elasticities of input demand. These definitions are analogous to those used in Chapter 3 when discussing consumer demand for final goods.

We can interpret the information presented in Table 5.7 as follows: a 1 percent increase in the price of land, for example, will decrease the quantity of land demanded for agricultural use by 0.15 percent. Similarly, a 1 percent increase (decrease) in the price of fertilizer will lead to a 0.54 percent decrease (increase) in the quantity of fertilizer demanded, and so on. The positive (negative) off-diagonal elasticities imply that these inputs are substitutes (complements). For example, according to these estimated elasticities, fertilizer and land are substitutes. A 1 percent increase in the price of fertilizer, *ceteris paribus,* will increase the quantity of land demanded by 1.05 percent as land is substituted for fertilizer. Capital (mainly machinery) and energy, on the other hand, are complements. A 1 percent increase in the price of energy will lead to a reduction in the demand for capital inputs by

| Input | Price of the input | | | | |
	Land	Labor	Fertilizer	Energy	Capital
Land	−0.15	0.12	1.05	0.56	−0.62
Labor	−0.12	0.00	−1.52	1.07	0.52
Fertilizer	0.10	0.14	−0.54	0.58	0.00
Energy	0.03	0.92	1.21	−1.65	−0.52
Capital	−0.02	−0.23	−0.21	−0.15	−0.60

Source: Derived from M. Leblanc, "Estimating Input Cost Shares for Agriculture Using a Multinominal Logit Framework," *Agricultural Economics Research,* 1982, pp. 23–31.

TABLE 5.7 INPUT DEMAND ELASTICITIES FOR SELECTED CATEGORIES OF INPUTS. The input demand elasticities presented in this table help us get a feeling for what would happen to the demand for these inputs their price should change. For example, if the price of energy rose by 1 percent, the demand for land would fall by 0.56 percent, the demand for labor would rise by 1.07 percent, the demand for fertilizer would rise by 0.58 percent, and the demand for energy and capital would fall by 1.65 percent and 0.15 percent, respectively.

0.15 percent. A 1 percent increase in the price of capital will result in a 0.5 percent decrease in the quantity of energy demanded—an even more dramatic effect.

Estimates of Product Supply Elasticity

It is frequently argued that farmers cannot respond immediately to an increase in the expected price of the commodity (Nerlov, 1956; Nerlove and Addison, 1958). As time passes, the quantity of the commodity supplied increases. This implies that the long-run elasticity of supply is greater than the short-run elasticity. Askari and Cummings (1977) summarized an enormous volume of previous studies based on Nerlove's approach. Table 5.8 reproduces several of the elasticities of supply found by Askari and Cummings for both the short run and the long run. As indicated, the long-run elasticities of supply are larger than their short-run counterparts. We can interpret

Commodity	Location	Own-price elasticity of supply	
		Short run	Long run
Pork	U.S.	0.24	0.48
Milk	California	0.38	2.54
Wool	U.S.	0.14	0.33
Coffee	Brazil	0.10	0.11
Soybeans	U.S.	0.84	0.84
Onions	U.S.	0.34	1.00
Lettuce	U.S.	0.03	0.16
Barley	Punjab	0.22	0.27
Wheat	Chile	0.37	3.65
Rice	Punjab	0.31	0.59
Cotton	Sudan	0.39	0.50
Carrots	U.S.	0.14	1.00

See H. Askari and J. Cummings, "Estimating Agricultural Supply Response with the Narlove Model: A Survey," *International Economic Review*, 1977, pp. 257–292.

TABLE 5.8 SUPPLY ELASTICITY ESTIMATES FOR SELECTED AGRICULTURAL PRODUCTS. The supply elasticities for the commodities presented here indicate the production response by farmers in various countries to a rise in the price they receive. For example, the supply of lettuce in the United States would be virtually unchanged (0.03 percent) in the short run (current year) if the price of lettuce increased by 1 percent. The supply response in the longer run would be somewhat higher (0.16 percent) but still relatively small when compared, for example, to the supply response for carrots in the United States.

these estimates as follows: a 1 percent increase in the price of pork, for example, will increase the supply of pork in the following year by 0.24 percent, all other things constant. As time passes and all adjustments have taken place, there will be a 0.48 percent increase in the supply of pork. More will be said about this lagged supply response when we examine the concept of market equilibrium for farm products in Chapter 9.

Let us examine a final example that illustrates the cross-price elasticity of supply at the sector level. In a study of corn and soybean acreage response in the Corn Belt, the elasticity of corn acreage with respect to its own price was estimated to be −0.50. (Houck and Subotnik, 1969). These elasticities must be interpreted under the assumption that government programs are held constant. The elasticity of soybean acreage with respect to the price of corn was estimated to be −0.50. Thus soybeans and corn are substitutes. A 1 percent change in the price of corn leads to a 0.5 percent decrease in soybean acreage. Similar results were found for corn acreage response.

SUMMARY

The purpose of this chapter was to characterize the economic dimension of the production decisions confronting a competitive firm. The major points made in this chapter can be summarized as follows:

1. The *isocost line* represents all possible input combinations that yield a given level of total cost. Its slope is the input price ratio, which measures the market rate of exchange among inputs.
2. The *least-cost input combination* for a particular level of output is characterized by the equality of the marginal rate of technical substitution and the input price ratio. This means that the *marginal benefits per dollar expended on all inputs are equal.*
3. Opportunity cost measures the benefits lost from a foregone opportunity. Cost of production include direct (accounting) expenses plus opportunity costs. *Economic efficiency* dictates that total costs for a given level of production be *minimized.*
4. *Marginal cost* is the change in total cost with respect to a change in output. *Average cost* is total cost divided by total output. *Fixed costs* are those costs that do not vary with output.
5. The *profit-maximizing* output of a competitive firm occurs where the *product price is equal to marginal cost.*
6. The supply curve represents the minimum price for which the farmer would produce and sell the product. The greater (smaller) the elasticity, the greater (smaller) the impact of a given percentage change on total farm revenue.

7. The quantity demanded of an input is determined by the equality of marginal value product marginal factor cost.
8. *Optimal product choice* is characterized by the *equality* of the *marginal rate of production transformation* and the negative of the *price ratio.* This suggests that the supply of each product depends on the price of other products as well.
9. The various revenue and cost concepts introduced in this chapter can be summarized as follows:

Total variable cost	=	wage rate $\times$ labor use
Total fixed cost	=	rental rate $\times$ capital use
Total cost	=	total variable cost + total fixed cost
Average total cost	=	$\dfrac{\text{total cost}}{\text{total output}}$
Average variable cost	=	$\dfrac{\text{total variable cost}}{\text{total output}}$
Average fixed cost	=	$\dfrac{\text{total fixed cost}}{\text{total output}}$
Marginal cost	=	$\dfrac{\text{change in total cost}}{\text{change in total output}}$
Total revenue	=	product price $\times$ total output
Marginal benefit (revenue)	=	$\dfrac{\text{change in total revenue}}{\text{change in total cost}}$
Average benefit (revenue)	=	$\dfrac{\text{total revenue}}{\text{total cost}}$
Accounting profits	=	total revenue accounting costs
Economic profits	=	accounting profit opportunity cost

DEFINITION OF TERMS

Least cost: achieving a given objective while minimizing cost. Generally this refers to choosing input combinations that minimize the total cost of producing a given output.

Maximum profit: input and output choices that maximize profit.

Price takers: when firms or consumers do not alter the prices they face, they are said to be price takers.

Isocost line: the locus of all input choices that yield a given level of total cost.

Opportunity cost: the implicit cost of an action that is the maximum forgone opportunity in an alternative activity. For example, the opportunity cost of using one's labor to farm may be the wage forgone elsewhere (e.g., in manufacturing).

Economics profits: total revenue or sales minus economic costs. These costs include accounting costs (cash costs plus depreciation) plus opportunity costs.

Accounting profits: total revenue or sales minus accounting costs.

Marginal cost: the change in total cost divided by the change in output.

Average cost: total cost divided by output.

Marginal benefit: the increment to total benefit (revenue) per unit increase in an activity (e.g., output).

Marginal net benefit: marginal benefit (revenue) minus marginal cost.

Fixed costs: those costs that do not vary with output changes.

Variable costs: costs that vary with output.

Elasticity of supply: a measure of the relative response of output supplied to a price change. It is the percentage change in the quantity of output supplied resulting from a 1 percent change in output price.

Producer surplus: the excess of market price over the minimum price necessary to bring forth the quantity supplied (supply price).

Isorevenue line: the locus of all output quantities of a multiproduct firm that yeild a given revenue or sales.

Cross-price elasticity of supply: the relative response of the supply of a good A as the price of good B changes. It is the percentage change in good A divided by the percentage change in the price of good B.

REFERENCES

ASKARI, H., and J. CUMMINGS, "Estimating Agricultural Supply Response with the Nerlove Model: A Survey," *International Economic Review,* 1977, pp. 257–292.

HOUCK, J., and A. SUBOTNIK, "The U.S. Supply of Soybeans: Regional Acreage Functions," *Agricultural Economics Research,* 1969, pp. 99–108.

LEBLANC, M., "Estimating Input Cost Shares for Agriculture Using a Multinomial Logit Framework," *Agricultural Economics Research,* 1982, pp. 23–31.

NERLOVE, M., "Estimates of the Elasticities of Supply of Selected Agricultural Commodities," *Journal of Farm Economics,* 1956, pp. 496–508.

NERLOVE, M., and W. ADDISON, "Statistical Estimation of Long Run Elasticities of Supply and Demand," *Journal of Farm Economics,* 1958, pp. 82.

SHUMWAY, C. RICHARD, HOVAV TALPAZ, and BRUCE R. BEATTIE, "The Factor Share Approach to Production Function Estimation: Actual or Estimated Equilibrium Shares?" *American Journal of Agricultural Economics,* 1979, pp. 561-564.

ADDITIONAL READINGS

HEADY, EARL O., *Economics of Agricultural Production and Resourse Use.* Englewood Cliffs, N.J.: Prentice-Hall, Inc., 1952.

KOHLER, H., *Intermediate Microeconomics: Theory and Applications.* Glenview, Ill.: Scott, Foresman and Company, 1982.

PETERSON, WILLIS L., *Principles of Economics: Micro,* 4th ed. Homewood, Ill.: Richard D. Irwin, Inc., 1980.

QUESTIONS

1. Fill in the blanks in the following table.

Output	Fixed cost	Total variable cost	Total cost	Marginal cost
0	$1,000	0	$ 1,000	
				$5,000
1	1,000	——	6,000	
2	1,000	$ 7,000	8,000	——
				3,000
3	1,000	10,000	——	
				5,000
4	1,000	15,000	16,000	
5	1,000	25,000	——	——
6	1,000	——	41,000	——
7	1,000	80,000	——	——

2. For the data in problem 1, calcualte average total, average fixed, and average variable costs. Why does average fixed cost decline as output expands?

3. If the price of output in problem 1 were $5,000, what level of output would maximize profit?

4. If technical change increased the marginal physical product in Table 5.5 by 20 percent, how would this alter the optimal level of lime usage?

5. If the price of breakfast oatmeal cereal increases, how will this affect the demand for oats?

6. Explain economic substitution as (1) the relative price of labor increases, and (2) the relative price of corn (ratio of corn to soybeans) increases. How might these concepts relate to public policies that alter prices?

7. Explain how the concepts of marginal benefit and marginal cost could be used to decide:
   (a) Whether to attend college
   (b) Whether to buy insurance
   (c) Whether to quit teaching and farm
   (d) Whether to add insulation to a home

ADVANCED TOPICS

Three additional subjects are covered in this section. The first two topics focus in more depth on input demand, while the third topic introduces the concept of producer surplus.

Substitution and Output Effects

How do input demands change in response to changes in the economic environment? If energy prices or agricultural wage rates rise relative to other input costs, what adjustments might we observe in the farmer's input use? Normally, a rise in an input's price increases marginal cost. This shifts the supply curve upward from S to S^* in Figure 5.11. The new profit-maximizing output level would be lower than it was previously. There are two adjustments to input use. The first occurs along an isoquant and is called the

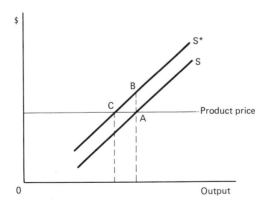

Figure 5.11 *Input Price Change and Farm Input Demand.* The total input demand response to a change in the price of an input can be broken down into a substitution effect occurs along an isoquant as one input is substituted for another. The net result is an increase in marginal cost from point A to point B. As output is reduced from point A to point C to maximize profits, less is used of all inputs. Both effects have a negative impact on demand.

substitution effect. As the wage rate rises, capital is *substituted* for labor. The net result is the increase in marginal cost from point *A* to point *B* in Figure 5.11.

A second effect is the *output effect.* As output is reduced from point *A* to point *C* to maximize profits, generally less is used of *all inputs.* Underlying this effect is a movement from one isoquant to another with input prices held fixed. The sum of the substitution and output effects gives the *total input response.* That is, the response of an input to a change in its price is the sum of the substitution and output effects. Both effects have a negative impact on input demand. As the price of an input rises (falls), both effects lead to reduced (increased) input use.

Derived Input Demand

Input demand curves are like consumer demand curves in that they are both downward sloping.[11] We see in Figure 5.12, for example, that at a wage of $6 per hour, four workers are hired; at $3 per hour, six workers are hired. Such an input demand curve is often called a *derived demand curve* because it depends in part on the product's price (i.e., conditions in the firm's product market). Let us assume that the product price increases and that, as a result, output expands from point *A* to point *D* in Figure 5.11. This,

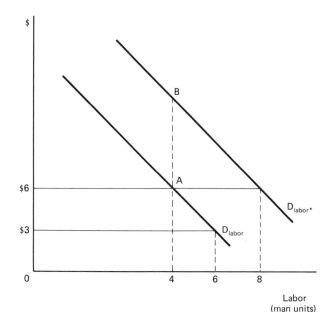

Figure 5.12 *Derived Demand for Labor.* The demand curve for inputs like labor is "derived" because it reflects conditions in farm product markets (i.e., the product price). An increase (decrease) in the product price will cause the input demand curve to shift to the right (left). Other factors causing this demand curve to shift are changes in the prices of other inputs. The direction of this shift depends on whether these inputs are substitutes or complements.

[11] Input demand elasticities can also be calculated as the percentage change in the quantity of the input demanded divided by the percentage change in an input price.

in turn, will increase the demand for labor. This is reflected by a shift in the demand curve for labor from D_{labor} to D^*_{labor} in Figure 5.12. At the higher output price and at a wage of $6, eight people would be hired. Input use expands because the initial marginal benefit from labor use exceeds the marginal cost (4), as shown by the gap between points B and A. Increased labor use from four to eight people reduces this marginal benefit until it equals the marginal cost of labor at $6.

The input demand curve will also shift as the prices of other inputs change. These effects can be decomposed into substitution and output effects, but the total effect cannot be determined except by empirical study. If a rise (fall) in the rental rate for capital increased (decreased) the demand for labor, these inputs (labor and capital) are said to be *substitutes*. If the opposite effect occurs, the inputs are said to be *complements*.

Finally, technological change will also shift the input demand curve. If prices were fixed and technology increased productivity, the input demand curves would all shift right. Thus a genetic improvement may lead to increased water use, fertilizer use, and so on.

Producer Surplus

Economic rent is the return to an input above the minimum price at which farmers would have supplied inputs to the market.[12] When economic profit exists, rents are accruing to farmers. We can measure these rents by examining the firm's short-run cost curves. Farmers will supply the first unit of output for the marginal cost of producing the first unit. If this marginal cost were $1 and the price of output were $4, the farmer would receive a $3 gain or *surplus* from producing and exchanging the commodity. Suppose that the marginal cost of producing the one-hundredth unit were $3; the gain would be $1 for producing this unit. By similar reasoning, the area above the supply curve and below the market price represents total producer surplus or rent. This surplus is represented by area ABC in Figure 5.13 when the product price is $4. If the product price rises to $6, producer surplus increases to area $CBDE$. These areas represent profit plus fixed costs.[13] Hence producer surplus is a measure of the economic welfare of producers.

---

[12] If the rents disappear with entry or exit, they are short-term phenomenan called quasi-rents.

[13] Since the producer surplus associated with a unit of output represents the marginal profit, total producer surplus represents total revenue minus total *variable costs*, or profit plus *fixed costs*.

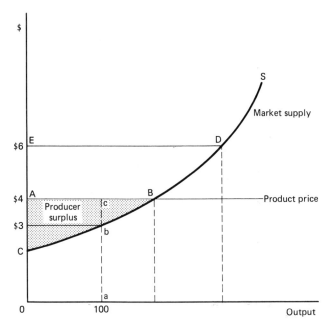

Figure 5.13 *Concept of Producer Surplus.* The change in the economic welfare of farmers can be approximated through the concept of economic rent or producer surplus. The value of this surplus is given by the shaded area in the figure, the area above the market supply curve and below the equilibrium market price for the product. This area reflects the revenue received by farmers above the minimum price they would have been willing to supply their products.

6

FARM MARKETING OPTIONS

While the point was made in earlier chapters that the competitive firm is a *price taker in the markets where it acquires its inputs and sells its products,* this does not mean that the individual farmer is without farm marketing options to choose from. For example, the farmer must decide sometime before the harvest of his crops or the finishing of his livestock whether he is going to (1) accept the prevailing price in the local cash market when production is completed, or (2) use one of several means available to negotiate a forward price for his product. Farmers producing such nonperishable commodities such as wheat are faced with the additional decision of whether to sell their production at harvest time or store the commodity on or off the farm in anticipation of future favorable price trends.

Before we leave the short run and focus on the long-run growth of the competitive firm, let us discuss the nature of the marketing options available to farmers. In the first section we discuss the importance of having a *marketing plan* and introduces the wide range of marketing options farmers should consider when developing their marketing plan. In the second section we take an in-depth look at specific marketing options, including the use of *production contracts* and *future contracts* as a means of determining in advance the ultimate market price for their output. In the third section we focus on the magnitude of storage activities by farm businesses and the factors they should consider when planning inventory buildups and purchasing of on-farm storage facilities.

THE MARKETING PLAN

When developing a marketing plan or strategy, farmers must have a clear idea of the objectives they wish to achieve. With these objectives in mind, farmers can select that marketing option which is best suited for their firm.

Objectives of Plan

The marketing plan for a farm business must reflect the objectives of the firm in its buying and selling activities. Does the farmer strive to minimize costs when he purchases inputs such as fertilizer and feed? Does the farmer choose those marketing strategies for his firm's output that maximizes cash receipts?

Although both of these objectives are no doubt paramount in the minds of many farmers, most farmers would probably confirm that they consider a variety of other factors as well when formulating their marketing plan. These additional objectives might include market freedom at harvest time, income stability, and firm growth. Often these factors are in conflict. For example, the strategy to maximize cash receipts from farm marketings may lead to high exposure to risk and thus be at odds with the desire to minimize exposure to market risk. The weights farmers place on these factors will have a definite effect on which marketing options they select.

Marketing Options

While the point was made in Chapter 5 that farmers are price takers, this does not mean that an individual farmer is necessarily limited to accepting the current cash market price. The following discussion summarizes the various options farmers have in the markets where they purchase their inputs and sell their output.

Input markets. The use of purchased production inputs has grown dramatically during the post–World War II period. The technology embodied in these inputs has increased farmers' production efficiency. The increased use of nonfarm inputs, however, has reduced farmers' self-sufficiency and links their economic performance more closely than ever before with events taking place elsewhere in the economy.

Farmers essentially have two marketing options when acquiring production inputs: (1) they can purchase these manufactured inputs *directly* from the merchant or (2) they can acquire these inputs through a *purchasing co-operative.* Farmers can enchance their net income prospects by sharpening their negotiating skills when directly acquiring production inputs. Larger farm businesses, for example, may be able to achieve volume discounts on

USDA Photo

The farmer should not wait until his crops are harvested to formulate his marketing plan. He may choose to accept the current price for his crop at harvest. Other options that should be carefully weighed, however, include signing a production contract, hedging in the futures market, and storing the crop either on or off the farm and then sequentially marketing out of storage over a period of time.

the unit price for specific inputs such as fertilizer. Purchasing cooperatives, however, enable their farmer-members to achieve better terms of exchange than they could otherwise because of the cooperative's relative market power. Farm purchasing cooperatives account for over 20 percent of total cash expenditures for feed in this country. They also account for about 40 percent of total cash expenditures by farmers for fertilizer and fuel. The Farm Credit System, a cooperative that acquires the funds it lends to its members in the nation's money markets, is the largest lender to the farm business sector.

Product markets. Farmers have considerably more options to choose from when it comes to when and where to market their current production. In addition to the decision of whether to market their crops individually or jointly through a marketing cooperative, farmers have the option of signing a *production contract* to deliver a certain quantity of a commodity for a predetermined price or to *hedge* part of their production in the *futures market.* Before going into the details of selected product marketing options, let us illustrate the range of marketing options available to farmers by identifying six different possiblities.

First, farmers can *accept the current price* when the crop is harvested or the livestock are finished. This is the price determined in a local cash or spot market for the commodity. In such markets, the commodity is actually physically exchanged at a fixed price per unit. This price is often below the average annual price and is free to fluctuate up or down as demand and supply conditions change. The decision as to *which* spot market to ship to will depend on the prices quoted in various spot markets and the costs farmers would incur by transporting their products to a different geographical location. In fact, the equilibrium price in two local markets should differ only by the costs of transporting these goods to the other market. It also follows that the central or terminal market price will be higher than the prices observed in any decentralized or local market. Thus the farther farmers are located from the central market, the lower the local spot market price for their product will be.

Second, farmers can *accept an average price* for their product by spreading the marketing of the commodity over a period of time. This *sequential marketing* of the firm's product must either be tied to a sequential production plan (e.g., selling and restocking a portion of feeder cattle in your feedlot) or to a sequential marketing of a nonperishable commodity initially stored at harvest time.

Third, farmers can *store their current production* of nonperishable commodities in storage facilities on or off the farm in anticipation of favorable future price movements. This option is often used by grain farmers with on-farm storage facilities. As we will discuss later in this chapter, the decision to follow this marketing option will depend on whether farmers expect the eventual market price to exceed the current market price plus the costs of storage. For those farmers participating in the federal farm program, there is also the option of the farmer-held reserve program, which we will examine in Chapter 10.

Fourth, farmers can *become members of a marketing cooperative* that markets the production of all of its members in a manner designed to achieve the best return. This pooling option allows inexperienced farmers to take advantage of the cooperative's marketing skills and spreads market risks over the cooperative's entire membership. Farmers who like to gamble or are confident of their own marketing abilities, however, may see this option as placing a ceiling on their total revenue.

Fifth, farmers can fix the price for their commondity by *signing a production contract* prior to the completion of the commodity. This contract may even be signed before production has begun. This option eliminates much of the price uncertainty farmers may face, but it is not without its disadvantages, as we will make clear when we examine this option in more depth later in this chapter.

Sixth, farmers can *hedge* their market position and lock-in a price for specific commodities such as corn and wheat by *selling a futures contract*. Like the production contract, this marketing option allows the farmer to "determine" the price of the product well before it is finished. The mechanics of this option and a discussion of its advantages and disadvantages are presented in a later section of this chapter.

The six marketing options identified above can be summarized as follows:

Options	*Action*
Accept current price	Sell in spot market at harvest
Accept average price over marketing year	Store at harvest and market sequentially in spot market
Accept later price	Store at harvest and sell entire crop later in spot market
Accept group sales price	Sell through marketing cooperative
Lock-in future price	Sign production contract prior to harvest
Lock-in future price	Sell futures contract for delivery at future time and location

These six marketing options do not represent an all-inclusive listing of the options available to all farmers. This list does represent the major options available to a majority of farmers, however. The farmer's choice of which option to use will depend on his objectives and understanding of their relative advantages and usage. As we shall underscore in Chapter 8, a profit-maximizing farmer will be indifferent to the market risks involved with selling output and would therefore wish to rule out those options that lower risk at the expense of placing a ceiling on potential returns. Farmers who are averse to accepting risks (to varying degrees) will rank those options differently than a farmer who is indifferent to risk would. Sale of commodities at current market price, either at the time the product is finished or later when nonperishable commodities are removed from storage, represents the most frequently used option.

In periods of price instability, however, there is greater interest in production contracts and future contracts. The applicability and relative advantages of these two options are discussed in the next two sections.

FUTURES MARKET CONTRACTS

Futures trading is a highly organized and regulated method of forward pricing selected farm products. It allows the farmer to *lock-in* the price he will receive when the commodity is eventually marketed. Futures markets exist for a wide range of commodities, including broilers, cattle, corn, eggs, milo, oats, orange juice, potatoes, soybeans, sugar, wheat, and wool (see Figure 6.1). The terms of a *futures contract* are highly standarized as to the quality and quantity of the commodity to be delivered as well as the location and data of delivery.

For example, suppose that the farmer wished to lock-in a price for his corn crop before it is harvested. This can be done by *selling* a futures market contract. This contract amounts to a promise to deliver a specific quantity of corn at harvest time for the current futures price associated with that date. Implicit in this decision is the determination that this price (less commission) would result in an acceptable profit level per unit of output.

The farmer can also choose to store his commodity at harvest time and sell a July futures contract for the following year. Let's assume that the futures market price is sufficiently above the current spot market price, thereby allowing him to lock-in a higher profit above brokerage commissions, interest charges, and storage costs. Before next July rolls around, he can (1) sell his corn crop on the spot market and (2) buy an *equal and offsetting* futures market contract. This transaction wipes out the farmer's futures market position. If the delivery date arrives and the farmer has not liquidated the contract through equal and offsetting purchases of futures contracts, the contract must be satisfied by actual delivery of the commodity at an approved warehouse. It is important that the farmer determine whether or not the futures price is sufficient to cover storage costs (including income forgone by not receiving current cash payment at harvest and investing these funds in the next best opportunity) before selling the futures contract.

FUTURES TRADING FACTS

COMMODITY	NAME OF EXCHANGE	TRADING HOURS N.Y. Time Mon. thru Fri.	CONTRACT	MINIMUM FLUCTUATION Per Lb., etc.	Per Contract	DAILY TRADING LIMITS (From Previous Close)
BROILERS, FRESH	Chicago Mercantile Exchange	10:10 A.M. - 2:00 P.M.	30,000 Lbs.	2½/100¢	$7.50	2¢
CATTLE (FEEDER)	Chicago Mercantile Exchange	10:05 A.M. - 1:45 P.M.	42,000 Lbs.	2½/100¢	$10.50	1½¢
CATTLE (LIVE BEEF)	Chicago Mercantile Exchange	10:05 A.M. - 1:45 P.M.	40,000 Lbs.	2½/100¢	$10.00	1½¢
COCOA	Coffee, Sugar & Cocoa Ex.	9:30 A.M. - 3:00 P.M.	10 Tonnes	$1.00/Tonne	$10.00	$88.00*
COFFEE "C"	Coffee, Sugar & Cocoa Ex.	9:45 A.M. - 2:28 P.M.	37,500 Lbs.	1/100¢	$3.75	4¢*
COPPER	Commodity Exch., Inc., N.Y.	9:50 A.M. - 2:00 P.M.	25,000 Lbs.	5/100¢	$12.50	5¢*
COTTON #2	New York Cotton Exchange	10:30 A.M. - 3:00 P.M.	50,000 Lbs.	1/100¢	$5.00	2¢*
Currencies BRITISH POUND		8:30 A.M. - 2:24 P.M.	25,000 BP	$.0005	$12.50	$.0500*
CANADIAN DOLLAR	International Monetary	8:30 A.M. - 2:22 P.M.	100,000 CD	$.0001	$10.00	$.0075*
DEUTSCHE MARK	Market of	8:30 A.M. - 2:20 P.M.	125,000 DM	$.0001	$12.50	$.0100*
JAPANESE YEN	Chic. Merc. Exch.	8:30 A.M. - 2:26 P.M.	12.5 Mil. JY	$.000001	$12.50	$.0001*
SWISS FRANC		8:30 A.M. - 2:16 P.M.	125,000 SF	$.0001	$12.50	$.0150*
GINNIE MAE MTGES.	Chicago Board of Trade	9:00 A.M. - 3:00 P.M.	$100,000 @ 8%	1/32 Pt.	$31.25	64/32*
GOLD	IMM—Chicago Merc. Exch.	9:25 A.M. - 2:30 P.M.	100 Troy oz.	$.10/Oz.	$10.00	$50.00
	Commodity Exch. Inc., N.Y.	9:25 A.M. - 2:30 P.M.	100 Troy oz.	$.10/Oz.	$10.00	$25.00*
	MidAmerica Com. Ex., Chi.	9:25 A.M. - 2:40 P.M.	33.2 Troy oz.	$.025/Oz.	$ 0.83	$50.00*
	Winnipeg Commodity Exch.	9:25 A.M. - 2:30 P.M.	20 Troy oz.	$.10/Oz.	$2.00	$30.00* (U.S.)
Grains-Chicago WHEAT, SOYBEANS, CORN, OATS	Chicago Board of Trade	10:30 A.M. - 2:15 P.M.	5,000 Bus.	1/4¢	$12.50	Wheat 20¢, Soybeans 30¢
	MidAmerica Com. Ex., Chi.	10:30 A.M. - 2:30 P.M.	1,000 Bus. (Oats-5,000)	1/8¢	$ 1.25 (Oats-$6.25)	Corn 10¢ Oats 6¢ *
Grains-Minneapolis WHEAT	Minneapolis Grain Exchange	10:30 A.M. - 2:15 P.M.	5,000 Bus.	1/8¢	$6.25	20¢*
Grains-Kansas City WHEAT	Kansas City Board of Trade	10:30 A.M. - 2:15 P.M.	5,000 Bus.	1/4¢	$12.50	Wheat—25¢
Grains-Winnipeg BARLEY, OATS, RYE, RAPESEED, FLAXSEED	Winnipeg Commodity Ex.	10:30 A.M. - 2:15 P.M.	20 Tonnes	10¢/Tonne	$2.00	Barley, Oats, Rye $5.00/Tonne (Cdn.) Rapeseed & Flaxseed $10.00/Tonne (Cdn.)
HOGS, (LIVE)	Chicago Mercantile Exchange	10:10 A.M. - 2:00 P.M.	30,000 Lbs.	2½/100¢	$7.50	1½¢
LUMBER	Chicago Mercantile Exchange	10:00 A.M. - 2:05 P.M.	130,000 Bd. Ft.	10¢/1000 Board Ft.	$13.00	$5.00
OIL, HEATING #2	N.Y. Mercantile Exchange	10:30 A.M. - 2:45 P.M.	42,000 gals.	1/100¢	$4.20	2¢*
ORANGE JUICE (Frozen Concentrate)	New York Cotton Exchange	10:15 A.M. - 2:45 P.M.	15,000 Lbs.	5/100¢	$7.50	5¢*
PLATINUM	N.Y. Mercantile Exchange	9:30 A.M. - 2:30 P.M.	50 Troy oz.	10¢	$5.00	$20.00*
PLYWOOD	Chicago Board of Trade	10:00 A.M. - 2:00 P.M.	76,032 Sq. Ft.	10¢/1000 Sq Ft.	$7.60	$7.00*
PORK BELLIES	Chicago Mercantile Exchange	10:10 A.M. - 2:00 P.M.	38,000 Lbs.	2½/100¢	$9.50	2¢
POTATOES	N.Y. Mercantile Exchange	10:00 A.M. - 2:00 P.M.	50,000 Lbs.	1¢/Cwt.	$5.00	50¢*
SILVER OLD	Commodity Exch., Inc., N.Y.	9:40 A.M. - 2:15 P.M.	5,000 Troy oz.	10/100¢	$5.00	50¢*
	Chicago Board of Trade	9:40 A.M. - 2:25 P.M.	5,000 Troy oz.	10/100¢	$5.00	40¢-80¢**
NEW	Chicago Board of Trade	9:40 A.M. - 2:25 P.M.	1,000 Troy oz.	10/100¢	$1.00	40¢-80¢**
	Winnipeg Commodity Exch.	9:40 A.M. - 2:25 P.M.	200 Troy oz.	1¢	$2.00	50¢* (U.S.)
SOYBEAN MEAL	Chicago Board of Trade	10:30 A.M. - 2:15 P.M.	100 Tons	10¢/Ton	$10.00	$10.00*
SOYBEAN OIL	Chicago Board of Trade	10:30 A.M. - 2:15 P.M.	60,000 Lbs.	1/100¢	$6.00	1¢*
SUGAR world #11 domestic #12	Coffee, Sugar & Cocoa Ex.	10:00 A.M. - 1:43 P.M.	112,000 Lbs.	1/100¢	$11.20	½¢*
SUNFLOWER SEED	Minneapolis Grain Exch.	10:25 A.M. - 2:20 P.M.	100,000 Lbs.	1¢/Cwt.	$10.00	50¢*
T - BILLS (13 weeks)	IMM-Chicago Merc. Exch.	9:00 A.M. - 2:40 P.M.	$1,000,000	.01	$25.00	.60*
	N.Y. Futures Exchange	9:00 A.M. - 3:00 P.M.	$1,000,000	.01	$25.00	1.00*
T - BONDS (Long Term)	Chicago Board of Trade	9:00 A.M. - 3:00 P.M.	$100,000 @ 8%	1/32 Pt.	$31.25	64/32*
	N.Y. Futures Exchange	9:00 A.M. - 3:00 P.M.	$100,000 @ 9%	1/32 Pt.	$31.25	96/32*

*Expanded limits go into effect under certain conditions.   **Limit based on price range and can be expanded under certain conditions.

Commissions and Margins: CONTACT YOUR BROKER FOR ALL INFORMATION.

All statements made herein, while not guaranteed, are based on information we consider reliable and accurate as of 4/2/81.

Figure 6.1 *Major Commodity Exchanges.* For the most part, commodity exchanges are located where a substantial portion of the commodities being traded pass through. For example, the largest commodity exchanges for grain are located in the Midwest (e.g., Chicago, Kansas City, and Minneapolis). The Chicago Mercantile Exchange is the principal commodity exchange for livestock.

Future market contracts are secured by what is known as *margin deposits*. Buyers and sellers of futures market contracts must place an original margin deposit with their broker, who, in turn, deposits these margins with the exchange's clearinghouse. The farmer may later have to make a *variation margin deposit* to cover his market position if the futures market price increases. More is said about these deposits later in this chapter and again in Chapter 8.

To illustrate the use of futures market contracts and their advantages and disadvantages, let us assume that Walt Wheaties expects in February 1984 that his wheat crop that year will be 10,000 bushels and that he can sell two 5,000-bushel futures contracts for a July 1984 delivery at a futures market price of $3.70. At this price, Walt knows that he can earn an acceptable profit on his wheat crop.

Let us assume for the moment that both the spot market price and the futures market price on an offsetting contract in July 1984 turn out to be $3.20. This means that Walt can sell the 10,000 bushels of wheat on his local spot market in July 1984 for $32,000. Two equal and offsetting futures market contract for July 1984 will also cost $32,000. Since he originally sold two futures market contracts for a total of 10,000 bushels for $3.70 per bushel, however, Walt has earned an extra $0.50 per bushel by hedging his wheat crop minus any transaction costs that he would have to pay. This transaction can be summarized as follows:

Item	Date of transaction	Effort of gross income
Cash market transactions: Sell 10,000 bushels of wheat at $3.20 per bushel	July 1984	+$32,000
Futures market transactions: Sell July 1984 futures contract for 10,000 bushels of wheat at $3.70 per bushel	February 1984	+$37,000
Buy July 1984 futures contract for 10,000 bushels of wheat at $3.20 per bushel	July 1984	−$32,000
Total gross income		$37,000

Thus Walt's total gross income from his wheat crop would be $37,000 rather than the $32,000 he would have received had he chosen not to hedge his wheat crop. Walt would have earned an additional income of $5,000 as a result of his hedging transactions.

There are also some potential disadvantages to using futures market contracts to lock in a forward price. First, futures market contracts place an effective ceiling on the gross income one can receive. Suppose, in the example above, that both the spot market and futures market prices in July 1984 had risen to $4 rather than falling to $3.20.

The effects of this price movement on Walt's gross income can be summarized as follows:

Item	Date of transaction	Effort of gross income
Cash market transactions:		
Sell 10,000 bushels of wheat at $4.00 per bushel	July 1984	+$40,000
Futures market transactions:		
Sell July 1984 futures contract for 10,000 bushels of wheat at $3.70 per bushel	February 1984	+$37,000
Buy July 1984 futures contracts for 10,000 bushels of wheat at $4.00 per bushel	July 1984	−$40,000
Total gross income		$37,000

Thus gross income from Walt's wheat crop would still be $37,000. Although he could sell his 10,000 bushels on his local spot market for $40,000, Walt would have to pay $0.30 more per bushel for an equal and offsetting contract than the price at which he originally sold the 10,000 bushels forward. Thus Walt's total gross income from his wheat crop would be $3,000 *less* than it would have been if he had *not hedged* his wheat crop.

Other factors to consider when deciding whether or not to hedge a commodity in the futures market include the problems associated with basis risk, yield risk, and the uncertainties associated with variation margin deposits. *Basis risk* refers to the risk that the basis (difference between the cash price and the futures price) will have widened by the time you finally sell the firm's production. This will cause the net effect of hedging on gross income to be less (remember, we assumed above that the basis was zero). This can occur if the quality of the product was to differ from the grade specified in the contract. *Yield risk* refers to the possibility that Walt's output may turn out to be less than what he originally expected when he sold a futures contract. If Walt had hedged his entire expected output and output turned out to be lower, he may have to "buy" his way out of the contract (i.e., purchase some of the commodity in the cash market at the going price). Finally, *variation margin deposits* place a strain on the farmer's cash and credit reserves to meet these calls. The effects of all three forms of risk will be assessed in more depth in Chapter 8.

Futures price quotations can be found in many major newspapers, including the *Wall Street Journal.* An examination of Figure 6.2 shows that the opening trade of the day on September 17 for a November feeder cattle contract on the Chicago Merchantile Exchange (CME) was $66.30 per hundred weight. The highest price was $66.55 and the lowest price was $65.65.

PRODUCTION CONTRACTS

A cash forward or *production contract* is a written agreement between the farmer and contractor. Processors or first handlers of commodities initiate these contracts with farmers. The contract specifies the terms of the delivery and acceptance of a specific product at a future date. Like a futures market contract, the farmer can typically lock in a fixed forward price.[1] As Table 6.1 indicates, the extent of forward contracting in the farm business sector varies considerably by commodity. Production contracts are typically used for perishable commodities such as vegetables and eggs. In addition, livestock processors often offer production contracts to farmers and ranchers to ensure a steady flow of livestock to their plants. These processors normally then turn around and hedge their market position by selling forward in the future market. Grain elevators may also offer production contracts to farmers and then hedge their position in the futures market.

Production contracts can be grouped into three broad categories: (1) market specification contracts, (2) production management contracts, and (3) resource provision contracts. *Market specification contracts* are normally signed *after* production has begun and specify the quantity (but not quality) of the commodity to be delivered. The farmer has title to the commodity until it is physically transferred to the contractor. He also supplies all the production inputs used to produce the commodity. Production contracts with farmers of grain, cotton, livestock, and other nonperishable commodities are usually of this type. *Production management contracts* are normally signed *before* production has begun and specify both the quantity and quality of the commodity under contract. The farmer continues to retain title to the commodity until delivery, but contractors may provide some inputs (i.e., seed, fertilizer). Contracts for vegetable commodities such as tomatoes, peas, sweet corn, and other perishable commodities are normally of this type. Finally, *resource provision contracts* call for most of the production inputs used by farmers to be supplied by the contractor. The farmer's role is to supply the land, labor, machinery, and buildings needed. Unlike the other two types of production contracts, the price paid to the farmer

---

[1] In some contracts, a formula stating the terms of compensation is employed instead of a fixed price.

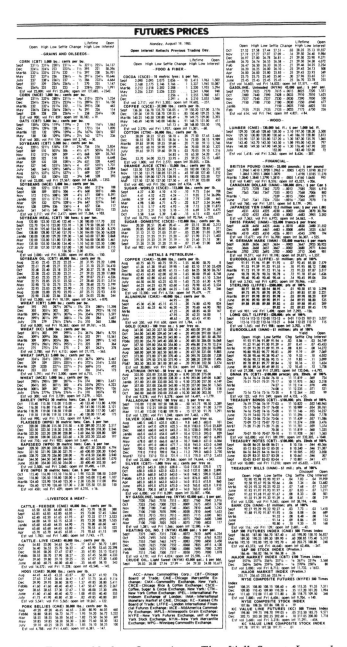

Figure 6.2 *Futures Market Quotations.* The *Wall Street Journal* and other daily news services provide commodity traders with up-to-date information on market developments. This figure shows the contract prices for specific commodities, including the high and low for the day and the closing price.

Commodity	Extent of contracting[a]
Crops	
Feed and food grains	Low
Vegetables for fresh market	Medium
Vegetables for processing	High
Potatoes	Medium
Citrus fruits	High
Sugar beets	High
Sugarcane	Medium
Cotton	Medium
Oil bearing crops	Low
Livestock or livestock products	
Feed cattle	Medium
Sheep, hogs	Low
Fluid-grade milk	High
Manufacturing-grade milk	Medium
Eggs	Medium
Broilers	High
Turkeys	Medium

[a] "Low" is between zero and 10 percent of output contracted; "Medium" is more than 10 but less than 50 percent of output contracted; "High" is 50 percent or more of output contracted.

Source: R. L. Mighell and W. S. Hoofnagle, *Contract Production and Vertical Integration in Farming,* 1960 and 1970, ERS–479, U.S. Department of Agriculture, ERS, April 1972.

TABLE 6.1 EXTENT OF OUTPUT PRODUCED UNDER CONTRACT. Production contracts are typically written for some commodities and not others. Large canning companies such as Del Monte and Green Giant, for example, frequently offer production contracts to growers who agree to produce such perishable commodities as peas, green beans, and sweet corn. Meat-packing companies also frequently offer production contracts to cattle feeders. This gives these processing firms an idea of the quantities they will have available as inputs to their own production processes.

is based on the volume of output, and managerial control is exercised by the contractor instead of the farmer. Finally, these contracts are signed *before* production is initiated. This form of contract is found in egg and broiler production. These and other features of production contracts are summarized in Table 6.2.

The problems of basis risk, variation margin deposits, and the existence of transaction costs associated with futures contracts (e.g., broker fees) are undoubtedly contributing factors to the relatively greater popularity of production contracts as a means of locking in a forward price.

Contract terms	Market specification contracts	Production management contracts	Resource provision contracts
Specified delivery schedule	Yes	Yes	Yes
Signed after production begins	Usually	No	No
Title of commodity with producer	Yes	Yes	No
Price to producer	Fixed[a]	Fixed[a]	Based on volume of output
Specifies quantity	Sometimes	Sometimes	Yes
Specifies quality	Usually	Yes	Yes
Specifies cultural practices	No	Some	Yes
Money advanced to producer by contractor	Few	Few	Sometimes
Input supplied by contractor	No	Some	Most
Inputs financed by producer	Yes	Most	Few
Examples in farm business sector	Grain, cotton, livestock	Vegetables for processing	Broilers, eggs

[a]Sometimes this price is determining a compensating formula.

Source: Adapted from R. L. Mighell and L. A. Jones, *Vertical Coordination in Agriculture,* Ag. Econ. Report 19, ERS, U.S. Department of Agriculture, February 1963, p. 13.

TABLE 6.2 CLASSIFICATION OF PRODUCTION CONTRACTS. There are essentially three forms of production contracts. Market specification contracts, for example, specify the quantity to be delivered. Production management contracts specify both the quantity *and* quality of the commodity in the contract. Finally, resource provision contracts specify the inputs to be supplied by both parties to the contract.

As was true with futures market contracts, production contracts can place a ceiling on the potential revenue to farmers. Farmers also face the possibility of having to buy their way out of a production contract if lower-than-expected yields cause production to fall below the quantity specified in the contract. To make up this difference, farmers would have to purchase more of the commodity in the cash market at the going price. This topic will be pursued in more depth in Chapter 8 when we look at marketing decisions under conditions of risk.

STORAGE OF FARM COMMODITIES

One of the marketing options available to farmers at harvest time is to store their current production for sale at a later date. This storage can take place either on the farm or off the farm in commercial elevators. Table 6.3 shows that the bulk of grain stored by farmers is stored in on-farm storage facilities. For example, 6 billion bushels of corn were stored on farms as of January 1, 1983, compared to 2.2 billion bushels stored off the farm. This carryover of stocks from the previous year is frequently as large or larger than the current year's production. As the year progresses, you can also see these stocks decline as farmers sell off a portion of these stocks during the year. Some of

Crop	Jan. 1, 1983	April 1, 1983	June 1, 1983	Oct. 1, 1983
Corn				
On-farm	5,936	4,242	3,094	1,510
Off-farm	2,269	1,956	1,830	1,610
Sorghum				
On-farm	268	150	96	60
Off-farm	543	471	433	340
Soybeans				
On-farm	1,008	643	425	119
Off-farm	755	505	366	226
	Oct. 1, 1983	Jan. 1, 1984	April 1, 1984	
Wheat				
On-farm	1,236	1,015	771	
Off-farm	1,719	1,311	985	
Barley				
On-farm	344	244	169	
Off-farm	172	123	99	
Oats				
On-farm	426	322	227	
Off-farm	79	56	43	

Note: Values in millions of bushels.

Source: U.S. Department of Agriculture, *Agricultural Statistics* (Washington, D.C.: U.S. Government Printing Office, 1984).

TABLE 6.3 DOMESTIC STOCKS OF SELECTED COMMODITIES. Major grain crops typically move into storage at harvest time for later utilization. On-farm storage of corn carried into 1983 was 6 billion bushels. Nine months later, these stocks had been depleted down to 1.5 billion bushels. While most corn is stored on farms, off-farm storage plays a significant role for such commodities as sorghum and wheat. Very few fruits and vegetables can be stored in a fresh state. Apples, onions, and potatoes can be stored for several months. Meat is consumed at roughly the rate at which live animals are marketed.

these grains, however, are feed grains that are being held for feeding through livestock rather than for sale.

In addition to grains, other commodities are stored on and off farms. Hay harvested during the summer months is stored either in barns or in the field until it is consumed. Very few fruits and vegetables, however, can be stored for sale later without serious damage. Finally, there is virtually no on-farm storage of livestock products once they are finished. Thus the storage requirements for farm products varies greatly depending on the nature of the product itself. The nature of the storage facilities may also vary from one farm to the next. For example, grains may be stored in either wood or metal cribs and bins, while hay bales may be stored in the field. In the remainder of this section we discuss the factors to be considered when deciding whether or not to store and the decision to invest in on-farm storage facilities.

Reasons for Storing

Let us assume for the moment that a farmer already has storage facilities on his farm and must decide whether to sell his crop at harvest time or to store the crop and sell at a later date. What factors should the farmer consider when making this decision? We can divide this discussion into those factors that affect costs and those that affect the returns from storage.

The *costs of storage* when the farmer owns his own storage facilities include such items as (1) the repair and maintenance costs associated with the usage of the facilities, (2) depreciation of the facilities, (3) property insurance on the facilities, (4) the interest on financing the planned inventory buildup (cost of borrowed capital and/or cost of using own funds, which represents income forgone by not being able to use the cash receipts from the stored commodity), and (5) the losses associated with deterioration of the commodity during storage.

The *returns from storage* come primarily from rising commodity prices over the storage period. An additional benefit accruing to farmers who recognize income for tax purposes when the output is sold is that they can postpone paying the tax liability associated with this output by storing the commodity until the next calendar (tax) year.

The farmer will benefit from storing his current output until a later date *if* the *returns* from storage *exceeds* the current price plus the *costs* of storage. Many farmers decide not to sell their output at harvest time in expectation of earning a net return from storage activities. If the farmer is leasing commercial storage for his commodities because he does not have his own on-farm storage facilities, one must merely substitute the commercial leasing fees for the costs associated with ownership of storage facilities identified in items 1 to 3 above. *The issue remains that of determining whether or not the returns from storage operations exceed the costs of storage.*

To illustrate, let's suppose that Walt Wheaties has the option of accepting a current price in the cash market of $3.50 per bushel or storing the commodity and selling it three months later for an expected price of $4 per bushel. If Walt's monthly storage cost (excluding the cost of any borrowed capital) is $0.12 per bushel, should Walt sell now or store the commodity and sell it three months from now? Thus far we can see that the returns from storage ($4.00 − $3.55 = $0.45) exceeds the storage costs ($0.12 × 3 = $0.36). It would therefore seem to benefit Walt under these circumstances to choose the storage option. There is an additional cost that Walt must consider because he is waiting three months to receive the $4 price per bushel: namely, the cost of capital.[2] If Walt must borrow to finance that portion of his operations normally financed by the proceeds from this sale, he must reflect this is in the per bushel cost of storage. Even if he does not borrow, Walt must still account for the opportunity cost (i.e., income forgone) of having to wait three months to receive the proceeds from this sale. Finally, there are price risks associated with storage: namely, the trend in the price of the commodity over the marketing period may turn out to be unfavorable. This topic and strategies for reducing the farmer's exposure to price risk while the commodity is in storage are addressed in Chapter 8. Federal farm programs that relate to the storage of specific commodities on farms after their harvest provide economic incentives for storing grain on farms. An in-depth discussion of the farmer-owned reserve program will be presented in Chapter 10.

On-Farm Storage Facilities

The capacity of on-farm storage facilities owned by farmers has increased substantially since 1977, when the Commodity Credit Corporation (CCC) initiated an expanded loan program to help farmers finance the construction of grain storage facilities. Before 1977, farmers were expanding their on-farm storage capacity by less than 200 million bushels per year during the seventies. After 1977, however, farmers doubled or tripled this annual rate of expansion. For example, farmers expanded on-farm storage capacity by 754 million bushels in 1978 and 685 million bushels in 1979. The availability of subsidized loans from the CCC and payments to cover interest on stored commodities made by the CCC no doubt contributed to this expansion. These programs will be discussed in Chapter 10. For now, let us discuss the factors that farmers consider when expanding their on-farm storage facilities.

---

[2] The cost of capital is normally accounted for by *discounting* the future cash flows back to the present period. The interested reader is referred to the Advanced Topic section at the end of Chapter 7 for further discussion of this topic.

USDA Photo

As indicated in Table 6.3, off-farm storage plays an important role in the marketing of raw agricultural products over time. There are approximately 15,000 elevators at country and terminal locations in the United States. Much of this storage space is devoted to facilitating the movement of grain; a given lot of grain may remain in this space for a short time period.

When deciding whether or not to expand their on-farm storage facilities, farmers must evaluate the costs associated with the investment with the returns it will generate over time. The costs involved with the investment decision include the purchase price of the storage facilities as well as the after-tax cost of capital to finance the investment (i.e., the cost of borrowed funds on the debt-financed portion plus the opportunity cost of the down payment and subsequent future receipts of net cash income). Other costs will include repairs and maintenance, depreciation, and property insurance. The returns from investment in storage facilities include the gains in returns from storage over the life of the investment as well as the tax benefits achieved by being able to postpone the recognition of income for tax purposes until a later date. If the returns exceed the costs, the investment is feasible from an economic standpoint. More will be said about this and other forms of investments in Chapter 7.

SUMMARY

The purpose of this chapter was to discuss the importance of the farmer having a marketing plan and to identify the marketing options available when formulating the marketing plan. The major points made in this chapter can be summarized as follows:

1. The *marketing plan* for a farm business should reflect the objectives of the firm in its buying and selling activities. These objectives will be influenced by the farmer's attitudes toward such factors as profit, income stability, and market freedom.

2. Two marketing options available to farmers when acquiring inputs include (1) purchase inputs *directly* from the merchant or dealer, and (2) purchase these inputs through a *purchasing cooperative.*

3. Farmers when selling their output also have the option of selling *individually* or through a *marketing cooperative.* In addition, farmers have the option of (1) signing a *production contract* to deliver a certain quantity of output for a fixed price, (2) *hedging* part of their output in the *futures market* for delivery at harvest at a fixed price, and (3) *storing* their production in anticipation of a more favorable market price at a later date.

4. While production contracts and hedging allow the farmer to lock-in a price for his output before harvest, they both have the disadvantage of effectively placing a ceiling on his potential income. Thus the farmer's attitude toward *risk* will have an effect on whether or not he utilizes these marketing options.

5. If the farmer expects the benefits from storing output rather than selling at harvest time to exceed the costs of storage, he can justify storing the crop in either on-farm or off-farm facilities until a later date. The costs of storage should include not only such costs as repair and maintenance costs for storage buildings (if applicable) and deterioration of the product, but the *cost of financing* the inventory buildup as well.

DEFINITION OF TERMS

Marketing plan: the farmer's marketing plan reflects his objectives when buying inputs and selling farm products. These objectives, in turn, will affect the farmer's choice among marketing options.

Market risk: risk that the market price and quantity will differ from that originally expected by the farmer.

Hedging: the process by which the farmer first sells and later buys a futures product contract for the expressed purpose of locking in a forward price for his products.

Futures contract: standardized agreement that spells out the quality and quantity of the commodity to be delivered as well as the location and date of delivery.

Production contract: written agreement between the farmer and contractor specifying the terms and acceptance of a specific product at a future date.

Purchasing cooperative: a farmer-owned cooperative formed principally to collectively purchase goods and services for its members.

Marketing cooperative: a farmer-owned cooperative formed principally to collectively market the output of its members.

Sequential marketing: acceptance of an average price for a product by spreading the marketing of the commodity over a period of time.

Spot market: market in which the commodity is actually physically exchanged for cash at a fixed price per unit.

Margin deposits: buyers and sellers of futures market contracts must place an original margin deposit with their broker, who, in turn, deposit these funds with the exchange's clearinghouse.

Variation margin deposits: the farmer may have to make an additional deposit to cover his market priorities if the futures market price increases.

Basis: difference between the cash price and the futures price at a specific point in time.

Basis risk: the risk that the basis will have widened by the time the farmer finally sells his output.

Yield risk: the risk that the farmer's output may turn out to be less than what he expected when he sold a futures contract.

Cost of capital: the after-tax cost of capital relevant to the decision of whether or not to expand on-farm storage facilities reflects the farmer's cost of borrowing, the opportunity rate of return on other uses of his equity capital, and his tax bracket.

Transactions costs: brokerage commissions and other fees standardly assessed when completing a market transaction.

Cost of capital: the after-tax cost of capital relevant to the decision of whether or not to expand on-farm storage facilities reflects the farmer's cost of borrowing, the opportunity rate of return on other uses of his equity capital, and his tax bracket.

Transactions costs: brokerage commissions and other fees standardly assessed when completing a market transaction.

REFERENCES

MIGHELL, R. L., and W. S. HOOFNAGLE, *Contract Production and Vertical Integration in Farming,* ERS–479, U.S. Department of Agriculture. Washington, D.C.: U.S. Government Printing Office, April 1972

MIGHELL, R. L., and L. A. JONES, *Vertical Coordination in Agriculture,* Agricultural Economics Report 19, ERS, U.S. Department of Agriculture. Washington, D.C.: U.S. Government Printing Office, February 1963.

U.S. Department of Agriculture, *Agricultural Statistics.* Washington, D.C.: U.S. Government Printing Office, 1981.

ADDITIONAL READINGS

HIERONYMUS, T. A., *Economics of Future Trading for Commercial and Personal Profit.* New York: Commodity Research Bureau, 1971.

KOHLS, RICHARD L., and JOSEPH N. UHL, *Marketing of Agricultural Products,* 5th ed. New York: Macmillan Publishing Company, 1980.

TOMEK, WILLIAM G., and KENNETH L. ROBINSON, *Agricultural Product Prices,* 2nd ed. Ithaca, N.Y.: Cornell University Press, 1981.

QUESTIONS

1. What are some of the likely objectives to be considered when formulating the farmer's marketing plan?

2. Describe the major marketing options available to farmers and their effects on the price the farmer expects to receive for his output.

3. Discuss the advantages and disadvantages to using futures market contracts to lock-in a forward price.

4. What are the different forms of production contracts available to farmers? What are the essential differences between them?

5. It was said that the farmer should assess the "net economic benefits" from storage for nonperishable commodities when formulating his market plan. Describe the factors that influence these net economic benefits.

7

GROWTH

OF THE COMPETITIVE FIRM

Now that we have an understanding of how profit-maximizing farmers organize their existing enterprises in the short run (Chapter 5) and the marketing options available to them (Chapter 6), let us turn our attention to the longer run where farmers can expand or contract the size of their firm. In this chapter we initially discuss the factors underlying the existence of returns to scale. The relationship between short-run and long-run average costs will then be explored in the context of the optimal size of the competitive firm. Having considered the production costs associated with larger firm sizes and the optimal size of the firm, we shall discuss the nature of farm investments and the factors that might limit the annual growth of the firm and thus affect the amount of time necessary to reach the desired size.

FACTORS INFLUENCING RETURNS TO SCALE

In the long run, everything is considered variable. The farmer can expand his production by acquiring and operating a larger firm. The distinction made between fixed and variable costs in Chapter 5 is no longer necessary since all resources (and hence all costs) can be varied. That is, farmers in the long run can expand their production by using more of *all* inputs—more labor, more equipment, and more land and buildings. If the increase in output turns out to be exactly proportional to the increase in the quantities of the inputs, the *returns to scale* are said to be *constant*. This means that a doubling or a tripling of inputs used by the farmer will result in a doubling or tripling of output.[1] If the increase in output, however, is *more (less)* than proportional to the increase in input use, we said the returns to scale are *increasing (decreasing)*. We will introduce the notion shortly that increasing (decreasing) returns to scale will exist if the farmer's long-run average costs are increasing (decreasing) as the farm is expanded.

Before turning to the shape of the long-run average cost curve and the role it plays in deciding just how large the farmer's business should be, let us examine some of the factors that help explain the existence of increasing returns to scale (or economies of scale) and decreasing returns to scale (or diseconomies of scale). While we shall focus primarily on the physical or *technical factors* that explain the existence of returns to scale, we shall also identify a major *pecuniary factor* affecting the shape of the farmer's long-run average cost curve.

Increasing Returns to Scale

Some of the physical causes of increasing returns to scale are purely *dimensional* in nature. For example, if the diameter of a pipe is doubled, the flow through it is more than doubled The carrying capacity of a truck also increases faster than its weight. After some point, however, such increases in dimensional efficiency come to an end. As the size of the pipe was increased, it probably had to be made out of thicker and stronger materials. The size of the truck will also be limited by the width of streets, the heights of overpasses, and the capacities of bridges.

A closely related technical factor that helps to explain the existence of increasing returns to scale is the *indivisibility* of inputs. In general, indivisibility means that equipment is available only in minimum sizes or in a specific range of sizes. As the scale of the farm's operations increases, the farmer can switch from using the minimum-sized piece of equipment to larger, more efficient equipment. Thus the larger the scale of the operation, the more the farmer will be able to take advantage of large-scale equipment that cannot be used profitably in smaller-scale operations.

Still another technical factor contributing to increasing returns to scale comes from the potential benefits from *specialization* of effort. For example, as the farmer hires more labor, he can subdivide tasks and thus gain in the efficiency of labor.[2] Furthermore, as he expands the size of his opera-

---

[1] A word of caution. You may have heard the phrase "the economies of mass production" before. This phrase carries several meanings, some of which are irrelevant here and therefore are potential sources of confusion. For example, the greater efficiency frequently observed for larger production units—in contrast to smaller ones—is often caused by the fact that the larger units are *newer* and use better production techniques than the older and smaller units. However important this may be, improvements in technology are *not* part of the concept of returns to scale. The concept assumes a given technology.

[2] The benefits gained from specialization are well known. Adam Smith in his book *The Wealth of Nations* published in 1776 addressed the gains from the division of labor.

tions, the farmer can buy specialized pieces of equipment as well as assign special jobs even to standardized types of machinery.

A frequently noted pecuniary factor that helps us explain the existence of increasing returns to scale is *volume discounts* on large purchases of such farm inputs as fertilizer. Lower input prices paid by larger farming operations could be a major reason why average costs decline as farm size is increased.

Constant Returns to Scale

Increasing returns to scale cannot go on indefinitely. Eventually, the farm will enter the phase of constant returns to scale, where a doubling of all inputs simply doubles output. The phase of constant returns to scale can be brief before decreasing returns to scale set in. As we will note shortly, empirical evidence suggests that the phase of constant or nearly constant returns to scale can be fairly long, typically covering a large range of output levels.

Decreasing Returns to Scale

Can a farmer keep on doubling his firm's inputs indefinitely and expect the firm's output to double? The answer is likely no. Eventually, there must be a *decreasing return to scale*. The farmer himself may actually represent the reason underlying decreasing returns to scale. That is, while all other inputs can be increased, his ability to manage larger operations may not. The managerial skills needed to coordinate efforts and resources likely increase proportionately with increases in the size of the farmer's operations.

THE LONG-RUN PLANNING CURVE

The firm's long-run average cost curve is often referred to as the *long-run planning curve*. In this section we examine the economic incentives for expanding the "capital input" held fixed until now, the measurement of the long-run average cost curve, and how to determine the optimal size of the competitive firm.

Expansion of Capital

The input "capital" held constant thus far is allowed to vary in the long run. This input can be thought of in the context of "plant size" (i.e., farm size as measured by land for a cropping operation). In the long run, capital can be adjusted to its least-cost level, which occurs where the *marginal rate of technical substitution of capital for labor is equal to the input price ratio*. This suggests that the short-run cost for a given level of capital exceeds the long-run cost except at one point. This is illustrated in Figure 7.1 with the use of isoquants.

Figure 7.1 shows that at 1 unit of capital, labor is at its least-cost level of use only when output is 10 units. At this output level, the least-cost combination of inputs would be 5 units of labor and 1 unit of capital (see point *A*). If an output of 20 units is desired, the least-cost combination of these inputs would occur at point *B*. Yet if capital is fixed at 1 unit in the short run, the only way this farmer can produce 20 units of output would be to employ 9 units of labor (point *C*). This means that the *total cost* of producing 20 units will be greater in the short run than it would be in the long run. Since the distance from isocost line *DE* to isocost line *FG* is indicative of long-run marginal costs, while the distance from isocost line *DE* to isocost line *HI* is indicative of short-run marginal costs, it follows that *short-run mar-*

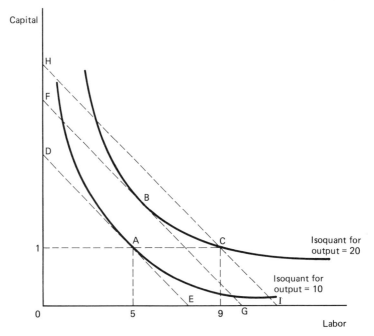

Figure 7.1 *Economic Incentive for Expanding Capital Input.* In the long run, the size of the farmer's operations can be expanded if the economic incentive to do so is there. This requires increasing the capital input to its least-cost level (i.e., where the marginal rate of technical substitution of capital for labor is equal to their price ratio). You will recall that this is the same stipulation made for the short-run case [see equation (5.4)]. Unlike Chapter 5, however, the farmer can now increase his use of capital beyond 1 unit. Producing 20 units of output instead of 10 units can be most efficiently done by operating at point *B,* not *C.*

ginal costs exceed long-run marginal costs. The same conclusion holds for comparisons of *average costs.* Therefore, there is economic incentive for the farmer desiring to produce 20 units of output to expand his use of capital to the level indicated by point *B*. Only at this point will he minimize his cost of producing 20 units of output.

Long-Run Average Cost Curve

Panel a in Figure 7.2 depicts three short-run average cost *(SAC)* curves. The presence of fixed inputs in the short run ensures that these short-run average cost curves are U-shaped. Each short-run average cost curve reflects the full average cost of the firm for three separate sizes. Farm size *A* is the smallest, with costs represented by SAC_a. This curve might correspond to the farmer using 1 unit of capital to produce 10 units of output in the example discussed above. Farm size *B* is somewhat larger and operates at much lower costs, owing to the presence of increasing returns to scale. Curve SAC_b is much lower, except at the extreme left end. This curve might reflect the capital needed to minimize the farmer's cost of producing 20 units of output in the example cited above. Farm size *C* is still larger, but the curve SAC_c is higher because decreasing returns to scale have begun to set in.

Clearly, the farmer will wish to operate farm size *A* in Figure 7.2 if an output equal to *OA* or less is desired. If output is, instead, desired in the *OB* or *OC* range, the farmer will prefer farm size *B* or farm size *C,* respectively. Notice that if the farmer desires to produce an output somewhat larger than *OA,* farm size *B* would be better than farm size *A* since its costs are lower. Take output *OA,* for example. This output represents the economic capacity of farm size *A* since it represents the farmer's minimum cost of operation. Obviously, it would be better—when producing *OA*—to select farm size *B* and operate it at less than its capacity than it would be to continue with farm size *A* since the farmer's costs of production would be lower. This proposition can be generalized. *When increasing returns to scale exist, the minimum cost of any output can be obtained by operating a larger firm at less than its capacity rather than operating a smaller firm whose minimum cost corresponds to the desired level of output.*

In deciding how big the firm should be, the farmer must consider a relevant range of minimum costs. The farmer may be aware of this range either from his own experience or from economic feasibility studies conducted for different types of farms in his particular area. The short-run average cost curves associated with different sizes of farms over this range enable the farmer to determine the firm's long-run average cost *(LAC)* curve. Often referred to as the *planning curve* for the firm, the long-run average cost curve illustrates to the farmer during the planning stage how varying the size of the firm will affect the firm's efficiency. It also indicates the minimum

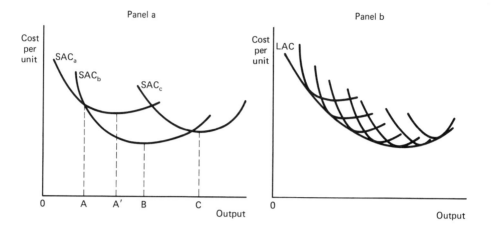

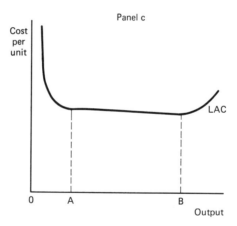

Figure 7.2 *Relationship between Short- and Long-Run Average Cost Curves.* The long-run average cost (*LAC*) curve plays a key role in determining the optimal size of the competitive firm in the long run. Often referred to as the "planning curve," the *LAC* curve represents an envelope of a series of short-run average cost curves, as illustrated in panels a and b. Increasing returns to scale exist over the declining portion of this curve. This suggests that the farmer can lower his costs per unit of output by expanding his operations. All points on this curve over this range represent least-cost combinations of inputs. Points *A* and *B* in Figure 7.1, for example, would lie on this curve. Beyond the minimum point on the *LAC* curve, decreasing returns to scale occur. Finally, the *LAC* curve in reality may look more like the one in panel c.

per unit cost at which any output can be produced after adjusting the firm's size. For example, the least-cost use of capital and labor indicated by points *A* and *B* in Figure 7.1 to produce 10 units and 20 units of output would represent two points along the long-run cost curve in panel b of Figure 7.2.

As panel b in Figure 7.2 illustrates, the long-run average cost curve is the "envelope" of the short-run average cost curves. That is, the long-run average cost curve is tangent to the short-run average cost curves to the left of their minimum points when the long-run average cost curve is declining. When the long-run average cost curve is rising, it touches the short-run average cost curves to the right of their minimum points. Only at the minimum point on the long-run average cost curve does it touch the short-run average cost curves at their minimum point.

The declining portion of the long-run average cost curve suggests the existence of increasing returns to scale. Beyond the minimum point on this curve, decreasing returns to scale exist. Economists are often concerned with the shape of the long-run average and marginal cost curves. The minimum point on the long-run average cost curve for various farm enterprises is of particular interest. It represents the most *efficient* firm or plant size in the long run in the sense that the farmer's average costs of production are minimized. More will be said about this topic in the next section.

An Empirical Example

The long-run cost curve depicted in panel b of Figure 7.2 reflects the conventional shape illustrated in most textbooks. While the long-run average cost curve no doubt decreases over some range of output before eventually turning up, its shape is unlikely to be perfectly U-shaped. In fact, empirical studies suggest that there may be some range of output over which the long-run average cost curve is relatively flat. Hall and LaVeen found in California, for example, that the long-run average cost curve becomes relatively flat after initially declining rapidly (Hall and LaVeen, 1978). They reported that the costs of producing highly mechanized crops generally continued to decline slowly over the entire range of surveyed farm sizes. For vegetables and fruit crops, however, Hall and LaVeen found little or no decline after the initial benefits from expansion were achieved. These findings are illustrated in Table 7.1. The economic efficiency (physical returns plus pecuniary returns to scale) of the farm sizes surveyed showed that the average cost of production (as measured by total cost divided by the value of output) declined sharply initially for all farm types and then flattened out before finally increasing for some farm types (e.g., fruit and nut farms). The economic efficiency associated with larger farm sizes is also illustrated by the increasing rate of return to land indicated by this table as farm size increases. Finally, Hall and LaVeen examined the *sources* of declining production

	Size of farm (value of output)				
Type of farm	$5,000– $9,999	$10,000– $19,999	$20,000– $39,999	$40,000– $99,999	$100,000 and over
	Production cost per dollar of output				
Cash grain farm	$1.070	$0.786	$0.703	$0.636	$0.550
Cotton farm	1.041	0.836	0.701	0.693	0.637
Sugar, hay, and other field crop farm	1.149	0.775	0.726	0.696	0.634
Vegetable farm	0.980	0.805	0.730	0.754	0.720
Fruit and nut farm	1.114	0.805	0.786	0.749	0.757
	Rate of return (%) to farmland[a]				
Cash grain farm	0.4	2.6	3.9	6.2	16.2
Cotton farm	1.4	4.3	7.6	9.0	17.3
Sugar, hay, and other field crop farm	−2.0	2.3	3.1	6.0	15.6
Vegetable farm	0.8	6.0	6.7	9.4	20.9
Fruit and nut farm	−0.9	2.0	4.9	6.8	9.5

[a]This rate of return was derived by dividing profits by total land value.

Source: B. F. Hall and E. P. LeVeen, "Farm Size and Economic Efficiency: The Case of California," *American Journal of Agricultural Economics,* 1978, pp. 589–600.

TABLE 7.1   FARM SIZE AND ECONOMIC EFFICIENCY. The empirical example presented above demonstrates what happens to the average cost of production as farm size is increased for different types of farms. We see the average cost of production drop off sharply as the size of the farmer's operations is increased for very small firms. As these farms increase in size, average cost continues to decline, although not as rapidly. For all but fruit and nut farms, however, decreasing returns to scale were not observed. The increasing rates of return reported in this table mirror the declining average cost of production reported in the top part of the table.

costs, concluding that management and resource quality may be just as important as the other technical causes of increasing returns to scale noted earlier.

Other studies, such as those by Faris and Armstrong (1963) and Kyle and Krause (1970), have alluded to significant pecuniary economies of scale for large firms. Kyle and Krause, for example, found that input prices may vary as much as 25 percent among grain farms of different size.

Panel c of Figure 7.2 illustrates the general nature of these findings. Between outputs *OA* and *OB,* the long-run average cost curve is relatively flat. Over this range, all farm sizes will achieve approximately the same costs. Thus the long-run average cost curve in agriculture is more L-shaped than U-shaped.

ADJUSTMENTS TO LONG-RUN EQUILIBRIUM

In the long run under conditions of perfect competition, existing firms will have time to expand (or contract) the size of their operations.[3] Suppose that the short run marginal cost and average cost curves for Frank Farmer's existing firm are represented in Figure 7.3 by SMC_1 and SAC_1, respectively. If the market price for the product is equal to P and the firm produced at the point where $P = SMC_1$, Frank's firm would sustain a small loss on each unit of output produced and sold. At this point, Mr. Farmer would have two

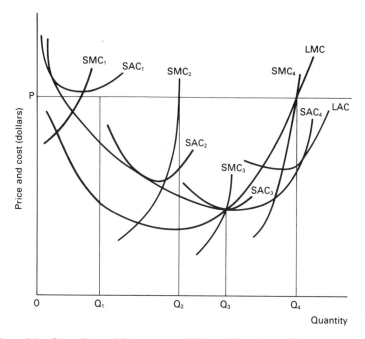

Figure 7.3 *Long-Run Adjustment of Firm Size.* A profit-maximizing farmer will desire to expand the size of his firm to that corresponding to the SAC_4 and SMC_4 cost curves given the level of product price P. As others respond to these profits, total output will expand and market price will fall. In a free-market setting, firms will cut back their output and eventually cut back on the size of their firm as best they can. Some firms will cease producing altogether. The sector will be in long-run equilibrium at the point where $P = LMC = LAC$, which would result in this farmer producing Q_3 units of output.

[3] We shall assume that the farm business sector is a "constant-cost" industry; that is, the entry and departure of firms will have no effect on resource prices and hence the location of their average total cost curve. For ease of expositon, we shall also adopt the conventional U-shaped long-run cost curves found in most textbooks.

options. He could go out of business, or he could expand the existing size of his firm, provided that he could convince his banker of the benefits from this expansion. If Frank expanded to the size represented by SAC_2 and SMC_2, his firm would produce quantity Q_2 and Frank would earn an economic profit per unit equal to P minus short-run average cost at quantity Q_2. A profit-maximizing farmer would want to expand the firm out to the size represented by SAC_4 and SMC_4. By producing Q_4, the firm would be operating at the point where P is equal to both SMC_4 as well as the firm's LMC curve. Thus it would appear that the optimum size of Mr. Farmer's firm in the long run under conditions of perfect competition (Q_4) is larger than the size associated with minimum unit costs, which occurs at output Q_3 where the LMC, long-run average cost, SMC_3 and SAC_3 curves intersect.

While this long-run adjustment for an existing firm is taking place, however, the *number* of firms may also increase as new firms enter due to the existence of economic profits, as we suggested in Chapter 5. Some of these entrants will be newly created firms, such as new feedlots in the cattle feeding industry. Others may be firms that have shifted out of less profitable enterprises. As these new and modified operations begin to produce output, the market supply of the product will increase. *This, in turn, will cause the price of the product to fall.* When each firm responds to the new lower market price, the output of each will be smaller than before. Those firms that were just preparing to expand their size in response to the earlier price will be able to adjust their size rapidly. Other firms that have just completed expansion of their firm will obviously respond more slowly. Those firms that cannot expand rapidly will lose more money than those that can. *This process conceivably will continue until economic profits have been reduced to zero and the incentive for additional firms to enter the sector have been eliminated.* Those existing firms losing money will eventually cease producing this product or leave the sector altogether.

At this point, the sector will be in *long-run equilibrium.* At the firm level, the product price will have fallen to the point where it is just equal to the short-run marginal and average total cost (SMC and SAC) as well as long-run marginal and average total cost (LMC and LAC). Figure 7.3 shows that the optimal size of the firm in the long run would see Mr. Farmer producing an output equal to Q_3.

NATURE OF INVESTMENT DECISIONS

As farmers expand the size of their current operations,, they are typically confronted by a wide variety of investment opportunities. A cornerstone to the success of the farmer's firm over time is his ability to make sound investment decisions. While an unwise production decision affects the *current* performance of the firm, an unwise investment decision will be reflected in the firm's performance over a period of *several years*. We can group the investment opportunities available to farmers into the following categories: (1) land, (2) depreciable assets, (3) inventories, and (4) financial assets. Each category is discussed in turn below.

Land

One of the most important decisions a farmer must make concerns the investment in farmland. The farmer must not only be able to evaluate its physical properties (e.g., soil productivity, drainage, and location), but the economic dimensions of the investment as well. An attractive tract of farmland down the road may have the physical attributes the farmer is looking for and yet still be infeasible from an *economic* standpoint. The farmer must be able to determine whether or not the current price being asked by the seller results in a *net economic benefit* to his firm. If additional machinery is needed to farm these acres, the farmer must examine the *joint* investment in both land and depreciable assets.[4]

Depreciable Assets

This category of investment opportunities encompasses the purchase of machinery and equipment, breeding livestock, and farm buildings (including on-farm storage facilities). The feasibility of investments in new or used depreciable assets also hinges on whether or not the investment results in a net economic benefit to the firm. The income tax laws pertaining to the *depreciation* of an asset (i.e., writing off the cost of the asset over time) and *investment tax credit* play a role in determining whether or not the farmer will realize a net economic benefit from the investment. More liberal tax policies (i.e., faster write-off of assets or a higher tax credit) will encourage investment in depreciable assets, as we will discuss in Chapter 13.

A related decision to the original purchase of depreciable assets is when the best time is to *replace* these assets. Knowledge of the optimal age to replace a tractor, a combine, or a dairy cow is just as important to the growth of the firm over time as its initial purchase was. The *optimal* replacement policy is determined by the age that results in the *lowest* replacement cost.[5]

[4] The determination of the *net economic benefit* for this and other investment opportunities discussed in this section requires one to account for the cost of capital and the time value of future cash flows. Due to the advanced nature of this topic, the interested reader is referred to the Advanced Topic section at the end of this chapter for a discussion of how to account for the *present value* of future cash flows when assessing the net economic benefit to the firm.

[5] These replacement costs should also reflect the affects of the time value of money (see the Advanced Topic section at the end of this chapter).

As noted in Table 2.3, real estate represents the largest category of assets on the balance sheets of farm businesses. Farmers must therefore be able to evaluate not only the physical attributes of a new tract of land but the "economics" of the investment decision as well. This includes being able to determine whether or not meeting the seller's asking price would result in a net economic benefit to the business (whether the marginal returns would exceed the marginal costs).

Inventories

Plans to build up inventories of the output produced by the firm for later sale or for use as inputs in later production also hinge on the expected costs and returns associated with these "investments." For example, the cost of storing grain for later sale (i.e., expected damage to the crop in storage plus the cost of financing this inventory buildup) must be less than the expected proceeds from the sale of these commodities.

Financial Assets

Farmers also typically invest in a variety of financial assets. These assets include commerical bank deposits, stocks and bonds, and other forms of financail claims on others. The decision to acquire these assets depends not only on income considerations, but also on the relative certainty associated with their returns and value as well as *liquidity* considerations (i.e., the ability to convert an asset to cash quickly with little or no loss in value and disruption to the firm's ongoing operations). The importance of diversifying asset holdings and being liquid will be stressed in Chapter 8 when we discuss decision making in an uncertain world.

CONSTRAINTS ON FIRM GROWTH

Profit-maximizing farmers will obviously desire to expand their operations as quickly as possible to take advantage of the expected economic profits associated with larger firm sizes. However, there are several factors that may impede the rate of growth of their firms. Some of these factors are external in origin, and thus beyond the control of an individual farmer. Other factors are influenced by the decisions made by the individual farmer.

External Constraints

An external constraint on the growth of the firm refers to those factors over which the farmer has no control. Three examples of such constraints are: (1) the amount of income tax the farmer must pay, (2) the interest rates farmers must pay when borrowing, and (3) the availability of loan funds.

Income taxes. The rate at which a farmer's income is taxed will have a direct bearing on the growth of his operations. The higher the farmer's effective tax rate—all other things constant—the lower the rate of growth of the firm. Efforts to obtain full tax credits, exemptions and deductions allowed by law, and planning production, marketing, and investment strategies with their tax consequences in mind will have a positive impact on the growth of the firm over time.

Interest rates. While farmers should shop around for the best loan terms in much the same way that they do when purchasing fertilizer and other production inputs, there is little an individual farmer can do to forestall the effects of rising interest rates. The level of interest rate farmers must pay for the use of loan funds will also have a direct bearing on the growth of the firm over time. The higher the interest rate the farmer must pay—all other things constant—the lower the rate of growth of the firm.

External credit rationing. The final external factor discussed here is the limitations placed on the farmer's ability to borrow by his lender. The issue here is what the growth of the firm would be if the farmer was limited to a particular financial leverage ratio (i.e., ratio of total liabilities to total net worth). The higher the financial leverage ratio permitted by a lender, the greater the rate of growth the firm will achieve. This assumes, of course, that the rate of return generated by the farmer's operations exceeds the interest rate on loan funds. Obviously, the use of loan funds in relation to the use of the farmer's own funds will have no impact on the firm's growth if these rates are equal.

There are other factors which are largely beyond the control of the individual farmer that can influence the growth of his operations over time. Examples of these additional external constraints on firm growth include unfavorable wheather conditions, low product prices, and high input prices. A summary of the effects of external constraints on firm growth is presented in Table 7.2.[6]

Internal Constraints

In addition to the external constraints on the growth of the firm identified above, there are several things farmers can do which limit the growth of their firm's operations. Two such constraints are discussed here: (1) income withdrawals to finance personal consumption and off-farm investments, and (2) internal rationing of the use of loan funds.

---

[6] For the reader interested in verifying these conclusions, consider the following growth model:

$$e = [r + (r - i) f] (1 - t)(1 - w)$$

where e represents the rate of growth in the firm's net worth, r is the before-tax rate of return on the farm business assets, f is the ratio of the firm's debt to net worth, i represents the rate of interest, t is the income tax rate, and w is the farmer's withdrawal rate. Try assuming a base set of values for these variables and then modify them to reflect the nature of the discussion above and observe the results. For example, if $r = 10$, $i = .08$, $f = 1.0$, $t = .30$, and $w = .60$, the rate of growth in the firm's net worth would be 3 percent. What happens if $i = .12$ instead?

Factor	Stimulate growth	Retard growth
External constraints:		
Income taxes	Decrease in taxes	Increase in taxes
Interest rates	Decrease in interest rates	Increase in interest rates
Availability of loan funds	Increase in availability	Decrease in availability
Farm product prices	High product prices	Low product prices
Farm input prices	Low input prices	High input prices
Weather conditions	Favorable	Unfavorable
Internal constraints:		
Income withdrawals	Decrease in withdrawals	Increase in withdrawals
Willingness to borrow	Willing	Unwilling
Quality of management	Good manager	Poor manager
Physical returns to scale	Increasing returns	Decreasing returns
Nonfarm investment opportunities	Unfavorable	Favorable

TABLE 7.2 FACTORS AFFECTING FIRM GROWTH. There are a number of factors that can influence the rate of growth of the firm. Some of these factors are beyond the control of the individual farmer (e.g., interest rates, income tax rates, input, and product prices). Weather is another external factor that can have a significant effect on firm growth. Those factors affecting growth over which the farmer can exert some influence include the level of income withdrawals for personal consumption and nonfarm uses, his attitude toward borrowing, and the quality of his managerial skills.

Income withdrawals. A farmer's willingness or ability to retain current after-tax income to finance the expansion of his firm's operations will have a definite effect on the growth of the firm. One frequently hears of young farmers in particular "living poor" to provide additional funds for their firm. If a farmer withdrew only 40 percent of his firm's after-tax income to finance personal expenditures, the growth of his firm's operations in the current period will obviously be greater than if he withdrew all of his firm's after-tax income, other things constant.

Internal credit rationing. Farmers can also inhibit the growth of their firm by their attitude toward borrowing. The consequences are identical to those expressed earlier in connection with *external* credit rationing. In addition to these factors, the farmer's managerial skills will also have an effect on the rate of growth of the firm. The effects of this and other internal constraints on growth are also summarized in Table 7.2. One item not identified in this table is the farmer's perceptions about the existence of risk and the effects this perceived risk has on his production, marketing, and investment decisions. The entire Chapter 8 is devoted to decision making in an uncertain world.

SUMMARY

The purpose of this chapter was to consider several long-run issues facing the farmer, including the optimal size of the firm and those factors that can impede the achievement of this firm size. The major points made in this chapter can be summarized as follows:

1. Farmers in the long run can expand the size of their operations by using more of *all* inputs. As farmers expand the *scale* of their operations, they will incur *returns to scale.*
2. If the increase in output is exactly proportional to the increase in input use, the returns to scale are *constant.* If this increase was more (less) than proportional to the increase in input use, returns to scale are *increasing (decreasing).* The firm will normally pass through a phase of increasing returns to scale or *economies of size* before encountering constant and then decreasing returns to scale, or *diseconomies of size.*
3. The long-run average cost curve, often referred to as the *planning curve,* illustrates how varying the size of the firm will affect its efficiency. The long-run equilibrium of the firm under conditions of perfect competition is that output level where the product price is equal to the firm's short-run marginal and average total costs as well as to its long-run marginal and average total costs.
4. The factors that can limit the rate of growth of the firm can be grouped into two categories: (1) external factors over which farmers have little or no control and (2) internal factors that farmers can control. The external factors that can impede firm growth include high income tax rates, high interest rates, external credit rationing by lenders, unfavorable weather conditions, low product prices, and high input prices. The internal factors discussed included withdrawals from the firm's after-tax income to finance personal expenditures and the farmer's attitude toward incurring debt (internal credit rationing).

5. The investment opportunities confronting farmers can be grouped into four categories: (1) land, (2) depreciable assets, (3) inventories, and (4) financial assets. The feasibility of these investments hinges on whether or not they are expected to result in a net economic benefit to the firm.

6. The long-run average cost curve for most types of farming operations in the United States is likely to be L-shaped rather than U-shaped. When diseconomies of scale are finally reached, it will likely be due to the farmer's inability to manage the larger operation.

DEFINITION OF TERMS

Returns to scale: change in output in relation to an expansion of the use of all inputs (more labor, more equipment, and more land and buildings). Returns to scale can be either constant, increasing, or decreasing nature.

Indivisibility: the indivisibility of an input refers to the fact that inputs like equipment are available only in specific sizes.

Specialization: the use of inputs to perform specific tasks or produce only certain products.

Expansion path: line connecting optimal input–input relationships.

Depreciable assets: specific assets with a useful life of more than one year that qualify for tax depreciation. This allowance enables the farmer to "write-off" the cost of the asset over time. Machinery and buildings are two general forms of depreciable assets. Land is not a depreciable asset.

Net economic benefit: total revenue less total costs of production.

Depreciation: the IRS tax code allows farmers and other businesses to write off the cost of depreciable assets over a specific period of time for the purpose of computing their tax payments.

Investment tax credit: a specific percentage of the value of qualified assets that can be deducted directly from the tax payment due.

Commercial bank deposits: demand deposits (i.e., checking account balances) plus time and savings accounts at commercial banks.

Liquidity: the ability to convert an asset(s) to cash quickly with little or no loss in value and disruption to the firm's operations.

Diversification of assets: holding a variety of physical and/or financial assets, as opposed to "holding all your eggs in one market."

Financial leverage ratio: an indicator of a firm's financial strength, this ratio is usually defined as debt-to-equity or net worth. A ratio of greater than

1 suggests that farmer's creditors have more invested in the farm than the farmer does.

Credit rationing: a limitation placed on the amount of borrowed funds used to finance a farmer's operations.

REFERENCES

FARIS, J. E., and D. L. ARMSTRONG, *Economics Associated with Size: Kern County Cash Crop Farms,* Giannini Foundation Research Report 269, University of California, Berkeley, 1963.

HALL, B. F., and E. P. LAVEEN, "Farm Size and Economic Efficiency: The Case of California," *American Journal of Agricultural Economics,* 1978, pp. 589–600.

KYLE, R., and K. R. KRAUSE, "Factors Underlying the Incidence of Large Farming Units: The Current Situation and Probable Trends," *American Journal of Agricultural Economics,* 1970, pp. 748–760.

PENSON, JOHN B., JR., DANNY A. KLINEFELTER, and DAVID A. LINS, *Farm Investment and Financial Analysis.* Englewood Cliffs, N.J.: Prentice-Hall, Inc., 1981.

SMITH, ADAM, *The Wealth of Nations,* Book I. New York, Random House, Inc., 1957.

ADDITIONAL READINGS

GARDNER, B. D., and R. D. POPE, "How Is Scale and Structure Determined in Agriculture," *American Journal of Agricultural Economics,* 1978, pp. 295–302.

HEADY, E. O., *Economics of Production and Resource Use.* Englewood Cliffs, N.J.: Prentice-Hall, Inc. 1952.

KOHLER, H., *Intermediate Microeconomics: Theory and Application.* Glenview, Ill.: Scott, Foresman and Company, 1982.

MADDEN, J., and E. J. PARTENHEIMER, "Evidence of Economies and Diseconomies of Farm Size," in *Size, Structure and Future of Farms,* ed. G. A. Ball and E. O. Heady. Ames, Iowa: Iowa State University Press, 1972.

PENSON, JOHN B., JR. and DAVID A. LINS, *Agricultural Finance Introduction to Micro and Macro Concepts.* Englewood Cliffs, N.J.: Prentice-Hall, Inc., 1980.

PETERSON, WILLIS, *Principles of Economics: Micro.* 4th ed. Homewood, Ill. Richard D. Irwin, Inc., 1980.

RAUP, P. M., "Some Questions of Value and Scale in American Agriculture," *American Journal of Agriculture Economics,* 1978, pp. 303–308.

QUESTIONS

1. Contrast the essential differences between constant, increasing, decreasing returns to scale. Describe some of the sources of increasing returns to scale.

2. Illustrate the relationship between the short-run and long-run average cost curve. Why is the long-run average cost curve referred to as the "planning curve"?

3. Describe the essential differences between the short-run and long-run equilibrium of the firm under conditions of perfect competition.

4. Outline the nature of the investment decisions farmers must make over a period of time. Describe the economic criteria for evaluating the merits of these types of investments.

5. What are the principal external constraints to firm growth? Internal constraints?

ADVANCED TOPICS

Two advanced topics are addressed in this section. The first topic deals with the need to account for the *time value of money* when assessing the net economic benefit of an investment to a farmer. The second topic pertains to the concept of an *expansion path*.

Time Value of Money

It is an economic fact that $1 paid to you today is worth more than the promise of a $1 payment at some future point in time. The reasoning underlying this statement has nothing to do with the integrity of the person making the promise, although this may be a factor to consider. Rather, it has to do with the *time value of money*, or the earnings potential of this $1 between now and the time when the payment will be received. The purpose of determining the *present value* of a sum of money to be received some time in the future is to account for the opportunity cost of waiting for your money, or the income forgone by not having this money to invest *now*. The process of calculating the present value of a future sum of money is called *discounting*.

One approach to determining present value of a future sum of money to be received n number of periods from now is to use the following generalized formula:

$$PV = FV_n \div (1 + r)^n \tag{7.1}$$

where PV represents the present value (i.e., the value of having this money now), FV_n represents a future sum of money received n number of periods from now, and r represents the discount rate, or per dollar cost of capital. For example, suppose that we wished to know the present value of $1,100 to be received one period from now ($n = 1$) if your discount rate was 10 percent ($r = 0.10$). Substituting this information into equation (7.1), we see that

$$\begin{aligned} PV &= \$1,100 \div (1.10)^1 \\ &= \$1,100 \div 1.10 \\ &= \$1,000 \end{aligned} \tag{7.2}$$

Thus the present value of $1,100 received one period from now is $1,000 if your discount rate is 10 percent.

If this sum of money was to be received at the end of two periods instead of just one, the present value would be

$$PV = \$1,100 \div (1.10)^2$$
$$= \$1,100 \div 1.210 \qquad (7.3)$$
$$= \$909.09$$

Thus $1,100 received two periods from now would be worth less than $1,100 received one period from now. This result can be generalized as follows: *the present value of a specific sum of money for any positive discount rate will decline in value as the payment is postponed further and further into the future.*

We can determine the net economic benefit or the *net present value* of an investment by subtracting the initial capital outlay from the *sum* of the present values of the periodic net cash flows generated by the investment, or

$$NPV = FV_1 \div (1 + r)^1 + \cdots + FV_n \div (1 + r)^n - I_0 \qquad (7.4)$$

Where NPV represents the net present value, FV_1 represents the future net cash flow received in period 1, FV_n represents the future net cash flow received in the last period, and I_0 represents the initial capital outlay.[7] As long as the net present value is positive (NPV is greater than zero), the investment is considered feasible from an economic standpoint.

The calculation of equation (7.4) is made simpler by the availability of *interest factor tables* for different discount rates *(r)* and number of periods *(n)*. This means, of course, that you do not have to calculate the values of $(1 + r)^1$ through $(1 + r)^n$ required by this equation. Table 7.3 reproduces part of such a table. Notice, for example, that the interest factor for a discount rate of 10 percent two years from now is equal to 1.210, which is identical to the value used in equation (7.3).

Expansion Path

In addition to the long-run average cost curve, we can examine the expansion of the firm by looking at its *expansion path* in either an input–input or a product–product setting. Beginning with the input–input case, we know that each point on the long-run average cost curve represents the least-cost combination of resources to produce a given level of output [i.e., where the conditions expressed in equations (5.4) and (5.5) hold for different plant sizes].

---

[7] For a further discussion of this topic, including the information needed in investment analysis and how to measure the discount rate, see Penson et al. (1981).

Year	Discount rate		
	5%	10%	20%
1	1.050	1.100	1.200
2	1.102	1.210	1.440
3	1.158	1.331	1.728
4	1.216	1.464	2.074
5	1.276	1.611	2.488
.	.	.	.
10	1.629	2.594	6.192
.	.	.	.
20	2.653	6.727	38.337

Source: John B. Penson, Jr. and David A Lins, *Agricultural Finance: An Introduction to Micro and Macro Concepts* (Englewood Cliffs, N.J.: Prentice-Hall, Inc., 1980.

TABLE 7.3 FUTURE VALUE OF $1 AT COMPOUND IN-TEREST. The person who coined the phrase "time is money" undoubtedly understood the concept of the time value of money. One dollar invested for one year at 5 percent interest, for example, would earn 5 cents in income and therefore be worth $1.05 one year from now. Two years from now, this investment would be worth $1.10. Twenty years from now this investment would be worth about $2.65. The higher the interest rate, the higher the future value will be. For example, one dollar invested for 20 years at 20 percent interest would be worth $38.34.

This same phenomenon holds along the expansion path in panel a of Figure 7.4 given by (1) the points of tangency between a set of isoquants for two inputs associated with different output levels, and (2) a set of isocost lines whose slope is given by the ratio of the prices for these inputs. Thus at all points along the expansion path in panel a, the conditions expressed in equations (5.4) and (5.5) hold for different plant sizes.

Panel b in Figure 7.4 illustrates the nature of the expansion path in a product–product setting. Rather than the single production possibilities curve depicted in Figure 5.7, we see a set of production possibilities curves associated with different levels of available resources. A line drawn through the points of profit-maximizing combinations of products also represents an expansion path. All points along this path satisfy the conditions for profit maximization expressed in equation (5.14). Any deviation from these combinations of products for specific levels of available resources will result in a reduction of the farmer's profits.

Panel a

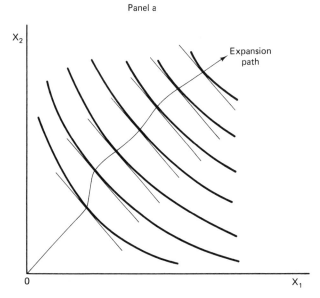

Panel b

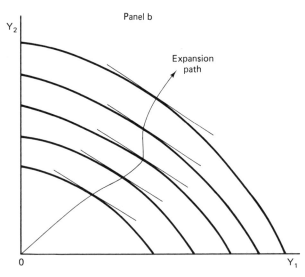

Figure 7.4 *Expansion Paths for Inputs and Outputs.* The long-run average cost curve was said to represent a path of points reflecting the least unit cost of producing specific rates of output. We can also look at the firm's "expansion path" in terms of the least-cost combination of inputs and profit-maximizing combination of products. Panel a shows that a line connecting a series of points given by the tangency of isocost lines and isoquants associated with different levels of output forms an expansion path. Panel b shows that a line connecting a series of points given by the tangency of isorevenue lines and production possiblities curves associated with different levels of available resources also forms an expansion path.

8

DECISION MAKING IN AN UNCERTAIN WORLD

The theory of consumer and producer behavior presented thus far in this part of the book assumed that both have perfect knowledge of future events. If this were really true, however, why would producers and consumers feel the need to purchase insurance, and how can we explain the existence of a futures market for agricultural commodities? These two observations should clearly demonstrate that the assumption of certainty utterly fails in the real world. By accounting for the existence of uncertainty and the attitudes toward uncertainty, virtually all agricultural decisions can be better understood.

In this chapter we explore the basics of measuring uncertainty and illustrate how it affects some of the decisions discussed in previous chapters where conditions of certainty were assumed. Since a majority of the uncertainty surrounding commercial agriculture involves producers rather than consumers, producer-oriented examples will be emphasized.

MOTIVATION TO STUDY UNCERTAINTY

To dramatize the need to study uncertainty, let us examine the following hypothetical situation. Suppose that you have $10,000 which you can allocate between three assets: stock A, stock B, and stock C. The returns per dollar invested in each stock are not known with complete certainty, but you expect the returns outlined as follows:

Asset	Expected return per dollar invested
Stock *A*	0.14
Stock *B*	0.12
Bond *A*	0.10

If there are no restrictions on how you can invest this money and you wish to maximize your expected returns, what investments would you make? The correct decision would be to invest your entire $10,000 in stock *A*. This would yield an expected return of $1,400 (i.e., 0.14 times $10,000). This exceeds the expected return from investing all your funds in stock *B* or in stock *C*. It also exceeds the expected return derived from any combination of these three stocks. In summary, you should specialize your investment "portfolio" by investing all your available funds in stock *A* if your goal is to maximize your expected return.[1]

Is this the behavior investors normally exhibit? Certainly not! The most commonly observed investment behavior is that of *diversification,* or the holding of several stocks. What, then, is wrong with our earlier statement that rational investors behave in a way that will maximize their expected return? Could it be that investors do not choose a portfolio with the sole objective of maximizing their expected return? Might some sense of variability of returns matter?

These questions should help you see the need to examine decision making under uncertainty. It is a vast subject, but we will attempt to cover the basics of behavior under uncertainty.[2]

MEASURES OF UNCERTAINTY

We have used the word "uncertainty" rather loosely thus far. Let us alter this situation by defining uncertainty as Webster does: *uncertainty involves any event where we are not sure of the outcome.* Generally, agricultural production and prices are not known with certainty when decisions are made. For example, a feedlot operator at the time he buys his feeder cattle does not know with certainty what the final weight gain for his cattle will be and what the price of cattle will be in the spot market when he eventually markets his cattle. Thus cattle prices as well as those factors affecting production (e.g., death loss, rates of gain, etc.) would represent uncertain variables in this example.

[1] The term "portfolio" simply refers to the *combination* of investments one chooses to hold.

[2] For a detailed analysis of agricultural decision making under uncertainty, see Anderson et al. (1980).

"And so, extrapolating from the best figures available, we see that current trends, unless dramatically reversed, will inevitably lead to a situation in which the sky will fall."

Drawn by Lorenz; © 1972 The New Yorker Magazine, Inc.

While the sky is unlikely to fall, the graph Chicken Little is pointing to looks like the fluctuations in prices and interest rates observed in the U.S. economy in the early eighties. With such fluctuations comes uncertainty about what the future will bring. Up to now we have assumed that farmers knew what these prices were going to be with perfect certainty when they made their production, marketing, and investment decisions. This assumption is relaxed in this chapter to show how the existence of risk and uncertainty affects the farmer's production, marketing, and investment decisions.

We shall assume that a farmer can form beliefs about a range of possible outcomes and express the strength of these beliefs in terms of the "probability" or *chance of occurrence* he assigns to each potential outcome. In assigning these chances, the farmer must follow a few rules. First, each percent chance must *lie in between zero and 100 percent.* Second, all percent chances must *sum to 100 percent.* For example, suppose that you are not sure whether the price of corn will be $2, $3, or $4 per bushel and that you expressed your beliefs about each possible outcome as shown in the box on page 226.

We can interpret these data as meaning that you believe that there is a 40 percent chance of receiving a price of $4, a 50 percent chance of receiving $3, and a 10 percent chance of receiving as little as $2 per bushel. This is in sharp contrast to our earlier assumption of certainty, where the farmer was

Corn price	Chances of occurrence (%)
$4	40
3	50
2	10

thought to be 100 percent sure of receiving a particular price (e.g., a 100 percent chance of occurrence would have been assigned to one of the prices above, while a 0 percent chance of occurrence would have been assigned to the other two prices).

Expected Prices

In the simple example presented above, how would you determine the *expected value* of the product's price? You might be inclined to respond that the expected price is $3 since it has the greatest chance of occurring. But this would ignore the fact that the price of corn could be as high as $4 per bushel or as low as $2 per bushel. Surely an expected price must consider the chances of these other possible outcomes occurring.

The expected price is instead equal to a weighted average of all possible prices. In the example in the preceding box, the expected price would be $3.30 [i.e., ($4.00 × 0.40) + ($3.00 × 0.50) + ($2.00 × 0.10)]. The expected price therefore represents a measure of central tendency but is *not necessarily* the price associated with the greatest chance of occurrence.

In conclusion, *the expected value is a weighted average reflecting the central tendency of an uncertain variable. The weights are the chances that the events could occur.*

Variability of Prices

A second concept we will need when assessing uncertainty is that of *variance.* Variance is a measure of the *dispersion* of the potential deviations from the expected value discussed above. Suppose that Frank Farmgate and Ralph Rancher perceived the following potential corn prices:

Corn prices	Chances of occurrence (%)	
	Frank's	Ralph's
$4	40	45
3	20	10
2	40	45

Examining this table, we see that both Frank and Ralph expect the price to be $3 per bushel. However, Ralph places greater likelihood on the other possible prices occurring than Frank. Hence, in Ralph's mind, there is a greater chance of the corn price being higher or lower than what Frank perceives. In such a case, we would say that Ralph's perceptions contain more *variance* than Frank's.

Formally, variance is obtained by multiplying each event's chance of occurring times the corresponding deviation from the expected price squared and then adding these terms together. For example, the variance of the price of corn as perceived by Frank is $0.80 [i.e., $0.40 \times (\$4.00 - 3.00)^2 + 0.20 \times (\$3.00 - \$3.00)^2 + 0.40 \times (\$2.00 - \$3.00)^2$]. The variance according to Ralph's perceptions would be $0.90.

In conclusion, *variance is a measure of the dispersion of the chances of occurrence and their respective events. The greater the variance, all other things constant (e.g., the expected value), the greater the likelihood that specific events will deviate from the expected value.*

A Measure of Risk

When measuring risk, it is important to assess the variability of an uncertain event in relation to its expected value. For example, the price of one product might be measured in "dollars per ton," while the price of another product might be expressed in "dollars per hundredweight." We obviously could not compare the relative variability of different production enterprises in this instance.

To overcome this shortcoming, we can relate the size of the *standard deviation* (i.e., the square root of the variance) to the size of the expected value.[3] This ratio is called the *coefficient of variation* and is a convenient "unit-free" measure of the relationship between the variability of returns and the expected return.

What does the coefficient of variation tell the farmer? Calculation of this coefficient for different crops, for example, tells the farmer something about the relative amount of uncertainty associated with each crop. To illustrate, suppose that corn returns have *more variability* than soybean production but both have the *same expected return.* Thus the coefficient of variation would be greater for corn than it would be for soybeans. This means that a farmer growing corn is more likely to experience "boom" and "bust" years than if he were to grow soybeans. If, instead, we assume that

[3] Most inexpensive hand calculators today have either a square-root key or an exponent key (any number raised to an exponent of 0.50 represents its square root), which greatly simplifies the calculation of the standard deviation. The standard deviation for the variance of the price of corn perceived by Frank would be the square root of the variance (i.e., $0.80) or $0.89.

corn has a *higher expected return* than soybeans, but both have *identical variances*, the coefficient of variation would now be greater for soybeans than for corn. This means that the likelihood of "bust" years would be greater for soybean production than for corn production.

The coefficient of variation by definition tells us something about the amount of *uncertainty per dollar of expected returns*. To illustrate, we know that Frank's coefficient of variation for corn in the example above would be 0.298 (i.e., 0.894 ÷ 3.00), while Ralph's coefficient would be 0.316 (i.e., 0.949 ÷ 3.00). Thus Ralph perceives a greater risk per dollar of expected returns than Frank. The importance of this perception will become clearer later in this chapter when we discuss different attitudes by farmers toward the trade-off between uncertainty and expected returns.

In conclusion, *the coefficient of variation is the ratio of the standard deviation (square root of the variance) divided by the expected value. It measures the risk per dollar of expected return.*

Relationship between Events

The relationship between two uncertain events is also an important concept. *Correlation* is a measure of association between two events. Rather than numerically illustrate the calculation of the correlation coefficient, we refer you to an introductory statistics textbook.[4] A few qualitative aspects of correlation need to be understood, however. As a farmer contemplates in the spring of the year whether to grow say all corn, all soybeans, or some combination of both crops, he does not know for sure what each commodity's price will be when these products are eventually marketed.[5] Most farmers know something about how these prices fluctuate in relation to one another, however. If the prices of soybeans and corn always move in the *same direction*, their *correlation is positive*. If these prices move in *opposite directions*, their *correlation is negative*.

The correlation coefficient reflects the degree of correlation and is bounded by –1 and +1. A value of +1 (–1) implies perfect positive (negative) correlation. Two uncertain events are *independent* if fluctuations in one uncertain event are unrelated to fluctuations in the other. Thus if corn and soybean prices are independent (i.e., their correlation coefficient is zero), the occurrence of a "high" corn price should have *no effect* on soybean prices.

In conclusion, *correlation is a measure of the association between two uncertain variables. It ranges in value from –1 to +1. A negative (positive) value implies that fluctuations of the two uncertain variables tend to be in*

---

[4] For example, see Wonnacott and Wonnacott (1976).

[5] This implicitly assumes that the farmer has not signed a forward contract or hedged his crop in the futures market. Both of these assumptions will be relaxed shortly.

the opposite (same) direction. A zero correlation implies no systematic relationship exists between the fluctuations of two uncertain variables.

These are the essential properties of uncertain events that we will need throughout the remainder of this chapter. In the theory and applications that follow, we will assume that the farmer has definite perceptions about the expected value, variances, and correlations of uncertain quantities and prices. These perceptions may be based on his subjective feelings only or they may be related to an analysis of historical data on prices and yields. Throughout the remainder of this chapter, the terms "risk" and "uncertainty" will be used interchangeably.[6]

RISK PREFERENCES AND BEHAVIOR

Why do some people choose to take a risk whereas others do not? Why do some farmers hedge their crop or buy crop insurance whereas others do not? And why do some fasten automobile seat belts whereas others do not?

Part of the answer to these questions hinges on differences in the *risk preferences* of the population. A crucial variable affecting a farmer's behavior is his assessment of the chances that different events have of occurring. If Frank Farmgate believes, for example, that there is a 20 percent chance of hail damage to his crop, while Ralph Rancher believes that there is a 50 percent chance, Ralph will have more incentive to purchase full-coverage hail insurance, all other things constant.[7]

Figure 8.1 illustrates three types of risk behavior with respect to wealth. For the risk-averse (preferring) farmer, the marginal utility of wealth decreases (increases) as his wealth increases. The risk-averse (preferring) farmer will require a positive (negative) risk premium or additional return before accepting the risk associated with a particular decision. The marginal utility of wealth for the risk-neutral farmer is constant. For him, every additional dollar gained has the same utility. Thus a dollar gained and a dollar lost cancel each other. The risk premium for a risk-neutral farmer will therefore always be zero. Uncertain fluctuations about a particular wealth level are of no concern to this farmer. What increases his utility is expected wealth. Thus a risk-neutral farmer will choose that action which maximizes his expected wealth. For example, a risk-neutral farmer will purchase hail insurance only if the insurance premium is *less than or equal* to the expected loss from hail damage. A risk-averse farmer, however, would be willing to

---

[6] In an earlier time, risk was defined using objective or actuarial probabilities, while uncertainty used subjective assessments. In modern theory, such distinctions are not usually made and hence will not be made in this chapter.

[7] The Advanced Topics section at the end of this chapter presents a theory that blends the farmer's risk perceptions with his risk preferences.

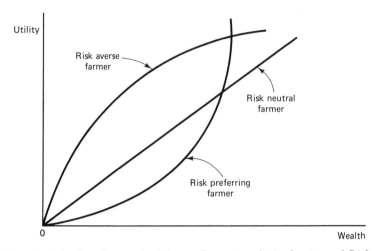

Figure 8.1 *Utility Curves for Three Alternative Attitudes toward Risk.*
There are three general categories of behavior toward risk: (1) risk
averse, (2) risk neutral, and (3) risk preferring. Most farmers are generally thought to be risk averse, reflecting the fact that the marginal
utility of wealth decreases as his wealth increases. He will assign a risk
premium to uncertain events. A risk-neutral farmer, on the other hand,
will always have a zero-risk premium. Uncertainty would be of no concern to him. Finally, a risk-preferring farmer would be willing to pay
for the opportunity to be exposed to risk.

pay something more than the expected loss from hail damage if necessary for
full insurance coverage.[8]

In general, risk-averse and risk-preferring individuals "care about" their
exposure to uncertainty. To illustrate, suppose that Frank Farmgate is faced
with the following characteristics:

Action	Outcome	Chance of occurrence (%)
1	Gain $3	50
	Lose $1	50
2	Gain $1	100

Which would Frank prefer? Using the utility function illustrated in
Figure 8.1, we can show that Frank would prefer action 2. Even though both
actions have the same $1 expected increases in wealth, a risk averter such as

[8] Much empirical research tends to support the notion that farmers are *risk averse*
for most risks. Along an individual farmer's utility curve, however, we may observe several types of behavior toward risk. That is, a decision maker may be risk averse for some
risks but risk neutral for others. See Young, et al. (1979).

Frank will always prefer certainty to uncertainty in such situations.[9] This notion has led many economists to characterize "risk taking" in terms of expected net wealth and the variability of wealth as measured by the variance defined earlier in this chapter. In such a setting, a risk-averse farmer will prefer activities with larger expected values and lower variances. In the case presented in the preceding table, for example, both actions have the same expected values, but action 1 has a higher variance. Thus action 2 would be preferred.[10]

SOME DECISIONS INVOLVING UNCERTAINTY

In this section we discuss selected decsions where uncertainty plays an important role. We briefly illustrate at least one situation involving uncertainty from each of the following areas: (1) production decisions, (2) marketing decisions, and (3) investment decisions.

Production Decisions

Since the environment in which farmers make decisions is clearly uncertain, the possible gain from considering risk and the risk-averse behavior of farmers is considerable. Decisions pertaining to insurance, crop and livestock production activities, input uses and valuation, participation in government programs, and geographical diversification of production are examples of production decisions involving uncertainty. In each of these situations, it is necessary to know how changes in production decisions will affect expected utility.

Generally, economic incentives can be characterized in terms of marginal benefits and marginal cost. A risk-averse farmer will maximize his expected utility or, alternatively, his certainty equivalent. This certainty equivalent, in turn, can be divided into the following components

$$\begin{matrix} \text{certainty} \\ \text{equivalent} \end{matrix} = \begin{matrix} \text{expected} \\ \text{revenue} \end{matrix} - \begin{matrix} \text{expected} \\ \text{cost} \end{matrix} - \begin{matrix} \text{risk} \\ \text{premium} \end{matrix} \qquad (8.1)$$

when both prices and output are uncertain.[11] Consider the farmer's choice of what level of fertilizer to use on a crop. Maximization of the certainty equivalent expressed in equation (8.1) suggests that the farmer should use

[9] That is, a risk averter would have to be paid the risk premium in order to be induced to take action 1 over action 2.

[10] A risk-neutral farmer would be indifferent between actions 1 and 2 since only expected values are relevant to him.

[11] A discussion of expected utility theory and the concept of certainty equivalents is presented in the Advanced Topics section at the end of this chapter.

an input up to the point where the marginal benefit exceeds marginal cost. In this case, marginal benefit is the expected marginal value product or the change in expected revenue as more fertilizer is applied. The marginal cost is now composed of two parts: (1) the direct input cost of the additional unit of fertilizer, plus (2) the marginal subjective cost associated with the uncertainty. The latter value is called the *marginal risk premium* and is the change in the risk premium as fertilizer use changes. Thus the optimal use of fertilizer (or any other variable input) is indicated by

$$\begin{matrix} \text{expected marginal} \\ \text{value product} \end{matrix} = \begin{matrix} \text{marginal factor} \\ \text{cost} \end{matrix} + \begin{matrix} \text{marginal risk} \\ \text{premium} \end{matrix} \qquad (8.2)$$

where the marginal risk premium is equal to the change in the risk premium divided by the change in fertilizer use. The intuitive reason why the farmer considers the marginal risk premium is that he is uncertain of the marginal benefit of applying additional fertilizer. Whether this is considered an increase in cost (as we have done here) or a decrease in revenue is immaterial.

The optimal level of fertilizer use is illustrated in Figure 8.2 for the case where increased fertilizer use leads to an increase in the risk premium. The optimal level of fertilizer use for a *risk-averse* farmer would occur at 0*A*. For a *risk-neutral* farmer, the marginal risk premium would be equal to zero and the optimal level of fertilizer use would occur at 0*B*. *Thus, fertilizer demand for a risk-averse farmer will be less than it would be for a risk-neutral farmer under conditions of uncertainty.* If fertilizer use marginally decreases the risk premium, the risk-averse farmer's fertilizer demand would be greater than it would be for a risk-neutral farmer. A similar analysis can be applied to the level of output as well. In such cases, the farmer would produce at the point where expected price equals expected marginal cost *plus* a marginal risk premium.

Another crucial production decision is *how to combine production enterprises* to obtain the highest expected total return and minimum total variance for the farm as a whole. For example, if a farmer combines corn and hog production, is this a better risk strategy than combining corn and soybean activities? The expected values, variances, and correlations of the net returns for each activity would be needed to answer this question. This decision is similar to the decision of what enterprises the farmer should invest in to maximize his expected utility.

The final production decision discussed here has to do with *participating in the government program* for specific crops and how this affects the expected value and variance the farmer perceives for these commodity prices. The specific features of these programs are spelled out in Chapter 10 and will not be introduced here. One feature of these programs, however, is that if the market price falls below the price the government has chosen to support prices, the farmer will receive the higher support price. While this feature rules out the chance of the participating farmer receiving a price

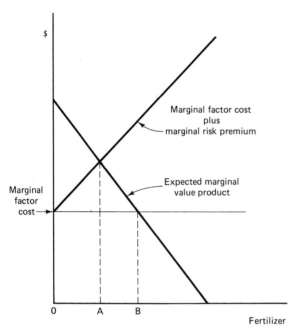

Figure 8.2 *Optimal Fertilizer Use under Risk-Averse and Risk-Neutral Behavior.* The existence of risk will cause a risk-averse farmer to purchase less production inputs than a risk-neutral farmer. By assigning a risk premium to this decision, the risk-averse farmer has in effect said that his costs of production are higher than the marginal factor cost. Equating total marginal costs with the expected marginal value product, he will purchase only quantity 0*A*. The risk-neutral farmer would purchase quantity 0*B*.

below the price support level, it *increases the expected price* and *reduces the variance*. The uncertainty per dollar of expected return (i.e., the coefficient of variation) would therefore be reduced. This will be important to risk-averse farmers, who are most apt to participate in the program.

Marketing Decisions

There are a host of marketing issues that involve uncertainty. In particular, the price of a commodity is inherently uncertain. Thus, even at the farm level, issues involving whether to use the futures market or production contracts to lock in a forward price for the commodity or to rely on the cash market are important.

Production contracts. Consider the production contract discussed in Chapter 6, in which the buyer of the product specifies the price at the contract date. The farmer must decide whether to accept the contract or wait and sell his crop later in the cash market. Let us suppose that the certainty equivalent of the random future cash price is $2.75. In other words, Frank Farmgate would be indifferent between the distribution of future cash prices presented in our earlier example or a certain price of $2.75. Hence, all other things equal, a production contract specifying a certain price exceeding $2.75 would be preferred to selling in the cash market. However, Ralph Rancher's perceptions and his certainty equivalent price are probably different.

Let us suppose Ralph's certainty equivalent price is $2.50. Their varying perceptions of the probabilities involved in their risk preferences may lead Frank to reject the forward contract and Ralph to accept the contract.[12]

Futures contract.   The use of the futures market also allows farmers to determine a forward price for their production. In Chapter 6 we illustrated how Walt Wheaties could sell two 5,000-bushel futures contracts in February for a July delivery at a futures price of $3.70 and thus protect himself from the prospect of the cash market price falling to $3.20. By doing so, we showed that Walt received a gross income of $37,000 rather than the $32,000 he would have received if he did not hedge his crop. Thus Walt substituted the certain income of $37,000 for an uncertain income, eliminating the risk associated with fluctuations in the price of the commodity. As long as the difference between the futures price and the transactions costs exceeds the certainty equivalent of the cash market price, hedging is a preferred marketing strategy.

As we hinted in Chapter 6, hedging is not without its potential disadvantages. For example, we illustrated how hedging placed a ceiling on Walt Wheaties' income. If the cash market price had risen to $4 per bushel instead of falling to $3.20, Walt would still receive a certain income of $37,000. We also eluded to several other potential disadvantages that should be considered when hedging, including basis risk, yield risk, and the uncertainties associated with variation margin deposits.

Basis risk refers to the risk that the basis (i.e., the difference between the cash price and the futures price) will have widened by the time the crop is finally sold. An illustration of the effects of basis risk on total gross farm income are illustrated in the example on page 235. In this example, we have assumed that Walt in February 1984 sold contracts totaling 10,000 bushels at $3.70 per bushel for July 1984 and the time has not come to sell his wheat and liquidate his futures market position. Returning to the original situation where the price of wheat in the cash market fell to $3.20, let us assume that the cost of buying an equal and offsetting futures market contract is now $3.35 instead of $3.20. Thus there is now a basis of $0.15 per bushel between what wheat is selling for and what it will cost Walt to liquidate his futures market position. In addition to the $32,000 gross income received from the sale of his wheat in the cash market, Walt would now receive only $3,500 from his futures market transactions (i.e., $37,000 − $33,500). Re-

---

[12] Since the level of initial wealth affects where a person is prior to the crop year, two people with identical utilities will behave differently if one is more wealthy. The impact of initial wealth is intriguing. The most widely believed hypothesis is that risk aversion (the risk premium) falls as one becomes more wealthy. This hypothesis is referred to as decreasing risk aversion. For a further discussion of these wealth effects, see the Advanced Topics section at the end of this chapter.

Item	Date of transaction	Effect of gross income
Cash market transactions:		
Sell 10,000 bushels of wheat at $3.20 per bushel	July 1984	+$32,000
Futures market transactions:		
Sell July 1984 futures contract for 10,000 bushels of wheat at $3.70 per bushel	February 1984	+$37,000
Buy July 1984 futures contract for 10,000 bushels of wheat at $3.35 per bushel	July 1984	−$33,500
Total gross income		$35,500

member that Walt received $5,000 from his futures market transaction when the basis was zero.

Yield risk refers to the fact that output is now known when the futures contract is sold. Thus there is a possibility that lower-than-expected output levels may force Walt to "buy" his way out of his futures market position. An example of the effects of yield risk is presented below. In this example we have assumed that the reason prices had increased earlier to $4 was that yields were lower because of unfavorable growing conditions. Since output is

Item	Date of transaction	Effect of gross income
Cash market transactions:		
Sell 5,000 bushels of wheat at $4 per bushel	July 1984	+$20,000
Futures market transactions:		
Sell July 1984 futures contract for 10,000 bushels of wheat at $3.70 per bushel	February 1984	+$37,000
Buy July 1984 futures contract for 10,000 bushels of wheat at $4 per bushel	July 1984	−$40,000
Total gross income		$17,000

not known when the two contracts for 5,000 bushels were sold in February 1984, let us see what happens to Walt's gross income if his wheat crop turns out to be 5,000 bushels instead of 10,000 bushels. Assuming a basis of zero once again, we see that Walt's gross income from his wheat production activities would fall from $37,000 to $17,000. To avoid this potential loss in gross income, Walt should have sold forward an amount *smaller* than his total expected output (perhaps two-thirds of what you expect output to be). For example, if Walt had sold only 5,000 bushels forward, the gross income from his wheat production activities would have fallen to only $18,500 instead of $17,000.

Finally, one may be reluctant to use the futures market because of the need to meet *variation margin deposit* calls. Let us suppose that Walt sold a futures market contract for 5,000 bushels of wheat at a futures price of $3.70. If the original margin deposit was 10 percent of the value of the contract, Walt would have had to post a $1,850 [i.e., 0.10 × ($3.70 × 5,000)] deposit with his broker at the time the transaction was completed. If the price of wheat futures suddenly rose to $3.80 per bushel, Walt would be required to post a variation margin deposit of $500 (i.e., 5,000 bushes times $0.10) with his broker to cover his *short position*. If the price had instead fallen to $3.60, Walt could have reduced the funds in his margin account by $500 (the buyer of Walt's contract in this instance would have to post a variation margin deposit of $500).

In summary, hedging their market position through the use of a futures market contract allows farmers to lock-in a forward price. However, hedging reduces but does not eliminate all risks to farmers.

There are other marketing strategies that one can adopt to reduce the effects of random fluctuations in commodity prices, including the sequential marketing of output throughout the year to achieve an *average annual price* rather than accept the market price at harvest time.[13]

Investment Decisions

It is important for risk-averse farmers to understand the effects that individual investment decisions have on their overall exposure to risk. The "portfolio return" consists of the return to a particular combination of asset holdings. Let us assume a beginning farmer is considering investing $350,000 in either enterprise *A* or enterprise *B*, or some combination of both enterprises.[14]

---

[13] The interested reader desiring a more in-depth coverage of these and other marketing strategies should consult a good agricultural marketing textbook. For example, see Kohls and Uhl (1981).

[14] The rate of return on an asset or group of assets is found by dividing the return by the initial investment. For example, if $1,400 is the expected return on $10,000, the expected rate of return would be 0.14.

The *portfolio's expected rate of return* can be found by computing the weighted average of the individual returns associated with these two enterprises just like any other expected value. To illustrate, suppose that the expected rates of return on enterprises A and B are 0.25 and 0.20, respectively. Thus, as the proportion of the $350,000 invested in enterprise A varies between 0 and 1, the expected rate of return on the total portfolio will vary between 0.20 and 0.25. Table 8.1 shows that when the portfolio consists of equal amounts of funds invested in enterprise A and enterprise B, the expected portfolio rate of return will be 0.225 (i.e., 0.50 × 0.25 + 0.50 × 20).

What happens to the *variance of the portfolio* as the proportion of funds invested in enterprise A is varied?[15] The variance of the portfolio for selected proportions invested in enterprise A and the correlation coefficient are also presented in Table 8.1. The first thing one notices in this table is that the variance of the portfolio is identical to the variance of the enterprise when the farmer specializes in a particular enterprise. If the farmer specializes in enterprise A, for example, the variance of the returns associated with enterprise B would be totally irrelevant, as would the correlation between the returns normally generated by these enterprises.

Now let us see what happens when we *diversify* the portfolio. Table 8.1 shows that when an equal amount of funds is invested in enterprises A and B, the variance of the portfolio of 0.0146 if the returns from these enterprises are perfectly positively correlated (i.e., the correlation coefficient is +1.0). In this instance, the variance of the portfolio is higher than the variance for enterprise B but lower than the variance for enterprise A. This occurs for two reasons. First, we were told that the variance of the returns from enterprise A was higher than the variance of the returns from enterprise B. Second, the returns on these two enterprises were *highly positively correlated*. Thus the sum of the returns is relatively stable. The portfolio variance will be relatively high when the returns on two enterprises are positively correlated.

What happens to the variance of the portfolio when the *correlation between these enterprises changes?* If the correlation were instead equal to zero, for example, the portfolio variance would be 0.0075, which is considerably less than the variance on either specialized portfolio. And if the correlation were instead perfectly negative, the portfolio variance would fall to 0.0005 since high (low) returns from one enterprise would cancel the low (high) returns from the other enterprise. The results presented in Table 8.1 therefore illustrate a valuable lesson: *The variance of the portfolio's return will decrease (increase) if there is a ceteris paribus reduction (rise) in*

---

[15] The calculation of this variance is somewhat more involved. The interested reader is referred to a financial management textbook for a discussion of where the procedures for calculating the portfolio's expected return and variance. For example, see Weston and Brigham (1978).

	Proportion of Funds in Enterprise A		
Correlation coefficient	Enterprise A only	50% Enterprise B and 50% Enterprise B	Enterprise B only
Expected Return			
+1.0	0.25	0.2250	0.20
0.0	0.25	0.2250	0.20
−1.0	0.25	0.2250	0.20
Variance of Portfolio			
+1.0	0.02	0.0146	0.01
0.0	0.02	0.0075	0.01
−1.0	0.02	0.0005	0.01
Coefficient of Variation			
+1.0	0.566	0.537	0.50
0.0	0.566	0.385	0.50
−1.0	0.566	0.099	0.50

TABLE 8.1 CHARACTERISTICS OF PORTFOLIO CONTAINING TWO ENTERPRISES. We can see the benefits from diversifying the operation of the farm as opposed to "putting all your eggs in one basket" with the help of the coefficients of variation presented above. This measure of risk is substantially lower (if these two enterprises are less than highly positively correlated) if the farmer avoids specializing in enterprise A or enterprise B. That is, putting 50 percent of his funds in enterprise A and 50 percent in enterprise B lowered his exposure to risk. The less correlated the returns from these two enterprises, the greater the reduction in risk realized from diversification.

the correlation among the returns from the enterprises in the farmer's portfolio. The less correlated these returns are, the lower the portfolio's variance will be.

An interesting special case worth noting is when the variance of individual enterprise returns are *equal and uncorrelated.* If there are four enterprises on the farm, for example, the variance of the farmer's portfolio will be minimized by *equally dividing* the portfolio among these four enterprises.

A risk-averse farmer will be interested in the *portfolio effects* on the coefficient of variation illustrated in Table 8.1. You will recall that we said earlier in this chapter that this coefficient tells us the uncertainty per dollar of expected return for each of these alternative combinations. Looking at this table, we see that *specialization* in either enterprise A or B would result *in the highest uncertainty per dollar of expected return.* The coefficient of variation for enterprise A would be 0.566, while the coefficient of variation for enterprise B would be 0.50. If the returns for these enterprises had been highly negatively correlated (i.e., the correlation coefficient was −1.0), the coefficient of variation for the portfolio made up of *equal* investments in both enterprises would have been only 0.099 [i.e., 0.0224 (the square root of the variance, or 0.0005) divided by the portfolio's expected rate of return of 0.225]. Thus *diversification* of enterprises on the farm, which involves both investment and production decisions, will have *the greatest impact on lowering the farmer's overall risk per dollar of expected return* when these returns are negatively correlated. This is again because the high returns on one enterprise *cancel or offset* the low returns on the other.

The risk-neutral farmer will be concerned only with the expected rate of return and will therefore *specialize* in enterprise *A* since it affords him the highest return (0.25). The risk-averse farmer, however, will be impressed by the lower risk per dollar of expected return provided by *diversification*, particularly if the returns on these two enterprises are negatively correlated.

A FEW EMPIRICAL EXAMPLES

In this part of the chapter we review several applications of decision making under risk which are designed to illustrate some of the basic concepts covered in this chapter. Each application is preceded by a brief review of the concept.

Risk Aversion and Input Demand

A substantial amount of the risk farmers face involves the uncertainty associated with production. For example, at planting time, the farmer does not know what the weather will be over the growing season and what effect this and other forces will have on his crop yields. Let us focus solely on production uncertainty. We shall presume that price uncertainty has already been resolved through the use of futures contracts as described earlier in this chapter.

From equation (8.2) we can see that the crucial effect the sign on the marginal risk premium has on input demand. *We will call an input marginally risk reducing (increasing) if it increases the expected output but decreases (increases) the variance of output at the margin.*

When an input is marginally risk reducing (increasing), the marginal risk premium is positive (negative). Referring back to Figure 8.2 for the moment, we see that a positive (negative) marginal risk premium implies increased (decreased) input demand for risk-averse farmers. This is in contrast to the neutral farmer, who has a marginal risk premium of zero. Thus, for marginally risk reducing (increasing) inputs, we might expect that the more risk averse the farmer is, the larger (smaller) his demand for this specific input will be. Also, the more an input marginally affects the variance of output, the greater the impact of risk aversion on input demand will be for a given farmer with a given level of risk aversion.

To illustrate, consider a study of California cotton farmers (Farnsworth and Moffitt, 1981). It was found that irrigation, labor, and capital were risk-increasing inputs, while fertilizer and labor were risk reducing.[16] Thus we might expect that as risk aversion decreases (increases), the use of labor, capital, and irrigation will increase (decrease). The reverse would apply to labor and fertilizer. The more (less) risk averse a farmer is, the larger (smaller) his use of fertilizer and labor will be. In a similar study of Australian wool production, buildings, land, and sheep were found to be risk-increasing inputs, while water, labor, and fencing were found to be risk reducing (Griffiths and Anderson, 1982). Thus we might expect that farmers with higher levels of risk aversion operate smaller operations in the sense of having fewer sheep on a given amount of land.

Crop and Marketing Choices

Much research on economic behavior under conditions of uncertainty employs the notion of *risk efficiency*. This notion addresses the question: Are there any production alternatives that can be eliminated from consideration? Consider a crop farm having 500 acres of tillable land. Among the potential crops that could be planted on this farm are potatoes and wheat. Let us assume that the returns per acre have the following expected values and variances:

Crop	Expected return per acre	Variance of return per acre
Potatoes	$ 75	$500
Wheat	100	300

Since potatoes have a smaller expected value and larger variance than wheat production, we can conclude that potato production is inefficient relative to wheat and should be discarded from further consideration by all risk-averse farmers. Indeed, even if the expected return per acre for potatoes were $100, risk efficiency dictates that potato production be discarded from further consideration. Every risk-averse farmer will prefer the crop with the lower variance if the expected returns are equal. Thus specialization in wheat production would be expected in the situation above.

Suppose that the data above were modified as follows:

[16] These input effects were estimated using objective data. We presume that the farmer's subjective evaluation of the chances of occurrence bear a close resemblance to their objectively estimated counterparts.

Crop	Expected return per acre	Variance of return per acre
Potatoes	$150	$500
Wheat	100	300

In this case, neither the production of potatoes or wheat is inefficient for risk-averse farmers. Risk-averse farmers may choose to specialize in either crop or perhaps plant a mixture of these two crops.[17]

A risk-neutral farmer will be concerned only with the expected return per acre. Thus wheat production would be inefficient for him in the second case and potatoes would be chosen instead. A highly risk averse farmer would be preoccupied with the large variance associated with potatoes and would prefer to produce wheat. Levels of risk aversion in between these two extremes will imply that a mixture of the two crops will be planted. The efficient mixture when returns are correlated will depend on the level of risk aversion, the expected returns per acre, the variance of returns per acre, and the correlation coefficient between the two returns.

In a study of risk efficiency in production and marketing in California, it was concluded that cotton hedging involves so much production risk and other costs that hedging is generally inefficient (Beick, 1981). The efficient set of production activities under risk aversion consisted of cotton and alfalfa for high levels of risk aversion. For lower levels of risk aversion, sugar beets, a higher-risk crop, was substituted for cotton. That is, sugar beets and alfalfa are mixed in the efficient crop combination. Finally, as risk aversion decreased even further, the extremely high risk (relatively large variance of return) crop, potatoes, became an efficient production choice.

In a complementary study, the impacts of changes in the expected return per acre and the variance of return per acre on crop acreage choices were estimated (Just, 1974). For example, it was estimated that the expected total revenue per acre for wheat in the Sacramento Valley rose from about $41 per acre in 1953 to $48 per acre in 1970, while expected total revenue per acre for grain sorghum rose from $77 per acre to $94 per acre over the same period. On the basis of this information alone, we see that sorghum has become more attractive since its relative expected return had increased from $77/$41 per acre in 1953 to $94/$48 per acre by 1970. However, during the same interval, the estimated variance of wheat revenue per acre rose from $211 to $238 while sorghum's variance per acre fell from $274 to $58. Thus the revenue variability of sorghum production had fallen.

To put these data in another perspective, the *coefficient of variation*

[17] Note that the coefficient of variation for potatoes would be equal to 0.149 now instead of the initial value 0.298, which is slightly less than the coefficient of variation for wheat of 0.173.

associated with these expected values and variances are as follows:

	Coefficient of variation	
Crop	1953	1970
Wheat	0.35	0.32
Sorghum	0.21	0.08

Thus, given the decreasing relative risk of sorghum, it is little wonder that the proportion of acreage devoted to sorghum acreage increased while wheat acreage decreased.

SUMMARY

The purpose of this chapter was to present some of the basic measurement concepts that help us understand uncertainty and to indicate how the precence of uncertainty can effect specific production, marketing, and investment decisions. The major points made in this chapter can be summarized as follows:

1. An *uncertain event* where we are not sure of the outcome. Examples of uncertain variables in agriculture include crop yields and commodity prices.
2. A *portfolio* refers to the combination of investments one chooses to hold or enterprises the farmer chooses to operate. A *diversified* portfolio refers to holdings of several investments or operation of enterprises while a specialized portfolio refers to a portfolio that includes only one investment or a farm that has only one enterprise.
3. The *expected value* is a weighted average of all possible outcomes, where the weights are the *probabilities* that these outcomes have of occurring.
4. The *variance* of returns is a measure of the dispersion of the probabilities and their respective outcomes. The greater the variance, the greater the likelihood of outcomes that *deviate* from the expected value.
5. The *coefficient of variation* is equal to the square root of the variance (i.e., standard deviation) divided by the expected value. This coefficient measures the uncertainty per dollar of expected return.
6. The *correlation* between two uncertain variables reflects the degree to which they fluctuate together. A negative (positive) correlation suggests that the variables fluctuate in the opposite (same) direction. A zero cor-

relation suggests there is no relationship between the fluctuations for these two variables.

7. The *expected utility theory* postulates that the farmer behaves in a manner that maximizes his expected utility.

8. The *certainty equivalent* of a risk refers to the sum of money it would take before you would be indifferent between a risky event and accepting this certain sum of money.

9. The *risk premium* is equal to the difference between the expected change in wealth and its certainty equivalent.

10. Three cases of behavior toward risk are possible: risk averse, risk neutral, and risk preferring. A farmer may be risk averse toward some risks and risk neutral toward others.

11. The existence of uncertainty has an effect on the farmer's production decisions. For example, farmers maximizing their expected utility will employ an input up to the point where its expected marginal value product is equal to its marginal factor cost *plus* the marginal risk premium.

12. The farmer's attitude toward risk will also affect his decisions of whether to participate in federal farm programs.

13. Risk-averse farmers will also reflect their attitude toward risk in their marketing decisions, where production contracts and hedging can be used to eliminate price uncertainty.

14. The investment decisions of risk-averse farmers will also be affected by the presence of uncertain returns. *Diversification* of investments or enterprises may lower the variance of the portfolio's returns. The lower the correlation between these enterprises, the greater the benefits from diversification.

DEFINITION OF TERMS

Uncertainty: when particular economic outcomes are not certain to occur. Certainty is characterized by a probability of 1 that an event will occur.

Expected value: a weighted average of outcomes where the weights are probabilities. It is a measure of central tendency and is also called the mean or average.

Variance: a measure of the dispersion of random or uncertain outcomes. It is defined as a weighted average of deviations from the mean where the weights are probabilities.

Coefficient of variation: a measure of dispersion per unit of expected value.

It is defined as the square root of the variance (the standard deviation) divided by the expected value.

Correlation: a measure of association of two random variables by –1 and⁻ +1, where +1 (–1) represents perfect positive(negative) correlation and a value of zero represents no association of the random variables.

Risk preference: a term denoting the propensity of a person to take risks. This propensity is implicitly defined by the utility of wealth schedule.

Risk neutral: a person exhibiting constant utility of wealth. That is, the person values a given gain and loss equally in absolute value. Hence fluctuations (variance) tend to be of little or no importance as compared to the average value.

Risk averse: a person exhibiting diminishing marginal utility of wealth. This implies that a person values a given gain less than a given loss in absolute value. Hence fluctuations (variance) and expected values are of concern to the person.

Risk preferring: a person exhibiting increasing marginal utility of wealth. Such a person values increments in wealth more than decrements in wealth (in absolute value).

Expected utility theory: a prominent theory of behavior under uncertainty which postulates that people choose actions so as to maximize the expected or average utility.

Certainty equivalent: a certain sum of money that makes a person indifferent to a given risk.

Risk premium: the expected value minus the certainty equivalent. It is positive, zero, or negative as a person, is, respectively, risk averse, neutral, or risk preferring.

Basis risk: the uncertain variation in the difference between the cash value and futures price.

Yield risk: the risk associated with an unknown relationship between inputs and output in agricultural production.

Random variable: a variable whose outcome is uncertain, such as the profit from growing an acre of corn.

Portfolio: a mixture of marketing, production, or investment activities. It is generally characterized by the proportion of invested wealth allocated to each activity.

Portfolio effect: the effect that an activity has in conjunction with other returns in an investment portfolio. Thus an activity may have a high variance but low correlation, so that including it in a portfolio may reduce the variability of the portfolio's return.

REFERENCES

ANDERSON, J., J. DILLION, and B. HARDAKER, *Agricultural Decision Analysis.* Ames, Iowa: Iowa State University Press, 1980.

BEICK, P., "Portfolio Theory and the Demand for Futures: The Case of California Cotton," *American Journal of Agricultural Economics,* 1981, pp. 466–474.

DILLON, J., and P. SCANDIZZO, "Risk Attitudes of Subsistence Farmers in Northeastern Brazil: A Sampling Approach," *American Journal of Agricultural Economics,* 1978, pp. 425–435.

FARNSWORTH, R., and L. J. MOFFITT, "Cotton Production under Risk: An Analysis of Input Effects on Yield Variability and Factor Demand," *Western Journal of Agricultural Economics,* 1981, pp. 155–163.

FRIEDMAN, M. and L. J. SAVAGE, "The Utility Analysis of Choices involving Risk," *Journal of Political Economy,* 1948, pp. 279–304.

GRIFFITHS, W., and J. A. ANDERSON, "Using Time-Series and Cross-Section Data to Estimate a Production Function with Positive and Negative Marginal Risks," *Journal of the American Statistical Association,* 1982, pp. 529–536.

HALTER, A., and R. MASON, "Utility Measurement for Those Who Need to Know," *Western Journal of Agricultural Economics,* 1978, pp. 99–109.

JUST, R. E., "An Investigation of the Importance of Risk in Farmer's Decisions," *American Journal of Agricultural Economics,* 1974, pp. 14–25.

KOHLS, RICHARD, and JOSEPH UHL, *Marketing of Agricultural Products.* New York: Macmillan Publishing Company, 1981.

WESTON, J. F., and E. F. BRIGHAM, *Managerial Finance.* Hinsdale, Ill.: Dryden Press, 1978.

WONNACOTT, T. H., and R. J. WONNACOTT, *Introductory Statistics for Business and Economics,* 2nd ed. New York: John Wiley & Sons, Inc. 1976.

YOUNG, D. L., W. LIN, R. POPE, L. ROBISON, and R. SELLEY, "Risk Preferences of Agricultural Producers: Their Measurement and Use," in *Risk Management in Agriculture Behavior, Managerial and Policy Issues,* Proceedings of the Western Regional Research Project W-149, Urbana, Ill.: University of Illinois, 1979.

ADDITIONAL READINGS

BARRY, PETER J., et al., *Foundations of Risk Analysis.* Ames, Iowa: Iowa State University Press, 1983.

QUESTIONS

1. University X is known to have an outstanding graduate program in your field but only one-half of the entrants complete the program. University Y has a program of less stature, but virtually all students admitted finish the program. Would you expect individuals to select between these programs based on risk preferences?

2. Given the following data, which of these activities would you choose if you must specialize?

	Average return per dollar invested	Variance of return per dollar invested
Machinery	$1.16	0.08
Land	1.16	1.20
Training	1.16	2.00

Does this help to visualize why stocks and bonds with high fluctuations or variances must have high equilibrium average returns? (*Hint:* Would any risk-averse people invest in "training"?)

3. Calculate expected profit, the variance of profit, and the coefficient of variation for the following two activities.

Profit outcomes	Probability Activity I	Activity II
$150	1/3	1/2
100	1/2	1/6
30	1/6	1/3

4. Firm X sells steel. Its profit tends to be "pro-cyclical" (moves with the business cycle). Why might this firm want to merge with a business whose profit moves countercyclically?

5. Can a purchaser of farm products essentially "lock-in" a forward price for his products? How does this affect the price the farmer would receive?

6. We see daily on television economic prophets forecasting the future. If any one of these forecasts were believed with certainty to be correct, how could you or they take advantage of this knowledge? Why does this suggest that such forecasts have little value?

7. Speculate on which of the following inputs in agricultural production are risk reducing:
   (a) Pesticide
   (b) Labor
   (c) Machinery
   (d) Water
   How do risk-reducing inputs alter input use for risk-averse decision makers?

ADVANCED TOPICS

In Chapter 3 we introduced the topic of utility theory when describing consumer behavior under conditions of certainty. In Chapter 5 we suggested that profit maximization and utility maximization were synonymous under conditions of certainty. The most commonly held theory of behavior where uncertainty *does* exist is *expected utility theory.* This concept rests on the assumption that the farmer or consumer chooses those actions that will maximize his or her expected utility. The term "expected" denotes the fact that we have relaxed the assumption of perfect certainty in this chapter.

In this section we focus specifically on farmer behavior under conditions of uncertainty or risk. Utility will be discussed in the context of how the farmer values wealth. Let us divide wealth into two categories: (1) that portion which is *certain* at the time a decision is made, and (2) that which is viewed as *uncertain.* For example, a farm or ranch might have a known market value of $500,000. Thus this component of the farmer's wealth is certain. On the other hand, the income the farmer expects to derive from this year's production is uncertain until the commodity is sold.[18]

Figure 8.3 presents a utility curve that reflects Frank Farmgate's risk preferences.[19] Note that this particular utility function exhibits *diminishing marginal utility.* This means that Frank values an additional dollar more at low levels of wealth than he does at high levels of wealth. It should be intuitively clear why low wealth levels are of greater concern and why losses are marginally more important than gains (in absolute terms). For example, a loss of $1,000 is of more significance to the average college student than it is to a multimillionaire.

To illustrate the nature of expected utility, assume that Frank Farmgate faces two possible wealth levels if he does not purchase insurance: (1) $90,000 if there is no hail damage to his crop, and (2) $40,000 if there is hail damage to his crop. Suppose that Frank perceives there is a 20 percent chance of it hailing. Expected utility, like any expected value, is equal to the weighted average of all possible events. Frank's expected utility in this example would be $280.[20] This level of expected utility is denoted by point *Y* in Figure 8.3.

What level of wealth can Frank expect if he does *not buy* hail insurance? On average, his expected wealth would be $80,000 (i.e., $90,000 × 0.8 + $40,000 × 0.2). Thus the expected loss from hail damage would be

---

[18] This ignores the possibility of forward or futures contracting.

[19] For illustration purposes, we have expressed Frank's preferences as a function of the square root of wealth (i.e., $U = \sqrt{W}$, where U represents utility and W represents wealth).

[20] Frank Farmgate's expected utility in this instance was found as follows: $280 = 0.8 \times \sqrt{90,000} + 0.2 \times \sqrt{40,000}$.

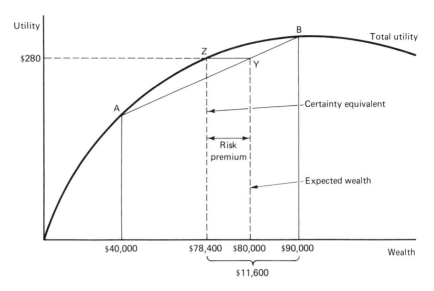

Figure 8.3 *A Risk-Averse Farmer's Utility Curve.* This utility curve reflects the attitude toward risk of someone who is risk averse. While the farmer in this example could receive a wealth of $90,000, there is a 20 percent chance of a loss due to hail damage that would lower his wealth to $40,000. The certainty equivalent, or value of wealth that would leave this farmer as equally well off as he would be by facing this uninsured risk, is equal to $78,400. The difference between what he could receive ($90,000) and the certainty equivalent ($78,400) is known as the risk premium ($11,600). If the cost of full coverage hail insurance carries a premium of $11,600, this farmer would be indifferent as to whether he should buy insurance. If the premium were less than $11,600, he would not buy the insurance.

$10,000 (i.e., $90,000 − $80,000). If full coverage hail insurance were available so that any loss would be covered, Frank could afford to pay an insurance premium of up to $10,000 and expect to break even (i.e., the point where the expected loss from hail damage equals the value of insurance premium).

If Frank Farmgate were interested only in expected wealth, he would buy insurance if the premium was *less than or equal to* the expected loss from hail damage. Would Frank ever be willing to pay *more than* $10,000 in insurance premium?

The Certainty Equivalent

To answer this question, we can focus on the value of wealth we know for certain would leave Frank Farmgate as *equally well off* as he would be facing the uninsured risk of hail damage. This certain sum of money is called the *certainty equivalent.* The certainty equivalent of a risk is the sum of money known with certainty that makes a person indifferent between a risky situation and having this sum of money. In general, the value of the certainty equivalent will depend on the farmer's level of certain wealth versus uncertain wealth as well as his attitude toward risk.

To illustrate, let us begin by varying the chance of hail damage between 100 and 0 percent. This will cause Mr. Farmgate's *expected wealth* to vary between $90,000 and $40,000. The *expected utility* for these combinations are given by points on line *AB* and the vertical axis in Figure 8.3. Their *certainty equivalent* is then found by (1) reading up from the expected wealth on the horizontal axis to a particular point on line *AB,* (2) moving horizontally from this point to the utility curve and (3) reading down to the horizontal axis again to find the corresponding certainty equivalent. For example, we showed earlier that the expected value of wealth when the chance of hail is 20 percent is $80,000. Reading up from $80,000 on the horizontal axis to point *Y* on line *AB* (which indicates the expected utility of $280 discussed earlier), reading over to the utility curve at point *Z,* and then down to the horizontal axis again, we see that the certainty equivalent would be $78,400. Thus Figure 8.3 suggests that $78,400 known with certainty would provide the *same* expected utility as facing the uninsured risk.[21]

Now let us assume that the insurance premium for full coverage hail insurance is $11,600. Would Frank prefer to purchase the insurance? Since the premium in this instance is exactly equal to the difference between receiving $90,000 and the certainty equivalent of $78,400, he would be *indifferent* between purchasing the insurance and not purchasing the insurance.

The Risk Premium

You may have noticed that the certainty equivalent of the risk in the example above was always lower than the expected wealth. When the chance of hail damage occurring was 20 percent, we said that Frank Farmgate's expected wealth was $80,000 (i.e., $0.20 \times \$40,000 + 0.80 \times \$90,000$) and that his certainty equivalent was $78,400. We are now in a position to define the risk premium: *the risk premium is equal to expected wealth minus the certainty equivalent.* In our example, the risk premium would be $1,600 (i.e., $80,000 – $78,400), as indicated in Figure 8.3. It represents the added value above the expected loss that Frank is willing to pay for insurance.[22] Note that for a

---

[21] When the prospective event is known for certain, the chance of this event occurring is 100 percent and all other events would have a zero percent chance of occurring. Hence expected utility and utility are equal.

[22] Expected loss is $10,000, while the maximum insurance premium Frank would be willing to pay is $11,600.

utility function which is bowed downward like Mr. Farmgate's illustrated in Figure 8.3, the risk premium is always *positive*. The risk premium would have been *zero* if his utility curve had been a straight line and *negative* if his utility curve has instead been bowed upward. These three cases correspond to what economists refer to as (1) risk-averse behavior, (2) risk-neutral behavior, and (3) risk-preferring behavior, respectively.

part III
FARM MARKET AND GENERAL EQUILIBRIUM

9

MARKETS AND THE MARKET

PRICE

Farm product and input markets and the intitutions that facilitate the flow of these goods and services through market channels provide an important bridge between farm businesses and such groups as the consumers of food and fiber products and the manufacturers of farm inputs. These markets, for example, send important signals to farm businesses on (1) *what* commodities they should produce, (2) *how much* of each commodity they should produce, (3) *how* these commodities should be produced, and (4) *where* these commodities should be distributed.

The marketing of farm products and inputs necessarily involves the services of many agribusiness entities which perform one or more market functions. For example, recent statistics reveal that the services of 8 to 10 million people are required to store, transport, process, and merchandize the output of farm businesses in this country. Another 3 million people are involved in providing the seed, fertilizer, and other inputs needed by farm businesses in their production operations. Approximately 140,000 of the latter group are involved in the production of farm tractors and other machinery and equipment purchased by farm businesses each year.[1] These statistics suggest that approximately one out of every five jobs in the private

[1] As further evidence of the linkages between the farm business sector and the rest of the economy discussed earlier in Chapter 2, it should be noted that it takes another 40,000 people to produce the steel necessary to manufacture this machinery and equipment.

sector of the U.S. economy is in one way or another tied to this nation's food and fiber system.

The purpose of this chapter is to introduce the field of marketing and illustrate how market prices are determined under different market settings. We shall begin with a discussion of how market prices are determined under conditions of (1) perfect competition and (2) imperfect competition. This discussion will build on the material presented in Chapter 3 (consumer behavior), Chapter 5 (economics of production), and Chapter 6 (farm marketing decisions). Following this discussion will be individual sections that focus on the concept of marketing margins and the role played by middlemen, the regulation of agricultural markets, and the role played by agricultural cooperatives in this country. We shall postpone until Chapter 10 a discussion of the impact of the relatively inelastic nature of the demand for farm products on farm revenue and the need for farm programs.

MARKET PRICE UNDER PERFECT COMPETITION

Firms in the economy can be grouped into two general categories: (1) perfectly competitive firms, and (2) imperfectly competitive firms. The latter group of firms encompasses a variety of firms with different degrees of competitiveness. In this section we concentrate on the determination of the market price in a perfectly competitive market.

Characteristics of Perfect Competition

What does it take to have a "perfectly competitive" market situation? Before we discuss how prices are determined in these markets, let us look at the economic environment we are talking about. A market structure can be classified as perfectly competitive if the following conditions hold:

1. The product sold by firms in a sector is *homogeneous.* In other words, the product sold by one firm is a *perfect substitute* for the product sold by the other firms. This enables buyers in the market to choose among a large number of sellers.
2. Any firm can enter or leave the sector without encountering serious barriers. That is, resources must be free to move into the sector without encountering barriers to entry. The same condition holds for resources leaving the sector.
3. There must be a large number of sellers and buyers in the market. No single buyer or seller should have a disproportionate influence on price.
4. Adequate information must exist for all participants regarding prices, quantities, qualities, sources of supply, and so on.

When all four conditions hold, we can say the market's structure is *perfectly competitive.* Firms participating in this market are also by definition perfectly competitive. Each firm, for example, is a *price taker,* or takes the price of the product as given. The discussion of producer behavior in Chapter 5 implicitly assumed the existence of perfect competition by assuming that the demand curve perceived by each farmer was completely horizontal. The farm business sector comes about as close as any sector in the U.S. economy to satisfying the conditions of perfect competition.

Determination of Market Price

You will recall from Chapter 5 that the *firm's* short-run supply curve is equal to that portion of its marginal cost curve which lies above the firm's average variable cost curve. We also said that the *sector's* short-run supply curve is given by the horizontal summation of the individual firm supply curves. Once we know the sector's supply curve and demand curve (discussed in Chapter 3), we are in a position to determine the equilibrium market price.

The equilibrium price in a perfectly competitive market is established by the point of intersection of the sector's demand and supply curve. Let *DD* represent the total demand "schedule" or curve for the sector's product and *SS* represent the total supply "schedule" or curve for all firms in the sector. Panel a in Figure 9.1 shows that the equilibrium price in this market would equal to P_e. At this price, firms would be willing to supply quantity Q_e and the buyers of this product would desire to purchase quantity Q_e. Thus P_e and only P_e is the price per unit that will "clear the market." There would be no excess quantity supplied or *surplus* like that which would have existed at price P_s (see panel b). And there would be no excess quantity demanded or *shortage* like that which would have existed at price P_d (see panel c). More will be said about shortages and surpluses later in this section when we focus on market disequilibrium.

Shifts in either the demand curve or the supply curve will result in a new equilibrium market price. Four possible events can occur which affect the market equilibrium price and quantity: (1) demand increases, shifting the demand curve to the right; (2) demand decreases, shifting the demand curve to the left; (3) supply increases, shifting the supply curve to the right; and (4) supply decreases, shifting the supply curve to the left. The effects of each situation on the equilibrium price that clears the market are illustrated in Figure 9.2. In panel a, for example, we see that an increase in demand (perhaps consumer disposable increased) will result in a higher market price (P_e^*). Buyers will now demand—and firms will supply—a quantity equal to Q_e^* instead of Q_e. The opposite effect occurs when demand decreases (see panel b).

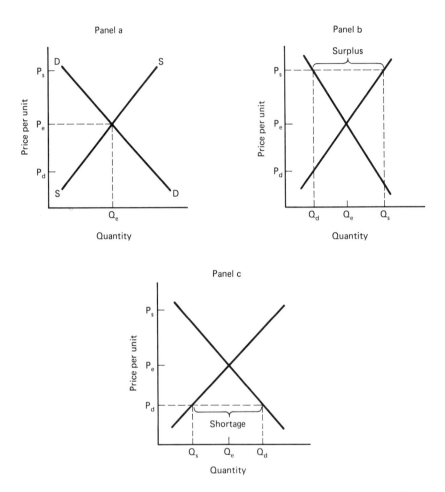

Figure 9.1 *Equilibrium Price, Surpluses, and Shortages.* The equilibrium price in a competitive market is given by the intersection of the market demand and supply curves. As shown in panel a, this would result in a price of P_e and quantity Q_e. If, instead, the price were equal to P_s, as shown in panel b, producers would be willing to supply more than consumers would demand. Not surprisingly, this phenomenon is referred to as a surplus. If the price were instead equal to P_d, the quantity demanded by consumers would be greater than the quantity producers would be willing to supply. This excess demand situation is commonly referred to as a shortage. Thus only quantity Q_e would clear the market.

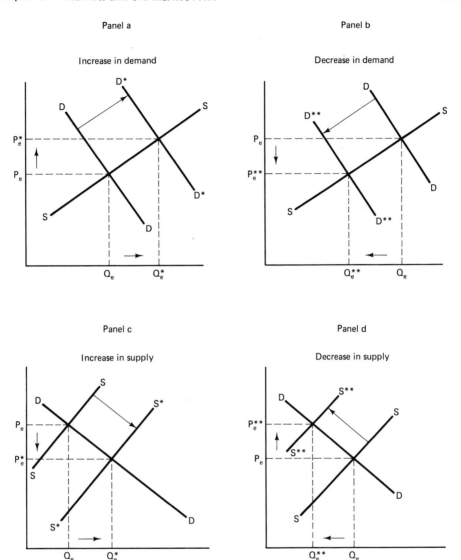

Figure 9.2 *Price Effects of Shifts in Supply and Demand.* It is important to distinguish between changes in supply or demand and changes in the quantity supplied or demanded. An increase in demand depicted in panel a increases the equilibrium price to P_e^* and quantity supplied to Q_e^*. Conversely, a decrease in demand in panel b shows the equilibrium price falling to P_e^{**} and quantity supplied falling to Q_e^{**}, Panel c shows that an increase in supply lowers the equilibrium price to P_e^* and increases the quantity demanded to Q_e^*. A decrease in supply in panel d raises the equilibrium price to P_e^{**} and lowers the quantity demanded by consumers to Q_e^{**}.

Turning to supply, let us assume that the supply of the product increases, or that the supply curve shifts to the right. Panel c in Figure 9.2 illustrates that this shift will lead to a decline in the market-clearing price from P_e to P_e^*. At this new price, firms will supply—and buyers will demand—a quantity equal to Q_e^*.[2] Panel d in Figure 9.2 shows that the opposite outcome will occur if there is a decrease in supply.

The elasticity of the demand and supply curves—a concept covered in earlier chapters—plays an important role in determining how much the equilibrium price will change if demand or supply changes. For example, the more inelastic the demand curve, the greater the rise (fall) in the market price will be for a given decrease (increase) in supply. The relatively inelastic nature of the demand for farm products, coupled with a volatile supply curve that can shift to the right or the left depending on the vagaries of weather, helps explain the high variability of farm income that we see in the farm business sector from one period to the next. More will be said about this when we discuss the traditional "farm problem" in Chapter 10.

Market Disequilibrium

At prices *above* the market-clearing price P_e, there would be an excess quantity supplied by farmers, or a *surplus*. At prices *below* the market-clearing price, an excess quantity demanded or *shortage* would exist. For example, panel b in Figure 9.1 shows that at price P_s, buyers would wish to purchase Q_d while sellers would want to supply Q_s. The difference between these two quantities $(Q_s - Q_d)$ represents the surplus available on the market at the price P_s. This suggests that the market is in disequilibrium rather than equilibrium since the market has not been cleared at this price. The opposite is illustrated in panel c of this figure. At a price of P_d, buyers would wish to purchase quantity Q_d while sellers would only want to supply quantity Q_s. Thus a shortage equal to $Q_d - Q_s$ would exist in the market at a price of P_d.

The existence of these disequilibrium situations will modify over time if prices and quantities are *free* to seek their equilibrium levels. If a *surplus* exists, for example, the inventories of unsold production will be unintentionally high. Farmers will have incurred costs but received no revenues for this unplanned inventory buildup. As long as these inventories remain unsold, farmers will also be incurring storage costs in one form or another. Since they are not maximizing their profits at this point, farmers will find it profitable to decrease their level of production and accept a lower price for their inventories. This adjustment process will stop after prices have fallen

---

[2] This is a good point to reemphasize the difference between the "change in demand" and the "change in quantity demanded." Since we are simply moving along the demand curve in panel c, there has been a change in the quantity demanded $(Q_e$ to $Q_e^*)$ but no change in demand. The latter phenomenon requires a *shift* in the demand curve.

from P_s to P_e.[3] If a *shortage* exists, buyers would compete for available supplies by offering to pay higher prices. This will encourage farmers to raise and market more of this commodity. This adjustment process will stop after prices have risen from P_d to P_e. At this point, the quantity demanded will be exactly equal to the quantity supplied, and market equilibrium will be restored.

The adjustment processes discussed above may suggest that the quantities demanded and supplied are both determined by *current* prices. In the farm business sector, however, adjustment to market equilibrium takes time. One reason is the biological nature of the production process itself. Once the crop has been planted, for example, little can be done to adjust the supply response of farm businesses until the next production season.[4] Furthermore, when farmers plant their crop, they do not know what the market price will eventually be when they sell their crop several months later.[5]

Let us assume for the moment that farmers base their production plans for *this year* on *last year's* price. This means that price and quantity are now sequentially rather than simultaneously determined. The price *last* year determines *this* year's production response. This year's quantity marked, however, will affect *this* year's price, which will affect *next* year's production, and so on.[6] If prices were high last year, for example, farmers under free-market conditions would respond by expanding their production activities with the anticipation of eventually marketing more output. The increased level of production will lead to lower prices, all other things constant. This pattern of price and quantity responses is therefore *cyclical in nature* over time.

To illustrate this market behavior, let us examine panel a in Figure 9.3. Given the demand and supply curves *DD* and *SS*, let's suppose that the price

---

[3] As we will discuss in Chapter 10, the price support system for selected farm commodities establishes a *minimum* price for these products. Farmers who cannot market their output at this price can in effect sell their surplus to the government.

[4] Livestock production response is also limited by biological factors. It takes time, for example, to build up beef cow herds in the cow–calf industry in response to an increase in the retail demand for beef. As a result of these and other factors, hog prices as well as cattle prices typically exhibit a cyclical behavior. For example, the hog cycle is generally thought to be four years (i.e., it takes four years to move from one price peak to the next).

[5] Farmers can determine the price they will eventually receive in some cases through the use of one or more of the marketing options discussed in Chapter 5. Futures market contracts, for example, allow a wheat farmer to lock-in a forward price for his wheat. Many wheat farmers as well as other farmers, however, choose instead to rely on the spot market because they feel accepting a forward price for their product will limit their potential revenue.

[6] The demand and supply functions in this instance would be given by $P_t = f(Q_t)$ and $Q_t = f(P_{t-1})$, respectively. The response to last period's price in the supply function is thus different from the response to current price assumed thus far.

Panel a

Panel b

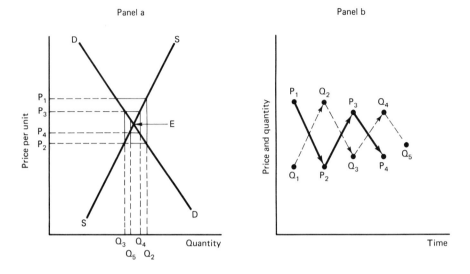

Panel c

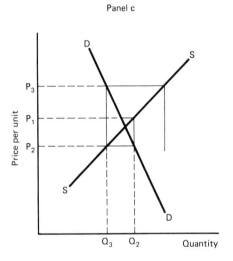

Figure 9.3 *Converging and Diverging Cobweb Market Behavior.* The prices for farm products are known for their cyclical behavior. This can occur because the adjustment to equilibrium is not simultaneous (i.e., current prices influence current production and current production influences current prices). Farmers, for example, may respond to last year's prices when planning this year's crop. High prices last year therefore would increase the quantity supplied this year, which lowers current prices. This pattern of price and quantity fluctuations is referred to as cobweb behavior. Panel a illustrates a "converging" cobweb, which shows prices and quantities converging to point E. The price and quantity fluctuations over time are illustrated in panel b. Note here that each price and quantity fluctuates less than it did the period before. Finally, panel c illustrates the nature of a "diverging" cobweb behavior, where prices and quantities are diverging away from point E.

of the commodity last year (year 1) is equal to P_1. Since farmers base their production for year 2 on P_1, they will produce Q_2 in year 2. This quantity, however, will cause prices in year 2 to fall to P_2. Farmers will respond to this lower price in year 3 by producing only Q_3, and so on.

This behavior of prices and quantities over time is referred to as a *cobweb* pattern after the cobweb-like nature of the solid lines tracing the movements of prices and quantities. Panel a in Figure 9.3 illustrates the nature of a *converging cobweb*. Here prices and quantities will eventually converge to a market equilibrium at point E. This cobweb pattern will occur when the slope of the *supply curve* is *steeper* or *more inelastic* than the slope of the demand curve. Panel b shows the cyclical pattern of prices and quantities associated with this converging cobweb. The quantity peak Q_4, for example, is lower than peak Q_2, and the price peak P_1 is higher than peak P_3. Thus, these oscillations are *dampening* over time as the market price converges to equilibrium. Panel b also represents the case where the length of the cycle (i.e., the time between peaks in the market) is two years. Panel c illustrates the nature of a *diverging cobweb,* which occurs when the slope of the *demand curve* is *steeper* or *more inelastic* than the slope of the supply curve.[7]

Events causing changes in demand or supply can cause an interruption to these cycles and lead to a new set of market adjustments over time. As we will discuss later in Chapter 10, federal programs exist for some commodities which are designed to modify the booms and busts associated with fluctuating prices and quantities.

MARKET PRICE UNDER IMPERFECT COMPETITION

Up to this point we have assumed that the conditions required for perfect competition set forth at the beginning of this chapter exist in the marketplace. The economy does not consist entirely of perfectly competitive firms, however. Although farm businesses generally satisfy the conditions of perfect competition, most of the firms farmers do business with in the food and fiber system do not. In this section we examine several forms of imperfectly competitive market structures and cite examples of each form in the U.S. food and fiber systems.

We can classify imperfectly competitive forms of market structure by (1) the number of firms, and (2) the nature of their product. For example, we said earlier that perfect competition is characterized by many firms in a sector producing and marketing a standardized product. We also included the proviso that there are no barriers to entry or exit. The farm business sector is characterized by many firms selling a standardized product. Furthermore, farm businesses are *relatively* free to enter or exit the sector as they wish.

[7] A persistent cobweb would occur if the demand and supply curves have identical slopes. This means that the market would continue to oscillate around the market's equilibrium, never converging or diverging.

Monopolistic Competition

If there are a large number of firms (a somewhat smaller number than exists in the case of perfect competition) selling a nonstandardized or *differentiated* product, we would say that *monopolistic competition* exists.[8] Retail farm input supply firms differentiating their products (e.g., branded feed supplements and branded hybrid seeds)—in the eyes of farm businesses—exemplify this type of market structure.[9]

Monopolistic competitors face the same average total cost *(ATC)* and marginal cost constraints as perfect competitors. By differentiating their product, however, monopolistic competitors face a downward-sloping demand curve (and a marginal revenue curve that reflects the change in total revenue at each output level).[10] Product differentiation can be accomplished by modifying the firm's product or through advertising and sales promotion activities. Such activities can be found in most markets in this country. The better the firm is at product differentiation, the greater its monopoly power will be.

The equilibrium values for price and quantity under monopolistic competition are determined by the intersection of the marginal cost curve *(MC)* and the marginal revenue curve *(MR)*. As shown in panel a in Figure 9.4, this occurs at quantity Q_e and price P_e.

A gap between the demand curve *(DD)* and the average total cost curve *(ATC)* at the point where monopolistic competitors are equating their marginal cost *(MC)* and marginal revenue *(MR)* represents their economic profits or losses. The existence of profits (losses) would result in the entry (exit) of additional monopolistic competitors until these monopolistic competitors found themselves making zero economic profits. Thus the situation depicted in panel a in Figure 9.4 suggests that the market is in *long-run equilibrium* since there is no gap between the demand curve and the average total cost curve at Q_e. Note that the equilibrium quantity here is less than what would have occurred under perfect competition. This is because monopolistic competitors choose to operate to the *left* of the point where the *MC* curve inter-

---

[8] A suffix "poly" refers to sellers, while "sony" refers to buyers. The prefix "mono" means one, while "oli" means few.

[9] The corollary to this form of market structure on the demand side of the market is referred to as *monoponistic competition,* where there are many buyers who perceive differences in the products they have to choose from.

[10] The relationship between the demand curve and marginal revenue curve is tied to the elasticity of demand along the demand curve. For example, *MR* is zero at the point of unit elasticity of demand (i.e., –1.0). Up to that point, the imperfectly competitive firm's total revenue was increasing as output increased. For the perfect competitor, $P = MR$ since the demand curve was perfectly flat. Since monopolistic competitors face downward-sloping demand, this is no longer true. Thus they must be aware of their *MR* curves declining nature and the possibility of negative *MR* at lower points on their demand curve.

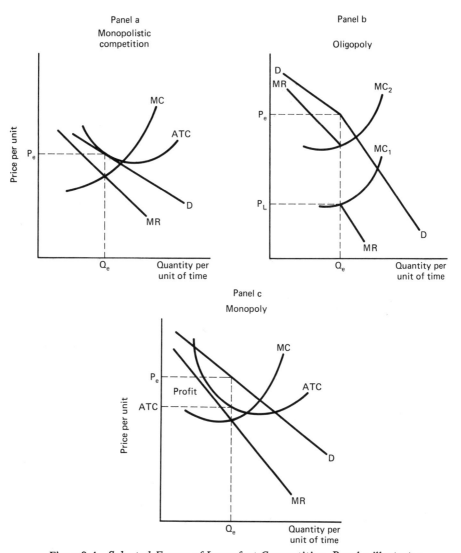

Figure 9.4 *Selected Forms of Imperfect Competition.* Panel a illustrates
the equilibrium price and quantity under conditions of monopolistic
competition. Monopolistic competitors equate marginal cost and marginal revenue. The situation depicted in panel a represents long-run
equilibrium since there are no economic profits to encourage further
entrants. Panel b illustrates the equilibrium price and quantity under
pure oligopoly. The fact that oligopolists match all decreases but not all
increases in price leads to a "kinked" demand curve. If the objective of
these oligopolists is to maximize their joint profits, their market behavior would instead take the form illustrated in panel c. These firms
would simply divide the monopoly profits among themselves. Finally,
a monopolist also equates marginal costs and revenue. The price charged
to consumers at this equilibrium quantity is read off the demand curve.
The monopolist differs from monopolistic competitors in that the
monopolist strives to block others from entering the market place.

sects the minimum point on the *ATC* curve. Monopolistic competition is therefore less efficient from society's viewpoint than perfect competition; its price is higher than marginal cost and its average total costs are higher than the minimum point on its *ATC* curve.

Oligopoly

If there are, instead, just a few firms selling a standardized product, a *pure oligopoly* is said to exist. These firms typically recognize their mutual inter-dependence and act in response to how they expect their fellow oligopolists to act. This is in contrast to perfect competitors, who ignore the actions of other firms because they expect they can sell all their output without affecting the going market price.

Since an oligopoly exists whenever a small number of firms control a large part of the total output in a particular industry, we can examine the existence of oligopolies by looking at the degree of industry concentration. For example, if there are 100 firms in an industry but only four firms account for a large share the industry's output, we would conclude that an oligopoly exists. The automobile industry and aircraft manufacturing industry are two nonagricultural examples of ologopolies. In agriculture, the farm machinery and equipment industry can be classified as an oligopoly since as we said in Chapter 2, the top four brands account for about 80 percent of all two-wheel tractor sales and 89 percent of all combine sales.

Because oligopolists take account of the reaction of other oligopolists, there is no single demand curve facing a particular oligopolist. Let us assume for the moment that oligopolies match all price *decreases* by their fellow oligopolists (they do not want to be undersold) but not all price *increases* (they want to capture a greater market share). The result of this assumption is a "kinked" demand curve like the one illustrated in panel b of Figure 9.4. At a price of P_e, the oligoplist firm would assume that if it raised its prices, other frims would *not* follow suit. Hence this portion of the demand curve *DD* is relatively *elastic*. If the oligopolist firm lowered its price below P_e, however, it would assume that other oligopolists would follow suit. Therefore, the demand curve below P_e is less elastic than the portion lying above P_e. The kink in the total demand curve occurs at the point corresponding to price P_e. The marginal revenue curve would be discontinuous between prices P_e and P_1 at output Q_e. Any shifts in the oligopolist's marginal costs between MC_1 and MC_2 will not cause their prices or output to change. The marginal revenue curve to the left of Q_e curve is associated with the portion of the kinked demand curve lying above price P_e. The marginal revenue curve to the right of Q_e, however, is associated with the less elastic portion of the demand curve lying to the right of Q_e and below P_e. In meeting demand along the lower segment of the kinked demand curve, the oligopolist firm will be *maintaining* his market share. If oligopolists respond under the assumptions outlined, there would be a tendency for prices to remain at P_e. If so, the oligopolist will earn an economic profit per unit of P_e minus his average total cost of production.

For a variety of reasons, including the inherent uncertainty of knowing how others will respond, oligopolists facing similar demand and cost conditions may instead behave in a collusive fashion (i.e., to arrange to charge the same price for their output). Their objective would be to maximize their *joint* profits. The prices and quantities observed when this occurs will be much the same as those charged by a pure monopolist, as we will soon see. Each oligopolist would charge price P_e, product its predetermined share of Q_e, and share in the monopoly profits. The market structure underlying this form of oligopolistic behavior would be identical to the monopolistic case presented in panel c.[11]

Pure Monopoly

If there is only *one* firm selling a unique product, we refer to this firm as a *monopolist* or a *pure monopolist*. A rural gas station 100 miles from the next gas station can be thought of as a monopolist. If you are low on gas, you have no choice but to buy gas at the prices established by its owner. Such a firm actively seeks to block other firms from entering the market. It strives to be the single supplier of the product.

The long-run equilibrium values for price and quantity under a pure monopoly are depicted in panel c of Figure 9.4. The monopolist will maximize profits by operating where MC equals MR and then determining the highest price for the firm's product. Panel c shows that this occurs at output rate Q_e and price per unit P_e. If the monopolist produces at a lower rate, the firm's profits would not be maximized (i.e., it could achieve additional profits by expanding its production rate to Q_e). If the monopolist produced at a higher rate, the costs of producing the additional units would exceed the revenue received from their sale.[12]

Economic profits will exist under a pure monopoly in the long run

---

[11] If there are a few number of firms buying a standardized product, they are referred to as a *pure oligopsony*. A pure oligopolist therefore participates on the supply side of a standardized product market, while the pure oligopsonist participates on the demand side. In those instances where a few firms are selling a *differentiated* product or buying a *differentiated* product, we would refer to them as *differentiated* oligopolies and oligopsonies, respectively.

[12] A smart monopolist will seek ways to discriminate efficiently among the buyers of the firm's products. In practice, price discrimination requires separating buyers into groups according to the elasticity of their demand curves. The monopolist then charges those with a less elastic demand curve more per unit than it does those with higher elasticities of demand. By doing so, the monopolist would earn a greater profit than that earned when all customers are charged the same prices per unit.

since there are likely both economic and legal barriers preventing other firms from entering the sector. The economic barriers might consist of prohibitive production costs or product prices, or outright restraints of trade. The legal barriers, on the other hand, might include patents on the design of specific products. Other laws may permit a group of firms to act as a monopolist. Electric power companies and telephone companies are two often-cited examples of pure monopolies. In agriculture, milk marketing orders permit the setting of minimum farmer price and allows for controls of the flow of products to specific markets (fluid milk versus manufactured milk markets). This enables dairy farmers to receive a total price they would not have otherwise received.[13] More will be said about marketing orders when we address farm program policy in Chapter 10.

Comparison of Market Structures

Table 9.1 summarizes the basic features of both the perfectly competitive and imperfectly competitive forms of market structure. For example, this table describes the number of sellers, ease of entry and exit, the ability to set market prices, the existence of economic profits in long-run equilibrium, and the extent of product differentiation. It also cites some examples of each market structure in the U.S. food and fiber system.

As with the oligopolist and monopolistic competitor, the pure monopolist will produce at a lower rate than would occur under perfect competition. Each of these imperfectly competitive firms prefers to operate to the left of the minimum point on their average total cost curve, where long-run equilibrium under perfect competition occurs. Thus there is a cost to society associated with all forms of imperfect competiton. The quantity supplied is smaller, unemployment of resources higher, and prices are higher than under perfect competition.[14]

MARKET INTERMEDIARIES

Farm businesses are linked with consumers by a complex marketing system for food and fiber products. Consumers spend over $200 billion for U.S. farm-produced foods. Approximately 70 percent of this total went toward moving this food from the farm to the consumers' table. This food had to be assembled, inspected, graded, stored, processed, packaged, transported,

---

[13] If only one *buyer* exists for a product, he or she is referred to as a *monopsonist*. A monopsonist has a negotiating edge over sellers in the market and actively seeks to block other buyers from entering the market.

[14] The effects that imperfect competition have on the economic well-being of producers and consumers are addressed in the Advanced Topics section at the end of this chapter.

Item	Market Structure			
	Perfect competition	Monopolistic competition	Oligopolies	Pure monopolies
Number of sellers	Numerous	Many	Few	One
Ease of entry or exit	Unrestricted	Unrestricted	Partially restricted	Restricted
Ability to set market price	None	Some	Some	Absolute
Long-run economic profits possible	No	No	Yes	Yes
Product differentiation	None	Yes	Yes	Product unique
Examples of U.S. food and fiber system	Corn producers	Feed manufacturers	Manufacturers of farm tractors	Fluid milk market

TABLE 9.1 ALTERNATIVE FORMS OF MARKET STRUCTURE. This table summarizes many of the features of the different market structures discussed in this chapter: (1) perfect competition, (2) monopolistic competition, (3) oligopolies, and (4) pure monopolies. The examples of each given at the bottom of this table should help you visualize their nature. There are numerous corn producers, for example, who sell an undifferentiated product and who individually have no ability to influence market prices. As indicated in Chapter 2, the four largest manufacturers of farm tractors account for 80 percent of total sales. These manufacturers do try to differentiate their product (e.g., different colors, model styles, etc.) and have some ability to influence the price of their product. Finally, milk producers collectivity, through federal milk marketing orders, behave as a pure monopoly and have absolute market power in setting the price for milk products.

and sold at the wholesale and retail levels. More than 400 million tons of food products flow annually over 201,000 miles of railroads, 3.2 million miles of intercity highways, and 26,000 miles of improved waterways. There are over 8,000 different forms of food and fiber that flow through supermarkets.

Involved at various stages of the flow of food and fiber products to their ultimate consumer is a network of intermediaries which facilitate this flow in one way or another. These intermediaries, or "middlemen" as they are frequently called, come in various forms. The purpose of this section is to identify the various types of market intermediaries between farm businesses and the consumers of food and fiber products and to illustrate the concept of marketing margins.

Middlemen

Middlemen are those persons or firms that perform one or more marketing functions associated with the buying and selling of goods as they move through marketing channels from farm businesses to their ultimate consumer. These functions may be directly related to either the actual buying and selling activities (exchange functions), the storage, transportation, and processing of food and fiber products (physical functions), or the standardization, financing, risk bearing, and market information activities (facilitating functions).

Figure 9.5 illustrates the nature of the product flows in the U.S. food and fiber system. After raw agricultural products are produced, they can go in any one of three different directions. They can be sold directly to consumers (e.g., roadside stands). They can be consumed directly by the farm household. The overwhelming share of farm production, however, is trans-

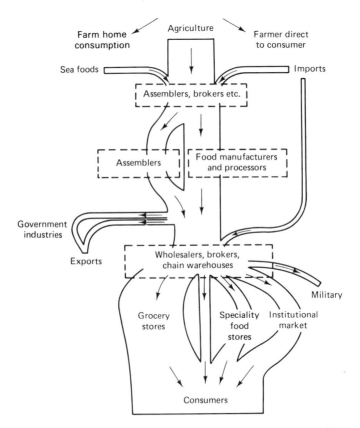

Figure 9.5 *Product Flow from Source to Destination.* This figure illustrates the channels through which food and fiber products flow. The width of these channels reflects their relative magnitude. For example, almost all raw agricultural products flow to brokers and other middlemen, who either pass it on to wholesalers or sell it to manufacturers and processors. The final middlemen, who interact directly with the consumer, include grocery stores and specialty food stores.

Speculative middlemen.   Speculative middlemen differ from merchant middlemen in that they do less in the way of merchandising and instead actively seek out and bear price risk in the hope of making a profit from favorable fluctuations in commodity prices. They often buy and resell commodities over a relatively short period of time (days). It is not unusual for a grain trader to buy and sell grain several times during the same day if price fluctuations are perceived to be favorable.

Food processors and manufacturers.   These middlemen may not only perform their obvious role of transforming raw farm products into final goods, but may also perform some of the functions identified above for merchant and agent middlemen to control their costs. For example, a meat packer may act as its own purchasing agent by buying feed livestock directly from farm businesses. They may also serve as their own wholesaler by dealing directly with retail stores. These processors and manufacturers often also communicate directly to the ultimate consumer of the product by advertising and other promotional means.

Facilitative organizations.   These organizations serve a variety of functions, including the gathering and distribution of market information as well as the establishment and enforcement of policies and standards for their trade. Grain exchanges, stockyards, and trade associations all represent facilitative organizations. Their income comes from fees paid for the use of their facilities or services.

Marketing Costs

The cost of marketing food and fiber products in the United States is a significant portion of the total price paid for these products by consumers, as you will soon see. Before proceeding further, we should define some key terms used when evaluating marketing costs.

The difference between the price consumers pay for final agricultural products and the price the farm business receives for raw agricultural products is called the *marketing margin*. To illustrate this concept, we must differentiate between the retail demand for food and fiber and farm level demand for raw agricultural products, which is *derived* from the retail demand. Let D_r in Figure 9.6 denote the demand for farm products at the retail level and let D_f denote the derived demand for farm products at the farm level. Finally, let S_r and S_f represent the supply of farm products at the retail and farm levels, respectively. An analysis of this figure suggests that P_{re} is the equilibrium price at the retail level and P_{fe} is the equilibrium price at the farm level. The difference between these two prices, or P_{re} minus P_{fe}, is the marketing margin. The shaded area represents the total

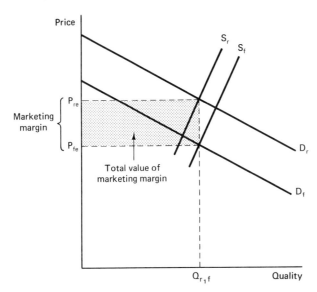

Figure 9.6 *Concept of Marketing Margin.* The marketing margin is equal to the difference between the retail price (P_{re}) and the farm price (P_{fe}) for food and fiber products. This margin represents the returns to the various forms of middlemen for their services. The shaded area represents the total value of the marketing margin. It represents the difference between total consumer expenditures on food and fiber products and what farmers received for the equivalent farm product.

value of the marketing margin, or the per unit value of this marketing margin multiplied by the quantities sold. This is the difference between total consumer expenditures on food and what farm business received for the equivalent farm products. This shaded area can be viewed in terms of the returns to factors of production (i.e., wages, interest, rent, and profits). Alternatively, the market margin can be viewed as the returns to middlemen (retailers, wholesalers, processors, brokers, commission men, and specific facilitating institutions) for their services.

The U.S. Department of Agriculture gathers and publishes a series called the *marketing bill* which is roughly equivalent to the total value of the marketing margin for *all* farm products. This marketing bill can be examined several different ways. For example, panel a in Figure 9.7 illustrates the growing nature of the marketing bill during the 1971–1984 period. Much of this growth can be attributed to rising costs of labor, transportation, food-packaging materials, and other inputs used in marketing relative to the growth in the revenue received by farm businesses. For example, about two-thirds of the increase in consumer expenditures on food during this period consisted of increases in the marketing bill.

Finally, panel b in Figure 9.7 illustrates the recent importance of the various components of the marketing bill. As you can see, 45 percent of the total was accounted for by labor costs. While part of the rise in the labor cost component was due to rising wage rates, the number of persons involved in the marketing process increased by about 30 percent during this period. Packaging and transportation costs together accounted for an additional 20 percent. Contrary to the popular belief that middlemen reap huge profits, only 6 percent of the marketing bill was accounted for by corporate profits.

Panel a

Marketing bill, farm value, and expenditures
for farm foods

$ billion

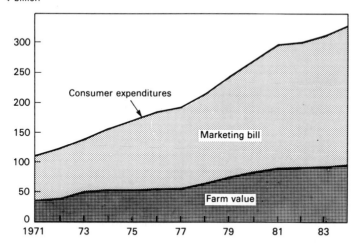

Components of the farm-food marketing bill

Panel b

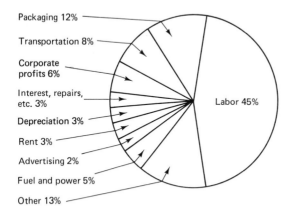

Figure 9.7 *Alternative Views of the Marketing Bill.* The marketing bill represents the total value of the marketing margin for all farm products. Panel a shows that the marketing bill has represented an increasingly larger component of total consumer expenditures for food items. Panel b shows the distribution of this marketing bill between various categories of expenditures and profit. For example, labor expenses account for approximately 45 percent of the total marketing bill, while corporate profits account for only 6 percent.

Source: U.S. Department of Agriculture

THE STUDY OF MARKETS

The preceding section identified the intermediaries active in the marketing channels which link farmers with the ultimate consumer of their products. With this in mind, let us focus on the various approaches traditionally taken to study markets and market activity. Three such approaches are discussed here: (1) the market structure approach, (2) the institutional approach, and (3) the functional approach. Each approach is discussed in turn below.

Market Structure Approach

The study of a market's structure entails examining the characteristics identified earlier in Table 9.1. These characteristics include (1) the number of sellers, (2) the ease of entry and exit, (3) the ability to set market price, (4) the prospect of long-run economic profits, and (5) the existence of product differentiation. Corn farmers were cited in Table 9.1 as an example of a perfect competitor because they are numerous in number, have no ability to set the market price, and do not sell a differentiated product. Manufacturers of farm tractors, on the other hand, were classified as oligopolies because a few firms account for a large proportion of total farm tractor sales. Furthermore, these firms do sell a differentiated product (e.g., they come in different models and colors) and do have some ability to set the price for their products.

These market structures in turn have a definite impact on the performance of these markets (e.g., the price of the product and the quantity of the product marketed). The norm for comparing different market structures is usually the price and quantity marketed achieved under perfect competition. That is, the price and quantity marketed under perfect competition is compared with prices and quantities marketed under other types of market structure. Each of the three market structures illustrated in Figure 9.4 would lead to higher prices and lower quantities marketed than would have occurred under perfect competition [i.e., where the intersection of demand *(D)* and supply *(MC)* curves determined the equilibrium price and quantity]. Hence market performance, particularly in the eyes of the buyers of these products, would be poorer under the various forms of imperfect competition depicted in Figure 9.4.

Institutional Approach

The institutional approach to studying markets focuses on the activities of the market intermediaries discussed in the preceding section. Middlemen, who were divided into merchant middlemen, agent middlemen, and speculative middlemen, represent one such intermediary. These middlemen perform one or more functions associated with the buying and selling of agricultural products as they move through marketing channels. In addition, other market intermediaries who perform specific functions that help in transforming and transferring food and fiber products to their ultimate consumer include food processors and manufacturers as well as such facilitative organizations as grain exchanges and stockyards.

This approach to the study of markets would center on the existence and quality of services performed by these intermediaries.

Functional Approach

The final general approach to studying markets is the functional approach, or the examination of the functions performed by markets and market intermediaries. To begin with, markets and market intermediaries perform *physical functions*. As raw agricultural products are transformed into their final form through processing and manufacturing processes, *form utility* or value is added to these products. Storage by farmers or by others along the marketing channel adds *time utility* or value to these products. Finally, transportation of products from the point of production to the point of consumption adds *place utility* or value to these products.

In addition to these physical functions performed along marketing channels, markets and market intermediaries provide *exchange functions*. These buying and selling functions include locating commodities in sufficient quantities and desired price and, through packaging and advertising, see to the sale of these products to their ultimate consumer. Finally, markets and market intermediaries provide *facilitating functions,* as discussed in the preceding section. These functions include the gathering and distribution of market information as well as the establishment and enforcement of policies and standards for their trade.

The existence of these functions and the quality and efficiency with which they are performed are of concern of economists taking a functional approach to studying markets.

MARKET REGULATION

Agricultural markets are subject to a variety of regulations, some which are specifically unique to agriculture and others which pertain to markets in general. Some of these regulations are *restrictive*. Such regulations are aimed at prohibiting monopoly practices, deceptive advertising, and price fixing. Antitrust laws apply equally to farm and nonfarm business activities. Some regulations are *permissive,* such as those which allow farmers to form cooperatives to purchase inputs and sell their products. And other regulations are *facilitative* in nature. That is, they set grades and standards for farm products which are enforced by inspection. They also regulate farm market news services.

Restrictive Regulations

There are a variety of regulations designed to either control or eliminate monopoly practices. The Sherman Antitrust Act of 1890 prohibits conspiracies among firms to restrain competition. The Clayton Act, passed in 1914, sought to prevent anticompetitive mergers. The Federal Trade Commission was also established in 1914 to prevent unfair trade practices. The Packers and Stockyards Act, passed in 1921, prevents unfair or deceptive acts in the marketing of livestock. The Robinson-Patman Act of 1936 sought to eliminate price discrimination unless products were of different grades or quality. The Wheeler-Lea Act, passed in 1935, made false and deceptive advertising illegal. These and other regulations are aimed at restricting the market freedoms of firms when the public interest is at stake.[15]

Permissive Regulations

Permissive regulations encourage rather than discourage imperfectly competitive market activities where it is deemed to be in the public interest. Federal farm programs that support farm prices and restrict input use, for example, are designed to take the "booms and busts" out of agriculture—maintaining a healthy farm business sector while holding down sharp increases in food prices. The Food Stamp program also falls in this category. The Morrill Land Grant College Act of 1862 fostered the establishment of our system of higher education as we know it today. The Hatch Act, passed in 1887, established agricultural experiment stations at these land-grant institutions. The Smith-Lever Act of 1914 established agricultural extension services. The Capper-Volstead Act and subsequent legislation permitted farmers to form cooperatives for the purpose of gaining marketing power in the purchase of inputs and the sale of products. More will be said about agricultural cooperatives in the final section of this chapter.

Facilitative Regulations

Regulations of this type are generally aimed at informing consumers about the nature and wholesomeness of the farm products they are purchasing. For example, the Meat Inspection Act of 1907 focused on the inspection of meat and meat packing firms to see to it that these products were fit for human consumption. This as well as the Pure Food and Drug Act and similar legislation is aimed at protecting the consumer. The Warehouse Act of 1916, the Produce Agency Act of 1927, and the Perishable Agricultural Commodities Act of 1930 dealt with the licensing of warehouses and middlemen. The es-

---

[15]An excellent review of these and other forms of market regulations can be found in Kohls and Uhl (1979, Chap. 22).

tablishment of grades and standards and the provision of market news services and market statistics also increases the efficiency of the marketing process by the information they communicate to both consumers and farmers.

COOPERATIVE BARGAINING

The Capper-Volstead Act and subsequent legislation have given monopoly powers to farm businesses by allowing them to bargain collectively for favorable terms of exchange in the product and input markets (including credit). Cooperatives are voluntary organizations designed to benefit their members. Five of every six farm businesses in the United States utilize the services of cooperatives for one reason or another, including (1) the marketing of their products, (2) the purchasing of input supplies, and (3) the purchasing of needed services. Figure 9.8 illustrates the number of farmer cooperatives and their membership by region.

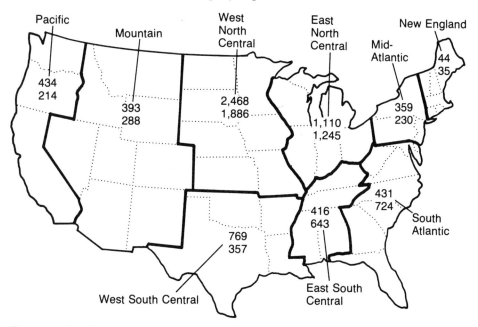

The top number in each region refers to the number of farmer cooperatives and the lower number refers to the number of memberships (in thousands), in farmer cooperatives Calendar year 1979.

Figure 9.8 *Farmer Cooperative Membership by Region.* Farmer cooperatives in this country play a major role in purchasing inputs and selling products for their farmer members. Five of every six farmers in the United States utilize the services of a farmer cooperative in one fashion or another. This figure shows that the largest concentration of farmer cooperatives is in the north central regions.

Marketing Cooperatives

This form of cooperative provides help to member-farm businesses when they sell their output. Some marketing cooperatives provide a wide range of functions (assembling, grading, packaging, etc.). Some may simply act as agent middlemen and never handle the product. Regardless of their physical association with the product flow, their purpose is to negotiate the best price for their members. Farm marketing cooperatives account for over 30 percent of the farm products marketed in his country. Some of the larger marketing cooperatives in the United States include Diamond Brand walnuts, Sun-Maid raisins, and Sunkist oranges.

Purchasing Cooperatives

Purchasing cooperatives are organized to purchase the input supplies needed by their members. These cooperatives may purchase the raw materials and manufacture the input (e.g., fertilizer and feed supplements) or they may simply act as merchant middlemen in acquiring and selling inputs to their members which are already in their final form. Many states have large statewide associations (e.g., Illinois Farm Bureau) which act in this manner. They supply fuel, fertilizer, chemicals, and other inputs. One of the largest purchasing cooperatives in the United States is Farmland Industry, headquartered in Kansas City. These cooperatives supply over 20 percent of the farm supplies purchased by farm businesses in this country.

Processing Cooperatives

These cooperatives are involved in processing and packing products produced by their members. Processing cooperatives are most prevalent in dairy products, fruits, and vegetables. In some instances, these cooperatives may also market the products they process. Their goal, like that of the other forms of cooperatives, is to negotiate the best possible price for their members.

Service Cooperatives

The final type of cooperative is organized to provide specific services to their membership. Rural electric associations supply power to their cooperative members, which include a large share of the rural population in this country. Mutual insurance companies also provide a wide range of insurance coverages to their members. Perhaps one of the most crucial service cooperatives to the growth of the farm business sector during the post–World War II period is the Farm Credit System, which acquires loan funds for its membership in the nation's money markets and distributes them efficiently to borrowers in all parts of this country. More will be said about the specific functions of the Farm Credit System banks in Chapter 17.

SUMMARY

The purpose of this chapter was to discuss the determination of the price of farm commodities in the marketplace and the roles played by market intermediaries in the nation's food and fiber system. The major points made in this chapter can be summarized as follows:

1. A market structure is classified as *perfectly competitive* as long as (1) the product is homogeneous, (2) there are no serious barriers to entry, (3) there is a large number of buyers and sellers, and (4) adequate information exists for all market participants.
2. The equilibrium price is a perfectly competitive is established by the intersection of the market demand and supply curves. Only at this price would there be no excess quantity supplied (surplus) and no excess quantity demanded (shortage).
3. The elasticity of supply and demand have an effect on the volitility of price movements. The *greater* the inelasticity of demand, the *greater* the decline (rise) in market price for an increase (decrease) in supply.
4. The area above the market supply curve and below the market demand curve represents the *consumer and producer surplus* of all market participants. Changes in the size of this area thus have direct implications for the economic welfare of these market participants.
5. The prices for several raw food and fiber products are known for their *cyclical behavior.* This occurs when producers base this year's production on *past* prices, while buyers purchase these goods based on this *this* year's prices. This behavior of prices and quantities is known as a *cobweb pattern.*
6. Imperfectly competitive forms of market structure can be classified by (1) the number of firms in the market, and (2) the nature of the product. If there is a relatively large number of firms *selling (buying)* a differentiated product, *monopolistic (monopsonistic) competition* is said to exist. If there are just a few firms *selling (buying)* a standardized product, a *pure oligopoly (oligopsony)* is said to exist. Finally, if there is only one firm *selling (buying)* a product, the firm is said to be a *monopolist (monopsonist).*
7. There is a network of market intermediaries at various stages of the marketing channel who perform specific functions. Middlemen perform *exchange, physical, and facilitating* functions. *Merchant middlemen* buy

and sell commodities for their own economic gain. *Agent middlemen* do not own the product they handle but rather serve as an agent for those who do. *Speculative middlemen* bear price risk in hopes of making a profit from favorable price fluctuations. *Food processors and manufacturers* and *facilitative organizations* such as grain exchanges also perform important roles as food and fiber products flow through market channels to consumers.

8. The *marketing margin* is the difference between the price paid by consumers and the price the producer receives. The *marketing bill* is roughly equivalent to the total value of the marketing margin for *all* food and fiber products.

9. Market regulations can be classified as to whether they are *restrictive, permissive,* or *facilitative* in nature. Restrictive regulations are aimed at prohibiting such things as monopoly practices and deceptive advertising. Permissive regulations are those which allow producers certain advantages in the marketplace, including the formation of marketing and purchasing cooperatives. Finally, facilitative regulations set grades and standards as well as regulate other market features.

10. The Capper-Volstead Act and later legislation allowed producers to gain monopoly market powers by forming a *cooperative*. Cooperatives can be classified by the functions they perform: namely, marketing cooperatives, purchasing cooperatives, processing cooperatives, and service cooperatives.

DEFINITION OF TERMS

Perfect competition: a sector is said to be perfectly competitive when (1) the product is homogeneous, (2) there are no barriers to exit or entry, (3) there are a very large number if sellers and buyers in the market, and (4) adequate market information exists.

Surplus: the excess quantity supplied at a particular price.

Shortage: the excess quantity demanded at a particular price.

Market-clearing price: the market price given by the intersection of the demand and supply curve (also referred to as the equilibrium price). This price clears the market of any excess demand (shortage) or excess supply (surplus).

Monopolistic competiton: a market structure where a large number of firms produce a differentiated product. It is relatively easy to enter such a sector.

Differentiated product: a product that is made different from others through advertising or quality variation.

Oligopoly: a market structure where there are a small number of sellers. Each seller (oligopolist) knows how the other sellers will respond to any changes in quantity marketed or prices he might initiate.

Pure monopoly: a market structure that has only one firm supplying products to buyers.

Middlemen: firms that perform one or more marketing functions associated with the buying and selling of goods as they move through marketing channels.

Marketing margin: the difference between the retail price and farm-level price for food and fiber products.

Marketing bill: equivalent to the total value of the marketing margin for all products taken together; consumer expenditures for food minus their farm value.

REFERENCES

KOHLS, RICHARD L., and JOSEPH N. UHL, *Marketing of Agricultural Products,* 5th ed. New York: Macmillan Publishing Company, 1979.

ADDITIONAL READINGS

DAHL, DALE C., and JEROME W. HAMMOND, *Market and Price Analysis: The Agricultural Industries.* New York: McGraw-Hill Book Company, 1977.

KOHLER, H., *Intermediate Microeconomics: Theory and Applications.* Glenview, Ill.: Scott, Foresman and Company, 1982.

RHODES, V. JAMES, *The Agricultural Marketing System,* Columbus, Ohio: Grid Publishing, Inc., 1978.

QUESTIONS

1. What are the characteristics of perfect competition? Discuss the determination of the market price under conditions of perfect competition.
2. What is the difference between a change in demand and a change in the quantity demanded? A change in supply and a change in the quantity supplied?
3. Describe the cobweb pattern of price and quantity responses in the marketplace.

Under what conditions will this pattern converge toward a market equilibrium price?

4. Describe the essential difference between perfect competition and monopolistic competition. Which form of competition is more efficient? Why?

5. Why do oligopolists and monopolists earn economic profits in the long run, whereas perfect competitors do not? Cite some examples of oligopolies and monopolies in the U.S. food and fiber system.

6. Does the existence of monopoly power guarantee the monopolist a profit? why?

7. Describe the major types of middlemen in the food and fiber system and the functions they perform.

8. What is the relationship between the marketing bill and the marketing margin?

9. What are the essential differences between the alternative approaches to the study of markets?

ADVANCED TOPICS

Two advanced topics are addressed in this section. The first topic pertains to the concept of *producer and consumer surplus.* The second topic deals with the *effects that imperfect competition* has on producers and consumers or the economic well-being of these market participants.

Producer and Consumer Surplus

You will recall the concepts of consumer and producer surplus were discussed in the Advanced Topics sections of Chapters 3 and 5, respectively. We know, for example, that consumer surplus is given by the area below the demand curve and *above* the equilibrium price, while producer surplus is given by the area above the supply curve and *below* the equilibrium price. These areas represent the *economic well-being* achieved by consumers and producers at the equilibrium or market-clearing price. If we add these two triangular areas together, the newly formed triangle represents the economic well-being achieved by *all* market participants in this particular market. Looking at panel a in Figure 9.9, we see that the summation of consumer surplus (area 1) plus producer surplus (area 2) represents the total area above the supply curve and below the demand curve, and hence the total surplus received by all market participants.

Now suppose that because of low yields, the supply curve in panel a shifts inward to the left, from SS to S*S*. Producer surplus would now be equal to area 4 plus area 6. Thus, if areas 4 plus 6 sum to less than areas 6 plus 7, we can conclude that the economic well-being of producers would have declined. We can also obviously conclude that consumer surplus declined since consumers received the equivalent of areas 3, 4, and 5 before but now receive only area 3. Finally, we can conclude that this decrease in

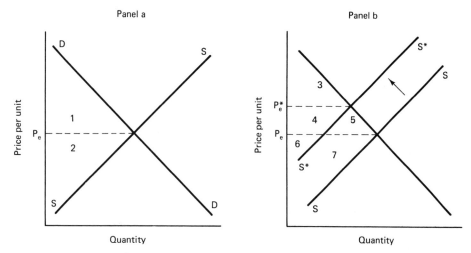

Figure 9.9 *Consumer and Producer Surplus.* In Chapters 3 and 5 we developed the concepts of consumer and producer surplus (see Advanced Topics sections). This figure brings both concepts together in the same graph. Area 1 in panel a represents consumer surplus and area 2 represents producer surplus. Panel b shows what would happen to the economic welfare of consumers and producers if, say, a drought caused the aggregate supply curve to shift from *SS* to *S*S**. Producer surplus would fall to now equal area 6 plus area 4 (area 6 plus area 7 in panel b is equivalent to area 2 in panel a). Consumer surplus would fall from area 1 in panel a to area 3 in panel b. Thus areas 5 and 7 represent welfare losses to society (i.e., producers and consumers collectively) as a result of the drought.

supply means that the economic well-being of market participants in general would have fallen by an amount equal to area 5 plus area 7. The concept of total producer and consumer surplus will be alluded to in later chapters when we examine the economic welfare implications of specific events.

Effects of Imperfect Competition

We can utilize the concept of producer and consumer surplus to discuss the economic welfare implications of imperfect competition in the long run. The point was made earlier in this chapter that imperfect competitors operate to the left of the minimum point on their average total cost curve. This, of course, differs from the behavior of the perfectly competitive firm, which will, in long-run equilibrium, operate where the product price is equal to its marginal cost at the minimum point on its average total cost curve. This difference occurs because of the downward-sloping nature of the imperfect competitor's demand curve and the desire of these firms (1) to operate at the point where their marginal costs are equal to marginal revenue, and (2) to price their product according to the demand curve that lies above the marginal revenue curve. What does this difference in market behavior imply about the economic well-being of producers and consumers?

We can assess the effects of imperfect competition on producers and consumers in a particular market by observing the change in producer and consumer surplus if we went from perfect competition to a monopoly. Figure 9.10 indicates that the market equilibrium price under perfect competition would be P_{pc} while the quantity marketed would be Q_{pc}. Total consumer surplus under these conditions would be equal to the sum of areas 1, 4, 5, 8, and 9. Total producer surplus would be equal to the sum of areas 2, 3, 6, and 7. If this market instead exhibited the characteristics of a monopoly, the equilibrium price would rise to P_m while the equilibrium quantity market would fall to Q_m (remember that S in this case is the monopolist's marginal cost curve). The monopolist would earn economic profits equal to the sum of areas 3, 4, 5, and 6. His total producer surplus would be equal to this economic profit plus area 7. Thus producers (even though there is now only one) gained areas 4 and 5 and lost only area 2. Since areas 4 and 5 exceed area 2, we can say that the monopolist would be economically better off than all producers were collectively under perfect competition.

Consumers, on the other hand, would be considerably worse off under

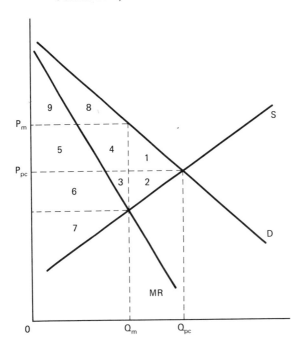

Figure 9.10 *Effects of Imperfect Competition.* Consumer surplus would be lower under a monopoly (areas 8 and 9) than it would be under perfect competition (areas 1, 4, 5, 8, and 9). Producers would have been willing to supply Q_{pc} at a price of P_{pc} under perfect competition. A monopoly however, would be willing to supply a quantity of Q_m at price P_m. Producer surplus would be higher under a monopoly (areas 3, 4, 5, 6, and 7) than it would be under perfect competition (areas 2, 3, 6, and 7). The economic welfare of society as a whole would decline by the sum of areas 1 and 2.

a monopoly than they would be under conditions of perfect competition. Total consumer surplus would fall by the sum of areas 1, 4, and 5 under conditions of pure monopoly, totaling only area 8 plus area 9. Thus, whereas producers gained areas 4 and 5 and lost only area 2, consumers gained nothing and lost areas 1, 4, and 5.

Society as a whole would therefore be a net loser if a market's structure were to switch from perfect competition to a pure monopoly. Society would gain nothing in terms of economic welfare and would lose areas 1 and 2. The sum of areas 1 and 2 is frequently referred to as a "dead-weight loss." These results support our earlier statements about the relative efficiency of perfect competition from the perspective of consumers and society as a whole.

10

FARM POLICY
AND MARKET EQUILIBRIUM

In the early twentieth century, the farm business sector enjoyed continuous prosperity. This period is often referred to as the "golden age of American farming." World War I, which occurred during this period, added to the prosperity by increasing the export demand for U.S. farm products as foreign countries sought to compensate for losses in production caused by an underutilization of resources. In fact, the 1910–1914 period later became the basis for the concept of *parity*, which seeks to compare prices in the current period with what they were during this "golden" period.[1]

The depression that occurred in 1920 brought the good times in the U.S. economy to a halt. Unfortunately, when the general economy picked up again in 1921 and continued strong during the "roaring twenties," the farm business sector did not participate in the renewed prosperity. Export demand for U.S. farm products fell as resources were more fully utilized again abroad. This country also placed high tariffs on imported goods, and because other countries were unable to export as many goods as before, they reduced their imports as well. The farm business sector in the United States during the twenties was therefore plagued with *surplus productive capacity, low farm prices, and depressed farm income levels.* Little did economists realize in the early twenties that the problem of excess capacity in the farm business sector would continue for the next 50 years.

[1] The basic idea behind the concept of parity is that if the farmer could exchange a bushel of corn for a pair of overalls in 1910–1914, he should be able to make the *same* exchange today. If this occurs, he has achieved 100 percent parity with the "golden" period used as the basis for analysis.

A variety of farm policies have been adopted at one time or another to support farm income levels in this country. The row of storage bins depicted above reflect an era that saw the federal government take ownership of surplus commodities accumulated by the Commodity Credit Corporation (CCC). During the fifties, the federal government acquired so much surplus wheat that it was spending over $1 million a day in storage costs. The switch to a market-oriented approach in the seventies brought about a switch from government-held to farmer-held reserves, causing the elimination of scenes like this. The problem of stocks of surplus commodities remains, however, as evidenced by the need for the payment-in-kind (PIK) program employed by the U.S. Department of Agriculture in 1983–1984 to reduce production and stocks of surplus commodities.

By the time the great depression hit in 1929, farmers were really hurting. Farm prices and income levels suffered even further declines. In response to this situation, the Federal Farm Board was created and charged with the responsibility to use its budget of $1.5 billion to begin stabilizing farm prices at specific levels. It did this by purchasing crops. Thus began a long history of government involvement in this sector of the economy.[2] Later other approaches would be instituted to see that the prices of wheat, feed grains, dairy products, cotton, rice, soybeans, sugar, peanuts, and tobacco would not fall below a specific level.

The purpose of this chapter is to illustrate the consequences of an inelastic demand for farm products and the nature and effects of government programs that have been used to stabilize farm prices and income. These programs have included *supply constraint* programs as well as *demand expansion*

[2] For an excellent review of the historical development of government programs for the farm business sector, see Cochrane and Ryan (1976).

programs. This discussion includes an examination of the effects these government programs have on market equilibrium. In the final section of this chapter we discuss the implications that a more elastic demand for farm products would have on farm revenue and the need for supply constraint programs.

INELASTIC DEMAND AND FARM INCOME

Most everyone knows that farm production is subject to the vagaries of climatological and biological phenomena. Wet springs, dry summers, and early frosts, together with such things as corn blight and cholera, will shift the supply curve to the left, while bumper crops and technological change will shift the supply curve to the right. Shifts in supply curves, coupled with the historically inelastic demand for farm products in general identified in Chapter 3, can lead to wide fluctuations in farm product prices and farm income levels.

To illustrate the effects of an inelastic demand on farm product prices, let us look at the effects of a change in supply for two different demand curves, one more inelastic than the other. Looking at panel a in Figure 10.1, we see that the market equilibrium price would decline from P_e to P_e* if the demand curve facing farmers were represented by curve DD and the supply curve were to shift from SS to $S*S*$. The point at which market equilibrium is attained would shift from E to $E*$. Now let us assume that the sector were instead confronted by a more inelastic demand curve, represented by $D*D*$. What happens to the product price if the supply curve were to shift by the *same* amount (i.e., from SS to $S*S*$)? The market equilibrium would now be $E**$ instead of $E*$ and the equilibrium price would fall all the way to P_e** instead of just P_e*.

We can conclude from panel a in Figure 10.1 that the more inelastic the demand for farm products, the greater the decline (rise) in market prices will be for a given increase (decrease) in supply. A bumper crop, for example, could cause farm product prices to drop sharply under these conditions. Conversely, a drought that shifts the supply curve leftward could lead to a substantial increase in farm product prices.

An inelastic demand for farm products and the ever-expanding level of annual farm output can lead to low returns to resources in agriculture in the absence of offsetting increases in demand. Why is this so? Any sector facing an inelastic demand for its products will suffer a *decrease* in its total revenue if market prices *fall*. We can see this by examining panel b in Figure 10.1. *Before* the shift in the supply curve from SS to $S*S*$, farmers were receiving a total revenue equal to the area formed by $OP_eE'Q_e$. *After* the shift in the supply curve to the right, however, farmers were receiving a total revenue equal to the area formed by $OP_e*E'Q_e*$. Obviously, the second area is

Panel a

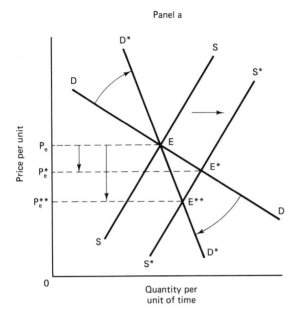

Panel b

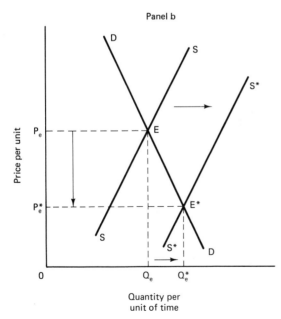

Figure 10.1 *Effects of inelastic demand for farm output.* Panel a illustrates an important phenomena of interest to farmers; namely, the more inelastic the demand for farm products (i.e., the steeper the demand curve), the greater the decline in market prices will be for a given change in supply. The equilibrium price will fall in panel a to P_e^{**} if the market demand curve is equal to D^*D^*, as opposed to only P_e^* if the demand curve were equal to DD. Panel b illustrates what happens to the total revenue received by farmers facing an inelastic demand for their products if the supply curve were to shift to the right. Total revenue would fall since area $0P_eEQ_e$ is greater than $0P_e^*E^*Q_e^*$.

smaller than the first, implying that the economic well-being of farmers would be diminished. Observed another way, market prices fell more (P_e to P_e^*) than quantities marketed increased (Q_e to Q_e^*).

Let us now turn to two general approaches to altering farm product prices through government intervention. One is to expand demand, thereby shifting the demand curve to the right and raising the equilibrium price. This general approach will be discussed later in this chapter. First, however, let us examine the second general approach, which consists of constraining the quantity of farm products reaching the market.

SUPPLY CONSTRAINT PROGRAMS

The historical problem of low returns to resources in agriculture has been dealt with in different ways over time by the federal government. The approach taken has depended in part on the nature of the conditions that existed at the time. As indicated earlier in this chapter, a system of price supports was instituted during the Great Depression to keep market prices from falling below a certain level. The approach taken in recent years has been to stabilize prices within a specific range.

In this section we look at the programs that have been employed by the federal government at one time or another to influence the quantities of farm products reaching the marketplace and the price farmers receive. These supply-oriented approaches can be categorized into the following groups: (1) the commodity acquisition approach, (2) the production control approach, and (3) the market-oriented approach. In addition, we shall also briefly discuss the payment-in-kind (PIK) approach to reducing inventories and raising farm prices.

Commodity Acquisition Approach

The U.S. Department of Agriculture began in the early thirties to purchase quantities of wheat and the other commodities identified earlier in this chapter. The objective was to keep the market price of these commodities from falling below a specific level. The more inelastic the demand was, the less the quantity marketed had to be reduced to achieve a certain increase in price.

To illustrate how this approach works, look at the market demand and supply curves for wheat presented in Figure 10.2. If competitive market forces were free to work, the market-clearing price would be P_e and the quantity marketed would be Q_e. Let us assume that the federal government wished to support prices at P_s, which we see lies above P_e (obviously, if the federal government set the support price below P_e, there would be *no change* in market prices and quantities marketed). The quantity demanded at price P_s would be Q_d, while the quantity supplied would be Q_s. As illustrated in

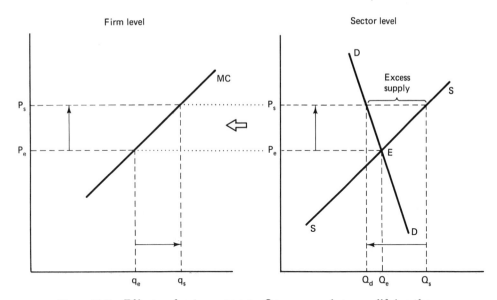

Figure 10.2 *Effects of price supports.* One approach to modifying the income levels of farmers has been the use of price supports. To achieve support prices of P_s, the federal government purchased the surplus or excess supply marketed by farmers at the announced support price level. This meant that the federal government became the owner of Q_s-Q_d bushels of the commodity. The price at which this commodity was supported is called the loan rate. The Commodity Credit Corporation (CCC) extended nonrecourse loans to farmers at a fixed price per unit (i.e., the loan rate). If P_s was greater than the actual market price (P_e), the farmer turned over the commodity pledged as security for the loan to the Commodity Credit Corporation as payment in full for this loan. This "repayment" feature represents the price support mechanism for this approach.

Figure 10.2, the individual farmer would produce output q_s, where his marginal costs *(MC)* equaled his marginal revenue (P_s). The difference between Q_d and Q_s at the sector level represents the excess supply or *surplus* at P_s the federal government had to purchase and store for later distribution if it desired to support prices at this level.

The Commodity Credit Corporation (CCC), a corporation operating within the U.S. Department of Agriculture, acts as the "purchasing agent" for the federal government. Under programs entailing government-held stocks, the CCC has been given a price it could offer for specific commodities.[3] It then accumulated surpluses through the extension of *nonrecourse* loans equal to P_s times the quantity of the commodity pledged as collateral.

[3] This price was tied to the concept of parity, which again relates the purchasing power of the current market price to purchasing power of market prices in the "golden age" of 1910-1914.

These loans were made at a *fixed price per unit* of the commodity called the *loan rate*. The interest rate charged on this loan, which should not be confused with the loan rate, was normally at or near the cost of money paid by the U.S. Treasury. The CCC allowed farmers participating in the program either (1) to sell the commodity at price P_s and repay the loan (which they would do if the market-clearing price P_e is greater than P_s), or (2) to turn the commodity over to the CCC as repayment for the loan including interest (which they would do if P_s is greater than P_e). The "foregiveness" feature of the latter option represents the *price support mechanism*. The commodities accumulated by the CCC under this option became government property and were held in storage.

There have been several problems associated with the commodity acquisition approach. For example, if the support price is higher than the marketing-clearing price, it entices higher production. The individual farmer will respond to the higher support price, as we see in Figure 10.2, by producing q_s instead of q_e. This, in turn, leads to greater government-held stocks and corresponding storage costs.[4] During the fifties, the government acquired so much surplus wheat that it was spending over $1 million a *day* in storage costs. These charges eventually reached $3 million a day (U.S. Department of Agriculture, 1981). In addition, since price supports aid farmers in direct proportion to their level of production, the owners of large cropping operations received the bulk of the program's benefits. Finally, the value of expected *future* benefits were "capitalized" in the market value of farmland, resulting in an additional benefit to large landowners.

Production Controls Approach

To combat the growing problem of government-held stocks, *production controls* were introduced. Their purpose was to constrain the annual production levels of those crops that were in excess supply. These controls took the form of *acreage allotments* and *marketing quotas*.

Acreage allotments restricted farmers in the number of acres they could plant to such crops as wheat, rice, cotton, peanuts, and tobacco.[5] A national acreage allotment was apportioned to individual farmers based on the number of acres they planted to this crop in previous years.

To illustrate how acreage restrictions work, look at Figure 10.3. Let *DD* and *SS* represent the market demand and supply curves for a commodity before acreage restrictions are implemented. The market would have cleared at

[4] This problem was solved by tobacco growers over 30 years ago by convincing Congress to enact legislative to enforce licensing and production quotas limiting the amount of land that could be used to raise tobacco.

[5] The program of acreage allotments continue to this day for peanuts and tobacco. The dairy program also involves regulation of the marketing of milk between fluid and manufacturing uses.

price P_e and quantity Q_e. Let us again assume that the government wants to support prices at P_s, which lies above P_e. At price P_s, the quantity demanded would be equal to $Q_s{}^*$ while the quantity supplied would be Q_s if farmers were free to produce all they desired. We know from the previous discussion that this would result in a surplus of $Q_s - Q_s{}^*$. The CCC, in the absence of production controls, would have had to accumulate these additional stocks if it wished to maintain the market price at P_s.

Let us now suppose that the federal government enacted production controls which restricted the amount of land that could be planted to a particular crop. This would result in a *new* marginal cost curve MC^* at the firm level and a *new* market supply curve S^*S^*. As we see in Figure 10.3, the individual farmer would produce $q_s{}^*$, where his marginal cost (MC^*) equaled his marginal revenue (P_s). The market supply curve would intersect the market demand curve at the point where the market-clearing quantity was exactly equal to the allotted acreage times the yield per acre. The new marginal cost and market supply curves are *steeper* than the old curves because land is now fixed. These new curves, however, are not identical to the old curves up to $q_s{}^*$ and $Q_s{}^*$ and then become perfectly elastic. Instead, both curves be-

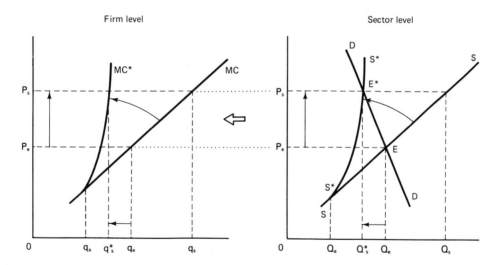

Figure 10.3 *Effects of acreage restrictions.* The production control approach to supporting farm prices involved removing the inputs from production that were contributing to the surplus. If the federal government announced support prices at P_s, the supply curve under the acreage restrictions approach would take on the properties of MC^* at the firm level and S^*S^* at the sector level, the individual farmer would produce q_s^* rather than q_e. Farmers can increase their profits by applying additional fertilizer and other inputs to increase their output from q_a (allotment times old yield) to q_s^* (allotment times new yield).

come more inelastic at q_a and Q_a as farmers apply *additional* fertilizer on their allotted acres in response to the higher price.[6]

Under the production control approach, the government essentially "rents" land from farmers. In other words, the federal government pays farmers *not* to use a specific quantity of land in production. The value of this rent at the sector level equals the difference between the areas formed by $0P_sE^*Q_s^*$ and $0P_eEQ_e$. The program required that farmers not use a certain percentage of their available land to produce a particular crop if they wished to receive the support price P_s. The hope of policy planners was that the quantity $Q_s - Q_s^*$ would effectively be removed from the market *without* having the CCC accumulate large stocks of commodities.

Because farmers responded to acreage restrictions by cropping their allotted acres more intensively (e.g., using more fertilizer) and by removing their worst land first, further reductions in acreage allotments were required to achieve a market price of P_s. *Marketing quotas,* which restricted the quantities of commodities farmers could place on the market, were also used in conjunction with acreage allotments.

Initially, these controls were mandatory, but that was found to be unconstitutional.[7] Under the Agricultural Adjustment Act of 1938, the Secretary of Agriculture was authorized to set the value of P_s at between 52 and 75 percent of *parity*. Marketing quotas were binding on *all* farmers only if two-thirds of farmers holding allotments voted for marketing quotas in a referendum.

This land retirement program, with its complicated system of allotments and quotas existed until 1956, when a voluntary land retirement program referred to as the *Soil Bank program* was established. The "diverted" land under the Soil Bank program had to be maintained in a soil-conserving use. This program resulted in whole farms being diverted from production and disrupted the social structure and economic climate of many rural areas. Over 63 million acres of farmland were retired by this program by the mid-sixties. The cost to the federal government under this program reached almost $1 billion by 1971 (U.S. Department of Agriculture, 1979).

The concept of "set-asides" was introduced in 1970. Here, farmers wishing to receive price supports had to agree to set aside some land. The major difference from earlier programs was that no *direct* rents were paid to farmers for setting aside land and prices were not supported for those farmers who chose not to participate in the program. This program suffered, however, from what is referred to as "slippage"; that is, not all farmers desired to participate in the program and those that did idled their marginal land first and more intensively cropped their remaining acres. Experience during the

---

[6] This reflects the assumption that input combinations can be varied, as opposed to being used in some fixed proportion (see Chapter 4).

[7] This form of control was first authorized by the Agricultural Adjustment Act of 1933 but was ruled to be unconstitutional in 1936.

seventies suggested that a 15 percent set-aside resulted in about a 3 percent reduction in farm output (Knutson et al., 1983).

Thus, despite a variety of efforts at controlling levels of production, the farm business sector's production capacity continued to expand and price support levels rose higher and higher. Even though large quantities of farmland were being retired, farm output was continuing to expand. Wheat output, for example, expanded 25 percent during the 1961–1972 period while corn output increased by 55 percent and soybeans increased by 87 percent (U.S. Department of Agriculture, 1981). Obviously something new was needed.

Market-Oriented Approach

The shift from a production control to a market-oriented approach was initiated by then Secretary of Agriculture Earl Butz. Congress passed a new farm bill in 1973 containing a system of *target prices* and *diversion payments*. Secretary Butz considered this bill a turning point in farm programs.[8] The transition to this market-oriented policy was smoothed by the expansion of the export demand for grains facilitated by a controversial subsidy (recall the 1972 "Russian wheat deal"?) and low grain harvests in other countries. Table 10.1 illustrates the substantial growth in the exports of selected farm products which began in 1972.

Target prices.   A major feature of the 1973 farm bill was the reintroduction of *target prices*. The concept of target prices was actually first proposed by Secretary of Agriculture Charles F. Brannen of the Truman administration back in 1949. As a key feature of the 1973 bill, the target price concept of income support called for direct payments to farmers based on the difference between the target price (P_t) and the average market price at which Q_t is sold (P_e^*) *if* P_t exceeded P_e for a certain length of time. For example, if the target price of wheat is \$5 per bushel and the market price at which Q_t clears the market is \$4 per bushel, farmers would receive a subsidy of \$1 for every bushel of wheat they produced.

This payment, which is made out of the general tax revenues of the federal government, is called a *deficiency payment*. A per unit maximum has been placed on this payment. This maximum is equal to the difference between P_t and the loan rate (P_l) on CCC nonrecourse loans.

[8] Even though policy instruments differ in general from the allotments and quotas used in the thirties, forties, fifties, and sixties, farm legislation today takes the form of amendments to the Agricultural Act of 1949. That is, farm bills today merely represent amendments to the 1949 Act and carry specific expiration dates. Thus if Congress were to fail to enact a new farm bill before the previous farm bill expired, we would revert to the allotments, quotas, and price supports of over 30 years ago.

Year	Corn	Wheat	Cotton	Soybeans
1970	517,000	741,000	3,740	433,801
1971	796,000	610,000	3,229	416,829
1972	1,258,000	1,135,000	5,000	479,443
1973	1,243,000	1,217,000	5,746	539,129
1974	1,149,000	1,018,000	3,746	427,342
1975	1,711,000	1,173,000	3,178	555,094
1976	1,684,000	950,000	4,565	564,071
1977	1,948,000	1,124,000	5,219	700,484
1978	2,133,000	1,194,000	5,850	739,154
1979	2,433,000	1,375,000	8,779	875,173
1980	2,355,000	1,514,000	5,639	724,295
1981	1,967,000	1,773,000	6,263	929,080
1982	2,050,000	1,525,000	N/A	N/A

Note: Calendar year. All quantities are expressed in 1,000 bushels except cotton (1,000 bales of 480 pounds each).

Source: U.S. Department of Agriculture, *Agricultural Statistics* (Washington, D.C.: U.S. Government Printing Office, 1983).

TABLE 10.1 EXPORTS OF SELECTED FARM PRODUCTS. One of the major factors that allowed the federal government to shift smoothly from a production control approach to a market-oriented approach was the expansion of the export demand for U.S. raw agricultural products. Beginning in 1972, the quantity of major crops such as corn and wheat exported really took off. Favorable exchange rates into U.S. dollars, trade concessions, and credit, as well as growing world-wide demand for these commodities in the seventies helped remove the "surpluses" from domestic markets, causing farm market prices to jump above price support levels. More will be said about this demand expansion in foreign markets at key points in this and later chapters.

To illustrate this market-oriented approach, let us examine Figure 10.4. The intersection of the market demand curve (DD) and supply curve (SS) at point E indicates the market-clearing price (P_e) and quantity (Q_e) that would have occurred *in the absence of government intervention.* Now let us assume that the federal government announces a target price of P_t for the coming year. If the market demand curve had been located far enough to the right of DD such that P_e was *greater than* P_t, we know that the individual farmer would produce at the point where his marginal costs equaled the higher P_e. Under these conditions, he would not have received a deficiency payment. In the event that the market-clearing price (P_e) is *less than* P_t, the individual farmer will respond by producing q_t, the output where his marginal costs equals P_t. As indicated in Figure 10.4, the quantity of production at the sector level would now be Q_t rather than Q_e. If we look at the market demand curve for this commodity, however, we see that a quantity Q_t can clear the market only if the price to buyers is P_e^*. This means that the federal government must pay a deficiency payment per unit of $P_t - P_e^*$ on each unit pro-

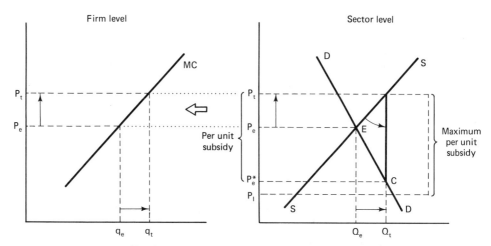

Figure 10.4 *Effects of target prices.* The switch to a market-oriented approach of supporting farm prices brought about the introduction of target prices and deficiency payments. If the price at which Q_t can be sold (i.e., P_e^*) is less than the target price of P_t, farmers are paid a subsidy or "deficiency payment" equal to the difference between these two prices (i.e., $P_t - P_e^*$ per unit). The maximum deficiency payment per bushel is equal to the difference between the target price and the loan rate P_1 established by the Commodity Credit Corporation. One advantage to this approach over the production control approach is the savings to the U.S. Treasury in periods of high prices (i.e., when P_e is greater than P_t).

duced and marketed. The total payment in this case would be equal to $P_t - P_e^*$ times the number of units sold (Q_t). The *maximum* per unit subsidy permitted by the 1973 bill would be the difference between P_t and P_l. Finally, the market supply curve in Figure 10.4 would be represented by the kinked *CS* curve instead of the original *SS* curve.

To further illustrate the calculation of the deficiency payment, consider the following numerical example. Assume that the target price for corn is $3 and the loan rate is $2.35. If the market-clearing price for corn actually fell to $2, the farmer would receive a deficiency payment of $0.65 per bushel (i.e., the target price of $3 minus the loan rate of $2.35). In addition, the farmer would keep the proceeds of the nonrecourse loan of $2.35 per bushel and turn his production over to the CCC. Thus the farmer would receive a total of $3 per bushel for his corn (i.e., the deficiency payment of $0.65 plus the nonrecourse loan of $2.35) even if the market-clearing price fell to $2 a bushel as long as he was participating in the program.

One of the chief challenges in administering a target price program is knowing where to set the target price. Initially, a measure of the national average costs of production for grains and cotton was used in lieu of parity to determine what target prices would have to be to cover costs (including a nominal return to land). The 1977 bill furthered this approach by allowing for annual adjustments based on cost of production studies. When the market-clearing price (P_e) fell below the target price (P_t) in the late seventies and early eighties, however, this approach to setting target prices came under heavy questioning. Congress finally ended up instituting its own judgment in setting target prices; the target prices set forth in the 1981 farm bill were based on political negotiations rather than cost of production measures.

If target prices are set too high, they encourage expansion of the sector over what it would otherwise have been. As illustrated in Figure 10.4, the individual farmer will respond to the higher target price by expanding his output to q_t. The resulting deficiency payments must be paid out of federal tax revenues, and thus may lead to either higher taxes or greater budget deficits during a period when neither are very popular with voters.

Farmer-owned reserve.   A second major feature of the 1973 farm bill was the switch from government-held to *farmer-owned reserves.* In return for placing commodities in the farmer-owned reserve program, farmers are granted a higher loan rate (P_r) or "entry price" (see panel a in Figure 10.5) at low or zero interest and storage costs.[9] Farmers entering this three-year program agree not to market a quantity equal to $Q_t - Q_r$ unless the market-clearing price reaches the *release price.* This, as shown in panel a, raises the market-clearing price to P_r. Panel b of this figure shows that stocks will be accumulated in this storage program as long as prices do not rise above P_r.

If the release price (P_m) is reached before this three-year period expires, farmers can sell their stored output if they wish to. If they choose to continue to store their output under this program, however, they may be asked to begin paying interest on the loan plus storage costs (both of which are incentives to sell.)[10] When farmers do sell their stored output and repay their loans, the market-clearing price is dampened. In theory, the release price (P_m) serves as a ceiling on the market-clearing price (hence the jagged price movements in both panels a and b once this price is reached) if the Secretary of Agriculture so wishes. There have been only six times since 1960 in which the market price has risen substantially above the release price (1966 and 1972–1976).[11] This can occur either because there are no more stocks available to release onto the market or because remaining stocks have been earmarked for other uses.

Finally, the market supply curve—now that we have introduced the Farmer-Owned Reserve program—begins at point R in panel a and is per-

[9] The entry price may be set equal to the regular CCC loan rate under certain circumstances [e.g., when the regular loan rate (P_l) exceeds the market clearing price (P_e^*)].

[10] Before the 1981 bill, this program also contained a *call price*, whereby farmers were *required* to repay their loans if this price was reached.

[11] U.S. Department of Agriculture (1981); and data supplied to the authors by the U.S. Department of Agriculture.

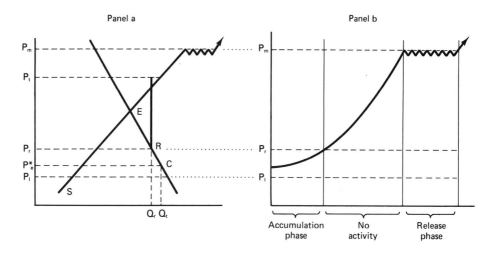

Figure 10.5 *The farmer-owned reserve, the market supply curve, and price movements.* A second feature of the market-oriented approach instituted in the seventies was the switch from government-owned to farmer-owned reserves. In return for the higher loan rate (P_r) shown in panel a, farmers agree to store output Q_t-Q_r for three years unless market prices rise above the release price (P_m). Stocks would cease being accumulated if market-clearing prices should fall in between P_m and P_r, as shown in panel b. The federal government can keep prices from rising above the release price level until stocks in this program have been depleted or reached a critically low level. After this point, however, market prices would be free to reach their "free market" level.

fectly inelastic up to the target price P_t, at which point it becomes discontinuous over to the original market supply curve (SS) and then follows the original market supply curve until the release price (P_m) is reached. This new market supply curve reflects the fact that quantity $Q_t - Q_r$ has been removed from the market for a period of three years unless the market clearing price reaches P_m.

Comparison with other approaches.   We can draw several conclusions from the market-oriented approach illustrated in Figures 10.4 and 10.5 as well as from our knowledge of what would have occurred under earlier forms of supply constraint programs. These conclusions are as follows:

1. There would be *no subsidies* to farmers if the market price is greater than the target price. Resource use would be responding to free market prices at that point and government involvement would be eliminated. This phenomenon occurred frequently during the seventies after 1972, and government payments to farmers fell sharply.

2. If the market price is less than the target price but greater than the loan rate, the amount of the deficiency payment would be equal to the difference between the target price and market price.

3. If the target price is greater than the market price, the *maximum* deficiency payment to farmers on a per unit basis would be the difference between the target price and the loan rate.

4. Target prices lead to a *greater* use of resources, *higher* output, and *more* consumption than would occur in the *free* market.

5. Target prices lead to *greater* use of resources, *higher* output, and *more* consumption than would occur under acreage restriction concepts to support income.

6. Target prices are *more cost efficient* to the federal government than acreage restrictions in those years when the market price is greater than the target price.

7. The farmer-owned reserve program brought to an end the costly practice of government-held stocks.

From both an efficiency and equity standpoint, the farm program that results in the lowest price to the consumer *and* a fair return to farmers' land, labor, capital, and management should be preferred over other alternatives. The current market-oriented approach, which works well in periods of demand expansion, has turned out to be costly to the U.S. taxpayer in recent years. Federal government outlays for farm price and income support programs in 1983 alone totaled $18.9 billion, a jump of some $12 billion over the outlays just two years earlier when export demand was stronger.

The Reagan Administration in early 1985 was proposing substantial cutbacks in price supports for farm commodities. While the exact design of the 1985 farm bill is not known at this time, two things are known for certain. First, there is general dissatisfaction with the current market-oriented approach. The Reagan Administration does not like it and farmers do not like it. It is entirely possible that Congress will settle for a temporary, patchwork extension of the current law. Second, the substantial cutbacks in price supports proposed by the Reagan Administration will substantially reduce net farm income at a time that many farm businesses are feeling a substantial cash flow stress.

Payment-in-Kind

Unfortunately, the worldwide recession in the early eighties, the high cost of importing U.S. commodities by other countries due to the relative strength of the dollar, and the record levels of crop production all served to increase carryover inventories of crops and depress farm prices. In an effort to reduce inventories of wheat, corn, sorghum rice, and cotton and lower resource use in the farm business sector—thus bolstering farm prices and net farm income —the Reagan administration in 1983 introduced a *payment-in-kind program.* The program represented an old twist to production set-asides designed to limit government spending.[12] A farmer who agreed not to plant a fraction of the acreage harvested the previous year would be given access to government stocks in roughly the amount he would otherwise have produced. The farmer could then use this commodity as livestock feed in the case of grain or sell it. This would reduce government inventories of grain and cotton, which have a depressing effect on market prices, and also reduce government expenditures by eliminating the need for CCC nonrecourse loans for the current crop year. The response to this program in 1983 was strong. Farm production expenses declined some 10 to 15 percent as farmers cut back their production of these crops. Government inventories also declined sharply. This program, while achieving many of its objectives, appears to be the most costly farm program to the U.S. Treasury in the history of this country. The cost of the PIK program in 1983 alone was $9.4 billion. This is in addition to the $18.9 billion spent on farm price and income support programs mentioned earlier. These programs together cost U.S. taxpayers approximately $12,000 per farm in 1983.

DEMAND EXPANSION PROGRAMS

Raising the level of farm income can also be accomplished through demand expansion, or shifting the demand curve for farm products to the right. The demand for farm products can be expanded in three different ways:

1. Programs to promote the *expansion of domestic demand* through school feeding and other nutrition service programs, advertising and promotional programs, and so on.
2. Programs to subsidize the *development of new uses* for farm products (e.g., as an intermediate good in the production of other goods). A recent example is the use of state and federal subsidies for the production of synthetic fuels.
3. Programs to promote the *expansion of export demand* for U.S. farm products through commercial channels as well as through aid programs and concessionary sales.

The first form of demand expansion program probably holds the *least* promise of the three in terms of its ability to alleviate the need for price sup-

---

[12] A payment-in-kind program was first introduced for feed grain in the 1961 Feed Grain Act.

Year ending June 30	Average monthly partici- pation	Value of coupons issued (thousands of dollars)		
		Total	Paid for by participants	Federal subsidy
1966	864,000	174,232	109,419	64,813
1967	1,447,000	296,106	190,556	105,550
1968	2,210,000	451,801	278,659	173,142
1969	2,878,000	603,351	374,532	228,819
1970	4,340,000	1,089,961	540,297	549,664
1971	9,368,000	2,713,273	1,190,524	1,522,749
1972	11,109,000	3,308,648	1,511,362	1,797,286
1973	12,166,000	3,883,952	1,752,547	2,131,405
1974	12,862,000	4,727,450	2,009,154	2,718,296
1975	17,064,000	7,265,642	2,880,141	4,385,501
1976	18,549,000	8,700,209	3,373,704	5,326,505
1977	17,077,000	8,351,112	3,284,162	5,066,950
1978	16,001,000	8,279,796	3,140,580	5,139,216
1979	17,653,000	7,225,499	745,310[a]	6,480,189
1980	21,071,000	8,685,379	0[a]	8,685,379
1981	22,431,000	10,629,913	0[a]	10,629,913
1982	21,716,000	10,208,300	0[a]	10,208,300
1983	21,621,000	11,153,867	0[a]	11,153,867
1984	20,867,000	10,711,000	0[a]	10,711,000

[a]Recipient payments phased out, but equivalent benefit levels were maintained without requiring cash outlay by the recipient.

Source: Food and Nutrition Service, U.S. Department of Agriculture.

TABLE 10.2 PARTICIPATION IN FOOD STAMP PROGRAM. The role played by the food stamp program since the mid-sixties has been significant regardless of whether we measure its activity in numbers of participants or dollar value of coupons issued.

ports in the farm business sector. With a declining rate of population growth in this country and our low income elasticity for food, it is difficult to foresee how advertising and promotional programs can lead to a significant increase in the domestic demand for food and fiber products over the long run. Furthermore, food and nutrition service programs are already in place. Table 10.2 shows, for example, that almost 21 million people were participating in the food stamp program in 1984 and that the federal government's expenditure on this program in 1984 had reached 10.7 billion. In addition, the federal government in 1984 also spent an additional $1.5 billion on commodity distribution programs for school feeding, institutions, and needy persons.

The effects of the second form of demand expansion programs are likely to be relatively minor given existing technologies unless the demand–supply conditions for industrial uses make it more economical for nonfarm businesses to utilize farm products in their production processes. If real energy prices increase, for example, biomass is likely to become an increasingly attractive input to liquid energy production. Another factor will be the nature of government policy incentives (i.e., subsidies) to produce ethanol for use in gasohol.

The third form of demand expansion programs appears to have the greatest potential for reducing the need for income support programs in the farm business sector. From the inception of P.L. 480, export subsidies have become an important demand expansion devise. The expanded sales of grain to the Soviet Union and other countries during the mid-seventies raised farmer's real gross income to its highest levels during the post–World War II period and greatly reduced the need for government support of farm incomes.[13] Some economists subscribe to the notion that we are entering an era of chronic scarcity of food.[14] To the extent that this is true, programs designed to make U.S. products more competitive in world markets will increase the level of farm revenue in this country.

As we will emphasize in Chapter 15, two factors that have a direct impact on U.S. exports are (1) the absence of a recession in importing countries, and (2) the relative cost of the U.S. dollar in foreign currency markets. Monetary policies designed to combat inflation in this country that result in high interest rates lead to (1) increases in foreign capital flowing into this country (which means that we are exporting recessionary pressures to other countries), and (2) a higher price for U.S. dollars in foreign currency markets (which means that it would now take more units of a foreign currency to buy the dollars necessary to purchase a given quantity of U.S. products). Therefore, expansionary monetary policies will have a positive impact on export demand, while contractionary policies will retard export demand.

EFFECTS OF A MORE ELASTIC DEMAND

As indicated in Chapter 3, the demand curve for raw agricultural products facing U.S. farmers became more elastic (less inelastic) during the seventies and early eighties. The primary reason for this was the growing export de-

[13] Public Law 480, or P.L. 480 as it is popularly referred to, is designed to export commodities to foreign countries under several different programs: long-term dollar and foreign currency sales (Title I sales), donations to other governments and various relief agencies to promote better diets and alleviate starvation (Title II donations), barter for strategic materials (Title III), or other foreign assistance programs. Almost 90 percent of P.L. 480 exports of wheat and flour, for example, are Title I sales.

[14] An argument can be made that developing countries will experience the highest rate of increase in population over the next 20 years. And because their income elasticity of demand for food is substantially higher than in the United States, the demand for food in these countries will increase rapidly.

USDA Photo

Public Law 480 provides for the use of a share of the funds generated by concessional sales to develop foreign markets for U.S. raw agricultural products. Export credits have also been an important tool to help move additional quantities of farm products. In 1981, for example, a total of $2.3 billion in credit guarantees to commercial banks were available for helping to finance agricultural exports.

mand for U.S. farm products.[15] To illustrate the importance of this development, let us examine why this is thought to have occurred and what this means for farmers and farm programs. We shall use wheat farmers and the wheat program in the numerical example developed in this section.

Increasing Importance of Export Demand

The own-price elasticity of demand for wheat can be partitioned into the contribution associated with the domestic use of the product and the contribution associated with exports as follows:

$$
\begin{array}{c}\text{own-price}\\ \text{elasticity of}\\ \text{total demand}\end{array} = \left[MS_d \times \begin{array}{c}\text{own-price}\\ \text{elasticity of}\\ \text{domestic demand}\end{array} \right] + \left[MS_e \times \begin{array}{c}\text{own-price}\\ \text{elasticity of}\\ \text{export demand}\end{array} \right] \quad (10.1)
$$

where MS_d and MS_e represent the market shares associated with the domestic use and exports of wheat, respectively.

The declining market share of total wheat output going to domestic use and corresponding increase in the share going to exports during the post-World War II period has led to an increased own price elasticity of the total demand for wheat. To illustrate, let us assume that the long-run own-price elasticity of domestic demand for wheat is –0.20 and that the long-run own price elasticity of export demand for wheat is –1.50.[16] We know that the domestic use of wheat output during the 1950–1959 period was 62.2 percent (i.e., MS_d = 0.622) while the amount of output going to exports was 37.8 percent (i.e., MS_e = 0.378). Thus the own-price elasticity for wheat during this period would have been

$$
\begin{array}{c}\text{own-price}\\ \text{elasticity of}\\ \text{total demand}\end{array} = 0.622 \times (-0.20) + 0.378 \times (-1.50) \qquad (10.2)
$$
$$
= -0.69
$$

Domestic use of total wheat output in the 1976–1982 period fell from 62.2 percent to 38.3 percent while export's share rose from 37.8 to 61.7 percent. Assuming for the moment that the values of E_{pd} and E_{pe} remain constant, the own-price elasticity for wheat during this period would have been

[15] The quantity of U.S. farm products shipped abroad tripled during the 1950–1980 period. During the decade of the seventies, approximately 40 percent of total U.S. production of grain and oilseed crops was exported.

[16] The long-run elasticity of demand is generally larger than the short-run elasticity of demand because of institutional constraints and other factors, such as the availability of transportation, which limit the quantity response in the short run (one year) to a given change in price. In the longer run, as these constraints are alleviated, the full quantity response to this price change is registered in the market, causing the elasticity to rise.

own-price
elasticity of $= 0.383 \times (-0.20) + 0.617 \times (-1.50)$ (10.3)
total demand
          $= -1.00$

The price flexibilities associated with these own-price elasticities would be −1.45 for the 1950–1959 period (i.e., $1.0 \div -0.69$) and −1.00 for the 1976–1982 period (i.e., $1.0 \div -1.00$). These flexibilities suggest that a 1 percent increase in quantities marketed will have reduced the price wheat farmers received for their product by 1.45 percent during the 1950–1959 period. During the 1976–1982 period, however, a 1 percent increase in quantities marketed would have had *no effect* on the price these farmers received for their wheat due to the growing importance of export markets for wheat and the more highly elastic nature of demand.

Implications for Farm Revenue

An increase in the own price elasticity of demand has important implications for total farm revenue.[17] As we will demonstrate shortly, a 1 percent increase in quantities marketed will result in *an increase* in total farm revenue if the own-price elasticity of demand is greater than 1.0. Let's suppose that the price of wheat is presently $4 per bushel and the quantity of wheat marketed is 2,500 million bushels. Total revenue would therefore be $10,000 million. Let's examine what happens to total revenue when we assume the own-price elasticities of demand reported in the first column of Table 10.3 when output increases by one percent.

Let's begin with the own-price elasticity of −0.69 given by equation (10.2). Looking at Table 10.3, we see that a 1 percent increase in the quantity marketed from 2,500 to 2,525 million bushels would cause the price per bushel to fall by 1.45 percent to $3.94 (remember the price flexibility associated with an elasticity of −0.69 is −1.45). Thus total revenue would be only $9,956 million (i.e., 2,525 million bushels times $3.94) instead of the original $10,000 million (i.e., 2,500 million bushels times $4.00) if the quantity marketed increased by 1 percent.

If the price elasticity is instead equal to −1.00 as given by equation (10.3), a 1 percent increase in the quantity marketed would result in no change in the total revenue of wheat farmers (i.e., $10,000 million earned here is identical to the original level of total revenue). Thus the gain achieved by the increased quantity would be exactly offset by the reduction in market price.

Further increases in the own-price elasticity of total demand given by

---

[17] The recent volatile nature of the export demand for U.S. farm products and some of the factors causing this variability will be explored in Chapters 15, 17, and 18.

equation (10.1) and corresponding decreases in the price flexibility would see wheat farmers achieving gains in total revenue from increases in quantities marketed. For example, if the own-price elasticity of total demand for wheat had been equal to –1.20, the corresponding price flexibility would have been –0.83 (i.e., –0.83 = 1 ÷ –1.20). If this were the case, a 1 percent increase in the quantity marketed would result in only a 0.83 percent decrease in price, which means that total revenue would be *higher* than it was originally. As shown in Table 10.3, total revenue under these conditions would be $10,024 million, or $24 million higher than the original level of total revenue.

Finally, let's look at the case where no wheat was exported (i.e., MS_e = 0.0). We know in this case that the total own-price elasticity would be –0.20 since MS_d would equal 1.0 and the second term in equation (10.1) would equal zero. Under these conditions, Table 10.3 indicates that a 1 percent increase in quantities marketed to 2,525 million bushels would cause prices to fall by five percent to $3.80 per bushel and total revenue to fall by $405 million to $9,696 million. Clearly, this case—and not the case above where the elasticity exceeded 1.0—is the basis on which the supply constraint programs discussed in this chapter have been justified.

Own-price elasticity	New quantity	New price	New revenue
–0.20	2,525	$3.80	$9,595
–0.69	2,525	3.94	9,956
–1.00	2,525	3.96	10,000
–1.20	2,525	3.97	10,024

TABLE 10.3 IMPORTANCE OF HIGHER PRICE ELASTICITY OF DEMAND. One important consequence of a rising own-price elasticity of demand is its effect on total revenue. Assume for the moment that farmers currently receive $4 per bushel for their wheat if a quantity of 2,500 bushels is marketed. Thus their total revenue would be $10,000 million. Now let's assume that the quantity marketed rises by 1 percent to 2,525 million bushels. This table shows what effect the new higher quantity marketed will have on farm prices and revenue under different price elasticity conditions. For example, if the elasticity is 0.20, prices will fall to $3.80 per bushel and total revenue will decline to $9,595 million. If the price elasticity were instead equal to 1.20, prices will only decline to $3.97 per bushel and total revenue will actually be higher than before (i.e., $10,024 million as opposed to $10,000 million). Thus the growth of farm export demand and its effect on the total own-price elasticity of demand for specific farm commodities is of considerable interest to farmers.

Implications for Policy

These observations have direct implications for the design of farm programs and conduct of macroeconomic and foreign policy. First, *if* the long-run own-price elasticity of wheat were to exceed 1, supply constraint programs such as those discussed in this chapter would restrict the total revenue of wheat farmers rather than support it. Total revenue would decline rather than increase if less wheat output is produced. Supply constraint programs and their attendant costs to the U.S. Treasury would therefore be counter-productive in the long run. If supply constraint programs in the example above had been enacted to hold quantities marketed at 2,500 million bushels to support prices at $4.00 when the own-price elasticity is –1.20, wheat farmers in general would have been penalized by $24 million (i.e., $10,024 – $10,000).

Second, the use of wheat as a foreign policy tool has the potential for reducing the quantity of wheat exports (embargoes not only have the rather obvious short-run effect of limiting the quantity shipped but also have the long-run effect of causing our export customers to lose confidence in the United States as a trading partner and either seek other trading partners or increase their own production for food security reasons). Furthermore, con-tractionary macroeconomic policies increase the value of the U.S. dollar, which, in turn, leads to higher exchange rates. This makes it more expensive for foreign customers to acquire the U.S. dollars needed to buy our wheat, thus lowering the export demand for wheat. Both policies, in turn, lower the value of MS_e and increase the value of MS_d in equation (10.1). This, in turn, lowers the own-price elasticity of demand and increases the need for supply constraint programs to support the income levels of wheat producers. These policies and their impact on the U.S. farm business sector will be discussed in depth in Chapter 15.

SUMMARY

The purpose of this chapter was to illustrate the economic consequences of the inelastic nature of the demand for farm products and the continuing expansion of the farm business sector's capacity to produce, and to discuss the government programs that have been used to affect the market price farmers receive for their products. The major points made in this chapter can be summarized as follows:

1. Changes in supply, coupled with the highly inelastic demand for raw food and fiber products, can translate into periods of booms and busts in farm income. The ever-expanding nature of annual farm output helps explain the low returns to resources observed historically in agriculture.

2. A short-run price elasticity of demand of –0.20 suggests a price flexibility (the reciprocal of the price elasticity) of –5.00. For farmers, this means that a 1 percent increase in the quantity they send to market will lower the market price they receive during the year by 5 percent, all other things constant.

3. One approach to dealing with the historical problem of low returns to resources is the implementation of *commodity supply programs.* The federal government has tried a variety of schemes, including price supports and acreage restrictions.

4. Since the mid-seventies, the concept of *target prices* and *farmer-owned reserves* have been used to support incomes. The target price concept calls for a direct *deficiency payment* to the farmer equal to the difference between the target price and the average market price when the target price is higher.

5. Raising the returns to resources in agriculture can also be accomplished by *demand expansion programs.* Domestic demand can be expanded by public (e.g., school lunch programs) and private (e.g., advertising) programs. The development of new uses for food and fiber products and expansion of export demand with export subsidies to importing countries also lead to higher domestic prices and farm income.

6. The level of export demand is important because it affects the elasticity of demand for certain farm products. While farm programs may be needed in the short run to alleviate economic stress, the continuation of farm programs when the elasticity of demand exceeds in the longer run may lower rather than raise farm revenue.

DEFINITION OF TERMS

Parity: a concept that expresses relative prices (price of farm products relative to input prices) in the current period as a ratio to relative prices in the 1910–1914 period. A parity price in the current period (i.e., ratio = 100) would mean that farmers are currently earning the same relative price as that received in this "golden era."

Soil bank: tillable land that farmers took out of production to qualify for price supports.

Price support: the minimized price or floor below which the government will not let the price of specific commodities fall. A variety of approaches have been taken to support prices at desired levels.

Market equilibrium: price and quantity given by the intersection of the market demand and supply curves.

Nonrecourse loan: an amount of money equal to support price times the quantity offered as collateral lent by the Commodity Credit Corporation (CCC). The loan is considered "paid in full" when turned over to CCC when the market price falls below the support price.

Commodity Credit Corporation: an agency within the U.S. Department of Agriculture that makes nonrecourse loans to farmers for the purpose of supporting prices at a specific level.

Slippage: extent to which farmers (1) participating in government programs "overproduce" by retiring marginal acres rather than highly productive acres, or (2) decide not to participate at all.

Set-aside: the amount of land that had to be "set aside"—either left idle or planted to another crop.

Target price: price set by government for selected commodities. This price is achieved by supplementing the market price with a deficiency payment.

Deficiency payment: value of payment per unit, equal to the difference between the market price and the target price. This payment is made to participating farmers.

Release price: the price ceiling for selected commodities enforced by the federal government by releasing reserves on to the market.

Payment-in-kind: the 1983–1984 PIK program called for payment of commodities to farmers roughly equal to the amount they would have produced had they not participated in this set-aside approach to support prices and reduce government stocks.

Tariff: a tax or duty placed on products imported into a country.

REFERENCES

COCHRANE, W. W., and M. E. RYAN, *American Farm Policy 1948–1973.* Minneapolis, Minn.: University of Minnesota Press, 1976.

HOUCK, J., and A. SUBOTNIK, "The U.S. Supply of Soybeans: Regional Acreage Functions," *Agricultural Economics Research,* 1969, pp. 99–108.

KNUTSON, R. D., J. B. PENN, and W. T. BOEHM, *Agricultural and Food Policy.* Englewood Cliffs, N.J.: Prentice-Hall, Inc., 1983.

RYAN, M., and M. ABEL, "Corn Acreage Response and the Set-Aside Program," *Agricultural Economics Research,* 1972, pp. 102–113.

U.S. Department of Agriculture, *Commodity Credit Corporation, History of Budgetary Expenditures.* Washington, D.C.: U.S. Government Printing Office, December 1979.

U.S. Department of Agriculture, *Agricultural Statistics.* Washington, D.C.: U.S. Government Printing Office, 1981.

ADDITIONAL READINGS

HALCROW, HAROLD G., *Food Policy for America.* New York: McGraw-Hill Book Company, 1977.

JOHNSON, GLENN L., "Supply Function—Some Facts and Notions," in *Agricultural Adjustment Problems in a Growing Economy.* Ames, Iowa: Iowa State University Press, 1958.

SCHULTZE, CHARLES L., *The Distribution of Farm Subsidies: Who Gets the Benefits?* Washington, D.C.: The Brookings Institution, 1971.

TWEETEN, LUTHER, "The Demand for U.S. Farm Output," *Food Research Institute Studies,* Vol. 7, 1967, pp. 343–369.

TWEETEN, LUTHER, *Foundations of Farm Policy,* 2nd ed. Lincoln, Nebr.: University of Nebraska Press, 1979.

QUESTIONS

1. Describe the consequences on an inelastic demand for farm products of:
   (a) A drought
   (b) A bumper crop

2. Discuss the commodity acquisition approach to supporting farm commodity prices. How does this approach support prices above market-clearing levels? What are the major drawbacks to the use of this approach?

3. Discuss the production controls approach to supporting farm commodity prices. How does this approach support prices above market-clearing levels? Why was it adopted in lieu of the commodity acquisition approach? What are the major drawbacks to the use of this approach?

4. Discuss the market-oriented approach to supporting farm commodity prices. How does this approach support prices above market-clearing levels? What are the major advantages and disadvantages to this approach?

5. Describe the nature of demand expansion programs and their impacts on the farm business sector.

6. Describe the importance of export demand to U.S. farm business. Why is the market share attributed to export demand so important? What are its implications for policy?

7. What will happen to farm revenue if the quantity marketed increases and the own-price elasticity of total demand is:
   (a) Less than 1.0?
   (b) Equal to 1.0?
   (c) Greater than 1.0?

ADVANCED TOPICS

A concept that has been widely used in understanding the impact of government programs on farmers' planting response is the *effective price support* originally proposed by Houck and Subotnik (1969). The minimum price that participating farmers realize for crops covered by government programs is not the announced price support (loan rate) but rather the effective price support. The purpose of their measure is to account for the effects of acreage restrictions (set asides) on the net price that farmers realize from program participation.[18]

Figure 10.6 illustrates this concept. The size of the gap between the announced price support and the effective price support is determined by the degree of acreage restrictions attached to the program. Let A_1 represent the acreage planted by farmers when there are no conditions attached to the price support. If policymakers wish to reduce participation in the program to, say A_2, they can either lower the *announced* price support or attach planting restrictions, which lowers the *effective* price support. If there are no acreage restrictions, these two price supports would be identical and the acres planted by farmers would be represented by A_1 in periods of low prices. If policymakers reduce program participation to A_2 through the use of acreage restrictions, however, the effective price support will be lower than the announced price support. The concept of effective price support helps explain the low participation in government programs by farmers in periods when market prices fall below the announced price support. Farmers respond to the effective price support when making planting decisions.

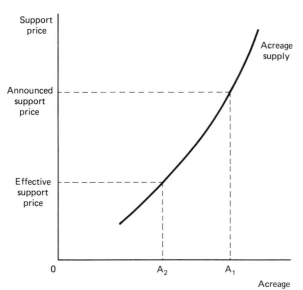

Figure 10.6 *The effective price support.* The effective price support takes into account the number of acres, if any, that have to be set aside as a requirement for participation in the farm program. If there are no acreage restrictions, the announced price support and the effective price support are the same. If farmers must restrict their acreage to A_2, however, the effective support price (i.e., take these acreage restrictions into account) when making their planting decisions.

---

[18] Ryan and Abel later extended this concept to the development of an *effective diversion payment* as well. See Ryan and Abel (1972).

11

MULTIMARKET RELATIONSHIPS

The discussion of market outcomes in the two preceding chapters was conducted within a *partial equilibrium* framework. That is, we implicitly assumed when studying the events taking place in the market for raw agricultural products that everything else in the economy would remain constant. The responses registered in all other markets to a new price for raw agricultural products were ignored. If we were to analyze the impact of a 1 cent per bushel tax on the production of corn in a partial equilibrium framework, for example, we would ignore the effects that this tax would have on such things as the federal budget deficit, national unemployment, and market interest rates. Also ignored would be the effects this tax would have on the prices for *other* raw agricultural products and what this may mean for the *corn* market. Implicit in an analysis of the equilibrium in a single market is the assumption that the indirect or "feedback" effects of this action from all other markets are so small that they can be ignored.

The concept of *general equilibrium,* on the other hand, regards all markets as being *interdependent.* Everything depends on everything else, to varying degrees, of course. The impact on the price of corn resulting from the effects of the tax on the prices of other goods and services in the economy would not be ignored. In short, all other things are no longer assumed to be constant. General equilibrium represents a bridge between microeconomics. This is because macroeconomic analysis simultaneously accounts for the principles of consumer behavior, the technology of production, and the principles of producer behavior as they affect outcomes in *all* markets in the economy.

The purpose of this chapter is (1) to illustrate how businesses and households are linked together through resource and product markets, (2) to acquaint you with the concept of general equilibrium, (3) to identify the ways in which the farm business sector is linked with other sectors in the domestic economy, and (4) to discuss the relationship between agricultural output and gross national product (GNP).

CIRCULAR FLOW OF PAYMENTS

Let us begin our discussion of multimarket relationships by assuming the existence of a barter economy where households and businesses exchange goods and services as a means for paying for their purchases. We will then relax this assumption by allowing for the presence of money as a medium of exchange. We shall also wait until this assumption is relaxed before we examine market interrelationships for inputs and outputs.

Barter Economy

In a barter economy, there is no money available for use as a medium of exchange. Households own all the primary resources (i.e., land, labor, capital, and management), which they in turn supply annually to businesses. Businesses need these resources to produce goods and services. As shown in the circular flow diagram in Figure 11.1, households receive payments in

Figure 11.1 *Simple flow diagram of a barter economy.* The business and household sectors in a barter economy interact with each other in the economy's resource and product markets. Businesses purchase the services provided by land, labor, capital, and management supplied by household in the resource market. Households "buy" the goods and services they need in product markets. Since there is no money in this economy, households barter among themselves and with businesses when exchanging goods and services. Bartering, of course, occurs even in a monetary economy. A plumber, for example, may do some plumbing work for a dentist in exchange for dental work of equal "value." The value of these services is considered income by the Internal Revenue Service, however.

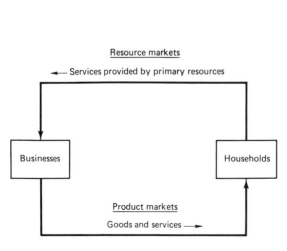

Resource markets

← Services provided by primary resources

Businesses   Households

Product markets

Goods and services →

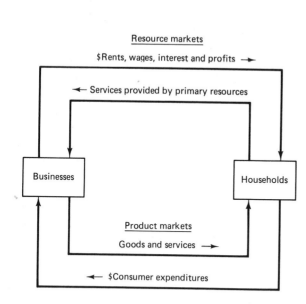

Figure 11.2 *Simple flow diagram for a monetary economy.* The major difference between the monetary economy depicted above and the barter economy illustrated in Figure 11.1 is that transactions are completed in dollars. When households provide labor and other services to businesses, they are compensated in the form of rents, wages, interest, and profits. When businesses sell goods and services to households, they are compensated by the value of private expenditures. The sum of rents, wages, interest, and profits received by households in the economy's resource markets represents its national income. The value of total expenditures by households represents gross national product.

kind; that is their wages are in the form of the products they helped produce.

Households, of course, would have to barter among themselves to obtain the mix of goods and services they desire. Can you imagine the difficulties that consumers and producers would encounter in an economy as complex as ours if bargaining between all parties was necessary to satisfy the demands for goods and services?

Monetary Economy

Now let's modify Figure 11.1 to reflect the fact that money is available for use as a medium of exchange. Continuing to assume that there are only households and businesses in our simplified economy, we see in Figure 11.2 that the household sector receives *monetary renumeration* in the form of rents, wages, salaries, and profits in exchange for providing the business sector with land, labor, capital, and management services. This figure also shows that businesses receive *monetary renumeration* in the form of consumer expenditures when they supply goods and services to households.[1] The sum of wages, rents, interest, and profits in the resource markets represents the economy's *national income.* The monetary value of the consumer goods flowing directly to households through the product markets in the economy represents its *national product.*

[1] The flow diagrams depicted in Figures 11.2 and 11.3 assume that businesses do not save (i.e., retained earnings are zero). Instead, all profits are paid out in the form of dividends to households that are assumed to own all primary resources in the economy. This assumption will be relaxed in Figure 11.4.

Figure 11.2 masks over the transactions that take place in the economy's input and output markets, however. Let us relax this constraint with the following example. Assume that the business sector produces two products—wheat and missiles. All income in this closed economy is spent on either of these two products. Also assume that the only resource needed to produce these two products is labor. We can now modify the circular flow diagram in Figure 11.2 to account specifically for the adjustment to equilibrium levels of wages paid to labor and the prices for wheat and missiles. This has been done for you in Figure 11.3. The equilibrium prices for wheat and missiles are represented by P_w, P_m, Q_w, and Q_m, respectively. The corresponding equilibrium wage rates and quantities of labor services are W_w, W_m, L_w, and L_m, respectively.

Short-run market adjustments.   To illustrate the interrelationships among resource and product markets, assume that something happens elsewhere in the world which causes our society to prefer more missiles and less wheat. This would be reflected by a shift to the right in the demand curve for missil~~ in panel c (from $D_m D_m$ to $D_m^* D_m^*$) and a shift to the left in the demand curve for wheat in panel d (from $D_w D_w$ to $D_w^* D_w^*$). Given the initial supply curve for missiles of $S_m S_m$, we see in panel c that the price for missiles would increase from P_m to P_m^*. This would cause the derived demand curve for labor in the missile industry illustrated in panel a to shift outward $d_m d_m$ to $d_m^* d_m^*$, and cause wage rates in this industry to increase from W_m to W_m^*. There would also be a decrease in the demand for labor to produce wheat from $d_w d_w$ to $d_w^* d_w^*$, as shown in panel b, resulting from the reduced demand for wheat. This would cause the wage rate in this industry to fall from W_w to W_w^* as shown in panel b.

General equilibrium.   The foregoing price and quantity adjustments represent the first in a series of events that can take place before an equilibrium is reached in all markets. For example, the disparity between the wage rates being paid in the missile and wheat industries (i.e., W_m^* is higher than W_w^*) will cause labor to flow out of the wheat industry, which is contracting, and into the missile industry, which is expanding. As these adjustments occur, the supply curve for missiles in panel c will shift outward from $S_m S_m$ to $S_m^* S_m^*$ while the supply curve for wheat in panel d will shift inward from $S_w S_w$ to $S_w^* S_w^*$. The product prices for these two goods will therefore adjust further to P_m^{**} and P_w^{**}, as shown in panels c and d, respectively. There will also be additional adjustments taking place in the labor markets. The new equilibrium wage rate will decline slightly in the missile labor market to W_m^{**}, as shown in panel a, and increase slightly in the wheat labor market to W_w^{**}, as indicated in panel b.

This process will continue until a *general equilibrium* is established in both the resource (labor) and product (wheat and missiles) markets. For example, the demand curves for labor in both markets will shift again in

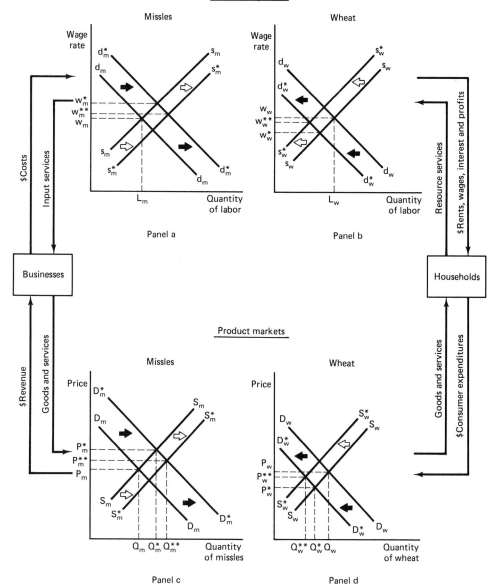

Figure 11.3 *Simple flow diagram for a two-product monetary economy.* Let us assume a monetary economy produces only two products (missiles and wheat). Also assume that something has occurred elsewhere in the world which causes the country to prefer more missiles and less wheat, as indicated by the black arrows in panels c and d. As a result, the derived demand for labor in the missile industry will increase (panel a), while the derived demand for labor by wheat producers will decline (panel b). In the longer run, supply shifts for both products and labor will occur, as indicated by the white arrows in all four panels, until an equilibrium is reached in all markets.

response to the new product prices for wheat (P_w^{**}) and missiles (P_m^{**}). If other products or resources had existed in the economy, we would have had to consider the effects of these goods and services as well. The conditions for general equilibrium will be covered in the next section. Before we identify these conditions, however, we should broaden our discussion of the circular flow of payments in an economy.

Other sectors.   You probably noticed that Figure 11.3 makes no mention of the economic role that *government* plays in the economy. This simplified flow diagram also ignores the possibility of *savings and investment.* And there is no mention of the role *financial markets* play in the economy.

To remedy these deficiencies, let us expand the simple flow diagram of a monetary economy presented in Figure 11.2 to include government and financial markets. This expanded flow diagram, which is illustrated in Figure 11.4, contains a financial market through which the savings of households are passed on by depository institutions, the bond market, and the stock market to businesses that must either borrow, issue bonds, or sell stock to finance their expenditures. The term "net saving" used in Figure 11.4 to describe the flow of money from households to financial markets and the term "net borrowing" used to describe the flow of money from financial markets to businesses signifies the fact that money is flowing in *both* directions (i.e., households also borrow from financial institutions, and businesses also save).

The production of goods and services in the monetary economy depicted in Figure 11.4 also generates income in the form of wages, rents, and interest. This income is captured at the bottom of this figure by the line drawn connecting the business and household sectors.[2] Businesses, of course, can decide to retain part of their profits (i.e., retained earnings) to help finance future expenditures.

The flow diagram depicted in Figure 11.4 also captures the flows of goods and services and flows of income and expenditures *between* government and businesses and households. For example, there is a flow of money from households to government in the form of tax payments. Households, in turn, receive money from the government in the form of Social Security payments, unemployment compensation, and other forms of payments (hence the use of the term "net taxes" here). Businesses also pay taxes as well as receive government payments. The government borrows in the nation's financial markets to finance its *budget deficits* (i.e., when expenditures exceed tax revenues). It does this through the sale of government securities by the U.S. Treasury. When the government has a *budget surplus,* which rarely happens at the federal level (this last occurred in 1969)

---

[2] For simplicity, only the money flows between the sectors are reflected in this figure, even though the physical flows of resource services and products continue to exist in the economy.

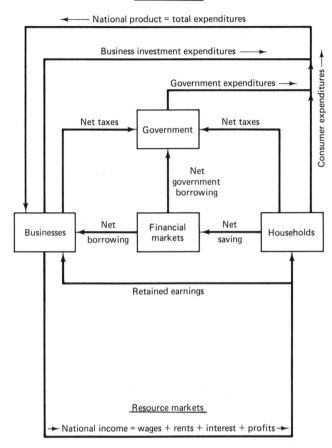

Product markets

National product = total expenditures

Business investment expenditures ⟶

Government expenditures ⟶

Consumer expenditures ⟶

Net taxes | Government | Net taxes

Net government borrowing

Businesses | Net borrowing | Financial markets | Net saving | Households

Retained earnings

Resource markets

National income = wages + rents + interest + profits ⟶

Figure 11.4 *Expanded flow diagram for a monetary economy.* This figure differs from Figure 11.2 in the sense that we have added a financial market sector and a government sector to the model. For example, households are now allowed to borrow and save. If their savings exceeds their borrowing, they are considered a net saver. Businesses are also allowed to borrow and save in financial markets. If their borrowing exceeds their savings, they are considered net borrowers. The government sector also borrows in the nation's financial markets to finance its budget deficits, as we will see in Chapter 12. The size of this deficit will be determined by the amount of government expenditures relative to tax receipts.

but does sometimes at the state and local level, it can buy back some of the securities it has issued. Finally, government expenditures for goods and services also represent a component of the *final demand* for the products produced by businesses. As such, these expenditures are included together with consumer expenditures and business expenditures for capital goods when measuring the nation's *gross national product* (GNP).

CONDITIONS FOR GENERAL EQUILIBRIUM

The foregoing discussion of multimarket relationships assumed the existence of a competitive economy. Profit-maximizing firms were assumed to maximize the revenue for the least-cost combination of inputs, which, for the economy in Figure 11.3, producing only missiles and wheat, would occur where the marginal benefits per dollar expended in competing activities are equal. This occurs where the slope of the isorevenue line (i.e., the product price ratio) is equal to the slope of the economy's production possibilities curve (i.e., the marginal rate of product transformation) for all producers taken together [see equation (5.14)]. Stated in the context of our missile–wheat example, production equilibrium would occur where

$$\frac{\Delta \text{ missiles}}{\Delta \text{ wheat}} = \frac{\text{price of wheat}}{\text{price of missiles}} \tag{11.1}$$

Panel a in Figure 11.5 illustrates the general equilibrium for production, which occurs at point C.

Consumers, on the other hand, were assumed to choose among goods and services in such a way that the marginal utility derived from the last dollar spent on each good and service and equal. This occurs in our two-product economy where the ratio of the prices of missiles and wheat is equal to the slope of the highest attainable indifference curve (i.e., the marginal rate of substitution for these products) for consumers as a whole [see equation (3.9)]. Stated in the context of our missile–wheat example, consumer equilibrium would occur when

$$\frac{MU_{\text{wheat}}}{MU_{\text{missiles}}} = \frac{\text{price of wheat}}{\text{price of missiles}} \tag{11.2}$$

Panel b in Figure 11.5 illustrates the general equilibrium of exchange that occurs at point C as well.[3]

The *economy* is in general equilibrium when producers taken together are operating at a point on their production possibilities curve that generates the highest attainable utility for consumers. This occurs at point C in panel c, where the producers' production possibilities curve and the consumers' highest attainable indifference curve are tangent. Producers would have no incentive to make further adjustments in the short run since they are operating at a point that maximizes their profits. Furthermore, consumers would have no incentive to change their minds since they are already maximizing their utility. Stated in the context of our missile–wheat example, general equilibrium will occur where

$$\frac{\Delta \text{missiles}}{\Delta \text{wheat}} = \frac{\text{price of wheat}}{\text{price of missiles}} = \frac{MU_{\text{wheat}}}{MU_{\text{missiles}}} \tag{11.3}$$

or where the marginal rate of product transformation for producers and the marginal rate of substitution for consumers are both equal to prevailing relative prices. *General equilibrium for the economy as a whole (i.e., both production and exchange) will therefore exist when a set of prices is found such that the demands of consumers are fulfilled by the quantities supplied*

---

[3] This should not suggest that we can obtain society's indifference curve by simply adding up the preferences of all consumers in the economy. The preferences of some people will "count" more than those of others because of differences in their budget constraints.

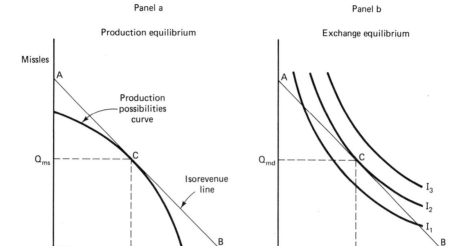

Panel a

Production equilibrium

Panel b

Exchange equilibrium

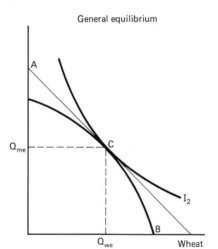

Panel c

General equilibrium

Figure 11.5 *Conditions for competitive general equilibrium.* General equilibrium conditions will be satisfied when both consumers and producers are in equilibrium. Focusing on producers first, we know from Chapter 5 that producers will be in equilibrium (i.e., at a point where they are maximizing their profits) when they are operating on their production possibilities curve and producing that combination of products that maximizes their profits. In a two-product economy, this would occur at point C in panel a, where the slope of the isorevenue line is equal to the marginal rate of product transformation. Consumers, in turn, would maximize their utility by purchasing that combination of these two products given by the equality if the ratio of their prices and the marginal rate of substitution. Panel b indicates that this would occur at point C as well. Finally, panel c suggests that the economy will be in equilibrium at point C.

by producers, who in turn are using all the inputs supplied at the going prices.
These conditions describe an economically efficient system. When these conditions are met, producers will be on their joint production possibilities curve rather than at some inefficient location inside this curve, and the economic welfare of society (producers and consumers) will be maximized.[4]

If the economy depicted in Figure 11.5 is *not* in equilibrium, market forces will be at work to reestablish general equilibrium. To illustrate, let us examine the process by which the general equilibrium price levels for missiles and wheat were determined. Let us assume that the initial set of prices were equal to those given by the isorevenue line *EF*, reflecting a lower relative price of wheat. Confronted with these relative prices, we see in Figure 11.6 that producers would want to produce Q_{ms} units of missiles and Q_{ws} units of wheat. But consumers would want to purchase Q_{md} units of missiles (remember that the government is a consumer) and Q_{wd} units of wheat. Thus both markets are in disequilibrium; there is a shortage of wheat (i.e., Q_{wd} exceeds Q_{ws}) and a surplus of missiles (i.e., Q_{ms} exceeds Q_{md}). At current prices, producers wish to produce Q_{ms} and Q_{ws} (point *G* in Figure 11.6). At current prices, consumers wish to buy Q_{md} and Q_{wd} (point *D* in Figure 11.6). Note this is not possible since point *D* lies beyond the production possibilities curve.

As the markets adjust as described earlier in Chapter 9, the price of missiles will fall and the price of wheat will rise. As these prices change, the slope of the isorevenue line *EF* adjusts toward the slope of the isorevenue line *AB* in Figure 11.5. The intercept of the isorevenue line on the missile axis, (revenue $\div$ P_m) rises from point *E* to point *A* as P_m declines. The interrupt on the wheat axis (revenue $\div$ P_w) shifts toward point *B* as P_w increases. Producers will respond by reducing their production of missiles from Q_{ms} toward Q_{md} and stepping up their production of wheat from Q_{ws} toward Q_{md}. This movement will continue until line *EF* rotates to exactly equal line *AB*. When this occurs, the quantity of missiles demanded will equal the quantity supplied (i.e., $Q_{md} = Q_{ms} = Q_{me}$) and the quantity of wheat demanded will equal the quantity supplied (i.e., $Q_{wd} = Q_{ws} = Q_{we}$).

In the real world, one can think of several examples of product and resource markets where imperfectly competitive behavior is practiced (see Chapter 9). This means that resources may be allocated *less efficiently* than they would have been under perfect competition. If producers of missiles formed a monopoly and thus ceased acting as perfect competitors, they would restrict the quantity of missiles produced to something less than Q_{me} in Figure 11.6. The economy would move to the right of point *C* in this

----

[4]While competitive behavior may be economically efficient, this does not mean that a competitive general equilibrium leads to socially desirable outcomes when factors other than economics are considered (e.g., existence of starvation). For a discussion of social benefits, costs, external economies (i.e., when marginal social cost differs from marginal private costs) see Ferguson and Maurice (1974).

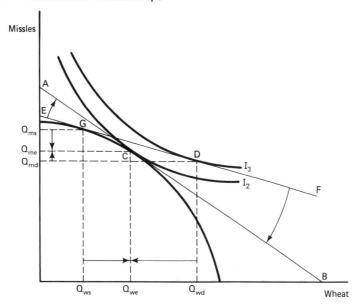

Figure 11.6 *Adjustment to general equilibrium.* Let us assume for the moment that a disequilibrium exists between production and consumption. Assume that the relative prices of the two goods produced in the economy are given by the slope of isorevenue line *EF* instead of *AB*. This results in a surplus of missiles and a shortage of wheat. Producers will respond to this situation by cutting back their production of missiles and expanding their production of wheat. This will cause the isorevenue line to rotate from line *EF* to line *AB*. The adjustment from disequilibrium to general equilibrium will be complete when line *AB* is reached. At this point, consumers will demand exactly what producers desire to supply: namely, a quantity of wheat equal to Q_{we} and a quantity of missiles equal to Q_{me}.

case since consumers would no longer be able to reach the I_2 indifference curve as before. As a result, the economic welfare of society will fall. Adjustments to general equilibrium prices and quantities may also be slow and continuous in nature. The economy in today's highly complex and integrated world may always be adjusting to new events. The study of multimarket relationships and general equilibrium is nonetheless useful for analysis purposes.

LINKAGES TO OTHER SECTORS

Now that we know we need to be aware of the interrelationships among markets if we want to fully understand the events taking place in the farm business sector, let us examine the linkages between this sector and other sectors of the economy. The farm business sector is linked with a number of other sectors in the domestic economy. For example, farm businesses purchase inputs from input supply firms and they sell raw farm products to processing and manufacturing firms, which in turn supply goods to wholesale and retail firms. These relationships were alluded to in an aggregate fashion earlier in Figure 2.1. In addition to these and other nonfinancial linkages, there are also a number of financial linkages between the farm business sector and the general economy.

Nonfinancial Linkages

Let us group input suppliers, processors, manufactures, and wholesalers and retailers of food and fiber products together with other firms into a single sector for the moment. We shall refer to this sector as the *nonfarm business sector,* a term frequently found in U.S. Department of Commerce publications. A major nonfinancial linkage between the farm and nonfarm business sectors takes place in the *domestic raw agricultural products markets,* where the supply of unprocessed output by farm businesses and the demand for these goods by nonfarm businesses and government are captured. Empirical studies have shown that approximately 54 cents out of every dollar's worth of agricultural output passes through this general market [44 of these 54 cents worth of product goes directly to processors (Penson et al., 1981)].

Another nonfinancial linkage is captured in the *manufactured farm inputs market,* where such goods as machinery and equipment, fertilizer and chemicals, fuel, and a variety of other products are sold to farm businesses. Over 20 percent of the production costs incurred annually by farm businesses are associated with goods purchased in this market (see U.S. Department of Agriculture, *Economic Indicators of the Farm Sector*).

The demand for and supply of farm real estate by farm as well as nonfarm businesses is captured in the *domestic farm real estate market.* For example, 86 percent of the acreage associated with farm real estate transfers in 1981 was acquired by buyers who intended to use this land in agriculture. The remaining 14 percent intended to use this land for other purposes (e.g., rural residences, recreation, subdivision, and commercial uses) (see U.S. Department of Agriculture, *Farm Real Estate Market Developments*). The quantities of land bought and sold foreign investors are also captured in this market.

Another example of a nonfinancial linkage between farm and nonfarm businesses takes place in the *farm input rental market.* Here, farm businesses lease the services of such items as machinery and equipment from nonfarm businesses as well as lease land and other farm assets from nonoperator landlords. The net rent paid to nonoperator landlords for the use of rented assets was $6.6 billion in 1981 (see U.S. Department of Agriculture, *Economic Indicators of the Farm Sector*). In addition to this return, nonoperator landlords also received approximately 30 percent of the annual capital gains accruing to farmland owners.

Other nonfinancial linkages include the supply of labor services by farm operator families and others in the *farm and nonfarm labor markets.* For example, farm operator families supply labor services demanded by farm businesses in the farm labor market. Some labor services provided by farm operator families is not paid a wage, however, and therefore do not appear in this market. Hired farm labor families and part-time laborers also supply labor services in this market. The total cash wages paid to hired labor amounted in 1981 to $9.3 billion (see U.S. Department of Agriculture, *Economic Indicators of the Farm Sector*). All of the labor groups above also supply labor services to nonfarm businesses and governments in the nonfarm labor market. During much of the post–World War II period, farm operator families as a whole received more income from off-farm activities than they did from their own farming operations.

As indicated earlier in Chapter 9, farmers are generally *price takers* rather than *price setters* in each of these markets. In other words, the relative market power of farmers is such that they generally must accept the price others offer to pay them for their product and pay the price others set for the inputs they use. Nonfinancial linkages between agriculture and the general economy are summarized in Table 11.1.

Financial Linkages

Farm businesses are financially linked to the general economy in a variety of ways (see Table 11.2). For example, farm operator families use part of their firm's current income to pay their income and Social Security taxes as well as to finance their personal consumption and other nonfarm uses of funds. The income remaining after these withdrawals is referred to as "retained earnings" and represents both an incremental change to the value of the firm as well as a means of financing investments by the farm business. A related financial linkage is the direct equity investments in farm business assets made by farm operator families *and* nonoperator landlord families. Nonoperator landlords are also financially linked to farm businesses through the rental income they receive from farmers.

Another financial linkage between farm businesses and the general economy is the *flow of new loans and loan repayments* between this sector and financial institutions. In 1981, the *net* flow of farm loan funds (i.e., new loans minus repayments) to farm businesses from private financial institutions amounted to $15.8 billion (see U.S. Department of Agriculture, *Economic Indicators of the Farm Sector*). The government also lends funds to farm businesses through Farmers Home Administration (FmHA) and Commodity Credit Corporation (CCC) programs. We devote an entire chapter to this important financial linkage (Chapter 16).

The *flow of deposits* from farm businesses to such depository institutions as commercial banks represents another form of financial linkage.

Activity	Good or services	Market	Other sectors involved
1. Sell output	Crops and livestock products	Domestic raw agricultural market	Food processors and manufacturers, exporters, consumers
2. Buy inputs	Machinery and equipment fertilizer chemicals, fuel	Manufactured farm inputs markets	Feed manufacturers, equipment manu- facturers, chemical and fertilizer manufacturers, oil and gas retailers
3. Buy real estate	Land and buildings	Domestic farm real estate market	Current owners of farmland, building manu- facturers
4. Rent inputs	Real estate and equipment	Farm input rental market	Current owners of farmland, equipment users (manufacturers, banks, etc.)
5. Hire labor	Labor services	Farm labor market	Farm and nonfarm households
6. Work off farm	Labor services	Nonfarm labor	Manufacturers, service industries

TABLE 11.1 NONFINANCIAL LINKAGES BETWEEN AGRICULTURE AND GEN-ERAL ECONOMY. Farm businesses interact with a variety of other sectors in the economy as they buy production inputs and sell their goods and services. Over one-half of farm business output is sold in domestic raw agricultural product markets (the remainder is sold to other farm businesses or directly to consumers). Farm businesses have dramatically increased their use of manufactured farm inputs during the post–World War II period as capital was substituted for labor. The value of farmland is influenced by demand and supply conditions in the nation's farm real estate markets. Farmers also rent inputs, hire farm labor, and provide labor services to nonfarm employers during periods of slack farm labor requirements.

These institutions also obtain funds in the form of deposits made by non-operator landlord families, farm operator families, and hired labor families, as well as from other sources. Other financial institutions, such as the Farm Credit System, obtain their new loanable funds from the *sale of debt securities* in the nation's bond market. A few farm businesses and many nonfarm businesses also obtain financing from the *sale of debt and equity securities* in nation's bond and stock markets.

   The final financial linkage between farm businesses and the general economy discussed here is the *flow of tax payments* from these firms and/or

Activity	Other sectors involved
1. Deposit funds in checking accounts or savings accounts	Banks, savings and loans, credit unions
2. Withdraw income from firm	Farm households and nonoperator landlords
3. Pay income, property, and Social Security taxes	Local, state, and federal government
4. Borrow	Private lenders (e.g., banks and Farm Credit System) and public lenders (e.g., Commodity Farmers Home Administration)
5. Buy stocks and bonds	Brokers, financial markets, nonfarm firms selling securities
6. Receive government payments	Federal government
7. Receive outside equity capital	Farm households, nonoperator landlords, and other investor groups
8. Withdraw equity capital	Discontinuing farm operators

TABLE 11.2   FINANCIAL LINKAGES BETWEEN AGRICULTURE AND GENERAL ECONOMY. Farm businesses also interact with other sectors in the nation's financial markets. For example, farm businesses place funds in checking accounts and time and saving accounts at banks and other depository institutions. Farmers also withdraw income from their farm businesses to finance their family's consumption expenditures. They also pay taxes, borrow funds to finance their business expenses and investments, buy stocks and bonds, and receive government payments (some even receive outside equity capital invested in their business). Finally, some farmers withdraw their equity in their business from the farm business sector when they sell out and leave farming.

farm operator families to the government and the reverse *flow of government payments* from the government to farm businesses and farm operator families. For example, farm businesses in 1982 received $0.9 billion in government deficiency payments, $0.8 billion in government storage payments, and $2.1 billion in government payments to dairy producers.

FARM OUTPUT AND GNP

Earlier we illustrated the relationship between households and businesses in a general equilibrium setting and how this led to the calculations of gross national product in this country. How can we assess the farm business sector's contribution to this often-quoted national statistic? To begin with, the total demand for a specific good or service can be divided into *intermediate demand* and *final demand*. The final demand for a particular sector's product refers to that portion of its total output that goes *directly* to (1)

USDA Photo by David Warren

The photo above depicts a roadside stand where a farm business sells specific types of products directly to consumers. Only 16 cents out of every dollar of total farm sales, however, represent sales of products by farmers directly to their ultimate consumer. The remaining 84 cents per dollar of total farm product sales goes to other business sectors in the economy for use as an input in their own production processes. For example, approximately 44 cents of every dollar of total farm product sales goes directly to food processors, which transform these raw agricultural products into a form desired by their eventual consumer.

household consumption, (2) business investment, (3) net exports, or (4) government expenditures. The remainder of the demand for this good or service is considered intermediate demand since it represents that portion of total output used by this and other sectors to *produce additional output.*

A recent empirical study showed that 84 cents out of every dollar's worth of farm output represents an intermediate good in that it is used as an input to produce another product (Penson et al., 1981). Thus 84 percent of *farm output goes to intermediate demand.* This means that only 16 cents (i.e., $1.00 – $0.84) out of every *dollar's worth of farm output goes directly to final demand.*

In recent years, agriculture (i.e., the farm business sector) has accounted for approximately 2.5 percent of this country's gross national product. The sector's contribution to GNP or its "value added" is found by subtracting the value of its purchases of intermediate goods and services from the value of its total output.[5] As Table 11.3 suggests, the sector's relative contribution in 1980 was only one-half of its contribution to GNP back in 1950. Thus, while the farm business sector's value added was growing, its *relative share* of GNP has been declining during the post–World War II period. One of the reasons underlying this declining contribution is the greater use of more expensive manufactured inputs and less reliance on inputs produced on the farm (e.g., more manufactured fertilizer and chemicals and less use of manure).

The discussion above should convince you that it is incorrect to think that the *nation's* output is equal to the sum of each sector's output. Such a notion would fail to recognize that a portion of each sector's output was

Year	Gross national product	Agriculture's contribution	Percentage contribution
1950	$ 534.8	$27.0	5.05
1960	737.2	29.2	3.96
1970	1,058.6	31.1	2.86
1980	1,480.7	35.2	2.38

Note: Values in billions of dollars of 1972 dollars.

Source: Economic Report of the President (Washington, D.C.: U.S. Government Printing Office (1982).

TABLE 11.3 AGRICULTURE'S CONTRIBUTION TO GROSS NATIONAL PRODUCT. The farm business sector's relative contribution to the nation's total output has been declining during the post–World War II period. While its contribution has increased from $27 billion in 1950 to $35 billion in 1980 (measured in constant dollars), its relative contribution to that made by other sectors in the economy has dropped in half. In 1950, the farm business contributed slightly more than 5 percent of the nation's gross national product. By the beginning of the eighties, however, this percentage had dropped to about 2.4 percent. One of the reasons for this decline is the sector's increased use of manufactured inputs (e.g., fertilizer and chemicals) and less reliance on its own by-products (e.g., manure).

[5] The interested reader is referred to the Advanced Topics section at the end of this chapter, where a more in-depth discussion of interindustry relationships and output–input analysis is presented.

used as an input to the production of other products in the economy during the year.

SUMMARY

The purpose of this chapter was to introduce the concept of general equilibrium, the relationship between sector output and GNP, and the physical and financial linkages between the farm business sector and the rest of the economy. The major points made in this chapter can be summarized as follows:

1. A *partial equilibrium* essentially assumes that other things will remain unchanged. In many situations, however, it is necessary to take into account events taking place simultaneously in other markets. When we do this, we are focusing on a *general equilibrium.*

2. A general equilibrium exists when all markets are in equilibrium. If some are not (i.e., shortages or surpluses exist), market forces will be at work to establish a general equilibrium.

3. A general equilibrium of *production* occurs when the marginal rates of technical substitution between pairs of inputs are the same for all producers. A general equilibrium of *exchange* exists when the marginal rates of substitution between every pair of goods is the same for all consumers.

4. The economy in today's interdependent world may always be reacting to events and thus continually be adjusting to, but rarely reaching, a general equilibrium in the economy.

5. The economy's GNP is not equal to the sum of each sector's output. Instead, GNP is given by the total final demands for the economy's goods and services less imports. The output of each sector can be divided into that part which is used to produce additional output (i.e., intermediate demand) and that part which goes directly to final markets (i.e., final demand), where it is purchased by consumers, investors, foreign countries, and government.

6. The linkages between the farm business sector and the rest of the economy can be grouped into *physical* linkages and *financial* linkages.

DEFINITION OF TERMS

Partial equilibrium analysis: assumes the events taking place outside the market under analysis remain constant.

General equilibrium analysis: regards all sectors of the economy as being interdependent. The events taking place in all markets are considered in the analysis.

Gross national product: referred to as the nation's output, GNP is equal to consumer expenditures, business investment, government spending, and net exports (exports minus imports).

Barter economy: money is not used as the medium of exchange. Instead, households and businesses "swap" goods and services in satisfying their needs.

Monetary economy: unlike a barter economy, money is used as the principal medium of exchange. Households receive remuneration in the form of wages, rents, interest, and profits. Businesses receive remuneration in the form of expenditures by households, businesses, government, and foreign countries.

Intermediate demand: the quantity of goods and services used to produce other products as opposed to going directly to final demand.

Final demand: expenditures by consumers, investments by businesses, government spending, and net exports. Stated another way, final demand is equal to total output intermediate demand.

Disequilibrium: if a market is not in equilibrium (quantity demanded equals quantity supplied at announced price), the market is in disequilibrium. The existence of surpluses and shortages in a market indicates the existence of disequilibrium.

Interdependent: when two or more prices or quantities or other factors dependent on one another, they are said to be interdependent.

Medium of exchange: the means by which goods and services are paid for represents the medium of exchange. Money in a monetary economy serves as the principal medium of exchange.

Gross national income: given by the income approach to measuring economic activity, national income is equal to the sum of wages, rents, interest, and profits.

National product: see gross national product.

Depository institution: a financial institution, such as a commercial bank or a savings and loan association, which accepts deposits in exchange for interest income.

Budget deficit: the excess of government spending over government receipts.

Budget surplus: the excess of government receipts over government spending.

REFERENCES

FERGUSON, C. E., and S. C. MAURICE, *Economic Analysis*. Homewood, Ill.: Richard D. Irwin, Inc., 1974.

PENSON, JOHN B., JR., HOVAV TALPAZ, and HENRY S. FOSTER, "Estimation of a Quadratic Input-Output Model for the U.S. Economy," *Proceedings of the Annual Computer Simulation Conference*, Society for Computer Simulation, July 1981, pp. 538–541.

U.S. DEPARTMENT OF AGRICULTURE, *Economic Indicators of the Farm Sector*, ERS, USDA Statistical Bulletin Series. Washington, D.C.: U.S. Government Printing Office, selected issues.

U.S. DEPARTMENT OF AGRICULTURE, *Farm Real Estate Market Developments*. Washington, D.C.: U.S. Government Printing Office, selected issues.

ADDITIONAL READINGS

LEONTIEF, WASSILY, *The Structure of the American Economy*. New York: Oxford University Press, Inc., 1951.

MIERNYK, WILLIAM H., *The Elements of Input–Output Analysis*. New York: Random House Inc., 1965.

PENSON, JOHN B., JR., "Capturing the Linkages between Agriculture and the Domestic Economy," in *Modeling Agriculture for Policy Analysis in the 1980s*. Kansas City: Federal Reserve Bank of Kansas City, pp. 47–64, 1981.

PENSON, JOHN B. JR., and MURRAY E. FULTON, *Description and Use of a Quadratic Input-Output Model for the Texas Economy*, DTR 79-5, College Station, Tex.: Texas Agricultural Experiment Station, 1979.

QUESTIONS

1. What are the principal differences between:
   (a) Partial and general equilibrium?
   (b) Barter and monetary economy?
   (c) National income and national product?
   (d) Budget deficit and budget surplus?

2. Describe the conditions necessary for a general equilibrium in the economy. How does this relate to the concept of economic welfare?

3. What are the major non-financial linkages between the farm business sector and the rest of the economy? Are farmers likely to be "price takers" or "price setters" in these markets? Why?

4. What is the difference between non-financial linkages and financial linkages?

5. Describe how you would measure the farm business sector's contribution to the country's gross national product. What has happened to this sector's relative contribution over time?

ADVANCED TOPICS

One approach to gaining a better understanding of the interdependencies among sectors in an economy is *input–output analysis.* First developed by Nobel laureate Wassily Leontief, input–output analysis centers around calculations made using data provided by an input–output table. An input–output table captures the distribution of a sector's current output between intermediate demand and final demand. It also captures a sector's use of inputs produced by other sectors.

Figure 11.7 helps us conceptualize each sector's relative share of total expenditures for goods and services. For example, the first *row* in this figure, when completed, would tell us where "agriculture's" output went to. The value in the "manufacturing" box in this row would represent the value of farm output used as an input in the manufacturing sector. The sum of the values recorded in the shaded boxes in the first row therefore represents the *intermediate demand* for farm output. The value of agricultural output going directly to final markets (i.e., persons, investors, foreigners, and governments) is reported in the nonshaded boxes in this row. If we summed all the final demands for goods and services in the economy, this is equivalent to the "expenditure approach" taken to measuring gross national product, which will be discussed in the next chapter.

The sum of all the boxes in the row for agriculture (which represents the sector's total output) minus the sum of all the boxes in the column for agriculture (the sector's use of intermediate goods and services) equals the *value added* by agriculture. Value added represents the compensation of employees, rent, interest, and profit. As such, it represents the "income approach" to measuring national income and product. The sum of the value added by each sector represents the nation's gross national product.

Input–Output Table

The input–output table is similar in design to Figure 11.7. In fact, the only major difference is the explicit accounting of value added by each production sector that appears in an input–output table. Table 11.4 presents an input–output table for the U.S. economy for 1972. The final demand for specific goods and services by persons, investors, foreigners, and government have been condensed into one column in Table 11.4, labeled "final demand."

The first row in this table shows that total production of raw agricultural products in the economy during that year was $92.08 billion, of which $39.8 billion was sold to the "Processed Foods and Tobacco" sector for further processing before going to final demand. Another $26.6 billion was retained by farm businesses for use in producing additional raw agricultural products (e.g., feed grain fed to livestock). Thus, only a small proportion of

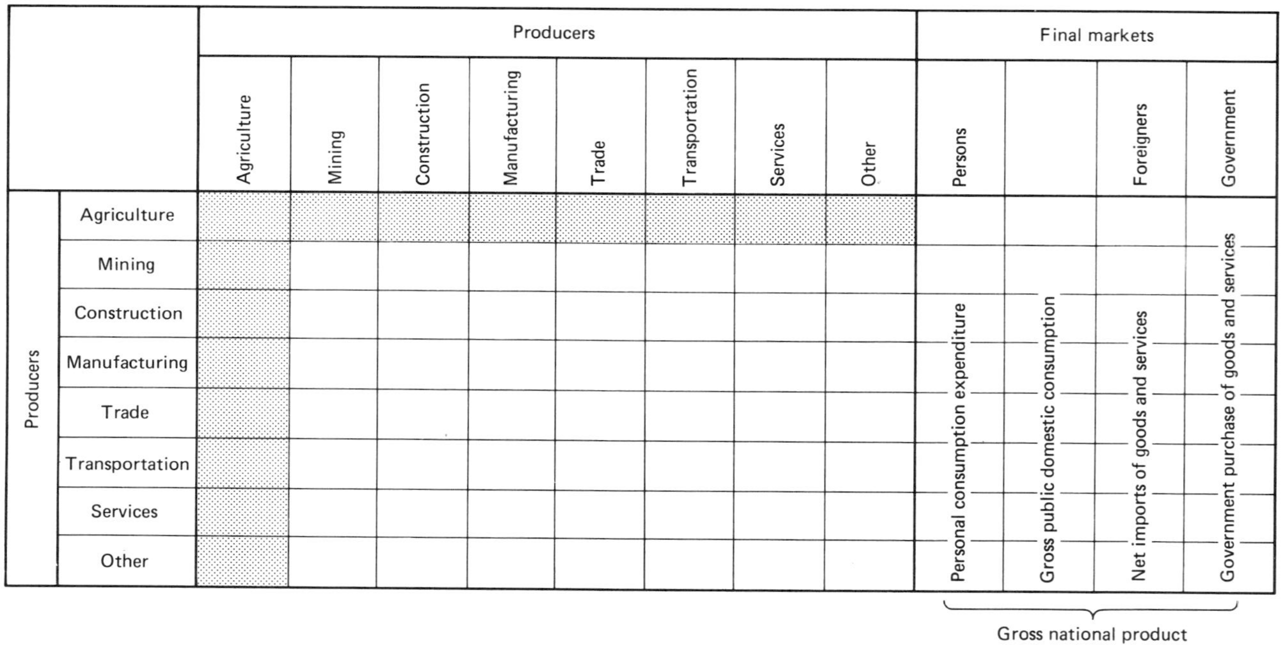

		Producers								Final markets			
		Agriculture	Mining	Construction	Manufacturing	Trade	Transportation	Services	Other	Persons	Foreigners		Government
Producers	Agriculture									Personal consumption expenditure	Net imports of goods and services	Gross public domestic consumption	Government purchase of goods and services
	Mining												
	Construction												
	Manufacturing												
	Trade												
	Transportation												
	Services												
	Other												

Gross national product

Figure 11.7 *Interindustry relationships in the general economy.* We can visualize the farm business sector's role in the economy and how to assess its contribution to the nation's gross national product with the help of this figure. The shaded row captures the products the sector supplies to other sectors (including itself), which are then used as inputs to produce other goods and services. The nonshaded boxes in this row represent sales by farm businesses directly to their final consumer. Only 16 cents out of every dollar's worth of farm output goes to the nonshaded boxes in this row. In other words, 84 cents goes to intermediate demand. The shaded column in this figure captures the purchases of inputs by farmers for use in their farming operations. The difference between the sum of all the boxes (both shaded and nonshaded) in the first row and the sum of all the boxes in the first column represents the "value added" by the farm business sector. As such, it represents the sector's contribution to the nation's total output or gross national product. The total gross national product can then be found by either summing all the boxes in the "final demand" columns or summing the value added by each sector.

Sectors producing

Sectors Purchasing	Raw agricultural products	Mining and quarrying products	Construction	Manufacturing	Processed foods and tobacco	Energy	Services	Trade and transportation	Final demand	Total sales
Raw agricultural products	26,642	0	390	3,637	39,823	76	5,053	362	14,111	90,084
Mining and quarrying products	167	1,819	1,333	7,206	104	22,441	680	68	1,427	35,245
Construction	680	801	44	2,890	393	2,209	17,001	2,980	139,003	166,001
Manufacturing	5,205	2,944	52,090	284,360	12,371	2,316	41,253	12,922	260,480	674,021
Processed foods and tobacco	4,001	0	0	1,754	24,002	50	5,897	1,607	94,430	132,701
Energy	2,287	803	3,304	12,409	1,254	15,002	10,510	9,053	40,598	96,020
Services	6,957	5,060	11,857	46,838	8,595	12,638	108,745	55,794	463,327	718,811
Trade and transportation	5,258	1,119	16,674	33,842	8,443	4,081	24,926	18,350	216,286	328,979
Imports	1,778	3,529	0	24,800	3,000	2,041	5,871	3,506		
Value added	36,149	19,170	80,309	256,295	34,636	34,366	499,897	223,537		
Total production	90,084	35,245	166,001	674,021	132,701	96,020	719,811	328,977		

TABLE 11.4 INTERINDUSTRY TRANSACTION TABLE, UNITED STATES. The dollar value of the product and input flows eluded to in Figure 11.7 are presented in this table. For example, we see that only $14.1 billion out of a total farm output of approximately $90 billion went directly to final demand. The largest buyer of raw agricultural products was the processed foods and tobacco sector ($39.8 billion). The sector's contribution to gross national product was said to be the difference between total sector output and its total purchases of intermediate goods and services, or value added. This table shows that the value added in the farm business sector was approximately $36 billion, or 3.05 percent of the economy's gross national product of $1,184 billion. The greatest contributors to GNP were the manufacturing and services sectors.

the total output of raw agricultural products in the 1972 U.S. economy went to final demand. A healthy farm business sector therefore would be extremely important not only to itself, but also to other sectors, such as the processed foods and tobacco sector, which acquires raw agricultural products as an input to its own production process.

Looking down the first column of this table, we see that the farm business sector purchased inputs from all other sectors in the economy, but in varying amounts. Note that total sales of $90,084 million minus purchases of inputs from domestic and foreign sources of $53,935 million results in a value added of $36,149 million in this sector. This value represents the returns to capital, labor, and management in this sector.

Another feature of this table is the measurement of the economy's GNP and the farm business sector's contribution to this total. If we sum each sector's value added reported in the last row of this input–output table, we can determine the economy's total output or GNP. Following this "income approach," we find a value of $1,184,337 million. We also see that the farm business sector's contribution in 1972 was 3.05 percent (i.e., $36,149 ÷ $1,184,337).

Finally, we can also determine the economy's GNP by summing the final demand for each sector's product and subtracting the sum of the imports row reported in this table. Doing this, we see that total final demand was $1,229,622 million, while the imports row totaled to $45,325 million. Thus the economy's GNP following this "expenditure approach" would also be $1,184,337 million (i.e., $1,229,622 − $45,325).

Thus an input–output table tells us something about the distribution of the sector's total sales and total purchases. It also allows us to assess each sector's contribution to the *economy's* total output.

Technical Coefficients

Another interesting feature of input–output analysis is the computation and interpretation of *technical coefficients.* These coefficients help us understand the relative factor shares associated with each sector's use of inputs. To obtain these technical coefficients for any particular sector, we must divide each purchase by the sector's total purchases appearing at the bottom of the column. For example, the technical coefficient for manufacturing inputs in the farm business sector would be 0.0587 (i.e., $5,285 ÷ $90,084).

These technical coefficients for the 1972 U.S. economy are reported in Table 11.5. Looking at this table, we see that approximately 30 percent of the farm business sector's total input purchases went toward acquiring intermediate products produced in this sector. Raw agricultural products also represented 30 percent of the inputs employed in the processed food and tobacco sector. Raw agricultural products do not represent a significant input in any of the other production sectors.

	Sectors producing							
Sectors Purchasing	Raw agricultural products	Mining and quarrying	Construction	Manufacturing	Processed foods and tobacco	Energy	Services	Trade and transportation
Raw agricultural products	0.2957	0.0000	0.0023	0.0054	0.3001	0.0008	0.0070	0.0011
Mining and quarrying products	0.0019	0.0516	0.0080	0.0107	0.0008	0.2337	0.0009	0.0002
Construction	0.0075	0.0227	0.0003	0.0043	0.0030	0.0230	0.0236	0.0091
Manufacturing	0.0587	0.0835	0.3138	0.4219	0.0932	0.0241	0.0573	0.0393
Processed foods and tobacco	0.0542	0.0000	0.0000	0.0026	0.1815	0.0005	0.0082	0.0049
Energy	0.0254	0.0226	0.0199	0.0184	0.0094	0.1562	0.0146	0.0300
Services	0.0772	0.1436	0.0714	0.0695	0.0648	0.1316	0.1511	0.1696
Trade and transportation	0.0584	0.0317	0.1004	0.0502	0.0636	0.0425	0.0346	0.0554

TABLE 11.5 TECHNICAL COEFFICIENTS, UNITED STATES. An important insight to the interrelationships between sectors of the economy is given by the technical coefficients provided by input-output analysis. These coefficients—found by dividing each input category by total output—show the relative contributions these inputs make in the sector's production process. For example, the largest technical coefficient in the agriculture column (0.2957) corresponds to its own products. Thus, the corn and other products fed to livestock and similar interrelationships show that this sector has a stake in its own performance as well as the performance of others. Other significant inputs are provided by the services (e.g., credit) sector.

Multipliers

Policymakers often want to know what the "multiplier" effects of a policy targeted for one sector are for *other* manufacturing sectors as well as households. Suppose that a program to promote the export demand for agricultural products by $10 billion is instituted. Multiplier analysis using the coefficients from an input–output table is one approach to providing this information. A "type II" *income multiplier* for agriculture of 3.12, for example, would suggest that the *direct effect* of a $10 billion increase in agricultural output on household income (payment for land, labor, capital, and management services) of $3.2 billion would have a *total effect* (i.e., direct, indirect, and induced) on the economy as a whole of $9.984 billion (i.e., $3.2 billion × 3.12).

part IV

MACROECONOMIC POLICY AND AGRICULTURE

12

MEASURING MACROECONOMIC PERFORMANCE

The application of macroeconomic policy to achieve specific goals for the economy requires vast amounts of information on the economy's current performance. Policymakers focusing on the economy as a whole are interested in the trends in such items as total consumption and investment expenditures. Policymakers with a particular interest in the health of the farm business sector want to keep abreast of fluctuations in farm cash receipts and net farm income. The federal government devotes a sizable amount of its resources annually to gathering information on the performance of the economy and publishing its findings for the benefit of policymakers and others.

The purpose of this chapter is (1) to introduce the general nature of the economic accounting system used by the federal govenment to determine the economy's performance at the national and sector levels, and (2) to discuss the economic consequences of fluctuations in business activity. Particular attention is given to assessing the farm business sector's contribution to the economy and to measuring unemployment and inflation.

NATIONAL ECONOMIC ACCOUNTING SYSTEM

The centerpiece of our country's national economic accounting system is the national income and product accounts published by the U.S. Department of Commerce. These accounts describe both the level and composition of our nation's gross national income and gross national product. In addition, the

Federal Reserve System publishes a balance sheet for the economy as well as a national flow-of-funds account. The discussion of these national accounts presented below focuses primarily on the income and product accounts.

Income and Product Accounts

The measurement of the nation's income and product (output) can be illustrated in the context of the relationship between (1) the flow of goods and services, and (2) the payments for the products and resource services depicted in Figure 11.4. The top portion of this figure, which accounted for the level of expenditures by households, businesses (inventory buildup and expenditures on new plant and equipment), and government for the goods produced by businesses, measures gross national product from an *expenditure point of view*. The value of the nation's gross national product in 1983, for example, was determined as follows:

	1983
Personal consumption expenditures	$2,155.9
Gross private domestic investment	471.3
Government purchases of goods and services	685.5
Net exports of goods and services	+ (8.3)
Gross national product	**$3,304.8**

which indicates that the value of the nation's output in 1983 was $3,304.8 billion. Nearly two-thirds of this total is accounted for by personal consumption expenditures.

The bottom portion of Figure 11.4, which accounted for payments for services provided by land, labor, capital, and management, measures gross national income from an *income point of view*. This requires totaling employee compensation, rent, profits, interest, indirect business taxes, and capital consumption allowances (depreciation). The value of gross national income is *identical* to the value of gross national product determined above.

While these aggregate measures of the economy's performance are informative, disaggregation of these statistics to determine consumer disposable income and saving gives economists further insight into the nature of the economy's performance.

Measurement of disposable income.   Any disaggregation of these accounts must begin with gross national product. The term "gross" in gross national product refers to the fact that we have not deducted the *depreciation* or wear-out of selected business assets (e.g., machinery) during the year. The U.S. Department of Commerce estimates the annual value of depreciation (also sometimes referred to as capital consumption allowances) to determine the economy's *net national product*, or

	1983
Gross national product	$3,304.8
Depreciation	– 377.1
Net national product	2,927.7

Net national product thus represents the economy's net output for the year.

To measure disposable personal income, we must first determine the economy's *national income.* This is done by subtracting total indirect business taxes from net national product, or

	1983
Net national product	$2,927.7
Indirect business taxes	– 281.0
National income	**$2,646.7**

where indirect business taxes includes excise taxes, sales taxes, and property taxes paid by businesses.

The next step in determining the annual level of disposable personal income requires the measurement of total personal income in the economy. This value is found by subtracting corporate profits, taxes, and Social Security contributions made by individuals from national income and then adding transfer payments (e.g., Social Security payments, food stamps, and welfare payments) or

National income	$2,646.7
Undistributed corporate profits	28.0
Corporate income taxes	75.8
Social security contributions	– 272.7
Subtotal	2,270.2
Transfer payments to individuals	+ 474.0
Personal income	**$2,744.2**

Finally, total personal income does not reflect the amount of personal tax and nontax payments individuals must pay to the government. To compute the *disposable* personal income earned by individuals during the year, we must calculate as follows:

	1983
Personal income	$2,744.2
Personal tax and nontax payments	– 404.1
Disposable personal income	**$2,340.1**

Thus individuals in 1983 had a disposable personal income of $2,340.1 billion, which they either used to finance consumption expenditures or to increase their personal savings. Knowing the value of disposable personal income helps economists explain current consumption expenditures in the economy, which, as we said earlier, comprises two-thirds of the nation's gross national product.

Table 12.1 presents the values of these income concepts for selected years during the 1940–1983 period. This table indicates that the level of personal disposable income increased about 30-fold during the 1940–1983 period. These values are expressed in current dollars or nominal terms, however. No adjustments have been made to reflect changes in the purchasing power of the dollar during this period.

Measurement of savings.   The level of savings in the economy plays an important role; it represents the amount of new capital available to finance investment expenditures. The level of annual personal saving in the economy is found as follows:

Disposable personal income	$2,340.1
Personal outlays	–2,222.0
Personal saving	**$ 118.1**

where personal outlays of $2,188.0 billion consist largely of personal consumption expenditures and interest paid by consumers to businesses. The level of personal saving above suggests a savings rate for individuals in 1982 of 5.0 percent (i.e., $118.1 billion ÷ $2,340.1 billion). The annual savings rate during the post–World War II period has varied from a high of 8.6 percent in 1973 to a low of 5.6 percent in 1960.

Accounting for inflation.   Can we compare the economy's historical gross national product with its current gross national product when assessing economic performance? The answer is no. If a pound of hamburger costs $1.50 this year, 10 pounds of hamburger would have a market value of $15.00. If next year a pound of hamburger costs $3.00, 10 pounds would have a market value of $30.00. Note there has been no change in quantity, only in price. If we apply this analysis to every product during the year, we see that gross national product measured in current dollars may distort our perception of the level of economic activity from one year to the next. Since economists are interested in the *real* growth of the economy, the U.S. Depart of Commerce also reports the level of gross national product in *constant dollars* (i.e., gross national product expressed in 1972 dollars). This adjustment is accomplished by dividing gross national product in current dollars by the U.S. Department of Commerce's *implicit GNP price deflator,* which is an index reflecting the weighted average of all prices in a particular year relative to a selected base period.

Item	1940	1950	1960	1970	1980	1981	1982	1983
Personal consumption expenditure	$71.0	$192.0	$324.9	$621.7	$1,668.1	$1,849.1	$1,984.9	$2,155.9
Gross private domestic investment	13.1	53.8	75.9	144.2	401.9	484.2	414.9	471.6
Government purchases of goods and services	14.2	38.5	100.3	220.1	537.8	596.5	650.5	685.5
Net exports of goods and services	1.8	2.2	5.5	6.7	23.9	28.0	19.0	(8.3)
Gross national product	100.0	286.5	506.5	992.7	2,631.7	2,957.8	3,069.3	3,304.8
Depreciation	-9.1	-23.5	-46.3	-88.1	-293.2	-330.3	-358.8	-377.1
Net national product	91.0	263.0	460.2	904.7	2,338.5	2,627.5	2,710.4	2,927.7
Indirect business taxes	-11.3	-25.4	-44.5	-94.0	-221.9	-263.7	-263.6	-281.0
National income	79.9	237.6	415.7	810.7	2,116.6	2,363.8	2,446.8	2,646.7
Undistributed corporate profits	2.6	14.1	9.9	11.3	67.1	60.0	22.4	28.0
Corporate income taxes	2.8	17.9	22.7	34.2	84.8	81.1	60.7	75.8
Social Security contribution	-2.3	-7.1	-21.1	-58.6	-203.7	-236.8	-251.3	-272.7
Subtotal	72.0	198.5	362.0	706.6	1,761.0	1,985.9	2,112.4	2,270.2
Transfer payments to individuals	5.9	28.7	40.3	104.5	404.3	443.6	472.2	474.0
Personal income	77.9	227.2	402.3	811.1	2,165.3	2,429.5	2,584.6	2,744.2
Personal tax and nontax payments	-2.6	-20.6	-50.4	-115.8	-336.5	-387.7	-404.1	-404.1
Disposable personal income	75.3	206.6	352.0	695.3	1,828.9	2,041.7	2,180.5	2,340.1

Source: *Economic Report of the President* (Washington, D.C.: U.S. Government Printing Office, 1985)

TABLE 12.1 MEASUREMENT OF PERSONAL DISPOSABLE INCOME. One of the key variables economists use to gain an understanding of annual consumer expenditures is the level of consumers' disposable personal income. This income concept reflects the amount of income that individuals have left over after taxes either to spend or to save. The annual values reported are expressed in billions of current dollars. Care should therefore be exercised in interpreting these values over time because they have not been adjusted to reflect changes in the purchasing power of the dollar during this period (i.e., they are not expressed in constant dollars).

To illustrate the effect adjusting for inflation can have, consider the following values published by the U.S. Department of Commerce for 1981 and 1982:

Year	Nominal GNP	Price Deflator	Real GNP
1981	$2,957.8	1.9560	$1,512.2
1982	3,069.3	2.0738	1,480.0

While nominal gross national product or our nation's output expressed in current dollars rose in 1982, we see that the economy's real gross national product actually fell. Only by accounting for the effects of inflation would we be able to see the negative growth that occurred in the economy during 1982.[1]

We stated in conjunction with Table 12.1 that the level of disposable personal income had increased almost 30-fold during the 1940–1983 period. Since these dollar amounts were expressed in current dollars, however, any differences between the purchasing power of a dollar earned in 1940 and the purchasing power of a dollar earned in 1983 were ignored. Dividing these two annual values by their appropriate price deflator (0.2906 in 1940 and 2.1534 in 1983), we see that real disposable income in 1983 of $1,086.7 billion is only four times greater than the real disposable income of $259 billion in 1940.

Other Accounts

In addition to the national income and product accounts summarized above, the federal government maintains a number of other economic accounts that give policymakers and economists an insight to the economy's performance. The Federal Reserve System publishes a balance sheet for the U.S. economy which captures the growth of the assets and liabilities of businesses and households.[2] An end product of this balance sheet is a measure of private wealth in the U.S. economy.

The Federal Reserve System also maintains a flow-of-funds account for the economy which captures the amount of funds flowing between sectors in

---

[1] The price deflator of 1.9560 for 1981 in the table above reflects the fact that the general price level in 1981 was 95.6 percent higher than what it was in the base period used to calculate this deflator. The Advanced Topics section at the end of Chapter 2 presents a discussion of aggregate output and price indices.

[2] Board of Governors of the Federal Reserve System, Division of Research and Statistics, *Balance Sheets for the U.S. Economy*, (Washington, D.C.: U.S. Government Printing Office, various issues).

the economy during the year.[3] The information contained in this economic account is indispensable to policymakers and economists desiring to understand the role that financial markets play in financing the production and investment activities of businesses and households.

The federal government and a number of public and private institutions gather additional information on other indicators of the economy's performance. The Federal Reserve System, the U.S. Department of Commerce, the Conference Board, and McGraw-Hill, for example, collect and analyze information on the economy's manufacturing capacity and its utilization. The U.S. Departments of Labor and Commerce gather information on the prices of goods and services in the economy and the relative importance of these products in the Consumer Price Index (CPI) and Producer Price Index (PPI). The Federal Reserve System, the Department of the Treasury, and others also collect and publish information on bond yields and interest rates.

In short, policymakers and economists are "blessed" with a wealth of information published by a variety of sources, which gives them an insight into current trends in the eoconomy's performance.

SECTOR ECONOMIC ACCOUNTING SYSTEM

Agriculture enjoys the most comprehensive economic accounting system of any sector in the economy. The principal accounts in this system are a sector balance sheet, a sector income statement, and a sector cash flow statement. The following discussion of these economic accounts focuses primarily on the sector income statement.

Farm Income Accounts

Perhaps one of the most widely quoted statistics published by the U.S. Department of Agriculture is *operator's net farm income.* This annual performance statistic initially requires the measurement of total cash farm receipts as follows:

	1983
Cash receipts from marketings	$138.7
Government payments	+ 9.3
Total cash farm receipts	**$148.0**

which we see was $148 billion in 1983. This value represents the cash

[3] Board of Governors of the Federal Reserve System, *Federal Reserve Bulletin,* various issues, Washington, D.C.

farmers receive from marketing their products as well as from the federal government in the form of deficiency payments (see Chapter 10).

We must also account for other farm sources of income, including the value of farm products consumed directly by the farm household, the net change in farm inventories, and income earned from machine hire and custom work. Adding these sources of income of total cash farm receipts, we can determine gross income from farming. In 1983, the level of gross income from farming was

Total cash farm receipts	$148.0
Nonmoney and other farm income	+ 3.4
Gross income from farming	**$151.4**

or $151.4 billion. This value represents the cash income farmers received during the year as well as any noncash adjustments to income, reflecting, say, an increase in unsold production inventories.

Finally, operators' net farm income is found by subtracting farm production expenses from gross income from farming, or

Gross income from farming	$151.4
Production expenses	-135.3
Operators' net farm income	**$ 16.1**

where farm production expenses captures both cash operating expenses as well as such noncash costs as depreciation.

The operators' net farm income of $16.1 billion observed in 1983 thus represents a measure of the economic performance of farmers in that particular year. Table 12.2 reports the annual values of operators' net farm income for selected years during the 1940–1983 period expressed in current dollars. A comparison of these annual performance statistics during the 1980–1983 period reflects the variable nature of returns in this sector from one year to the next.

Since these annual values are expressed in current dollars, they have not been adjusted for changes in the purchasing power of the dollar over time. Thus it is difficult to compare the level of operators' net farm income of $4.4 billion achieved in 1940 with the value of $16.1 billion achieved in 1983. If we divide these two annual values by an appropriate price deflator (i.e., the index value of 0.2906 in 1940 and 2.1534 in 1983 used earlier to compute real GNP), however, we see that operators' *real* net farm income in 1983 of $7.5 billion (i.e., $16.1 billion ÷ 2.1534) is actually less than the operators' real net farm income of $15.2 billion in 1940 (i.e., $4.4 billion ÷ 0.2906). This illustrates the fact that an income of $4.4 billion in 1940 would buy more goods and services than $16.1 billion would have in 1983. You may recall that we presented a graph in Chapter 2 which showed the trend in net farm income in both current dollars and constant dollars (see

Item	1940	1950	1960	1970	1980	1981	1982	1983
Cash receipts from marketings	$ 8.4	$28.5	$34.2	$50.5	$140.5	$142.6	$144.8	$138.7
Government payments	0.7	0.3	0.7	3.7	1.3	1.9	3.5	9.3
Total cash receipts	9.1	28.8	34.9	54.2	141.8	144.5	148.3	148.0
Nonmoney and other farm income	2.2	4.4	3.9	4.6	8.4	3.4	3.6	3.4
Gross income from farming	11.3	33.2	38.9	58.8	150.2	167.9	161.9	151.4
Production expenses	− 6.9	−19.4	−27.4	−44.5	−128.9	−136.9	−139.5	−135.3
Operators' net farm income	4.4	13.7	11.5	14.4	21.3	31.0	22.4	16.1
Personal income from farm sources[a]	4.8	14.1	11.1	12.9	17.9	25.3	18.8	13.6
Personal income from nonfarm sources	+ 2.8	+ 6.3	+ 7.2	+14.5	+ 28.5	+ 29.9	+ 30.4	+ 33.3
Total personal income	7.6	20.4	18.3	27.4	46.4	55.2	49.2	46.9
Less personal tax and nontax payments	−0.3	−1.9	−2.3	−4.0	−7.2	−8.8	−7.7	−6.9
Disposable personal income	7.3	18.5	16.0	23.5	39.2	46.4	41.5	40.0
Farm as percentage of total disposable income	9.8%	9.0%	4.6%	3.4%	2.1%	2.3%	1.9%	1.7%

[a]Equals operators' net farm income less net income of nonresident operators plus wages, salaries, and other labor income of farm resident workers less contributions of farm resident operators and workers to social insurance.

Source: U.S. Department of Agriculture, Economic Indicators of the Farm Sector (Washington, D.C.: U.S. Government Printing Office, various issues).

TABLE 12.2 MEASUREMENT OF OPERATORS' NET FARM INCOME. A key performance statistic for agriculture is operators' net farm income, reported here in billions of current dollars. Care should again be exercised in comparing these statistics over time unless they are expressed in constant dollars (see Figure 2.3). We can compare the disposable personal income of the farm population with the total disposable personal income in the economy over time, however, because they are valued in identical dollars (by being expressed as a percentage of each other). We see at the bottom of this table that the farm population's contribution to the economy-wide total has been declining over time.

Figure 2.4).[4] This figure showed that while net farm income in current dollars had been rising, albeit in an uneven fashion, real net farm income has been trending downward.

Table 12.2 also reports the calculation of the disposable personal income earned by farm residents for selected years during the 1940–1983 period. Also reported here is the percentage that these annual values were of total disposable personal income in the economy reported at the bottom of Table 12.1. These annual percentages show, for example, that disposable personal income of farm residents in 1940 was 9.8 percent of total disposable personal income in the United States. By 1983, this percentage had fallen to 1.7 percent. This decline reflects the declining relative performance of the farm business sector of the economy over time. Since the number of farm families declined over this period, however, the individual buying power of the farm population did not fall quite so rapidly.

Other Accounts

In addition to the sector income statement, the U.S. Department of Agriculture maintains a sector balance sheet and cash flow statement. The sector balance sheet was presented in Table 2.3 and was discussed there. The cash flow statement reports the sources of cash in the sector (e.g. cash farm income, off-farm income, loan funds) and the uses made of this cash. This economic account allows economists to observe the relative role credit has played in financing annual farm investments expenditures over time.

In addition to these accounts, the U.S. Department of Agriculture publishes information on the costs of production, the productivity and efficiency of farming operations, and the prices that farmers receive for their products and pay for inputs, among other things. The publication *Agricultural Statistics* published annually by the U.S. Department of Agriculture provides a comprehensive collection of information on the structure and performance of this sector (see the Reference section).

AGRICULTURE'S CONTRIBUTION TO U.S. ECONOMY

How important is the farm business sector in today's highly developed economy? We can provide some insight to this question by examining this sector's contribution to several key national statistics. These statistics are the nation's (1) gross national product, (2) civilian labor force, (3) business inventories, (4) fixed business investment, and (5) merchandise exports (see Table 12.3).

---

[4] Equation (2.6) described the conversion of net farm income in current dollars to net farm income in constant dollars. Considered an "advanced topic" at that point, we now suggest that you review this topic in the Advanced Topics section at the end of Chapter 2 if you do not understand this procedure to adjustment for inflation.

Item	1950	1960	1970	1981
Gross national product	5.1	4.0	2.9	2.5
Business inventory	22.0	19.0	15.0	13.0
Fixed business investment	14.7	8.3	6.5	6.2
Civilian labor force	12.2	8.3	4.4	3.3
Business debt outstanding	7.5	8.1	7.3	9.0
Merchandise exported	28.4	24.4	17.2	18.0

Note: Values in percent.

Source: U.S. Department of Agriculture, *Agricultural Statistics* (Washington, D.C.: U.S. Government Printing Office, 1981).

TABLE 12.3 AGRICULTURE'S CONTRIBUTION TO KEY NATIONAL STATISTICS. There are several ways in which we can assess agriculture's role in the U.S. economy. For example, we discussed the calculation and trend in agriculture's contribution to the nation's GNP in Table 11.3. We said there that although agriculture's total output has increased during the post–World War II period, it has grown more slowly than the output of the economy as a whole. We also see that agriculture's share of business inventories, fixed business investment (buildings and equipment), and the civilian labor force have declined over this period. Agriculture has the dubious honor of accounting for a growing share of the nation's business debt outstanding. Finally, the sector continues to play a significant role in the nation's exports.

While the farm business sector's contribution to the country's real GNP has increased 11-fold during the 1950–1981 period, we know from the discussion in Chapter 11 that this sector's *relative* contribution to this national statistic has fallen.[5] For example, the farm business sector's contribution to the country's real GNP in 1981 was 2.5 percent. This is in sharp contrast to the 82.3 percent contributed by the nation's nonfarm business sectors. The farm business sector's contribution to GNP in 1950 was 5.1 percent. This percentage fell to 4.0 percent by 1960 and 2.9 percent by 1970.

Turning to the civilian labor force, the farm business sector employed 7.2 million workers in 1950, which represented 12.2 percent of the total civilian labor force. By 1981, the farm business sector was employing only 3.4 million workers, which represented only 3.3 percent of the total civilian labor force. This declining trend serves to underscore the extent to which capital has been substituted for labor in this sector, a trend eluded to earlier in Chapter 2.

[5] The term "real" GNP once again conveys the fact that the annual GNP figures measured in current dollars have been adjusted for inflation.

Inventories of unsold production (i.e., business inventories) in the farm business sector have also been increasing in absolute terms during the 1950–1983 period. However, it too has been declining in relative terms compared with the inventories of nonfarm businesses. As a percentage of total real business inventories, the farm business sector accounted for 22 percent of total business inventories in 1950, 19 percent in 1960, 15 percent in 1970, and 13 percent in 1981. This is further evidence of the continuing relative development of the nonfarm business sector during the post–World War II period.

Total fixed business investment represents the capital expenditures by businesses for buildings as well as for machinery and equipment. While the level of fixed business investment in the farm business sector has increased during the 1950–1981 period, it has been declining as a percentage of total fixed business investment in this country. In 1950, for example, fixed business investment in the farm business sector represented 14.7 percent of total fixed business investment in the United States. This percentage fell to 8.3 percent in 1960, 6.5 percent in 1970, and 6.2 percent in 1981.

One area where the farm business sector's contribution to a key national statistic remained significant is that of merchandise exports. In 1970, for example, agricultural exports represented 17 percent of total U.S. exports. On the other hand, agricultural exports accounted for 18 percent of the total value of merchandise exported. We can also look at the agricultural trade balance, or the amount by which exports exceed imports. In 1950, for example, this trade balance was a negative $1.1 billion, which means that the value of agricultural products imported into this country exceeded agricultural exports by over $1 billion. This trade balance was positive in 1960 ($1.0 billion) and 1970 ($1.5 billion), however. During the seventies, as new markets opened up for U.S. agricultural products, our agricultural trade balance grew substantially. By 1981, this trade balance was a positive $26.5 billion. This positive development helped partially to offset the negative trade balance for nonagricultural goods experienced during this time period, and served as a source of foreign currency accumulation.

A final comparison of the relative magnitude of the farm business sector's contribution to the macroeconomy is in its use of debt. For example, farm business debt outstanding grew 15-fold during the 1950–1981 period. To see how this stacks up against the use of debt by other businesses, let's examine the percentage that farm business sector indebtedness is of total business indebtedness (excludes the liabilities of financial institutions). In 1950, for example, the farm business sector accounted for 7.5 percent of total business debt outstanding. By the end of 1980, this figure had risen to 9.0 percent.

In summary, the farm business sector registered a declining relative share of total output, inventories, and fixed business investment, but a greater relative share of total private debt during the 1950–1981 period—hardly an enviable record when compared with that achieved by nonfarm businesses in general.

FLUCTUATIONS IN BUSINESS ACTIVITY

The nation's economy traditionally goes through periods of ups and downs in the level of its business activity. These *business fluctuations,* referred to by some as *business cycles,* are typically thought of in terms of movements in the economy's GNP, interest rates, or the unemployment rate. The purpose of this section is to discuss the nature of business fluctuations in the general economy, the major indicators of this activity, and the policy actions normally taken to modify these fluctuations.

Nature of Business Fluctuations

Figure 12.1 illustrates the general nature of business fluctuations in the economy. There are four distinct phases to a business cycle. Periods of *recession* and *expansion* occur between *peaks* of these cycles. As the cycle reaches a *trough* or "bottoms out" and the recovery begins, the economy enters another expansionary period. these exapansionary periods are often referred to as "booms" in business activity. Not every expansionary period reaches a new high. An expansionary period may end prematurely for one or more reasons and a new recessionary period begin. If the level of business activity falls sharply enough, it may be classified as a *depression* rather than as a recession. Of course, nothing in modern U.S. economic history rivals the depths of the Great Depression of the thirties.

Four of the last seven periods of expansion in the economy coincided with this country's participation in war activities, the last period of expansion being that associated with the Vietnam War. The biggest swing from peak to peak during this century occurred during the 1929–1945 period, beginning with the Great Depression and ending with the boom associated with World War II business activity. Finally, the U.S. economy experienced an unprecedented period of expansion during much of the 30-year period beginning in 1950.

There are alternative definitions of what constitutes a recession. The U.S. Department of Commerce, for example, concludes that the economy is in a recession when it experiences two consecutive quarters of negative growth.[6] The National Bureau of Economic Research (NBER) has long devoted a considerable amount of its resources of defining and measuring

---

[6] Here and elsewhere, we are concerned with the *real* as opposed to *nominal* growth of the economy, which means that we have deducted the effects of inflation to focus on the growth of the economy's purchasing power (i.e., its real gross national product).

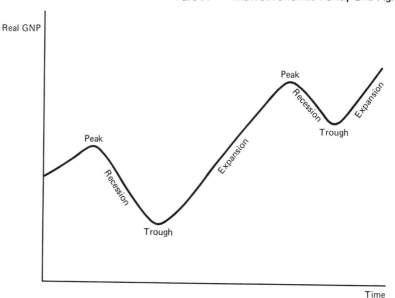

Figure 12.1 *Four phases of a business cycle.* The tradıtıonal business cycle (or fluctuation) has four phases: (1) an expansionary phase, (2) a peak which marks the end of the expansionary phase, (3) a recessionary phase, and (4) a trough which marks the end of the recessionary phase. Most cycles result in a higher peak in economic activity during a period of prolonged economic growth in the economy. This need not always be true, however. During the thirties, the recessionary phase became so pronounced that it was labeled the "Great Depression."

business fluctuations in the economy. After studying business activity "after the fact" the NBER defines the "official" timing of the recession. The NBER's identification of recessions does not necessarily have to contain two consecutive quarters of negative real economic activity.

Indicators of Economic Activity

Businesses and policymakers of course cannot wait for the NBER to tell them that the economy experienced a recession 12 months ago. Some follow indicators of business activity that are either (1) coincident with, (2) lag behind, or (3) lead business fluctuations in the economy. The U.S. Department of Commerce regularly publishes a series of lagging, coincident, and leading indicators that serve to tell businesses and policymakers what is happening in the economy and what is likely to happen in the future.

Coincident indicators. Coincident indicators move concurrently with business activity in the economy. Examples of such indicators include information on current industrial production, the number of employees on payrolls, personal disposable income, and manufacturing sales. These indicators help explain *current* business activity.

Lagging indicators.   Lagging indicators of business activity usually indicate a change in economic activity about one quarter (i.e., three months) *after* the fact. Examples of lagging indicators include business inventories, labor cost per unit of output, the average duration of employment, and the average interest rate that banks charge their best customers (i.e., the prime rate).

Leading indicators.   Finally, the leading indicators of business activity are defined so as to indicate business fluctuations *before* they occur (Figure 12.2). That is, they are expected to peak approximately one to two quarters before business activity actually peaks in the economy. Examples of

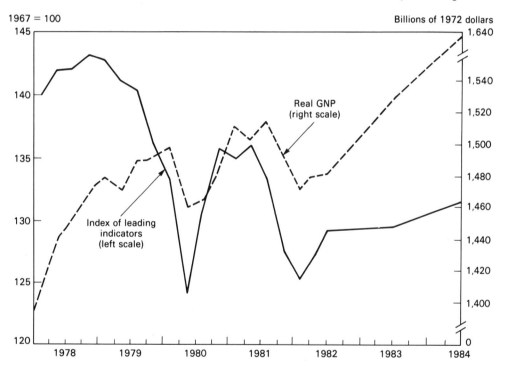

Source: Department of Commerce.

Figure 12.2 *Index of leading indicators and real gross national product.* The index of leading indicators given by the solid line "indicates" business fluctuations before they actually occur. While not a perfect indicator of future events, this index correctly signaled many of the directions in business fluctuations of real gross national product (given by the dashed line) during the 1978–1983 period.

leading economic indicators include new orders for consumer goods, new building permits, new investment in plant and equipment, and changes in selected prices and the money supply.[7]

Forecasting models. As an alternative to using leading indicators to make forecasts of what will happen to the economy in the future, many businesses and policymakers employ the services of sophisticated computer models. These models reflect the relationships between past economic behavior of producers and consumers and selected prices, interest rates, and other variables thought to explain their behavior. The creditability of these models depends largely on their ability to make accurate forecasts.

There are numerous commercial and government-sponsored models that are capable of projecting events in the economy in general and the farm business sector in particular.[8] Their major advantage is their ability to examine "what would happen if" conditions were to take on alternative values. This gives businesses and policymakers a feeling for the *range* of outcomes that are likely to occur under specific sets of conditions.

CONSEQUENCES OF BUSINESS FLUCTUATIONS

Two consequences of fluctuating business activity are *unemployment* and *inflation.* Unemployment will rise in periods of recession, while inflation generally rises in periods of economic expansion. It is often said that the goal of monetary and fiscal policy is to eliminate inflation and unemployment in the economy. Yet the terms "unemployment" and "inflation" are frequently used without the benefit of a precise definition of their meaning or measurement. Let us now define these two terms, discuss their measurement, and indicate how policy actions affect business fluctuations in general and unemployment and inflation in particular.

Unemployment

Unemployment, broadly defined, refers not only to the idling of part of the civilian labor force but the idling of plants and equipment as well. Unem-

[7] The U.S. Department of Commerce regularly publishes a set of indices capturing these and other indicators in the publication *Business Conditions Digest*. These include an index of twelve *leading* indicators, an index of four *coincident* indicators, and an index of six *lagging* indicators.

[8] Examples of commercial models of the U.S. economy which contain a farm sector are the models developed by Chase Manhattan Bank and Wharton Econometric Forecasting Associates. An example of a government-sponsored model of the U.S. economy containing a farm business sector is the COMGEM model developed initially by the U.S. Department of Agriculture and Texas A&M University.

ployment of part of the nation's scarce resources results in the loss of output and savings, both of which affect the potential future growth of the economy as well as the suffering of those workers and business managers whose resources as unemployed.

Unemployment of labor is measured by subtracting the total number of people not in the labor force (housewives, students, those physically unable to work, and others who do not wish to work) from the total noninstitutional population (excludes individuals in prisons as well as persons under 16 years of age). This difference represents the *total labor force,* which totaled 113.2 million people in 1983. From this figure we subtract the members of the armed services (1.7 million) to determine the *total civilian labor force* (111.5 million). Finally, unemployment (10.7 million) is found by subtracting the number of employed persons in the economy (100.8 million) from the total civilian labor force.

The *unemployment rate* is then found by dividing the number of unemployed persons by the size of the total civilian labor force, or

$$\begin{matrix} \text{annual} \\ \text{unemployment} \\ \text{rate} \end{matrix} = \frac{\text{number of unemployed persons}}{\text{size of total civilian labor force}} \quad (12.1)$$

In 1983, for example, the unemployment rate was 9.6 percent (i.e., 0.096 = 10.7 ÷ 111.5). Figure 12.3 shows what has happened to the unemployment rate since the thirties. This figure shows that the unemployment rate reached almost 25 percent during the Great Depression.[9]

The equivalent concept for capital (i.e., plant and equipment) is the *manufacturing capacity utilization rate* published by the U.S. Department of Commerce, or actual output divided by current manufacturing capacity. The lower the capacity utilization rate, the higher the unemployment of capital.

There are several unemployment concepts frequently referred to in the press and elsewhere. *Frictional unemployment,* for example, refers to the continuous flow of people who are changing jobs and thus are currently unemployed. Another concept, *full employment,* refers to the employment of labor and capital when the economy is producing at its maximum noninflationary level of output. In recent years, full-employment GNP has been thought to occur at an unemployment rate for labor of about 5 percent and a capacity utilization rate for capital of 86 percent. *Cyclical unemployment* refers to unemployment associated with business fluctuations. *Seasonal unemployment* refers to unemployment associated with changes in business

---

[9] Some argue that this unemployment rate understates the "true" unemployment rate because it does not account for discouraged workers who are no longer seeking employment and therefore are not included in the total civilian labor force (the denominator in the unemployment rate). This phenomenon is referred to as *hidden unemployment.* The *labor force participation rate* reflects the percentage of available people of working age who are actually in the civilian labor force.

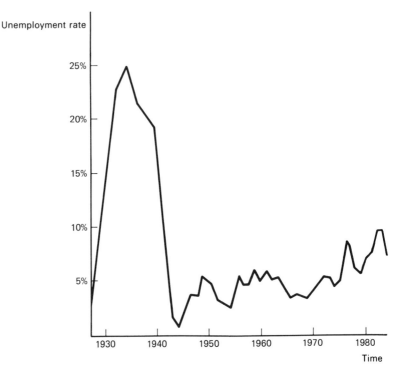

Figure 12.3 *Annual unemployment rate.* Compared to the 25 percent unemployment rate observed during the Great Depression, today's unemployment rates seem rather small. The unemployment rate is determined by dividing the number of unemployed persons by the total civilian labor force. Some argue that during a recession, hidden unemployment occurs because workers are discouraged from seeking work. Therefore, the true unemployment rate would be understated.

conditions which are seasonal in nature. Workers in fruit- and vegetable-processing plants and construction workers in northern states are two examples of workers who may be seasonally unemployed. Finally, *structural unemployment* refers to those workers who are unemployed due to structural changes in the economy brought about by technological change that does away with their job. Farm laborers whose jobs have been replaced by tomato pickers are examples of structurally unemployed workers.

Inflation

Inflation is generally defined as a sustained rise in the general price level (i.e., weighted average of all prices). Two key terms in this definition require special emphasis. First, the term "sustained" rules out a *temporary* rise in prices. Second, the term "general price level" rules out the use of the term "corn price inflation" or "fuel price inflation." The rise in the price of a single commodity need not be inflationary, particularly if the price of substitute goods or services have fallen. Instead, only a sustained rise in the general price level as measured by, say, the Consumer Price Index (CPI), which accounts for changes in the prices of all goods and services purchased by consumers, represents their inflation. The inflation *rate* for consumer can be measured by the computing percentage change in the CPI from one period to the next, or

$$\begin{array}{c} \text{annual} \\ \text{inflation} \\ \text{rate} \end{array} = \frac{\text{current CPI} - \text{previous CPI}}{\text{previous CPI}} \quad\quad (12.2)$$

Panel a in Figure 12.4 shows what happened to the rate of inflation during the 1950–1982 period. For example, we see the upward trend in inflation that occurred during the seventies and early eighties.[10]

The U.S. Department of Commerce also prepares a Producer Price Index (PPI), which measures changes in the average prices of goods and services purchased by producers. The *rate* of inflation for producers, as measured by the percentage change in the PPI from one period to the next, is illustrated for the 1950–1984 period in panel b of Figure 12.4. This index is calculated in the same manner as the CPI; it uses base-year quantities at *current* prices and compares them with base-year quantities at *base-year* prices. For example, suppose that the base year for computing this index is 1972. This means that the value of this index *in 1972* would be 100. This is because current prices and base-year prices *in that year* would be the same. If the weighted-average price of goods and services purchased by producers in 1983 is 85 percent higher than it was for the same bundle of goods and services purchased in 1972, the PPI would be equal to 185.

The cost of unemployment, is clear, particularly to those who are unemployed. Unlike unemployment, however, inflation affects all of us in a direct and immediate way. It reduces the purchasing power of consumers' disposable income and producers' profits. Consider the example presented in Table 12.4 of what your salary would have to be in the future if you currently earn $20,000 and inflation occurs at an annual rate of 10 percent. This table suggests that your salary would have to be $51,875 by the year 1994 if you wish to be able to buy the same bundle of goods and services

---

[10] The decline in the rate of inflation for consumers as measured by the percentage change in the CPI noted during the 1971-1972 period illustrated in this figure was the result of the price controls put into place by President Nixon. The effectiveness of price and wage controls in general and the lessons learned in the seventies are discussed in the Advanced Topics section of Chapter 15.

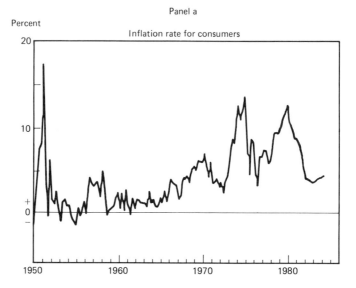

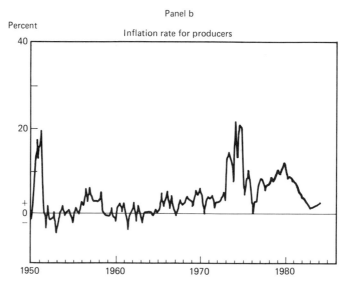

Figure 12.4 *Annual percentage change in the CPI and PPI.* Inflation is defined as a sustained rise in general price levels. The annual percentage change in the Consumer Price Index (CPI) measures the consumer's inflation rate. The annual percentage change in the Producer Price Index (PPI) represents the rate of inflation for producers in the economy.

Year	Salary required
1984	$20,000
1985	22,000
1986	24,200
1987	26,620
1988	29,282
1989	32,210
1990	35,431
1991	38,974
1992	42,872
1993	47,159
1994	51,875

TABLE 12.4 SALARY NEEDED TO STAY EVEN WITH 10 PERCENT INFLATION. To see the effects of inflation on the purchasing power of the dollar, let's examine the table. Suppose that you earned a salary of $20,000 in 1984. To be able to buy the same bundle of goods and services in 1994 if inflation occurs at an annual rate of 10 percent, you would have to earn a salary of at least $51,875. This underscores the problems faced by those on fixed incomes or those who receive annual pay raises that are less than the rate of inflation.

that $20,000 bought in 1984.[11] Persons hurt by inflation therefore include: (1) those whose salary does not increase enough to offset the effects of inflation (e.g., those on a fixed income), (2) lenders who make loans at fixed interest rates who are unfavorably "surprised" by the extent of inflation, (3) those who sign contracts that do not account for inflation, and (4) those who hold money rather than other assets which go up in value with inflation.

Like unemployment, there are also several types of inflation. When the aggregate demand for goods and services is rising and the economy is approaching full employment, *demand-pull inflation* will occur. The result is a rise in the general price level.[12] We can illustrate this phenomenon by the use of Figure 12.5. Let us assume that the SS curve represents the economy's current aggregate supply curve and D_1D_1, D_2D_2, and so on, represent a

[11] This ignores the fact that income is currently taxed in current dollars rather than after the effects of inflation have been accounted for. Thus if your salary rose just enough to offset the rate of inflation, your *after-tax* or disposable income would have declined in "real terms," or in what it can buy in the way of goods and services. This is due to the progressive nature of the current income tax system and the fact that income is valued in nominal rather than real terms when computing the tax due. Beginning in 1985, however, income tax rates will be adjusted to account for inflation.

[12] This also corresponds to the inflationary gap discussed in Chapter 13 and 14, where desired expenditures are greater than the economy's full-employment output.

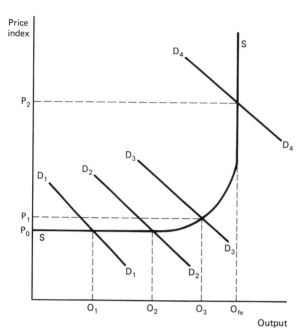

Figure 12.5 *Increase in demand and demand-pull inflation.* Demand-pull inflation occurs when changes in demand result in a sustained rise in the general price level. The increase in aggregate demand from $D_1 D_1$ to $D_2 D_2$ was not inflationary. The increase in aggregate demand from $D_2 D_2$ to $D_3 D_3$, however, was mildly inflationary since the general price level rose from P_0 to P_1. Finally, the increase in aggregate demand from $D_3 D_3$ to $D_4 D_4$ would be highly inflationary. The general price level rose from P_1 to P_2 while the output response was limited by the productive capacity of the economy.

series of alternative aggregate demand curves.[13] This figure suggests that if the aggregate demand curve were to shift from $D_1 D_1$ to $D_2 D_2$, there would be virtually no change in the general price level. If the aggregate demand curve instead shifted from $D_1 D_1$ to $D_3 D_3$, we see that the general price index increased from P_0 to P_1. Thus this increase in demand is inflationary, although mildly so.[14] The inflation rate in this instance would be equal to $(P_1 - P_0) \div P_0$. Finally, if the aggregate demand curve were to shift from $D_1 D_1$ to $D_4 D_4$, we see that the economy would have reached its full-employment output (O_{fe}). This desired level of expenditures would be highly inflationary since the general price index would increase from P_0 to P_2. In the last two situations, increases in demand would be "pulling up" the general price level.

A second form of inflation, which occurs when the economy is not at full employment, is *cost-push inflation*. This form of inflation occurred, for example, in 1969–1970 and again in 1973–1975. In both instances, prices were rising even though the economy was nowhere near full employment.

---

[13] These aggregate supply and demand curves are plotted with price rather than total expenditures are the vertical axis and thus look more like the traditional market demand and supply curves discussed in Chapters 3 and 5 than the aggregate demand and supply curves described in Chapters 13 and 14.

[14] It is important to note that demand-pull inflation begins to occur before full employment of the nation's resources is achieved. Some economists refer to this as *premature inflation*.

Cost-push inflation, sometimes referred to as *market power inflation,* can arise for at least two reasons: (1) union monopoly power, and (2) business monopoly power. For example, some unions may have enough bargaining power in the labor market to impose wage increases on employers, who in turn raise their prices to maintain current profit margins. This *wage–price spiral* results in a rise in the general price level. Businesses with monopoly powers such as those discussed in Chapter 9 can also raise their prices if they desire higher profits. Workers will then demand higher wages to compensate for losses in their standard of living (they no longer can buy the same bundle of goods as a result of this price increase). This, in turn, causes the monopolist to raise his prices further to secure his desired profit margin. This *price–wage spiral* thus also results in a rise in general price levels.

A new phenomenon experienced in the late seventies and early eighties has been assigned the name *stagflation.* The term refers to the existence of increasing inflation during a period when the economy is experiencing rising unemployment. This term originates from the combination of economic stagnation and inflation. Obviously, different macroeconomic policies are needed in each of the foregoing situations if policymakers desire both to promote the growth of the economy and to stabilize prices (i.e., eliminate inflation).

WHAT'S AHEAD IN COMING CHAPTERS

Now that we have an understanding of various measures of the economy's performance, we can turn our attention to the tools of macroeconomic policy and how their application affects the farm business sector. In Chapter 13 we describe the fiscal policy instruments available to the federal government and how they can be used to achieve the economy's current potential output. In Chapter 14 we focus on the Federal Reserve System and how it can use the monetary policy instruments at its disposal to achieve the economy's current potential output. Finally, in Chapter 15 we focus on the macroeconomic policy responses to the business fluctuations discussed in this chapter and how these policy responses can affect the farm business sector.

SUMMARY

The purpose of this chapter was to introduce the general nature of the economic accounting system used by the federal government to determine the economy's performance at the national and sector levels and to discuss the economic consequences of fluctuations in business activity. The major points made in this chapter can be summarized as follows:

1. The national economic accounting system includes the national income and product accounts published by the U.S. Department of Commerce and the national balance sheet and flow-of-funds account published by the Federal Reserve System.

2. The sector economic accounting system for agriculture consists of a sector balance sheet, income statement, and cash flow statement. All of these accounts are published by the U.S. Department of Agriculture.

3. The farm business sector's contribution to such key national statistics as the nation's GNP, civilian labor force, and fixed business investment have declined over time. The second, however, has played an important role in the nation's balance of trade.

4. There are four phases to a business cycle: (1) expansion, (2) peak, (3) recession, and (4) trough. Farmers generally fare well as the economy enters a recovery period and inflation is low. When anti-inflationary policies are instituted, however, and interest rates rise, farmers fare rather poorly.

5. Businesses and policymakers often study published indicators of economic activity. *Leading indicators,* for example, are expected to indicate business fluctuations *before* they occur. Computer forecasting models are also often used for this purpose.

6. Two consequences of fluctuating business activity are *unemployment* and *inflation.* Unemployment rises during periods of recession, while inflation rises in periods of expansion.

7. The unemployment rate reflects the percentage of the total civilian labor force that is unemployed. The equivalent concept for capital is the manufacturing capacity utilization rate.

8. Inflation is defined as a sustained rise in the general price level. The inflation rate for consumers is measured by the percentage change in the Consumer Price Index (CPI). The inflation rate for producers is measured by the percentage change in the Producer Price Index (PPI).

9. When the aggregate demand for goods and services is rising and the economy is at full employment, *demand-pull inflation* will occur. *Cost-push inflation,* also referred to as market power inflation, occurs when unions or imperfectly competitive firms impose an increase on the prices they charge for their goods or services.

10. The term *stagflation* refers to the existence of increasing inflation during a period when the economy is experiencing rising unemployment.

DEFINITION OF TERMS

Fixed business investment: capital expenditures by business for plant and equipment (e.g., buildings, tractors) during the year.

Business inventories: unsold output from current or past production activities.

Civilian labor force: total noninstitutional population (e.g., excludes people in prisons) minus total number of people not in the labor force (e.g., housewives, students) as well as members of the armed services.

Balance of trade: the difference between a nation's total exports and its total imports is referred to as the balance of trade. If exports are greater than (less than) imports, a nation is said to have a balance of trade surplus (deficit).

Business cycle: reflects the pattern of movements in the economy's real output, interest rates, or unemployment rate (also referred to as business fluctuations).

Recessionary period: phase of business cycle during which the nation's output is declining.

Expansionary period: phase of business cycle during which the nation's output is expanding.

Lagging indicators: indicators of changes in economic activity about one or two quarters after they occur.

Leading indicators: indicators of changes in economic activity about one or two quarters before they occur.

Coincident indicators: indicators of changes in economic activity that reflect current activity.

Unemployment rate: number of unemployed persons divided by the size of the total civilian labor force.

Cost-push inflation: rise in general price level resulting from businesses and unions raising their prices and wage requests (also referred to as market power inflation).

Demand-pull inflation: rise in the general price level which occurs when aggregate demand for goods and services is rising and the economy is approaching full employment.

Stagflation: existence of increasing inflation during a period when the economy is experiencing rising unemployment.

Manufacturing capacity utilization rate: actual output of nation's manufacturing firms divided by their potential output.

Frictional unemployment: persons who are changing jobs and thus are currently unemployed.

Full employment: high degree of employment of nation's resources (an unemployment rate of 5 to 6 percent for labor and a capacity utilization rate for capital of 86 to 88 percent is generally thought to constitute full employment).

Producer Price Index (PPI): weighted average of the prices producers pay for goods and services.

Consumer Price Index (CPI): weighted average of the prices consumers pay for goods and services.

REFERENCES

BOARD OF GOVERNORS OF THE FEDERAL RESERVE SYSTEM, *Chart Book,* various issues, Washington, D.C.

U.S. DEPARTMENT OF AGRICULTURE, *Agricultural Statistics.* Washington, D.C.: U.S. Government Printing Office, 1982.

U.S. DEPARTMENT OF AGRICULTURE, *Economic Indicators for the Farm Sector.* Washington, D.C.: U.S. Government Printing Office, various issues.

U.S. DEPARTMENT OF COMMERCE, *Business Conditions Digest.* Washington, D.C.: U.S. Government Printing Office, various issues.

ADDITIONAL READINGS

DERNBURG, THOMAS F., and DUNCAN N. MCDOUGALL, *Macroeconomics,* 6th ed. New York: McGraw-Hill Book Company, 1980.

PENSON, JOHN B., JR., and DAVID A. LINS, *Agricultural Finance: An Introduction to Micro and Macro Concepts.* Englewood Cliffs, N.J.: Prentice-Hall, Inc., 1980.

PRENTICE, PAUL T., and LYLE P. SCHERTZ, *Inflation: A Food and Agricultural Perspective,* AER-463, USDA, ERS, February 1981.

QUESTIONS

1. Discuss the various phases of a business cycle. How are these phases identified? What are the major consequences of business fluctuations?

2. Describe some of the approaches that businesses can take to understand what is happening in the economy and what is likely to happen in the future.

3. If the total labor force is 110 million people and there are 3 million members of the armed services, what is the unemployment rate if there are currently 100 million people employed in the economy?

4. Describe the essential differences between the Consumer Price Index (CPI) and the Producer Price Index (PPI). If the CPI were to increase from 175 to 189 over a 12-month period, what is the annual rate of inflation?

5. Define and contrast the following concepts of inflation:
   (a) Demand-pull inflation
   (b) Cost-push inflation
   (c) Stagflation

13

NATIONAL INCOME AND FISCAL POLICY

Hardly a day goes by when you do not either read on the front page of the newspaper or hear on television statements made by government officials concerning what is needed in the way of monetary or fiscal policy to stimulate the growth of the economy, reduce unemployment, balance the budget, and/or eliminate inflation. Some experts, for example, might recommend that a specific set of monetary policy actions be implemented by the Federal Reserve System. Other experts might recommend that a specific set of fiscal policy actions be implemented by Congress and the President. Sometimes the recommendations of experts are conflicting; that is, they would work against each other rather than work in harmony. In analyzing these policy recommendations, should agricultural economists limit their attention to the *direct* effects on farm businesses, or should they also be concerned with the *indirect* effects of these policies as they affect other segments of the domestic economy and export markets as well? In light of the increased use of manufactured inputs and outside financing by farm businesses and the increasing importance of export markets documented in Chapter 2, we know the farm business sector is increasingly susceptible to the effects that monetary and fiscal policies will have on the economy in general.

The purpose of this chapter is to introduce the determination of equilibrium national income and the nature of the fiscal policy instruments that can be used to move the U.S. economy toward its current potential output. Specifically, this chapter will (1) acquaint you with the determinants of aggregate demand and supply, (2) discuss why inflationary and recessionary gaps are undesirable, and (3) identify how fiscal policy actions can be used to eliminate these gaps and thereby achieve the economy's current potential output. The topic of monetary policy is postponed until Chapter 14.

CONSUMPTION, SAVINGS, AND INVESTMENT

There are two things that households can do with a dollar of disposable income (income after taxes): they can "consume" the dollar or they can save it. If the dollar is used to finance consumer expenditures, it is gone forever. However, if the dollar is saved, it will be available to finance future consumption and will earn interest in the meantime. We can state this relationship in equation form as follows:

$$\text{saving} = \text{disposable income} - \text{consumer expenditures} \qquad (13.1)$$

When households make consumer expenditures, they are purchasing what are normally referred to as *consumer goods*. If the good has a life of less than one year, it is called a *nondurable* good. If it is consumed over a longer period of time, however, it is a *durable* good. Food is an example of a nondurable good, and a house or car is an example of a durable good.

Investment, on the other hand, refers to expenditures by businesses on *capital goods*, such as the purchase of a new machine or a new building. Investment is normally separated into fixed investment and inventory investment. In the remainder of this section we shall identify the factors that influence the level of planned consumption expenditures by households and planned investment expenditures by businesses.

Determinants of Planned Consumption

The major determinant of planned consumption by households was identified by Keynes in 1936. Keynes suggested that people "increase their consumption as their income increases, but not by as much as the increase in their income." In other words, there is a relationship, but not a one-to-one correspondence, between the planned consumption expenditures by households and their current level of disposable income. As the household's disposable income goes up, its planned consumption goes up as well. This relationship represents the household's *consumption function.*[1]

Consumption function.   Figure 13.1 illustrates an annual consumption function for a hypothetical household. The 45-degree line eminating from the origin illustrates what the household's annual level of consumption

[1] The term "function" refers to the fact that there is causal relationship between income and consumption; if income increases, consumption will also increase. If consumption is said to be a function of income, this means that the level of consumption depends on "the level of income."

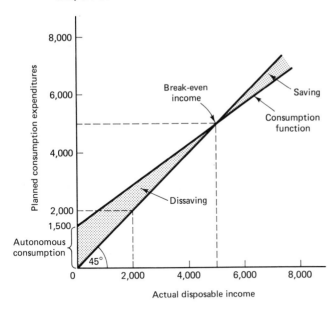

Figure 13.1 *The planned consumption function.* The relationship between actual disposable income and planned consumer expenditures by households illustrated here suggests that households will consume $1,500 per year if their income after taxes were actually zero (this is known as autonomous consumption). Not until their disposable income reaches $5,000 per year would households stop spending more than they are earning. At higher levels of disposable income, households would plan to save a part of their take-home pay rather than consume the entire amount.

would be if there *were* a one-to-one correspondence between actual disposable income and planned consumption expenditures. For example, point *A* on this line suggests that the household would plan to spend $2,000 annually on consumer goods if its current disposable income were $2,000.

As Keynes suggests, however, planned consumption expenditures rarely change by the same amount as a change in consumer disposable income. The hypothetical annual consumption function depicted in Figure 13.1, for example, suggests that planned consumption would be approximately $1,500 even if actual disposable income were zero. This level of consumption expenditures is referred to as *autonomous consumption.* For example, our hypothetical household would consume $1,500 during the year even if it did not receive any disposable income. Notice that our household's planned consumption expenditures exceed its actual disposable income up to the point where the household brings home $5,000 per year. Prior to that point, the household planned to spend more on consumer goods than it was currently receiving in the way of after-tax income. Such spending would be financed by *dissaving,* or by using previously accumulated wealth to finance currently planned consumption. Conversely, if the household received more than $5,000 annually, it would plan to spend less than that amount on consumer goods. The difference between the household's consumption function and the 45-degree line beyond this level of income therefore represents *planned saving.* More will be said shortly about the topic of saving.

Slope of consumption function. The household sector's consumption behavior can be assessed by looking at their *marginal propensity to consume,* where the term "marginal" once again refers to an "incremental change."

The marginal propensity to consume, which represents the slope of the planned consumption function, is defined as follows:

$$\begin{array}{c} \text{marginal} \\ \text{propensity to} \\ \text{consume} \end{array} = \dfrac{\begin{array}{c}\text{change in planned}\\ \text{consumption}\end{array}}{\begin{array}{c}\text{change in actual}\\ \text{disposable income}\end{array}} \qquad (13.2)$$

This statistic tells us the percentage of an increase in disposable income that would go toward financing planned consumption expenditures. For example, if the household's marginal propensity to consumer were 0.9, it would apply 90 percent of the next dollar's worth of disposable income it received toward the purchase of additional consumer goods. Thus, if the household's annual disposable income was $10,000 and it received a raise that increased this figure to $10,500, the household would increase its planned consumption expenditures by $450 (i.e., 0.90 × $500).[2]

Shifts in consumption function.   While changes in the level of income correspond to movements along the consumption function in Figure 13.1, other determinants of consumption expenditures will shift the consumption function. An increase in the *wealth* status of a household, for example, should shift its consumption function upward.[3] This implies that the household with a given level of income has a greater basis from which to spend than does a household with less wealth. A specific component of the household's wealth position—its holding of *liquid assets*—may be of special importance to the household when formulating its spending plans. A liquid asset is an asset that can be converted into money quickly with little or no loss in value. Cash is obviously a perfectly liquid asset. Other liquid assets include government bonds, shares in savings and loan associations, and savings accounts at commerical banks.

Expectations may also affect how much a household with a given level of current disposable income is willing to spend, particularly in the short run. For example, if a household expects a higher income in the near future, it may increase its current consumption expenditures. Conversely, the same household may decide to postpone consumption (and increase its savings) if it is pessimistic about the near future.

---

[2] An alternative measure of income in the consumption function is given by the *permanent income hypothesis*. This theory implies that planned consumption expenditures depend not on current income, but on a measure of expected or "permanent income" over, say, the next 3 to 5 years. In other words, current planned consumption would not change substantially if current actual disposable income changes unless this change is expected to continue over time.

[3] This measure of wealth should include the current market value of the household's physical and financial assets less debt outstanding, and should be adjusted for inflation.

Changes in the household's wealth or its expectations of income in the near future will *shift* the household's consumption function illustrated in Figure 13.1. An increase (decrease) in wealth or expected income in the near future will shift the consumption function in an upward (downward) fashion. Remember that only a change in current disposable income will cause the household to move along its consumption function.

Determinants of Planned Saving

Planned saving was defined above as the difference between actual disposable income and planned consumption expenditures. If you refer back to Figure 13.1 for a moment, you will see that the break-even level of actual disposable income was $5,000. Let this level of income serve as the reference point for plotting our hypothetical household's planned savings function. This suggests that the planned savings function must pass through the horizontal axis in Figure 13.2 at the $5,000 disposable income level since the household's savings at this income level would be zero. We also know from

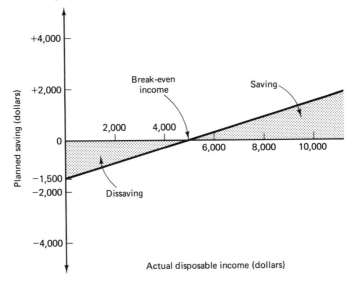

Figure 13.2 *The planned savings function.* We can examine in another way the planned savings of households referred to in Figure 13.1. We see here that a disposable income of $5,000 a year leads to planned savings equal to zero (i.e., planned consumption expenditures are exactly equal to disposable income). At income levels below $5,000 dissaving (consuming out of previously accumulated wealth) would take place. At income levels above $5,000, savings (additions to previously accumulated wealth) would occur. The relationships depicted in these two graphs allow us to conclude that savings is equal to disposable income minus consumption.

Figure 13.1 that the level of dissaving when disposable income is equal to zero is $1,500. Thus the planned savings function in Figure 13.2 must begin at –$1,500 on the vertical axis. The planned savings function can be determined by drawing a line connecting these two points and extending this line upward to the right to reflect the effects of higher positive levels of disposable income.

The household's change in planned savings for a given change in disposable income represents its *marginal propensity to save.* Stated in equation form, the household's marginal propensity to save is given by

$$
\begin{matrix} \text{marginal} \\ \text{propensity to} \\ \text{save} \end{matrix} \quad = \quad \dfrac{\begin{matrix}\text{change in}\\\text{planned savings}\end{matrix}}{\begin{matrix}\text{change in actual}\\\text{disposable income}\end{matrix}} \qquad (13.3)
$$

This value indicates the percentage change in the household's disposable income that would go into savings rather than consumption.[4] If the household's marginal propensity to save were 0.1, it would save 10 cents out of the next dollar of disposable income it received. Since planned consumption plus planned saving must equal actual disposable income, we can state that

$$
\begin{matrix}\text{marginal propensity} \\ \text{to save}\end{matrix} + \begin{matrix}\text{marginal propensity} \\ \text{to consume}\end{matrix} = 1.0 \qquad (13.4)
$$

from which we can infer that

$$
\begin{matrix}\text{marginal propensity} \\ \text{to save}\end{matrix} = 1.0 - \begin{matrix}\text{marginal propensity} \\ \text{to consume}\end{matrix} \qquad (13.5)
$$

Thus if the marginal propensity to consume is 0.90, the marginal propensity to save must necessarily be equal to 0.10.

Finally, because the level of planned savings is influenced by the level of planned consumption, those nonincome factors (e.g., wealth and expectations) which were said to affect planned consumption must also necessarily affect planned savings. Those factors that cause an upward shift in the planned consumption function will result in an equal *downward* shift in the planned savings function. The opposite is also true. That is, those factors that cause a downward shift in the consumption function will result in an equal *upward* shift in the planned savings function.

Determinants of Planned Investment

Business investment was defined earlier as business expenditures on new buildings and equipment plus net additions to their production inventories.[5]

---

[4] This value also represents the slope of the planned savings function.

[5] Purchases of land or used capital goods at the aggregate level are not considered as investment because they do not represent capital goods formed in the *current* period.

The level of planned investment in the current period is determined by a number of factors. Keynes (1936) for example, states that the "inducement to invest depends partly on the investment demand schedule and partly on the rate of interest."

Planned investment function.   The investment demand schedule that Keynes was referring to reflects the investment plans of businesses associated with specific rates of interest. The cost of acquiring the funds needed to finance these investments, for example, is an important determinant of investment. The higher the rate of interest, the higher the cost of making the investment will be. The opposite is also true. The lower the cost of investment funds, the lower the costs of making the investment will be. The planned investment function, therefore, should reflect this inverse relationship between the cost of investment funds (i.e., the rate of interest) and the level of planned investment.

A hypothetical annual planned investment function is presented in Figure 13.3. If the rate of interest in the current period were 13 percent, this planned investment function would suggest that businesses would plan to invest $300 billion in the current period. If the interest rate were 17 percent, our hypothetical firms would plan to invest only $200 billion. Notice that this planned investment schedule is downward sloping, like the demand curves derived in previous chapters.[6]

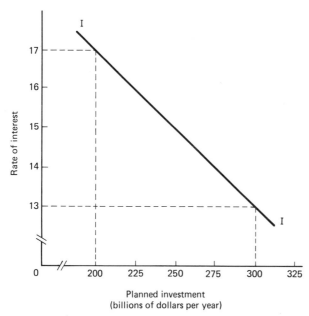

Figure 13.3 *The planned investment function.* The relationship between the market rate of interest and planned investment expenditures for new buildings and equipment is referred to as the planned investment function. This relationship has a negative slope. That is, the lower (higher) the rate of interest, the higher (lower) the level of planned investment expenditures. This planned investment function will shift to the right (left) if farm and nonfarm businesses expect the returns on investment to be more (less) favorable.

[6] These interest rates would reflect the required rates of returns of lenders and investors given the risks associated with the planned investment expenditures.

Shifts in investment function.   Other determinants of planned investment cause this investment schedule (II) to shift outward to the right or inward to the left. For example, a business must project the profitability of an investment alternative over the life of the investment. Thus its *expectations* about the *future prices* that it will receive for its product and pay for such nondurable inputs as labor and fuel will affect the firm's decision as to whether or not it should make a particular investment in the *current period.* If a business is optimistic about its future profit picture, the planned investment function will be positioned farther to the right for each interest rate than it would be if these same businesses had a pessimistic view of future profit levels.

The *purchase price of new capital goods* also represents a determinant of planned investment expenditures by businesses. If the cost of new buildings and equipment were suddenly to increase relative to the prices at which businesses expect to sell their output, we would expect the planned investment schedule depicted in Figure 13.3 to shift inward to the left. The opposite shift would occur if the relative cost of capital goods were suddenly to fall.

The *technology* embodied in new capital goods also has an effect on planned investment expenditures. Improvements in the productive services provided by equipment and innovations that affect the functions performed by capital should shift the planned investment function depicted in Figure 13.3 to the right. In other words, planned investments at each rate of interest should now be greater than before as firms seek to become more efficient in their operations.

Finally, the level of *business taxes* will also affect planned investment expenditures since businesses evaluate investment decisions on the basis of their expected after-tax return. If there is a decrease in effective tax rates (i.e., deductions and credits are liberalized), we would expect businesses to expand their expenditures for new capital goods. The opposite would be true if tax rates were increased (i.e., deductions and credits were tightened).

EQUILIBRIUM NATIONAL INCOME AND OUTPUT

To determine the equilibrium level of national income and output in the ecomony, we must employ the relationships discussed above for household and business expenditures. The total value of planned consumption, investment, government spending, and net exports in an economy is often referred to as *aggregate demand.* To determine the equilibrium level of national income and output, we must also incorporate the concept of *aggregate supply* in our discussion. When aggregate demand equals aggregate supply, national income and output will be in equilibrium.

The purpose of this section is to discuss the determination of the nation's potential output and the concepts of inflationary and recessionary gaps. In the discussion to follow, we shall employ some simplifying assumptions. First, we shall assume that annual taxes paid by businesses are exactly offset by government payments to businesses. Second, we shall assume that businesses distribute their entire current profits to their shareholders. Finally, we shall assume that there is no depreciation. These assumptions enable us to use the terms "disposable income," "national income," and "national output" or product (GNP) interchangeably.

Aggregate Demand

You will recall that earlier we related a household's planned consumption expenditures to the level of its current disposable income. In this section we consider aggregate consumption expenditures to fluctuate in direct proportion with national income. We shall capture all other factors that were said earlier to influence planned consumption in *autonomous consumption*. This relationship is illustrated in panel a of Figure 13.4. Changes in taxes, wealth, expectations, and so on, will once again result in shifts in the aggregate consumption function.

The planned investment function depicted in Figure 13.3 was not directly a function of national income. Therefore, *all* the determinants of business investment expenditures identified earlier (including the rate of

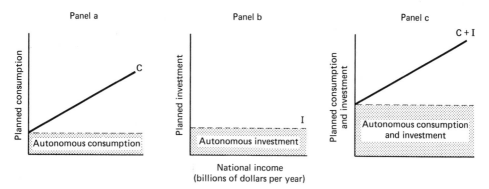

Figure 13.4 *Total planned consumption and investment.* Let us assume for ease of presentation that whereas consumption includes both an autonomous component and a component that increases as national income increases, investment is entirely autonomous. Thus when we add consumption expenditures in panel a and investment expenditures in panel b, we get the total planned private expenditures of businesses and households depicted in panel c. The curve labeled "*C + I*" in this panel can be thought of as the total private aggregate demand in the economy for the goods and services it produces. It also represents the "final demand" for goods and services by the domestic economy's private sectors. As such, it excludes businesses' "intermediate demand" for goods and services that they use as inputs in their production processes.

interest are captured in *autonomous investment*. This results in an aggregate investment function such as the one depicted in panel b in Figure 13.4, which runs parallel to the horizontal axis since it is not dependent on the level of national income. Changes in interest rates and other determinants of investment will, instead, result in *shifts* in this new aggregate investment function.

Assuming for the moment that aggregate demand consists entirely of consumption and investment expenditures, we can obtain an aggregate demand curve for the economy by adding these expenditures. That is, we can horizontally sum the planned consumption curve in panel a and planned investment curve in panel b to get the aggregate demand curve depicted in panel c. The curve labeled *"C + I"* in panel c represents an aggregate demand curve which includes only consumption *(C)* and investment *(I)*. If we continue to ignore government and net export expenditures, this curve represents a definition of gross national product.

Aggregate Supply

Aggregate supply is defined as the total value of all final goods and services supplied by businesses in the economy. The aggregate supply function therefore indicates the output that businesses are willing to offer to consumers, investors, governments, and foreigners. This willingness will depend on the expectation that businesses will receive $1 of revenue for $1 of output. By definition, if businesses produce $500 billion of output, they incur $500 billion worth of factor costs (i.e., wages, rents, interest and profits which were identified on lines 1 through 6 in Table 11.1 as comprising gross national income). Thus, we can represent the economy's aggregate supply function using by a line eminating from the origin at a 45 degree angle as illustrated in panel b of Figure 13.5. At all points along this line, the condition that the value of production equals total factor costs is satisfied.[7]

Equilibrium Income and Output

We can now determine the level equilibrium of national income and output in the product market of the economy by bringing the aggregate demand and supply functions together. The aggregate demand function in panel a of Figure 13.5 depicts total consumption, investment, *and* government expenditures *(G)*, where government expenditures, like investment expenditures *(I)*, are assumed to be completely autonomous.[8]

---

[7]While the simple model of income determination discussed here is valued in nominal terms, all prices are fixed.

[8] Although government spending is now included in final demand along with investment and consumption, we shall, for ease of presentation, continue to exclude net exports until Chapter 14 (i.e., we are assuming a closed economy).

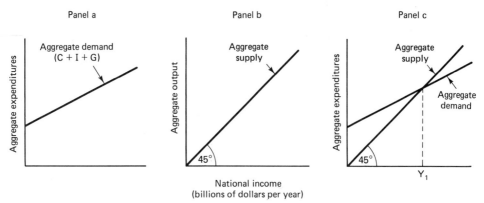

Figure 13.5 *Aggregate demand, supply, and equilibrium national income.* Panel a presents the aggregate demand curve for goods and services in the economy. It reflects the consumption and investment functions assumed in Figure 13.4 plus the additional assumption of autonomous government spending (*G*). Panel b reflects the aggregate supply curve, where aggregate output is exactly equal to national income at all points along this curve. Finally, panel c shows that the economy would be in equilibrium at a national income of Y_1, where the aggregate demand curve intersects the aggregate supply curve.

The intersection of the aggregate demand function and aggregate supply functions in panel c of Figure 13.5 represents the *equilibrium in the nation's product markets.* A line drawn down to the horizontal axis from this point indicates the equilibrium level of national income and output. At output Y_1, firms are selling all the products they produce and consumers, investors, and government are able to buy all the products they need.

If we were to vary the levels of autonomous consumption, investment, or government spending, we would observe different equilibrium levels of national income and output. For example, if we increased *I* in panel b of Figure 13.4, the aggregate demand curves in panels a and c in Figure 13.5 would shift upward. This, of course, would mean that the equilibrium level of national income and output would now lie to the right of Y_1.[9] An in-

---

[9] The change in the equilibrium level of national income will be greater than the change in autonomous spending. This phenomenon is referred to as the *multiplier effect.* This multiplier is equal to the reciprocal of the marginal propensity to save, or

$$\text{multiplier} = \frac{1.0}{1.0 - MPC}$$

where *MPC* represents the marginal propensity to consume. Thus the greater the marginal propensity to consume (the smaller the marginal propensity to save), the larger the multiplier will be. This value is multiplied by the change in autonomous spending to determine the change in the equilibrium level of national income. The multiplier is larger than 1.0 since a given change in say investment expenditures "induces" further consumer expenditures as consumers respond to the higher income level.

crease in autonomous consumption or government spending would have produced a similar result.

Potential Output of the Economy

The current potential output of the economy in our simplified model can be defined as the output producers could produce given the technology embodied in their existing resources, the "full employment" of the country's labor force, and existing plant capacity. Let us assume that we know the full-employment level of national income, and that it is represented by level of national output associated with Y_{fe} in Figure 13.6. If the aggregate demand curve intersects the aggregate supply curve at full employment of the economy's resources as it does in panel b, there would be no gap between actual and potential output. Panel a, on the other hand, illustrates the case where aggregate supply exceeds aggregate demand at full-employment output. This difference is normally referred to as a *recessionary gap*. It suggests that the economy was capable of producing more than was demanded and that its resources were being underutilized. Finally, aggregate demand exceeds aggregate supply in panel c at full-employment output. This difference is called an *inflationary gap*. It suggests that planned expenditures exceed the economy's current capacity to meet this demand.

There is no guarantee that the economy will be at Y_{fe}. There is more apt than not to be a gap between actual and potential output. One of the prime objectives of fiscal policy is to eliminate recessionary and inflationary gaps.

FISCAL POLICY INSTRUMENTS

Fiscal policy refers to the act of changing of government spending and/or taxes to achieve specific policy goals, such as promoting economic growth and price stability. To achieve these goals, Congress and the President have certain fiscal policy instruments at their disposal.

Let us divide our discussion of these fiscal policy instruments into two distinct categories: (1) *automatic* fiscal policy instruments, and (2) *discretionary* fiscal policy instruments. Automatic instruments are those that take effect without an explicit action by the President or Congress. Discretionary instruments, on the other hand, require the legislative and executive branches of government to take explicit policy actions that would not occur otherwise (e.g., pass a law). In the discussion to follow, we shall assume that the relevant goal for fiscal policy is to eliminate inflationary and recessionary gaps.

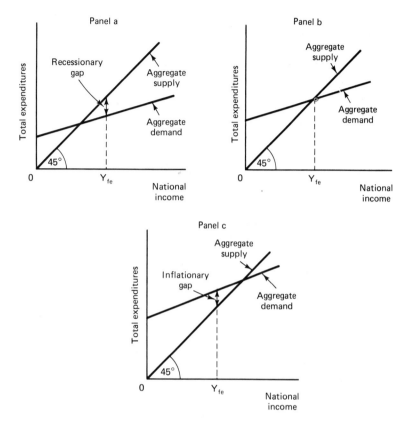

Figure 13.6 *Inflationary and recessionary gaps.* Let Y_{fe} represent the level of national income where the economy achieves full employment (i.e., the nation's labor and capital resources are at their natural rate of employment or the rate desired by laborers and owners of capital). Panel b represents the case where the economy is in equilibrium at full-employment output. Since aggregate supply exceeds aggregate demand at Y_{fe} in panel a, the economy here is suffering from a recessionary gap. This gap is equal to the difference between the potential quantity supplied and the planned quantity demanded at Y_{fe}. Finally, panel c reflects the existence of an inflationary gap, where planned quantities demanded exceeds the potential quantity supplied at Y_{fe}.

Automatic Instruments

There are several types of automatic fiscal policy instruments which are constantly at work in our economy. They act as built-in stabilizers, automatically watering down the punch bowl just when the party suddenly picks up steam (i.e., economy suddenly enters into a boom period) and automatically spiking the punch when the party is moving too slowly (i.e., economic activity suddenly starts to slow down).

The progressive income tax system in the United States serves the function of a built-in stabilizer. As taxable income goes up in a boom period, the marginal tax rate also increases. As illustrated in Table 13.1, the maximum marginal tax rate on taxable income for individuals is 50 percent. This causes aggregate demand to be less than it would have been in the absence of such a progressive tax rate structure. If the economy should instead suddenly slow down, where workers are no longer putting in as much overtime as they were and others who were laid off have had to settle for lower-paying jobs, taxable income would fall and thus be taxed at a lower rate than before. As a result, aggregate demand will not fall by as much as it would have if we did not have such a progressive tax system. In short, the existence of our progressive income tax system tends to stabilize any sudden changes in economic activity.[10]

Unemployment compensation also serves automatically to stabilize aggregate demand. When economic activity slows down, any workers who have been laid off automatically become eligible to receive unemployment compensation from their state government. This keeps their disposable income from dropping to zero until they find other work. When economic activity is strong, however, there is less unemployment, which means that fewer unemployment payments would be necessary.

Both built-in stabilizers tend to dampen the effects of sudden changes in disposable income and hence shifts in the equilibrium level of national income. Because automatic fiscal policy instruments may remove only part of a recessionary or inflationary gap in the economy, their use is normally complemented by *discretionary* policy instruments.

Discretionary Instruments

A tax cut or change in government spending are examples of discretionary fiscal policy instruments or actions. A recent example of discretionary fiscal policy is the Economic Recovery Tax Act of 1981. This Act introduced major changes in U.S. fiscal policy. For example, the Act sought to reduce individual taxes by (1) providing across-the-board rate reductions and indexation of tax brackets, (2) reducing the maximum tax rate on taxable income,

---

[10] An interesting phenomenon has been associated with this stabilizer during periods of inflation. Because the progressive income tax system is geared to nominal income, a rise in nominal income will cause taxes to rise even though the *purchasing power* of income may be falling. This phenomenon is normally referred to "bracket creep." Congress has agreed to index the tax brackets and personal expenditures to reflect changes in inflation as measured by changes in the Consumer Price Index so as to avoid bracket creep beginning after December 31, 1984.

MARRIED INDIVIDUALS FILING JOINT RETURNS
AND SURVIVING SPOUSES

For taxable years beginning in 1983:

If taxable income is:	The tax is:
Not over $3,400	No tax.
Over $3,400 but not over $5,500	11% of the excess over $3,400.
Over $5,500 but not over $7,600	$231, plus 13% of the excess over $5,500.
Over $7,600 but not over $11,900	$504, plus 15% of the excess over $7,600.
Over $11,900 but not over $16,000	$1,149, plus 17% of the excess over $11,900.
Over $16,000 but not over $20,200	$1,846, plus 19% of the excess over $16,000.
Over $20,200 but not over $24,600	$2,644, plus 23% of the excess over $20,200.
Over $24,600 but not over $29,900	$3,656, plus 26% of the excess over $24,600.
Over $29,900 but not over $35,200	$5,034, plus 30% of the excess over $29,900.
Over $35,200 but not over $45,800	$6,624, plus 35% of the excess over $35,200.
Over $45,800 but not over $60,000	$10,334, plus 40% of the excess over $45,800.
Over $60,000 but not over $85,600	$16,014, plus 44% of the excess over $60,000.
Over $85,600 but not over $109,400	$27,278, plus 48% of the excess over $85,600.
Over $109,400	$38,702, plus 50% of the excess over $109,400.

For taxable years beginning in 1984:

If taxable income is:	The tax is
Not over $3,400	No tax.
Over $3,400 but not over $5,500	11% of the excess over $3,400.
Over $5,500 but not over $7,600	$231, plus 12% of the excess over $5,500.
Over $7,600 but not over $11,900	$483, plus 14% of the excess over $7,600.
Over $11,900 but not over $16,000	$1,085, plus 16% of the excess over $11,900.
Over $16,000 but not over $20,200	$1,741, plus 18% of the excess over $16,000.
Over $20,200 but not over $24,600	$2,497, plus 22% of the excess over $20,200.
Over $24,600 but not over $29,900	$3,465, plus 25% of the excess over $24,600.
Over $29,900 but not over $35,200	$4,790, plus 28% of the excess over $29,900.
Over $35,200 but not over $45,800	$6,274, plus 33% of the excess over $35,200.
Over $45,800 but not over $60,000	$9,772, plus 38% of the excess over $45,800.
Over $60,000 but not over $85,600	$15,168, plus 42% of the excess over $60,000.
Over $85,600 but not over $109,400	$25,920, plus 45% of the excess over $85,600.
Over $109,400 but not over $162,400	$36,630, plus 46% of the excess over $109,400.
Over $162,400	$62,600, plus 50% of the excess over $162,400.

TABLE 13.1 PROGRESSIVE INCOME TAX RATE STRUCTURE. The taxation of personal and corporate income in the United States reflects a progressive tax system. Looking at the personal income tax table for married persons filing joint returns and surviving spouses, we see that income is taxed at higher rates as total taxable income rises. The maximum tax rate was 50 percent on income earned in excess of $162,400 in 1984.

and (3) mitigating the so-called marriage penalty. Specific incentives for savers, including the "all savers" certificate, were also a part of this Act. Major changes were also made in the estate and gift tax rules to lessen the tax burden on smaller estates, such as farm-related estates. The Act also contained provisions for businesses such as the Accelerated Cost Recovery System, which allows businesses to recover the cost of eligible assets more quickly than was previously allowed.[11] This Act was accompanied by cuts in government spending for specific programs but increased spending for others. The aim of the Reagan administration was to lessen the tax burden on savings and investment and thus promote economic recovery. The hope was that a revitalized economy would eventually result in an increased individual and corporate tax base that could offset or exceed the projected tax revenue losses from the lower tax rates.[12]

The Economic Recovery Tax Act of 1981 provided the largest overall tax reduction in U.S. history. The size of the ensuing federal budget deficits gave rise to a number of significant tax reforms. The Tax Equity and Fiscal Responsibility Act of 1982 turned out to be the largest revenue-generating bill in this country's history. And the Tax Reform Act of 1984 was the most comprehensive and complex revision of the federal tax system that had ever been attempted. Finally, several legislative proposals were made in 1985 to create a fairer and simpler tax system that would not inhibit economic growth. These proposals among other things called for a reduction of the number of tax brackets appearing in Table 13.1 down to 3–5 brackets. The Accelerated Cost Recovery System contained in the 1981 Act would also be scrapped in favor of the Real Cost Recovery System which adjusted the cost of business assets for inflation. Thus, discretionary fiscal policy is general and tax policy in particular is an ongoing process that requires close attention by farmers.

Effects on Output Gaps

To illustrate the relationship between fiscal policy and the elimination of inflationary and recessionary gaps, let us turn our attention to Figure 13.7. Panel a suggests that the economy currently is plagued by the fact that ag-

---

[11] For a more complete description of the Act, see *Handbook on the Economic Recovery Tax Act of 1981.*

[12] The notion that a reduction in tax rates will actually lead to an increase in government tax revenues has been promoted by Arthur Laffer, a chief proponent of "supply-side" economics. The Laffer curve captures the relationship between tax rates and tax revenues, and reflects the notion that a specific tax rate will maximize tax revenues. It rests on the assumption that a cut in tax rates will lead to an increase in tax collection resulting from an increase in work effort, saving, and investment as well as a decrease in tax avoidance. See the Advanced Topics section at the end of Chapter 15 for a discussion of the Laffer curve.

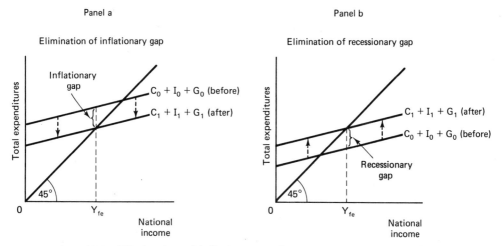

Figure 13.7 *Elimination of inflationary and recessionary gaps.* One of the goals of macroeconomic policy is to promote economic growth in the economy and to stabilize prices. This therefore requires the elimination of both inflationary gaps (excessive aggregate demand) and recessionary gaps (insufficient economic growth). Panel a indicates that inflationary gaps can be eliminated in the short run by lowering total expenditures through higher taxation (which lowers C) and reduced government spending (G). Panel b, on the other hand, indicates that recessionary gaps in the economy can be eliminated in the short run by raising total expenditures through lowering taxes (which raises C) and increasing government expenditures (G).

gregate demand represented by $C_0 + I_0 + G_0$ exceeds aggregate supply at full-employment output.[13] This inflationary gap can be eliminated through cuts in government spending and/or increases in taxes (tax increases would reduce planned consumption and investment expenditures). Both actions, in other words, would lower aggregate demand. The goal is to achieve the aggregate demand associated with $C_1 + I_1 + G_1$. At that point, the equilibrium in the nation's product markets would be achieved *at the same time* that the economy's resources are fully employed.

The opposite steps are necessary if fiscal policy is to be used to eliminate a recessionary gap. Panel b shows an economy currently underutilizing its resources, since aggregate demand, which is represented by $C_0 + I_0 + G_0$, is less than aggregate supply at full employment. To eliminate this gap, fiscal policy must be oriented toward cutting taxes to increase consumption and

---

[13] Such a situation would lead to "excess demand" inflation, where inflation once again is defined as a sustained rise in the general price level (change in the CPI). Here, goods and services are in short supply because the economy is being "fully utilized." We can, of course, observe inflationary pressures before full-employment output is reached. One reason for this might be "cost-push" inflation as resources available at specific prices become scarce.

investment or increasing government spending. The tax cuts, for example, would lead to shifts in the planned consumption and investment expenditures function. The goal would be to shift the aggregate demand curve up to $C_1 + I_1 + G_1$. The problems with both cutting taxes *and* increasing government spending are discussed later in this chapter.

FISCAL POLICY AND THE BUDGET

Much of the current debate in fiscal policy centers around the existence and magnitude of federal *budget deficits.* A budget deficit occurs when government spending exceeds government revenues. Some economists believe that the federal budget should be balanced. These economists, for example, may argue that the budget should be balanced annually. Others may prefer a cyclically balanced budget which requires that deficits incurred during recessionary times (when taxes were cut and/or government spending was increased) be offset later out of budget surpluses. Other less conservative positions are taken by other economists.[14]

Regardless of one's preference regarding balanced versus unbalanced budgets, it is important to understand the major effects of an unbalanced budget. When government spending *(G)* exceeds its revenues *(T),* the government must finance the resulting deficit *(G − T).* This deficit can be financed by the U.S. Treasury selling government bonds to the nonbank public and depository institutions (i.e., banks, savings and loans, etc) in the nation's financial markets. This generally curves interest rates in these markets to rise, however. This rise in interest rates, in turn, usually means that fewer planned investment expenditures *(I)* are undertaken by both farm and nonfarm businesses because of the higher cost of financing these expenditures. When government borrowing leads to higher interest rates and causes planned private investment expenditures *(I)* to be postponed, this effect is referred to by economists as the *crowding-out effect.*

Fiscal policy debates in the past have frequently revolved around the level of government spending and what the *net* effect of higher levels of government spending and lower levels of private spending on the level of national income.[15] If interest rates rise as the Treasury sells new bonds to finance the deficit associated with increased government spending, the expansionary effect of government spending will be offset to some degree by the reduced levels of planned investment expenditures. To this fiscal pol-

[14] Another budgetary proposal is the insistence on a balanced full-employment budget (i.e., what the budget would be if the economy were operating at full employment).

[15] That is, does the multiplier effects of increased government spending on national income outweigh the "crowding-out" effect? The role of the multiplier was discussed in footnote 9.

This cartoon unfortunately falls under the general heading of "funny but true." It is difficult to balance the budget and at the same time promote increased government spending and lower taxes. We have seen this firsthand thus far during the eighties. The "huge subsidies for tobacco growers," the "billions in price supports for dairy farmers," and the "massive federal grants for water projects" referred to by the speaker here are all reflected in government spending (G). Yet a balanced budget requires that tax revenue (T) equal government spending. Since it has been shown to be far easier to cut taxes than to cut government spending during the decade of the eighties, we have seen substantial growth in budget deficits ($G-T$).

icy debate in recent years has been added the growing nature of the federal budget deficit and what this means for servicing the national debt in future years and the subsequent need for higher taxes. This, in turn, will have a depressing effect on planned consumption expenditures.

Figure 13.8 summarizes the chain of events that take place from the point where government spending exceeds taxes to the point where private investment is crowded out by higher interest rates. As we will discuss in Chapter 14, the Federal Reserve System has the option of buying government bonds in the nation's financial markets, thereby "monetizing" part

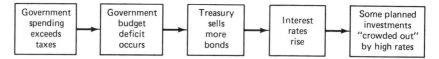

Figure 13.8 *Budget deficits and the "crowding-out" effect.* The series
of boxes illustrate the chain of events that generally lead to a "crowding out" of private planned investment expenditures. When government
spending (G) exceeds government revenue (T), a budget deficit $(G - T)$
occurs. The U.S. Treasury responds to this deficit by selling more
government bonds to finance the imbalance in its checkbook. Assuming
for the moment that the Federal Reserve System does not "monitize"
this deficit by buying additional government bonds, interest rates will
rise (bond prices will fall, which increases the yield to bondholders)
and businesses will be faced with having to pay more than before for
financial capital. At the margin, this may mean that some planned investment projects are no longer feasible.

or all of the deficit and offsetting part or all of the "crowding-out" effect
mentioned above. This monetary action would have the effect of reinforcing
the Administration's fiscal policies by holding interest rates relatively constant and thus preventing declines in planned private investment expenditures.

SUMMARY

The purpose of this chapter was to introduce the factors that determine
aggregate demand and supply in our nation's economy and to illustrate
how fiscal policy instruments can be used to eliminate any inflationary
or recessionary gaps that might exist. The major points made in this chapter can be summarized as follows:

1. Saving as defined as disposable income (income after taxes) minus consumption expenditures. The determinants of planned consumption
   expenditures by households include their disposable income, their
   wealth, and their expectations. A household's *marginal propensity to
   consume* represents the fraction of an increase in disposable income
   that it would use to finance additional consumption expenditures.
   One minus this marginal propensity to consume indicates the fraction
   of each additional dollar in disposable income the household would
   save, or its *marginal propensity to save.*
2. The determinants of planned investments expenditures by businesses
   include the rate of interest, their expectations about future profits,
   the cost of new capital goods, the technology embodied in these
   capital goods, and the level of business taxes.

3. The equilibrium level of national income is determined by the inter-section of the economy's aggregate demand and supply curves. Aggre-gate demand incorporates the levels of planned consumption expendi-tures by households, planned investment expenditures by businesses, government expenditures, and net exports (exports minus imports). If aggregate demand exceeds aggregate supply when the economy's resources are fully employed, an *inflationary gap* is said to exist. If aggregate demand is less than aggregate supply at full employment, the economy is suffering from an *recessionary gap.*

4. Fiscal policy is the act of government spending and/or taxation to eliminate inflationary or recessionary gaps whenever they exist in the economy. Fiscal policy instruments used to eliminate these gaps can be either automatic or discretionary in nature. *Automatic policy instruments* are those that take effect without an explicit action by the Congress or the President. Our progressive tax system is an example of an automatic fiscal policy instrument. *Discretionary policy instru-ments,* on the other hand, require Congress or the President to take an explicit policy action (e.g., pass a law).

5. If the economy is currently experiencing an inflationary gap, this gap can be eliminated by reducing government spending and/or increasing taxes. If a recessionary gap currently exists, however, increased govern-ment spending or tax cuts can be used to expand the economy's use of its resources.

6. A side effect of fiscal policy actions is the existence and magnitude of the *federal budget deficit.* Such a situation occurs when government expenditures exceed government revenues. When financed with the sale of government bonds, such deficits can lead to the *crowding out* of planned business expenditures.

DEFINITION OF TERMS

Planned consumption: amount of income households plan to spend on new goods and services during the year.

Savings: value of saving accumulated at a particular time (i.e., annual saving over a period of years represents your savings).

Marginal propensity to consume: ratio of change in planned consumer ex-penditures to the change in disposable income (income after taxes).

Nondurable good: a good that is consumed during the year.

Durable good: a good that is "consumed" over a period of several years.

Autonomous consumption: portion of total consumer expenditures that does not depend on the level of disposable income.

Dissaving: amount by which planned consumption exceeds disposable income.

Planned saving: the difference between disposable income and planned consumer expenditures or consumption.

Permanent income hypothesis: notion that consumption is dependent on household's long-run expected income.

Aggregated demand: dollar value of planned expenditures for all fixed goods and services during the year.

Aggregated supply: dollar value of all final goods and services supplied to consumers, investors, government, and foreigners during the year.

Autonomous investment: portion of total investment expenditures that does not depend on the level of disposable income.

Recessionary gap: value of output gap when economy's current potential output exceeds planned expenditures.

Inflationary gap: value of output gap when planned expenditures exceeds the economy's current potential output.

Automatic instruments: do not require action on the part of government to take effect (an example is the progressive nature of the income tax system in the United States).

Discretionary instruments: do require action on the part of government to take effect (opposite of automatic instruments).

Budget deficit: the excess of government spending over government revenues.

Crowding-out: the postponement of planned private investment expenditures caused by high interest rates brought about by government borrowing.

Inflation: a sustained rise in the general price level.

Multiplier: effect that a change in autonomous consumption or investment will have on equilibrium income. The investment multiplier, for example, is equal to the reciprocal of the marginal propensity to save.

Potential output: nation's gross national product when its labor and capital resources are "fully employed" (i.e., 5 to 6 percent unemployment rate for labor and 86 to 88 percent capacity utilization rate for capital). Also referred to as full-employment output.

REFERENCES

DERNBURG, THOMAS F., and DUNCAN N. MCDOUGALL, *Macroeconomics,* 6th ed. New York: McGraw-Hill Book Company, 1980.

Handbook on the Economic Recovery Tax Act of 1981. Englewood Cliffs, N.J.: Prentice-Hall, Inc., 1981.

KEYNES, JOHN MAYNARD, *The General Theory of Employment, Interest and Money.* New York: Harcourt, Brace & World, Inc., 1936.

ADDITIONAL READINGS

LINDAUER, JOHN, *Macroeconomics: A Modern View.* New York: Holt, Rinehart and Winston, 1979.

PECHMAN, JOSEPH A., *A Federal Tax Policy.* 3rd ed. Washington, D.C.: The Brookings Institution, 1977.

PENSON, JOHN B., JR. and DAVID A. LINS, *Agricultural Finance: An Introduction to Micro and Macro Concepts.* Englewood Cliffs, N.J.: Prentice-Hall, Inc., 1980.

QUESTIONS

1. Describe the relationship between savings, consumption, and income.
2. What are the determinants of investment? Of consumption?
3. Complete the following table.

Disposable income	Planned consumption	Planned saving
$1,000	$1,100	$_____
1,100	1,150	_____
1,200	1,200	_____
1,300	1,250	_____
1,400	1,300	_____
1,500	1,350	_____

In addition, plot the planned consumption and saving functions on graph paper and calculate the marginal propensity to consume.

4. Under what conditions is national income equal to national output or product?
5. What are the appropriate fiscal policy actions to eliminate an inflationary gap? A recessionary gap?
6. Why is it said that a progressive income tax system and unemployment compensation are "built-in stabilizers?"
7. Describe the process by whch a change in fiscal policy is transmitted to agriculture.

ADVANCED TOPICS

We indicated earlier in this chapter than when total government spending exceeds total government revenues from taxes and other sources, a *budget deficit* is incurred. We also indicated that this deficit can be financed by the U.S.

Treasury selling government bonds in the nation's financial markets. Since this amounts to borrowing from the private sectors of the economy, the government has incurred a debt. This debt is normally referred to as the *public debt* or the *national debt*.

Growth of Public Debt

One often hears references to the growing public debt in this country, which now exceeds $1 trillion expressed in current dollars. It is true that the size of the public debt has been growing at a rather healthy rate during the post-World War II period. However, the absolute level of this debt is not necessarily the best way to analyze the growth of this debt. Two alternatives are (1) expressing this debt in real terms on a per capita basis, and (2) expressing the interest paid on this debt as a percentage of the nation's gross national product.

Panel a in Figure 13.9 illustrates that while the per capita public debt of the federal government expressed in constant dollars rose sharply during the World War II period, it has declined by more than 50 percent since then. Thus while total public debt has been rising steadily in current dollars since the thirties, its real burden per capita is down sharply from the World War II period. Panel b in Figure 13.9 focuses on the interest payments on public debt expressed as a percentage of the nation's GNP. Looking at panel b, we see that while the interest payments paid to the private sector have been increasing as a percentage of GNP, this percentage remains extremely small.

The annual federal budget deficits apparently will continue to be in the range $100 to $200 billion well into the mid-eighties. The interest payments associated with the rise in public debt that will probably be needed if contractionary monetary policies are followd will probably continue to increase, possibly even when expressed as a percentage of GNP. It is important to note, however, that as long as this debt is held by U.S. citizens, it is one that we as a nation owe to ourselves. Under these circumstances, the future interest income received by certain segments of the private sector will have been paid in part by future taxes levied on the private sector. Therefore, this represents a transfer of wealth among segments of the private sector. One flaw in all of this is the fact that foreign ownership of the public debt of the United States has been rising in the late seventies and early eighties, accounting for 10 percent of this debt. Thus the interest payments on this debt leave the United States, returning only if reinvested by foreign investors in this or other forms of investments in the United States.

Burden on Future Generations?

Does an increase in public debt mean that future generations are forced to pay for our current budget deficits? When the federal government borrows from the private sector to cover its budget deficits, this means that the private sector, which is comprised of consumers and producers, are forgoing

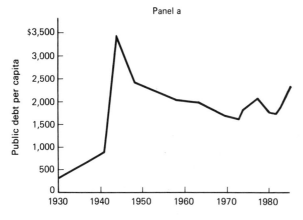

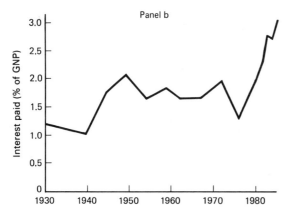

Figure 13.9 *Alternative views of the magnitude of the national debt.* In addition to examining the dollar value of our national debt, we can examine its importance in other ways. One is to look at the constant dollar level of public debt per capita, which is shown in panel a to be high but not nearly as high as it was during the World War II period. Panel b shows that interest payments on this debt are rising as a percentage of our gross national product, but still represent a small fraction of GNP.

current consumption and investment expenditures. That is, they have chosen to lend a certain sum of money to the federal government rather than use these funds for some other purpose. Thus future generations will not be paying for the government resources purchased today. If the government controls $1 trillion in resources but part of these resources were acquired through deficit spending, this does not alter the fact that the government still controls $1 trillion worth of resources. Think of it another way: if you borrow $1,000 and use these funds to purchase as asset worth $1,000, your net worth (assets minus debt) will be unchanged. If these assets represent dams, power plants, and other items that provide services to producers and consumers, future generations may be better off even after we account for the higher taxes required to pay the interest on foreign-owned debt.

The IS Curve

A simple static Keynesian model of an economy contains an *IS* curve and an *LM* curve. An *IS* curve represents a series of market equilibriums in the nation's product market, while an *LM* curve represents a series of market equilibriums in the nation's money market. Since fiscal policy is directly related to the *IS* curve, we shall introduce this relationship here. The relationship between the *LM* curve and monetary policy will be explored in the Advanced Topics section in Chapter 14. Finally, both curves will be brought together in the Advanced Topics section in Chapter 15, where the effects of policy actions on the general equilibrium interest rate and output will be explored.

Figure 13.1 highlighted the positive relationship between consumer disposable income (i.e., income after taxes) and the level of consumption expenditures. This figure suggested that the higher the level of disposable income, the greater consumer expenditures will be. Exactly how much greater will depend on the slope of the curve in Figure 13.1, or the consumer's marginal propensity to consume. We can write this consumption function as follows:

$$\text{consumption} = \underset{\text{sumption}}{\underset{\text{mous con-}}{\text{autono-}}} + \underset{\text{consume}}{\underset{\text{propensity to}}{\text{marginal}}} \times \underset{\text{income}}{\underset{\text{disposable}}{\text{consumer}}} \qquad (13.6)$$

Figure 13.3 illustrated the negative relationship between the rate of interest and the level of investment expenditures. This figure suggested that the higher the rate of interest were, the lower investment expenditures will be. Exactly how much lower will depend on the slope of Figure 13.3 or investor's interest sensitivity of demand. We can express this investment function as follows:

$$\text{investment} = \underset{\text{vestment}}{\underset{\text{mous in-}}{\text{autono-}}} - \underset{\text{demand}}{\underset{\text{sensitivity of}}{\text{interest}}} \times \underset{\text{rate}}{\underset{\text{interest}}{\text{level of}}} \qquad (13.7)$$

Assuming that government expenditures for fixed autonomously and ignoring net export demand, we can conclude that equilibrium in the nation's product market is satisfied by the condition that the use of resources in the private sector to produce output not sold to consumers (i.e., planned investment and government expenditures) must equal the amount of income that consumers do not spend (i.e., planned savings plus taxes). Under these conditions, substituting equations (13.6) and (13.7) into this equilibrium condition and solving for income under different interest rates would tell us what the nation's income would have to be for there to be an equilibrium in the product market.[16] Figure 13.10 illustrates this relationship for three alternative interest rates, (i.e., i_1, i_2, and i_3). The lower the interest rate, the greater income must be to increase planned savings to the point where it equals the larger volume of planned investment, thereby ensuring product

---

[16] For a more technically precise explanation of this procedure, see John B. Penson, Jr., and David A. Lins, *Agricultural Finance,* (Englewood Cliffs, N.J.: Prentice-Hall, Inc., 1980) pp. 404–406.

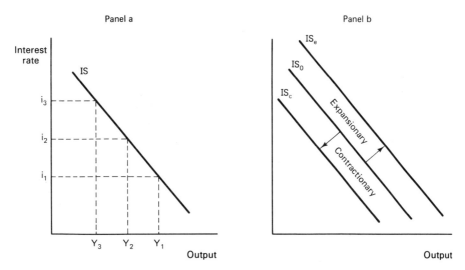

Figure 13.10 *The IS curve.* The *IS* curve illustrates a series of market equilibriums in the nation's product market associated with a particular interest rate and level of output. At each point, planned investment and government purchases equals planned saving (disposable income minus consumption) and tax revenues at that level of output. Panel a shows that at a market interest rate if i_3, an output of Y_3 would be needed to ensure an equilibrium in the product market (i.e., to shrink planned savings to the point where it equals planned investment at this high rate of interest). At an interest rate of i_1, however, more output would be needed for planned savings to equal planned investment at this lower rate of interest. Panel b in this figure shows that expansionary fiscal policy will shift the *IS* curve to the right (from IS_0 to IS_e) while contractionary fiscal policy will shift the *IS* curve to the left (i.e., from IS_0 to IS_c).

market equilibrium. A line passing through these points satisfying the investment equals savings equilibrium conditions is referred to as the *IS curve.* Each and every point along this curve represents an equilibrium in the nation's product market associated with a particular interest rate and level of outcome. At each point, planned investment and government purchases equals planned saving and tax revenues at that level of output.

Expansionary fiscal policy actions (i.e., a tax cut that raises consumer disposable income or increases government spending) will shift the *IS* curve to the right, implying that more outcome will be needed for planned savings to equal planned investment at each interest rate. Conversely, contractionary fiscal policies (i.e., a tax rise that reduces consumer disposable income or decreased government spending) will shift the *IS* curve to the left. This implies that less outcome will be needed for savings to equal planned investment at each interest rate.

14

MONEY AND MONETARY POLICY

It is difficult to imagine a large, highly integrated economy like that of the United States without the existence of money. Money is perhaps the most important invention created by human beings. Bartering is both time consuming and costly. Can you imagine a manufacturer of combines trying to exchange his product for the goods and services needed to manufacture additional combines? Workers certainly would not want to be paid off in combines, nor would the utility company supplying electrical power to the firm. Our willingness to accept money made of paper or specific metals allows households and businesses in various regions of the country to specialize in the goods or services they provide despite a local noncoincidence of wants. Given the critical role played by money in modern economies, it is important that we understand the factors that influence its demand and supply.

The purpose of this chapter is to discuss (1) the characteristics of money, including the functions it performs and how it differs from credit; (2) the Federal Reserve System and its role in our monetary economy; (3) the monetary policy instruments the Federal Reserve can use to transmit its monetary policies; (4) the determinants of equilibrium in the money market; and (5) how monetary policy can be used to help achieve the economy's current potential output.

CHARACTERISTICS OF MONEY

Money is generally thought of in terms of the change in your pocket or the bills in your wallet. Money includes more than *currency*. At a minimum, it

The home of the Board of Governors of the Federal Reserve System is located in Washington, D.C. The Board of Governors has general supervisory responsibility over the 12 district Federal Reserve Banks located throughout the country. It also directs the operations of the Federal Open Market Committee, which daily affects the nation's money supply.

also includes your checking account balance, which is referred to as a *demand deposit.* Money can be defined by the functions it performs.

Functions of Money

Money traditionally performs three functions. We have already discussed its role as a *medium of exchange.* Money allows us to specialize in endeavors where we have a comparative advantage by facilitating payments to others for the goods and services they have provided and payments from others for our labor.

Money also serves as a *unit of accounting.* That is, it provides a basis with which we can compare the relative value of goods and services in the economy. For example, we discussed the level of gross national product and national income in previous chapters in terms of billions of dollars. Physical measures of aggregate statistics such as these would be confronted with the age-old problem of "adding apples and oranges." Money also serves as the unit of accounting for assessing the profitability of businesses and household budgets.

Finally, money is an asset and as such has a *store of value.* You could store all your wealth in strawberries, for example. One problem with this is that these strawberries will eventually rot. The purchasing power of money also may "rot" or erode during periods of inflation. Strawberries also may not be very *liquid,* or cannot be easily disposed of without a transactions cost and with relative certainty as to their market value. Money, on the other hand, is the most liquid asset there is, and can easily be converted into other forms of assets if so desired. It is partially for this reason that households and businesses store at least part of their wealth in money. The *cost* of holding money is the income forgone by not using these funds in an alternative opportunity, such as a savings account earning a positive return and where funds can be transferred to your checking account only as needed (this is referred to as an automatic transfer system or ATS account).

In summary, money serves as (1) a medium of exchange, (2) a unit of accounting, and (3) a store of value.

Money versus Near Monies

If we define money by the functions it performs, currency and demand deposits definitely would be considered as money. As illustrated in Figure 14.1, this constitutes the narrowest definition of money, a definition labeled M1 by the Federal Reserve System. Until the eighties, only commercial banks could offer demand deposits. Today there are a variety of checking-type accounts offered by a variety of financial institutions (e.g., savings and loans, credit unions, etc). Some examples are negotiable orders of withdrawal (NOW) accounts, the ATS accounts described above, and share draft accounts. The definition of M1 balances was expanded by the 1980 Depository Institu-

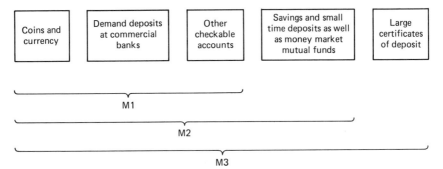

Figure 14.1 *Definition of monetary aggregates by the Federal Reserve System.* There is not complete agreement on just how to define the nation's money supply. The narrowest definition of money is referred to a "M1 balances" and includes coins and currency (paper money), demand deposits (checking account balances) at commercial banks, and checkable accounts in the economy. Some financial economists, including Milton Friedman, have argued for broadening the definition of the nation's money supply like that of "M2 balances" to include such near monies as savings accounts, small time deposits, and money-market mutual funds on the premise that they are nearly perfect substitutes for money narrowly defined.

tions Deregulations and Monetary Control Act to include these additional checkable accounts as well as demand deposits at mutual savings banks.

Other forms of assets may be considered *near monies* because of their relatively high liquidity and no-risk-of-loss value. Time deposits, which must be held for a specific time before being converted to money, fall into this category. Savings accounts are particularly liquid. Although a 30-day notice of intent to withdraw funds from a savings account is required, such notice in practice is rarely required. Shares in money-market mutual funds, which represent interests in holdings of government and corporate bonds, can also be classified as near money. Some of these funds allow one to write checks on the shares they own in the fund.

As we can see in Figure 14.1, the Federal System includes these near monies together with those assets previously captured in M1 in their definition of M2. Also included in M2 are certain specialized overnight assets.[1] Certificates of deposits (CDs) at all depository institutions issued in denominations of $100,000 or more is the major factor distinguishing the Federal Reserve System's M2 and M3 definitions of money.[2]

[1] These include overnight repurchase agreements issued by commercial banks as well as overnight Eurodollar deposits held by U.S. nonbank residents at Carribean branches of U.S. banks.

[2] Also included in M3 are term repurchase agreements issued by commercial banks and savings and loan associates. The Federal Reserve System also publishes a definition of liquid assets *(L)* which includes everything in M3 as well as such financial instruments as bankers acceptances, commercial paper, savings banks, and liquid Treasury obligations.

Backing of Money

What makes a piece of paper with green ink and a few numbers on it acceptable to us as payment for our labor services, for example? Monetary economies such as ours rest on what is termed a *fiduciary monetary system.* That is, the value of money rests on the public's belief that this piece of paper with green ink on it can be exchanged for the goods and services we buy. Take a dollar bill from your wallet or purse. See if there is a promise to exchange the dollar for a specific quantity of gold. You will not find one.

There are three principal reasons why money in a fiduciary monetary system has a positive value. First, money is acceptable by others when purchasing goods and services. Second, demand deposits and currency have been designated as legal tender by the federal government. Most paper money will contain the phrase "this note is legal tender for all debts public and private" in the upper left-hand corner. Thus it must be accepted for payment of debts. Finally, money also is a predictable value in *nominal* terms. A dollar is worth a dollar. Although the *purchasing power* of this dollar will decline in periods of inflation, you would not refuse to accept it in exchange for goods or services.

Now that we have an understanding of what money is, let us turn our attention to the Federal Reserve System and the concept of fractional reserve banking.

FEDERAL RESERVE SYSTEM

Congress passed the Federal Reserve Act and it was signed into law by President Woodrow Wilson on December 23, 1914. The Federal Reserve System began operation in the fall of 1914 as this country's central bank. Its principal domestic goals were to encourage economic growth and combat both inflationary and recessionary tendencies in the domestic economy. As we will see in this chapter, the Federal Reserve accomplishes these goals by regulating the quantity and cost of credit in the economy. The purpose of this section is to discuss the organization of the Federal Reserve System, the function it performs, its relationship to the banking system in this country, and the policy instruments that is has at its disposal.

Organization of the Fed

The Federal Reserve System is organized around a Board of Governors, located at the System's headquarters in Washington, D.C. The Board of Governors consists of seven full-time members appointed by the President and approved by the Senate. As Figure 14.2 illustrates, the Board of Governors exerts general supervision over the 12 district Federal Reserve Banks, which are located in selected major cities in the United States. The location

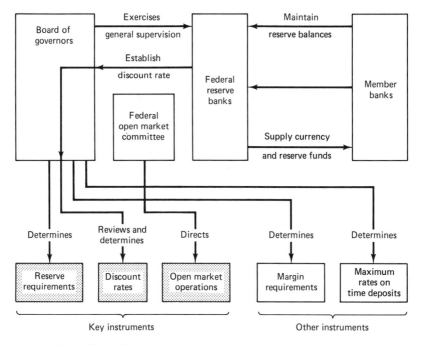

Source: Federal Reserve System

Figure 14.2 *Organization and functions of the Federal Reserve.* The Federal Reserve System consists of the Board of Governors, the Federal Open Market Committee, the 12 district Federal Reserve Banks, and the approximately 5,600 member banks located throughout the country. The 1980 Depository Institutions Deregulation and Monetary Control Act virtually eliminated the distinction between member and nonmember banks, however, by extending the Federal Reserve's reserve requirements to all depository institutions (nonmember commercial banks, savings and loan associations, and credit unions). In addition to establishing these requirements, the Board of Governors determines the discount rate charged to banks that borrow from it and directs the buying and selling of government bonds it owns through its open market operations.

of these district banks and their branches (25 in all) is shown in Figure 14.3. The Board, as we describe more fully later in the chapter, determines reserve requirements, reviews and determines the discount rate, determines margin requirements on stock market credit, and determines the ceilings on the yields paid by banks to their depositors (these ceilings are being phased out over time). Each governor on the Board serves one 14-year term and cannot be associated in any other way with banking during his or her term. In addition, no two governors may come from the same Federal Reserve district. Finally, the Board has a chairman and a vice-chairman. Both are appointed by the President of the United States to serve a 14-year term. These

Figure 14.3 *District bank boundaries in the Federal Reserve System.*
The geographical boundaries of the 12 district Federal Reserve Banks
are illustrated above. These banks serve as the repository for required
reserves of the depository institutions in its district, lend to (discount
paper of) member banks, and supply currency to the nation's banking
system. They also assist in the clearing of checks written on different
banks in the economy. Most of these district banks have one or more
branch banks located in large metropolitan areas within their boundaries. These district banks supply five members (usually the bank president) to the membership of the Federal Reserve System's Federal Open
Market Committee.

officers may be reappointed over the course of their 14-year term on the
Board.

The Federal Open Market Committee (FOMC), which is composed of
the seven members of the Board of Governors and five representatives of
the district banks, meets periodically to determine the desired future growth
of the money supply and other important issues. As suggested by Figure
14.2, this committee issues directives to the manager of the System Open
Market Account, who is located in New York and is responsible for seeing
that the appropriate buying or selling actions are taken in the government
securities market. The nature of these actions is also described later in the
chapter.

Each of the 12 district Federal Reserve Banks mentioned above is a
federally chartered corporation. Its stockholders are the member banks in
that district. These member banks pledge up to 6 percent of their own capital and surplus in reserve stock. The district banks are not profit-maximizing

businesses, however. Rather, their objective is to service and discipline member commercial banks in their districts. Each bank is managed by a nine-member Board of Directors serving in staggered terms. The role of these directors is to appoint the president of the district bank (with approval of the Board of Governors) and to serve in an advisory capacity to the bank on economic and financial conditions in the district.

Of the approximately 15,000 commercial banks in this country, about 5,600 are members of the Federal Reserve System. *National banks,* which receive their charter from the Comptroller of the Currency, are required to be members. There are about 4,600 national banks in this country. The remaining 1,000 member banks are *state banks.* They receive their charter from their respective state governments, but have elected to be members of the Federal Reserve System for one reason or another. Usually, this decision is based on weighing the cost of membership (e.g., the requirement of nonincome-producing reserve requirements) and the returns (e.g., the ability to borrow from the Federal Reserve's discount window and the use of its check-clearing facilities and teletype wires to transfer funds).[3]

Functions of the Fed

Now that we have an understanding of the organization of the Federal Reserve System, let us examine the functions it performs. One of the Fed's functions noted in Figure 14.2 is to supply the economy through the district banks with paper currency called Federal Reserve notes. Take a dollar bill or any higher domination of paper currency out of your wallet or purse. You will see the term "Federal Reserve Note" printed on it. Each district Federal Reserve bank must have enough paper currency to accommodate the demands for money in its district. Although this paper currency is printed in Washington by the Bureau of Printing and Engraving, it bears the code of the originating district bank.

The Federal Reserve System also supervises its member banks, as does the Comptroller of the Currency and the Federal Deposit Insurance Corporation (FDIC). Among the things that the examiners look at are the types of loans made, the backing, or collateral for these loans, and who borrowed these funds.

A third function performed by the Federal Reserve System is to provide check collection and clearing services. All member banks and depository institutions can send deposited checks to their district Federal Reserve Bank, who compete with private clearinghouses for their business. Suppose

---

[3] The Depository Institutions Deregulation and Monetary Control Act of 1980 virtually eliminates any differences between member and nonmember banks in the eyes of the Federal Reserve System. This act extends reserve requirements to *all* depository institutions (commercial banks, savings and loan associations, credit unions, etc.) but makes its services available to all these institutions.

that Ralph Rancher who owns a farm in the Kansas City Fed's district travels to San Francisco to attend a convention. While there, Mr. Rancher writes a check to Wally's Wharf resturant for $50. Now let us assume that Wally deposits these funds in his checking account at his commercial bank in San Francisco. Wally's bank would then deposit the check in its reserve account at the San Francisco district Federal Reserve Bank. The San Francisco Fed would then send this check to the district Federal Reserve Bank in Kansas City, which would deduct $50 from the reserve account of Ralph's bank and then send this check to his (Ralph's) bank. The final step sees Ralph's bank deducting $50 from his checking account and sending the canceled check to Ralph.

Another function performed by the Federal Reserve System noted in Figure 14.2 is that each district bank maintains the reserve balances of depository institutions in its territory as required by law. As we shall discuss in more detail later in this chapter, depository institutions are required to keep a certain fraction of their deposits on reserve.

The Federal Reserve System also lends to (discounts the paper of) depository institutions. The interest rate charged on these loans is called the *discount rate*. Those banks with a heavy seasonal demand for loans like rural commerical banks, which make a significant volume of loans to farm businesses, may qualify for special borrowing privileges.

The Federal Reserve System also acts as the federal government's banker and fiscal agent. The U.S. Treasury has a checking account with the Fed. In addition, the Fed helps the federal government collect tax revenues from businesses and aids in the purchase and sale of government bonds.

Finally, the Federal Reserve System regulates the money supply to achieve its goals of promoting economic growth and price stability. This function has received national attention in recent years of high interest rates. The monetary policy instruments the Federal Reserve System has at its disposal are discussed below.

Monetary Policy Instruments

As Figure 14.2 suggested earlier, the Fed has three major monetary policy instruments it can employ to regulate the growth of the nation's money supply. These instruments are (1) changes in reserve requirements, (2) changes in the discount rate, and (3) changes in the direction or magnitude of its open market operations.

Reserve requirements. The Federal Reserve System alters the supply of money by changing the amount of reserves in the banking system. One way to accomplish this is to change the requires reserves at depository institutions, which are required to maintain a specific fraction of their customers' deposits as reserves. Total reserves can be divided into three categories.

Legal reserves for member banks consist of deposits held at the institution's district Federal Reserve bank plus vault cash.[4] *Required reserves* represent the minimum weekly average legal reserves that a depository institution must hold. This requirement is expressed as a ratio. The minimum and maximum reserve requirement ratios for depository institutions permitted by law are given in Table 14.1. The final category of reserves is *excess reserves,* the difference between total reserves and required reserves. The level of excess reserves determines the extent to which depository institutions can make loans. Thus manipulation of the reserve requirement ratio will either expand or contract the level of excess reserves at depository institutions and hence their ability to make new loans. We will see shortly how this translates into expansion or contraction of the money supply.

Discount rate.   As indicated earlier, the discount rate represents the interest rate the Fed charges for lending reserves to depository institutions. If a depository institution wants to increase its loans but does not have any excess reserves at the moment, it can borrow reserves from the Fed at its "discount window."[5] The Fed does not have to lend all the reserves these institutions need every time they want them, however. As an alternative, banks can borrow funds on a short-term basis to meet reserve requirements, for example, from the *federal funds market.* This is a interbank market trafficing in reserves. Banks with excess reserves can lend to banks that are short on a 24-hour basis (usually overnight) at what is known as the *federal funds rate.*

Open market operations.   The third way the Federal Reserve System can alter the volume of reserves at depository institutions is by the sale or purchase of government securities. The directive by the Federal Open Market Committee (FOMC) to *sell* off government securities results in a decrease in reserves at depository institutions as deposits are withdrawn from these institutions to pay for these securities. This lowers the level of reserves in the banking system and hence its ability to make loans. The opposite occurs when the FOMC issues the directive to *buy* government securities. This results in an *increase in reserves* in the banking system. This is by far the most frequently used monetary policy instrument.

Other instruments.   The Fed also has several other policy instruments it can employ to regulate the expansion of credit in the nation's economy.

---

[4] Nonmember banks and other depository institutions may treat as reserves their deposits with a correspondent depository institution holding required reserves, with the Federal Home Loan Bank (savings and loan associations), or with the National Credit Union Administration central liquidity facility (credit unions), as long as these reserves are passed on to a Federal Reserve bank.

[5] These reserves are referred to as borrowed reserves. Excess reserves minus these borrowed reserves are often referred to as *free reserves.*

	Net demand deposits (%)[a]		Time deposits (%)		
	Under $25 million	Over $25 million	Savings deposits	Other under $5 million	Other over $5 million
Actual	3	12	3	3	6
Legal minimum	3	3	0	0	0
Legal maximum	14	14	9	9	9

[a] Equal to gross deposits minus cash items in the process of collection and balances due from other banks.

Source: Federal Reserve System.

TABLE 14.1 RESERVE REQUIREMENT RATIOS FOR DEPOSITORY INSTITU-TIONS. There is no single reserve requirement ratio for demand deposits and time deposits at depository institutions. Instead, there are a set of reserve requirement ratios that vary according to the size of the bank in question. For example, we see here that banks with net deposits over $25 million must meet a ratio of 12 percent as opposed to only 3 percent for smaller banks. This table also reports the legal maximum and minimum for these ratios that serve as the boundaries for the Federal Reserve System's use of these ratios to change the nation's money supply.

As Figure 14.2 suggests, the Fed determines the margin requirements (i.e., down payment required) for loans made by stockbrokers to customers desiring to purchase stock, as well as the maximum rates banks can pay depositors on specific types of deposits.

Let us now turn to the topic of the money supply and illustrate how the monetary policy instruments described above affect its magnitude.

CHANGING THE MONEY SUPPLY

At the end of the preceding section, we discussed how a change in reserves in the banking system brought about by the implementation of any one of three monetary policy instruments described above will affect the ability of depository institutions to make loans. How does this affect the money supply? To address this question, we must first discuss the process of money creation. Then we can discuss how changes in the three major monetary policy instruments shift the supply curve for money.

Creation of Deposits

There is an important relationship between the level of reserves in the banking system and the money supply. In the discussion to follow, let us focus on the M1 definition of the money supply: coins and currency in circulation plus checkable deposits at depository institutions. Part of this money supply consists of coins and currency which are physical units that can be carried around in a purse or wallet. The deposits in M1, on the other hand, are merely entries in an account at depository institutions.

New deposits can be created, and the money supply expanded, by increasing the level of excess reserves in the banking system. If the level of excess reserves at depository institutions is zero, there can be no further expansion of the money supply. No new loans can be made at that point.

To see how deposits can be expanded when excess reserves are greater than zero, let us examine the greatly simplified balance sheet of a hypothetical bank presented in Table 14.2. Let us assume that the bank's assets consist entirely of reserves and loans, while its liabilities consist entirely of deposits. If the reserve requirement ratio is 0.20, this bank must hold at least $2 million of its $10 million of deposits in reserves. If bank A already had loan outstanding of $8 million, as shown in Table 14.2, the bank would be fully "loaned up." That is, it could not increase its loan volume any further because it has no excess reserves.

Now let us assume that the depositors at this bank sell $1 million in government securities to the FOMC and deposit the checks they received from the Federal Reserve System in bank A (Table 14.3). As a result of these deposits, bank A's total deposits would increase to $11 million and its required reserves would have to increase to $2.2 million (i.e., its initial $2 million requires reserves plus 20 percent of its new $1 million deposit). Assuming that it has not had time to make any new loans, the bank would have excess reserves of $800,000.

Banks desire for profit-maximizing reasons to keep their excess reserves as low as possible. These reserves represent idle balances that are earning no in-

Assets		Liabilities	
Reserves:		Deposits	$10,000,000
Required	$ 2,000,000		
Excess	0		
Total	$ 2,000,000		
Loans	8,000,000		
Total	$10,000,000	Total	$10,000,000

TABLE 14.2 BANK A'S BALANCE SHEET BEFORE $1 MILLION DEPOSIT. To illustrate the effects of a deposit in a commercial bank and its effects on the makeup of its reserves, let's assume that $1 million is deposited in bank A. The partial balance sheet for this bank indicates that the bank had no excess reserves before this deposit. This suggests that the required reserve ratio in this simplified example was 20 percent (i.e., $2 million divided by $10 million). Finally, this bank had no ability to make any additional loans to its customers (i.e., it was fully "loaned up"), since the bank's excess reserves were zero.

Assets		Liabilities	
Reserves:		Deposits	$11,000,000
Required	$ 2,200,000		
Excess	800,000		
Total	3,000,000		
Loans	8,000,000		
Total	$11,000,000	Total	$11,000,000

TABLE 14.3 BANK A'S BALANCE SHEET AFTER $1 MILLION DEPOSIT. The bank's total deposits rise to $11 million as a result of the new $1 million deposit. Assuming that the required reserve ratio remained at 20 percent, the bank's required reserves will increase by $200,000 to $2.2 million. If the bank had not made any new loans, it would have excess reserves totaling $800,000. These are monies that can continue to be held in idle cash balances or used to make new loans. The bank's total loan volume under these conditions could increase to as much as $8.8 million.

terest income.[6] Let us assume for the moment that bank A lends its entire excess reserves of $800,000. The bank would then be fully loaned up again and would remain that way until new activities altered its balance sheet position. Now let us further assume that the proceeds of the loans made by bank A wind up as deposits in another bank. For example, assume the $800,000 lent by bank A shows up as deposits in bank B.[7] Given a required ratio of 20 percent, bank B must now hold $160,000 in additional reserves (i.e., 0.20 × $800,000) and can now make loans of $640,000 (i.e., $800,000 – $160,000). Table 14.4 shows how the initial deposit of $1 million in bank A has been used by the banking system to expand the deposits that appear in the M1 definition of the money supply.

If we look at the totals at the bottom of Table 14.4, we see that the deposits of the entire banking system have increased by a multiple of the initial $1 million change in reserves at these depository institutions brought about by the depositors of bank A selling $1 million in government securities to the Fed. If you divide the change in deposits ($5 million) by the change in reserves ($1 million) reported at the bottom of Table 14.4, we see that the change in the money supply was five times greater than the change in reserves. From this example we can make a generalization about the extent to which the money supply will increase when the banking system's reserves are increased. If we assume that banks will minimize their holdings of excess reserves and that all the proceeds from loans are deposited in the banking

[6] For reasons of safely and liquidity, banks normally hold some idle balances, however.

[7] This process could just as well occur without all these loan proceeds showing up in *different* banks.

Bank	Change in deposits	Change in loans	Change in reserves
A	$1,000,000	$ 800,000	$ 200,000
B	800,000	640,000	160,000
C	640,000	512,000	128,000
D	512,000	409,600	102,400
E	409,600	327,680	81,920
F	327,680	262,144	65,536
G	262,144	209,715	52,429
H	209,715	167,772	41,943
I	167,772	134,218	33,554
Subtotal	$4,463,129	$3,570,503	$ 892,626
Other banks	536,871	429,497	107,374
Total	$5,000,000	$4,000,000	$1,000,000

TABLE 14.4 CHANGE IN DEPOSITS IN THE BANKING SYSTEM AFTER $1 MILLION DEPOSIT. Let's suppose that the $1 million deposited in bank *A* was the result of a purchase of government bonds held by its depositors and sold by the Federal Reserve System. Also assume that bank *A* uses its newly found excess reserves to make loans and that the proceeds of these loans wind up in another bank. For example, the $800,000 in new loans made by bank *A* wind up as deposits in bank *B*. Bank *B* must hold 20 percent of these new deposits in reserve ($160,000), while the remainder can be used to make loans to its customers ($640,000). If we follow this process until the total change in reserves in the last column reached $1 million, we see new loans totaled $4 million and the total change in deposits equals $5 million. Thus the initial injection of $1 million in reserves was "multiplied up" by the banking system to a $5 million change in the nation's money supply.

system (none are hidden in tin cans in the backyard), we can assert the following:

$$\frac{\text{money}}{\text{multiplier}} = \frac{1}{\text{required reserve ratio}} \qquad (14.1)$$

This equation states that the *money multiplier* is equal to the reciprocal of the required reserve ratio. In our example above, where the required reserve ratio was 20 percent, the money multiplier would be 5 (i.e., 1.0 ÷ 0.20). Thus an increase of $1 million in reserves would expand the money supply to $5 million under the assumptions outlined above ($1 million × 5.0).[8] Note that this is identical to the total change in the money supply reported at the bottom of Table 14.4.

[8] The reverse of this conclusion is also true. That is, a $1 million *decrease* in reserves in the banking system will *reduce* the money supply by $5 million if the money multiplier is 5.0.

In the real world, the money multiplier normally ranges between 2.0 to 3.0, as illustrated in Figure 14.4. Thus a $1 million increase in reserves will increase the money supply by $2 million to $3 million. There are several factors that cause the money multiplier to be below the reciprocal of the required reserve ratio. These include *currency drains* (sometimes called leakages), which refers to individuals' desire to hold currency rather than deposit these funds in a bank or other depository insitution. When this occurs, these funds remain outside the banking system. If, in our previous example of the depositors at bank *A* receiving $1 million from the sale of securities to the FOMC, these depositors had chosen instead to hide these funds in their mattress, the level of deposits at bank *A* would not have changed and the money supply would not have expanded by $4 million. Thus the greater the incidence of currency drains, the smaller the multiplier will be. Banks' desire to hold idle excess reserves for reasons of safety and liquidity will also lower the value of the money multiplier. The greater the level of excess reserves, the lower the money multiplier will be.

Monetary Policy and the Money Supply

Now that we see how a change in reserves affects the money supply, let us go back to the monetary policy instruments available to the Fed and exam-

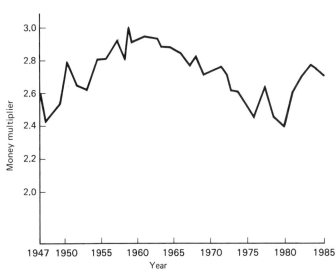

Figure 14.4 *Annual fluctuations in the money multiplier.* The money multiplier in the U.S. economy has varied between 2.0 and 3.0 during the post–World War II period. The higher the money multiplier, the greater the effect an injection of $1 million in reserves into the banking system will have on the nation's money supply. A money multiplier of 2.0 would suggest that a $1 million increase in reserves will increase the money supply by $2 million. If the multiplier were equal to 3.0, the money supply would increase by $3 million. Two factors that influence the size of the multiplier in addition to the required reserve ratio are currency drains (people desire to hold currency instead of checking account balances) and excess reserves (banks prefer to hold some idle balances rather than be fully loaned up).

Source: Board of Governors of the Federal Reserve System.

ine their effect on the money supply curve. The money supply curve M_sM_s pictured in Figure 14.5 reflects a policy that is invariant (i.e., unaffected by) the level of interest rates. That is, a change in interest rates is assumed to have no effect on the money supply.

In the discussion to follow, let us separate expansionary applications of these instruments from contractionary applications.

Expansionary applications.   A change in open-market operations, a change in reserve requirements, and a change in the discount rate can all have an effect on the money supply. The following applications of these monetary policy instruments will have an expansionary effect on the nation's money supply:

Expansionary actions	Effects of action
Fed purchase securities in the open market	Increases total reserves
Fed lowers the discount rate	Increases total reserves
Fed reduces the required reserve ratios	Increases the money multiplier

When the Fed purchases government securities in the open market, it increases the level of total reserves at depository institutions, which will cause the money supply curve depicted in Figure 14.5 to shift to the right. The new money supply would be equal to the money multiplier times the new higher level of total reserves.

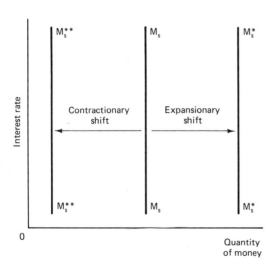

Figure 14.5 *Expansionary and contractionary shifts in the money supply.* Expansionary monetary policy actions (i.e., the Federal Reserve buys government bonds, lowers the discount rate, or decreases the required reserve ratio) will lead to increases in the money supply. This is illustrated graphically here by the outward shift in the money supply curve. Contractionary monetary policy actions (i.e., the Federal Reserve sells government bonds, raises the discount rate, or increases the required reserve ratio) will lead to decreases in the money supply. This will cause an inward shift in the money supply curve.

Lowering the discount rate will make it cheaper for depository institutions to borrow from the Fed and should thus increase the level of total reserves in the banking system. This, too, will cause the money supply to shift outward to the right. The new money supply would again be found by multiplying the existing money multiplier by the new level of total reserves.

Finally, a reduction of reserve requirements will mean that depository institutions have to hold a smaller fraction of their deposits in reserves. This will increase the money multiplier [see equation (14.1)]. This is also an expansionary application of monetary policy and would cause the money supply curve to shift from M_sM_s outward toward $M_s^*M_s^*$. The new money supply can be found by multiplying the existing level of total reserves times the new higher money multiplier.

Contractionary applications.   In contrast to the expansionary applications of the Fed's major monetary policy instruments, these same instruments can be used to contract the money supply. These contractionary applications include:

Contractionary action	Effects of action
Fed sells securities in open market	Reduces total reserves
Fed increases the discount rate	Reduces total reserves
Fed increases the required reserve ratios	Decreases the money multiplier

When the Fed sells securities in the open market to private investors, it reduces the total reserves in the banking system, which in turn leads to a *multiple* decrease in the money supply. Thus the money supply curve in Figure 14.5 will shift back to the left, from M_sM_s toward $M_s^{**}M_s^{**}$.

An increase in the discount rate by the Federal Reserve means that it is now more costly for banks to borrow reserves through the Fed's discount window. This also reduces total reserves and leads to a *multiple* decrease in the money supply.

Finally, an increase in the reserve requirement ratio reduces the money multiplier [see equation (14.1)], which means that existing total reserves will expand by a smaller multiple than before. If the Fed should increase its reserve requirements at a time when *all* depository institutions were fully loaned up (i.e., each had zero excess reserves), these institutions would either have to call in loans or decrease their investments to be in compliance.

Now that we have an understanding of the money supply and the factors that cause this curve to shift to the right or the left, let us look at the equilibrium in the money market by adding the demand for money curve and then see how the interest rates in this market affect national income and output.

MONEY-MARKET EQUILIBRIUM

Why do individuals prefer to hold part of their wealth in money rather than place all their wealth in income-earning assets? What happens to the interest rate if the demand for money increases or decreases? To answer these questions, we must understand the demand for money.

Demand for Money

Economists often identify three reasons why we hold money. The first represents our *transactions demand* for money. Households and businesses hold a certain amount of money because it is a widely accepted medium of exchange. Since their receipts of money income do not match the timing of their expenditures, households and businesses maintain some holdings of money to help finance these expenditures. The cost of not having transactions balances is the rate of interest households and businesses would have to pay when borrowing funds to finance these expenditures.

The second reason we hold money represents our *precautionary demand* for money. Some households and businesses may wish to hold money to meet unplanned expenditures when life's little surprises arise. This may be associated with an unexpected illness or unemployment.

The third and final reason that we hold money represents the *speculative demand* for money. Some households may wish to hold money when the prices of *other* assets are falling since the nominal value of money is *fixed*. One hundred dollars in cash will always be worth $100, but $100 invested in common stock could be worth less than that tomorrow. Thus in a recessionary economy when asset prices are falling, the speculative demand for money should increase.

Thus the demand for money reflects the "liquidity preferences" of households and businesses. The lower the rate of interest, the lower the opportunity costs of holding cash will be. Hence a larger quantity of money should be demanded. Panel a in Figure 14.6 illustrates this inverse relationship between the demand for money and the rate of interest. As the returns on assets in general and interest rates in particular fall, households and businesses will attempt to substitute cash for such financial assets as stocks and bonds.

The Keynesian notion that the demand for money is inversely related to interest rates and income is somewhat at odds with other theories of the demand for money. The Cambridge demand for money function—developed by classical economists at Cambridge, England—suggests that the demand for money is equal to some constant fraction of the nominal level of income. This is the simplest of all monetarist positions. Modern monetarists such as Milton Friedman argue that the demand for money is a function of alternative rates of return, nominal income, and the expected rate of inflation.

Determination of Interest Rates

Panel b in Figure 14.6 brings together the demand and supply curves for money. The intersection of the M_dM_d curve and the M_sM_s curve in panel b determines the equilibrium rate of interest. As we see here, this interest rate would be 10 percent.

EFFECTS OF MONETARY POLICY ON ECONOMY

We now know that the money supply affects the level of interest rates. A shift to the right of the money supply curve in panel b of Figure 14.6 would *lower* the interest rate below 10 percent, while a shift to the left would raise the market interest rate. You will recall from our discussions in Chapter 13 that the rate of interest has an effect on the level of planned investment and hence the equilibrium level of national income. An increase in interest rates would lower planned investment, while a lower interest rate would increase planned investment. For example, we would expect that

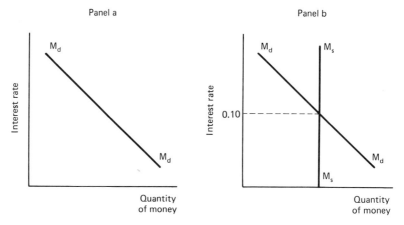

Figure 14.6 *Adding the demand for money.* Before we can determine the market rate of interest in the economy, we must know the demand for money. Panel a indicates that the demand for money function is downward sloping. That is, the higher (lower) the rate of interest, the lower (higher) the quantity of money demanded. This interest rate reflects the opportunity cost of holding money rather than an income-earning asset. The higher the expected income forgone by holding money, the lower the quantity of money demanded will be. Panel b shows that the market rate of interest is determined by the intersection of the money demand and supply curves. Thus an increase in the money supply will in the short run lower interest rates, while a reduction in the money supply will raise interest rates.

the demand for new machinery by farm business would be far greater if the prevailing market interest rate were 8 percent than if it were 16 percent.

Effects on Output Gaps

Let us suppose for the moment that the inflationary gap illustrated in panel a of Figure 14.7 exists in the economy.[9] Total planned expenditures are represented by $C_0 + I_0 + G_0$. Now let's assume that the Fed uses a contractionary application of monetary policy (i.e., sell securities, raise discount rate, and/or increase reserve requirements). This will shift the money supply curve inward to the left and cause interest rates to rise. As planned investment falls from I_0 to I_1, the aggregate demand curve will fall, hopefully to the

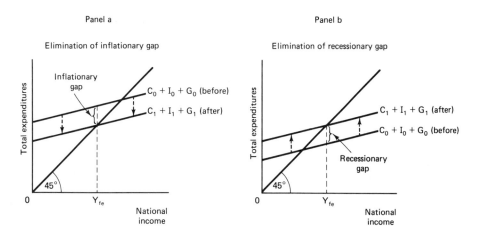

Figure 14.7   *Elimination of inflationary and recessionary gaps.* In Chapter 12 we said that the role of macroeconomic policy is to promote economic growth and stabilize prices. If an inflationary gap exists in the economy [i.e., aggregate demand exceeds aggregate supply at full-employment income (Y_{fe})], contractionary monetary policy which leads to higher interest rates and hence lower investment expenditures will lower aggregate demand and eliminate the inflationary gap. This case is illustrated in panel a. If the economy is suffering from a recessionary gap (i.e., aggregate demand is less than aggregate supply at full employment), expansionary monetary policy which leads to lower interest rates and hence higher investment expenditures will increase aggregate demand and eliminate the recessionary gap. This case is illustrated in panel b.

[9] The same assumptions as those underlying Figure 13.7 are employed in the discussion of Figure 14.7.

point where the aggregate demand curve intersects the aggregate supply curve at full employment (Y_{fe}). At this level of gross national product, the economy's resources will be fully employed (i.e., the inflationary gap will have been fully eliminated). If the economy had instead been experiencing a recessionary gap such as the one illustrated in panel b of Figure 14.7, the Fed could have followed expansionary policies. These policies would increase reserves, shift the money supply curve outward to the right, and increase planned investment. The objective would be to shift the aggregate demand curve upward to the point where it intersects the aggregate supply curve at Y_{fe}.[10]

Transmission of Policy

Figure 14.8 summarizes the mechanism through which changes in monetary policy are transmitted through to the nation's income and product. The change in policy first shows up in the money market, where it affects interest rates. This, in turn, affects the equilibrium in the product market through investment and through the income multiplier discussed in Chapter 13, the equilibrium level of national income. To the extent that the demand for money is affected by this level of income, we must account for the *simultaneous interaction* between the money and product markets when determining the general equilibrium level of income and interest rates.

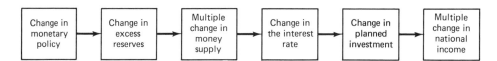

Figure 14.8 *Effects of a change in monetary policy on GNP.* This figure illustrates the chain of events that takes place when a change in monetary policy is made. A change in monetary policy will directly affect the reserves depository institutions like banks are required to hold. This, in turn, will affect the banks' excess reserves and therefore their ability to make new loans, which ultimately affects the size of the money supply. An increase (decrease) in the money supply will put downward (upward) pressure on interest rates. A decline (rise) in interest rates will encourage (discourage) further investment expenditures by businesses in the economy. Finally, we know from Figure 13.7 that an increase (decrease) in total expenditures will increase (decrease) national income.

---

[10] A comparison of Figures 13.7 and 14.7 shows that expansionary monetary policy has the same general effect on recessionary gaps as expansionary fiscal policies. Similarly, contractionary monetary policies have the same general effect on inflationary gaps as contractionary fiscal policies.

Potential Problems in Policy Implementation

Four problems encountered when using monetary policy to eliminate such gaps are (1) knowing the value of money multiplier, (2) knowing the exact size of the inflationary or recessionary GNP gap, (3) knowing whether fiscal policy will also be used to eliminate such gaps, and (4) knowing how long it will take for these policies to be fully reflected in the product markets. For example, if it takes more than one year before a contractionary monetary policy is fully reflected in the economy, conditions might have changed by then for other reasons. Thus a policy designed to move the economy to full employment can actually be inflationary if, for other reasons, aggregate demand had shifted upward before then.

SUMMARY

The purpose of this chapter was to acquaint you with the functions of money in a monetary economy, the role of our central bank (the Federal Reserve System) in regulating the supply of money to achieve specific national economic objectives, how interest rates are influenced by expansionary versus contractionary monetary policies, and the effect of interest rates on national income. The major points made in this chapter can be summarized as follows:

1. Money serves as (1) a medium of exchange, (2) a unit of accounting, and (3) a store of value. These functions help us define money. Money has value because it is widely acceptable in exchange for goods and services and because its nominal value is fixed.

2. The *Federal Reserve System* is comprised of the Board of Governors, the 12 district Federal Reserve Banks, and it member banks. An omnibus banking act in 1980 gave the Fed regulatory powers over the reserves held by all depository insititutions in this country, including savings and loan associations and credit unions.

3. The Fed performs the following functions: (1) it regulates the supply of money to the private sector, (2) it holds the reserves required of depository institutions, (3) it provides a system of check collection and clearing, (4) it supplies fiduciary currency (Federal Reserve notes) to the economy, (5) it acts as the banker and fiscal agent for the Treasury, and (6) it supervises the operations of its member banks.

4. Money is created by the banking system through the *multiple expansion of deposits.* The full effects of an increase in reserves is found by multiplying these new reserves by the *money multiplier,* which is equal to the reciprocal of the reserve requirement ratio. The Fed can therefore influence the money supply by changing the *reserve requirement*

ratios for deposits. It can also use the *discount rate* as well as its open market transactions for government securities to influence the level of reserves and hence the money supply.

5. A decrease in the discount rate, a lowering of reserve requirements, or the purchase of government securities by the Fed all represent a expansionary monetary policy in that they will expand the money supply. Conversely, an increase in the discount rate, a raising of reserve requirements, or the sale of government securities by the Fed all represent a contractionary monetary policy.

6. Monetary policy affects aggregate demand in the economy and hence eliminates inflationary or recessionary gaps in the economy through the rate of interest. The higher the rate of interest, the lower aggregate demand will be, and vice versa. The effectiveness of monetary policy will be reduced by the presence of currency drains and bank holdings of excess reserves.

DEFINITION OF TERMS

Store of value: value of holding money as an asset.

Unit of accounting: money provides a basis with which the relative value of goods and services can be assessed and with which the profitability and financial position of businesses can be assessed.

Medium of exchange: money allows businesses and individuals to specialize in their endeavors and to purchase the goods and services they need with money they receive for their efforts.

Near monies: assets that are almost money or can be converted to money quickly with little or no loss in value.

Fiduciary monetary system: value of currency issued by government based on the public's faith that currency can be exchanged for goods and services.

Federal Open Market Committee: consists of members of the Board of Governors of the Federal Reserve System plus selected district Federal Reserve Board presidents who meet periodically to assess the appropriate action the Fed should take (buy or sell) in the open or private secondary bond market for government securities.

Reserve requirements: fraction of its deposits that banks and other depository institutions must hold in reserve (i.e., held on deposit at its district Federal Reserve Bank or in vault cash).

Discount rate: rate the Federal Reserve charges when it lends to member commercial banks (all national banks plus those state banks that choose to be members of Federal Reserve System).

Open market operations: buying or selling of government securities in the Federal Reserve's portfolio on the open market to achieve specific policy objectives.

State bank: bank that is chartered by a state government.

National bank: bank that is chartered by the federal government.

Legal reserves: deposits at district Federal Reserve banks plus vault cash.

Required reserves: minimum amount of deposits that banks and other depository institutions must hold in reserve (*see* reserve requirements).

Excess reserves: difference between legal reserves and required reserves.

Federal funds market: an interbank market in which banks borrow the excess reserves of other banks to meet their own reserve requirements.

Money multiplier: the reciprocal of the fractional required reserve ratio if there are no currency drains and no excess reserves.

Currency drain: currency (paper bills and coins) held by the public, whether it is in their wallets or stored in a nonbank location (e.g., hidden in a mattress).

Transaction demand for money: demand to hold money to pay for expected expenditures.

Speculative demand for money: demand to hold money as an asset in expectation that other asset prices will fall.

Precautionary demand for money: demand to hold money to pay for unexpected expenditures that may arise.

REFERENCES

BOARD OF GOVERNORS OF THE FEDERAL RESERVE SYSTEM, *Federal Reserve Bulletin,* Washington, D.C., various issues.

BOARD OF GOVERNORS OF THE FEDERAL RESERVE SYSTEM, *The Federal Reserve System: Purposes and Functions,* 6th ed. Washington, D.C.: 1974.

FRANCIS, DARRYL R., "Impact of Monetary Actions on Farm Income and Finance," *American Journal of Agricultural Economics,* December 1974, pp. 1047–1055.

LINS, DAVID A., "Monetary Policies of the Federal Reserve System and Their Impact on the Farm Sector," *Agricultural Finance Review,* November 1979, pp. 61–71.

ADDITIONAL READING

AUERNHEIMER, L., and R. B. EKELUND, JR., *The Essentials of Money and Banking.* New York: John Wiley & Sons, Inc., 1982.

DERNBURG, THOMAS F., and DUNCAN N. MCDOUGALL, *Macroeconomics,* 6th ed. New York: McGraw-Hill Book Company, 1980.

PENSON, JOHN B., JR., and DAVID A. LINS, *Agricultural Finance: An Introduction to Micro and Macro Concepts.* Englewood Cliffs, N.J.: Prentice-Hall, Inc., 1980.

QUESTIONS

1. What are the functions performed by money, and what is its backing?
2. Which Federal Reserve district are you located in? What role do the district Federal Reserve banks play in our banking system?
3. If the legal reserves held by depository institutions is $200 billion and required reserves are $150 billion, what is the level of excess reserves in the economy? Can excess reserves ever be negative? Why?
4. If the fractional reserve requirement ratio is equal to 0.20 percent and total reserves in the economy are $250 billion, what is the value of the money supply? How would your answer be affected by currency drains or banks' desire to hold excess reserves?
5. How do expansionary and contractionary monetary policy actions affect the rate of interest in the short run? Why is the money supply curve highly inelastic?
6. Discuss the process by which a change in monetary policy affects national income and output.
7. How can monetary policy be used to eliminate inflationary gaps in the economy? Recessionary gaps? What happens in both cases if monetary policymakers overreact? How is agriculture affected by these actions?
8. Why might it be appropriate to term the money multiplier given by equation (14.1) as the "maximum deposit expansion multiplier"?

ADVANCED TOPICS

A topic that normally comes up when discussing the effects of using monetary policy to eliminate inflationary and recessionary GNP gaps in the economy is the trade-off between the rate of unemployment and the rate of inflation. Some 20 years ago, the British economist A. W. Phillips observed an inverse relationship between the unemployment rate and the rate of inflation. This relationship has come to be known as the *Phillips curve.*

Let us examine the hypothetical Phillips curve illustrated in Figure 14.9. This figure shows that a 7 percent inflation rate is associated with a 5 percent unemployment rate. Thus if we wish to lower the rate of inflation to 5 percent, we as a society must be willing to live with an unemployment rate

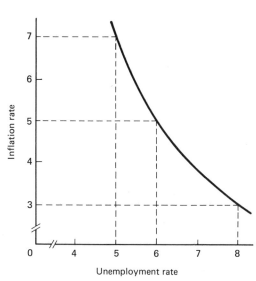

Figure 14.9 *The Phillips curve.* The relationship between the unemployment rate and the rate of inflation was originally observed by the British economist A. W. Phillips. He noted that efforts to combat inflation will lead to higher unemployment. That is, there is a trade-off between unemployment and inflation. While there was a relative stable Phillips curve in the U.S. economy during much of the fifties and sixties, the relationship implied by this curve has changed sharply since then. Factors causing this curve to change include changes in the composition of the labor force, an increase in the labor force participation rate, and increass in unemployment compensation.

of 6 percent. This curve suggests that we cannot have a decrease (increase) in the unemployment rate without an increase (decrease) in the inflation rate. Policymakers are thus faced with the prospect of determining what constitutes an "acceptable" rate of unemployment and rate of inflation rate.

The Phillips curve can shift to the right over time as specific factors in the economy change. For example, if unemployment compensation and welfare benefits increase, unemployed workers will take longer in searching for a new job at a given rate of inflation. An increase in the participation rate in the labor force, which requires the economy to absorb a greater percentage of the population, will also translate into a higher unemployment rate for a given rate of inflation. This will also cause the Phillips curve to shift to the right. Changes in the composition of the labor force (e.g., more unskilled teenagers) and an increase in the minimum wage rate will also shift this curve to the right, all other things constant.

Critics of the Phillips curve argue that this analysis ignores the public's expectations of future inflation rates, on which they base their decisions, since the actual inflation rate is used on the vertical axis in Figure 14.9. They argue that the only way that a permanent reduction in the unemployment rate can be "bought" by an increase in the inflation rate is if laborers consistently underestimate the actual rate of inflation.[11]

---

[11] For a further discussion of this point, see Alan S. Blinder, *Economic Policy and the Great Stagflation* (New York: Academic Press, Inc., 1979).

Others point to the empirical fact that while the data on inflation and unemployment during the sixties formed a reasonably smooth curve such as the one illustrated in Figure 14.9, this was hardly the case in the seventies. Whereas there appeared to be a substitution relationship between inflation and unemployment in the sixties, the economy registered increasing inflation *and* unemployment during the seventies (i.e., stagflation). Two factors thought to have caused this are: (1) the existence of cost-push inflation (higher oil prices), and (2) high wage settlements in labor contract negotiations. Both of these factors shift the curve to the right. In other words, movement along the curve captures only demand-pull inflation. These issues will be defined and discussed further in Chapter 15.

The LM Curve

The Advanced Topics section at the end of Chapter 13 referred to the *LM* curve found in the traditional static Keynesian model of an economy. Unlike the *IS* curve, which is directly affected by fiscal policy, the *LM* curve is directly affected by the monetary policy actions discussed earlier in this chapter.

Figure 14.6 illustrated the nature of the equilibrium in the nation's money market. While the money supply was set autonomously in this market, the demand for money was said to be negatively related to the rate of interest and positively related to the level of income. This suggests that the higher the rate of interest and lower the level of income, the lower the demand for money would be. The slope of this demand curve reflects the interest sensitivity of the demand for money, while the degree to which this demand curve shifts to the right (left) as income rises (falls) depends on the income sensitivity of the demand for money.

By varying the level of income (i.e., Y_1, Y_2, and Y_3) and observing the resulting interest rate (i.e., i_1, i_2, and i_3) in this market, we can obtain a series of equilibriums in the nation's money market.[12] Figure 14.10 illustrates this relationship. The higher the level of income, the higher the interest rate must be if the demand for money is to remain equal to the supply of money. A line passing through these points represents different equilibriums in the nation's money market associated with these levels of national income. This locus of points is referred to as the *LM curve*. At each point along this curve, liquidity preferences (i.e., the demand for money) in the economy will equal the money supply.

Expansionary monetary policy actions (i.e., lowering the reserve requirement ratio, lowering the discount rate, or buying more bonds by the

[12] For a more precise description of this procedure, see John B. Penson, Jr., and David A. Lins, *Agricultural Finance,* (Englewood Cliffs, N.J.: Prentice-Hall, Inc., 1980), pp. 402–404.

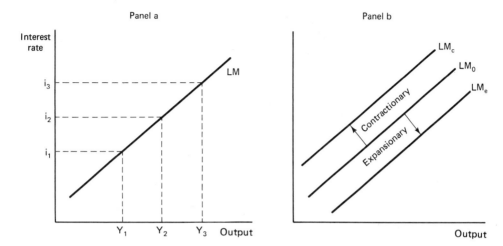

Figure 14.10   *The LM curve.* The *LM* curve illustrates a series of market equilibriums in the nation's money market associated with a particular interest rate and level of output. At each point on this curve, the demand for money equals the supply of money. Panel a shows that at a market interest rate of i_1, an output of Y_1 would be needed to ensure equilibrium in the money market. At a market interest rate equal to i_3, a greater amount of output (i.e., Y_3) would be needed to offset the negative effects of the higher interest rate on demand and leave the quantity demanded unchanged. Panel b illustrates that expansionary monetary policy actions will shift the *LM* curve to the right, while contractionary monetary policy actions will shift the *LM* curve inward to the left.

Fed) will shift the *LM* curve to the right. This implies that only a higher level of income would keep interest rates from falling. Conversely, contractionary monetary policy actions (i.e., raising reserve requirement ratios, raising the discount rate, or selling bonds by the Fed) will shift the *LM* curve to the left. This implies that only a lower level of national income would keep interest rates from rising.

15

MACROECONOMIC POLICY AND AGRICULTURE

The goals of macroeconomic policy are to promote employment, price stability, and economic growth. The general economy, as we all know, experiences rising unemployment, inflation, and economic stagnation from time to time. It is therefore the job of macroeconomic policymakers to use the monetary and fiscal policy tools available to them to cure these economic ills. The purpose of this chapter is to examine the nature of fluctuations in business activity, the potential macroeconomic policy responses to these fluctuations, the channels through which these policy actions affect agriculture, and the major macroeconomic problem confronting the farm business sector in the early eighties.

POLICY RESPONSE TO BUSINESS FLUCTUATIONS

The role of macroeconomic policy can be likened to being the host of a party; that is, policymakers should know when to remove the punch bowl before the party gets out of hand and know when to bring the punch bowl back before the party gets too dull. In economic jargon, policymakers attempt to promote the economic growth of the economy without stimulating inflation. If inflation begins to rise, policy actions can be taken to dampen aggregate demand for goods and services, which reduces inflationary pressures but slows economic growth if the economy is not at full employment. Conversely, if unemployment begins to rise, policy actions can be taken to stimulate aggregate demand. These actions will reduce unemployment but may be inflationary if the economy is approaching full employment. The purpose of this section is to discuss the nature of the actions that policy-makers can take to combat inflation and unemployment, how these policy actions are transmitted to the farm business sector, and how this sector is affected as these policies are put into place.

In discussing the expected effects of selected policy actions in the general economy, we shall describe those general policy actions that can (1) combat unemployment, (2) combat inflation, and (3) combat stag-flation.

Policies to Combat Unemployment

Monetary and fiscal policies of the federal government can be designed to reduce unemployment. Assuming that unemployment is the only problem, *expansionary monetary policies* leading to an increase in the money supply will make lower cost credit available to consumers and producers.[1] This will expand consumption and investment expenditures, which in turn will increase the need for more workers to help produce these additional goods and services. *Expansionary fiscal policies* that lead to greater government spending or lower taxes paid by consumers and producers will also stimulate aggregate demand in the economy and promote the employment of workers currently seeking jobs.

To illustrate, let's examine the aggregate demand and supply curves depicted in Figure 15.1. If expansionary monetary and fiscal policies shifted the aggregate demand curve from $D_1 D_1$ to $D_2 D_2$, output will increase from O_1 to O_2. Additional workers will be needed to produce this additional output. Note that because there was plenty of slack in the economy, these policies were not inflationary (i.e., prices remained at P_0).

Policies to Combat Inflation

Monetary and fiscal policies can also be designed to reduce inflation. Assuming that inflation is the only problem, *contractionary monetary policies* that lead to a decrease in the money supply will result in higher real interest rates, which will dampen consumer and producer expenditure plans. This reduction in demand will put a downward pressure on prices. *Contractionary fiscal policies* which reduce government spending and increase the tax bur-

---

[1] For those readers interested in a discussion of the specifics of implementing expansionary and contractionary monetary and fiscal policies, see Chapter 13 (fiscal policy) and Chapter 14 (monetary policy). In addition, the Advanced Topics section of this chapter discusses how expansionary monetary policy actions will lead to lower interest rates and a higher gross national product.

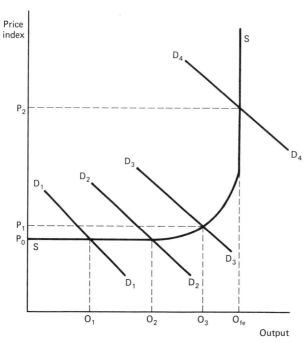

Figure 15.1 *Elimination of inflation and unemployment.* Monetary and fiscal policies have traditionally been used to expand or contract aggregate demand to promote economic growth and price stability. Some economists in recent years have proposed the use of policies that would expand supply to achieve greater economic growth and price stability. The aggregate demand and supply curves depicted above differ from those presented in Chapters 13 and 14. This is because price rather than total expenditures is plotted on the vertical axis in this figure.

den placed on consumers and producers will also dampen aggregate demand and put a downward pressure on prices.[2]

To illustrate, let's look again at Figure 15.1. Assume that aggregate demand in the economy is represented by the $D_4 D_4$ curve. If contractionary monetary and fiscal policies brought about a shift in this demand curve from $D_4 D_4$ to a demand curve that intersects the supply *(SS)* curve at an output of O_{fe}, prices would fall substantially without causing a reduction in output or less than full employment of the nation's labor and capital. If policymakers dampened demand to the point where the demand curve shifted back to $D_3 D_3$, prices would fall further, to P_1. But output would fall from O_{fe} to O_3, thereby reducing the employment of our nation's resources below full-employment levels.

Policies to Combat Stagflation

The monetary and fiscal policies to reduce either inflation or unemployment discussed above may have unacceptable results when the economy is exper-

[2] The policy of "jawboning" businesses and labor unions has been used in the past to combat cost-push inflation. Recent presidents, including Kennedy, Johnson, and Nixon, used jawboning to achieve certain aims. Perhaps the most memorable was the jawboning of U.S. Steel in 1962 by President Kennedy, which was successful in getting this major steel producer to cancel an announced price increase.

iencing inflation and unemployment at the same time. Contractionary macroeconomic policies designed to dampen aggregate demand in an effort to bring down inflation will further add to existing recessionary pressures (i.e., lead to higher unemployment of labor, lower utilization of existing plant capacity, and reduced plant expansion). Furthermore, expansionary policies designed to stimulate demand in an effort to reduce unemployment may further add to the inflationary pressures that currently exist in the economy.

One approach suggested to overcome the inability of these demand-oriented macroeconomic policies to deal with the problem of stagflation is *supply-side economics*. For example, increases in productivity (output per unit of input) brought about by laborers, savers, and investors reacting rationally to a reduction in marginal tax rates is thought to shift the aggregate supply *(SS)* curve in Figure 15.1 to the right. If this occurs, as argued by supply-side economists, employment will increase and inflationary pressures in the economy will decrease.[3]

TRANSMISSION OF POLICY ACTIONS TO AGRICULTURE

There are numerous channels through which changes in monetary and fiscal policies can be transmitted to the farm business sector. In the discussion to follow, we shall divide these channels into (1) direct effects, and (2) indirect effects.

Direct Effects on Agriculture

The initial effects of monetary and fiscal policies are felt by all consumers and producers, including farmers. Expansionary (contractionary) monetary policies, for example, will increase (decrease) the *money supply*. The presumably means that more (less) credit will be available to farmers. Expansionary (contractionary) fiscal policies will increase (decrease) *federal budget deficits* by cutting (raising) taxes and/or increasing (decreasing) government spending. Lower (higher) tax rates would appear to increase (decrease) the current after-tax net income available to farmers which they can either reinvest in their business or use to finance their consumption expenditures. These policies may also mean a decrease (increase) in the after-tax cost of capital over the life of the investment opportunities farmers are currently considering, thereby making these opportunities more (less) attractive. Finally, these policies may mean higher (lower) government payments to farmers, as described in Chapter 10. This, too, will have a direct effect on the decisions made in the farm business sector.

[3] The Advanced Topics section at the end of this chapter presents a discussion of the Laffer curve, which is at the heart of the supply-side prescriptions for the economy.

The terms "presumably," "would appear to," and "may" were used here when describing the direct effects these policies will have upon the farm business sector. Since these policies also have an effect on other sectors of the economy who deal in one way or another with the farm business sector, we must also account for the indirect effects they have upon the sector.

Indirect Effects on Agriculture

In addition to the effects described above, there are several ways in which monetary and fiscal policy actions can indirectly affect the farm business sector. To begin with, the *prices farmers receive for their products* are affected by the impacts that these macroeconomic policies have on the domestic and export demand for farm products. Expansionary (contractionary) monetary policies, for example, will increase (decrease) domestic demand by increasing (decreasing) consumer disposable income and lowering (raising) interest rates. These policies will also increase (decrease) export demand by lowering (raising) the strength of the dollar and thus, exchange rates.[4] While the net effects of these monetary policy actions on farm product prices are straightforward, Table 15.1 suggests that this is not the case for fiscal policy. As equation (10.1) suggests, the net effects of fiscal policy actions on the prices of exportable farm products will depend on what happens to the market shares associated with domestic and export demand and their respective own price elasticities of demand. For those products with a relatively high export market share, however, we can conclude that contractionary (expansionary) fiscal policy actions will probably raise (lower) farm product prices due to their effects on exchange rates.

Another indirect effect of these policy actions is on the *prices farmers pay for their inputs.* Expansionary (contractionary) monetary and fiscal policies will increase (decrease) the demand for inputs used by farm and non-farm businesses in the economy. In the short run, input manufacturers will increase (decrease) the quantity of these inputs supplied [i.e., capacity utilization rates will rise (fall)] as the prices for these inputs rise (fall). *Farmland*

---

[4] Why does the strength of the dollar affect exchange rates and export demand for farm products? To buy U.S. farm products, a foreign firm must pay for these products in U.S. dollars. This means that this firm, which we shall assume is located in France, must use its country's currency (francs) to buy U.S. dollars. If interest rates on U.S. government securities are relatively high (low), the demand for U.S. dollars in foreign currency markets will be relatively strong (weak). Thus it will take more (less) francs to buy one dollar than it would if the demand for U.S. dollars in foreign currency markets were weak (strong). The exchange rate in this case is simply the price of U.S. dollars divided by the price of the French franc. The higher (lower) the exchange rate, therefore, the more (less) francs this French firm will need to acquire the necessary number of dollars required to purchase the desired quantity of U.S. farm products.

	Expansionary monetary policy	Expansionary fiscal policy	Contractionary monetary policy	Contractionary fiscal policy
Macro impact of policy action	Increase money supply	Increase budget deficit	Decrease money supply	Decrease budget deficit
Policy effects on:				
Farm product prices				
Domestic demand	Raise	Raise	Lower	Lower
Export Demand	Raise	Lower	Lower	Raise
Net impact on price	Raise	Uncertain	Lower	Uncertain
Farm input prices	Raise	Raise	Lower	Lower
Real interest rate	Lower	Raise	Raise	Lower
Inflation	Raise	Raise	Lower	Lower

TABLE 15.1 SHORT-RUN EFFECTS OF POLICY ACTIONS ON KEY ECONOMIC VARIABLES. Expansionary and contractionary applications of monetary and fiscal policy affect the farm business sector indirectly through the prices farmers receive for their products and pay for their inputs as well as through the nominal interest rates (real rate of interest plus the rate of inflation) they are charged on new loans.

values will also rise (fall) as both returns and inflationary expectations are rising (falling).

Finally, the *interest rates that farmers are charged on loans* are also indirectly affected by the demand for capital by the Treasury to finance budget deficits, the demand for capital by nonfarm businesses and consumers, and the inflationary expectations of lenders. For example, expansionary (contractionary) monetary policies, by expanding (contracting) the supply of credit, will lower (raise) the real rate of interest on loans to all producers and consumers (including farmers and their families). As purchases of goods and services by producers and consumers increase (decrease) in response to the lower real interest rates, however, upward (downward) pressure will be placed on all prices. This rise in general price levels may increase (decrease) the future inflationary expectations of lenders, who must worry about what will happen to inflation over the life of the loan. When making fixed-rate loans, lenders must charge a nominal interest rate that reflects what they expect to happen to inflation over the life of the loan. In the case of variable-rate loans, however, any increases in nominal interest rates will automatically be passed along to the farmer in the form of higher interest payments. Expansionary (contractionary) fiscal policies will probably require the Treasury to increase (decrease) their borrowing from the private sector to finance budget deficits. As a result, real interest rates (i.e., the nominal interest rate minus the rate of inflation) will rise (fall) even further and private invest-ment (including that by farmers) will decline (rise).[5]

Fluctuations, Policy and Agriculture

The farm business sector experiences many of the same fluctuations as those registered by the *domestic* economy. Let us examine *one possible scenario* or series of events. As the economy enters an expansionary period, the domestic demand for farm products is expanding somewhat (remember that the in-come elasticity of demand for farm products however is quite small in the United States) and net farm income is increasing somewhat. Inflation pressures have just begun to build, so that farmland values are not becoming increas-ingly burdensome to those farmers who must pay the going price for land when expanding the size of their operations. At the point where stagflation in the domestic economy sets in, however, the farm business sector becomes caught in a cost–price squeeze which sees farm expenses rising faster than farm revenue, thereby causing net farm income to decline.[6] Farmers are still continuing to receive returns in the form of unrealized capital gains on assets such as farmland, since inflation, which is rising, is now built into everyone's expectations. Unfortunately, these increases in net worth are not available to help finance current farm expenses unless farmers are willing to pay the going rate of interest to borrow against them.

As inflationary pressures mount, policymakers begin to feel pressure to implement anti-inflationary policies. The enactment of contractionary macroeconomic policies will eventually restrain aggregate demand in the domestic economy, and it enters a recession. Unemployment rises as firms, facing lower demands for their products, cut back their production and lay off workers. Firms also begin to sell off their inventories, accepting lower prices to move their products, and inflation begins to decline.

Farmers suffer economically during this period. The extent of this suffering will depend in part on how long stagflation has existed and on what combination of macroeconomic policies are implemented. Long peri-ods of stagflation, for example, may have enticed some farmers to borrow against unrealized capital gains on farmland to the point where even cautious farmers increase their borrowing.[7] If contractionary monetary policy is

[5] Note that a contractionary monetary policy and an expansionary fiscal policy both lead to an increase in real interest rates. This phenomenon, which is discussed in depth in the Advanced Topics section at the end of this chapter, helps explain the histor-ically high real interest rates observed during the early eighties.

[6] This stagflation may have been brought about by workers realizing the effects that inflation is having on the purchasing power of their wages and thus demanding higher wages. Output will decline during this period while inflation continues to grow.

[7] Some farmers, confronted with declining farm prices, may seek in the longer run to increase the size of their operations in an effort to lower their unit costs of production and thereby offset the effects of lower product prices on their profit margins.

used to fight inflation at the same time that expansionary fiscal policies are being followed, the impact of slowing inflation is large on those farmers with substantial debt. Nominal interest rates remain high (real interest rates are forced high by these macroeconomic policies, while inflationary pressures continue to exist due to expansionary government spending and the uncertainty associated with the eventual financing of the budget deficits). In addition, the farm income needed to make loan payments is also declining because the high real interest rates contribute to a strong dollar in foreign currency markets, thereby keeping exchange rates high and reducing export demand for farm products. Higher interest payments are also driving up production expenses, which further reduces net farm income. Farmland values are probably also declining under these circumstances.

Finally, as the trough of the cycle is reached in this scenario and the economy enters the expansionary phase of a new business cycle, relief in the form of increased demand is provided to nonfarm businesses and—to some extent—to farm businesses as well. The extent of the relief experienced by farmers will depend on the nature of the monetary and fiscal policies employed at this time and how they affect (1) the interest payments made by farmers, (2) the cost of manufactured inputs, and (3) the export demand for farm products.

This scenario represents a series of events that *could* take place in the domestic and world economies and their potential effects on agriculture. We should not be surprised to observe some departures from the nature and timing of the events decribed above. For example, the statement was made earlier that net farm income is probably increasing in the early stages of an expansionary period. This need not be the case if the economies of other countries are in a relatively weakened condition, whereby a relatively strong U.S. dollar further weakens the buying power of importing nations. This would cause exports of U.S. farm exports to drop, U.S. farm product prices to decline, and both to total farm revenue at net farm income to fall. This did not occur until later in the initial scenario described above when contractionary measures were taken to work domestic inflation.

MACROECONOMIC POLICY: A FARM PROBLEM?

The definition of what constitutes the "farm problem" has changed over time. For much of the century, many economists concluded that the major problem confronting the farm business sector was excess resources committed to the production of farm output and the lack of mobility of these resources out of the sector. Simply put, the excess supply of farm products was caused by the demand for these farm products growing more slowly than their supply. The production controls approach to farm policy discussed in Chapter 10 was designed specifically to attack this problem.

The decade of the seventies, however, saw a sharply higher export demand for farm products on top of a domestic demand for food and fiber that was growing at an annual rate of about 2 percent. The rest of the world also increasingly looked to the U.S. farm business sector for a larger and larger share of its food supplies during this decade. By the late seventies, excess capacity in the U.S. farm business sector had declined to the point where meeting domestic and foreign demand depended on further productivity gains, additional land being brought into production, and favorable weather.[8] In 1980, for example, the output form more than 2 of every 5 acres planted in this country was exported. As a result of this strong export demand, the level of farm revenue received by most farmers was high enough to more than cover the scheduled loan payments on the debts they incurred when expanding the capacity of their operations during the seventies.

Unfortunately, foreign demand for U.S. farm products, which was largely responsible for the elimination of excess capacity and improved farm incomes in the seventies, has proven to be both volatile and uncertain. U.S. exports of farm products declined from $44 billion in the 1980-1981 marketing year to less than $35 billion in 1982-1983, a decline of about 20 percent in current and 33 percent in constant dollars. The economic havoc caused by this decline was great enough to place many farmers under severe financial stress and give rise to the PIK program, described in Chapter 10 as the most costly farm program in the history of this country.

Some economists have thus concluded that the major problem confronting the sector during the eighties is likely to be one of *instability of returns* and the effects that this has on farmers who have borrowed large amounts of capital to acquire, expand or modernize their business. The purpose of this section is to discuss the nature of this problem and its causes.

Nature of Problem

Farming is a capital-intensive economic activity. To attract and maintain an economically-feasible farming operation using today's technology, farmers usually must borrow large sums of money. Because of the long-term nature of these debt commitments and the relative immobility of assets out of this sector as returns decline, farmers have a difficult time adjusting to rapidly changing demand conditions.

Many farmers did accumulate sizable amounts of debt during the relatively prosperous decade of the seventies. Table 15.2 shows that total farm business debt in this country rose from $50.5 billion at the beginning of the seventies to $201.0 billion by the beginning of 1984. This represents a 237

---

[8] One segment of the farm business sector continues to suffer from overcapacity is milk production. Approximately 10 percent of annual milk production has had to be removed from the market in the early eighties to support the income of dairy farmers.

Year	(1) Total farm debt Dec. 31 (billions of dollars)	(2) Net farm income (billions of dollars)	(3) Years required to repay debt (years)
1970	50.5	14.4	3.5
1971	55.3	13.6	4.1
1972	60.2	18.6	3.2
1973	68.1	31.0	2.2
1974	75.8	28.9	2.6
1975	85.1	25.6	3.3
1976	96.8	20.1	4.8
1977	114.7	19.8	5.8
1978	131.7	27.7	4.8
1979	154.9	32.3	4.8
1980	170.0	21.2	8.0
1981	188.5	31.0	6.1
1982	202.8	22.3	9.1
1983	201.0	16.1	12.5

Source: U.S. Department of Agriculture, *Economic Indicators of the Farm Sector* (Washington, D.C.: U.S. Government Printing Office, various issues).

TABLE 15.2   YEARS REQUIRED TO REPAY DEBT. The information presented in this table provides further insight to the problem facing many farmers in the eighties. If we divide total farm debt outstanding at the first of the year by net farm income received during the year, we can approximate the number of years it would take to repay this debt if net farm income remained constant and was used only for this purpose. In the favorable net farm income years during much of the seventies, it would have taken two to four years to retire total farm debt. By 1983, however, it would have taken roughly 13 years to repay total farm debt outstanding. Thus there is increased pressure on farm sources of income to service farmers' growing indebtedness.

percent increase in farm debt during the seventies and a 300 percent increase during the entire 1970-1983 period.

A large share of these loans were made with variable rather than the fixed interest rates called for in the loan agreement. This means that the interest portion of their loan payments will go up (down) as nominal interest rates in financial markets rise (fall). Thus as net farm income declined in the early eighties when product prices fell, prices paid for inputs rose, and nominal interest rates remained high, those farmers with substantial debts found themselves under severe cash flow stress.[9] In other words, their loan pay-

[9] Total interest payments on farm debt in 1983 amounted to $21 billion compared to only $19 billion in 1983. Expressed as a percentage of total cash operating expenses, interest payments accounted for 5 percent of total farm expenses in 1973 compared to only 8 percent in 1973.

Des Moines
Sunday Register

$1.00 single copy from dealer or vendor
■ Des Moines, Iowa ■ March 25, 1984   ■ 85¢ by motor route; 50¢ by carrier

SECTION A

THE WEATHER — Increasing cloudiness. Highs 48 to 54s; lows in 28s to 40s. Sunrise 6:30 a.m.; sunset 6:33 p.m. Details 2B.

Economic squeeze may force thousands of farmers off land

Big debts, high interest, falling prices create chaos

The headline in the newspaper clipping helps underscore the problem confronting many farmers across the country in the early and mid-eighties. Those farmers who accumulated substantial amounts of debt during the decade of the seventies have encountered substantial difficulties in making their loan payments in the eighties. As farm exports declined, commodity surpluses grew, and net farm incomes measured in constant dollars of purchasing power fell to levels not experienced since the thirties, these farmers were placed under severe cash flow stress. Declining farm land values added to the problems many farmers have had in obtaining further extensions on their overdue loan balances.

ments remained high at a time when their ability to make these loan payments (justified on earlier cash flow expectations) was declining. The declining levels of net farm income in the early eighties, coupled with declining farmland prices, seriously affected the strength of many farmers' net worth position.[10]

One way to assess the increasing burden of these farm debt levels on farmers is to relate the size of the debt to the level of net farm income. This ratio provides a crude approximation of the number of years it would take to repay these debts if all net farm income were used for this purpose, all other things constant. Column (3) of Table 15.2 shows that it would have

[10] You will recall that in Chapter 2 we made the observation that forms in the "$40,000–$99,999" category and the "$100,000 and over" category recorded the largest gain in total farm assets in the seventies. They also account for over 70 percent of the sector's total farm debt outstanding.

taken between 2 and 5 years during the decade of the seventies to retire total farm debt if income had remained constant. This is in sharp contrast to the experience in the early eighties, during which time we saw continued increases in farm debt even though net farm income was falling. Table 15.2 shows that it would have taken roughly nine years to retire total farm debt in 1982 and almost 13 years in 1983 if net income remained constant and was used entirely for this purpose.[11]

Surveys showed that two to three times the normal proportion of farmers are leaving the sector, either voluntarily or through forced sales in the mid-eighties. Farm loan losses at banks and the Farm Credit System also grew dramatically. Delinquencies at the Farmers Home Administration exceeded 30 percent. Approximately 6 percent of all farms in this country were technically insolvent at that time. Another 7 percent were moving rapidly toward insolvency. And an additional 20 percent were in serious fianancial condition, but should be able to survive a few more unfavorable years. These three groups of farmers represent one-third of all farms, but owe over two-thirds of all farm debt outstanding.

The deterioration of farm financial conditions in this country during the mid-eighties also had serious spin-off affects for agricultural lenders and rural communities. Commercial banks, which hold nearly 20 percent of all farm debt, experienced sharp increases in delinquencies and loan losses during this period. Twenty-three agricultural banks, for example, failed in 1984. An additional 8 agricultural banks failed in the first two months of 1985. Agriculture banks comprised 40 percent of the "problem" institutions monitored by the Federal Deposit Insurance Corporation during that period. The Farm Credit System, which holds over 30 percent of all farm debt, experienced significant net operating losses in the mid-eighties. Life insurance companies and the Farmers Home Administration were also experiencing special problems and difficulties. Finally, many rural communities which were closely tied to agriculture experienced economic problems as well. Mount Ayr, a town of 1,900 people in Iowa, lost three farm implement dealers, its major department store, one of its two banks and its grain elevator in 1984.

Underlying Causes

There are two major factors that have contributed to the instability of returns and resulting cash flow stress experienced particularly by farmers who accumulated sizable debt commitments during the seventies. One is the nature of the macroeconomic policies followed during the seventies and

---

[11] It is interesting to note that those farmers who did not substantially expand their indebtedness during the seventies were under less cash flow stress in the early eighties than were those farmers who did borrow extensively.

early eighties. The other is the trade policies practiced during this period. These factors are discussed in turn below.

Macroeconomic policies.   The supply of money in circulation in the private sectors of the economy has a positive influence on the rate of inflation and a negative influence on the real interest rates (i.e., nominal interest rates minus lower real interest rates.[12] This relationship was used to determine the "appropriate" level of the money supply in the economy until 1979. Up to that time, the Federal Reserve pursued those policy actions that would smooth out fluctuations in GNP. This meant that in the expansionary phase of a business cycle, the money supply was constrained to raise real interest rates, dampen planned investment expenditures, and slow inflation. Nominal interest rates eventually fell as inflationary pressures subsided. During the recessionary phase of a business cycle, the money supply was expanded to bring down real interest rates, encourage planned investment expenditures, and thus stimulate growth in GNP. Nominal interest rates eventually rose as inflationary pressures rose. Interest rates were therefore the target to be monitored when designing policies to achieve a steady growth in the economy.

It is a political fact of life that it is easier in the short run to expand the money supply and lower interest rates than it is to contract the money supply and raise interest rates. The result of the Federal Reserve's operating policies for managing the money supply during the seventies were low real interest rates, which encouraged a substantial growth in farm debt outstanding. The excessive growth in the use of credit by other producers and consumers as well in response to low (sometimes negative) real interest rates brought about an unsustainable expansion of aggregate demand and resulted in excess demand inflation such as that illustrated in Figure 15.1. These inflationary pressures in turn put an upward pressure on nominal interest rates, causing the Federal Reserve to expand the money supply further to keep interest rates as low as possible.

The Federal Reserve switched its operating procedures in 1979 to emphasize monitoring the growth of the money supply instead of monitoring interest-rate movements. Once real interest rates were allowed to seek their own level, they rose substantially, as illustrated in Table 15.3. By focusing on controlling the growth of the money supply, however, the Federal Reserve was successful in reducing inflation and nominal interest rates by 1983.

To the monetary policy actions practiced in the early eighties must be added the fiscal policies put into practice at that time. We have said that contractionary monetary policies in the early eighties resulted in higher real interest rates, which eventually helped lower inflation. The expansionary fiscal policies followed by Congress and the President during this period (tax cuts without offsetting cuts in government spending) placed further up-

---

[12] The manner in which this effect takes place was discussed in Chapter 14.

	(1) Real interest rates	(2) Inflation rate, %ΔCPI	(3) Nominal prime rate charged by banks, (1) + (2)	(4) Trade-weighted exchange rate
1973	1.83	6.2	8.03	98.8
1974	–0.19	11.0	10.81	99.2
1975	–1.24	9.1	7.86	93.9
1976	1.04	5.8	6.84	97.3
1977	0.33	6.5	6.83	93.1
1978	1.36	7.7	9.06	84.2
1979	1.37	11.3	12.67	83.2
1980	1.77	13.5	15.27	84.8
1981	8.47	10.4	18.87	100.8
1982	8.76	6.1	14.86	111.7
1983	7.59	3.2	10.79	117.3

Source: Economic Report of the President (Washington, D.C.: U.S. Government Printing Office, 1984).

TABLE 15.3 INTEREST-RATE AND EXCHANGE-RATE MOVEMENTS. The switch from expansionary monetary policy, where farmers accumulated sizable outstanding debt at cheap interest rates, to contractionary monetary policy, where farmers had to pay higher interest rates on variable rate loans, has caused severe cash flow problems for many farmers. The rise in real interest rates has also made the U.S. dollar attractive in foreign currency markets and driven up exchange rates for our trading partners. This has dampened export demand for U.S. farm products and further weakend net farm income.

ward pressure on real interest rates.[13] We know from our earlier discussion that higher real interest rates in turn place further upward pressure on the value of the U.S. dollar in foreign currency markets, thereby raising exchange rates and dampening export demand. As shown in Table 15.3, this occurred in the early eighties, where contractionary monetary policies coupled with expansionary fiscal policies led to historically high real interest rates and exchange rates.[14]

How do these events affect the farm business sector? One hears the following rules of thumb kicked around by policy analysts: (1) a 1 percent increase in nominal interest rates raises farm production expenses by $4 billion, and (2) a 1 percent increase in exchange rates due to a rise in the value of the dollar lowers the price of specific export crops by as much as $0.10 per

[13] Figure 15.2 suggested that both a contractionary monetary policy and an expansionary fiscal policy would put upward pressure on real interest rates. This helps explain the high real interest rates observed during the early eighties in Table 15.2.

[14] The growing budget deficits that exist during this scenario also contribute to higher long-term interest rates if financial markets expect the Federal Reserve to "accommodate" or monetize those deficits by expanding the money supply (see Chapter 14).

bushel on world markets. Whether these rules of thumb are completely accurate or not, they do indicate the magnitude that monetary and fiscal policies (which we said directly affect interest rates and exchange rates) can have on farmers.

The monetary policies followed during the seventies, which led to high annual rates of inflation, contributed to sharp increases in farm production expenses. This placed many farmers in a cost-price squeeze that only a strong export demand in selected years could offset. Farmland values were still rising prior to 1979, however, and many farmers used these unrealized capital gains as collateral when borrowing the additional funds which they needed to finance their farming operations. The change in Federal Reserve operating procedures in 1979 and high nominal interest rates that ensued in subsequent years led to sharply higher interest payments required of farmers, thereby driving farm production expenses to historically high levels. The efforts by the Federal Reserve to combat inflation, coupled with the expansionary fiscal policies of Congress and the President, placed upward pressure on real interest rates in the early eighties and dampened export demand (exchange rates rose in response to higher interest rates). The decrease in export demand for farm products, combined with continued high farm production expenses, contributed to the sharply lower net farm incomes (see Table 15.2) and lower farm asset values observed in the early eighties.

In conclusion, macroeconomic policies that lead to high interest rates and a strong dollar overseas hurt U.S. farmers, particularly those who owe a substantial amounts of debt on variable interest rate loans. The combination of "big debts, high interest rates, and falling prices" referred to earlier in the newspaper clipping have resulted in a financial stress being placed on many farmers from which some may not survive. Farmers are probably beginning to realize that they have a large stake in the macroeconomic policies adopted in Washington in addition to their traditional interest in farm program policy.

Agricultural trade policies.   Another factor adding to the variability of returns in the farm business sector is the nation's foreign trade policy. Past presidents have had to make tough foreign trade policy decisions, such as vetoing legislation calling for meat import quotas. Perhaps no action created more controversy, however, than the suspension of U.S. farm product sales to the Soviet Union in January 1980 in response to their invasion of Afganistan. Many farm groups at the time called for the resignation of the Secretary of Agriculture. The USDA responded by buying additional grain from farmers that had been earmarked for shipment to the Soviet Union. However, this embargo and other attempts to embargo nonfarm product sales to the Soviet Union undermined the confidence that our trading partners had in our desire to honor trade agreements.

A related issue is the growth in farm exports during the seventies financed by credit extended by the federal government and commercial banks. The worldwide recession encountered in the early eighties along with high U.S. interest rates have made it difficult for many of these countries to service their debts. This source of export stimulant therefore will probably be used with far more moderation during the remainder of the eighties. The topic of agricultural trade policies is addressed in considerable more depth in Part IV.

SUMMARY

The purpose of this chapter was to examine the nature of fluctuations in business activity, the potential macroeconomic policy responses to these fluctuations, the channels through which these policy actions affect the farm business sector, and the major problem confronting many farmers in the early eighties. The major points made in this chapter can be summarized as follows:

1. Expansionary monetary and fiscal policies can be employed to combat unemployment, while contractionary monetary and fiscal policies can be used to combat inflation.
2. Supply-side economists have proposed in recent years that these "demand management" policies cannot attack the problems of stagflation. These economists have proposed tax cuts to shift the supply curve to the right to lower both unemployment *and* inflation.
3. The direct effects of macroeconomic policy on the farm business sector are transmitted by the availability of credit, the marginal tax rates on taxable income, and government payments.
4. The sector is indirectly affected by these policies as they affect the prices farmers receive for their products, the prices they pay for their inputs, and the interest rates they are charged on loans.
5. The major problem likely to be confronting farmers in the eighties is the *instability of returns.* The "roots" of the instability of returns observed in the late seventies and early eighties were the nature and variability of macroeconomic policy (which orignially allowed inflation to get out of hand and then applied contractionary policies which raised interest rates and exchange rates) and agricultural trade policies (originally to extend credits and later to institute trade embargoes).

DEFINITION OF TERMS

Expansionary policies: monetary and fiscal policies that lead to greater economic growth of the economy.

Contractionary policies: monetary and fiscal policies that lead to reduced economic growth of the economy.

Economic growth: increase in the economy's real level of output (real gross national product).

Price stability: minor increases in the general price level as aggregate demand increases (i.e., low or zero rate of inflation).

Supply-side economics: promotion of macroeconomic policies that increase productivity and thereby shift the current aggregate supply curve to the right. This is thought to promote higher output at lower price levels.

Federal budget deficit: amount by which government spending during a period exceeds govenment revenues.

Plant capacity: maximum outuut technically possible by a frim given its existing plant size (e.g., number of acres) and technology.

Trade-weighted exchange rate: price of foreign currencies in terms of the U.S. dollar weighted by the relative importance of trade flows with our leading trading partners.

Cash flow stress: combination of economic factors that hamper farmers' ability to cover their cash uses of funds (including interest payments) with their cash sources of funds.

Nominal interest rate: market rate of interest unadjusted for the current rate of inflation.

Real interest rate: nominal interest rate minus the rate of inflation.

REFERENCES

Economic Report of the President. Washington, D.C.: U.S. Government Printing Office, various issues.

U.S. DEPARTMENT OF AGRICULTURE, *Agricultural Statistics.* Washington, D.C.: U.S. Government Printing Office, 1982.

U.S. DEPARTMENT OF COMMERCE, *Business Conditions Digest.* Washington, D.C.: U.S. Government Printing Office, various issues.

ADDITIONAL READINGS

DERNBURG, THOMAS F., and DUNCAN N. MCDOUGALL, *Macroeconomics,* 6th ed. New York: McGraw-Hill Book Company, 1980.

LINDAUER, JOHN, *Macroeconomics: A Modern View.* New York: Holt, Rinehart and Winston, 1979.

PENSON, JOHN B. JR., "Capturing the Linkages between Agriculture and the Domestic Economy," *Modeling Agriculture for Policy Analysis in the 1980s,* Kansas City: Federal Reserve Bank of Kansas City, pp. 47–64, 1981.

PENSON, JOHN B., JR., and DEAN W. HUGHES, "Endogenizing Linkages between Agriculture and the General Economy," *American Journal of Agricultural Economics,* December 1980.

PRENTICE, PAUL T., and LYLE P. SCHERTZ, *Inflation: A Food and Agricultural Perspective,* AER-463, USDA, ERS, February 1981.

QUESTIONS

1. What policies can the federal government adopt to combat:
   (a) Unemployment? (b) Inflation? (c) Stagflation?
2. Describe in general terms how macroeconomic policy is transmitted to agriculture.
3. Outline what is happening to agriculture as macroeconomic policies are implemented to achieve a steady rate of growth in the economy (i.e., control nature of business fluctuations).
4. What has been the major farm problem confronting agriculture in the early eighties? What were the underlying causes of this problem?

ADVANCED TOPICS

Two additional topics are covered in this section. The first topic discussed pertains to the Laffer curve and its relationship to supply-side economics. The second topic has to do with the effectiveness of wage and price controls as a means of controlling inflation.

The Laffer Curve

Supply-side economics stresses that "aggregate demand management" macroeconomic policies have neglected the possible effects of these policies on aggregate supply. These economists argue that workers, savers, and investors react rationally to marginal tax rates. That is, lower marginal tax rates will encourage workers to work more, savers to save more, and investors to invest more—all of which will lead to shifts in the aggregate supply curve to the right. An important component of supply-side economics is the Laffer curve, named after its founder, Arthur Laffer.

As illustrated in Figure 15.2, the Laffer curve rests on the notion that tax revenues are determined by multiplying the tax rate by the tax base. This suggests that a given level of tax revenue can be raised by (1) a relatively high tax rate and low tax base, or (2) a relatively low tax rate and high tax base. Looking at Figure 15.2, we see that there is a *maximum collectible tax revenue* equal to T_1. If the government insists on a tax rate of say t_2 instead

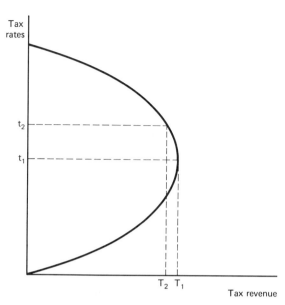

Figure 15.2 *The Laffer curve.* The relationship between tax rates and tax revenues collected by the Treasury is named after its creator, Arthur B. Laffer. This curve suggests the popular supply-side notion that a cut in tax rates from, say, t_2 to t_i will lead to an increase in tax revenues from T_2 to T_1. This reasoning led to the tax cuts called for in the 1981 Economic Recovery Tax Act and other legislative initiatives. Laffer's proposition is not without its critics, however, who point to the need to know exactly where the economy is on this curve when the tax cut is enacted.

of t_1, the tax revenue collected by the government would fall to T_2. This suggests, as supply-side economists have argued in recent years, that a reduction in tax rates will lead to an increase in tax revenues received by the government.

This curve is not without its critics, however, who point out the critical need to know where the economy is on the Laffer curve. For example, if the tax rate is currently equal to t_1 and the government institutes a tax cut, this curve suggests that tax revenues will fall (i.e., people will work less, investors will invest less, etc.)

Wage and Price Controls

One alternative to the use of contractionary macroeconomic policies to combat inflation is to institute *price and wage controls.* This proposition rests on the assumption that the actual rate of inflation is determined primarily by the levels of inflation that consumers and producers expect to occur and that what is needed is something to break these inflationary expectations. By breaking these expectations, it is thought that inflation can be slowed without increasing unemployment.

A fundamental problem with such controls is that they do not allow the economy to function and can lead to *black markets.* To illustrate, let's examine the market situation depicted in Figure 15.3. The market demand curve is represented by the *DD* curve and the market supply curve is represented by the *SS* curve. The market equilibrium price would be equal to P_e. Now let's suppose that the government imposes a maximum price of P_m in this market. At this lower price, the quantity demanded would be equal to

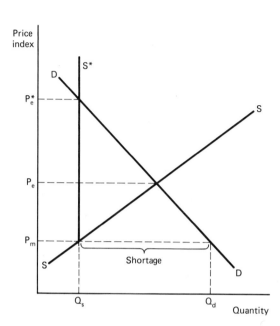

Figure 15.3 *Effects of price controls.* Do price and wage controls work in controlling inflation? History says no. Wage and price controls ignore the problems that led to rising prices to begin with. Furthermore, by placing a ceiling of P_m on prices in a particular market, a shortage equal to Q_d-Q_s will develop. They also can lead to black markets, where quantities of this good would sell at a price of P_e^* per unit. When these controls are eventually lifted, prices generally jump above what they were before the price controls were initiated. There are plenty of historical examples that can be cited to support this position. The price controls enacted by President Nixon on August 15, 1971, represent one of the latest examples of the failure of such a policy. Shortages occurred during the period and prices jumped sharply afterward.

Q_d while the quantity supplied would be Q_s. This means that a shortage equal to Q_d -Q_s would exist in this market. Furthermore, the price ceiling would cause a black market to develop.

The existence of this black market would mean that the supply curve takes on the characteristics of SS^* curve and that the equilibrium price would be P_e^*. These prices would include an under-the-counter payment to the seller equal to $P_e^* - P_m$. Thus there is no guarantee that such ceilings will work. In fact, they often result in higher actual prices rather than lower prices.

Another problem with price and wage controls is that they avoid tackling the underlying problems in the economy. Furthermore, they may permit policymakers ignoring these problems to implement expansionary macroeconomic policies to increase employment. As shortages of goods become more visible and policymakers decide to lift the price controls, a period of rapid inflation is likely to follow. For example, President Nixon instituted a 90-day freeze on wages, prices, and rents in August 1971. These controls were later extended and finally lifted in 1973. These controls seemed to work; the inflation rate actually dropped in 1971 and 1972. Expansionary macroeconomic policies were also adopted during this period to reduce the unemployment rate. When these controls were finally lifted in 1973, however, the annual inflation rates in this and subsequent years jumped well above the rate of inflation before these controls were imposed.

IS-LM Analysis

The Advanced Topics sections at the end of Chapters 13 and 14 introduced the existence of an *IS* curve representing market equilibriums in the product market and an *LM* curve representing market equilibriums in the money market. These two curves were illustrated in Figures 13.10 and 14.10, respectively. Specific statements were made in both instances about how each curve would shift if fiscal policy actions (the *IS* curve) or monetary policy actions (the *LM* curve) were taken. Nothing was concluded about what

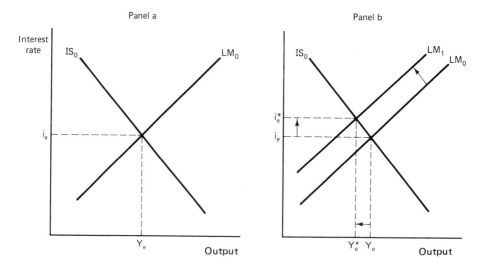

Figure 15.4 *General equilibrium in the product and money markets.* The intersection of the *IS* and *LM* curves in panel a identifies a unique market interest and level of output which results in both the money and product markets being in equilibrium (i.e., i_e and Y_e). The *IS-LM* curves can be used to determine the short-run impacts of changes in monetary and fiscal policy on market interest rates and national output and product. Changes in monetary policy shift the *LM* curve, while changes in fiscal policy shift the *IS* curve. Panel b, for example, shows that a contractionary monetary policy that shifts the *LM* curve to the left (i.e., from LM_0 to LM_1) results in a new general equilibrium in the nation's money and product markets. Interest rates will be higher than before (they have increased from i_e to i_e^* and the nation's output and product will be less than before (Y_e^* instead of Y_e). Expansionary monetary policy actions would have shifted the *LM* curve to the right. Expansionary fiscal policy actions would have shifted the *IS* curve to the right, while contractionary fiscal policy actions would have shifted the *IS* curve to the left of IS_0.

would happen to interest rates or the economy's income and product as a result of these actions being taken.

By combining the *IS* and *LM* curves in a single graph and focusing on the *general equilibrium* in the nation's product and money markets, however, we can address this topic. Figure 15.4 illustrates the equilibrium interest rate and output given by the intersection of the *IS* and *LM* curves. Only at this point would *both* the product and money markets be in equilibrium.

Expansionary (contractionary) monetary policies that shift the *LM* curve to the right (left) will in the short run lead to lower real interest rates and a higher gross national income and product. This assumes, of course, that there is slack in the economy's capacity to supply these additional goods and services. Expansionary (contractionary) fiscal policies that shift the *IS* curve to the right (left) will in the short run lead to higher real interest rates and a higher gross national income and product under the assumptions outlined above. Given the expansionary fiscal policies (which shift the *IS* curve to the right) and contractionary monetary policies (which shift the *LM* curve to the left) in the early eighties, it is no wonder that we observed the historically high real interest rates that we did during this period.[15]

[15] For a more precise description of *IS-LM* analysis, see John B. Penson, Jr. and David A. Lins, *Agricultural Finance* (Englewood Cliffs, N.J.: Prentice-Hall Inc., 1980). pp. 406–420.

16

SCARCE RESOURCES
AND THE ENVIRONMENT

When we discussed the concept of resource scarcity in Chapter 1, we divided resources into three categories: (1) natural resources, (2) human resources, and (3) manufactured resources. We said that these resources were considered scarce because nature does not freely provide as much of them as we would like. The U.S. farm business sector is well endowed in each of these resource categories, particularly if we compare this sector to similar sectors in other countries. The quality of these resources and the quantity available are influenced by such important issues as the conservation of natural resources, the capacity of the sector to supply food and fiber products, and environmental regulations related to the use of the resources in the farm business sector.

The purpose of this chapter is to inventory the scope and magnitude of scarce resources in the U.S. farm business sector, the issues related to the conservation of natural resources, and the measurement and importance of the sector's productive capacity. The chapter concludes with the topic of environmental regulations. This discussion focuses on the difference between private versus social costs, the concept of externalities, and the "economics" of pollution.

SCARCE RESOURCES IN AGRICULTURE

In this section we inventory the scarce resources that the farm business sector has available to produce raw agricultural products. This discussion

The Soil Conservation Service (SCS), an agency in the U.S. Department of Agriculture, gives technical assistance to farmers and other groups to reduce erosion and sedimentation as well as to conserve water and improve its quality. There are approximately 2,950 local conservation districts located throughout the country to assist in this effort. The Agricultural Conservation Program (ACP), administered by the Agricultural Stabilization and Conservation Service (ASCS), also provides assistance to farmers in carrying out measures to prevent soil loss from wind and water erosion, address water conservation and quality problems, conserve wildlife, and preserve forest resources. The ASCS is also an agency of the U.S. Department of Agriculture.

focuses on the three groups of scarce resources identified above, as well as on the productivity of these resources.

Natural Resources

Land, its natural fertility and mineral deposits, water, and the weather or climate in which raw agricultural products are raised represent the major natural resources in the U.S. farm business sector. Table 16.1 shows that the total land in farms used as cropland is largely within the range 360 to 380 million acres. Land in farms, however, has changed regionally. Some land has gone out of agricultural use in the Northeast and the South. Offsetting these losses are new lands in agricultural use in the Southeast and in the Mississippi Delta. Cropland used only for pasture is also approximately what it was in the twenties.

Major land uses	1920	1930	1940	1950	1959	1969	1974	1978	1982
Cropland used for crops[a]	368	382	368	377	359	333	361	370	383
Idle cropland	34	31	31	32	33	51	21	26	21
Cropland used only for pasture	78	67	68	69	66	88	83	76	65
Grassland pasture[b]	652	652	650	631	633	604	598	587	597
Forest land[c]	602	601	608	601	728	723	718	703	655
Special uses[d]					147	171	182		
Other land	170	171	179	194	305	291	301	502	544
Total land areas[e]	1,904	1,904	1,904	1,904	2,271	2,264	2,264	2,264	2,265

Note: Values are given in millions of acres.

[a]Cropland harvested, crop failure, and cultivated summer fallow.

[b]Grassland and other nonforest pasture and range.

[c]Excludes reserved forest land in parks and other special uses of land. Includes forested grazing land.

[d]Includes urban and transportation areas. Federal and state areas used primarily for recreation and wildlife purposes, military areas, farmsteads, and farm roads and lanes.

[e]Remeasurement and increases in reservoirs account for changes in total land area except for the major increase in 1959 when data for Alaska and Hawaii were added.

Source: Economic Research Service. Estimates based on reports and records of the U.S. Departments of Agriculture and Commerce, and public land administering and conservation agencies.

TABLE 16.1 **LAND UTILIZATION IN THE UNITED STATES.** The number of acres devoted to cropland use in the United States has remained relatively constant over much of this century. The decline noted in 1969 is explained by the acreage restriction programs which were then used in agriculture to support prices (see Chapter 10). The increase in total land area that initially appears in the table in 1959 is explained by the statehood of Hawaii and Alaska.

Texas leads the nation with 138 million acres of land in farms. Other leading states are Kansas (48 million acres), Montana (62 million acres), and Nebraska (48 million acres). Rhode Island has the fewest acres of land in farms (75 thousand acres). Kansas and North Dakota, however, lead the nation in the number of acres *used for crops.* California, Texas, and Nebraska lead the nation in the number of acres of *irrigated land.* Finally, it is estimated that 43 million acres of cropland need improved drainage. Another potential 11 million acres of wet forest and pastureland could be converted to cropland (Stultz, 1979).

The other major natural resource discussed here is water. Water comes in two forms: (1) rainfall, and (2) irrigation. Approximately 4.7 billion acre-feet or 1,531,730 billion gallons of rainwater falls each year in the 48 contiguous states. About two-thirds of this total is lost through evaporation or transpiration from plants. The remaining one-third replenishes our streams, lakes, and underground aquifers.

Approximately 50 million acres of land in farms is irrigated. Irrigation practices are particularly important in the production of vegetables, fruits, cotton, rice, and other high-value crops. Approximately 50 percent of the total fresh water withdrawn for use in this country is accounted for by irrigation practices in the farm business sector. Interestingly, annual domestic (i.e., household) use of fresh water is only 8 percent of total withdrawals. Steam generation of electricity accounts for an additional 29 percent, while another 10 percent goes is accounted for by commercial and manufacturing uses (Stultz, 1979). Finally, of the total withdrawals of fresh water for use in agriculture, 56 percent is consumed (i.e., used up forever), while the remaining 44 percent is returned to surface water and ground water for subsequent reuse.

Human Resources

Approximately 2.7 percent of the U.S. population resided on farms in 1980 compared to approximately twice that percentage during the sixties. Not surprisingly this decline reflects the decline in the number of farms in the farm business sector noted earlier in Chapter 2. There were 2.4 million family workers (farmers and farm family members) working on farms in 1980, as indicated in Table 16.2. Another 1.3 million hired laborers were needed in 1980 to help with the production of raw agricultural products during the year. Since the size of the hired labor force remained relatively constant during the seventies, the declines noted in the total labor force in the farm business sector were therefore the result of the decline in number of farms and, correspondingly, the number of farmers themselves.

In comparison with other segments of the U.S. population, the farm population is largely (92 percent) white and non-Hispanic. Hired laborers, on the other hand, are often blacks, hispanics, or members of other minority groups (Beale, 1979).

Young farmers today are more highly educated than were the young farmers of past generations. A 1970 survey revealed, for example, that 72 percent of all farmers aged 55 to 64 had not finished high school. This same survey revealed, however, that only 12 percent of all the farmers aged 20 to 24 had not finished high school and that 25 pecent actually had some college training (Beale, 1979). Finally, there was a direct correlation noted in this survey between the size of the famer's operation and his degree of formal education; that is, the higher the farmer's level of education, the larger the size of his farm.

Year	Total workers	Family workers	Hired workers
1970	4.52	3.45	1.17
1971	4.44	3.28	1.16
1972	4.37	3.23	1.15
1973	4.34	3.17	1.17
1974	4.39	3.07	1.32
1975	4.34	3.03	1.31
1976	4.37	3.00	1.37
1977	4.15	2.86	1.31
1978	3.96	2.69	1.27
1979	3.77	2.50	1.27
1980	3.71	2.40	1.31
1981	3.33	2.20	1.10
1982	4.00	2.50	1.50

Source: U.S. Department of Agriculture, *Agricultural Statistics.* (Washington, D.C.: U.S. Printing Office, 1981).

TABLE 16.2 ANNUAL AVERAGE NUMBER OF WORKERS ON FARMS. The annual average number of workers employed in the farm business sector declined from 4.52 million people in 1970 to 3.71 million at the beginning of the eighties. Approximately two-thirds of the 1.31 million workers employed annually in 1980 were short-term seasonal workers employed for a period of approximately three months or less. The decline in the annual average employment of family workers (i.e. farm operators and family members) over the decade of the seventies reflects the decline in the number of farms over this period.

Manufactured Resources

Figure 2.3 illustrated the growing use of manufactured resources (i.e., capital) and declining use of labor in the farm business sector during the post–World War II period. Included in panel a of this figure was an illustration of the growth in tractor horsepower on farms during the 1950–1980 period. This substitution of manufactured resources for labor in the farm business sector has led to a large outmigration of farmily labor during the post–World War II period, as noted above. The new technologies embodied in manufactured resources contributed to a cutback in the amount of labor required to produce raw agricultural products by more than one-half.

Table 16.3 presents a disaggregation of the input "capital," indicating that some manufactured resources (e.g., chemicals) grew in use much faster than others (e.g., machinery). The rising use of chemicals in the sector represents approximately 60 percent of the sector's total energy needs, the remaining 40 percent being associated with direct energy use in the form of gasoline, diesel and fuel oil, liquid petroleum gas, natural gas, coal, and elec-

Year	Farm labor	Farm machinery	Farm chemicals
1970	126	85	75
1971	123	87	81
1972	117	86	86
1973	115	90	90
1974	112	92	92
1975	107	96	83
1976	103	98	96
1977	100	100	100
1978	95	104	107
1979	93	107	118
1980	92	104	120
1981	90	103	121
1982	86	99	111

Source: U.S. Department of Agriculture, *Agricultural Statistics.* (Washington, D.C.: U.S. Government Printing Office, 1981).

TABLE 16.3 GROWTH OF MANUFACTURED AND HUMAN RESOURCES. The downward trend in the index of farm labor and upward trend in the index of farm machinery and chemicals in the table above reflects the general substitution in favor of manufactured resource which has taken place during the post–World War II period. This substitution is one of the main reasons for the rapid strides in output per worker-hour in recent years. Today, the average horsepower of tractors per farm is almost double what it was a decade earlier. This substitution was discussed in earlier chapters (see Chapters 2 and 5).

tricity. Gasoline and diesel and fuel oil account for slightly more than two-thirds of direct energy use in the farm business sector. The sector's total energy needs, however, represents only about 3 percent of the total energy consumption in the United States.

Productivity of Scarce Resources

Table 2.2 demonstrated the rapid growth in the productivity ratio, or total farm output divided by total farm inputs. For example, the productivity ratio was shown to have grown by 142 percent during the 1929–1981 period. Increased merchanization, the development of hybrids and improved seed varieties, the development of new commercial chemicals (i.e., fertilizers, pesticides, etc.), and the use of irrigation all contributed to the productivity gains noted over this period. The availability of relatively cheap credit to finance the purchase of manufactured resources also facilitated this transformation.

The extent to which the productivity of inputs in the sector continues to expand and what forms it will take is, of course, unknown at this point. Much of the past productivity gains noted in Table 2.2 were the result of abundant and cheap sources of energy. That is, low-cost energy helped influence the development of machinery and equipment, which replaced relatively high-priced labor (i.e., reduced the number of farms) as well as the development of new energy-based chemicals. In light of the rising cost of energy and the increased uncertainty associated with its availability during the seventies, new technological progress will probably take the form of energy-saving or energy-producing production activities.

CONSERVATION OF NATURAL RESOURCES

The energy crisis initiated by the OPEC cartel in 1973–1974 awoke the American public to the fact that we live in a world of limited resources and that conservation efforts are needed. In this section we define what is meant by the term "conservation" and discuss how price affects the depletion of nonrenewable resources.

What Does Conservation Mean?

One possible definition of "conservation" is the optimal timing of the use of proven reserves of resources given existing and expected technology and preferences. Let us look more closely at the various components of this definition. To begin with, the "optimal timing" refers to the utilization of resources in a manner that maximizes the *present value* of the annual net returns expected to be generated by the resource. The term "present value" refers to the fact that we have netted out the *opportunity cost* or income forgone by having to wait to receive these net returns.[1] The further these net returns are in the future, the lower their present value.

The second component of this definition refers specifically to "proven reserves of resources." Reference to the proven reserves of a particular resource does not necessarily refer to its remaining supply. Instead, it refers to the known reserves that can be utilized profitably. Use of the resource is being *optimized* in an economic sense rather than maximized in an engineering sense. As the relative price of the resource rises, known resources generally rise as marginal lands are brought into production, exploration increases and so on.

The final component of our definition has to do with the fact that "existing and expected technology and preferences" are assumed. Deviation from these levels of technology, for example, which allows us to reclaim resources more cheaply, should change the level of known reserves. Similarly,

[1] In the Advanced Topics section of Chapter 7, we discussed the notion of *discounting* and the calculation of the net present value.

deviation from these levels of tastes and preferences to a philosophy of "use less now" will also affect the level of proven reserves.

Depletion of a Nonrenewable Resource

A nonrenewable resource refers to a resource that once exhausted, cannot be restored. Two examples of nonrenewable resources are coal and oil. Such resources are available in a fixed amount. The faster we use them, the quicker they will be gone.

When a resource is exhaustible, we must question ourselves as to how we should use this nonrenewable resource. Using nonrenewable resources efficiently involves the issue of "timing," or how fast it should be used. The optimal use of a nonrenewable resource is much like that of any other scarce resource—using up nonrenewable resources efficiently involves correct timing. In other words, the value of such resources is maximized if they are used over time such that the present value of the net returns is maximized.

Does this lead to the depletion of this resource? Consider the downward-sloping demand curve for a nonrenewable resource depicted in Figure 16.1. The inverse relationship between the price of this resource and the quantity demanded suggests that as the price of this resource increases, less will be demanded. Thus if we continued to use up the nonrenewable resource at the old rate, we may indeed eventually deplete this resource. The point, however, is that the upward-sloping *DD* demand curve suggests that if its price increases—reflecting its increasing scarcity—we will use less of the resource. In this sense, we may never "run out" of a nonrenewable resource. Its use may become so unprofitable that only small quantities will be demanded.

When substitutes exist for a nonrenewable resource, their demand will increase as the own price of the nonrenewable resource rises. If we choose not to use natural gas because its price increases, it may be because we chose

Price

D

D

Quantity per
unit of time

Fiure 16.1 *Demand for nonrenewable resources.* The demand for nonrenewable resources is like the demand for any other asset; it is downward sloping. The higher the per unit cost of such resources, the fewer units will be demanded. As a resource becomes increasingly scarce, therefore, its per unit cost may become so high that its use is largely unprofitable.

to use more coal, oil, or some other form of energy. This, of course, means that *these* nonrenewable resources will be depleted more quickly than before. Thus restrictions placed on the use of one nonrenewable resource (e.g., natural gas) may simply mean that some other nonrenewable resource (e.g., coal) may be used up more quickly. The alternative is to use less of *all* nonrenewable resources, which means a return to a simpler way of life without as many material goods.

In summary, conservation does not mean limiting the use of our nonrenewable resources. Instead, it means maximizing the present value of the net returns associated with these resources.[2]

SECTOR CAPACITY AND POPULATION GROWTH

Another dimension of the presence of scarce resources is the productive capacity of the farm business sector, its ability to meet the demand for its products. In this section we discuss the measurement of the sector's productive capacity, the growth of the world's population, the Malthusian cycle, and the importance of changes in technology.

Productive Capacity

The current productive capacity of an individual farm can be defined as the maximum level of output that it is technically possible to produce given normal operating practices, the farm's current size, and current technology. In terms of the farm's cost curves, it is that output where the farm's supply curve (i.e., its marginal cost curve) becomes almost completely vertical, or where the level of output is very unresponsive to further increases in product price.

This relationship is illustrated in Figure 16.2. In panel a of this figure, for example, we see that the productive capacity of farm 1 is equal to quantity of Q_1. This farm could not supply any additional quantities beyond this point no matter how high prices rose. Let us assume that these are only two farms in the sector, the second farm having a productive capacity equal to Q_2. We know from Chapter 5 that the market supply curve is equal to the horizontal summation of the individual farm supply curves. This means that the farm business sector's productive capacity must be equal to the sum of

[2] Another dimension of resource depletion is the property rights in these resources. There are two categories of property rights in resources: (1) private property resources, and (2) common property resources. A common property resource is one (like air, oceans, etc) that no one owns. Property rights in common property resources are either indefinite or nonexistent.

[3] The summation of each sector's productive capacity is technically applicable only at the subsector level (e.g.; the cow–calf subsector, the corn subsector, etc.). This is be-

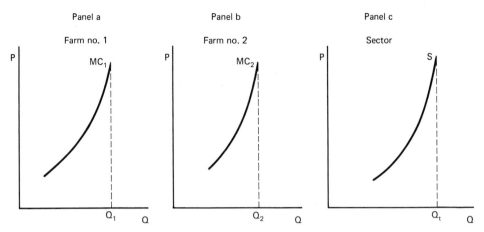

Figure 16.2 *Productive capacity at the firm and sector level.* The point at which the firm's marginal cost curve (i.e., its supply curve) becomes almost completely vertical represents the firm's productive capacity in the short run. Further increases in demand and hence the price the farmer takes from the market place will do little in bringing forth additional current output. The horizontal summation of firm-level supply curves represents the sector's supply curve. Hence the highly inelastic portion of this curve represents the sector's current productive capacity. In this example of a two-firm sector, the sector's productive capacity (Q_t) is equal to farm no. 1's productive capacity (Q_1) plus farm no. 2's productive capacity (Q_2).

the productive capacities of the individual farms in the sector. Hence Q_t in panel c, which represents the *sector's* productive capacity, is equal to Q_1 in panel a plus Q_2 in panel b.[3]

Capacity Utilization

Productive capacity as defined above is a short-run concept based on each farm's current size and existing technology. It reflects the output *technically* possible and thus bears no relationship to prices of farm inputs and the prices of farm products. *Economic* or "preferred" capacity is that quantity of output that farmers desire to produce in the current period in light of current prices for production inputs and product prices.

The *preferred capacity utilization rate* captures the relationship between economic capacity and productive capacity. If farm 1 in panel a prefers to produce less than Q_1, its preferred capacity utilization rate would be less than 1.0. If all farmers are operating collectively at less than Q_t in panel

cause some subsector products are used as inputs by other subsectors and therefore should not be counted when describing the entire sector's capacity. This point is similar to the discussion of the sector's contribution to the economy's GNP in Chapter 11.

c, the economic signals received by farmers are causing them to produce less than they technically can in the current period.

When this occurs, physical resource scarcity per se is not bottlenecking the output of the sector, although resource prices do affect preferred capacity utilization. If this utilization rate is equal to 1, however, physical resource scarcity is bottlenecking the sector's ability to meet the demand by others for raw food and fiber products.

Population Growth

A major reason for our concern over the productive capacity of the farm business sector is its ability to assist other surplus-producing nations to meet the world's food needs. The Presidential Commission on World Hunger in 1980 concluded that a major world food crisis appears likely by 1990. To dramatize the potential magnitude of the problem, they characterized this crisis as having the potential of being worse than the energy crisis during the seventies (see Johnson, 1975).

Annual population growth rates are often translated by population experts into what is known as *doubling time.* This statistic tells us how many years it would take for the country's population to double at current growth rates. As shown in Table 16.4, the range of doubling times is substantial; with its low annual growth rate in population, it would take Sweden 327 years before its population would double. At the other end of the spectrum are countries such as Venezuela and Pakistan. With their high annual growth rate in population, it would take only 23 years at current growth rates for their population to double.

In 1798, English economist Thomas Malthus published a 50,000-word treatise which argued that population, left unchecked, goes on doubling every 24 years, thereby increasing geometrically. He argued that food production, on the other hand, increases arithmetically. These general relationships are depicted in Figure 16.3. This figure shows a population increasing at an increasing rate while food production increases at a constant rate. Eventually, Malthus hypothesized, population will outstrip available food supplies.

Malthus assumed that "passion between the sexes" would cause the family size to increase as long as they had enough food to feed a growing family. This relationship is illustrated in Figure 16.4. Population is plotted on the horizontal axis and the real wage rate (after adjustments for inflation) is plotted on the vertical axis. The real wage rate indicates the family's ability to purchase the goods and services it needs. Malthus suggested that "positive checks" on the growth of the population in the form of starvation and disease would begin to occur at point *A* in Figure 16.4, where the real wage rate per family falls below the subsistence level. This "positive check" on population growth is frequently referred to as the *Malthusian cycle.*

Country	Doubling Time (years)
Sweden	327
Denmark	180
United States	180
France	176
Japan	164
Canada	109
Soviet Union	99
Poland	85
Iceland	56
Israel	38
Mexico	25
Venezuela	23
Pakistan	23

Source: Statistical Office of the United Nations, 1980.

TABLE 16.4 DOUBLING TIME IN SELECTED COUN-TRIES. A country's "doubling time" refers to the number of years it would take for a country's population to double at current growth rates. The table shows that it would take 327 years for Sweden (which has a low annual population growth rate) to double, while it would taken only 23 years for Venezuela's and Pakistan's population to double. The lower the doubling time, the greater the strain placed on the country's resources to meet the needs of its future population.

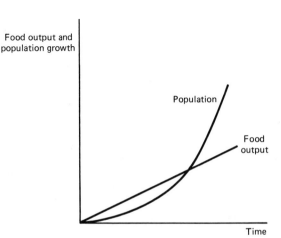

Food output and population growth

Population

Food output

Time

Figure 16.3 *Growth of population and the food supply.* One of Malthus's concerns at the beginning of the nineteenth century was that population grew at a geometric rate (e.g., 1, 2, 4, 8, 16, . . .) while food production grew at an arith-metic rate (e.g., 1, 2, 3, 4, 5, . . .). Based on this concept, he con-cluded that the food needs of the population would eventually outstrip a country's ability to meet these needs (i.e., where the two curves in the figure cross). Malthus overlooked the possibilities of the food supply curve shifting in response to new technology developments, however.

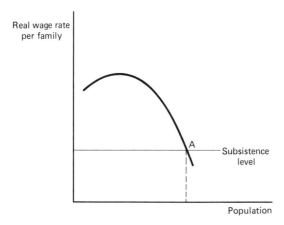

Figure 16.4 *The Malthusian cycle.* Malthus argued that only "positive checks" on population growth could keep the situtuation in Figure 16.3 from getting completely out of hand. Malthus's positive checks consisted of the starvation and other problems that occur when the real wage rate falls below the family's subsistence level.

Factors Affecting Analysis

A key assumption made by Malthus was that technology was fixed. Another was that population size was a function of real wage rates alone. Although technological change was slow back in the late eighteenth century when Malthus developed his theory, we know that technological change both within and outside the farm business sector has increased tremendously in most industrialized countries since then. When the technology of production is improved, the curve in Figure 16.4 shifts upward to the right.[4] If these gains in productivity rise fast enough, the country's population can grow without real wages falling below subsistence levels. Thus there need not be a "Malthusian positive check" as long as the real wage rate curve keeps shifting upward.

Other factors may also affect population growth. For example, family size may stabilize and even decline over time as income levels rise beyond certain levels. Another factor affecting Malthus's theories is the zero population growth movement (ZPG). ZPG advocates argue that the only way to control pollution in this country is to control the size of the population.[5] Another factor, which offsets the affects of ZPG, is the improvement in health care, which allows people to live longer lives. Both of these factors lead to increases in the average age of the population.

ENVIRONMENTAL REGULATIONS

Thus far we have discussed only the market prices that the farmer must pay when using resources to produce raw food and fiber products. These prices

[4] Increases in technology will also shift the firm's supply curve to the right as these technologies are adopted over time. In the context of Figure 16.2, this means that the sector's productive capacity will increase.

[5] One can argue that the quantities produced and consumed in the country and not the size of the population that influences pollution.

are frequently referred to as *private costs.* Private costs are considered internal to the farmer's business, in that he must explicitly account for them when making production and investment decisions. In this section we introduce the notion of *social costs* and discuss the economics of pollution.

Social Costs

Crop and livestock production practices can result in environmental damage. Approximately 95 percent of the nation's hydrologic river basins have some degree of water pollution, where farming activities are fingered as the major contributor.[6] Rainfall and irrigation runoff can carry soil, salts, animal wastes, nutrients, and farm chemicals into groundwater or streams. Polluted waters can create hazards to fish and wildlife, recreation facility users, freshwater production, and agricultural uses of water. Such pollution also increases the cost of purifying water for consumption in rural communities. Obviously, costs are involved when this occurs. These costs are not incurred directly by the farmer, but rather are external to the nature of his farming operations.

The sum of these external costs plus all internal or private costs represents *social costs.* When private costs are less than social costs, we usually refer to this as a problem of *externalities.* That is, some of the costs associated with production are external to the production decisions discussed in Chapter 5. The full cost of using a scarce resource is borne by someone. Society must pay that part of the full cost of production activities not borne directly by farmers.

Effects of Accounting for Social Costs

Figure 16.5 presents the demand curve *(DD)* and supply curve *(SS)* for a particular product, where *SS* represents the summation of the *private costs* borne by farmers. In this case, market equilibrium would occur at price P_e and quantity Q_e. Now let us assume that the full costs of production, including the costs external to the farmers' business, result in a social cost represented by *S*S** in Figure 16.5. This suggests the corrected market equilibrium would suggest that the equilibrium price would rise to P_e^* and the equilibrium quantity would fall to Q_e^*. This suggests that production of Q_e is *excessive* when we account for the full costs of the production activity borne by society.

One approach to "internalizing" these external costs on the production decisions of farmers is to institute a tax equal to the economic damages caused by their production activities. This would leave farmers with two choices: (1) they could alter their production practices to cut down on the amount of pollution generated by their operations, or (2) they could cut back their level of production and continue to use their current production practices. In either case, the farmer would be modifying his economic

[6] Draft RCA report on the Potential Problem Areas of Water Quality, July 13, 1979.

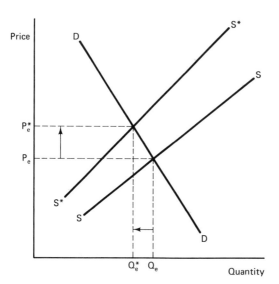

Figure 16.5 *Effects of external costs on market equilibrium.* The supply curve *SS* represents the summation of each firm's marginal cost curve in the sector. It therefore represents the total private costs associated with the supply of these goods. The difference the *S*S** curve and the *SS* curve represents the additional costs extended to production that must be borne by society. The *S*S** curve therefore represents the total social costs associated with the supply of specific quantities of this product. An equilibrium quantity of Q_e would be viewed excessive if these external costs or "externalities" are accounted for.

behavior from what it would have been if he were not forced to account for these externalities.

Abatement Regulations and Programs

There is a long history of abatement regulations and programs designed to reduce pollution generated by farm business operations. Early legislation includes the Federal Insecticide, Fungicide and Rodenticide Act of 1947, the Clean Water Restoration Act of 1966, and the National Environmental Policy Act of 1970, which established the Environmental Protection Agency (EPA).

Farm production activities are affected primarily by the following regulations and programs: pest control, feedlot waste disposal, nonpoint pollution abatement, and soil and water conservation. For example, the 1972 Pesticides Act authorizes the EPA to regulate the use of pesticides in crop production. The Federal Water Pollution Control Act of 1972 addresses surface-water pollution from point sources, including feedlots. The term "point source" refers to a single, identifiable source of pollution, such as feedlot drainage. Nonpoint pollution, on the other hand, cannot be traced to a single point or source. It may stem from rainfall or irrigation runoff which carries pesticides, fertilizers, salts, and other substances into streams and lakes. Although no mandatory controls exist yet for nonpoint pollution in the sector, the 1972 amendments to the Water Pollution Control Act established a planning process for environmental action programs. Finally, U.S. Department of Agriculture programs for soil and water conservation have been voluntary thus far, relying on low-interest loans and technical assistance as incentives.[7]

Economics of Abatement Programs

One approach to deciding how much pollution is acceptable is to assess the *marginal social cost of pollution* and the *marginal cost of abatement.* To begin with, the marginal social cost of pollution would probably be quite small at low levels of pollution and increase at an increasing rate as the quantity of pollution increases. Thus if we plotted this relationship, as we have done in panel a of Figure 16.6, we would expect the resulting curve (MC_p) to be upward sloping like the marginal cost curves developed in Chapter 5.

Turning to the marginal social cost of abatement, it seems reasonable that it would be relatively cheap to reduce or eliminate the first few units of pollution. Because some pollution abatement regulations will require substantial capital outlays (e.g., scrubbers for smokestacks at steel mills), the

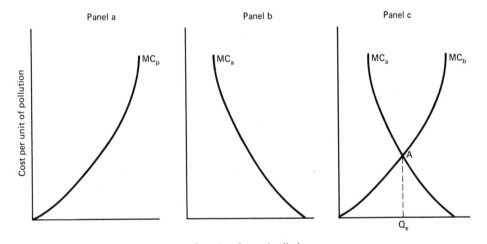

Quantity of annual pollution

Figure 16.6 *Determination of optimal level of pollution.* We can study the problem of pollution and its abatement in the context of economics. Assume that MC_a curve in panel a represents the marginal social cost of pollution, or the additional social cost associated with an increase in pollution. The MC_a curve in panel b represents the marginal cost of pollution abatement, or the cost of eliminating another unit of pollution. The "optimal" level of pollution would be given the intercept of these two years marginal cost curves, which occurs at point *A* in panel c and results in an equilibrium quantity Q_e.

---

[7] For a review of empirical studies of the effects of environment regulations on the structure of the sector see Magleby and Gadsby.

marginal social cost of eliminating additional units of pollution will be lower. Thus one can argue that the marginal social cost of abatement will decrease at an increasing rate, giving us a curve (MC_a) like the one plotted in panel b.

We can now determine the acceptable level of pollution from an economic standpoint. It is given by the point of intersection of these two marginal social cost curves in panel c, or point A. The optimal level of pollutions from an economic standpoint would therefore be Q_e. If we sought to lower pollution below this quantity, the marginal social costs of the abatement program would actually exceed the marginal social cost of the pollution itself. Thus pollution abatement programs can be seen as a trade-off with pollution levels. We are trading off less production for less pollution.[8]

SUMMARY

The purpose of this chapter was to inventory the scope and magnitude of scare resources in the farm business sector as well as to discuss the issues related to the conservation of natural resources, population growth, the measurement and importance of the sector's productive capacity, the existence of environmental regulations in the sector, and the economics of pollution. The major points made in this chapter can be summarized as follows:

1. The major natural resources in the farm business sector include farmland and its natural fertility and mineral deposits, water, and the climate in which farmers raise their products.

2. Total cropland in the United States has remained largely the same over the last 60 years. The distribution of land in farms has changed regionally, however. Water used in the sector comes in two forms: (1) rainfall, and (2) irrigation. About one-half of the total fresh water withdrawn for use in this country is accounted for by irrigation practices.

3. The decline in farm population closely follows the decline in the number of farms in the farm business sector. The hired labor force remained relatively constant during the seventies. Young farmers today have more formal training than did young farmers of past generations. Farm size is positively related to the extent of a farmer's formal education.

4. The substitution of manufactured resources for labor has led to the out-migration of family labor during the post–World War II period. Sixty percent of the sector's total energy use takes the form of farm chemicals. The remaining 40 percent is accounted for by fuel and utilities. The sector's total energy use, however, represents only 3 percent of the nation's total energy use.

[8] Some will argue, of course, that society's goal should be to eliminate all pollution. Although it is difficult to argue with the desirability of a pollution-free environment, it is important that we understand the economics of pollution abatement programs.

5. *Conservation* is defined as the optimal timing of the use of proven reserves of resources given existing and expected technology and preferences.

6. The optimal use of nonrenewable resources, like other resources, involves maximizing the present value of annual net returns. This will not lead to the depletion of these resources, since their price will rise as they become more scarce and make further use uneconomical.

7. The *productive capacity* of an individual farm refers to the maximum output technically possible given the farm's current size and technology. The *sector's* productive capacity is equal to the horizontal summation of each farm's marginal cost curve at the point where they become highly inelastic. The *preferred capacity utilization rate* captures the relationship between the *economic* or "preferred capacity" and productive capacity.

8. Malthus argued that the population increases at an increasing rate and therefore will eventually outstrip the food supply, which increases at a constant rate. Malthus suggests that "positive checks" on population will occur in the form of starvation and disease as the family's real purchasing power falls below the subsistence level. This check on population growth is known as the *Malthusian cycle.* However, Malthus overlooked the possibility that technological change could result in output growing faster than population.

9. *Social costs* capture the *private costs* of production internal to the farmer's decision-making process *plus* such external costs as pollution. When private costs are less than social costs, economists refer to this as a problem of *externalities.*

10. There are many abatement regulations and programs designed to abate the pollution generated by farming operations. These regulations and programs focus on pest control, feedlot waste management, nonpoint pollution abatement, and soil and water conservation.

11. The acceptable level of pollution from an economic standpoint occurs where the *marginal social cost of pollution* is equal to the *marginal social cost of abatement.*

DEFINITION OF TERMS

Natural resources: land and mineral deposits (the original fertility of land or land without fertilization is included here).

Manufactured resources: also referred to as capital, manufactured resources include such things as tractors and combines, which are combined with land, labor, and management to produce goods and services.

Human resources: labor and management used together with land and capital to produce goods and services.

Scarce resources: at any time there exists only a finite quantity of natural, manufactured, and human resources in the environment.

Productivity ratio: ratio of output to input.

Conservation: optimal timing of the use of proven reserves of resources given existing and expected technology and preferences.

Present value of returns: the future returns discounted back to the present by an appropriate cost of capital (e.g., the opportunity cost of capital). A dollar in benefits in the future is worth less than it would be worth today.

Opportunity cost: the rate of return on the best alternative or "opportunity" use of funds.

Nonrenewable resource: a scarce resource that cannot be reproduced (e.g., mineral deposits).

Productive capacity: the maximum output technically possible in the short run given available resources and existing technology.

Economic capacity: the desired output in the short run given available resources, technology, and existing economic conditions.

Preferred capacity utilization rate: ratio of economic capacity to productive capacity.

Malthusian cycle: the "positive check" on population growth in the form of starvation and disease when real wage rate per family falls below the subsistence level.

Doubling time: the number of years it would take for a country's population to double at its current growth rate.

Private costs: costs incurred by individuals when using scarce resources. The private costs of operating a tractor include the fuel and maintenance expenses associated with its use.

Social costs: costs incurred by society when a resource is used. The social cost of operating a tractor is equal to the private costs plus any additional cost that society bears, including air pollution.

Externalities: difference between social costs and private costs.

Marginal social cost of pollution: increase in the social cost of pollution caused by an annual increase in pollution.

Marginal social cost of abatement: increase in the cost of pollution abatement practices associated with an annual increase in pollution.

Proven reserves: known reserves that can be extracted or used profitably.

REFERENCES

BEALE, CALVIN L., "Demographic Aspects of Agriculture Structure," in *Structure Issues of American Agriculture,* ed. Lyle P. Schertz et al., Agricultural Economic Report 438, ESCS, U.S. Department of Agriculture, 1979.

JOHNSON, D. GALE, *World Food Problems and Prospects.* Washington, D.C.: American Enterprise Institute, 1975.

MAGLEBY, RICHARD, and DWIGHT GADSBY, "Environmental Regulations: Impacts on Farm Structure," in Structure Issues of American, ed. Lyle P. Schertz et al., Agricultural Economic Report 438, ESCS, U.S. Department of Agriculture, 1979.

STULTZ, HAROLD, "Water Use and Water Use Policy," in *Structure Issues of American Agriculture,* ed. Lyle P. Schertz et al., Agricultural Economic Report 438, ESCS, U.S. Department of Agriculture, 1979.

U.S. Department of Agriculture, *Agricultural Statistics.* Washington, D.C.: U.S. Government Printing Office, 1981.

ADDITIONAL READINGS

EHRLICH, PAUL R., and ANNE H. EHRLICH, *Population, Resources, Environment,* 2nd ed. San Francisco: Freeman, Cooper & Company, 1972.

KNEESE, A. V., and C. L. SCHULTZE, *Pollution, Prices, and Public Policy.* Washington, D.C.: The Brookings Institution, 1979.

QUESTIONS

1. Will the world run out of crude oil in your lifetime? Why?
2. Give several examples of the following categories of scarce resources.
   (a) Manufactured
   (b) Natural
   (c) Human
3. What is meant by the term "productivity of scarce resources"? What is the difference between productive capacity and economic capacity? Would they ever be the same?
4. Fully describe the meaning of the term "conservation." Does this term apply to both renewable and nonrenewable resources?
5. Malthus predicted that food supplies would be outstripped by population growth. What caused Malthus to reach this conclusion? What factors have caused Malthus's predicition not to materialize in most countries?
6. Are the concepts of pollution and population related? Why or why not?
7. Describe the concept of optimum pollution and the economic factors that determine this level.

17

SUPPLY OF LOAN FUNDS
TO AGRICULTURE

The farm business sector was shown in Chapter 2 to have significantly expanded its use of loan funds during the seventies. Farmers and ranchers will probably continue to be heavy users of loan funds during the remainder of the eighties, although it is unlikely to expand at the rate observed during the seventies and early eighties. These loan funds are provided by a wide variety of private lenders, including commercial banks, the Farm Credit System, and life insurance companies, to name a few. Government lenders such as the Farmers Home Administration also represent a significant source of loan funds to a specific segment of farmers and ranchers.

Many of these lenders experienced some difficulties with the performance of the farm loans in their loan portfolio during the mid-eighties. The purpose of this chapter is to identify the major groups of lenders who are supplying these funds and to outline the environment in which they operate. This discussion will focus on (1) the role these lenders play, (2) where *they* obtain their loanable funds, and (3) what factors affect their market share.[1] For example, we already know from Chapter 14 that monetary policy has a direct effect on the amount of loanable funds (i.e., excess reserves) at depository institutions such as commercial banks. Each of the lender groups supplying loan funds to the farm business sector operates in a somewhat different environment. Those differences must be understood if we are to understand the cost and availability of loan funds from these various lender groups.

[1] The term *loanable funds* differs from *loan funds* in that it refers to the pool of funds lenders have available to lend. *Loan funds,* on the other hand, refer to the funds lent to borrowers.

PROCESS OF FINANCIAL INTERMEDIATION

The process by which loanable funds are transferred from savers to borrowers in exchange for securities is known as *financial intermediation*. Figure 17.1 illustrates the general nature of this process. On the left-hand side of this figure, we see that lenders receive loanable funds from savers in exchange for securities (e.g., certificates of deposit). By the time the security matures, the saver will have been repaid the amount of money he "lent" to the lender *plus* interest. On the right-hand side, we see that lenders use the loanable funds they receive from savers to lend to borrowers. By the time the loan matures, the lender will have been repaid the money he lent to the borrower *plus* interest.

Savers are made up of individuals, businesses, and even local, state, and federal governments. Savers consider the rate of return, liquidity, and risk of alternative financial assets. Some savers, for example, save for long-term reasons (e.g., persons accumulating wealth for their retirement years). Others save for short-term reasons (e.g., businesses may have a temporary surplus of funds). These liquidity needs have an effect on the maturities of the securities offered by lenders. In general, however, we can say that the borrowing needs of farmers to finance their capital purchases extend over terms longer than the maturity desired by many savers. Most loans also contain more risk than many savers would normally desire.

It is up to lenders to meet the needs of both savers and borrowers. To do this, the lender may have to pool the loanable funds by many savers to meet the needs of just one borrower. Furthermore, since these savings deposits and other funds will probably mature long before intermediate- and long-term farm loans are repaid, lenders count on these savers to reinvest their funds once the security matures or new savers to provide the funds necessary to pay off those savers who choose to place their funds elsewhere upon maturity. Lenders also use a variety of means to modify savers' exposure to risk [e.g., bank depositors are guaranteed up to a specific amount by the Federal Deposit Insurance Corporation (FDIC)].

Figure 17.1 *Financial intermediation process.* Lenders serve as an intermediary between savers and borrowers. That is, they obtain loanable funds from savers in exchange for a security or financial asset of one form or another. Lenders then provide loan funds to borrowers in exchange for a note or mortgage. Since the needs of savers are different from those of borrowers, it is the role of lenders to satisfy the needs of both groups.

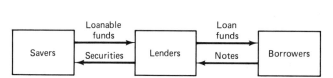

Lenders therefore provide an important service to borrowers by accumulating the loanable funds provided by savers into amounts and maturities desired by borrowers.

HISTORICAL PERSPECTIVE

Before we focus on specific characteristics of the various lender groups that provide loan funds to farm businesses, let us take a moment to gain a historical perspective on the relative market shares achieved by specific groups of lenders.

The Farm Credit System is the largest supplier of farm loan funds. As shown in Table 17.1, Federal Land Banks account for approximately 40 percent of the real estate loan funds market, and Production Credit Associations and Federal Intermediate Credit Banks together accounted for one-fourth of the non-real estate market. Commercial banks are also a significant supplier of non-real estate loan funds (approximately 38 percent of the market) but are a far less significant supplier of real estate loan funds to farm businesses.

It is fairly apparent from the data presented in Table 17.1 that Federal Land Banks have represented a substitute source of financing for life insurance companies in the real estate loan funds market. We can see this by examining the following data. Life insurance companies achieved a market share of about 23 percent in 1960. Federal Land Banks recorded a 19.3 percent share at that time. By the mid eighties, however, life insurance companies' share fell to 11 to 12 percent, while the Federal Land Bank's share increased to 41 to 43 percent. To a lesser degree, Federal Land Banks also compete with, or substitute for, the other nongovernment lenders identified in Table 17.1.

With respect to non-real estate loans, Production Credit Associations appear to have gained a higher market share at the expense of individuals and others, which includes merchant-dealer financing of machinery and equipment sales.

The relative market shares for the specific groups of lenders identified in Table 17.1 are anything but stable. To understand the forces behind shifts in these relative market shares, we must understand the differences in the regulatory and funding environments in which these lenders operate. The remainder of this chapter is devoted to a lender-by-lender examination of the sources of loanable funds and the factors that influence their involvement in supplying loan funds to farm businesses.

COMMERCIAL BANKS

A commercial bank is a privately owned, profit-seeking institution. As indicated in previous chapters, a commercial bank accepts deposits against which

Lender	1960	1970	1980	1981	1982	1983	1984
			Real estate debt (%)				
Federal Land Banks	19.3	22.9	34.7	37.6	41.3	43.1	42.9
Farmers Home Administration	5.6	7.8	8.3	8.1	8.3	8.3	8.4
Life insurance companies	23.3	19.6	14.3	13.5	12.4	11.7	11.4
Commercial banks	12.6	21.1	10.1	9.2	7.9	7.7	8.3
Individuals and others	39.2	37.5	32.6	31.6	30.1	29.2	28.9
	100.0	100.0	100.0	100.0	100.0	100.0	100.0
			Non-real estate debt (%)				
Commercial banks	38.0	43.3	38.6	36.5	34.3	33.8	38.0
Production Credit Association	10.7	18.9	22.4	22.7	21.9	18.8	18.2
Federal Intermediate Credit Banks	0.7	0.9	0.8	0.9	0.9	0.8	0.8
Farmers Home Administration	3.1	3.3	11.2	13.6	15.0	13.8	14.2
Individuals and others	38.3	22.4	20.7	20.5	19.6	18.3	18.4
Commodity Credit Corporation[a]	9.2	11.2	6.3	5.8	8.3	14.4	10.5
	100.0	100.0	100.0	100.0	100.0	100.0	100.0

[a]Price support and storage loans made or guaranteed by the Commodity Credit Corporation.

Source: Economic Indicators of the Farm Sector, various issues, U.S. Department of Agriculture.

TABLE 17.1 DISTRIBUTION OF FARM DEBT OUTSTANDING BY LENDERS. Federal Land Banks have become the major supplier of real estate loans during the post–World War II period, while commercial banks continue to account for the largest share of the non-real estate loan market. Individuals and others (which includes seller financing supplied by discontinuing farmers) have traditionally represented a major source of real estate financing in the farm business sector.

the depositor may write checks (i.e., a demand deposit). This check instructs the bank to transfer deposits from the depositor's account either to another account at that bank or to an account at an entirely different depository institution. In addition, commercial banks accept time deposits, which yield a specified return when held until maturity. Commercial banks will also automatically transfer funds from time deposits to demand deposits to cover checks written by the customer when instructed to do so. Finally, commercial banks serve as a *financial intermediary,* using the deposits of savers to make loans to borrowers.

The 15,000 commercial banks in this country play a major role in funding the capital needs of farm businesses. As shown in Table 17.1, they represent the largest single institutional source of non-real estate loan funds for farm businesses, but play a relatively minor role in providing real estate loan funds. In this section we examine the topics of bank structure, the regulatory environment in which banks operate, and their sources of loanable funds.

Banking Structure

As indicated earlier, banks can be categorized by whether they are *national banks* (and thus automatically a member of the Federal Reserve System) or *state banks.* All national banks contain the word "national" in their title. They are regulated by federal authority. State banks have the option of belonging to the Federal Reserve System. They are regulated by national *and* state authorities.

Banks are physically structured along specific lines depending on the state in which they are located. Some states have no limitations on *branch banking.* In these states, one is apt to see a relatively small number of banks, each having a large number of branch offices. Branch banking is permitted on a statewide basis in the District of Columbia and in 21 states, including California, New York, New Jersey, and Virginia. *Limited branch banking* is allowed in 17 other states. Here, a limitation is placed on the geographical locations of branches and/or the number of branches themselves. Included in this category are such states as Florida, Iowa, Michigan, Georgia, Pennsylvania, and Wisconsin. There are some states that specifically prohibit branch banking in any form. Instead they allow *unit banking,* where each banking location is a separate business entity. Included among the 12 unit banking states in this country are Texas, Illinois, Minnesota, Kansas, and Nebraska.

Regulatory Environment

There are a variety of regulations that affect the lending and investment behavior of commercial banks. We discussed the issue of *legal reserves* in Chapter 14. A bank's legal reserves are the amount of its deposits that the bank must hold either in valut cash or on deposit at the Federal Reserve Bank in its district. An increase in the reserves required by the Federal Reserve System will have a direct effect on the bank's lending behavior. If forced to increase its holdings of required reserves when its excess reserves (total reserves minus required reserves) are equal to zero, for example, the bank would face the prospect of selling part of its holding of government securities or calling in some of its existing loans.

There are also regulation that affect bank safety. In response to the massive bank closings in the late twenties and early thirties, a number of bank reforms were passed. These included (1) a deposit insurance require-ment of member banks and the provision of insurance facilities at other depository institutions, (2) tighter regulation of bank holding companies, (3) maximum interest-rate ceilings on time and savings deposits paid by commercial banks (and more recently savings and loan associations), and (4) the prohibition of interest paid on demand deposits.[2] The deposit insurance requirements for the banking system are managed by the Federal Deposit Insurance Corporation (for banks), the Federal Savings and Loan Insurance Corporation (for savings and loan associations and mutual savings banks), and the National Credit Union Administration (for credit unions). The Federal Reserve also regulates the types of business in which the bank may engage and the maximum interest rates that banks can pay depositors on specific categories of time and savings deposits. The latter regulation was proposed to protect the financial system against price competition. The pro-hibition of paying interest on demand deposits was also designed to prevent banks from becoming embroiled in unsound business practices. With the advent of the Depository Institutions Deregulation and Monetary Control Act of 1980, such price controls either have been or are being eliminated. For example, deregulation of interest rates paid on deposits at all depository institutions will gradually be "phased out" by 1986 under the guidance of the Depository Institutions Deregulation Committee. Emerging from all this is the existence of competitive interest rates paid to small savers (banks for some time were free to adjust upward the yields on time deposits of over $100,000) as well as interest-paying checkable deposits.

Perhaps the most common form of business regulation is the controls placed on the entry of new firms. Freedom of entry in many sectors of the economy is normally controlled through licensing, franchising, or charters. In banking, prospective commercial banks must initially show why a new bank is needed in their locale. It must also demonstrate its financial and managerial capabilities not only to the appropriate chartering body, but also to the Federal Deposit Insurance Corporation. Other regulatory character-istics of banking include regulations of bank mergers and the controls placed on the operations of bank holding companies.

There are also legal limitations placed on loans made by commercial banks. For example, there are legal maximums placed on the total amount that a bank may lend to an individual borrower. Banks are also restricted in the amount they may lend to one of their officers. They are also prohibited against accepting their own stock as collateral for a loan. Some states also dictate the maximum interest rates on loans to *individuals* through what is termed "usury" laws. Such regulations vary depending on the type of loan involved. A three-year moratorium on state usury ceilings was enacted by the

[2] A bank holding company is a corporation that controls the stock of one or more banks and possibly that of other related corporations. These companies are found most notably in unit banking states, where branch banking has been prohibited.

Depository Institutions Regulations and Monetary Control Act of 1980.[3] The high interest rates in the early eighties brought about a proposal that would lead to a *national usury law.* This and similar legislation has yet to be enacted, however.

Finally, commercial banks are profit-seeking corporations and as such are subject to the payment of income tax on their taxable corporate profits. This is an important regulation to remember because another financial intermediary providing loan funds to farm business (i.e., Federal Land Banks and Federal Land Bank Associations) are *exempt* from federal, state, and local income taxation.

Sources of Loanable Funds

The major source of loanable funds for commercial banks are demand deposits and time and savings deposits. Banks do borrow to meet their reserve requirements from other banks in the *federal funds market.* However, these loans are extremely short term in nature (12 to 24 hours). As such, they do not represent a source of loanable funds for banks. Small banks can "participate" with larger banks to meet the borrowing needs of their larger customers. Or several banks similar in size in the region may jointly participate in making such a loan. Banks can also borrow from the Federal Reserve System for short periods of time to meet their seasonal borrowing needs. In addition, banks can either discount loans with the Federal Intermediate Credit Bank in their district, provided that certain requirements are met, or participate with Production Credit Associations. Banks also sometimes sell the guaranteed portion of a loan guaranteed by one of several government agencies in secondary markets, retaining only the responsibility for servicing of the loan. Finally, agricultural credit corporations offer a way for a single bank or group of banks to obtain loanable funds from nondeposit sources. The bank or banks supply capital to the corporation, which then either (1) makes loans and discounts them with the Federal Intermediate Credit Bank in its district, or (2) makes loans with funds obtained from the sale of money-market instruments such as its own commercial paper.[4]

In short, the availability of loan funds to farm businesses at commercial banks will depend on the bank's level of excess reserves, its legal lending limits, and the degree to which the bank is able to obtain loanable funds

---

[3] Under Title V of this act, provisions regulating maximum amounts of interest were preemptied with respect to loans, mortgages, and credit sales after March 31, 1980, that are secured by first liens on residential property or other designated collateral. A state could reinstate usury limitations before April 1, 1983, if it adopted a law that preempted the federal usury override.

[4] Commercial paper refers to unsecured notes that indicate a promise to pay, issued by well-known companies with good credit reputations, which carry maturities of up to 270 days.

from nondeposit sources. The interest rates on loans to farm businesses will reflect the bank's cost of funds plus a margin when usury ceilings permit.

FARM CREDIT SYSTEM

The Farm Credit System is a member-owned lending cooperative. The system has its roots in the establishment of the Federal Land Bank System in 1916. With the help of "seed" capital provided by the federal government, which has since been repaid, the Federal Land Banks began making long-term real estate loans to farmers. The Federal Intermediate Credit Banks were established in 1923 for the purpose of discounting short-term loans made by commercial banks as mentioned above. It was not until 1933 that Production Credit Associations were established to make short- and inter-mediate-term loans to farmers. The Federal Intermediate Credit Banks and it its Production Credit Associations together comprise the Production Credit System. The Banks for Cooperatives were also established in 1933. Their role is to provide a source of loan funds to farmer-owned marketing, supply, and service cooperatives. The Federal Land Bank System, the Production Credit System, and the Banks for Cooperatives constitute the three major branches of the Farm Credit System as we know it today. Currently, the system is entirely owned by its members, the seed capital originally provided by the federal government having been retired many years ago.

Structure of System

Figure 17.2 illustrates the overall organizational structure of the Farm Credit System. The System is operated as a cooperative under the supervision of the Farm Credit Administration, an independent government agency located in Washington, D.C. The Farm Credit Administration consists of the Federal Farm Credit Board, the Governor, and staff. The Board is made up of 13 members, one from each of the 12 Farm Credit Districts in this country, and one appointed by the Secretary of Agriculture. The 12 district representatives are appointed for six-year terms by the President of the United States and must be approved by the U.S. Senate. The Board appoints a governor to direct the operations of the Farm Credit Administration and also to act on policy directives for the Farm Credit System as a whole. The governor of the Farm Credit Administration and staff are responsible for the examination and supervision of the System. A field staff of examiners checks the records of local associations to see that their policies and lending practices are consistent with the System's regulations. Other staff are responsible for funding and administrative activities.

As Figure 17.2 suggests, there are 12 district Federal Land Banks (FLBs), 12 district Federal Intermediate Credit Banks (FICBs), and 12 dis-

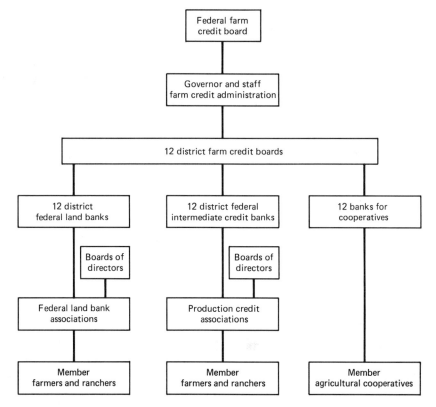

Figure 17.2 *Organizational structure of Farm Credit System.* The Farm Credit System consists of 12 districts, each of which contains a Federal Land Bank, a Federal Intermediate Credit Bank, and a Bank for Cooperatives. A cooperative wholly owned by its member-borrowers, the Farm Credit System is directed by the Federal Farm Credit Board and supervised by the Farm Credit Administration located in Washington, D.C.

trict Banks for Cooperatives (BCs). There also is a Central Bank for Cooperatives located in Denver, which acts as a clearinghouse on loan funds for those district Banks for Cooperatives experiencing temporary surpluses or shortages of funds. There are 494 Federal Land Bank Associations (FLBAs) and 424 Production Credit Associations (PCAs) located through the 12 districts.

The Farm Credit System is controlled largely by its member borrowers through their elected representatives. Members in each FLBA and PCA holding voting stock (borrowers must purchase either voting stock or participation certificates equal to a certain percentage of the amount of the loan at the time the loan is made) and elect a board of directors. The District Farm Credit Board is comprised of seven members; two are elected by PCA borrowers, two are elected by FLBA borrowers, two are elected by BC borrowers, and one is appointed by the governor of the Farm Credit Administration.

Regulatory Environment

The FLBs, FLBAs, FICBs, PCAs, and BCs are private organizations that are completely owned by their member-borrowers. Each operates under a federal charter, the Farm Credit Act of 1971 and subsequent amendments. As indicated above, these lending cooperatives operate under the supervision of the Farm Credit Administration, which sees to it that the System complies with the Act's regulations.

The Farm Credit Act of 1971 and subsequent amendments lay out specific operating guidelines for the System. These guidelines include regulations regarding the size of loans, term of loans, and valuation of collateral, among other things. For example, FLB loans can be written for maturities ranging from 5 to 40 years. The size of the loan cannot exceed 85 percent of the real estate offered as security. FLBs also can accept only first mortgages on real estate.

The FLBs and FLBAs are exempt from usury ceilings enacted by state governments on loans made to individuals. The FLBs and FLBAs are also exempt from all federal, state, and local taxes, except on the real estate they hold. Life insurance companies argue that this enables FLBs to lower their interest rates by ½ to 1 percent, thereby forcing other lenders to lower their interest rates on loans to compete effectively. These companies also point to the fact that FLB interest rates are exempt from state usury laws, whereas life insurance company loans are not. This helps explain some of the substitution noted between the market shares of FLBs and life insurance companies noted in Table 17.1. The FLBs, however, feel their tax-exempt status is justified because they must operate in uneconomical areas where profit-oriented lenders may choose not to serve.

PCAs are also exempt from state usury laws, but they are subject to federal income taxation. Finally, although the FICBs are not subject to income taxation, they must pay property taxes on their holdings of real estate and other property.

Source of Loanable Funds

The Farm Credit System obtains loanable funds by selling *system-wide bonds* and *discount notes* in the nation's financial markets through the System's fiscal agency located in New York City. The system-wide bonds are sold through a nationwide network of securities dealers. These bonds have maturities ranging from six months to 20 years and are issued in $1,000 amounts or multiples thereof. The discount notes are sold to a limited number of dealers in New York City for maturities ranging from 5 to 270 days in denominations of $50,000, $100,000, $1,000,000, and $5,000,000. The dealers identified above may either hold these securities for their own portfolios or sell them to the general public. Because these dealers *guarantee* to make a market for the System's bonds and notes, the System is ensured of a reliable source of loanable funds, even in periods of tight money.

The major buyers of these bonds and notes are commercial banks. Other large buyers include state and local governments, life insurance companies, and pension funds. The proceeds from the sale of these bonds and notes are then distributed to each district FLB, FICB, and BC as illustrated in Figure 17.3. The district FICBs then distribute these funds to the PCAs, who lend directly to the borrower. The district FLBs make the loan to borrowers, with the FLBAs processing the necessary paperwork. The district BCs lend directly to agricultural cooperatives.

OTHER LENDERS

The remainder of the lenders providing loan funds to farm businesses have unique and often fluctuating commitments to financing this sector. We can

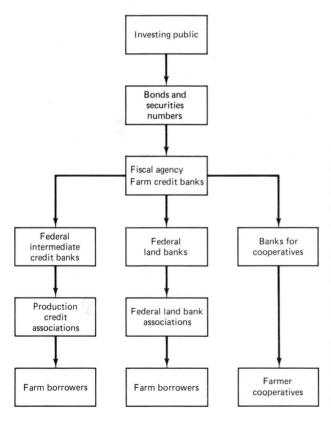

Figure 17.3 *Distribution of proceeds from bonds and notes.* The loan funds supplied to farm borrowers and farmer cooperatives by the Farm Credit System are obtained by the sale of consolidated system-wide bonds to the investing public. These funds are then distributed to the district bank according to their initial requests. The Production Credit Associations (PCAs) and Federal Land Bank Associations (FLBAs) represent the local contact point for loan requests by farmer borrowers, while farmer cooperatives deal directly with their district Bank for Cooperatives.

categorize these lenders into two groups: (1) other private lenders, and (2) government lending agencies. The lenders in each group are discussed below.

Other Private Lenders

The remaining nonpublic lenders providing loan funds to farm businesses include life insurance companies, merchants and dealers, and individuals. Collectively, these lenders are shown in Table 17.1 to have achieved a 17 percent market share for non-real estate loans and a 43 percent market share for real estate loans in 1981.

Life insurance companies. Life insurance companies are an important supplier of real estate loan funds to specific categories of farm businesses and regions of the country. Life insurance companies tend to focus their lending efforts on large farm businesses. At least one company reportedly will not make a real estate loan for less than $250,000. The average-size life insurance company loan in recent years has been two to three times the average-size Federal Land Bank loan. Although relatively inactive in the Northeast part of the country, life insurance companies have relatively high market shares in the Corn Belt as well as in the southern and western parts of the country. Their market shares range all the way from zero percent in Rhode Island and Alaska to roughly 30 percent in such states as Arizona and Nevada. The five highest states in terms of the dollar volume of life insurance company farm debt outstanding in 1981 were California, Texas, Illinois, and Nebraska, in that order.

Farm mortgages traditionally account for 2 to 3 percent of the total investments made by life insurance companies. These companies compare the returns, safety, and liquidity of farm mortgages with the features of their other opportunities when selecting which investments to make. Most life insurance company loans are first mortgages to finance the purchase of farmland. It is not uncommon for commercial banks to "originate" a loan for a life insurance company if it is unable to make the loan itself. The bank merely serves as a middleman. The life insurance company decides on the merits of the loan and supplies the loan funds. Their primary source of loanable funds are the life and health insurance premiums paid by their policyholders and annuity payments by private pension plans and individual retirement plans.[5] Other sources include the investment income received by life insurance companies from their holdings of government and corporate securities.

The market shares accounted for by life insurance companies are therefore influenced by the feasibility of their other investment opportunities. Another factor affecting their market share is the presence of usury ceilings

---

[5] An annuity is a life insurance contract under which the insured receives a specified periodic payment for the remainder of his or her life or for a stated number of years.

in periods of high interest rates. These ceilings regulate the maximum rates these companies can charge on loans to individuals (remember, we stated earlier that Federal Land Banks are not affected by these laws). If these companies can make a higher return on another investment than that permitted by these usury ceilings, we would expect their market share in farm loans to decline.

Finally, life insurance company activities are regulated by specific agencies within state governments (usually termed departments of insurance). Many states, for example, regulate the maximum size of loan made by life insurance companies to a specific percentage (e.g., 75 percent) of the appraised value of the farmland being financed. Many life insurance companies set a self-imposed maximum loan *per acre* that it will lend in a particular area.

Merchants and dealers.   Captured in the "Individuals and others" category in Table 17.1, merchants and dealers often use financing as a means to help sell their products. Financing normally is offered when farm businesses acquire feed, seed, fertilizer, chemicals, machinery, and many other inputs. Credit from merchants selling annual operating inputs (e.g., fertilizer, chemicals, fuel) is generally extended using an *open account.* This allows farm businesses to charge purchases of thse inputs instead of paying cash. The merchant then bills the farm business at a future date (normally after 30 days). This form of credit may be in short supply during periods of tight money or when supplies of the input are scarce (i.e., when credit programs are not needed to move inventories).

Many manufacturers of farm machinery and structures have established credit subsidairies which supply credit through their dealers. The term of these loans is often longer than the terms available from other lenders, but the interest rates are normally higher as well.

The source of these loanable funds vary. Local merchants may arrange for financing with a local bank, while the funds extended by dealers may have originated with the issuance of bonds by the parenting manufacturing company.

Individuals.   Often, sellers of farmland and other farming assets provide credit to the producers purchasing these assets. Sometimes these transactions are merely sales among relatives. Sellers disinvesting from farming normally provide real estate financing in two major ways: (1) installment land contracts, and (2) mortgages. The installment land contract is the more popular of the two. Frequently, the buyer can acquire farmland with a lower down payment under a land contract than conventional lenders would require. Use of a land contract also affords the seller certain tax advantages. Finally, buyers and sellers can negotiate the possibility for a lower interest rate (which helps the buyer) in exchange for a higher sales price (which benefits the seller).

Government Lending Agencies

There are three agencies that provide loan funds to farm businesses: the Farmers Home Administration, the Commodity Credit Corporation, and the Small Business Administration. Some of these agencies also provide financial assistance to rural businesses and communities when funds from private sources are unavailable.

Farmers Home Administration.   The Farmers Home Administration (FmHA) is an agency of the U.S. Department of Agriculture. It provides financial assistance to farm businesses in three ways: (1) grants, (2) insured loans, and (3) guaranteed loans. Grants are direct government subsidies to the recipient and represent a very small proportion of the total funding providing by FmHA. Insured loans, on the other hand, constitute about 85 percent of the total funds provided by FmHA. These are loans made and directly serviced by this agency. Finally, guaranteed loans are not loans made by the FmHA, but rather, represent FmHA guarantees against default on loans to farm businesses made by *other* lending institutions.

The loanable funds required to finance these FmHA programs are acquired from two major sources: (1) congressional appropriations, and (2) the sale of certificates of beneficial ownership (CBOs). Most of its funding is provided by sales of CBOs. CBOs are purchased by the Federal Financing Bank, an agency of the U.S. Treasury, which in turn raises funds through the sale of Treasury notes and bonds in the nation's money markets.

The FmHA offers a variety of programs. For example, farm ownership loans can be made up to $200,000 (insured loan) or $300,000 (guaranteed loan) for a term of as long as 40 years. This agency also makes farm operating loans which can be used to finance the purchase of livestock, machinery, and other production inputs. These loans may not exceed $100,000 (insured loan) or $200,000 (guaranteed loan) and can be made at subsidized rates of interest under specific conditions. To be eligible for either of these loan programs, producers must prove that (1) they are unable to obtain sufficient credit elsewhere at reasonable rates and terms, (2) they are a citizen of the United States, (3) they have sufficient training/experience to ensure the success of the operation, and (4) they are or plan to become the operator of a family farm business.[6] FmHA can also provide farm loans to producers in areas hard hit by either a natural or an economic disaster. This requires either the President or Secretary of Agriculture to designate the area as a disaster area eligible for emergency loans.

Commodity Credit Corporation.   The Commodity Credit Corporation (CCC) is a federally chartered corporation in the U.S. Department of Agri-

---

[6] Once the borrower has advanced to the point where other lenders are willing to provide adequate financing, the borrower must refinance, thereby graduating from FmHA.

culture. Its purpose is to support prices for certain farm commodities and to provide interim financing so that farmers are not required to sell their product at harvest time. The CCC makes two types of loans to farm businesses: *nonrecourse loans* and *recourse loans.* Nonrecourse CCC loans are available on a wide variety of products. At the option of the borrower, the product can be forfeited as full payment of principal and interest on the loan. For example, if the "loan rate" on corn is $2.40 and the current market price for corn is only $2.20, the farmer would want to forfeit his product as payment in full for the loan (i.e., exercise the nonrecourse feature of the program). If the current market price was $2.70, however, the borrower would want to sell his crop and pay off the loan. Farm businesses can also obtain CCC recourse loans to finance the purchase of storage and drying facilities on the farm. Such a loan *cannot* be repaid by forfeiting current production, but rather must be retired through conventional means.

Small Business Administration.   The Small Business Administration (SBA) is also a federal agency. It has a brief history in providing financial assistance to farmers and farm-related firms. Most SBA lending activity in agriculture has been in helping farmers overcome natural disasters. The SBA has supported the elimination of their authority to make loans to farm businesses provided that comparable lending authority is granted to FmHA.

SUMMARY

The purpose of this chapter is to provide a historical perspective on the relative market shares achieved by lenders supplying loan funds to farm businesses and discuss the environment in which they operate. The major points made in this chapter may be summarized as follows:

1. The Farm Credit System is the largest supplier of loan funds to farm businesses. Commercial banks are also a significant supplier of loan funds, but they tend to concentrate their lending efforts on short- and intermediate-term loans.
2. Both the Farm Credit System and commercial banking system are regulated by one or more authorities, which, among other things, limit the maximum loan size per customer. These two lenders acquire their loanable funds in different ways, however. While commercial banks depend largely on deposits for their lending base, the Farm Credit System obtains its funding needs by selling debt instruments (bonds and notes) to a network of securities dealers, who in turn sell them to the investing public.
3. The Farm Credit System has certain legal features (e.g., exemption from state usury laws) that other lenders, such as life insurance com-

panies, argue give it an unfair advantage in making farm loans. This and other factors have caused the relative market shares of the different farm lender groups to shift during the post–World War II period.

4. Merchants and dealers, as well as farmers financing the sale of their assets, are also sources of debt financing to farm businesses.

5. In addition to these private lenders, several public agencies provide loan funds to farmers under specific circumstances. These include the Farmers Home Administration, the Commodity Credit Corporation, and the Small Business Administration.

DEFINITION OF TERMS

Financial intermediation: process of channeling funds and securities between savers and borrowers.

Loanable funds: pool of funds available for lending to borrowers.

Loan funds: funds lent to borrowers.

Real estate debt: debt outstanding on loans and secured by real estate (i.e., farm mortgage loans).

Non-real estate debt: debt outstanding other than that secured by real estate (e.g., chattel mortgage loans).

Financial intermediary: firm or institution that provides financial intermediation services (*see* financial intermediation).

National bank: bank that is chartered by the federal govenment.

State bank: bank that is chartered by a state government.

Branch banking: no specific constraints are placed on the geographical structure of the bank's property (*see* unit banking).

Limited branch banking: limitation placed on the geographical location of branches and/or the number of branches themselves.

Unit banking: each banking location is considered a separate business entity (no branch banking permitted).

Usury: concept of limiting the rate of interest charged on loans.

Federal funds market: an interbank market in which banks lend excess reserves to other banks on a extremely short term basis (e.g., 12 to 24 hours).

Farm Credit Administration: an independent government agency located in

Washington, D.C., which supervises the operation of the Farm Credit System.

Farm Credit System: a member-owned lending cooperative which consists of the Federal Land Bank System, the Federal Intermediate Credit Bank System, and the Banks of Cooperatives.

Open account: line of credit extended to businesses that charge purchases.

Farmers Home Administration: an agency of the U.S. Department of Argiculture which provides financing assistance to farmers in the form of grants, insured loans, and guaranteed loans.

Commodity Credit Corporation: a federally chartered corporation in the U.S. Department of Agriculture whose purpose is to support prices through its nonrecourse loan program (see Chapter 10).

REFERENCES

BARRY, PETER J., JOHN A. HOPKIN, and C. B. BAKER, *Financial Management in Agriculture,* 2nd ed., Danville, Ill.: The Interstate Printers and Publishers, 1979.

ADDITIONAL READINGS

PENSON, JOHN B., JR., and DAVID A. LINS, *Agricultural Finance: An Introduction to Micro and Macro Concepts.* Englewood Cliffs, N.J.: Prentice-Hall, Inc., 1980.

PENSON, JOHN B., JR., DANNY A. KLINEFELTER, and DAVID A. LINS, *Farm Investment and Financial Analysis.* Englewood Cliffs, N.J.: Prentice-Hall, Inc., 1982.

QUESTIONS

1. Describe the role that lenders play in linking the funds provided by savers with the borrowing needs of farmers.

2. Which lender represents the largest source of real estate loans to farmers? Non-real estate loans?

3. What are the essential differences between branch banking and unit banking? Which is the more widely practiced form of bank structure?

4. How does the Farm Credit System obtain its loanable funds?

5. In addition to commercial banks and the Farm Credit System, what other private lenders service farmers' borrowing needs?

6. Describe the loan programs designed for farmers by agencies of the federal government. Why are these agencies needed, given the numerous private lenders servicing the borrowing needs of farmers?

ADVANCED TOPICS

Reference was made in this chapter to usury laws, which limit the interest rates life insurance companies and other private lending institutions can charge on loans to individuals. The term "usury" suggests lending money at "unreasonable" prices. Usury laws have been with us since biblical times. The Bible, for example, states that "Unto a stranger thou mayst lend upon usury; but unto thy brother thou shalt not lend upon usury" (Deuteronomy 23:19–20). The philosopher Aristotle felt that "breeding of money from money" (i.e., charging interest on loans) was unnatural.

A popular misconception on the part of some is that usury laws benefit borrowers in general. Recently, legislation calling for a national usury ceiling was proposed. The purpose of this section is to examine the economics of usury laws and to determine who benefits from them.

Equilibrium Interest Rate

Let the demand for loan funds be represented by the DD curve in panel a of Figure 17.4, and let the supply of loan funds be represented by the SS curve. The demand curve is downward sloping, reflecting the fact that the quantity of loan funds demanded will increase if the interest rate declines. The supply curve, on the other hand, is upward sloping, reflecting the fact that lenders

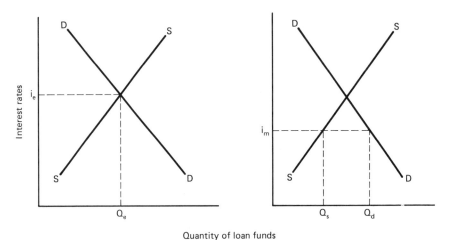

Quantity of loan funds

Figure 17.4 *Demand and supply of loan funds and the effects of a usury ceiling.* The imposition of usury ceilings on a loan funds market distorts the free-market interest rate (i_e) and creates a market disequilibrium. At the ceiling of i_m, borrowers will wish to borrow quantity Q_d, while lenders will wish to supply only Q_s. Thus, although the lower interest rate (i_m) may appear to do borrowers a favor, a usury ceiling will create a shortage in the market equal to Q_d-Q_s.

will prefer to supply a greater quantity of loan funds at higher interest rates. The equilibrium quantity of loan funds demanded would be Q_e and the equilibrium interest rate would be i_e. At higher interest rates, lenders would be willing to supply more loan funds than Q_e, but borrowers would demand less than Q_e.

Effects of Usury Ceiling

Now let us impose a legal maximum interest rate of i_m, as shown in panel b of Figure 17.4. At this interest rate, there would be an excess quantity demanded equal to $Q_d - Q_s$. That is, borrowers would want to borrow Q_d at this interest rate, while lenders would only be willing to supply quantity Q_s.

How will this disequilibrium situation be resolved? Lenders will look for ways to get around the ceiling, such as by charging specific fees at loan closings. They will also look for ways to reduce their operating costs, such as by making fewer but larger loans (which would cut their costs per dollar lent). Life insurance companies may reduce the number of local field representatives and perhaps rely more on participating with banks in making a loan. Efforts to cut costs will shift the SS curve to the right and thereby reduce the magnitude of the excess demand initially observed. Borrowers, on the other hand, will seek to borrow loan funds from those lenders who are not restricted by the maximum interest rate. An example in agriculture is the Farm Credit System, which is exempted from usury laws because of its federal charter. This action will shift the demand curve DD in the restricted market to the left, further reducing the excess demand depicted in panel b. During periods of high interest rates during the sixties and seventies, we saw the Federal Land Bank's share of the farm real estate loan funds market increase at the same time that the share accounted for by life insurance companies declined. During this period, life insurance companies consolidated their loan offices and increased the value of their minimum-sized loans.

The larger borrower will therefore benefit from the usury ceiling. He will be able to obtain financing at the maximum interest rate. The smaller borrower, on the other hand, may have to seek financing from lenders who can charge market interest rates.

part V
AGRICULTURE AND THE WORLD ECONOMY

18

INTERNATIONAL AGRICULTURAL TRADE

The factors that influence the economic well-being of U.S. farmers have become increasingly international in nature during the past two decades. The economic and political events occurring in the United States and seemingly unrelated parts of the globe since then have transformed the world agricultural economy in fundamental ways.

The purpose of this chapter is to review the trends in trade flows of U.S. agricultural commodities, examine their significance to the U.S. economy and the farm business sector, and answer the important question of "Why all this trade?"

RECENT TRENDS IN AGRICULTURAL TRADE

Although many elements contribute to the agricultural transformation referred to above, several stand out. These are (1) the rising expectations of people around the world, (2) the role played by the United States in meeting these expectations, and (3) the increasing interdependencies in the world economy. Under normal circumstances, these developments would have been welcomed by most Americans. They served the economic, foreign policy, and humanitarian objectives of the United States. But the decade of the seventies and the experiences in the early eighties do not represent normal economic conditions.

Whether importing or exporting, all countries benefit from international agricultural trade. Agricultural products account for approximately one-fifth of our nation's total exports. Roughly 40 percent of these agricultural exports consist of grain and feed. One-half of our agricultural exports go to other developed economies. As emphasized in Chapter 10, U.S. farmers have a large stake in a strong export demand for their products, due to the elastic nature of this demand. A strong export demand may mean the difference between an increase in quantities marketed raising or lowering total farm revenue.

Rising Expectations

The rate of growth in world food production in the late sixties was greater than the rate of growth in international trade for raw food and fiber products. But since 1970, this relationship has been reversed. By the early eighties, international trade in raw food and fiber products was 140 percent more than what it had been in 1970, whereas world production of food and fiber was only 120 percent more than what it was in 1970. Among other things, this trend is an indication of growing food and fiber interdependence among the nations of the world. In numerous centrally planned and developing nations, imports have been growing faster than exports, while the opposite has been true in most industrialized countries. The drive for food self-sufficiency in some importing countries, however, has led to cutbacks in their imports of food and fiber.

Role of the U.S.

For the past 30 years, the role of the United States in world agricultural trade has been growing in importance. As population and food requirements increased, most of the world's nations have found it increasingly difficult to satisfy domestic demand from internal production. As a result, these food-deficit countries have had to look toward the major exporting nations, including the United States. In 1950, the United States exported 10 percent of all of the agricultural goods traded in world commerce. By the early eighties, the U.S. share of world agricultural trade had increased to 17 percent. Between 1960 and 1980, world agricultural trade increased by 100 percent, from 150 million metric tons to 300 million metric tons. During this period, grain as a component of total agricultural trade increased from 49 percent to 76 percent. As grain took a larger share of the volume and value of world trade, the U.S. share rose. In 1970, the United States exported one-half of all the world's grain. By the early eighties, this figure had reached almost 60 percent before dropping slightly again in 1985.

As indicated in Table 18.1, the dollar value of U.S. agricultural exports increased from $6.9 billion in 1970 to $40.5 billion in 1980—an almost sixfold increase. Nonagricultrual exports also increased fivefold during the same period. U.S. agricultural exports reached a record level of $43.8 billion in 1981 before decreasing to $38 billion in 1984. The percentage that U.S. agricultural exports represent in total U.S. merchandise exports has remained relatively constant, however.

Grains and oilseeds together accounted for 66 percent of the total value of exports by the United States in 1983–1984. The growing importance of grains is in large part a response to increased demands for more grain-fed animal protein in the diets of the Japanese, Europeans, Soviets and more

	Agricultural exports	Nonagricultural exports	Total exports	Percentage that agricultural is of total
1970	$ 6,958	$ 34,337	$ 41,295	17
1971	7,955	35,928	43,883	18
1972	8,242	36,633	44,875	18
1973	14,984	47,759	62,743	24
1974	21,608	68,823	90,431	24
1975	21,854	82,180	104,034	21
1976	22,760	88,520	111,280	21
1977	23,974	94,311	118,285	20
1978	27,290	103,906	131,196	21
1979	31,975	135,631	167,606	19
1980	40,480	173,500	214,000	19
1981	43,780	185,426	229,206	19
1982	39,092	176,311	215,403	22
1983	36,099	159,870	195,969	18
1984	37,825	174,232	212,057	19

Source: U.S. Foreign Agricultural Trade Statistical Report, Fiscal Year, 1982, USDA, ESCS, *Business Conditions Digest,* Department of Commerce, October 1982.

TABLE 18.1 VALUE OF U.S. FOREIGN TRADE. Both agricultural and nonagricultural exports expanded substantially during the seventies and early eighties as illustrated here in billions of current dollars. Agricultural exports reached almost one-fourth of total U.S. exports during 1973–1974, which reflects the effects of the "Russian wheat deal."

recently dynamic middle-income countries such as Taiwan and Korea. Livestock and cotton are also important, accounting for approximately 10 and 6 percent, respectively, of the total value of U.S. agricultural exports. Even though grain dominates the value and volume of U.S. agricultrual exports, the greatest percentage increases during the 1976–1984 period were in livestock, cotton, and oilseed products.

The export market has increasingly become a growth market for domestic raw food and fiber production. A slowdown in population growth and achievement of relatively high per capita income and consumption levels are limiting growth in the U.S. domestic food and fiber market. Table 18.2 shows that domestic use of wheat, corn, and soybeans increased by 20, 79, and 301 percent, respectively, between 1950 and 1980. Yet export placement for these commodities grew at the remarkable rates of 296, 2060, and 2875 percent, respectively, during this period. Corn provides an interesting but not abnormal example of this phenomenon. In 1950, the United States exported 4 percent of its corn production. By 1980, the United States ex-

Commodity	1950	Production (million metric tons) 1960	1970	1980	Percent increase from 1950 to 1980
Soybeans					
Production	8.1	15.1	30.7	48.3	496
Domestic use	7.4	12.1	22.4	29.7	301
Exports[a]	0.8	3.7	11.8	23.8	2875
Corn					
Production	70.2	99.2	105.5	164.1	134
Domestic use	69.9	86.0	101.0	124.8	79
Exports	3.0	7.4	13.1	64.8	2060
Wheat					
Production	27.7	36.9	36.8	64.3	132
Domestic use	18.8	16.1	21.0	22.6	20
Exports	9.3	17.8	20.2	36.9	296

[a] Does not include soybean meal, which amounted to 7.2 million metric tons exported in 1980.

Source: U.S. Foreign Agricultural Trade Statistical Report, Fiscal Year, 1980, USDA, ESCS, Outlook for U.S. Agricultural Exports, November 17, USDA World Food and Agricultural Outlook and Situation Board, and Business Conditions Digest, Department of Commerce, October 1980.

TABLE 18.2 DISAPPEARANCE OF SELECTED AGRICULTURAL COMMODITIES. The rising importance of foreign markets for the major U.S. crop commodities is illustrated in the table. The 1950–1980 period saw a declining proportion of soybean, corn, and wheat production going to domestic uses and an increasing proportion going to meet the export demand for these crops.

porting almost 40 percent of domestic corn production. It is important to note that domestic production for wheat, corn, and soybeans increased 132, 134, and 496 percent, respectively, during this 30-year period. This dramatic increase in domestic production, due largely to productivity gains, was not matched by growth in domestic consumption for grains and oilseeds. The slow rate of growth in the U.S. domestic demand during this 30-year period, accompanied by large gains in U.S. production and liberalization of government policies led to the enormous growth in export sales and an increasing interest in foreign market opportunities.

Increasing Interdependencies

U.S. producers of raw food and fiber products are becoming increasingly dependent on foreign markets as an outlet for their expanded production. As growth in agricultural production exceeds the growth of domestic demand for food and fiber, dependence on foreign markets becomes increas-

Commodity	Percentage of production exported	Commodity	Percentage of production exported
Sunflower seeds	72	Tobacco	39
Wheat	59	Corn	45
Almonds	74	Grain sorghum	50
Rice, milled basis	71	Lemons, fresh	21
Cotton	87	Soybeans	45

Source: Foreign Agricultural Trade of the United States FATUS, USDA, ESCS, Washington, D.C., 1985.

TABLE 18.3 IMPORTANCE OF EXPORT MARKETS FOR SELECTED AGRICULTURAL PRODUCTS. The importance of a strong export demand for agricultural products varies from commodity to commodity, as indicated above. Almost 87 percent of total U.S. cotton production in 1983–84 was exported compared to about 45 percent for corn and 21 percent for fresh lemons.

ingly apparent. Agricultural exports as a share of production increased throughout the seventies and early eighties. Harvested crop acreage going to export markets increased from 25 percent in 1970 to 34 percent in 1980. Table 18.3 shows, for example, that almost 80 percent of the sunflower seeds, 50 to 70 percent of wheat and almonds, and 60 percent of rice and cotton produced in the United States during 1980–1984 period were exported.

Increased dependence on foreign markets has made domestic markets more sensitive to world commodity supplies, competitor nations export policies, importing country economic and political behavior, and world commodity prices. This increase in price uncertainty and variability demands that the U.S. producer and participants in the exporting process be more concerned and informed about world demand–supply conditions, agricultural export policies, U.S. macroeconomic policies, and changing food and fiber trade patterns. In general, the U.S. farm business sector has adapted well to the phenomenon of increased variability associated with increased exports. The instability of the early seventies was magnified by a number of unique events. These events included:

1. The collapse of the Bretton Woods international monetary system and the ensuing adjustments in which exchange rates ended an overvaluation of the dollar, which resulted in an increase in foreign demand for U.S. exports, including food and fiber.

2. A move toward a more market-oriented agriculture, including more flexible farm program policies.

3. Traditional customers (e.g., Japan and the European community) and

some new customers (e.g., China and the Soviet Union) insulate their domestic consumers from world market prices, transferring instability to the international markets and in turn to countries that were more open to market forces.

The initial shock of these three forces has not been registered in the U.S. export sector's "learning curve." Later in this chapter and in Chapter 19, the international monetary exchange rate and domestic agricultural policy aspects of these shocks will be dealt with in greater detail. In the remainder of this section we concentrate on understanding some of the changes taking place in world agricultural trade patterns.

Trade flows for U.S. agricultural exports changed significantly during the seventies. Table 18.4 shows, for example, that Asia and Western Europe, followed by Latin America and Eastern Europe, are the leading regional markets for U.S. raw food and fiber products. All regional markets increased

	1970		1980	
Region	Value	Percent of U.S. exports	Value	Percent of U.S. exports
Western Europe	$2.369	35.2	$12,569	31.0
Eastern Europe	0.133	2.0	2.449	6.0
Soviet Union	0.017	0.3	1.457	3.6
Asia	2.452	36.5	14.298	35.2
Japan	1.089	16.2	5.775	14.3
China	0.000	0.0	1.957	4.8
Other	1.363	20.3	6.506	16.1
Canada	0.767	11.4	1.830	4.5
Africa	0.229	3.4	2.277	5.6
Latin America	0.649	9.7	5.482	13.5
Oceania	0.056	0.8	0.189	0.5
Other	0.050	0.7	—	—
TOTAL	6.721	100.0	40.480	100.0

Sources: USDA, Outlook for U.S. Agricultural Exports, November 17, 1980 and U.S. Foreign Agricultural Trade Statistical Report, Fiscal Year, Washington, D.C., December 1971.

TABLE 18.4 DESTINATION FOR U.S. AGRICULTURAL EXPORTS. Western Europe and selected Asian countries such as Japan represent the major importers of U.S. agricultural products. Japan, for example, imported $5.8 billion worth of U.S. agricultural products, or 14.3 percent of the total. Although a declining market, approximately one-third of the total value of U.S. agricultural products were imported by Western European countries.

their dollar value of agricultural imports from the United States during the 1970-1980 period, with the Soviet Union, China, Eastern Europe and Latin America making the largest percentage gains. The early eighties have seen China and Eastern Europe decrease from these earlier gains.

Asia showed a slight decline in share since 1970, from 36.5 to 35.2 percent. There were significant changes within the area. In 1980, China emerged as the fourth most important customer of U.S. agricultural products. The growing economies of Taiwan and South Korea also emerged as important commercial importers during the seventies and continued to do so in the early eighties.

Western Europe imported $12.6 billion in 1980, up from $2.4 billion in 1970, but showed a significant decline in market share during the seventies, down from 35 to 31 percent. Eastern Europe increased its share from 2 to 6 percent in the late seventies but had dropped to 2 percent again by 1982. Poland had become the major market in this area.

Mexico, the third largest importer of U.S. agricultural products by 1980, and Brazil led the growth experienced in Latin America during the seventies and early eighties.

The Soviet Union became a major agricultural trading partner of the United States during the seventies. Soviet imports at the beginning of the seventies were insignificant, but in 1980, even after the U.S. embargoed grains and oilseeds, the Soviets imported food and fiber valued at almost $1.5 billion. The distinguishing feature of Soviet imports from the United States is their extreme variability. This has been demonstrated by a decrease in Soviet imports from the U.S. in 1982, but record increases in 1983 and 1984.

The chronic inability of the agricultural sector of Africa to ease demand pressures necessitated a steady increase in the imports of basic foodstuffs. Egypt and Nigeria are the two largest importers of U.S. agricultural products in this area.

Canada remains one of our most important food importers. But Canada's relative importance as an importer of U.S. food and fiber decreased as its market share dropped from 11.4 percent during the seventies to 4.5 percent during the early eighties.

Another way of looking at the change in trade patterns is to divide the world into industrialized (developed), developing, and centrally planned economies. In the past fifteen years, the share of U.S. agricultural exports destined for the industrialized nations (Japan, Europe, and Canada) decreased from 63 percent to 50 percent. The centrally planned and developing countries have increased their market share from 2 to 33 percent, respectively, to more than 14 to 35 percent, respectively. China has also become a major purchaser of U.S. cotton in recent years. Another recent trend is the increase in agricultural imports, particularly grains, oilseeds, and cotton, by the major "takeoff" developing countries, such as South Korea, Taiwan and Mexico.

TRENDS IN TRADE PERFORMANCE

International trade is becoming increasingly important in the U.S. economy. The ratio of U.S. exports to the gross national product has risen steadily, from 4.2 percent in 1972 to 8.5 percent in 1980, declining slightly since then. The ratio of imports to GNP has climbed from 5.1 percent in 1972 to 10 percent in 1984.

The trade balance, particularly the merchandise trade balance, is a commonly used mesure of a country's overall trade performance. The merchandise trade balance is the difference between total revenues earned from exports and total spending on imports. When exports exceed imports, we have a *trade surplus;* when imports exceed exports we have a *trade deficit.* During the fifties and sixties, the United States generally enjoyed a moderate surplus in its merchanidse balance of trade. This trend was reversed during

Year	Merchandise exports	Merchandise imports	Merchandise trade balance	Agriculture trade balance
1960	$ 19.6	$ 14.6	$ 5.0	$ 1.0
1965	26.5	21.5	5.0	2.1
1970	42.5	39.9	2.6	1.5
1971	43.3	45.6	−2.3	1.9
1972	49.4	55.8	−6.4	2.9
1973	71.4	70.5	0.9	9.3
1974	98.3	1036.0	−5.3	11.7
1975	107.1	98.0	9.1	12.6
1976	114.7	124.1	−9.4	12.0
1977	120.2	1517.0	−31.5	10.2
1978	142.1	175.8	−33.7	14.6
1979	184.5	211.9	−27.4	18.0
1980	223.9	249.3	−25.4	23.9
1981	236.3	264.1	−27.8	26.6
1982	211.2	247.6	−36.4	21.4
1983	200.3	261.3	−61.1	19.9
1984	220.3	327.8	−107.4	18.5

Source: Federal Reserve Bank of St. Louis, "International Economic Conditions," various issues.

TABLE 18.5 TOTAL MERCHANDISE AND AGRICULTURAL TRADE BALANCE. While the United States has been running a trade deficit during most of the seventies and early eighties (i.e., the value of merchandise imported exceeds the value exported), we have seen a trade surplus for agricultural products. For example, total merchandise imported into the United States of $327.8 billion in 1984 exceeded the value of total merchandise exported of $220.3 billion. This represents a trade deficit of $107.4 billion. In contrast, agricultural exports exceeded agricultural imports in that year by $18.5 billion.

the seventies, and by 1982, the United States has registered its eighth consecutive yearly deficit of greater than $25 billion, as seen in Table 18.5.

Since 1970, the United States has experienced only two years in which it accumulated a merchandise trade surplus, 1973 and 1975. A number of factors have led to the deterioration of the U.S. merchandise balance: (1) the increased dependence of the United States on imported raw materials, particularly petroleum; (2) more rapid economic growth and technological advances in foreign countries than in the United States; (3) an exchange rate structure which gave a strong competitive advantage to foreign countries; (4) the adverse shift in the terms of trade of the United States since 1969; (5) a prevailing domestic orientation of U.S. firms and trade policy resulting in less emphasis on export markets compared to attitudes and policies in other exporting countires, and (6) foreign tariff and nontariff trade barriers which discriminate against some products in which the United States has a significant competitive advantage.

The performance of the U.S. agricultural trade sector during this same period was most impressive, however. When the balance of payments is constructed, the value of agricultural exports and imports is accounted for in the merchandise trade balance. During the seventies, agriculture registered increasingly significant trade surpluses as shown in Table 18.5. Since 1974 both export volumes and prices for agricultural exports have generally risen rapidly, pushing the value of agricultural exports to a record $43.8 billion in 1981, then decreasing to $37.8 billion in 1984. Although agricultural imports also increased significantly between 1973 and 1984, the increase was significantly less than the growth of exports. By 1984, the United States had a $18.5 billion surplus in its agricultural trade balance.

WHY ALL OF THIS AGRICULTURAL TRADE?

We have spent a considerable amount of time discussing the trends in world agricultural trade and the performance of the United States in international trade. Now let us examine the forces that influence the magnitude of these trade flows and discuss who gains from trade.

Determinants of Agricultural Trade

International commerce benefits a country because it allows nations to specilize in the production of those goods in which they are relatively more efficient and to take advantage of the more efficient production techniques of other countries by importing those products in which the country is not as productive. International trade also enables countries that are not well endowed with sufficient domestic quantities of essential raw materials for industrial and agricultural production to obtain these supplies from overseas.

The export of agricultural goods represents foreign demand for U.S. production and as such, depends on the overall level of economic activity in other nations. But U.S. cotton, hides, and other agricultural goods compete in those foreign markets with agricultural supplies from Argentina, Canada and many other food and fiber exporting countries as well as domestically produced agricultural products. The extent to which U.S. agricultural goods remain competitive in terms of both price and non-price factors will determine the share of U.S. commodities in foreign markets.

When goods are produced and sold in competitive markets, the price at which they sell in the international marketplace reflects in the long run the costs of the human, natural and manufactured resources used in the production of these products. There *are* market imperfections though, and differences between the production cost and the market price do occur. For example, some countries subsidize the export of commodities, like the European Economic Community does for wheat, where the export price is lower than the cost of resources used in their production. On the other hand, if the structure of a market permits (i.e., monopoly or cartel), it is possible to export a good for more than the production costs. The most common example of this type of discrepancy between production costs and market price in international trade is the crude oil market, where the 1984 U.S. import price averaged about $28 per barrel and the cost of production was less than $1 per barrel.

However, the price of most manufactured goods and agricultural commodities traded in international markets reflect production costs.[1] A nation will therefore be most competitive in those products it can produce at a relatively lower cost than other countries and least competitive in those goods that have a relatively higher cost in other countries.

The key concept in understanding the gains from international trade is the following: *Countries export those goods they are relatively most efficient in producing (those requiring least resources) and import those commodities they are relatively least efficient at producing.* By concentrating its production activities in those areas in which it is relatively most efficient, a country increases the amount of goods and services available for it to consume from its available resources than it would if it did not trade internationally.

It is important to remember that gains from trade do not depend on a nation being absolutely more efficient than other countries in producing some goods and absolutely less efficient in producing other goods. Rather, gains from trade occur when a country is *relatively* more efficient in the production of some goods than others. This concept is called the *law of comparative advantage.* An example will help us understand this elusive and somewhat counterintuitive concept.

Suppose that the world economy is comprised of two countries, Mexico and the United States. Each country produces two goods, tomatoes and

---

[1] Further exceptions to this statement will be discussed in Chapter 19.

wheat, and uses only one input (labor). International trade depends on domestic exchange ratios or *opportunity costs,* which can be defined in this context as *the output of one product sacrificed to produce more of another.* In Mexico, for example, the opportunity cost of producing one more bushel of wheat might be the sacrifice of 2 tons of tomato production. Let us further assume that the opportunity cost of producing 10 tons of wheat in the United States is 2 tons of tomato production. Thus the United States produces more wheat than Mexico for an equal sacrifice of tomatoes. Because the transfer of a unit of resources from tomato production to wheat production in these two countries involves unequal opportunity costs, trade could be mutually beneficial to both countries. Specialization and international trade could increase total world output even though one nation might be more efficient in producing both products, provided that the opportunity cost ratios associated with these two products differ between the two countries. So we have concluded that the concept of opportunity costs provides the basis for trade. For a clearer understanding, let's investigate further the concepts of absolute and comparative advantage.

Absolute Advantage

An absolute advantage exists if one country can produce a commodity *less expensively* than another. This is often possible because of differences between nations with respect to (1) natural, human, and manufactured resource endowments, such as climate, land area and quality, capital, and labor; (2) industrial organization; and (3) relative prices. Let's look at our example. Suppose that one resource unit (worker-day) in Mexico is being used to produce 3 tons of wheat and another worker-day is being used to produce 12 tons of tomatoes. For the United States, let us assume that one worker-day is being used to produce 15 tons of wheat and another worker-day is being used to produce 5 tons of tomatoes. Table 18.6 shows that total production in the two countries together equals 18 tons of wheat and 17 tons of tomatoes, or a total of 35 tons of raw food and fiber products when they do not trade. However, Mexico is more efficient in using a resource unit to produce tomatoes (one worker-day produces 12 tons of tomatoes compared to 5 in the United States) and less efficient in wheat production (3 tons compared to 15 in the United States per worker-day). Therefore, Mexico has an *absolute advantage* in tomato production and the United States has an absolute advantage in the production of wheat.

What would happen if these two nations specialized and traded wheat and tomatoes? By transferring one worker-day of labor from wheat to tomatoes in Mexico and one worker-day from tomatoes to wheat in the United States, total output in the two countries would increase. With Mexico producing only tomatoes and the United States only wheat, and if each nation uses two worker-day units, total output would be 24 tons of tomatoes (i.e.,

	Wheat (tons) Produced by 1 Man Day	Tomatoe (tons) Produced by 1 Man Day	Total
Before trade:			
Mexico	3	12	15
United States	15	5	20
Total	18	17	35
After trade:			
Mexico	0	24	24
United States	30	0	30
Total	30	24	54

TABLE 18.6 HYPOTHETICAL TRADE EXAMPLE FOR THE U.S. AND MEXICO. Specialization in production and subsequent international trade can benefit society. In the two-country example above, the U.S. has an absolute advantage in producing wheat (one man unit can produce 15 tons of wheat in U.S. as opposed to 3 tons in Mexico). Mexico, however, has an absolute advantage in tomatoes (one man unit can produce 12 tons of tomatoes in Mexico as opposed to only 5 tons in the U.S.). If both countries had only two man units available to producing these products, total output in Mexico would be 15 tons while total output in the U.S. would be 20 tons. If both countries specialized in producing what they have an absolute advantage in and traded with the other, the U.S. could produce 30 tons of wheat and Mexico could produce 24 tons of tomatoes. Thus, world output would jump from 35 tons to 54 tons—a gain of 19 tons of output.

2 resource units times 12 tons of tomatoes per unit) and 30 tons of wheat (i.e., 2 resource units times 15 tons of wheat per unit). By concentrating on their absolute advantages, these two nations together would increase the total output of the world economy by 19 tons (i.e., 54 tons – 35 tons). Thus under these circumstances, both nations could benefit from the opening of trade.

Comparative Advantage

The principle of comparative advantage explains how gains from trade are possible even when one nation can produce all products more efficiently than another because of differences in the opportunity costs among countries. Let's assume that the efficiency of tomato production in the United States suddenly increases such that a one-man day can now produce either 15 tons of wheat or 15 tons of tomatoes. We shall continue to assume that a one-man day in Mexico can produce either 3 tons of wheat or 12 tons of tomatoes. Thus, with two resource units available in each country and *no special-*

ization, world output would be 18 tons of wheat and 27 tons of tomatoes. You have probably already noticed that the United States has a greater productive capacity than Mexico in both commodities. The United States is 5 times (15 to 3) more efficient in producing wheat and 1.25 times (15 to 12) more efficient in producing tomatoes.

Because of the law of comparative advantage, it would be beneficial for each of these nations to specialize and trade (assuming no transportation costs). The United States's *greatest comparative advantage* would be in wheat and Mexico's *smallest comparative disadvantage* would be in tomatoes. By specializing on this basis, world output in this two-country example would still increase by 9 tons (i.e., 54 tons − 45 tons). *The key point to remember is that even if a nation has an absolute advantage in both products, total world output can be increased if the opportunity costs differ among countries.* Work through an example when the opportunity costs in two countries are equal to see if you completely understand this concept.

An Expanded Example

The key to the law of comparative advantage is that relative costs make specialization and trade a viable way of raising output. Let us continue to assume that the U.S. can produce 15 tons of wheat or 15 tons of tomatoes with one resource unit. Thus the relative cost ratio (i.e., ratio of the opportunity costs) in this instance would be 1:1. Let us also continue with our assumption that the only other country in the world is Mexico and that it can produce 3 tons of wheat or 12 tons of tomatoes with one resource unit. Thus its relative cost ratio would be 1:4. Remember that the basis for specialization, the law of comparative advantage, prevails when the relative costs (relative cost ratios) for two or more nations differ. Since the U.S. ratio is 1:1 is not the same as Mexico's ratio of 1:4, we know that total output could be increased by specialization and trade. Two final assumptions are required: (1) the production possibilities curves for wheat and tomatoes depicted in Figures 18.1 and 18.2 exist in the United States and Mexico, and (2) the United States has 10 resource units available for producing these products whereas Mexico has 20 resource units available.[2]

Production possibilities. If the United States used its 10 resource units to produce just wheat, it could produce 150 tons of wheat (i.e., 15 tons of wheat per resource unit times 10 units). This production possibility

---

[2] These figures assume a constant relative cost ratio (or marginal rate of product transformation using the terminology developed in Chapter 4) to keep matters simple. As such, these two production possibilities curves are directly comparable to the "perfectly substitutable outputs" case presented in panel b of Figure 4.7. This simplifying assumption allows us to avoid having to keep track of changing relative costs in our discussion which would have little or no effect on the validity of our conclusions.

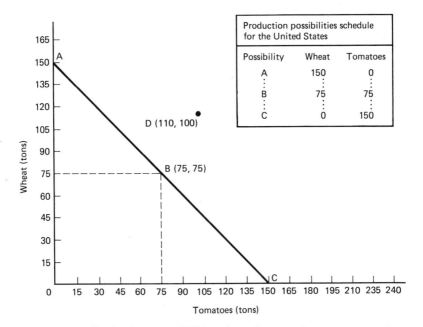

Figure 18.1 *Production possibilities for wheat and tomatoes in the United States.* If we assume that one-man unit can produce either 15 tons of wheat or 15 tons of tomatoes and that there are 10 man units available in the United States, then we can conclude that a maximum of 150 tons of wheat (point *A*) or 150 tons of tomatoes (point *C*) can be produced. Assuming a constant relative cost ratio, a line connecting points *A* and *C* would represent the country's production possibilities curve. Any point along line *AC*—such as point *B*—represents an efficient use of this nation's resources.

is denoted by point *A* in Figure 18.1. If all of these resources were instead used to produce tomatoes, the United States could produce 150 tons of tomatoes, which is denoted by point *C* in Figure 18.1. The United States could also efficiently produce any combination of these two commodities that lies on the production possibility curve *AC*. The slope of *AC* is equal to 1.0 (i.e., the relative cost ratio, where the cost of one additional ton of tomatoes in the United States is the sacrifice of 1 ton of wheat.

We already know that Mexico can produce 3 tons of wheat or 12 tons of tomatoes with one man unit. Since Mexico has 20 man units available, it can produce a maximum of 60 tons of wheat or 240 tons of tomatoes (points *O* and *Q* in Figure 18.2). Or it can efficiently produce any combination of wheat and tomatoes lying along the production possibility curve *OQ* in Figure 18.2. The slope of this curve is 0.25 (i.e., to increase wheat production by 1 ton, Mexico has to sacrifice 4 tons of tomatoes).

Figures 18.1 and 18.2 indicate that the United States has an absolute

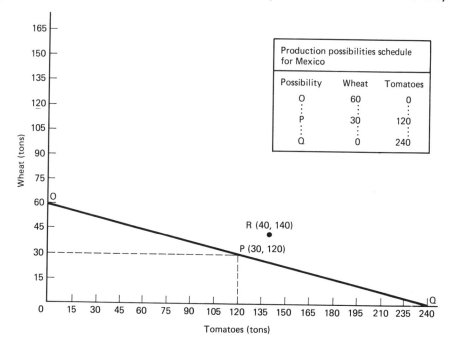

Figure 18.2 *Production possibilities for wheat and tomatoes in Mexico.*
Assuming that one man unit can produce either 3 tons of wheat or 12
tons of tomatoes in Mexico, we know that the maximum output of
wheat would be 60 tons (point *O*) and the maximum output of tomatoes would be 120 tons (point *Q*) if there are 20 man units of labor
available. Like Figure 18.1, a line connecting points *O* and *Q* accounts
for the nation's production possibilities curve under conditions of constant relative costs. Any point along this curve—like point *P*— represents
an efficient use of Mexico's resources.

advantage in both wheat and tomatoes as well as a comparative advantage in
wheat. Mexico has the smallest comparative disadvantage in tomatoes. Without international trade, supply and demand forces in each domestic economy
would determine the equilibrium price and quantity of both wheat and tomatoes. Let us assume that prices suggest the use of the 10 man units in the
United States (full employment of the nation's labor force) distributed
equally between the production of wheat and the production of tomatoes.
This allocation would lead to the production of 75 tons of wheat (5 man
units times 15 tons of wheat per man unit) and 75 tons of tomatoes (5 man
units time 15 tons of tomatoes per man unit). This product combination
is denoted by point *B* in Figure 18.1. Let us assume that Mexico's 20 man
units are also fully employed and divided equally between these two products. This would result in 30 tons of wheat (10 man units times 3 tons per
man unit) and 120 tons of tomatoes (10 man units times 12 tons per man

unit). This product combination is denoted by point P in Figure 18.2. Total world output would thus be equal to 105 tons of wheat (75 tons in the United States and 30 tons in Mexico) and 195 tons of tomatoes (75 tons in the United States and 120 tons in Mexico), as indicated on line 2 in Table 18.7.

We know that an opportunity for trade exists because of the differences between the relative cost ratios in these two countries (see line 1 in Table 18.7). We also know that the United States has the comparative advantage in the production of wheat, and Mexico has the smallest comparative disadvantage in the production of tomatoes. The two countries would therefore specialize accordingly. The United States would give up 1 ton of tomatoes to produce an extra ton of wheat, while Mexico would forgo 1 ton of wheat to produce 4 extra tons of tomatoes. The United States would therefore produce 150 tons of wheat and Mexico would produce 240 tons of tomatoes. Total world output would be 45 tons of wheat and 45 tons of tomatoes greater than it was before specialization and trade. If trade can be consummated, both nations would benefit. The key question now becomes: At what price do they trade or, rather, *what will the terms of trade be?*

Item	United States	Mexico	Total
1. Relative cost ratio of wheat *(W)* to tomatoes *(T)*	1:1	1:4	2:5
2. Before trade production and consumption of wheat and tomatoes	$75W + 75T$	$30W + 120T$	$105W + 195T$
3. Production after specialization	$150W + 0T$	$0W + 240T$	$150W + 240T$
4. Exports	$40W$	$100T$	
5. Imports	$100T$	$40W$	
6. Total consumption	$110W + 100T$	$40W + 140T$	$150W + 240T$
7. Gains from trade	$35W + 25T$	$10W + 20T$	$45W + 45T$

TABLE 18.7 PRODUCTION AND CONSUMPTION BEFORE AND AFTER TRADE. The difference between the relative cost ratios for the United States and Mexico suggests that it is in the best interest of both countries to specialize in "what they do best" and trade with each other. By growing only wheat and exporting 40 tons to Mexico in exchange for 100 tons of tomatoes increases total consumption of both products over what it was before trade. Point D in Figure 18.1 lies above the U.S. production possibilities curve, reflecting the totals on line 6 above. Mexico also gains from trade. Point R in Figure 18.2 lies above Mexico's production possibilities curve as well. It also reflects the totals on line 6 in the table. Finally, this two-country world is 45 tons of wheat and 45 tons of tomatoes better off than before, as shown in the "total" column on line 7.

Terms of trade.   The domestic opportunity costs in each nation set the upper and lower limits to the terms of trade. For example, the upper price limit for wheat is Mexico's relative cost ratio of 4 tons of tomatoes for 1 ton of wheat, whereas the lower price limit for wheat is the U.S. ratio of 1 ton of tomatoes for 1 ton of wheat. The maximum possible gain for Mexico from exporting tomatoes to the United States is obtained by importing of 4 tons of wheat in exchange for 4 tons of tomatoes. Mexican exports of 1 ton of tomatoes can finance imports of 1 ton of wheat, whereas domestic production of 1 ton of wheat in Mexico costs 4 tons of tomatoes. *This would benefit Mexico and leave the United States no worse off than if it produced its own tomatoes.* On the other hand, if the United States could export 1 ton of wheat in exchange for 4 tons of tomatoes, *it would benefit significantly while Mexico would be no worse off than if it produced its own wheat and tomatoes.*

The equilibrium terms of trade will lie somewhere between the two limits set by each nation's domestic opportunity costs. The relative strengths of the demand forces in these two countries for tomatoes and wheat will play a key role in determining the final terms of trade. Trade terms will favor Mexico if tomatoes are in greater demand than wheat, and vice versa.

Let us assume that trade opens at an exchange ratio of 2 tons of wheat to 5 tons of tomatoes and that each specializes according to its comparative cost advantage. This would result in the United States producing 150 tons of wheat and exporting 40 tons of this wheat to Mexico in exchange for 100 tons of tomatoes. Mexico, on the other hand, would produce 240 tons of tomatoes and export 100 tons of these tomatoes to the United States in exchange for 40 tons of wheat (see lines 3, 4, and 5 in Table 18.7). The U.S. consumption of wheat and tomatoes would rise to point *D* in Figure 18.1, where it would be consuming 110 tons of wheat and 100 tons of tomatoes (see line 6 in Table 18.7). Both levels exceed the amounts consumed in the United States before specialization and trade (35 tons more wheat and 25 tons more tomatoes) and exceeds the country's current productive capacity. Mexico's consumption would increase from 30 to 40 tons of wheat and 120 to 140 tons of tomatoes (point *R* in Figure 18.2), for a net gain of 10 tons of wheat and 20 tons of tomatoes. This again exceeds this country's productive capacity.

The example above worked through a very simple and abstract case of comparative advantage. The subsequent discussion moves us closer to the real world. The normal operation of the price mechanism would move resources into production and the export of those products in which the nation has a comparative advantage and out of those traded goods in which it does not. This assumes, of course, that there are no distortions caused by government intervention. This is especially true when the comparative advantage of a nation changes over time; some industries may become "uncompetitive," causing domestic production in these industries to decline.

Other domestic industries normally will be expanding sufficiently to absorb the labor and capital released from the declining industries.

Often, however, adjustment problems arise in transferring those resources into industries in which the nation's comparative advantage and competitiveness are increasing, resulting in short-run unemployment for some of the factors of production in the declining industries. This has happened in the steel, textile, and automobile industries in the United States in the early eighties. In agriculture, the production of sugar and some manufactured dairy products are under the same pressure. Although it is usually futile and economically wasteful to resist the transfer of resources out of industries declining in competitiveness, the United States provides some forms of compensation and assistance to the owners of unemployed resources.

The final question that needs to be answered, then, is: What determines the relative efficiency with which nations produce goods? In general, nations tend to be most efficient in those products that require the largest proportion of resources—labor, capital, land, entrepreneurial skills, and technology—that they posses in relatively the largest amounts. For example, countries with very large quantities of labor and little capital and scientific skills will tend to be "relatively" more efficient in the production of goods that intensively utilize large amounts of unskilled or semiskilled labor, such as footwear, apparel, and simple consumer electronics.

Although the United States possesses large quantities of all types of labor and capital, its most abundant factors of production are its supplies of highly skilled labor, technological and entrepreneurial skills, and its natural resources, combined with highly favorable climate conditions. It would be expected, then, that the United States would have a comparative advantage in products where these factors are intensively employed. The results of a recent Department of Labor study verify that the United States does have a comparative advantage in capital-intensive and high-skilled labor economic activities. These factors have led the United States to have large trade surpluses in three product categories: capital equipment goods, high-technology products (many of which are also capital godos), and agricultural products. Continued adaptation of new technology and adherence to the concept of comparative advantage are major sources of real productivity growth in an economy, and productivity growth in agriculture as well as other sectors of the economy is the source of continued improvement in our standard of living.

Productivity and Agricultural Exports

As you will recall from Chapter 2, productivity is defined as a measure of output (e.g., wheat) per unit of some input (e.g., labor). There are other measures of productivity, but the use of labor productivity is the most common. Increases in labor productivity generally indicate that (1) more capital per worker is used in production (an example in farming might be the investment in tractors with greater horsepower), (2) technological improvements (such as the adoption of hybrid seeds) have caused an increase in the output derived from given amounts of labor and capital inputs, and (3) the quality and quantity of some other input has increased (such as fertilizer, irrigation, or agricultural chemicals). All three of these factors have contributed to increased productivity in agriculture.

Figure 18.3 illustrates the effects that a technological advancement which doubles the amount of wheat that can be grown with the resources currently available would have on Mexico's production possibilities curve in the hypothetical example used earlier. This change may have been the result of a new seed variety of wheat that now allows producers to double their yields. The new production possibilities curve would now be *NQ* instead of *OQ*.

In the United States, the average annual growth rates of productivity

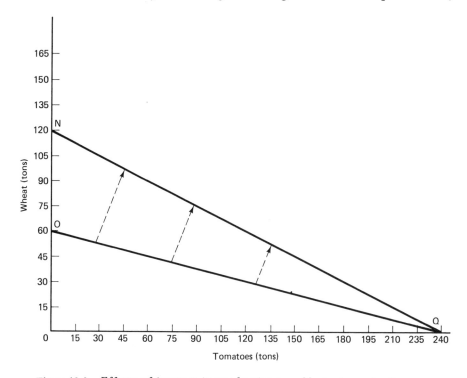

Figure 18.3 *Effects of increase in productivity on Mexico's production possibilities curve.* Let us assume that Mexico can suddenly grow twice as much wheat per man unit as it could before in Figure 18.2. That is, it can now raise 6 tons of wheat per man unit instead of 3 tons. This would cause this country's production possibilities curve to shift upward from line *OQ* to line *NQ* as illustrated above.

vary considerably among the various sectors. In a recent Trade Polcy Staff Committee Study, it was estimated that agriculture's labor productivity was led by an annual average increase 7.3 percent in cotton, 7 percent in poultry and dairy, 5.8 percent in food and feed grains, and 5.3 percent in the meat and livestock sectors. In contrast, the average annual growth rate of labor productivity in overall manufacturing was only 2.9 percent during this period.

These productivity gains led to an increase in agricultural production which the domestic U.S. food and fiber markets were unable to absorb. Nevertheless, expanding world demand and the shift toward a one-price domestic commodity policy in the early seventies permitted the United States to channel this production into export markets.

WHO GAINS FROM U.S. AGRICULTURAL TRADE?

In Chapter 19 we will examine the welfare aspects of international trade policies and examine in more depth the impact of these policies on the economic well-being of producers and consumers. However, in this section we want to examine briefly some of the impacts of agricultural trade.

Employment Benefits of Agricultural Trade

An important benefit generated by export activity by the U.S. food and fiber system is in the employment area. In a recent USDA study, Schluter traced the impact of 1979's agricultural exports (value $34.7 billion, calendar year) through the U.S. economy. The study estimated that more than 1 million full-time jobs were related to agricultural exports in 1979. Of the 1 million jobs, nearly 500,000 workers—15 percent of the farm labor force—were employed in the production of food and fiber commodities for export. In the other segments of the U.S. food and fiber system, more than 630,000 jobs were directly or indirectly related to assembling, processing, and distributing agricultural commodities and products for export. Approximately 60,000 workers were employed in the food-processing sector, 300,000 in transportation and trade, 120,000 in other manufacturing sectors, and 150,000 in related services.

Income Benefits of Agricultural Exports

Additionally, agricultural exports generate output and income in other sectors of the economy. According to Schluter, of the $34.7 billion of the food and fiber products exported in 1979, the farm value of raw agricultural exports totaled $20.2 billion and the value of processed products, transportation, trade, and other services accounted for the remaining $14.5 billion. Furthermore, the sale of this $34.7 billion of agricultural exports produced additional spending power. This impact is created by the economic multiplier effect. This effect takes into account both direct (income going directly to farmers, ranchers, and providers of services directly involved in the export process) and indirect (income going to producers of goods and services that these farmers, ranchers, and providers of services purchased) impacts. For every dollar of agricultural exports sold by the United States in 1979, it is estimated that the sale actually added $2.05 to the U.S. economy. If we use this same multiplier for 1984, we would conservatively estimate that the $37.8 billion in farm exports in 1984 resulted in approximately $77.5 billion in total U.S. business activity. This additional $39.7 billion was distributed throughout various sectors of the economy. It is estimated that $10.0 billion went to farmers through farm-to-farm transactions, $3.0 billion to food processors, $12.5 billion to other manufacturing sectors, $3.2 billion for trade and transportation, and $10.9 billion for various other services. *It can be observed, then, that in recent years 75 cents of every additional dollar generated by food and fiber exports goes to* the nonfarm business sectors of the U.S. economy.

Agricultural exports have therefore had positive impacts on the U.S. economy in the form of increased income, more employment, and strengthening of the trade balance. But rising agricultural exports have produced some concerns, particularly among domestic food consumers.

Effects of Agricultural Exports on Food Prices

A concern of American consumers over expanded agricultural exports is that exports increase domestic food prices. Sudden increases in agricultural exports can augment commodity prices in the short run, and these higher prices eventually work their way through the marketing system and are reflected in grocery prices at the supermarket. However, this relationship between food and fiber exports and consumer food prices is much more complex than this common perception suggests.

A recent study focusing on the question "What would be the economic impact of a 50 percent increase in wheat exports?" provides an example of the complexity of this relationship. The results indicated that wheat prices would increase by approximately 43 percent over the two-year period from what they would have been otherwise. This was estimated to increase retail food prices by an average of 0.8 percent over the period due to increased prices of cereal and bakery products. Since the food category enters the Consumer Price Index with an approximate weight of 20 percent, the inflation rate in the economy would have increased by only 0.2 percent.

Consumers were shown to derive some benefits from this sharp increase in exports. For example, the increase in agricultural dollar exports reduced the U.S. net exports deficit by 52 percent. This improvement in the balance of trade, combined with increased purchases by farmers of tractors, cars, and other items stimulated by the 36 percent increase in farm income, more than offset the negative impacts from the increase in food prices. The net positive impact from the improved farm income and trade balance was estimated to boost employment by 20,000 and increase real GNP by 0.1 percent in the first year.

The relatively small increase in the overall inflation rate can be explained by the fact that the farm portion of the food prices consumers pay is quite small—one third on average. Approximately two-thirds of what consumers pay for food covers the costs of transportation, processing, packaging, wholesaling, and retailing of foodstuffs after they leave the farm gate.

Another factor that is generally not recognized when concern is generated about sudden and drastic increases in commodity prices is the point that Americans consume very little grain or oilseeds directly. Most grain reaches the dinner table as animal products made in part from feeding grain and protein meal. This indirect pattern of grain consumption softens the impact of grain price increases. A 10-cent-per-bushel increase in the price of corn, for example, increases the cost of producing beef less than 1 cent a pound. For poultry, a 10-cent increase in the price of corn would increase the cost of producing poultry by less than ½ cent per pound.

When discussing the relationship between exports and increased food prices, it is also important to distinguish between the short-run and long-run effects of higher commodity prices. A review of pricing commodity patterns shows that shortfalls in crop production caused by such factors as inclimate weather, cause sudden—but often temporary—increases in farm-level commodity prices. As stated previously, these higher farm prices are eventually reflected in higher retail food prices. Nevertheless, increased prices accomplish the important short-run tasks of allocating available supplies and stimulating increased production in the next growing season.

If, on the other hand, higher farm prices are caused by market forces that are viewed to be more-or-less permanent, their long-run effect on consumers may be beneficial. The likelihood of greater profitability caused by steadily rising export demand, for example, might induce producers to expand their operations and adopt the latest production practices. This, in turn, would mean greater efficiency and more output. Over a period of time, this may result in a relatively lower level of consumer spending on food. For example, between 1970 and 1980, the volume of agricultural exports increased 2.5 times, farm production efficiency rose steadily, and the share of consumer disposable income spent on food and nonalcoholic beverages consumed at home declined modestly. A recent USDA study estimates that in 1977, the latest year for which complete data were available for countries other than the United States, only 16.5 percent of U.S. private consumption expenditures went for food, tobacco, and beverages. This represents a continuation of a downward trend that has seen the share spent on food fall from 20 percent in 1965, to 18 percent in the early seventies, to 17 percent in 1976. More recent U.S. Department of Commerce data show that this share has dropped further, to 15.6 percent in 1982. Table 18.8 shows that the average share of disposable income spent on food by the

Country	National disposable income per capita (U.S. dollars)	Consumption expenditures on food, beverages, and tobacco (%)
United States	$7,666	16.5
Canada	7,482	21.0
Belgium	7,394	26.0
Switzerland	8,823	29.0
Finland	6,160[a]	35.0
Italy	3,440[a]	35.0
Greece	2,810[a]	40.0
Poland	3,150[a]	45.0
Soviet Union	3,020[a]	45.0
Portugal	1,890[a]	50.0
Jordan	710[a]	55.0
Sri Lanka	200[a]	65.0

[a]World Bank estimates for 1977.

Source: Arthur B. Mackie and Michael Allan, "U.S. Consumers Spend Less of Their Income on Food than the Rest of the World," *Foreign Agriculture,* November 1980

TABLE 18.8 SHARE OF DISPOSABLE INCOME SPENT ON FOOD. The United States is by far the leader in the lowest share of consumer disposable income spent on food. This is despite the fact that other nations, such as Switzerland, have a higher per capita disposable income. This reflects the efficiency and productivity of American farmers in meeting our nation's food and fiber needs.

U.S. consumer in 1977 was the lowest of any nation in the world, including nations, such as Switzerland, which have higher per capita incomes than we do in the United States.

COMPARATIVE ADVANTAGE AND THE U.S. DOLLAR

Although the principle of comparative advantage generally determines which products are exported and imported, the general competitiveness of a nation's exports also depends on the prevailing exchange rates and domestic money wages and prices compared to those in other countries producing and exporting similar products.

The relationship between the exchange rate and domestic prices is influenced by a variety of factors, including economic conditions in the United States and abroad, the response of policymakers to fluctuations in the exchange value of the dollar, and expectations of future economic and political events. These considerations complicate efforts to measure the inflationary/

deflationary impacts of changes in the value of the dollar. In the mid and late 1970s the nominal value of the U.S. dollar relative to other major currencies declined. From 1980 through early 1985 the nominal value of the U.S. dollar appreciated. Let's examine these events.

As the value of the dollar *declines,* foreign costs of production rise when measured in terms of dollars.[3] Stated another way, *the dollar buys less of the foreign product.* The resulting squeeze on earnings from goods exported to the United States tends to induce foreign producers to boost the dollar price of their exports. Viewed from the American perspective, the depreciation of the U.S. dollar raises the price of the goods we import. That is, it takes more dollars to purchase the same amount of goods than it did before depreciation. The decline in the value of the dollar may raise the level of prices in three ways: (1) by increasing the price of imported goods, (2) by exerting new demand pressure for domestically produced goods, and (3) by encouraging workers to demand increased wages.

Domestic consumer prices increase through two different channels because of a rise in import prices. First, increases in the prices of imported consumer goods are reflected directly in consumer prices in the United States. Second, American companies that rely on imported materials attempt to pass through to consumers the prices they pay for their supplies.

When the dollar depreciates, the dollar price of foreign goods rises relative to the price of domestically produced substitutes. U.S. imports tend to fall as Americans switch from the now more expensive foreign goods to American products. Our exports tend to rise as foreign purchasers do the same. Conseqently, the *demand for domestically produced items increases.* In competitive sectors of the economy where prices are determined by the forces of supply and demand, the prices of domestically produced goods and services normally will be bid up as demand shifts toward U.S. markets. Of course, in the real world all of this is much more complicated by the ability of domestic producers to expand supplies and conflicting government policies. An example demonstrates the complexity. To boost farm incomes in 1978, set-aside programs were activated for several commodities. At the same time, however, the dollar was declining in value, providing foreign governments with incentives to increase imports. As a result, the limitation of supplies and the increased foreign demand pressure resulted in a significant jump in food prices in the United States during 1978.

The third impact of a decline in the value of the dollar occurs when the initial round of higher prices induces workers to attempt to recoup their lost purchasing power by demanding higher wages. In unionized sectors, these forces are often intitutionalized by the provision in labor agreements of cost-of-living escalators or "reopener" clauses. Additional pressures on wages is also created in domestic industries that compete with foreign producers.

---

[3] The opposite effects noted in this section will occur if the value of the dollar *appreciates.* For example, the dollar would buy more of a foregin product than before. And it would take more units of a foreign currency to buy U.S. products.

Following a depreciation of the dollar, as exports rise and imports fall, domestic firms experiencing increased demand for their goods need additional labor to expand production. If the unemployment rate is low and there is not a ready supply of qualified workers, employers in the expanding sectors may have to offer wage increases in excess of the general rise in prices to attract the requisite number of extra workers.

During the first half of the 1980s we have experienced just the opposite economic phenomenon—the appreciation of the U.S. dollar relative to other foreign currencies. A number of economists (Schuh, Chattin and Lee) suggest that it is this increase in the dollar's value that has caused the leveling off and decline of U.S. agricultural exports during the first five years of the 1980s.

There are numerous others that suggest that there is not a clear and simple relationship between the value of the dollar and volume of U.S. agricultural exports. These economists (Batten and Belongia) argue that the previous arguments did not recognize the important distinctions between nominal and real exchange rate changes. Nominal changes in exchange rates occur when the rates of inflation differ among countries. Real exchange rate changes reflect changing relative prices brought about by major economic structural changes among nations. These economists argue that there is a weak link between U.S. money growth and real exchange rates. They further argue that the major factor that determines the level of a nation's imports of U.S. agricultural products is the rate of growth in real GNP—not exchange rates in the foreign (importing) country.

SUMMARY

The purpose of this chapter was to review the major trends in trade flows for U.S. agricultural products, assess the performance of agricultural exports relative to other commodities, and examine the economic benefits from international trade. The major points made in this chapter can be summarized as follows:

1. Rising world expectations for agricultural products during the seventies and early eighties have generated increases in world food and fiber production and increases in world agricultural trade.

2. The increasingly important role played by the United States in meeting the world's food and fiber needs during the seventies is reflected in dramatic increases in the value and volume of U.S. agricultural exports. The exports of each major U.S. food and fiber product increased during the seventies.

3. U.S. food and fiber producers are becoming *increasingly dependent* on foreign markets as an outlet for their expanded production. Further-

more, international trade has become increasingly important to the U.S. economy. Agricultural exports play a major role in this regard.

4. Countries export those goods in which they are relatively most efficient in producing and import those commodities in which they are relatively least efficient at producing. Gains from trade occur when a country is *relatively* more efficient in some goods than others. This concept is called the *law of comparative advantage.*

5. The price at which goods that were produced and sold under competitive conditions sell for in international markets reflect the costs of resources used to produce these goods. Market imperfections such as government intervention cause market prices to differ from production costs.

6. The *production possibilities curve* for two commodities in a country reflects the combinations of products it can supply efficiently with its given endowment of resources. This curve will shift outward as *productivity* increases.

7. Employment and national income benefit from agricultural exports. While domestic food prices will increase somewhat, consumers as a group derive some benefits from an expanded general economy.

8. The general competitiveness of a nation's exports depends not only on its competitive advantage in production, but also on such factors as the prevailing foreign exchange rates and the prices of producing and exporting similar products in other countries.

9. As the value of the dollar (i.e., its *purchasing power after adjustment for inflation*) declines, it will buy fewer foreign products, and thus U.S. imports will tend to fall. Exports will rise, however, because U.S. products can now be purchased with cheaper dollars relative to other currencies.

DEFINITION OF TERMS

Self-sufficiency: refers to the ability of a country to meet its domestic needs for a product without importing quantities from other countries.

Trade balance: value of products bought and sold in international markets.

Trade surplus (deficit): amount by which exports are greater than (less than) imports.

Comparative advantage: ability of a country to produce a product at a lower opportunity cost than another country can.

Absolute advantage: ability of a country to produce more of a product with its existing resources than other countries can.

Exports: quantities of products sold and shipped to foreign countries.

Imports: quantities of products purchased from foreign countries and shipped to the United States.

Opportunity cost of production: the production of one product sacrificed by choosing to produce more of another product.

Relative cost ratio: represents the ratio of the opportunity costs of producing one product in lieu of another.

Production possibilities curve: represents all possible combinations of total output that could be produced given the efficient use of existing resources.

REFERENCES

BATTEN, DALLAS S., and MICHAEL T. BELONGIA, "The Recent Decline in Agricultural Exports: Is the Exchange Rate the Culprit?" in *Federal Reserve Bank of St. Louis,* October 1984.

CHATTIN, BARBARA, and JOHN E. LEE, JR., "United States Agricultural Policy in a Managed Trade World" in *United States Farm Policy in a World Dimension,* Special Report 305, Agricultural Experiment Station, University of Missouri, November 1983.

MACKIE, ARTHUR B., and MICHAEL ALLAN, "U.S. Consumers Spend Less of Their Income on Food than the Rest of the World." *Foreign Agriculture.* November 1980.

SCHUH, G. EDWARD, "Future Directions for Food and Agricultural Trade Policy." *American Journal of Agricultural Economics* (May 1984) pp. 242–247.

U.S. DEPARTMENT OF AGRICULTURE. *Foreign Agriculture Trade of the United States.* ESCS, Washington, D.C., various issues.

U.S. DEPARTMENT OF AGRICULTURE, *U.S. Foreign Agricultural Trade Statistical Report,* ESCS, Washington, D.C., various fiscal and calendar years.

U.S. DEPARTMENT OF COMMERCE, *Business Conditions Digest.* Washington, D.C.: U.S. Government Printing Office, various editions.

U.S. DEPARTMENT OF COMMERCE, *The Export Imperative.* Report to the President, submitted by the Presidents Export Council, December 1980, Washington, D.C.

ADDITIONAL READING

CAVES, RICHARD E., and RONALD W. JONES, *World Trade and Payments: An Introduction,* 2nd ed. Boston: Little, Brown and Company, 1977.

QUESTIONS

1. Should international trade be encouraged or discouraged? How does trade affect our nation's gross national product?

2. Why is international trade particularly important to U.S. farmers? (*Hint:* You may wish to review the discussion of the total elasticity of demand in Chapter 10 before you complete your answer.)

3. What role has U.S. agriculture played in our nation's trade balance in recent years?

4. Assume a two-country world where each country produces two commodities: guns and butter. What conditions are necessary for international trade between these two countries? Assuming that these conditions are met, how would the production and trade decisions in these two countries be determined?

5. Given your response to question 4, what can you say about the terms of trade between these countries?

6. What affect would an increase in the productivity of a country have on its production and trade decisions?

7. Describe the relationship between the principle of comparative advantage, a nation's exports, and the value of its currency.

19

AGRICULTURAL TRADE POLICY

In previous chapters the determination of the equilibrium price for a particular commodity in single and multiple markets was discussed. The law of comparative advantage was also introduced in Chapter 18 to explain production efficiency, trade flows, and exchange ratios in a two commodity–two country world. In this chapter we initially deal specifically with *prices* for a single commodity in several spatially separated markets and the *flows* of a single commodity in international trade. The implications of these flows for the exporting and importing nation's farm business sector are then analyzed. After evaluating the cost of adjustment created by the introduction of international trade, arguments pro and con for agricultural protection are presented. In the second section of this chapter we explain the economics of protectionism and some of the import and export control policies utilized in distorting trade flows. In the final section we deal with the formulation, history, and concerns relating to current agricultural trade policy.

ECONOMICS OF INTERNATIONAL TRADE FLOWS

In Chapter 18 we evaluated the advantages to two countries of specializing in the production and exporting of a commodity in which they have a comparative advantage and importing the commodity in which they have a comparative disadvantage. In doing so, we determined only a range of prices (exchange ratios). In this chapter we will become more specific about prices and quantities.

Photo by F. Iovino

A session during the "Tokyo Round" of the GATT negotiations on international trade. The General Agreement on Tariffs and Trade (GATT) organized in 1947 is a multilateral treaty dealing with international trade. The agreement contains a code of principles and rules, and provides a continuing forum for consultation and dispute settlement. The GATT also initiates periodic negotiating conferences called by member nations, the most recent being the Tokyo Round 1973–1979. More than 80 governments, including the United States, participate fully; others have observer or partial status.

To begin with, let us assume there are two "countries": the United States (U.S.) and the "rest of the world" (ROW). Let us also assume that both countries produce and consume wheat. We will use a technique called a "back-to-back" diagram to analyze the trade flow between these two countries. The supply and demand curves for the ROW in Figure 19.1 are plotted on the right side of this figure in conventional form. *The supply and demand curves for the U.S. have been reversed on the left side of this figure, however.* Quantities are measured to the right of the origin *(O)* for the ROW and to the left of the origin for the U.S. In the absence of trade between these two countries, these curves determine the price for the commodity in each country. In the ROW, the demand curve D_{ROW} and supply curve S_{ROW} intersect at a point that results in a competitive price for *OA*. In the U.S., on the other hand, we see the demand and supply

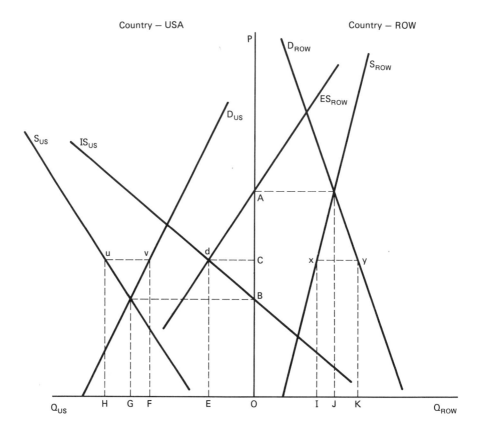

Figure 19.1 *Impacts of trade on producers and consumers.* This "back-to-back" diagram illustrates the determination of the equilibrium market price in a two-country world before and after the opening of international trade. The equilibrium price before trade in the United States (U.S.) would be price *OB*, while the equilibrium price before trade in the rest-of-the-world (ROW) would be price *OA*. After the opening of trade, quantity *HF* of wheat will be exported from the U.S. to the ROW. This will cause prices in the U.S. to rise to price *OC* while the price in the ROW will fall to price *OC*. Producers in the U.S. and consumers in the ROW will benefit from trade, while producers in the ROW and consumers in the U.S. will be less well off.

curves (D_{US} and S_{US}) intersect at price *OB*. In the absence of trade between the U.S. and the ROW, these competitive prices and the respective quantities of wheat produced and consumed would represent market equilibrium conditions.

Now assume that traders from the ROW venture into the U.S. and discover that the price *OB* for wheat in the U.S. in much lower than it is in the ROW (which we said is price *OA*). Ignoring transfer costs for the moment, traders will realize that they can buy wheat in the U.S. and sell it in the ROW for a profit. These traders will therefore engage in this arbitrage to their own profit. As supplies of wheat are exported from the U.S. to the ROW, the price in the ROW begins to decline while the price of wheat in the U.S. increases. This arbitraging will continue as long as the price in ROW exceeds the price in the U.S. Eventually, however, the flow of the commodity from the U.S. to the ROW will be just large enough to result in identical wheat prices in both countries and the establishment of a single market.

Let's examine where this equilibrium will occur in Figure 19.1. First, we need to plot "excess supply" curves for these two countries. Excess supply curves indicate the amount by which the quantity offered for sale exceeds the quantity demanded at various price levels. Let ES_{ROW} and ES_{US} represent the excess supply curves for the ROW and the U.S. in this figure. Figure 19.1 indicates that these two curves intersect at point d. This suggests that the equilibrium price when international trade is allowed between the ROW and the U.S. would be equal to price OC. This intersection will *always* lie in between the prices that would occur in both countries in the absence of trade (price OA in the ROW and price OB in the U.S.). Furthermore, shipments of the commodity will always flow from the low-price country to the high-price country. In our example, wheat was exported from the U.S. to the ROW, where the price was higher. The amount of wheat exported from the U.S. in Figure 19.1 is equal to quantity HF, while the quantity imported by ROW is equal to quantity IK. Note that the distances OE, HF, and IK are all identical. They are also identical to quantity uv (the amount of the excess supply in the U.S. exported to the ROW at price OC) and quantity xy (the amount of excess demand met by imports from the U.S.).

The opening of trade between the U.S. and the ROW has numerous impacts on the production and consumption in these two countries. First, we see that the production of wheat in the U.S. increases from quantity OG to OH—an increase of quantity GH—because producers are responding to the higher price offered for wheat. At the same time, consumers in the U.S. are also reacting to the higher price for wheat by decreasing their consumption from quantity OG to OF, a decrease of quantity GF. Of course, the difference between production OH and consumption OF at the equilibrium price OC in the U.S. is the quantity exported HF.

In the ROW the impacts are quite different. Because of the opening of trade between the two countries and our assumption of zero transportation costs, the equilibrium price OC (which was lower than the price OA before trade began) will force producers and consumers in both countries to reallocate their resources. First, because of lower prices, consumers of wheat in the ROW will increase their consumption from quantity OJ to OK, an increase of quantity JK. Producers in the ROW will cut back their production of wheat from quantity OJ to OI. The amount imported from the U.S. at price OC would be quantity IK.

In summary, the producers in the U.S. and consumers in the ROW will benefit from open trade. Producers in the ROW and consumers in the U.S. on the other hand, must make adjustments. Obviously, some resistance to such changes may arise in the real world as producer groups fight to protect their domestic markets from foreign producers. Meanwhile, consumers may become quite vocal in the exporting country as they adjust to higher prices. These conclusions represent some of the reasons why the notion of "protectionism" is often attractive to specific producer and consumer groups.

FREE TRADE OR PROTECTIONISM?

The two country–one commodity partial equilibrium case presented in Figure 19.1 suggests that international trade in agriculture can have serious implications for national economies. Even though the formulation of trade policy has a considerable impact on many sectors and interest groups, its formulation is usually limited to a few participants. This is because the effect of any given trade policy to the majority affected is usually indirect and slow in coming. But those groups that are immediately affected become very vocal. They are the ones that generally seek protection.

Trade policy is formulated in the "national interest," that is, developing a policy that (1) maintains certain industries in the interest of national security—steel, aviation, merchant marine, and so on; (2) seeks to stabilize economic activity; (3) does not have a negative impact on the balance of payments; (4) safeguards consumer costs; (5) increases or maintains employment; and (6) does not have a skewing effect on income distribution. When formulating trade policy two schools of argument immediately emerge: those that favor free trade and those that favor some degree of distortion from absolute free trade. Let's briefly examine some of the reasoning behind these two schools of thought.

Arguments against Protectionsim

In Chapter 18 and earlier in this chapter, we explored the key to the free-trade argument, the *law of comparative advantage.* Emanating from the law of comparative advantage is the concept of specialization and that society gains economically from specialization. It is further argued that if international markets are not obstructed by protectionistic measures and private entrepreneurs were allowed to pursue their interests, resource allocation would be optimized and overall welfare would be maximized. In essence, the free-trade argument says that resources will adjust *across* national boundaries as well as *within,* so that marginal-value products for land, labor, and capital will be equal in all uses, and the result will be optimum welfare for the world in total.

Noneconomic Arguments for Protectionism

There are two major types of arguments against free trade: *noneconomic* and *economic.* The noneconomic arguments for protectionism center around the need (1) to maintain a level of self-sufficiency in the production of certain products and commodities for defense reasons, (2) to maintain a diversity of production to guard against emerging situations, and (3) to maintain industries vital to survival in the case of war or embargoes.

General Economic Arguments for Protectionism

The general economic arguments against free trade can be categorized into three groups: (1) the *infant industry* argument, (2) the *balance of payment/ monetary flow* argument, and (3) the *unfair competition argument.*

The "infant industry" argument contends that when an industry is in its infancy stage its per unit costs are greater because of insufficient volume produced because of lack of demand or of investment capital. The argument states that infant industries should be protected for a period of time so that they are not eliminated before they become operationally efficient. Over time these industries will expand in size and achieve economies of scale equivalent to those in foreign industries. Although the infant industry argument is accepted as valid where appropriate, it can serve to perpetuate and maintain inefficient industries. The United States originated this argument in its early years to protect itself from the more developed European industries.

The second economic argument against free trade suggests that free trade can lead to excessive imbalance of payments and resources imbalances during adjustment periods. The need for this kind of protection is closely related to the development of national economic policies which emphasize goals such as growth and employment rather than efficiency, which is the fundamental goal of international specialization (free trade). Countries outside the International Monetary Fund (IMF) coordinated international monetary system and numerous third- and fourth-world countries will use this argument for many years to come.

The third general argument for protectionism is that foreign countries implement unfair trade practices. Currently, this is the argument against the "invasion" of Japanese automobiles and European dairy products in the United States. The argument suggests that coordination between governments, firms, and banks which offer excessive subsidies is unfair competition for the "unprotected" U.S. industries. Another argument advanced by "protectionists" is that developed-country industries cannot compete against low-wage countries, particularly in the production of labor intensive products. This is an argument currently being used by the U.S. textile and footwear industries against low-cost Asian and Latin American producers.

Economic Arguments for Protectionism in Agriculture

In addition to the foregoing arguments for protection, agricultural interest groups and policymakers throughout the world have argued that agriculture has several unique characteristics that necessitate protection of this sector. These inherent characteristics are (1) a slow growth in the demand for food, (2) an inelastic supply, and (3) an inelastic demand for agricultural commodities. These factors make agriculture particularly sensitive to changes in supply and prices, creating considerable need for risk management. Governments have taken it upon themselves to manage this risk through the income support programs discussed in Chapter 10. These programs have helped create major distortions in agricultural prices, protection, consumption, and trade flows.

BARRIERS TO TRADE

The forms of protection utilized by national governments are innumerable. Sorenson defines five major methods: those that (1) change market price and thus influence domestic production and consumption, (2) influence production only, (3) influence consumption and utilization only, (4) influence imports, and (5) influence exports. We concentrate on the latter two groups of controls in this section.

Import Controls

For discussion purposes, let us divide the general category of import controls into (1) tariff barriers, and (2) nontariff barriers.

Tariffs. Tariffs act as a tax on the imported product by raising the purchasing price and therefore decreasing the quantity demanded. A tariff imposed by the United States on an imported product raises the price that U.S. consumers must pay for this product, regardless of whether the product came from foreign or domestic sources. To see this, let us examine the effects of a tariff as illustrated in Figure 19.2. The domestic demand curve for this product is denoted by DD and the domestic supply curve for this product is represented by SS. The market equilibrium for this product *in the absence of trade* would be represented by price P_e and quantity Q_e.

Now let us assume that the world price is equal to P_w. Left unchecked, foreign countries would have an economic incentive to export quantities of this product to the United States until the price in U.S. markets fell to the world price.[1] If we accounted for foreign supply as well as domestic supply,

---

[1] For simplicity, this discussion ignores the transportation costs associated with shipping these goods to the United States.

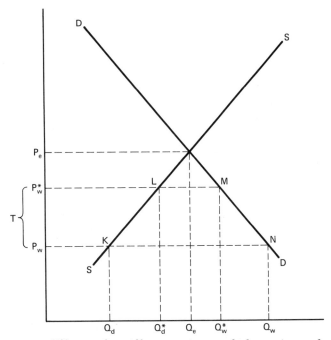

Figure 19.2 *Effects of tariffs on prices and domestic production.*
Assume that the world price is equal to P_w and the domestic equilbrium price is equal to P_e. The opening of free trade would see quantity
Q_w-Q_d imported into the United States and domestic production fall
to Q_d. The imposition of a tariff equal to T dollars per unit, however,
would reduce imports to Q_w^*-Q_d^* and increase domestic production to
Q_d^*. Thus the tariff protects domestic producers (their total revenue
would be higher than it would be without the tariff) but results in a
higher price to consumers in this country. A tariff greater than T dollars
per unit would be needed to bar imports altogether.

the total supply curve (not drawn) would shift outward to the point where
it intersected the domestic demand curve *(DD)* at price P_w and quantity
Q_w.
    To illustrate the effects of a tariff, let T represent the value of a tariff
established by the United States on each unit of this good entering the
country. The U.S. Treasury would collect T dollars per unit on quantities of
this product imported from other countries, but it would not collect a similar
tax on quantities of this good produced domestically. This policy would reduce the quantities of this product entering the country by an amount equal
to the difference between Q_w and Q_w^*. That is, foreign countries would now
export quantities of this product to the United States only until the price
in the domestic market fell to P_w^* instead of P_w. Thus the tariff of T dollars
per unit would effectively kept quantity Q_w-Q_w^* from entering the U.S.
market. Domestic consumers would desire to purchase only Q_w^* at price

P_w^*. Obviously, a higher tariff would be needed to keep foreign products out entirely.

What will domestic producers be doing while all this is going on? With the advent of trade and market price falling to price P_w, domestic producers would cut their production from Q_e to Q_d. The imposition of the tariff and increase in price from P_w to P_w^* would mean that domestic producers now would be able to justify increasing their production from Q_d to Q_d^*. The tariff would thus increase the economic well-being of producers.[2] The value of this increase would be represented by the area formed by $P_w^* LKP_w$.

The cutback in the quantity of this product entering the U.S. market from foreign countries, however, means that the economic well-being of consumers would decline.[3] This loss would be represented by the area formed by $P_w^* MNP_w$. As we will discuss later, the imposition of a tariff may result in retalitory measures by U.S. trading partners. Thus the imposition of a tariff on foreign goods is not without its costs.

The United States over time has relied on tariffs to varying degrees. The highest tariff rates were observed in the depression years of the early thirties to protect domestic producers. These tariffs were set forth in the Smoot-Hawley Tariff enacted by Congress in 1930. In recent years, as a result of the General Agreement on Tariffs and Trade (GATT) agreements, tariff rates in this country have been historically low. The GATT is discussed in the next section.

Nontariff barriers.   The protection of agricultural products through tariffs is not as important nor as widespread now as it was prior to World War II. Protection in the postwar period has taken a much more sophisticated form—that of nontariff devices. According to Hillman, the term "nontariff barriers" has come to mean all those restrictions other than traditional customs duties which distort international trade. These include restrictions at national borders and domestic laws and regulations of all types which discriminate against imports.[4]

A well-known nontariff approach to implementing trade barriers is to impose a *quota* on the quantity (or value) of a product that can enter the importing country. In the United States, for example, there is an annual quota on the quantities of certain meat products that can enter the country.

---

[2] For a discussion of the concept of producer surplus, see the Advanced Topics section at the end of Chapter 5.

[3] For a discussion of the concept of consumer surplus, see the Advanced Topics section at the end of Chapter-3.

[4] There are also many government programs that provide unusual subsidies to exports, including direct price guarantees or export restitutions, tax incentives, favorable financial rates for exports, and domestic programs or assistance to production which not only help substitute for imports but also promote exports.

The effects of a quota on the domestic economy are much the same as those just identified for a tariff. For example, suppose that the United States imposed an import quota of $Q_w^* - Q_d^*$ on the product illustrated in Figure 19.2. This quota would prevent the price of this product from falling below P_w^*. Domestic producers would gain from the quota since prices would have fallen to the world price P_w if there was no quota. Consumers lose from the imposition of quotas in exactly the same way that they lost from the use of tariffs in the previous discussion.

Another well-known nontariff instrument adapted to protect a domestic agricultural industry is the European Economic Community's (EEC) *variable levy system.* The EEC's common agricultural policy establishes a minimum price at which imported agricultural commodities can enter the community. If the import price is below the minimum price, a levy (tax) is imposed that equals the difference between the minimum price and the import price. The minimum price for corn set by the EEC on June 21, 1983, was $5.55 per bushel. On the same day the world price (import price, C.I.F. Rotterdam) was $3.67 per bushel. So the EEC placed a levy of $1.88 per bushel on corn to bring the selling price on the European market to $5.55 per bushel. Therefore, the European buyer on June 21, 1983, paid 150 percent of the world price and the quantity he bought was much less than if the variable levy had not been invoked. More recently the difference between the world price and the minimum price has narrowed considerably.

There are many other types of nontariff policies imposed by food-importing countries. Japan has a *quarantine prohibition* against imports of in-shell peanuts because of the possible entry of the burrowing nematode. One reason given for the maintenance of this restriction is to protect the Japanese citrus industry from the nematode, although a definite link between the worm and the plant has never been established. These restrictions and quotas appear to be working quite well for the Japanese citrus industry, as the price of oranges in mid-1984 was 20 cents on the deck and over $1 at the retail level. Other importing nations have adopted standards and practices for red meat. For example, the EEC has adopted a variety of meat import requirements, including separate slaughter facilities for suspect animals, physical separation of rooms for cutting and packaging, ante-mortem inspection by licensed veterinarians, and inspection of lymph glands for tuberculosis. Literally thousands of other examples could be given to demonstrate the ingenious methods by which nations attempt to protect their domestic agricultural industries from the competitiveness of free trade.

Domestic subsidies.   A third form of import control is domestic subsidization. Domestic subsidization of agriculture occurs in varying forms and degrees in all exporting and importing countries. They normally take the form of policies that (1) change market price and thus influence domestic production and consumption, (2) directly influence production only, and

(3) influence consumption and utilization only. These subsidies take the form of direct price payments, deficiency payments, subsidies on inputs such as fertilizer or credit and food stamps, and other demand–creating policies. Domestic subsidization has the same negative impact on trade as tariffs and nontariff trade barriers. That is, it distorts the flow of agricultural trade and encourages the inefficient allocation of resources. Many nations attempting to meet national goals other than efficiency have complicated and subsidized domestic food systems.

No subject in trade negotiations creates as much emotion as do subsidies and countervailing duties. Since all nations protect their agriculture to one degree or another, efforts to liberalize trade are often regarded not as a trade-neutral measure but as a direct political and economic attack on the sovereign policies of the subsidizing country.

Export Controls

Earlier in this section the term "trade barrier" was used to signify controls over imports that impede or bar access to markets. However, events during the seventies and early eighties, such as the oil and food crisis, the surge in worldwide inflationary pressures, and diplomatic confrontations, centered on the opposite problem—that of controls over exports that impeded or prevented access to supplies.

Export controls are undertaken for a number of reasons. Some of these include: (1) to avoid "unacceptable" domestic price rises; (2) to improve the terms of trade of the producing country, or at least to keep them declining, by forcing up world prices for its commodity exports; (3) to conserve limited resources, especially for countries reliant on a single commodity; (4) to develop domestic processing industries rather than exporting raw materials; (5) to avoid physical shortages; (6) to limit the military and economic capability of other countries; and (7) for foreign policy reasons, in an effort to induce the denied consumer to change his policy.

The use of numerous export controls during the seventies and eighties has become widespread. In the United States, export goods have become more visible as a foreign economic policy tool. In 1973, soybeans were embargoed to avoid unacceptable increases of domestic food prices. In 1974 and 1975, similar actions were taken with respect to grain export sales to the Soviet Union. The bilateral trade agreement between the U.S. and the Soviet Union made export demand management by the U.S. government a regular feature of trade with the Soviets. In January 1980, the United States suspended exports of numerous agricultural products to the Soviet Union for diplomatic reasons. In 1983 and 1984 the Brazilians temporarily suspended exports of soybean products to enhance the terms of trade.

The implementation of export controls on agricultural goods and the use of food as a diplomatic weapon have a number of negative impacts on market-oriented trade flows: (1) It decreases the perception of the export nation as a reliable supplier of agricultural export commodities, and this increases the uncertainty in the importer's decision-making process. The importer therefore seeks substitutes and alternative sources of supply. (2) It increases the variability of the volume of agricultural exports and therefore increases the uncertainty at every level in the production and marketing system. This uncertainty may create inefficiency and a misallocation of resources that in the long run can lead a nation toward a comparative disadvantage in the production of its export commodities. (3) Export controls generally depress farm-level prices, which in the long run may cause inefficient allocation of resources.

The domestic cost of export controls is always high; and when a sensitive and highly complex economic sector such as agriculture is forced to bear the burden of such policies, the ultimate loser is the consumer. The international costs and ramifications of export controls must also be considered from a variety of perspectives. For Example, export controls spawn defensive export controls or import controls on other commodities. They also injure the reputation of the implementing country as an advocate of free trade. This is particularly important to U.S. agriculture, which for many years has insisted that major food importers reduce their import controls. Export controls encourage the use or formation of other exporter controls or cartels by implicitly sanctioning the use of such a policy tool. World inflation is also fueled by export controls, particularly if implemented by major suppliers of inelastically demanded goods, such as food. Ultimately, export controls can in some circumstances produce resutls contrary to humanitarian goals. This is particularly true with controls on food sales, which can lead to severe malnutrition and even starvation if imposed when world food supplies are tight.

FORMULATION OF AGRICULTURAL TRADE POLICY

Presently, the international agricultural trade policy under which trade constraints can be removed is the General Agreement on Tariffs and Trade (GATT). GATT was created in 1947 by the United States and 22 other nations to secure a substantially free and competitive world market as the best means of conducting international trade and serving the best interests of all nations.

General Agreement on Tariffs and Trade

GATT has five basic principles: (1) trade must be nondiscriminatory, meaning that all contracting parties receive equal treatment regarding import and export duties and charges; (2) domestic industries receive protection mainly by tariffs (agriculture, however, receives special treatment in that import quotas are allowed if domestic supply management restrictions are in force); (3) agreed-upon tariff levels bind each country, whereby if tariff levels are raised, compensation must be made to injured countries; (4) consultations are provided to settle disputes; and (5) when warranted by economic or trade circumstances (such as balance of payments problems), GATT procedures may be waived if other members agree and compensation is made to them.

Since its inception in the late forties, seven major negotiating conferences have been held by GATT. The first significant achievement was to bind (prevent the raising of) existing tariff levels. Each subsequent round of negotiations reduced industrial tariffs substantially. In the early years, the problems of agriculture and the developing countries received very little attention. In the more recent negotiations, some progress has been made regarding trade problems in agriculture.

The fifth round, called the Dillion Round (1960–1961) was called to prevent discrimination by the European Economic Community (EEC) against nonmembers. The non-EEC members were unsuccessful in their challenge and the EEC became a reality. The United States did achieve one significant concession for agriculture in this round. Soybeans, soybean meal, other oilseeds, and cotton were granted virtually duty-free entry to the EEC.

In the Kennedy Round (1963–1967), agriculture negotiations led to the Interntational Grains Agreement, and some tariff concessions were made on a wide range of farm products. Even though tariff reductions on farm products were generally smaller than those for industrial products, they were significant in that GATT, for the first time, seriously attempted liberalization of agricultural commodity trade.

These six general tariff-bargaining negotiations from 1947 to 1967 led to the reduction of customs duties on thousands of products traded among member countries. However, by the early seventies it had become apparent that the trading system was coming under new pressures that threatened a proliferation of new barriers to international trade, many in the form of quantitative import restrictions and other nontariff barriers. The GATT, moreover, was less and less able to deal with problems not directly related to tariff reduction.

A seventh general negotiation, now known as the Tokyo Round, was the result. Conducted between 1973 and 1979, 99 countries participated, compared with 40 in the Kennedy Round and 20 in the Dillon Round. Let us examine the U.S. role in the Tokyo Round in greater depth.

U.S. Agricultural Trade Policy

U.S. agricultural trade policy during the post-World War II period can be divided into two general periods, 1945–1965 and 1965 to the present. There is a high degree of interplay between domestic agricultural policy and trade policy during both periods. The U.S. position between 1945 and 1965 can be characterized as more protectionistic than the years since 1965. Until the mid-sixties, the United States sought and obtained GATT exceptions and exclusions for agriculture. The United States utilized the import protection and export disposal provision of the 1935 Agricultural Adjustment Act in harmony with high domestic support price systems to maintain a relatively well protected agriculture. But by the mid-sixties, major shifts occurred in both U.S. agricultural and trade policies. The high price supports for the major export crops of cotton, feed grains, and wheat were eliminated. In 1973 the two-price system was terminated and the direct conflict between U.S. domestic policy and export objectives was eliminated. These policy moves made the U.S. agricultural production system more sensitive to international markets. This was a major turning point for U.S. agriculture.

The adoption of these market-oriented domestic agricultural policies made the United States take an even more aggressive stand on liberalized trade in the Tokyo Round of the multilateral trade negotiations.

The U.S. approach to agricultural negotiations in the Tokyo Round was based primarily on a growing concern over nontariff barriers, such as import quotas, discriminatory measures favoring other exporters, and devices leading to unfair competition in third-country markets. The U.S. negotiating strategy was to seek improved export opportunities and stability through improved trading rules and workable consultative arrangements. At the same time, tariff concessions were sought on products with a high growth potential. These included products such as high-quality beef, port, poultry, variety meats, tallow, tobacco, fresh and canned fruits and juices, vegetable oils, and vegetable protein products. Other important concessions involved soybeans, rice, and cotton.

The trade coverage of agricultural products on which the United States received concessions amounted to the equivalent of 16 percent of agricultural exports and almost one-fourth of U.S. farm exports subject to foreign barriers. The value of the concessions was $4 billion in 1976 trade.

Concessions from industrialized countries accounted for over three-fourths of the trade concessions. Japan accounted for about one-third of the coverage of trade offers to the United States, the European Economic Community for 28 percent, and Canada for 13 percent. Mexico, the Philippines, Korea, Taiwan, and India together accounted for almost all of the value of trade offers that the United States received from developing countries.

The United States offered tariff concessions on products covering about $2.7 billion in U.S. agricultural imports in 1976. Approximately one-fourth of this was in fresh or frozen beef, lamb meat and wool, live cattle, and certain grain products, in which concessions were offered to industrialized countries. Most of the remainder was in vegetable oils, inedible molasses, fruits and vegetables, and preserved beef, in which concessions were offered to developing countries.

The United States also expanded quotas on cheese. Certain countries would be allowed to increase their exports of cheese to the United States by about 15 percent over 1978 levels. At the same time, however, the most important of these cheeses not previously subject to import quotas were made subject to quota for the first time. This resulted in about 85 percent of cheese imports being covered by the quota system, compared with 50 percent previously.

Even more important in the long term was the negotiation of a series of codes that extended the GATT trading system into areas where it had not previously reached and which elaborate on existing rules and procedures. These will help create an improved climate for export expansion in the decades ahead. New consultative arrangements were also agreed on for meat and dairy products.

These actions suggest that the general direction of U.S. agricultural policy is to continue pushing for a more liberalized agricultural trade. The policy in many industrialized and developing countries is quite the opposite, and if the United States seeks to gain greater access to food and fiber markets, significant challenges lie ahead for U.S. trade policymakers. What follows is a brief review of some of their concerns.

U.S. AGRICULTURAL TRADE POLICY CONCERNS

There are two general trade policy phenomena that could have an important impact on the future direction of U.S. agricultural exports. The first is the slowness with which progress is being made in liberalizing world agricultural trade. The second phenomenon that demands attention is the increasingly protectionist actions of many industrialized nations, including the United States.

Slow liberalization of trade. Despite limited success on two developments in the recent round of multilateral trade negotiations, a code of conduct on export subsidies, and some progress on label and standard codes, agriculture did not become a full-fledged participant in liberalized trade. The notion that agricultural trade policies are an outgrowth of domestic policies and should be subservient to them appears to be the prevalent mood in most countries. Another factor adding to the reluctance in establishing a more liberalized trading system is the increasing pressure of developing countries to construct, through the auspices of UNCTAD, a new international economic order. This is being carried out in the context of a series of discussions, dialogues, consultations, charges, and countercharges, all of which have become known as the North–South dialogue.

Some of the main issues and activities under consideration in this context that have a direct impact on agricultural trade include (1) further negotiation on commodity agreements, (2) continued negotiation on a common fund, (3) the need to increase the flow of technology transfers from developed to developing countries, (4) a call by developing countries to transfer many of the GATT trade functions to UNCTAD, (5) a proposal to extend general system preference to all export of developing countries, and (6) proposals to allow for greater trade preferences among developing countries. This persistent and ardent call for a more controlled system is of concern to the U.S. agricultural sector.

Protectionistic actions.   Unemployment and other macroeconomic ills currently being experienced in the economically advanced countries are due partly to a slowing of world wide economic growth rates. The resumption of economic growth cannot be advanced by protection. But growth means disruption and inconveniences, and as countries become richer, they start to trade off growth for convenience and efficiency for stability. This is an illusion. The trade-off can be made in the short run but not in the long run. For economies like the United States to maintain solid economic growth, a shift must occur in the manufacturing sector. The high technology and high productivity sectors must replace low technology and low productivity industries. Potentially, one of the greatest constraints to expanded agricultural exports is the increasing threat of a move toward protectionism in the United States. If the United States limits industrial imports from major customers of the United States' agricultural sector, soon those clients will be unable or unwilling to purchase U.S.-produced agricultural commodities.

Despite the essentially free market stance of U.S. agricultural trade policy, protectionist measures are utilized to isolate certain segments of U.S. agriculture from volatile international forces. These include section 27 provisions, meat import legislation and tariffs. U.S. tariffs on raw materials are, in general, quite low, but they tend to escalate for processed products. Coffee beans, for example, enter the United States with no tariffs but processed coffee beans have a 60 percent tariff. Unfortunately, the incidence of these escalating tariffs is on producers of labor-intensive commodities which might well have a comparative advantage in the U.S. market.

SUMMARY

The purpose of this chapter was to discuss how various forms of trade policies can be used to constrain the free flow of goods between importing and exporting countries. The major points made in this chpter can be summarized as follows:

1. The *free trade* argument says that resources will adjust *across* national boundaries as well as *within* so that marginal value products for land, labor, and capital will be equal in all uses, and the result will be *optimum welfare* for the world in total.

2. *Partial equilibrium analysis* demonstrated that the producer in the low cost exporting country and the consumer in the high cost importing country have the most to gain in opening up their frontiers to free trade in a one commodity-two country world.

3. Most *noneconomic* arguments *against free trade* center around a nation's need for self-sufficiency, diversity, and national security.

4. Most *economic* arguments *against free trade* center around a) infant industry concept, b) the balance of payments argument, and c) the unfair competition argument.

5. A *tariff* represents a tax on imported goods. This tariff or duty raises the prices of the product in domestic markets and therefore decreases the quantity demanded.

6. A *quota* acts much the same as a tariff in that it results in lower quantities marketed. There are a variety of other nontariff barriers to trade which restrict the free flow of trade. The EEC's *variable levy system,* for example, establishes a minimum price at which a particular good can enter the country. Japan has a *quarantine* prohibiting imports of in-shell peanuts.

7. A third form of import control is *domestic subsidies* of production. Such subsidies distort the flow of agricultural trade by modifying the free-market price.

8. Export controls are used to control domestic prices, conserve limited resources, develop domestic industries, and avoid domestic shortages. They may also be used for foreign policy reasons.

9. The use of *export controls* have a undesirable effects of damaging the country's reputation as a reliable trading partner, increasing uncertainty in commodity markets, and depressing farm prices.

10. The *general agreement on tariffs and trade* or GATT was created to promote a free and competitive world market.

11. U.S. trade policy concerns include the slow liberalization of trade flows among important and exporting nations and the protectionistic actions taken by specific trading partners.

DEFINITION OF TERMS

Protectionism: act on the part of policymakers to protect a country's industry by modifying the terms of trade for importing countries, either making their goods more expensive or barring them all together.

Free trade: refers to an absence of goverment intervention which alters free-market prices and quantities marketed.

Tariff: tax or duty placed products imported into a country.

Quota: limit on quantity or value of imports permitted to enter a country during the year.

Variable levy system: based on the minimum price at which non-EEC member commodities can be imported into a country. If the import price is below this minimum, a levy (tax) equal to this difference is imposed on the product.

Quarantine prohibition: absolute restriction place on the entry of imported goods into a country; designed implicitly to protect domestic agricultural commodities.

European Economic Community: group of European countries that act in unison to discriminate against non-EEC countries by placing duties or levies on imported products.

General Agreement on Tariffs and Trade: created by the United States and 22 other nations in 1947 to secure a substantially free and competitive world market.

Liberalization of trade: refers to the removal of restrictions on imports.

Excess supply curve: derived from the difference between quantities of product supplied domestically and quantities demanded at prices above the domestic equilbrium market price.

UNCTAD: United Nations Conference on Trade and Development, which focuses particular attention on the trade and development problems of poor countries.

REFERENCES

BRESSLER, RAYMOND G., and RICHARD A. KING, *Markets, Prices, and Interregional Trade.* New York: John Wiley & Sons, Inc., 1970.

HILLMAN, JIMMYE S. *Nontariff Agricultural Tariff Barriers.* Lincoln, Nebr.: University of Nebraska Press, 1978.

JABARA, C., "Commodity Policy Issues in Developing Country Trade," International Economics Division, ESS, U.S.D.A., Washington, D.C., 1981.

JOHNSON, D. GALE., "Agriculture in the International Economy," in Tarliffs, *Quotas and Trade: The Politics of Protectionism.* San Francisco: Institute for Contemporary Studies, Calif. 1978.

SORENSON, V. L., *International Trade Policy: Agriculture and Development.* Michigan State University, International Business and Economic Studies, East Lansing, Mich. 1975.

TWEETEN, LUTHER G., "Agriculture Policy: A Review of Legislation, Programs, and Policy," in *Food and Agricultural Policy.* Washington, D.C.: American Enterprise Institute for Public Research, 1977.

U.S. DEPT. OF AGRICULTURE., *FAS Report Foreign Agricultural Service.* Washington, D.C.: U.S. Government Printing Office, various issues.

ADDITIONAL READINGS

BRANDOW, GEORGE E., "Policy for Commercial Agriculture, 1945–1971", in *A Survey of Agricultural Economics Literature,* Vol. I, ed. L. Martin. Minneapolis, Minn.: University of Minnesota Press, 1977.

GARDNER, BRUCE, and JAMES RICHARDSON, eds., *Consensus and Conflicts in United States Agriculture.* College Station, Tex., Texas A&M Press, 1979.

KNUTSON, R. D., J. B. PENN, and W. T. BOEHM, *Agricultural and Food Policy.* Englewood Cliffs, N.J.: Prentice-Hall, Inc., 1983.

PAARLBERG, DONALD, *Farm and Food Policy: Issues of the 1980's.* Lincoln, Nebr.: University of Nebraska Press, 1980.

SCHULTZ, THEODORE W., ed., *Distortions of Agricultural Incentives.* Bloomington, Ind.: Indiana University Press, 1978.

QUESTIONS

1. Describe the concept of the excess supply curve and the role it played in Figure 19.1.
2. Describe how the internal equilibrium for a commodity is established under conditions of free trade. How is this equilibrium modified if a country utilizes a tariff to protect its producers?
3. What are the arguments for free trade? Those against free trade? How are these arguments related to the law of comparative advantage?
4. What are the economic arguments for protectionism in general? What special characteristics might apply in making a case for protectionism for agriculture?
5. How high would the tariff in Figure 19.2 have to be to keep imports of this commodity off the domestic market depicted in this figure? Besides tariffs, what other forms of barriers to trade can a country employ to protect an industry?
6. What are some of the current U.S. agricultural trade policy concerns?

20

FUTURE CLIMATE FOR INTERNATIONAL TRADE

The purpose of this chapter is to identify the environment in which international trade is conducted, to discuss the factors that expand export demand for agricultural products, and to assess the current implications that these demand forces will have on international trade in the foreseeable future. Included in this discussion is an assessment of world economic conditions in light of the purchasing power of importing countries, U.S. trade policies, and exchange rates.

INTERNATIONAL EXPORT–IMPORT SYSTEM

The facsimile of the world export–import system presented in Figure 20.1 helps illustrate that the marketing channel, which both adds value to and facilitates the flow of agricultural commodities from producers through the exporter to the importer, is influenced by two sets of environments. On the export side (let us assume that the United States is the exporting nation), the participants along the U.S. market channel (i.e., input suppliers, producers, handlers and exporters) are influenced by the economic, agricultural, foreign, and trade policies of the U.S. government as well as the policies of the market institutions themselves. The same set of policy considerations also influence economic behavior in the food-and-fiber importing nation. The domestic environment of the exporter and importer are further influenced by world economic, political, trade, and monetary conditions.

As with any complex system, numerous impediments exist as to the optimal performance of the world's food and fiber export–import system.

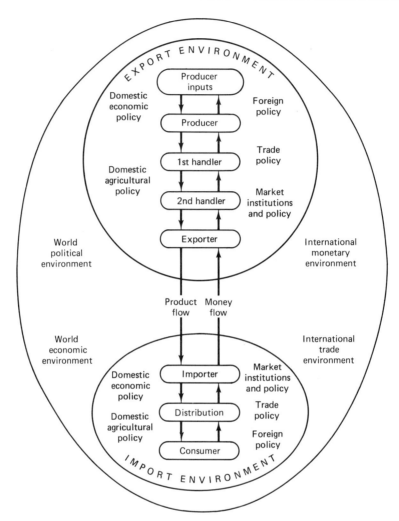

Source: Cook, Michael L. *U.S. Farm Export Strategies for the
         Eighties*, Agricultural Council of America, Washington,
         D.C., February, 1981.

Figure 20.1 *World export–import system.* The flow of food and fiber
products from the producer to consumers in other countries is affected
by two sets of environments, domestic and international. The domestic
environment generally consists of agricultural, economic, market, trade,
and foreign policies. The international environment is made up of political, economic, monetary, and trade elements. The same set of forces
also influences the food and fiber importing nation.

From a supply point of view, there are several potential constraints to in-reasing exportable supplies of agricultural commodities. Some of these con-straints include (1) maintenance of an adequate and quality land and water base, (2) domestic agricultural productivity, (3) the level of government in-volvement in domestic programs, and (4) concerns about transportation and other infrastructure systems. From a demand point of view, there are con-straints to increasing foreign demand for agricultural products. These con-straints include (1) the state of the world economy, (2) protectionist trade policies of exporting and importing countries, (3) congested infrastructure in major importing nations, (4) the rate of population growth, and (5) pres-sures to adopt a more protectionist trade policy in the United States.

The emergence of the United States as a net agricultural exporter since 1963 is due to five major factors: (1) its natural resource endowment coup-led with a highly favorable climatic condition; (2) the dramatic and consis-tent productivity gains in the domestic farm business sector; (3) liberalized agricultural price, income, and exchange-rate policies, resulting in significant resource adjustments within the farm business sector; (4) the development of a highly efficient export marketing infrastructure; and (5) large increases in the foreign demand for food and fiber. Previous chapters addressed many of the factors affecting the export availability of food and fiber supply. There-fore, the emphasis in this chapter is on factors affecting changes in demand.

EXPORT DEMAND EXPANSION

The dramatic growth in U.S. agricultural exports during the seventies and early eighties was not an aberration from a normal trend but rather, repre-sented an unambiguous indication of increasing global food and fiber inter-dependence. This increasing interdependence complicates the predictability of policy changes when attempting to understand the factors that determine the export demand for U.S. food and fiber products. Let us take a look at these factors considered to be important in determining future export de-mand for U.S. food and fiber products. Some of the major factors are des-cribed in this section.

Population Growth and Wage Distribution

World population is presently expanding at a net rate of 230,000 people daily and is projected to grow at an annual rate of 1.5 to 2.0 percent—similar to that in recent years. The rate of population growth is expected to be greatest in Africa, Latin America, the Middle East, and certain parts of Asia. The average age in these rapidly expanding countries is at or ap-proaching the age of maximum caloric intake. Both of these factors sug-gest that there is potentially a strong demand for food and feedstuffs in much of the world, particularly in the development economies during the next 20 years.

Per Capita Income

Per capita income growth and the rate at which food consumption and demand increase given an increase in income are another set of important factors that influence the aggregate demand for food. The relationship between consumption and increases in income is measured by the concept of income elasticities, as explained in Chapter 3.

Developing economies, in contrast to developed countries, tend to be characterized by high levels of incremental consumption of food out of additional income (i.e., high income elasticities). According to Josling, the range of income elasticities for food products extends 0.9 at the high extreme to not much above 0.1 at the other.[1] Income growth therefore has very different implications for the food sector in different countries. A country such as the United States, with an income elasticity for food products of 0.08 means that a 10 percent increase in disposable income for U.S. consumers would result in less than a 1 percent increase in the demand for food products. On the other hand, if the disposable income of people in India was to increase by 10 percent, the quantity of food products demanded would increase by 8 percent since the income elasticity of demand for food in that country is 0.8.

Income growth and population increases are related to a country's stage of economic development. There appears to be a tendency for population to increase somewhat faster in the rapid-growth state of development at the same time as income growth is high. As an economy matures, population growth rates drop significantly, as does total income growth, although per capita incomes often continue to rise. The effect of the combination of such factors on the demand for agricultural commodities (particularly food products) is illustrated in Table 20.1.

In general, one would expect to see demand for food in low-income countries growing at about 3 percent, the rapid-growth-rate countries' food demand increasing at approximately 4.3 percent, and the industrialized countries' demand for food growing below 2 percent.

It is evident that the performance of the world economy will have a considerable impact upon world food and fiber demand. Projections indicate that the worldwide growth of gross national products will be somewhat lower than that of the past two decades. This impact is discussed in more detail in the section on world economic conditions.

---

[1] The income elasticity of demand was defined in Chapter 3 as the percentage change in the amount of a good purchased divided by the percentage change in income. If this elasticity is less than 1, there will be a less than 1 percent increase in quantity demanded for every 1 percent increase in income.

Income Distribution

Another major factor that affects the demand for U.S. agricultural exports is the income distribution in importing countries. Just as income elasticities vary between countries, they vary among different income groups within any given country. It is generally found that the lower-income groups have the high income elasticities for food. Therefore, the dispersion of any income growth in a country is very important for the prospects of increased food imports. In general, the broader the distribution of any gain in income, the greater the demand for food.

Foreign Production

The final major factor influencing import demand of food and fiber of any country is the ability of that country to increase its supply relative to any increase in demand. On a world level, total food production increased at an annual 2.6 percent rate during the seventies, similar to growth rates experienced in the sixties. This overall rate of growth conceals substantial differences among the developing regions. In the period 1974-1978, agriculture production in the Asian Far East rose 4.3 percent annually, while African production over the same period increased by 1.6 percent. Developed economies' food production increased at 2.3 percent for the period 1974-1978.

There is little evidence that the 1973 world food crisis had a positive impact on world food production or capital investment in agriculture production or capital investment in agriculture production and marketing systems. Investment has increased, though, in land, labor, and other inputs (e.g., fertilizer) in most nations since 1973.

IMPLICATIONS FOR U.S. AGRICULTURAL EXPORTS

With a number of exceptions, the growth rate in the demand for food in the developed market economies (Europe, Japan, and Canada) during the late eighties is not expected to duplicate their past growth rates. These countries have low population growth rates, low income elasticities for food products, and a projected decline in the rate of real economic growth. The exceptions, though, are important for a number of commodities. Increased demand for specialty food such as apricots, pecans, and processed foods, together with animal proteins and accompanying inputs, will continue. It is estimated that in Japan, for example, the income elasticities for beef, veal, and pork will be above 1 for the next five years and that its income elasticities for dairy products and chicken will approach 0.6.

The centrally planned economies found in socialistic countries are also beginning to show decreased rates of economic growth. It should be noted that economic growth in ce trally planned countries is not highly influenced by import demand. With the exception of China, the increase in demand for food and fiber products is expected to become more moderate. China is project to experience real economic growth and is expected to continue its appetite for both food and fiber. In Eastern Europe and the Soviet Union, however, import demand growth rate is expected to decline slightly.

The third-world countries in the "takeoff" stage of development and oil-exporting nations, with capital surpluses, are expected to maintain economic growth rates between 3 to 6 percent during the late eighties.[2] These areas, Mexico, Brazil, Venezuela, Nigeria, East Asia, North Africa, and the Middle East, are projected to increase their demand for most food and fiber products and will experience even greater increases in demand for animal-protein-related food products.

The lower-income third-world countries and the fourth-world countries are expected to experience small to decreasing gains in the rate of economic growth. Combined with increasing population growth and minor increases in agricultural productivity, the pessimistic income outlook suggests a grave decade ahead. Food demand will increase but will be met only if increased food aid, credit, and developmental assistance are forthcoming. The prospect that many of these nations will reach the take off stage of economic development during the next decade is also dim.

ROLE OF WORLD ECONOMIC CONDITIONS

It should be clear from the discussion in the preceding section that the demand for U.S. exports is dependent on the nature of world economic conditions. In this final section we examine world economic conditions from the following perspectives: (1) the ability of importing countries to pay for U.S. food and fiber products, (2) the U.S. role in world economic conditions, and (3) exchange rates.

Purchasing Power

Purchasing power as defined in the context of this chapter refers to a country's ability to pay for imported food and fiber products. Factors most important in influencing the ability of a nation to pay for imports include (1) income growth, (2) export earnings, and (3) external debt. Each factor is discussed in turn on the next few pages.

---

[2] Rostow's theory of development assumes that all nations pass through five stages of development (i.e., traditional, preconditions, take off, drive to maturity, and high mass consumption) as they move along the path of economic progress. See W. W. Rostow, *The Stages of Economic Growth* (London: Cambridge University Press, 1960).

Income growth. The economic environment of the next 10 to 20 years will be heavily influenced by the events that occurred in the seventies and early eighties. Given these developments, the world faces a series of adjustments over the decade of the eighties. While this adjustment process is going on, the world economy and most developing countries are likely to grow more slowly than they did during the seventies and early eighties.

One of the adjustment that must take place is the adjustment to higher energy costs. Higher oil prices have clearly improved the prospects of those developing countries with oil to export, where a fifth of the developing world's population lives. Their per capita gross national product grew 2.8 percent a year in the sixties, compared with 3.1 percent for the oil-importing developing countries. In the seventies the oil exporters accelerated to an annual 3.5 percent growth, while the oil importers slowed to 2.7 percent (the disparity was even larger when GNP is adjusted for changes in the purchasing power of their exports). With increased oil revenues, the oil exporters' growth will be contrained more by the productivity of domestic investment than by their ability to borrow abroad.

There is concern about the rate of economic growth in both the industrialized and the developing world. The industrialized economies face more serious difficulties than in the mid-seventies, when adjustment tended to be viewed as a phase from which they would quickly recover. But the growth of the sixties and early seventies has not been regained, and although their slowdown may not be as marked as it was in 1974-1975, the recovery outside the United States has been slow. It is also important to remember that even though food income elasticities are low in the industrialized nations, they are not in the developing economies. Therefore, it is important for food-and-fiber-exporting nations such as the United States to be particularly concerned not only about industrialized markets that presently import 50 percent of the U.S. agriculture exports but also the increasingly important developing-country importer. Their economic growth becomes a vital factor to prospects for U.S. agricultural exports.

The economic health of industrialized countries is a key determinant of the growth prospects of developing nations. Industrialized countries are the principal markets for exports from developing countries and their main suppliers of external capital and technology. By the early eighties, industrialized countries purchased two-thirds of all merchandise exports from developing countries; the share was 70 percent for fuel, 65 percent for other primary commodities and 60 percent for manufacturers. The chief concern regarding the economic growth of the developing countries is whether they can sustain the high annual growth rates of 2.6 and 3.2 percent per capita gross national produc rather than the slower annual rates of 2.0 to 2.4 percent. The difference for the agricultural export sector is substantial.

Export earnings. The ability to generate export earnings is the second important factor in being prepared to pay for inccreased imports of food and fiber. Trends in the rate of growth of world trade comprise an aggregate indicator of changes in export earnings. During the seventies and early eighties, annual world trade growth averaged 5.7 percent. But estimates for the middle and late eighties suggest a slower rate of gain.

The trade outlook differs sharply between oil exporters and oil importers—underlining the important effects of terms-of-trade changes. In the seventies and early eighties, export volume for oil-exporting developing countries great at about two-thirds the rate achieved by oil importers, but because the price of their exports rose so much faster, their import volume was able to grow twice as fast. For oil exporters with capital surpluses, the terms-of-trade benefits were even greater.

The second area of concern is that of sufficient export earnings. The potential purchasing power of a food-and-fiber-importing nation depends not only on economic growth rates, but also on the growth in export earnings. Two specific areas are of interest: the level of and the variability of export earnings. World Bank projections suggest that the average annual growth rate for export earnings will increase for all the developing countries from their 1973-1983 average of 5.0 percent to 5.5 to 6.5 percent per year. Yet there is concern about these countries developing trade policies that are more biased toward import substitution than export expansion. Frequently, such policies have been introduced in response to temporary balance-of-payments crises but then maintained for long periods. They result in misallocated resources and create a constituency for retaining protection.

The other area of concern regarding export earnings is their high degree of variability. Historically, most developing countries have depended on primary mineral and/or agricultural commodity exports. The nature of the fluctuating international prices, and therefore variable export earnings, has introduced a degree of risk that few domestic eonomies can adjust to consistently. This, in turn, leads to a highly protectionist import-substitution-oriented trade policy to save on outflows of scarce foreign currency. The end result is again the development of inefficient manufacturing industries that are often unable to compete in international markets.

External debt.   The extent of external debt outstanding is a third measure of determining a potential importing nation's purchasing power. Borrowing abroad to supplement domestic savings has been a feature of most countries at some point in their historical development. The United States was a net capital importer until around the turn of the twentieth century. In more recent times flows of capital across international boundaries have reached unprecedented levels, spurred by high levels of economic growth in the industrialized countries (hence a supply of capital) and the attempt of most governments in the developing world to accelerate the pace of economic development (hence a demand for capital).

These tendencies were promoted and facilitated by the generally liberal climate of the international economy since World War II, particularly in the removal of restrictions on payments and financial transfers. In the past 12 years, there has been a dramatic increase in borrowing and external debt brought about by these factors, together with the sudden phenomenon of large surpluses in oil-exporting countries. The level of outstanding public debt in the developing countries (including the undisbursed element) rose from $75 billion in 1970 to over an estimated $700 billion in 1984. The debt accumulated by these trading partners and the size of their annual debt servicing commitment is illustrated in an example for three of these nations in Table 20.2.

Not only have the debt problems of many non-oil-exporting developing countries become more acute since 1982, but there has also been mounting concern about the external debt of other countries, including some developed countries. The long-term external debt of non-oil-exporting developing countries increased by over 50 percent between 1980 and 1983. Meanwhile, their debt service ratio on long-term foreign borrowing—loan payments expressed as a percentage of exports of goods and services—rose from 18 to 22 percent, and much more so for some individual countries.

The problem with foreign laons is that they must be repaid, even if this is done through new borrowing. If a country is unable to service its debt and to raise new capital, debt-servicing problems will arise. The enormous surge in borrowing during the past decade outstripped the economic performance—in particular, the export growth—of some developing countries, straining the debt-servicing ability of these countries even though in global terms, because of inflation, the growth of exports by all developing countries has been in line with the growth of indebtedness during the last decade. However, there has been a large increase in the number of countries encountering external debt problems during this period. Between 1975 and 1984, the number of countries that experienced arrears on their external debt rose 4 to 28. The need for borrowing by developing countries is not likely to abate in the middle to late eighties. On the contrary, given the needs of development,the necessity of servicing the outstanding foreign debt, and financial requirements of meeting anticipated current account balance of payments deficits—particularly serious in view of the sharp increase in energy prices and the slowdown in the world economy—the need to borrow abroad is likely to increase. If there is a further increase in such borrowing, the prospect is for more countries to face difficult debt-servicing situations. This enhances the need for appropriate policies on the part of the borrowers to avoid difficulties.

Role of the United States

The economic health of the United States which is vitally important to the growth prospects for other nations of the world is the second major area we will explore in this section. The United States is a principal market for exports from industrialized and developing countries and is a major supplier of external capital and technology. In 1980, for example, the United States imported 50 percent of the total manufactured products exported by the developing countries to the industrialized countries. The United States imported 10 percent of the manufactured exports of the industrialized countries in the early eighties. The United States and the industrialized countries to gether imported almost 70 percent of all merchandise exports from developing countries; the share was 70 percent for fuel, 65 percent for other primary commodities, and 60 percent for manufactures.

Will the United States be able to maintain the role of a world economic catalyst, and does it matter for the U.S. farm business sector? World economic conditions and the vital role that the U.S. plays in them will heavily influence not only the future demand for food and fiber but also the ability of the U.S. to supply the growing demand. The answer to the first part of this question is a subject of much recent debate.

During the past several years, numerous sectors of the American economy have experienced a marked deterioration of competitive vigor. This interruption in a trend of consistent economic growth that was blamed on (1) declining investment, (2) slow growth in technological development, (3) decreasing rates of productivity growth, and (4) foreign trade barriers.

U.S. industrial capital expansion has lagged behind that of our major foreign competitors. During the last twenty years, capital resources available per worker in the United States grew by less than 2 percent per year. In contrast, capital available per worker in Japan and Korea increased by more than 10 percent per year. In Europe and many developing countries, the growth in capital per worker was more than 4 percent. A a result, the United States dropped from first to sixth place in the ranking of countries according to the amount of capital available per worker. This more rapid growth of capital per worker by other countries has expanded their capabilities to supply and compete in those markets for traditionally strong U.S. exports. Thus the relative role of the United States in world trade has declined and it is meeting increased competition for the sale of its traditional export products.

The absolute size of expenditures on research and development in the United States still constitutes a majority of such expenditures by the developed countries. However, other countries, especially Japan and West Germany, have increased their research and development efforts substantially in proportion to their GNP, while U.S. research and development expenditures as a percentage of GNP have declined in recent years. Because U.S. exports of of manufactures are dominated by high-technology products, a future decline in U.S. research and development expenditures in absolute terms or even relative to foreign competitors would threaten the United States with a loss of foreign markets for U.S. manufactured exports. Japan has already joined the United States in having a competitive advantage in a number of high-technology products, and intense competition between the two countries will undoubtedly continue in the future.

U.S. productivity growth in manufacturing has lagged behind that of all of our major foreign competitors except the United Kingdom. Over the last decade, manufacturing productivity in the United States increased by an average of 2.5 percent per year. In Japan, the average increase was 5 percent; in West Germany, 5.5 percent; in France, 4.5 percent; and in Canada, 4 percent. The comparatively high productivity growth rates in Japan and most of Europe have permitted more rapid increases in real wage rates in these countries than in the United States. These charges in productivity are consistent with more rapid growth of capital and technological capabilities abroad.

Exchange Rates

The third important element that needs at least a brief mention as a key factor in explaining the role of world economics is the exchange-rate issue. The present international money system is a piecemeal arrangement that has grown out of the breakup in 1971–1973 of the Bretton Woods Agreement negotiated in 1944. The Bretton Woods System created the *International Monetary Fund* (IMF). This fund was originated to develop and maintain an orderly and stable international monetary system which would permit expansion of world trade and economic growth for its member nations. The regulatory procedures agreed upon formed a sharp contrast to the automatic process once provided by the gold standard. Its guiding principles have been consultation, cooperation, adaptability, and flexibility. These principles originated from recognizing that fundamental disequilibrium among economies of the world can and does occur as nations develop at differing rates and with different policies. The need for adjustment is evident in balance-of-payments surpluses or deficits. For instance, a nation with continuing deficits can lose its international liquidity (funds to settle its international accounts), which triggers a lack of confidence in its currency. Consequently, IMF provisions were made for temporary and permanent adjustments in exchange rates.

Students of the international monetary system recognized that the system needed reform, yet no acceptable solution was in the offing in the seventies or early eighties. Several steps to mitigate emerging problems had been taken in the sixties. For instance, the fund enlarged its pool of gold and currencies by raising members' quotas. Special arrangements also were made to permit borrowing of currencies. "Special Drawing Rights," sometimes called "Paper Gold" or SDRs were created to supplement national currencies and gold and create liquidity. All of these measures aided members in managing their balance of payments.

These measures alleviated but did not resolve underlying weakness eroding the original IMF system. The system broke down in 1971 when the United States suspended its commitments to the IMF and called for reform. This marked the end of the original post–World War II or Bretton Woods

Monetary scheme. Lack of confidence in the dollar and the U.S. action reflected the inability of the original system to adjust international monetary relations to changing international economic conditions.

The crisis created by the U.S. action stimulated other nations to agree to substantial revisions in the world monetary system. The value of the U.S. dollar relative to other currencies had gotten seriously out of line. Disparities were greatest between the dollar and the yen and the mark. The dollar was devalued twice: 8 percent in August 1971 and 10 percent in February 1973. These realignments proved inadequate, so world monetary managers agreed to a further step away from the stable exchange rate system. Exchange rates are now allowed to fluctuate (or "float"), letting the market determine their relative values.

It is argued that the move toward a flexible exchange rate released the dollar from being overvalued and therefore decreased the price of U.S. goods in terms of foreign currencies. According to this school of thought, the adoption of the managed floating system led to the expansion of food and fiber exports throughout the seventies and into the eighties. In the mid-eighties, the reverse has been the case, and it is argued that the overvalued dollar has led to a decrease in farm exports.

However, another school of researchers suggests that devaluation or revaluations have only small impacts on changes in agricultural trade, especially in the short run. This argument is based on a number of empirical findings and theoretical analyses related to import demand and export supply elasticities.

It can be concluded, nevertheless, that failure to stabilize the foreign exchange markets may encourage a return to a policy of fixed exchange rates.

SUMMARY

The purpose of this chapter was to identify the environment in which international trade is conducted, to discuss the market forces that expand the export demand for U.S. agricultural products, and to assess the effects that these forces will have on future trade levels. The major points made in this chapter can be summarized as follows:

1. The world *export–import system* for food and fiber products operates in the world *political* environment, the world *economic* environment, the *international monetary* environment, and the *international trade* environment.

2. Potential constraints on the quantities of agricultural products available for export include the availability of natural resources such as water, the productivity of the farm business sector, the intervention of govern-

ment, and the capacity of the marketing infrastructure in the United States.

3. The factors potentially limiting the growth of export demand for U.S. agricultural exports include the state of the world economy, the protectionistic policies of importing nations, the growth of the world's population, and the capacity of the marketing infrastructure in importing countries.

4. Developing countries are characterized by relatively high income elasticities for food. This fact and the income distribution in importing countries are major factors affecting imports of food and fiber products in these countries.

5. Lower population growth rates, low income elasticities, and projected declines in real economic growth in developed market economies suggests a slower growth in export demand for U.S. food and fiber products in these markets. Other economies are also projected to experience slower rates of economic growth. These and other factors, such as the external debts of many importing countries, contribute to a pessimistic outlook for export growth.

6. In addition to the decreased purchasing power of importing countries and their external debt, exchange rates also affect the export demand for U.S. commodities. A relatively strong dollar makes it more costly for importing countries to buy U.S. commodities.

DEFINITION OF TERMS

Third-world countries: middle-income countries (relatively better off than fourth-world countries but relatively less well off than industrialized economies). Examples include Egypt, Brazil, Thailand, Jordon, Mexico, and South Korea.

Fourth-world countries: low-income countries characterized by a low adult literacy rate, a low life expectancy, and a low caloric intake. Examples include India, Sudan, Chad, Sri Lanka, and Ghana.

Industrialized economies: high-income countries exhibiting high per capita income together with high adult literacy rates, high life expectancy rates, and a high caloric intake. Examples include United States, France, Canada, Japan, Italy, the United Kingdom, and West Germany.

Public debt: also referred to as national debt (see Chapter 12).

Debt service ratio: ratio of loan payments to exports of goods and services.

Productivity: level of output per unit of inputs.

Exchange rate: price of foreign currency in terms of domestic currency.

International liquidity: ability of nations to meet payments quickly without converting capital assets to cash or borrowing.

Special drawing rights: an amendment to the articles of the IMF to lend foreign exchange.

Marketing infrastructure: as described in Chapter 9, refers to the marketing intermediaries and facilities that transport commodities from producers to consumers.

Gold standard: an international monetary system in which each country values its currency in terms of a specific quantity of gold. This fixes exchange rates in relationship to each other.

Takeoff stage: period of several decades during which an economy transforms itself such that economic growth becomes more or less automatic; industry blossoms, stimulated by the availability of surplus labor.

Flexible exchange rates: exchange rates that are allowed to fluctuate in the open market in response to the demand and supply of foreign currencies.

Fixed exchange rates: exchange rates requiring government actions rather than market conditions to change.

Devaluation: a loss in the value of a domestic currency in terms of foreign currencies.

World Bank: located in Washington, D.C., it is a source of development finance and expertise on development policy.

Import substitution: replacing imports by domestic production under protection of tariffs and quotas.

REFERENCES

BHATWATI, JAGDISH, *Anatomy and Consequences of Exchange Control Regimes.* Cambridge, Mass.: Ballinger Publishing Co., 1978.

CLARKE, STEPHEN V. O., "Perspective on the United States External Position Since World War II," Federal Reserve Bank of New York, *Quarterly Review,* Summer 1980.

JABARA, C., ET AL., "The Relationship between Economic Growth and Trade," International Economic Division, ESS, USDA, Washington, D.C., 1982.

JOSLING, TIMOTHY, "World Food Production, Consumption, and International Trade: Implications for U.S. Agriculture," paper presented to the American Enterprise Institute, Conference on Food and Agricultural Policy, October 1980.

WORLD BANK, World Development Report 1984. The International Bank of Reconstruction and Development, Washington, D.C., 1984.

ADDITIONAL READINGS

BALDWIN, ROBERT E., "Determinants of Trade and Foreign Instruments, Further Evidence," *Review of Economics and Statistics,* February 1979.

COOK, MICHAEL L., *U.S. Farm Export Strategies for the Eighties.* Washington, D.C.: Agricultural Council of America, February 1981.

KOST, WILLIAM E., "Effects of an Exchange Rate Change on Agricultural Trade," *Agricultural Economics Research, 28 (3),* July 1976.

SCHUH, C. EDWARD, "The Exchange Rate and U.S. Agriculture," *American Journal of Agricultural Economics, 56 (1),* 1974.

VILLIANITIS-FIDAS, AMALIA, "The Impact of Devaluation on U.S. Agricultural Exports," *Agricultural Economic Research, 28 (3),* July 1976.

QUESTIONS

1. Describe the potential constraints to supplies of exportable food and fiber products. What affect would they have on a country's comparative advantage?

2. What are the major constraints to the export demand for U.S. food and fiber products?

3. Suppose that the income elasticity of the demand for food in a country is equal to 0.75. What will happen to the quantity of food demanded in this country if the disposable income of its consumers rose by 10 percent? How would this differ from what would occur in the United States?

4. Describe the various factors that influence thepurchasing power of a country in terms of its ability to pay for imported food and fiber products.

5. What is the difference between fixed and flexible exchange rates? How do exchange-rate movements help explain changes in the export demad for food and fiber products?

GLOSSARY

Absolute advantage: ability of a country to produce more of a product with its existing resources than other countries can.

Accounting profits: total revenue or sales minus accounting costs.

Aggregate demand: dollar value of planned expenditures for all fixed goods and services during the year.

Aggregate supply: dollar value of all final goods and services supplied to consumers, investors, government, and foreigners during the year.

Agricultural economics: the study of (1) the production, processing, marketing, and consumption of food and fiber products, and (2) the interrelationship between agriculture and the general economy and the direct and indirect effects of macroeconomic policies.

Asset: something of value owned by a farm business. Assets are generally divided into either (1) physical and financial assets, or (2) current (short-term) and fixed (intermediate- and long-term) assets.

Automatic instruments: do not require action on the part of government to take effect (an example is the progressive nature of the income tax system in the United States).

Autonomous consumption: portion of total consumer expenditures that does not depend on the level of disposable income.

Autonomous investment: portion of total investment expenditures that does not depend on the level of disposable income.

Average cost: total cost divided by output.

Average physical product: total physical produce or output divided by the input level.

Balance of payments: value of production, financial assets, and all other transactions in the world market.

Balance of trade: the difference between a nation's total exports and its total imports is referred to as the balance of trade. If exports are greater than (less than) imports, a nation is said to have a balance-of-trade surplus (deficit).

Balance sheet: a financial statement reporting the value of real estate (land and buildings), non-real estate (machinery, breeding livestock, and inventories), and financial (cash, checking account balance, and common stock) assets owned by farm businesses as well as these firms' debt outstanding. The difference between total farm assets and total farm debt outstanding represents the firms' net worth.

Barter economy: money is not used as the medium of exchange. Instead, households and businesses "swap" goods and services in satisfying their needs.

Basis: difference between the cash price and the futures price at a specific point in time.

Basis risk: the risk that the basis will have widened by the time a farmer finally sells his output.

Branch banking: no specific constraints are placed on the geographical structure of the bank's property (see unit banking).

Budget constraint: defined by the income available for consumption and the prices that a consumer faces. This constraint defines the feasible set of consumption choices facing a consumer.

Budget deficit: the excess of government spending over government revenues.

Budget surplus: the excess of government receipts over government spending.

Business cycle: reflects the pattern of movements in the economy's real output, interest rates, or unemployment rate (also referred to as business fluctuations).

Business inventories: unsold output from current or past production activities.

Capital gains: the gain in the value of an asset (sales price minus basis for tax purposes). This gain is considered a capital gain rather than as ordinary income if the asset is held for a specific length of time (usually 12 months).

Capitalism: an economic system where individuals own resources and have the right to employ their time and resources however they choose, with minimal legal constraints from government.

Cash flow stress: combination of economic factors that hamper farmers' ability to cover their cash uses of funds (including interest payments) with their cash sources of funds.

Certainty equivalent: a certain sum of money that makes a person indifferent to a given risk.

Change in demand: a shift in the demand curve caused generally by changes in the prices of complements or substitutes, income, and tastes.

Change in quantity demanded: a movement along a demand curve indicating the consumption response as its own price changes, holding the prices of complements or substitutes, income, and tastes constant.

Civilian labor force: total noninstitutional population (e.g., excludes people in prisons) minus total number of people not in the labor force (e.g., housewives, students) as well as members of the armed services.

Coefficient of variation: a measure of dispersion per unit of expected value. It is defined as the square root of the variance (the standard deviation) divided by the expected value.

Coincident indicators: indicators of changes in economic activity that reflect current activity.

Commercial bank deposits: demand deposits (i.e., checking account balances) plus time and savings accounts at commercial banks.

Commodity Credit Corporation: an agency within the U.S. Department of Agriculture that makes nonrecourse loans to farmers for the purpose of supporting prices at a specific level.

Comparative advantage: ability of a country to produce a product at a lower opportunity cost than another country can.

Complements: goods *A* and *B* are complements if the cross-price elasticity of demand is negative.

Concentration: refers to the number and market power of firms marketing their products in a particular market. A market characterized by a small number of firms accounting for the majority of total sales is said to have a high degree of concentration.

Conservation: optimal timing of the use of proven reserves of resources given existing and expected technology and preferences.

Constant dollars: the valuation of assets and income in terms of some base period's prices (i.e., 1967) as opposed to today's prices (*see also* purchasing power).

Consumer equilibrium: the consumption bundle that maximizes total utility and is feasible as defined by the budget constraint. The marginal utilities per dollar spent on each good or service must be equal.

Consumer Price Index (CPI): weighted average of the prices consumers pay for goods and services.

Consumption bundles: quantities of various goods or services that a consumer might potentially consume.

Contractionary policies: monetary and fiscal policies that lead to reduced economic growth of the economy.

Correlation: a measure of association of two random variables by −1 and +1, where +1 (−1) represents perfect positive(negative) correlation and a value of zero represents no association of the random variables.

Cost of capital: the after-tax cost of capital relevant to the decision of whether or not to expand on-farm storage facilities reflects the farmer's cost of borrowing, the opportunity rate of return on other uses of his equity capital, and his tax bracket.

Cost-push inflation: rise in general price level resulting from businesses and unions raising their prices and wage requests (also referred to as market power inflation).

Credit rationing: a limitation placed on the amount of borrowed funds used to finance a farmer's operations.

Cross-price elasticity: a measure of the response of consumption of a good or service to changes in the price of another good or service. It is defined as the percentage change in the quantity of good A demanded divided by the percentage change in the price of good B.

Cross-price elasticity of supply: the relative response of the supply of a good A as the price of good B changes. It is the percentage change in good A divided by the percentage change in the price of good B.

Crowding-out effect: the postponement of planned private investment expenditures caused by high interest rates brought about by government borrowing.

Currency drain: currency (paper bills and coins) held by the public, whether it is in their wallets or stored in a nonbank location (e.g., hidden in a mattress).

Current dollars: the valuation of assets and income in terms of current or this year's prices as opposed to some base period's prices.

Debt service ratio: ratio of loan payments to exports of goods and services.

Deficiency payment: value of payment per unit, equal to the difference between the market price and the target price. This payment is made to participating farmers.

Demand-pull inflation: rise in the general price level which occurs when aggregate demand for goods and services is rising and the economy is approaching full employment.

Depository institution: a financial institution, such as a commercial bank or a savings and loan association, accepts deposits in exchange for interest income.

Depreciable assets: specific assets with a useful life of more than one year that qualify for tax depreciation. This allowance enables the farmer to "write off" the cost of the asset over time. Machinery and buildings are two general forms of depreciable assets. Land is not a depreciable asset.

Depreciation: the IRS tax code allows farmers and other businesses to write off the cost of depreciable assets over a specific period of time for the purpose of computing their tax payments.

Devaluation: a loss in the value of a domestic currency in terms of foreign currencies.

Differentiated product: a product that is made different from others through advertising or quality variation.

Discount rate: rate the Federal Reserve charges when it lends to member commercial banks (all national banks plus those state banks that choose to be members of Federal Reserve System).

Discretionary instruments: do require action on the part of government to take effect (opposite of automatic instruments).

Disequilibrium: if a market is not in equilibrium (quantity demanded equals quantity supplied at announced price), the market is in disequilibrium. The existence of surpluses and shortages in a market indicates the existence of disequilibrium.

Dissaving: amount by which planned consumption exceeds disposable income.

Diversification of assets: holding a variety of physical and/or financial assets, as opposed to "holding all your eggs in one market."

Doubling time: the number of years it would take for a country's population to double at its current growth rate.

Durable good: a good that is "consumed" over a period of several years.

Economic capacity: the desired output in the short run given available resources, technology, and existing economic conditions.

Economic growth: increase in the economy's real level of output (real gross national product).

Economic profits: total revenue or sales minus economic costs. These costs include accounting costs (cash costs plus depreciation) plus opportunity costs.

Economics: a social science that studies how consumers, producers, and societies choose among the alternative uses of scarce resources in the process of producing, exchanging, and consuming goods and services.

Elasticity of supply: a measure of the relative response of output supplied to a price change. It is the percentage change in the quantity of output supplied resulting from a 1 percent change in output price.

European Economic Community: group of European countries that act in unison to discriminate against non-EEC countries by placing duties or levies on imported products.

Excess reserves: difference between legal reserves and required reserves.

Excess supply curve: derived from the difference between quantities of export product supplied domestically and quantities demanded at prices above the domestic equilibrium market price.

Exchange rate: price of foreign currency in terms of domestic currency.

Expansionary period: phase of business cycle during which the nation's output is expanding.

Expansionary policies: monetary and fiscal policies that lead to greater economic growth of the economy.

Expansion path: line connecting optimal input–input relationships.

Expected utility theory: a prominent theory of behavior under uncertainty which postulates that people choose actions so as to maximize the expected or average utility.

Expected value: a weighted average of outcomes where the weights are probabilities. It is a measure of central tendency and is also called the mean or average.

Exports: quantities of products sold and shipped to foreign countries.

Externalities: difference between social costs and private costs.

Factors of production: the inputs in a production process.

Farm business sector: one of the sectors comprising the food and fiber system is the farm business sector. This sector represents an aggregation of firms that produce raw agricultural products (i.e., farms and ranches).

Farm Credit Administration: an independent government agency located in Washington, D.C., which supervises the operation of the Farm Credit System.

Farm Credit System: a member-owned lending cooperative which consists of the Federal Land Bank System, the Federal Intermediate Credit Bank System, and the Banks for Cooperatives.

Farmers Home Administration: an agency of the U.S. Department of Agriculture which provides financing assistance to farmers in the form of grants, insured loans, and guaranteed loans.

Federal budget deficit: amount by which government spending during a period exceeds government revenues.

Federal funds market: an interbank market in which banks lend excess reserves to other banks on a extremely short term basis (e.g., 12 to 24 hours).

Federal Open Market Committee: consists of members of the Board of Governors of the Federal Reserve System plus selected district Federal Reserve Board presidents who meet periodically to assess the appropriate action that the Fed should take (buy or sell) in the open or private secondary bond market for government securities.

Fiduciary monetary system: value of currency issued by government based on the public's faith that currency can be exchanged for goods and services.

Final demand: expenditures by consumers, investments by businesses, government spending, and net exports. Stated another way, final demand is equal to total output intermediate demand.

Financial intermediary: firm or instituation that provides financial intermediation services (see financial intermediation).

Financial intermediary: process of channeling funds and securities between savers and borrowers.

Financial leverage ratio: an indicator of a firm's financial strength, this ratio is usually defined as debt-to-equity or net worth. A ratio of greater than 1 suggests that a farmer's creditors have more invested in the farm that the farmer does.

Fixed business investment: capital expenditures by business for plant and equipment (e.g., buildings, tractors) during the year.

Fixed costs: those costs that do not vary with output changes.

Fixed exchange rates: exchange rates requiring goverment actions rather than market conditions to change.

Flexible exchange rates: exchange rates that are allowed to fluctuate in the open market in response to the demand and supply of foreign currencies.

Food and fiber system: consists of business entities that are involved in one way or another with the supply of food and fiber.

Fourth World Countries: low-income countries characterized by a low adult literacy rate, a low life expectancy, and low caloric intake. Examples include India, Sudan, Chad, Sri Lanka, and Ghana.

Free trade: refers to an absence of goverment intervention which alters free-market prices and quantities marketed.

Frictional unemployment: persons who are changing jobs and thus are currently unemployed.

Full employment: high degree of employment of nation's resources (an unemployment rate of 5 to 6 percent for labor and a capacity utilization rate for capital of 86 to 88 percent is generally thought to constitute full employment).

Futures contract: standardized agreement that spells out the quality and quantity of the commodity to be delivered as well as the location and date of delivery.

General Agreement on Tariffs and Trade: created by the United States and 22 other nations in 1947 to secure a substantially free and competitive world market.

General equilibrium analysis: regards all sectors of the economy as being interdependent. The events taking place in all markets are considered inthe analysis.

Gold standard: an international monetary system in which each country values its currency in terms of a specific quantity of gold. This fixes exchange rates in relationship to each other.

Gross farm income: annual level of income received from farming activities before farm expenses, taxes, and withdrawals have been deducted.

Gross national income: given by the income approach to measuring economic activity, national income is equal to the sum of wages, rents interest and profits.

Gross national product: referred to as the nation's output, GNP is equal to consumer expenditures, business investment, government spending, and net exports (exports minus imports).

Hedging: the process by which the farmer first sells and later buys a futures product contract for the expressed purpose of locking in a forward price for his product.

Human resources: the services provided by laborers and the entreprenuership services provided by management represent the two major forms of human resources.

Human resources: labor and management used together with land and capital to produce goods and services.

Imports: quantities of products purchased from foreign countries and shipped to the United States.

Import substitution: replacing imports by domestic production under protection of tariffs and quotas.

Income elasticity: a measure of the relative response of demand to income changes. It is defined as the percentage change in the quantity demanded divided by the percentage change in income.

Indifference curve: a graph of the locus of consumption bundles that provide a consumer a given level of satisfaction.

Indivisibility: the indivisibility of an input refers to the fact that inputs such as equipment are available only in specific sizes.

Industrialized economies: high-income countries exhibiting high per capital income together with high adult literacy rates, high life expectancy rates, and low caloric intake. Examples include United States, France, Canada, Japan, Italy, the United Kingdom, and West Germany.

Inferior goods: goods whose consumption falls (rises) as a consumer's income increases (decreases).

Inflation: a sustained rise in the general price level.

Inflationary gap: value of output gap when planned expenditures exceeds the economy's current potential output.

Interdependent: when two or more prices or quantities or other factors dependent on one another, they are said to be interdependent.

Intermediate demand: the quantity of goods and services used to produce other products as opposed to going directly to final demand.

International liquidity: ability of nations to meet payments quickly without converting capital assets to cash or borrowing.

International Monetary Fund: institution designed to manage international monetary system. It arose from the 1944 Bretton Woods Agreement.

Investment tax credit: a specific percentage of the value of qualified assets that can be deducted directly from the tax payment due.

Isocost line: the locus of all input choices that yield a given given level of total cost.

Isoquant: all input combinations that lead to a given level of output.

Isorevenue line: the locus of all output quantities of a multiproduct firm which yield a given revenue or sales.

Lagging indicators: indicators of changes in economic activity about one or two quarters after they occur.

Law of diminishing marginal returns: eventually successive increments in an input lead to correspondingly lower increments to output (i.e., marginal physical products eventually fall with increased input quantities).

Law of diminishing marginal utility: marginal utility declines as more of a good or service is consumed during a specified period of time.

Leading indicators: indicators of changes in economic activity about one or two quarters before they occur.

Least cost: achieving a given objective while minimizing cost. Generally this refers to choosing input combinations minimize the total cost of producing a given output.

Legal reserves: deposits at district Federal Reserve banks plus vault cash.

Liability: a liability or debt outstanding refers to the amount *owed* by the farm business to others.

Liberalization of trade: refers to the removal of restrictions on imports.

Limited branch banking: limitation placed upon the geographical location of branches and/or the number of branches themselves.

Liquidity: the ability to convert an asset (s) to cash quickly with little or no loss in value and disruption to the firm's operations.

Loanable funds: pool of funds available for lending to borrowers.

Loan funds: funds lent to borrowers.

Macroeconomics: branch of economics that focuses on broad aggregates such as the growth of gross national product and the money supply as well as the stability of prices and the level of employment.

Malthusian cycle: the "positive check" on population growth in the form of starvation and disease when real wage rate per family falls below the subsistence level.

Manufactured resources: also referred to as capital, manufactured resources include such things as tractors and combines which are combined with land, labor, and management to produce goods and services.

Manufacturing capacity utilization rate: actual output of nation's manufacturing firms divided by their potential output.

Marginal benefit: the increment to total benefit (revenue) per unit increase in an activity (e.g., output).

Marginal cost: the change in total cost divided by the change in output.

Marginal net benefit: marginal benefit (revenue) minus marginal cost.

Marginal physical product: the increment to efficient output, or total physical produce when an input is varied while other inputs are held fixed.

Marginal propensity to consume: ratio of change in planned consumer expenditures to the change in disposable income (income after taxes).

Marginal rate of product transformation: measures the minimum possible reduction of the output of good *A* as the output of good is expanded by unit.

Marginal rate of substitution: the subjective rate of exchange of pairs of consumption goods or services so as to leave utility or satisfaction unchanged, or the absolute value of the slope of an indifference curve.

Marginal rate of technical substitution: the rate that the usage of one input must decline as another input expands by 1 unit so as to leave output unchanged.

Marginal social cost of abatement: increase in the cost of pollution abatement practices associated with an annual increase in pollution.

Marginal social cost of pollution: increase in the social cost of pollution caused by an annual increase in pollution.

Marginal utility: the increment to utility or satisfaction as consumption of a good is increased by 1 unit.

Margin deposits: buyers and sellers of futures market contracts must place an original margin deposit with their broker, who, in turn, deposit funds wit the exchange's clearinghouse.

Market-clearing price: the market price given by the intersection of the demand and supply curve (also referred to as the equilibrium price). This price clears the market of any excess demand (shortage) or excess supply (surplus).

Market equilibrium: price and quantity given by the intersection of the market demand and supply curves.

Marketing bill: equivalent to the total value of the marketing margin for all products taken together; consumer expenditures for food minus their farm value.

Marketing cooperative: a farmer-owned cooperative formed principally to collectively market the output of its members.

Marketing infrastructure: as described in Chapter 9, refers to the marketing intermediaries and facilities that transport commodities from producers to consumers.

Marketing margin: the difference between the retail price and farm-level price for food and fiber products.

Marketing plan: the farmer's marketing plan reflects his objectives when buying inputs and selling farm products. These objectives, in turn, will affect the farmer's choice among marketing options.

Market risk: risk that the market price and quantity will differ from that originally expected by the farmer.

Maximum profit: input and output choices that maximize profit.

Medium of exchange: the means by which goods and services are paid for represents the medium of exchange. Money in a monetary economy serves as the principal medium of exchange.

Medium of exchange: money allows businesses and individuals to specialize in their endeavors and to purchase the goods and services they need with money they receive for their efforts.

Mircroeconomics: branch of economics that focuses on the economic actions of individuals or specific groups of individuals.

Middlemen: firms that perform one or more marketing functions associated with the buying and selling of goods as they move through marketing channels.

Mixed economic system- markets are not entirely free to determine price in some markets but are in others. Government controls in selected markets and welfare programs are indicative of a mixed economic system.

Monetary economy: unlike a barter economy, money is used as the principal medium of exchange. Households receive renumeration in the form of wages, rents, interest, and profits. Businesses receive renumeration in the form of expenditures by households, businesses, government and foreign countries.

Money multiplier: the reciprocal of the fractional required reserve ratio if there are no currency drains and no excess reserves.

Monopolistic competition: a market structure where a large number of firms produce a differentiated product.

Multiplier: effect that a change in autonomous consumption or investment will have upon equilibrium income. The investment multiplier, for example,, is equal to the reciprocal of the marginal propensity to save.

National bank: bank that is charted by the federal government.

National product: see gross national product.

Natural resources: includes such resources as land and its mineral deposits that are available without additional effort on the part of the owners.

Near monies: assets that are almost money or can be converted to money quickly with little or no loss in value.

Net economic benefit: total revenue less total costs of production.

Net farm income: gross farm income minus farm expenses and taxes.

Nominal interest rate: market rate of interest unadjusted for the current rate of inflation.

Nondurable good: a good that is consumed during the year.

Non-real estate debt: debt outstanding other than that secured by real estate (e.g., chattel mortgage loans).

Nonrecourse loan: an amount of money equal to support price times the quantity offered as collateral lent by the Commodity Credit Corporation (CCC). The loan is considered "paid in full" when turned over to CCC the market price falls below the support price.

Nonrenewable resource: a scarce resource that cannot be reproduced (e.g., mineral deposits).

Normal goods: goods whose consumption rises (falls) as a consumer's income increases (decreases).

Normative economics: focuses on determining "what should be" or "what ought to be" issues and questions. Unlike positive economics, it interjects the values with specific goals or objectives.

Oligopoly: a market structure where there are a small number of sellers. Each seller (oligopolist) knows how the other sellers will respond to any changes in quantity marketed or prices he might initiate.

Open account: line of credit extended to businesses that charge purchases.

Open market operations: buying or selling of government securities in the Federal Reserve's portfolio on the open market to achieve specific policy objectives.

Opportunity cost: the rate of return on the best alternative or "opportunity" use of funds.

Opportunity cost: the implicit cost of an action which is the maximum forgone opportunity in an alternative activity. For example, the opportunity cost of using one's labor to farm may be the wage forgone elsewhere (e.g., in manufacturing).

Opportunity cost of production: the production of one product sacrificed by choosing to produce more of another product.

Own-price elasticity: a measure of the relative response of consumption of a good or service to changes in its price. It is defined as the percentage change in the quantity demanded divided by the percentage change in price.

Parity: a concept that expresses relative prices (price of farm products relative to input prices) in the current period as a ratio to relative prices in the 1910-1914 period. A parity price in the current period (i.e., ratio = 100) would mean that farmers are currently earning the same relative price as that received in this "golden era."

Partial equilibrium analysis: assumes that events taking place outside the market under analysis remain constant.

Payment-in-kind: the 1983-84 PIK program called for payment of commodities to farmers roughly equal to the amount they would have produced had they not participated in this set-aside approach to support prices and reduce government stocks.

Perfect Competition: a sector is said to be perfectly competitive when the product is homogeneous, (2) there are no barriers to exit or entry. (3) there are a vary large number if sellers and buyers in the market, and (4) adequate market information exists.

Performance: the efficiency and profitability of a farm business's production activities are typical barometers of the sector's performance.

Permanent income hypothesis: notion that consumption is dependent upon household's long-run expected income.

Planned consumption: amount of income households plan to spend on new goods and services during the year.

Planned saving: the difference between disposable income and planned consumer expenditures or consumption.

Plant capacity: maximum output technically possible by a firm given its existing plant size (e.g., number of acres and technology).

Portfolio: a mixture of marketing, production, or investment activities. It is generally characterized by the proportion of invested wealth allocated to each activity.

Portfolio effect: the effect that an activity has in conjunction with other returns in an investment portfolio. Thus an activity may have a high variance but low correlation, so that including it in a portfolio may reduce the variability of the portfolio's return.

Positive economics: focuses on "what is " and "what would happen if" questions and issues. Does not involve value judgements or policy.

Potential output: nation's gross national product when its labor and capital resources are "fully employed" (i.e., 5 to 6 percent unemployment rate for labor and 86 to 88 percent capacity utilization rate for capital). Also referred to as full-employment output.

Precautionary demand for money: demand to hold money to pay for unexpected expenditures that may arise.

Preferred capacity utilization rate: ratio of economic capacity to productive capacity.

Present value of returns: the future returns discounted back to the present by an appropriate cost of capital (e.g., the opportunity cost of capital). A dollar in benefits in the future is worth less than it would be worth today.

Price stability: minor increases in the general price level as aggregate demand increases (i.e., low or zero rate of inflation).

Price support: the minimized price or floor below which the government will not let the price of specific commodities fall. A variety of approachs have been taken to support prices at desired levels.

Price takers: when firms or consumers do not alter the prices they face, they are said to be price takers.

Private costs: costs incurred by individuals when using scarce resources. The private costs of operating a tractor include the fuel and maintenance expenses associated with its use.

Producer Price Index (PPI): weighted average of the prices producers pay for goods and services.

Producer surplus: the excess of market price over the minimum price necessary to bring forth the quantity supplied (supply price).

Production contract: written agreement between the farmer and contractor specifying the terms and acceptance of a specific product at a future date.

Production function: a mathematical or functional relationship between the maximum possible output associated with a given level of input use.

Production possibilities curve: represents all possible combinations of total output that could be produced given the efficient use of existing resources.

Productive capacity: the maximum output technically possible in the short run given available resources and existing technology.

Productivity: level of output per unit of input.

Productivity ratio: ratio of output to input.

Profitability: returns on capital invested in farm business assets represents a measure of profitability. Profitability may be express in dollar terms (i.e., net farm income) or in percentage terms (i.e., rate of return on farm capital).

Protectionism: act on the part of policymakers to protect a country's industry by modifying the terms of trade for importing countries, either making their goods more expensive or barring them altogether.

Proven reserves: known reserves that can be extracted or used profitably.

Public debt: also referred to as national debt (see Chapter 12).

Purchasing cooperative: a farmer-owned cooperative formed principally to collectively purchase goods and services for its members. Crop yields per acre are a measure of productivity.

Purchasing power: the purchasing power of money reflects what $1 today would have purchased in goods and services in a particular base period. Inflation is said to erode the purchasing power of money over time.

Pure monopoly: a market structure that has only one firm supplying products to buyers.

Quarantine prohibition: absolute restriction placed on the entry of imported goods into a country; designed implicity to protect domestic agricultural commodities.

Quota: limit on quantity or value of imports permitted to enter a country during the year.

Random variable: a variable whose outcome is uncertain, such as the profit from growing an acre of corn.

Real estate debt: debt outstanding on loans and secured by real estate (i.e., farm mortgage loans).

Real interest rate: nominal interest rate minus the rate of inflation.

Recessionary gap: value of output gap when economy's current potential output exceeds planned expenditures.

Recessionary period: phase of business cycle during which the nation's output is declining.

Relative cost ratio: represents the ratio of the opportunity costs of producing one product in lieu of another.

Release price: the price ceiling for selected commodities enforced by the federal government by releasing reserves on to the market.

Required reserves: minimum amount of deposits that banks and other depository institutions must hold in reserve (*see* reserve requirements).

Reserve requirements: fraction of its deposits that banks and other depository institutions must hold in reserve (i.e., held on deposit at its district Federal Reserve Bank or in vault cash).

Returns to scale: change in output in relation to an expansion of the use of all inputs (more labor, more equipment, and more land and buildings). Returns to scale can be either constant, increasing, or decreasing in nature.

Risk averse: a person exhibiting diminishing marginal utility of wealth. This implies that the person values a given gain less than a given loss in absolute value. Hence, fluctuations (variance) and expected values are of concern to the person.

Risk neutral: a person exhibiting constant utility of wealth. That is, the person values a given gain and loss equally in absolute value. Hence, fluctuations (variance) tend to be of little or no importance compared to the average value.

Risk preference: a term denoting the propensity of a person to take risks. This propensity is implicity defined by the utility of wealth schedule.

Risk preferring: a person exhibiting increasing marginal utility of wealth. Such a person values increments in wealth more than decrements in wealth (in absolute value).

Risk premium: the expected value minus the certainty equivalent. It is positive, zero, or negative as a person is, respectively, risk averse, neutral, or risk preferring.

Savings: value of saving accumulated at a particular time (i.e., annual saving over a period of years represents your savings).

Scarce resources: a resource is said to be scarce if only a finite quantity of the resource exists. Nature does not freely provide as much of these resources as we would like.

Self-sufficiency: refers to the ability of a country to meet its domestic needs for a product without importing quantites from other countries.

Sequential marketing: acceptance of an average price for a product by spreading the marketing of the commodity over a period of time.

Set-aside: the amount of land that had to be "set aside"—either left idle or planted to another crop.

Shortage: the excess quantity demanded at a particular price. It is relatively easy to enter such a sector.

Slippage: extent to which farmers (1) participating in government programs "overproduce" by retiring marginal acres rather than highly productive acres, or (2) decide not to participate at all.

Social costs: costs incurred by society when a resource is used. The social cost of operating a tractor is equal to the private costs plus any additional cost that society bears, including air pollution.

Socialism: resources are generally collectively owned and government decides through central planning how human and nonhuman resources are to be utilized in different sectors of the economy. Prices are largely set by the government and administered to consumers and producers.

Soil Bank: tillable land that farmers took out of production to qualify for price supports.

Special drawing rights: an amendment to the articles of the IMF to lend foreign exchange.

Specialization: the separation of productive activities between persons or geographical areas in such a manner that none of these persons or regions is completely self-sufficient. For example, some people specialize by learning to be plumbers. Others choose to be lawyers or even agricultural economists.

Speculative demand for money: demand to hold money as an asset in expectation that other asset prices will fall.

Spot market: market in which the commodity is actually physically exchanged for cash at a fixed price per unit.

Stages of production: classification of production as to whether marginal physical products are rising, falling, or are negative.

Stagflation: existence of increasing inflation during a period when the economy is experiencing rising unemployment.

State bank: bank that is chartered by a state government.

Store of value: value of holding money as an asset.

Structure: the composition or makeup of a sector can be assessed by examining its physical and financial structure. Physical structure is assessed by looking at such things as the number and size of farms, their ownership and control, and the ease of entry and exit from the sector. Financial structure is evaluated by looking at the composition of a sector's balance sheet.

Substitutes: goods A and B are substitutes if the cross-price elasticity of demand is positive.

Supply-side economics: promotion of macroeconomic policies that increase productivity and thereby shift the current aggregate supply curve to the right. This is thought to promote higher output at lower price levels.

Surplus: the excess quantity supplied at a particular price.

Takeoff stage: period of several decades during which an economy transforms itself such that economic growth becomes more or less automatic; industry blossoms, stimulated by the availability of surplus labor.

Target price: price set by government for selected commodities. This price is achieved by supplementing the market price with a deficiency payment.

Tariff: a tax or duty placed on products imported into a country.

Technical efficiency: the maximum possible output for a given input level or the minimum possible input use for a given level of output.

Technological change: also referred to as technical change and technical progress, technological change reduces the quantity of inputs required to produce a given level of output.

Third-world countries: middle-income countries (relatively better off than fourth-world countries but relatively less well off than industrialized economies). Examples include Egypt, Brazil, Thailand, Jordan, Mexico, and South Korea.

Total physical product: efficient output for a given level of input use. As inputs are varied, the total physical product curve is traced out.

Total utility: the total satisfaction derived from consuming a given bundle of goods and services.

Trade balance: value of products bought and sold in international markets.

Trade surplus (deficit):   amount by which exports are greater than (less than) imports.

Trade-weighted exchange rate: price of foreign currencies in terms of the U.S. dollar weighted by the relative importance of trade flows with our leading trading partners.

Transactions costs: brokerage commissions and other fees standardly assessed when completing a market transaction.

Transactions demand for money: demand to hold money to pay for expected expenditures.

Uncertainty: when particular economic outcomes are not certain to occur. Certainty is characterized by a probability of 1 that an event will occur.

UNCTAD: United Nations Conference on Trade and Development, which focuses particular attention on the trade and development problems of poor countries.

Unemployment rate: number of unemployed persons divided by the size of the total civilian labor force.

Unit banking: each banking location is condiered a separate business entity (no branch banking permitted).

Unit of accounting: money provides a basis with which the relative value of goods and services can be assessed and with which the profitability and financial position of businesses can be assessed.

Usury: concept of limiting the rate of interest charged on loans.

Utility function: a mathematical or functional representation of the satisfaction that a consumer derives from a consumption bundle.

Utils: units of satisfaction derived from consumption of goods or services.

Variable costs: costs that vary with output.

Variable levy system: based on the minimum price at which non-EEC member commodities can be imported into a country. If the import price is below this minimum, a levy (tax) equal to this difference is imposed on the product.

Variance: a measure of the dispersion of random or uncertain outcomes. It is defined as a weighted average of deviations from the mean where the weights are probabilities.

Variation margin deposits: the farmer may have to make an additional deposit to cover his market priorities if the futures market price increases.

World Bank: located in Washington, D.C., it is a source of development finance and expertise on development policy.

Yield risk: the risk associated with an unknown relationship between inputs and output in agricultural production. Also refers to situation where a farmer's output may turn out to be less than what he expected when he sold a futures contract.

INDEX